A PRACTICAL GUIDE TO Cyber Insurance *for* Businesses

Lauren D. Godfrey,
Michael Menapace,
Toni Scott Reed, and
Larry P. Schiffer,
Editors

AMERICAN BAR ASSOCIATION
Tort Trial and Insurance
Practice Section

Cover design by Amanda Fry/ABA Design

Printed in the United States of America.

26 25 24 23 22 5 4 3 2 1

ISBN 978-1-63905-136-6

e-ISBN: 978-1-63905-137-3

Discounts are available for books ordered in bulk. Special consideration is given to state bars, CLE programs, and other bar-related organizations. Inquire at Book Publishing, ABA Publishing, American Bar Association, 321 N. Clark Street, Chicago, Illinois 60654-7598.

www.shopABA.org

TABLE OF CONTENTS

Preface

There are lots of books about cybersecurity, data privacy and related issues but there are very few, if any, books about cyber insurance. This book, A Practical Guide to Cyber Insurance for Businesses, was created to fill that void and provide a practical look at cyber insurance for different types of businesses.

The book is divided into two parts. The first eight chapters focus on the development of cyber insurance and various aspects and elements of cyber insurance that affect all industries, including how cyber insurance interacts with other commercial insurance coverage. Chapters nine through twenty-five take a closer look at the cyber risks and cyber insurance coverage needs for specific industries. In this way, the unique characteristics of each industry segment are highlighted and a review of cyber insurance for that industry segment is more focused. While not every possible industry segment is covered, the broadness of the industries covered should provide guidance to any business.

Our goal is that this book will become a practical guide for insurance brokers, underwriters, risk managers and businesses as each of these constituencies work with each other to choose the right cyber insurance product for commercial businesses. Cyber insurance, like the cyber risks it seeks to protect against, is ever-evolving and changing as new risks arise and as claims flow through the judicial system making new law. Nevertheless, the fundamental concepts contained in these twenty-five chapters should stand the test of time.

The idea for this book came about during the early days of the COVID-19 pandemic. Toni Reed, a member of the Cybersecurity and Data Privacy Committee of the American Bar Association's Tort, Trial and Insurance Section ("TIPS"), happens to be a member of the TIPS Book Publishing Board. She approached Larry Schiffer, then Chair of the Cybersecurity and Data Privacy Committee, and suggested that the Committee consider writing a cyber book. An editorial committee was formed with Larry, Toni, then Chair-Elect Michael Menapace and then Chair-Elect Designee Lauren Godfrey. The editorial committee decided that a book about cyber insurance for commercial businesses was a logical way to proceed.

The Cybersecurity and Data Privacy Committee reached out to its committee members, across TIPS and its various committees, and outside of TIPS to recruit authors with industry expertise. Each of the editors was responsible for shepherding multiple chapters by working with the authors to keep to a rather aggressive timeline. The result of the fabulous work by our many authors and our editors is set out in the pages that follow.

The editors would like to thank all the authors and their assistants in making this book a reality. We would also like to thank Hailey Hillsman, a student at Cleveland-Marshall College of Law, for her citation assistance. Finally, the editors would like to thank Christine Grey from Clark Hill, who put this book into camera-ready art, which allowed for the timely publication of this work.

We hope you will find this book useful in both understanding cyber insurance and in assisting in evaluating the right coverage for businesses you are assisting.

Editors:

LAUREN D. GODFREY
MICHAEL MENAPACE
TONI SCOTT REED
LARRY P. SCHIFFER
November 2021

CONTRIBUTORS

EDITORS

Lauren D. Godfrey—Partner in Lewis, Brisbois, Bisgaard & Smith LLP. B.A., Drew University; M.S., University of Scranton; J.D., New York Law School; Health/Hospital Law Certificate, Seton Hall University Law School; CIPP/US, EU from IAPP. Chair-Elect of the ABA/TIPS Cybersecurity & Data Privacy Committee.

Michael Menapace—Partner in Wiggin and Dana LLP. B.M., The Hartt School, University of Hartford; J.D., Quinnipiac University School of Law. 2021-22 Chair of the ABA/TIPS Cybersecurity & Data Privacy Committee.

Toni Scott Reed—Partner in Clark Hill. B.A. and B.B.A., *summa cum laude*, Southern Methodist University; J.D., *cum laude*, Dedman School of Law—Southern Methodist University. Past Chair, ABA-TIPS Fidelity & Surety Law Committee; Vice Chair, ABA/TIPS Cybersecurity & Data Privacy Committee; Member, ABA Book Publishing Board.

Larry P. Schiffer—President of Schiffer Law & Consulting PLLC. B.A., *magna cum laude*, Brooklyn College City University of New York; J.D., *cum laude*, Albany Law School. Immediate Past Chair, ABA/TIPS Cybersecurity & Data Privacy Committee; Member of the ABA Cybersecurity Legal Task Force; Past Chair, ABA/TIPS Excess, Surplus Lines & Reinsurance Committee; Past Chair, ABA/TIPS Technology Committee.

AUTHORS

Ross Benson—Associate at McGlinchey Stafford. B.A., University of Alabama; J.D., University of Alabama School of Law.

Rafae Bhatti—Founder and Managing Partner at Brightline Law. PhD., Purdue University; J.D., Santa Clara University School of Law. Vice-Chair of the ABA/TIPS Cybersecurity & Data Privacy Committee.

KYLE BLACK—Associate in Buchanan Ingersoll & Rooney PC; B.S., Emory University; J.D., University of Pittsburgh School of Law; CIPP/US; CIPP/E; CIPM.

ELIZABETH BRUSA—Associate at Bradley Arant Boult Cummings LLP. B.A., Northern Illinois University; M.Ed., Univerity of Illinois; J.D. University of Illinois Chicago School of Law.

KRISTIN L. BRYAN—Senior Associate at Squire Patton Boggs (US) LLP; B.A., Dartmouth College; J.D., Columbia Law School. Vice Chair of the ABA-TIPS Cybersecurity & Data Privacy Committee.

DANIEL COTTER—Partner at Howard & Howard Attorneys, PLLC. B.A., Monmouth College; J.D., The John Marshall Law School.

DEBBIE CROCKETT—Shareholder in Cheffy Passidomo, P.A. B.A., Salisbury University; J.D., University of Baltimore.

GLENN E. DAVIS—Partner in HeplerBroom, LLC. B.A., DePauw University, J.D., Washington University, JD 1982. Member—ABA/TIPS Cybersecurity & Data Privacy Committee.

ANDREW DEUTSCH—Senior Contract and Compliance Manager, Intact Insurance Specialty Solutions. B.A., University of Minnesota—Duluth; J.D., University of Minnesota Law School. Member of ABA-TIPS Cybersecurity & Data Privacy Committee.

APRIL FALCON DOSS—Executive Director of the Georgetown Institute for Technology Law and Policy. B.A., Yale University; M.F.A., Goucher College; J.D., University of California, Berkeley.

CHAD ECKHARDT—Attorney at Frost Brown Todd LLC. B.A. and M.A., University of Kentucky; J.D., Northern Kentucky University—Salmon P. Chase College of Law.

AARON GARAVAGLIA—Lawyer at Arthur Cox LLP; B.A., San Jose State University; J.D., *cum laude*, American University.

DANIEL B. GARRIE—Founder of Law & Forensics, LLC. Neutral with JAMS. Professor at Harvard and Adjunct Professor of Law at Rutgers

School of Law. B.A., Brandeis University; M.A., Brandies University; J.D., Rutgers School of Law.

Lauren D. Godfrey—Partner in Lewis, Brisbois, Bisgaard & Smith LLP. B.A., Drew University; M.S., University of Scranton; J.D., New York Law School; Health/Hospital Law Certificate, Seton Hall University Law School; CIPP/US, EU from IAPP. Chair-Elect of the ABA/TIPS Cybersecurity & Data Privacy Committee.

Joe Gunset—Of Counsel at McGlinchey Stafford. B.A., Fordham University; J.D., Fordham University School of Law.

Peter A. Halprin, FCIArb, FAiADR—Partner in Pasich LLP. B.A., McGill University, First Class Joint Honours; J.D., Benjamin N. Cardozo School of Law; PGDip, Queen Mary School of Law, University of London.

Stan Johnson—Senior Managing Director with Ankura Consulting. B.A., University of Georgia; CPA; CFF.

Laurie Kamaiko—Partner in Saul Ewing Arnstein & Lehr LLP. B.A., Vassar College; J.D., Boston University School of Law.

Dennis Logan, Jr.—Chief Architect, Cyber Safety Architects. B.A., Bucknell University.

Greg Mantych—Associate at Mendes & Mount LLP. B.A., Saint Louis University; J.D., Fordham University School of Law.

Albert F. Moran—iStaff Attorney, Litigation for UHS of Delaware, Inc. B.A., University of Pennsylvania; J.D., Temple University Beasley School of Law.

Michael Nitardy—Member in Frost Brown Todd LLC. B.B.A., *summa cum laude*, Marshall University; J.D., *summa cum laude*, Salmon P. Chase College of Law, Northern Kentucky University.

Renier P. Pierantoni—Partner at Cooper, LLC. B.S., St. John's University; J.D., Yeshiva University—Cardozo School of Law. Member—ABA/TIPS Cybersecurity & Data Privacy Committee.

DANA POST—Senior Legal Editor, Privacy & Data Security, Thomson Reuters. B.A., Emory University; J.D., University of Maryland School of Law.

DR. BONNIE REAGAN-AYLOR—Founding President of BFC Analytics; A.A.; B.A.; M.S.; M.B.A; PhD.; J.D., Mitchell Hamline School of Law.

TONI SCOTT REED—Partner in Clark Hill. B.A. and B.B.A., *summa cum laude*, Southern Methodist University; J.D., *cum laude*, Dedman School of Law—Southern Methodist University. Past Chair, ABA-TIPS Fidelity & Surety Law Committee; Vice Chair, ABA/TIPS Cybersecurity & Data Privacy Committee; Member, ABA/TIPS Book Publishing Board.

MARGARET A. REETZ—Partner in Mendes & Mount, LLP. B.A., University of Illinois; J.D., DePaul College of Law. Member—ABA/TIPS Cybersecurity & Data Privacy Committee.

KRISTI W. RICHARD—Member at McGlinchey Stafford. B.S., Louisiana State University; M.B.A, Louisiana State University; D.C.L and J.D., Louisiana State University Paul M. Hebert Law Center.

JULY SELBY—Partner in Kennedys. B.S., College of Mt. St. Vincent; J.D., Brooklyn Law School.

JOHN F. STEPHENS—Of Counsel at Hendricks Law, P.C. B.S., Rutgers, The State University of New Jersey; J.D., Rutgers Law School—Camden. Vice Chair, ABA/TIPS Cybersecurity & Data Privacy Committee.

ROBERT STINES—Partner in Freeborn & Peters LLP. B.F.A., New York University; J.D., Stetson University College of Law; MSc, University of South Florida; Vice Chair, ABA/TIPS Cybersecurity & Data Privacy Committee.

MICHELLE WORRALL TILTON—Cyber Product Specialist, Zurich NA. B.S., University of Kansas; J.D., University of Kansas Law School. Past Chair, ABA/TIPS Cybersecurity & Data Privacy Committee.

ANDREW TUGGLE—Associate at Bradley Arant Boult Cummings LLP. B.S., University of Alabama; J.D., University of Alabama School of Law.

HEATHER WRIGHT—Partner at Bradley Arant Boult Cummings LLP. B.A., Sewanee: The University of the South; J.D., Wake Forest University School of Law.

DEBORAH YUE—Owner, Law Office of Deborah Yue LLC. B.S., Carnegie Mellon University; J.D., Cleveland-Marshall College of Law. Chair, TIPS Automobile Litigation Committee; Co-Chair, TIPS Law Practice & Legal Department Management Task Force; Diversity Vice-Chair, TIPS Women Trial Lawyers; Diversity Vice-Chair, TIPS Cybersecurity & Data Privacy Committee; Member of the ABA House of Delegates.

J. PAUL ZIMMERMAN—Attorney at Christan & Small LLP. J.D., University of Alabama.

Chapter 1

History/Development of Cyber and Network Security Risk and Insurance*[1]

The term "cyber" has been with us for many years, originating from the word cybernetics.[2] According to research, the term "cybersecurity" was coined in 1989.[3] For cyber insurance, there is much debate when it began,[4] but as early as the late 1990s there were some insurance policies[5] that covered some elements of cyber and network security risks.[6] Until

---

* By Daniel Cotter.

1 The author acknowledges the substantial assistance and work by Ariane M. Janz on this chapter.

2 *See, e.g.,* Alpine Security, *What is the Origin of the Word 'Cyber'?*, (Jan. 1, 2021, 11:06AM), *available at* https://alpinesecurity.com/blog/what-is-the-origin-of-the-word-yber/#:~:text=Cyber%20came%20from%20cybernetics,or%20cybersecurity%2C%20there%20was%20cybernetics.&text=Cybernetics%20derived%20from%20the%20Greek,governance%E2%80%9D%20and%20applies%20to%20leadership (Before there was cyberpunk or cybersecurity, there was cybernetics. In the late 1940s, cybernetics arose as the study of control systems and communications between people and machines.")

3 *Id.*

4 In an interview with Bob Parisi, currently Head of Cyber Solutions- North America at Munich Re, on January 27, 2021, by the author, Parisi discussed his time at AIG and the emphasis and development of cyber insurance. Parisi stated, "There were several forces driving [cyber insurance's] birth and growth and several more factors that drove its evolution over that past few decades." Notes of interview in possession of author, Dan Cotter. ("Parisi Interview.")

5 In an interview with Tracey Vispoli, currently President of Berkley Cyber Risk Solutions, on November 23, 2020, by the author, Vispoli discussed her time at Chubb Insurance and the early 2000s. She stated in the interview, "Around 2000, real cyber insurance started. People will tell you 1990s, may have been technologyesque policies back then, but what see today, real roots of what seeing today in early 2000." Notes of interview in possession of author, Dan Cotter. ("Vispoli Interview.")

6 *See, e.g.,* ColonyWest, *A History of Cyber Liability Insurance*, (Jan. 21, 2021, 11:08AM) *available at* https://colony-west.com/a-history-of-cyber-liability-

recently, the appetite for cyber insurance has not grown as rapidly as the risks presented by cyber attacks. This chapter gives a brief history of cyber risk and insurance and provides a basic history and general development of the market. Other chapters in the book go into greater detail about cyber insurance and industry-specific risks and considerations.

A. Privacy vs. Cybersecurity

As noted above, the term "cybersecurity" was coined in the late 1980s.[7] Often, the terms "privacy" and "cybersecurity" are used interchangeably, but there are differences. One excellent explanation of what the two terms mean is:

> Cybersecurity refers to the measures taken to protect a computer or computer system against unauthorized access from a hacker. On its most basic level, data privacy is a consumer's understanding of their rights as to how their personal information is collected, used, stored and shared.[8]

The two are connected, but not directly the same. In many instances, while the consumer expresses concern about how her information is being used, the user often believes that she has little control over how her information is used or protected.

Privacy as a concept has been around for much longer than cybersecurity, with Louis Brandeis writing an article in 1890 with his partner at the time, Samuel Warren. In the Harvard Law Review article,

---

insurance/ ("In the 1990s, the earliest form of cyber liability insurance generally included polices that covered online media or errors in data processing.").

7 *See supra, n 2.*

8 AmTrust Financial, *Cybersecurity v. Data Privacy*,(Jan. 21, 2021, 11:10 AM) available at https://amtrustfinancial.com/blog/small-business/cybersecurity-vs-data-privacy#:~:text=Data%20Privacy%3A%20Cybersecurity%20refers%20to,%2C%20used%2C%20stored%20and%20shared.

"The Right to Privacy,"[9] Warren and Brandeis argued for a "right to be left alone":

> These considerations lead to the conclusion that the protection afforded to thoughts, sentiments, and emotions, expressed through the medium of writing or of the arts, so far as it consists in preventing publication, is merely an instance of the enforcement of the more general right of the individual to be let alone. It is like the right not be assaulted or beaten, the right not be imprisoned, the right not to be maliciously prosecuted, the right not to be defamed.[10]

The authors also wrote, well ahead of the modern technology era:

> Recent inventions and business methods call attention to the next step which must be taken for the protection of the person, and for securing to the individual . . . the right 'to be let alone' . . . Numerous mechanical devices threaten to make good the prediction that 'what is whispered in the closet shall be proclaimed from the house-tops.'[11]

In the United States, there is no right to privacy explicitly set forth in the Constitution. However, when Brandeis became a Justice of the Supreme Court, he used this lens to address items such as surveillance and wiretapping, arguing for the right to be left alone in a dissent.[12] The

---

9 Samuel D. Warren & Louis D. Brandeis, *The Right to Privacy*, HARVARD LAW REVIEW 4, no. 5 (1890): 193-220 (Jan. 17, 2021), *available at* https://www.cs.cornell.edu/~shmat/courses/cs5436/warren-brandeis.pdf.

10 *Id.*

11 *Id.*

12 *See Olmstead v. United States*, 277 U.S. 438, 478 (1928) (J. Brandeis, dissenting) ("They sought to protect Americans in their beliefs, their thoughts, their emotions and their sensations. They conferred, as against the Government, the right to be let alone—the most comprehensive of rights, and the right most valued by civilized men. To protect that right, every unjustifiable intrusion by the Government upon the privacy of the individual, whatever the means employed, must be deemed a violation of the Fourth Amendment.").

Supreme Court would first find a right to privacy in the penumbras[13] of the Constitution in *Griswold v. Connecticut,*[14] with the Court holding:

> The foregoing cases suggest that specific guarantees in the Bill of Rights have penumbras, formed by emanations from those guarantees that help give them life and substance. Various guarantees create zones of privacy. . . . We have had many controversies over these penumbral rights of 'privacy and repose.' These cases bear witness that the right of privacy which presses for recognition here is a legitimate one.[15]

The basic framework for privacy and how organizations handle a customer's data originates from the work done by the Organization for Economic Co-operation and Development ("OECD")[16] in 1980, when it published the "OECD Guidelines on the Protection of Privacy and Transborder Flows of Personal Data" (the "OECD Privacy Guidelines").[17] The OECD Privacy Guidelines included the following principles or guidelines:

1. Collection Limitation Principle;
2. Data Quality Principle;
3. Purpose Specification Principle;
4. Use Limitation Principle;
5. Security Safeguards Principle;
6. Openness Principle;

---

13 The term penumbra was first used in astronomy. *See, e.g.,* Merriam-Webster Dictionary, Penumbra, https://www.merriam-webster.com/dictionary/penumbra (last visited Jan. 21, 2021).

14 *Griswold v. Connecticut,* 381 U.S. 479 (1965).

15 *Griswold v. Connecticut*, 381 U.S. at 484-85 (case citations omitted).

16 The OECD "is an international organisation that works to build better policies for better lives. Our goal is to shape policies that foster prosperity, equality, opportunity and well-being for all." OECD, *Who we are*, https://www.oecd.org/about/ (last visited Jan. 21, 2021).

17 OECD, *OECD Guidelines of the Protection of Privacy and Transborder Flows of Personal Data,* http://www.oecd.org/sti/ieconomy/oecdguidelinesontheprotectionofprivacyandtransborderflowsofpersonaldata.htm (last visited Jan. 21, 2021).

7. Individual Participation Principle; and,
8. Accountability Principle.[18]

If these principles or guidelines look familiar, it is because every cybersecurity and data protection law and framework is built on these key principles.[19] For cybersecurity and protection of data, as defined above,[20] the "Security Safeguards Principle" is particularly relevant, providing:

> Personal data should be protected by reasonable security safeguards against such risks as loss or unauthorised access, destruction, use, modification or disclosure of data.[21]

Cyber insurance policies have been designed with this framework in mind and based the ways in which the data can be impacted by wrongful acquisition.

B. The Beginning of Cyber Insurance

Memory has a way of blurring when something began.[22] Although the emergence of the cyber insurance industry is less than twenty-five years old, much has happened, and the cyber risk area of insurance has evolved with fits and starts along the way. In the late 1990s, the insurance industry and the rest of the world were focused on the potential doom that was

---

18 *Id.*

19 *See, e.g.,* California Consumer Privacy Act, CAL. CIV. CODE §§ 1798.100-1798.199.100, *available at* http://leginfo.legislature.ca.gov/faces/codes_displayText.xhtml?division=3.&part=4.&lawCode=CIV&title=1.81.5, which has these principles contained within its language.

20 *See supra n.33.*

21 *See supra* n. 42.

22 In the Vispoli Interview, she noted the developments and work in financial services. Vispoli Interview. But Parisi told the author, "Vispoli was there at the beginning with us. Chubb along with AIG and Lloyds had the earliest cyber policies. AIG was the first carrier to flesh out the coverage and create a true cyber policy that blended liability and first party risks backed up by an underwriting team (ProTech & NetAdvantage). Marsh brought a product out called NetSecure that was supported by myself at AIG, Vispoli and a since closed Lloyds syndicate." Parisi Interview.

going to strike on January 1, 2000, when the clocks turned over and for the first time since programmers wrote code, the current date represented by two digits, or "00," was less than the year in two digits that preceded it, or "99." The impending doom and calamity were referred to as "Y2K."[23] Once Y2K was over, businesses started to see their systems being hacked by outside intruders, along with the explosion of the internet and the dot.com emergence.[24]

Today, almost every person in the United States has ready access to the internet and the tools we use to make our lives more convenient, which during the COVID-19 pandemic allowed many to work from home. But before 1995, Amazon and eBay did not exist. In the history of the internet, "[a] watershed year for the internet comes in 1995: Microsoft launches Windows 95; Amazon, Yahoo and eBay all launch; Internet Explorer launches; and Java is created, allowing for animation on websites and creating a new flurry of internet activity."[25] In 1999, the "first internet virus capable of copying and sending itself to a user's address book is discovered."[26] With the emergence of the internet, cyber insurance began to develop:

> In response to the dot-com bubble in the 1990s, cyber liability insurance gained popularity as a layer of protection for these new companies against unauthorized system access, computer viruses

---

23 "Y2K is the shorthand term for 'the year 2000.'" Clay Halton, *Y2K*, INVESTOPEDIA, https://www.investopedia.com/terms/y/y2k.asp#:~:text=Y2K%20is%20the%20shorthand%20term,the%20turn%20of%20the%20Millenium (last visited Jan. 21, 2021).

24 For perspective, the company that millions of users use every day for basic internet searches, Google, was founded on September 4, 1998. According to Alphabet Inc.'s 10-K, "Google was incorporated in California in September 1998 and re-incorporated in the State of Delaware in August 2003." United States Securities and Exchange Commission, *Form 10-K: Alphabet Inc.*, *available at* https://www.sec.gov/Archives/edgar/data/1652044/000165204419000004/goog10-kq42018.htm.

25 Jefferson Online, *From Arpanet To World Wide Web: An Internet History Timeline*, https://online.jefferson.edu/business/internet-history-timeline/#:~:text=The%20internet%20as%20we%20know,Research%20Projects%20Agency%20(ARPA) (posted on Nov. 22,2016).

26 *Id.*

> and data loss. Back then, companies had it easy compared to the cybercrime and data breaches that organizations deal with today.[27]

While some policies were issued prior to 2000,[28] such as AIG that "had a whole unit writing cyber before the end of the century,"[29] momentum started to drive the cyber insurance line in the early 2000s, when companies like AIG and Chubb[30] were starting to focus on financial institutions exposures.[31] Cyber insurance policy drafting by insurers such as Chubb and AIG[32] began in earnest, and then the tragic attack of 9/11 happened.[33] In the early 2000s, post-9/11, the insurance industry turned its attention and focus to terrorism and property coverages, and the focus on cyber insurance was not a priority.[34]

Things remained relatively quiet in the ensuing decade or so in the cyber insurance market. That started to change in the mid-2010s, because:

> [W]e've seen a massive increase in cyber attacks due to social engineering, ransomware and malware. As more and more businesses become heavily reliant on technology, these attacks continue to evolve. Because of these exposures, cyber liability

---

27 See *supra* n.4.

28 *See, e.g.*, ProWriters, *The History of Cyber Insurance: The Evolution of Cyber Products*, https://prowritersins.com/wp-content/uploads/2018/09/The-History-of-Cyber-Insurance-041316V1.pdf (last visited Jan. 21, 2021).

29 Parisi Interview.

30 Chubb, *available at* https://www.chubb.com/us-en/ (last visited Jan. 21, 2021 at 11:45AM). However, in the Parisi Interview, he made it very clear, "Chubb initially had a very narrow focus and their cyber form was primarily a variation on a theme of fidelity coverage. AIG, ACE and Lloyds had true cyber policies. Chubb eventually abandoned its fidelity cyber approach. Today's cyber insurance policies evolved from the AIG, ACE and Lloyds forms not Chubb."

31 *See supra* n.3.

32 AIG, *available at* https://www.aig.com/ (last visited Jan. 21, 2021, 11:50AM).

33 In my interview with Vispoli, she noted the impact of 9/11 on cyber insurance writing, stating, "Just after Y2K, we started drafting right after that, then 9/11 hit. The focus then was on property and terrorism, with much less focus on cyber insurance, there was not a real drive to get those products on the market. Massive issues on world peace." *Supra* n.3.

34 *Id.*

> insurance companies are being forced to develop new policies that are broad enough to cover a variety of attacks while providing certain protections against business interruption risks rather than just data breach exposure.[35]

Despite the increasingly connected world resulting in more and more exposure, the level of uptake of cyber insurance remains relatively stable. While the increase in the market for cyber insurance has grown exponentially in recent years, the total volume of premium is still relatively small compared to other common lines of insurance. For example, in 2018, property and casualty premiums by commercial line of insurance included:

- Commercial multi-peril—$41.8 billion;
- Ocean and inland marine—$27.3 billion;
- Workers' compensation—$61.2 billion.[36]

By comparison, the premium in the United States for cyber insurance was approximately $2.03 billion.[37] While expectations are that the cyber insurance market will, in the next five years, increase to $20 billion,[38] that number still is not as large as might be expected given the increased cyber threats to every organization's security. The mantra, "it is not a matter of if, it is a matter of when," remains true when it comes to cybersecurity and cyber attacks on an organization's network.

---

35 *See supra* n.4.

36 National Association of Insurance Commissioners, Report Card, (2019), *available at* https://www.naic.org/state_report_cards/report_card_tx.pdf.

37 Aon, *US Cyber Market Update, 2018 US Cyber Insurance Profits and Performance*, Thought Leadership, (June 2019), *available at* http://thoughtleadership.aon.com/Documents/201906-us-cyber-market-update.pdf.

38 *See infra n. 80.*

In 2017, the OECD[39] published a report, "Enhancing the Role of Insurance in Cyber Risk Management,"[40] which posited that "insurance coverage for cyber risk can make an important contribution to the management of cyber risk by promoting awareness about exposure to cyber losses, sharing expertise on risk management, encouraging investment in risk reduction and facilitating the response to cyber incidents."[41] According to the OECD Report, "[a]n estimated USD 9 trillion to USD 21 trillion of economic value creation globally between 2015 and 2022 could depend on the robustness of the cybersecurity environment."[42] Notwithstanding this dependency on strong cybersecurity, the uptake and limits of cyber insurance coverage do not appear to match this reliance on secure systems. For instance, in November 2013, Target[43] experienced a massive cyber security breach when its HVAC vendor was hacked.[44] Target had approximately $100 million of cyber insurance, but more than $300 million in cyber exposure.[45]

Target is not alone in facing large cyber losses and potentially not having sufficient limits. In late 2018, Marriott Bonvoy[46]announced a

---

39 The OECD is an economic group of more than 30 countries. More information about the OECD can be found at its website *available at* www.oecd.org. In 1980, in a much different environment for privacy and data securities, the OECD established seven principles for the protection of private data. All privacy frameworks have as their base those seven principles.

40 OECD, *Enhancing the Role of Insurance in Cyber Risk Management*, OECD PUBLISHING, (published Dec. 8, 2017), available at http://dx.doi.org/10.1787/9789264282148-en.

41 *Id* at p. 7.

42 *Id* at p. 11.

43 TARGET, https://www.target.com/ (last visited Jan. 21, 2021 at 12:01 PM).

44 Gregory Wallace, *HVAC vendor eyed as entry point for Target breach*, CNN BUSINESS, The Cybercrime Economy, *available at* https://money.cnn.com/2014/02/06/technology/security/target-breach-hvac/index.html (published Feb. 7, 2014).

45 Craig A. Newman, *Target's Cyber Insurance: A $100 Million Policy vs. $300 Million (So Far) In Costs*, Patterson Belknap Data Security Law Blog, *available at* https://www.pbwt.com/data-security-law-blog/targets-cyber-insurance-a-100-million-policy-vs-300-million-so-far-in-costs#:~:text=As%20of%20January%202016%2C%20Target,be%20covered%20by%20cyber%20insurance (published Apr. 7, 2016).

46 MARRIOTT, https://www.marriott.com/default.mi (last visited Jan. 21, 2021).

major breach of one of its reservation systems, with an estimate of "insurable loss from the Marriott breach . . . between $200 million and $600 million, a particularly wide range that highlights the uncertainty in these cyber risk losses."[47] Marriott had procured a large tower of cyber insurance, with "a specific cyber insurance tower that provides at least $250 million, up to as much as $350 million, of affirmative cyber insurance cover."[48]

In its first annual report, or 10-K,[49] filed after the 2013 data breach, Target disclosed:

> As previously disclosed, we experienced a data breach in which an intruder stole certain payment card and other guest information from our network (the Data Breach). Based on our investigation to date, we believe that the intruder accessed and stole payment card data from approximately 40 million credit and debit card accounts of guests who shopped at our U.S. stores between November 27 and December 15, 2013, through malware installed on our point-of-sale system in our U.S. stores. On December 15, we removed the malware from virtually all registers in our U.S. stores. Payment card data used in transactions made by 56 additional guests in the period between December 16 and December 17 was stolen prior to our disabling malware on one additional register that was disconnected from our system when we completed the initial malware removal on December 15. In addition, the intruder stole certain guest information, including names, mailing addresses, phone numbers or email addresses, for up to 70 million individuals. Our investigation of the matter is

---

47 Steve Evans, *Marriott breach cyber industry loss could be up to $600m: AIR*, REINSURANCE NEWS, *available at* https://www.reinsurancene. ws/marriott-breach-cyber-industry-loss-could-be-up-to-600m-air/ (published Dec. 18, 2018).

48 *Id.*

49 A 10-K is defined by the SEC as "a comprehensive overview of the company's business and financial condition and includes audited financial statements." Investor.gov, *Form 10-K*, U.S. SECURITIES AND EXCHANGE COMMISSION, *available at* https://www.investor.gov/introduction-investing/investing-basics/glossary/form-10-k.

> ongoing, and we are supporting law enforcement efforts to identify the responsible parties.[50]

Cyber exposures create unique challenges for the cyber insurance market, as the types of losses include a vast array of direct and indirect losses and exposures to the insured:

> Cyber risks cause not only economic losses—damages to be paid due to loss of customer data, notification costs, credit monitoring costs, regulatory expenses, extortion, business interruption, loss of intellectual property, product or service failure, and website downtime—but also intangible losses—reputation damage, customer turnover, and increased costs of customer acquisition.[51]

The economic impact of cybercrime is staggering, with cybercrimes having an enormous economic impact costing "the global economy approximately $445 billion annually."[52]

Unlike Marriott and Target, with more than a hundred million in total cyber insurance limits, according to The Council of Insurance Agents & Brokers' ("CIAB")[53] seventh biannual Cyber Insurance Market Watch Survey,[54] the average limit was $2.8 million per policy.[55] But the CIAB

---

50 United States Securities and Exchange Commission, *Form 10-K: Target Corporation* (2014), p. 17, *available at* https://www.sec.gov/Archives/edgar/data/27419/000002741914000014/tgt-20140201x10k.htm#s31B3C3D2E932BBE0CDAEB8F76ED9DFD7.

51 The American Risk and Insurance Association, ,*Cyber Insurance Supply and Performance: An Analysis of the U.S. Cyber Insurance Market*, *available at* https://www.aria.org/wp-content/uploads/2020/06/Cyber InsuranceARIA2019.pdf (published Feb. 14, 2019).

52 *Id.*

53 The CIAB is "a high-touch member-based trade association for 200 of the world's top commercial insurance and employee benefits brokerages." CIAB, *What Drives Us*, https://www.ciab.com/about/who-we-are/ (last visited Jan. 21, 2021).

54 The CIAB, *Cyber Insurance Market Watch Survey: Executive Summary* (February 2019), *available at* https://www.ciab.com/download/16876/.

55 *Id.*

survey also noted that two respondents reported clients with $500 million towers.[56]

C. The Cyber Insurance Market

The cyber insurance market has grown from an estimated market of less than $1 billion prior to 2012[57] to an estimated market in 2025 of more than $20 billion.[58] That is an incredible level of growth. As noted, the United States cyber insurance premium market was "less than $1 billion in premium in 2012"[59] and is growing exponentially.

In 2015, the National Association of Insurance Commissioners (the "NAIC")[60] "created the Cybersecurity and Identity Theft Coverage Supplement, which requires insurance companies to report financial data on cyber risk coverage."[61] The intent was to track coverages offered and assess the market. More recently, the New York Department of Financial Services ("NYDFS") issued Insurance Circular Letter Number 2 (2021)

---

56 *Id.*

57 Interview with Nate Stortzum, Vice President, M&A, Alliant Insurance Services, Inc. (Jan. 14, 2021). Finding the numbers prior to that time is a difficult proposition.

58 Statista, *Estimated value of cyber insurance premiums written worldwide in 2018, 2020 and 2025(in billion U.S. dollars)*, Statista Research Department, *available at* https://www.statista.com/statistics/976526/global-cyber-insurance-market-size/#:~:text=Global%20cyber%20insurance%20market%20size%202018%2C%202020%20and%202025&text=This%20statistic%20shows%20the%20estimated,20%20billion%20U.S.%20dollars%20globally (last visited Jan. 21, 2021)

59 Sasha Romanosky, Lillian Ablon, Andreas Kuehn, Therese Jones, *Content analysis of cyber insurance policies: how do carriers price cyber risk?*, JOURNAL OF CYBERSECURITY, Vol. 5, Issue 1, (2019), *available at* https://doi.org/10.1093/cybsec/tyz002.

60 The National Association of Insurance Commissioners is "the U.S. standard-setting and regulatory support organization created and governed by the chief insurance regulators from the 50 states, the District of Columbia and five U.S. territories." More information can be found at NAIC, www.naic.org (last visited Jan. 21, 2021).

61 The American Risk and Insurance Association, *Cyber Insurance Supply and Performance: An Analysis of the U.S. Cyber Insurance Market*, *available at* https://www.aria.org/wp-content/uploads/2020/06/CyberInsuranceARIA2019.pdf (published Feb. 14, 2019).

("Cyber Insurance Framework Letter") on February 4, 2021,[62] which outlines important steps for ensuring that property and casualty insurance companies have effective policies and procedures in place to understand and assess their cyber insurance risk

The NYDFS Cyber Insurance Framework Letter, which was directed to all authorized property/casualty insurers, recognized that there is great importance in "a sustainable and sound cyber insurance market," and that "cybercrime becomes more common and costly," The Cyber Insurance Framework was designed to help ensure the sustainable and sound market that Superintendent Lacewell referred to in the opening paragraph of the Cyber Insurance Framework Letter. Property and casualty insurers authorized in New York will have to review and "employ the practices identified [in the Framework]."

Despite the growth in the cyber insurance premiums, in a study conducted in 2014 by Aon Benfield, only approximately one-third of United States businesses had purchased some form of cyber insurance.[63] The percentage continues to remain relatively small. But the uptake and coverages for cyber insurance "vary dramatically by industry and revenue size."[64] According to a recent CyberScout[65] survey:

> This was made abundantly clear in the results of a recent survey by CyberScout, a global leader in cybersecurity and identity theft resolution services, which revealed that 76% of US small and medium-sized businesses (SMBs) experienced some form of cyberattack in 2019, but only 31% had cyber insurance coverage.[66]

---

62 https://www.dfs.ny.gov/industry_guidance/circular_letters/cl2021_02.

63 Aon Benfield, *Insurance Risk Study—Growth, Profitability, and Opportunity*, (2014), *available at* http://thoughtleadership.aonbenfield.com/documents/20140912_ab_analytics_insurance_risk_study.pdf.

64 Parisi Interview.

65 CYBERSCOUT, https://cyberscout.com/en (last visited Jan. 21, 2021)

66 Bethan Moorcraft, *US insurance market not keeping up with cyber risk needs for small businesses*, (Nov. 19, 2020), *available at* https://www.insurancebusinessmag.com/us/news/cyber/us-insurance-market-not-keeping-up-with-cyber-risk-needs-for-small-businesses-239608.aspx#:~:text=This%20was%20made%20abundantly%20clear,31%25%20had%20cyber%20insurance%20coverage.

While many small and mid-sized companies are not buying cyber insurance, hackers realize that larger organizations "can devote more attention and resources to security and employee training. This makes smaller firms and high-net-worth individuals lower-risk targets for criminals."[67]

Yet, for many small companies, cyber insurance is not something they buy. A survey of small and mid-sized companies revealed the following reasons for not purchasing cyber insurance:[68]

1. Costs too much (42%);
2. Risk profile doesn't warrant coverage (35%);
3. Risks handled sufficiently internally (27%); and,
4. Too many exclusions (17%).[69]

D. A Tale of Market Growth

In 2015, there were 119 cyber insurers.[70] Three years later, that number had nearly doubled, to 184.[71] In that short period, standalone cyber insurance nearly tripled, from $488 million to $1.126 billion.[72] While some predicted in 2002 that the global premium for cyber insurance would be $2.5 billion, the market globally did not hit that number until 2015.[73] The uptake and interest in companies for standalone cyber insurance policies did not develop as quickly as anticipated.

---

67 Insurance Information Institute and J.D. Power, *2019 Small-Business Cyber Insurance and Security Spotlight Survey*[SM], *available at* https://www.iii.org/sites/default/files/docs/pdf/small_business_cyber_wp_102319.pdf *(the "III/J.D. Power Study").*

68 *Id* at p. 6, Figure 1.

69 *Id.*

70 *Supra* n.60.

71 *Id.*

72 *Id.*

73 Martin Eling & Jingjing Zhu., *Which Insurers Write Cyber Insurance? Evidence from the U.S. Property and Casualty Insurance Industry*, 41 *J. of Insurance Issues* 22(Spring 2018), *available at* http://www.jstor.org/stable/26441191 (last visited Jan. 14, 2021)

E. Type of Coverages

In insurance, there are two types of coverage on the property and casualty side: 1) first party coverage; and 2) third party coverage. First party coverage covers the insured for its own losses, and third party coverage defends and indemnifies the insured from claims by third parties alleging the insured harmed them. The same is true for cyber liability insurance.[74] Back in the cyber insurance infancy era, the types of policies were mostly limited to coverage for third party hacks.[75] While "first party coverage was there, [it was] not as popular as the liability. Several reasons for that: the AP for the first party coverage was high, the brokers selling cyber were financial lines brokers with little experience selling first party cover and the traditional property market had yet to start excluding or being express that cyber risks were excluded."[76]

Hacks have grown substantially. From January 1, 2005 until May 31, 2020, the total number of reported data breaches was 11,762 with 1.7 billion records exposed.[77] As major breaches have been publicized and more businesses have become aware of the risks, the demand for cyber insurance has increased. 2014, "The Year of the Retail Breach,"[78] featured the famous Target hack that occurred in 2013,[79] with tens of

---

74 TECHINSURANCE, *First-party vs. third-party cyber liability insurance*, https://www.techinsurance.com/resources/first-party-vs-third-party-cyber-liability-insurance.

75 *See supra* n.52 ("Some of the first stand alone products only covered liability from a Hack of a 3rd Party").

76 Parisi Interview.

77 IDENTIFY THEFT RESOURCE CENTER, *Data Breaches*, https://www.Idtheft center.org/Data-Breaches/.

78 PROWRITERS, *The Evolution of Cyber Insurance*, Cyber Insurance Blog, https://www.idtheftcenter.org/Data-Breaches/.

79 Verdict, *Cyber Insurance: Timeline*, Comment Wire (last updated June 29, 2020), *available at* https://www.verdict.co.uk/cyber-insurance-timeline/ ("US retailer Target suffered a data breach whereby the personal data of 40 million credit card customers was compromised").

millions of its customers impacted.[80] The next year was "The Year of the Healthcare Breach."[81]

F. Evolution of Language and Coverages

Early on, cyber and network security coverages were limited in what they protected and what was offered. Today's cyber insurance offerings are more cafeteria style,[82] with the coverages including:

1. Cyber incident response;
2. Legal and regulatory costs;
3. IT security and forensic costs;
4. Crisis communications;
5. Privacy breach management;
6. Third party privacy breach management;
7. Post breach remediation;
8. Fund transfer fraud;
9. Theft of funds held in escrow;
10. Theft of personal funds;
11. Extortion;
12. Corporate identity theft;
13. Telephone hacking;
14. Push payment fraud; and,
15. Many more.[83]

---

80 Maggie McGrath, *Target Data Breach Spilled Info On As Many As 70 Million Customers*, FORBES (Jan. 10, 2014) *available at* https://www.forbes.com/sites/maggiemcgrath/2014/01/10/target-data-breach-spilled-info-on-as-many-as-70-million-customers/?sh=3477a02e79 54.

81 *Supra* n.98.

82 Cafeteria style refers to the ability of the insured to select the coverages that make up the cyber insurance policy. *See, e.g.*, CENTRAL INSURANCE, *Cyber Liability Insurance*, https://centralins.com/business-insurance/cyber-liability/ ("Other policies allow the insured to choose, cafeteria style, the types of loses that appear to be most likely.")

83 *See, e.g.*, PROWRITERS, Cyber Private enterprise, *available at* https://cdn.prowritersins.com/wp-content/uploads/2020/07/CFC-Policy-Cyber-Private-Enterprise-US-v3.0.pdf (ProWriters' cyber insurance policy sample).

The offerings differ from insurer to insurer.[84] For many insurers, cyber is not offered on a standalone basis, but as part of a package policy.[85] A package policy is a single "combination policy providing several different coverages."[86] When the policy is a package policy, the cyber coverages might be embedded within the overall policy. For example, many small businesses purchase a businessowners policy, or BOP.[87]

For many small businesses, "[s]tandalone cyber policies for small business are just not the right fit. They're simply not being purchased."[88] Instead, for small businesses, adding an endorsement to a BOP policy might make more sense:

> Adding cyber coverage to small commercial package policies via endorsement is a much better fit for a small business. The market has to meet them where they're at, versus trying to sell them something that they're never even going to consider purchasing

84 For a Beazley Management Liability Cyber Policy, *see* BEAZLEY, Beazley Execuguard—Management Liability Insurance Policy Declarations, available *at https://www.beazley.com/documents/Management%20Liability/Beazley%20ExecuGuard%20-%20London.pdf.*

85 According to a September 12, 2019, Memorandum to the Innovation and Technology (EX) Task Force from the NAIC and The Center for Insurance Policy and Research ("CIPR"), in the four years that in the four years the NAIC has collected data on cyber insurance writings, the package premiums changed from $932.6 million to $1.3 billion, while standalone premiums in the same timeframe increased from $483.2 million to $2.3 billion. NAIC, *2019 Cybersecurity Supplement Report*, *available at* https://content.naic.org/sites/default/files/inline-files/Cyber_Supplement_2019_Report_Final%20%281%29.pdf.

86 INTERNATIONAL RISK MANAGEMENT INSTITUTE, INC. ("IRMI"), *Package Policy*, definition, https://www.irmi.com/term/insurance-definitions/package-policy#:~:text=Package%20Policy%20%E2%80%94%20a%20combination%20policy,allowed%20to%20reflect%20cost%20efficiencies (last visited Jan. 21, 2021).

87 *See, e.g.,* INVESTOPEDIA, *Business Owner Policy—BOP,* https://www.investopedia.com/terms/business-owners-policy.asp#:~:text=A%20business%20owner%20policy%20(BOP,cost%20of%20the%20individual%20coverages (defining a "BOP" policy).

88 *Supra* n.87 (quoting Matt Cullina, managing director of Global Markets at CyberScout).

> based on how they typically buy insurance today. The standalone products are almost a non-starter for most small businesses.[89]

Unlike many other lines of insurance, where policies are often standardized,[90] "cyber insurance "policy language is not standardized. The types of risks covered under cyber insurance vary significantly across policies and businesses, and insurers do not always agree on what loss events are covered under those policies."[91]

Part of the reason for this is that the types of losses and risks that the various cyber insurance policies cover continue to evolve. According to one article:

> The first cyber policy was written in 1997 through AIG by Steve Haase, an agent who was recently awarded the 'Advisen Cyber Legend Award.' Though groundbreaking as the first to address cyber security, it was a third party liability policy only and was basically a 'hacker policy.'[92]

As the market continues to mature, the language and offerings likely will become somewhat more uniform. That is not the current market. Another reason why cyber policy language is not being standardized might well be the early leadership of Beazley in the cyber insurance market. Beazley is "a proud participant in the Lloyd's market, the largest and oldest insurance

---

89 *Id.*

90 Some companies draft their own policy language, but many property and casualty insurers use utilize licensing services. The two largest providers of policy language services are the Insurance Services Office, or ISO, and American Association of Insurance Services, or AAIS. Known as "ratings bureaus," subscribers to ISO or AAIS use policy language and rates submitted by these ratings bureaus. More information about ISO can be found at VERISK, https://www.verisk.com/insurance/brands/iso/ (last visited Jan. 21, 2021) and more information about AAIS can be found at AAIS, https://aaisonline.com/ (last visited Jan. 21, 2021).

91 Andrew Granato and Andy Polacek, *The Growth and Challenges of Cyber Insurance*, Chicago Fed Letter, No. 426 (2019), *available at* https://www.chicagofed.org/publications/chicago-fed-letter/2019/426.

92 Brian D. Brown, *The Ever-Evolving Nature of Cyber Coverage*, INSURANCE JOURNAL (Sept. 22, 2014) *available at* https://www.insurancejournal.com/magazines/mag-features/2014/09/22/340633.htm.

market in the world."[93] Lloyd's syndicates writing United States risks are subject to oversight, but generally have more flexibility in policy language and pricing.

In addition, insurance policies are generally written on an admitted basis or surplus lines basis. Admitted insurers must submit policy forms and rates with the insurance regulators in each state where they do business, except for very large commercial insureds. On the other hand, surplus lines insurers, which include Lloyd's syndicates, generally have more flexibility in policy language and have less regulation by the individual state:

> [W]here the licensed insurers will not accept a risk because it does not meet their internally established guidelines. The risk may be too big, too unusual or substandard. In these cases, a specially licensed producer called a surplus line producer gets involved. Their special surplus line license allows them to procure a policy for you from an insurer that is not licensed in your state.
>
> Since this insurer is not licensed in your state, they are not regulated by your state's Department of Insurance in the same way licensed insurers are regulated (they are, however, regulated in the state or country where they are domiciled or located). Since they are not strictly regulated by your state, they are generally free from the form or rate regulations imposed on licensed insurers. This gives them the freedom to maintain broader internal guidelines for accepting risks. They have more flexibility to design and price their policies and can, therefore, accept risks that licensed insurers will not.[94]

In 2018, according to an NAIC Memorandum submitted by the NAIC and the Center for Insurance Policy and Research ("CIPR"), the total admitted

---

93 BEAZLEY, *Who we are*, https://www.beazley.com/who-we-are (last visited Jan. 21, 2021).

94 SURPLUS LINES ASSOCIATION OF ILLINOIS, *Frequently Asked Questions (FAQs): What is surplus lines insurance?*, https://www.slai.org/faq/insured_06.html.

written premium for standalone and package cyber policies combined was $2.0 billion, while the total for surplus lines was $1.6 billion.[95]

G. The Rise of Ransomware

In recent years, one of the biggest kinds of cyber attack is "[r]ansomware. Extortionists take advantage of Bitcoin and other crypto-currencies that allow ransom demands to be made and paid anonymously."[96] Bitcoin[97] permits the hackers to remain anonymous and obtain bitcoin.

Recently, the Indiana Supreme Court heard oral arguments in the case, *G&G Oil Co. of Indiana v. Continental Western Insurance Co.*,[98] involving a multi-peril commercial policy that included a computer fraud provision as part of the commercial crime coverage part. According to the Court of Appeals decision:

> A hijacker had gained access to G&G's computer network, encrypted its servers and most workstations, and password protected its drives. The hacker demanded a ransom, and in exchange for payment, agreed to send G&G the passwords and restore its control over its computer servers.[99]

The hijackers of G&G's computers demanded payment in Bitcoin, first demanding three coins and then demanding an additional coin:

> The hijacker demanded payment in bitcoin. G&G made the payment demanded, but the hijacker refused to restore G&G's control over its computer servers and demanded additional bitcoin. Ultimately, G&G paid $34,477.50 for the four bitcoins it

---

95 *Supra* n.105.

96 *Supra* n.88, p. 4.

97 Bitcoin is a form of cryptocurrency that it describes as "an innovative payment network and a new kind of money." BITCOIN, https:// bitcoin.org/en/ (last visited Jan. 21, 2021).

98 *G&G Oil Co. of Ind. V. Cont'l W. Ins. Co.*, 145 N.E.3d 842 (Ind. Ct. App. 2020), *available at* https://www.in.gov/judiciary/opinions/pdf/03312001 pdm.pdf.

99 *Id* at para. 5.

> sent to the hijacker. After receiving the fourth bitcoin, the hacker gave G&G the passwords enabling it to decrypt its computers and regain access to its servers.[100]

At issue in the Indiana Supreme Court was whether the payment of ransom outlined above satisfied the wording of the policy for computer fraud, that the policy would pay for losses and damages "resulting directly from the use of any computer to fraudulently cause a transfer of that property from inside the 'premises' or 'banking premises.'"[101]

Depending on the timing of the ransomware demand and the payment of the ransom by the impacted organization, the price of the Bitcoin can vary significantly.[102] Ransomware will continue to grow as a means by which hackers can obtain financial reward for attacking vulnerable networks. Insureds will continue to need insurance protecting them against these attacks.

H. Conclusion

While the market for cyber insurance is expected to increase to $20.4 billion by 2025,[103] there are concerns that the continued small number of insureds buying large coverages exposes this sector of the insurance industry to major losses. According to a recent Harvard Business Review article,[104] "[w]ith around 250 companies buying at least $200 million in

---

100 *Id* at para. 6.

101 *Id* at para. 4.

102 A historical pricing by day of Bitcoin can be found at YAHOO! FINANCE, *Bitcoin USD*, *available at* https://finance.yahoo.com/quote/BTC-USD/history/. For example, the chart shows that on January 17, 2021, Bitcoin closed at $36,272.46. On December 17, 2020, it was $22,805.16. During that one month period, it closed at over $40,000 on two days.

103 James Coker, *Cyber Insurance Market Expected to Surge in 2021*, INFO SECURITY, https://www.infosecurity-magazine.com/news/cyber-insurance-market-surge-2021/.

104 Tom Johansmeyer, *Cybersecurity Insurance Has a Big Problem*, Harvard Business Review, Strategy, (Jan. 11, 2021), *available at* https://hbr.org/2021/01/cybersecurity-insurance-has-a-big-problem.

protection, it would only take five insured losses of a bit more than that amount to wipe out an entire year's premium."[105]

As is discussed in much more detail in Chapter 9,[106] companies have increasingly included cyber risk and exposures in their enterprise risk management programs.

Cyber insurance has grown from a "nice to have" to, in many cases, "a must have" part of a risk management portfolio as the attacks on company computer systems increase and the costs of the attacks and intrusions multiply. Yet, as this chapter makes clear, this "must have" part of an effective risk management program varies significantly across the economy and penetration varies widely among businesses.

---

105 *Id.*

106 *See* Chapter 9, Risk Management for Private and Publicly Traded Companies.

Chapter 2

Overview of Types of Insurance Coverage Available for Cyber Risks*

Cyber insurance can provide much needed tactical and financial support to firms confronted with a cyber or privacy incident. This support is particularly valuable for small and midsized firms that may not be well equipped to respond to or survive such a mishap.

Scores of insurers offer some type of coverage for cyber risks for data breaches and other incidents. Recent policy iterations offer protection against a wide range of cyber and privacy threats including cyber extortion, social engineering, senior executive losses, corporate identity theft, "bricking" of corporate electronic devices, and contingent business interruption. Some of today's most innovative new coverages are discussed in more detail in this chapter.

But like cyber and privacy risks themselves, cyber coverage is constantly changing and evolving as underwriters endeavor to address new and pressing cyber and privacy exposures and legal and regulatory requirements. Comparing policies and selecting appropriate cyber coverage is rarely straightforward given the lack of policy standardization and the complex nature of data risks.

A. The Current Market

More than 150 insurers currently sell cyber coverage, and each has its own policy form, utilizing its own unique policy language. This creates challenges for companies trying to compare one cyber insurance policy with another. For example, two forms may use the same terms, such as "security event" or "regulatory investigation," but they will define those terms differently, creating significant differences in the scope of coverage provided.

Coverage differences across policies can be substantial and may include variations in the following:

---

* By Dana Post and Judy Selby.

- The triggering of notice requirements.
- Scope of coverage, including for regulatory exposures.
- Aggregate policy limits and sub-limits.
- Self-insured retentions.
- Coverage periods, including retroactive coverage.

The lack of standardization means that potential insureds should proactively ensure that they purchase cyber policies appropriate for their specific cyber risk profile. For example, if a company entrusts data to third parties, it will want coverage for that third-party risk. If it maintains an active social media presence, it will want media liability coverage. And as more jurisdictions across the globe enact cyber security and data-handling practices regulations, obtaining comprehensive coverage for a wide variety of regulatory violations (not just security breaches) and fines is increasingly important for many companies. Given the complexities of today's cyber insurance market, entities should work with knowledgeable insurance professionals to assist with procurement of appropriate coverage.

Currently there is a relative dearth of judicial decisions interpreting and applying cyber-specific policies. However, over the next couple of years, the pace of judicial decisions under cyber policies will likely increase markedly and provide additional guidance on coverage language.

B. Cyber Insurance Policies

Unlike other types of insurance policies, cyber insurance policies typically provide both first-party and third-party coverages. Generally, a cyber policy's first-party coverage applies to costs incurred by the insured itself when responding to a covered cyber event. Third-party coverage protects companies against liability to others stemming from or related to a cyber incident.

The main types of coverage discussed in this chapter are typically present in a stand-alone cyber policy. However, certain of these coverages may also be found as endorsements or additional coverages in certain types of business policies. Every potential insured must be careful to examine the full scope of coverages that are included in each type of policy, including optional endorsements.

1. *First-Party Coverage*

Various events may trigger first-party coverage including the theft or disclosure of protected information, malicious destruction of data, accidental damage to data, IT system failure, cyber extortion, viruses, and malware.

First-party coverage typically is available for the following:

- Legal and forensic services following a data breach or other covered event.
- Data breach notification costs.
- Call center costs.
- Business interruption.
- Restoration of the insured's data.
- Public relations and crisis management costs.
- Ransom payments.

In the event of a covered event, first-party cyber insurance typically provides for the retention of an attorney or other professional, a so-called breach coach, to coordinate the insured's cyber incident response. An experienced coach can build an effective team of specialists and efficiently guide companies through the forensic, regulatory, public relations, and legal issues arising from a security incident.

Given the complexities of the various US and global laws governing data breach notification, the increasing demands of regulators, and the scrutiny of the media and class action bar, coverage for the retention of a skilled breach coach is perhaps the greatest benefit of cyber insurance. By retaining an attorney to quarterback the incident response process, the insured will also have a better chance of protecting post-incident documents and communications from discovery in the event of subsequent litigation.

2. *Third-Party Coverage*

Third-party coverage typically applies to the following:

- Costs to defend consumer class action and other lawsuits.
- Credit card issuer lawsuits following a credit card data breach.

- Regulatory investigations and fines.
- Lawsuits alleging defamation or slander from the insured's website content.
- Claims based on the insured's transmission of virus to third parties.

Third-party coverage can be implicated in various ways, including by claims against the insured for breach of privacy, misuse of personal data, or the transmission of malicious content.

Third-party coverage generally covers legal defense costs, settlements, or damages the insured must pay after a breach, and electronic media liability, including infringement of copyright, domain name and trade names on an internet site, and regulatory fines and penalties.

3. Newer Cyber Insurance Coverages

Fortunately for today's businesses, recent iterations of cyber policies go far beyond data breach coverage and offer protection against a wide range of the most vexing cyber threats affecting companies in every business sector. Some key cyber exposures for which coverage may be available include:

- **Bricking.** Although cyber policies typically exclude coverage for damage to tangible property, some carriers have introduced endorsements that are triggered when a hacking event causes the "bricking" (loss of use or functionality) of the insured's computer hardware or electronic equipment by maliciously reprograming the software installed on that hardware or equipment. Bricking coverage applies to the costs to repair or replace the affected hardware or equipment when it would cost more to reinstall software.
- **Consequential Reputational Loss**. This coverage indemnifies the insured for lost income during a defined period of time (for example, 30 days) following a covered information security or privacy event.
- **Contingent Business Interruption**. Many insurers offer coverage for loss of business income, forensic expenses, and extra expenses caused by an unintentional and unplanned interruption of computer systems operated by a third party that contractually

provides necessary products or services to the insured. This coverage is especially valuable for companies operating in today's digital and interconnected economy.

- **Corporate Identity Theft Coverage.** This may be available for losses incurred as a result of fraudulent use of the company's electronic identity, including the establishment of credit in the company's name, electronic signing of contracts, and the creation of a website designed to impersonate the company.
- **Invoice Manipulation Loss.** At least two insurers provide coverage to companies that cannot collect payment for their goods and services as a result of an "invoice manipulation loss." Invoice manipulation means the release or distribution of a fraudulent invoice or payment instruction resulting from a security or privacy breach. The policies generally cover the insured's net cost to provide the goods or services, exclusive of profits.
- **Loss Adjustment Costs**. Calculating the costs associated with a system damage or business interruption insurance claim can be complicated, particularly when costs must be allocated to an uninsured waiting period designated in the policy form. Some cyber carriers offer coverage for the cost to retain professionals, such as forensic accountants, to assist the insured in the calculation of its financial loss.
- **Management Liability**. Cyber coverage may be available for directors, officers, managers, and business entities that are faced with cyber liability in connection with governance or management activities.
- **Property Damage and Bodily Injury**. At least one carrier currently offers coverage if a cyberattack causes damage to property of the insured or third parties, or injury to the insured's customers or other third parties.
- **Senior Executive Losses**. At least one insurer provides coverage for identity theft and theft of funds from executive officers' personal bank accounts resulting from a third-party breach of the company's network security.
- **Social Engineering**. Some insurers offer coverage under cyber policies for email phishing or other attacks that induce an insured to transfer company funds to unintended third parties. This often occurs when the insured company's employee receives a

fraudulent email instruction to change bank wire instructions for payment. These coverages frequently are available as endorsements to Cyber, Commercial Crime, or Fidelity policies. Endorsement may be titled "Social Engineering," "Fraudulent Funds Transfer," "Fraudulent Impersonation," "Business Email Compromise," or something conveying a similar meaning.

- **Telephone Hacking**. Companies may be able to obtain coverage for losses resulting from the hacking of their telephone system, including reimbursement of costs for unauthorized calls and use of the company's bandwidth.

The coverages described above may not be available from all insurers, and not all insureds will qualify for all types of coverage. In addition, some coverages may be subject to sub-limits and important conditions, such as requiring the insured to obtain the insurer's consent before expending funds in connection with an event covered by the policy.

Even if a carrier does not proactively offer any of these emerging coverages, organizations should request any desired coverage from the insurer and notify the insurer that competitors offer the coverage.

4. Regulatory Coverage

Cyber insurance policies typically provide broad coverages for a wide range of cyber and privacy risks, but that doesn't mean that every claim involving information misuse will be covered under every policy. As new and comprehensive privacy and cyber regulations proliferate across the globe, corporations carefully must consider whether their cyber insurance policies cover claims for regulatory investigations, privacy litigation, fines, and penalties. The costs associated with these items can be high.

The scope of personal information covered by emerging privacy laws has expanded significantly beyond the limited categories of personally identifiable information covered by early data breach notification laws and may now include broad categories of information such as the following:

- Browsing history.
- Biometric information.
- Geolocation information.
- Audio, visual, thermal, and olfactory information.

For example, with some enumerated exceptions, the California Consumer Privacy Act (CCPA)[1] protects "personal information," defined to include 11 separate categories of information that directly or indirectly:

- Identifies, relates to, or describes a particular consumer or household.
- Is reasonably capable of being associated with or could reasonably be linked to a particular consumer or household.

In addition, more recent United States privacy laws govern how covered entities treat protected information throughout its entire lifecycle, from collection or creation, through use, retention, security, and ultimate disposition. They may create disclosure obligations concerning the entity's information-related practices and actionable rights for affected individuals. Some laws require companies to create certain roles such as a data protection officer or a chief information security officer, and establish requirements concerning corporate board oversight. They also may mandate creation of specific internal or publicly-facing written policies and procedures. In addition to empowering enforcement by a state attorney general or other regulatory agency, these new laws and regulations sometimes provide a private right of action to affected individuals, pursuant to which they can seek actual and statutory damages.

Organizations handling non-U.S. personal information may also be subject to other countries' privacy laws. For example, the EU's General Data Protection Regulation (Regulation (EU) 2016/679) (GDPR) may apply to US organizations handling EU personal information. The applicability and scope of the GDPR is quite broad and organizations may face costs or liability for numerous violations beyond traditional data breaches including failure to do the following:

- Maintain records of processing activities (Article 30, GDPR).
- Conduct a data protection impact assessment (Article 35, GDPR).
- Enter into valid data processing contracts (Article 28, GDPR).
- Appoint a data protection officer (Article 37, GDPR).

---

1 Cal. Civ. Code § 1798.140(o)(1)(A) to (K).

Moreover, the GDPR contemplates three different types of personal data breach:

- A confidentiality breach, which involves disclosure of personal data.
- An availability breach, where personal data cannot be accessed or is destroyed.
- An integrity breach, where there is an unauthorized or accidental alteration of personal data.

Cyber insurance policies may or may not provide coverage for each of these incidents. Most cyber insurance policies provide excellent first, third-party, and regulatory coverage for a confidentiality data breach. Depending on the cause of an availability breach, such as a ransomware or a denial of service (DDoS) attack, coverage is generally available. Some insurers provide coverage for an integrity breach, but organizations must carefully examine the policy language to understand the scope of this coverage.

Achieving and maintaining compliance with complex and constantly evolving privacy and security obligations can create both budgetary and operational challenges for many entities. Mistakes and mishaps are inevitable, even for those entities that fully embrace their obligations in good faith. Incidents can arise when entities act negligently or recklessly, or if they intentionally elect not to comply with legal requirements.

This backdrop is leading to a higher frequency of regulatory actions and private lawsuits against covered entities that are quite different from "typical" data breach claims. How any given cyber insurance policy will respond to claims arising out of these information misuse claims requires a thoughtful analysis of the precise facts giving rise to the claim, the terms of the policy at issue, and the applicable law.

(a) Regulatory Coverage Checklist

When considering whether any given claim falls within a cyber insurance policy's regulatory coverage, the following issues should be considered:

- **Scope of Coverage**
  - Is coverage limited to only security events or breach/disclosure incidents, or is coverage triggered by, for example, claims arising out of an actual, alleged, or suspected breach of statutes or regulations governing the confidentiality, access, control, and use of protected or confidential information?
  - Does the policy apply to claims arising out of an alleged violation of a privacy or cyber law anywhere in the world or is coverage limited to specific laws or geographic areas?
  - Does the policy limit coverage to only specified violations of certain laws? For example, a policy may provide coverage for violations of the GDPR or CCPA, but limit that coverage to violations of only certain parts of those laws such as their information security provisions.
- **Scope of Covered Information**
  - The policy may limit the scope of information for which coverage is provided. For example, the policy may only apply to information specified in breach notification laws, or it may cover information that is the subject of any law or regulation related to information security or privacy.
- **Equitable Relief**
  - Does the claim arise out of a demand for equitable or injunctive relief?
  - Consider how the policy defines terms like "loss" or "damages."
  - Does the policy expressly preclude coverage for costs to establish or improve privacy or security practices?
  - Are costs for audit, reporting, and compliance specifically excluded?
- **Compensatory Damages**
  - Does the policy limit coverage to "compensatory" damages? If so, statutory damages that do not require the calculation of any actual damages to the claimant may not be covered.

5. *Coverage for Fines and Penalties*

Although cyber policies typically provide coverage for regulatory fines and penalties, the policy may limit covered fines to those arising only from certain types of regulatory violations. Thus, if only a data breach or a security event trigger a policy's regulatory coverage, the policy likely will not cover a fine arising out of some different type of noncompliance claim. In addition, some cyber policies provide that fines and penalties are insurable only if the law in the jurisdiction issuing the regulation allows for such coverage.

State law governs insurance disputes and the substantive laws vary significantly from state-to-state. Organizations should work with their counsel to examine the best forum and law for litigating coverage disputes and negotiate to have that choice of law included in the policy. Even if a policy contains no choice of law clause, organizations should negotiate to include this clause in their favor.

Organizations must also examine whether the policy provides coverage for fines that are considered punitive under the law governing the policy. Many jurisdictions preclude coverage for punitive damages on public policy grounds. For global organizations, GDPR Article 83 requires supervisory authorities to ensure that administrative fines imposed are effective, proportionate, and dissuasive. Insurers may argue that the imposition of a fine under Article 83 is punitive in nature depending on the facts.

(a) Fines and Penalties Coverage Checklist

When considering whether a cyber insurance policy covers fines and penalties, the following issues should be considered:

- Does the policy expressly provide coverage for fines and penalties?
- Consider the applicable law:
  - Does the policy contain a choice of law provision?
  - Is coverage for fines and penalties dependent on the law of a specific jurisdiction, such as the fining jurisdiction, the jurisdiction that most favors coverage, or the jurisdiction with a substantial relationship to the insured, the insurer, the policy, or the claim?

- Is the fine or penalty at issue punitive in nature?
    - If so, does the applicable law preclude coverage, even if the liability is vicarious?
- Does the claim arise out of intentional acts?
    - Does an intentional acts exclusion apply?
    - Is there an exclusion for knowing or willful violations of statutes?
    - Consider the application of imputation of knowledge provisions.
    - Does the applicable law prohibit coverage for intentional or non-fortuitous acts?

6. *Claims-Made and Retroactive Coverage*

Unlike traditional commercial insurance policies, which are available on either a claims-made or occurrence-based coverage structure, cyber coverage is currently only available on a claims-made basis. Under a claims-made policy, the trigger for coverage is a claim made against the policy holder during the policy period.

Because many cyber intrusions go undetected for months or even years, businesses should consider that they may already have an undetected data breach when they apply for coverage and attempt to secure coverage that might apply to any undetected events. In some cases, insurers may be willing to provide retroactive coverage for up to two years before writing the policy. However, whether or not an insurer will offer retroactive coverage is highly dependent on the insurer and the potential insured's unique risk profile.

7. *Typical Exclusions*

Because the primary purpose of cyber insurance is to protect against the loss of intangible data and the exposure of personal information, cyber policies generally exclude damages arising out of the following categories:

- Bodily injury.
- Property damage.

Cyber policies also typically exclude coverage for claims arising out of various violation categories, such as:

- Employment practices.
- Pollution.
- Antitrust violations.
- Employment Retirement Income Security Act (ERISA) violations.
- Telephone Consumer Protection Act violations.

In addition, policies may exclude coverage for broader conduct including:

- Directors' and officers' intentional acts, regardless of whether they acted outside the scope of their employment and intended to harm the company.
- Unlawfully collecting personally identifiable non-public information.
- Negligent information security practices, such as failing to install software patches for known software vulnerabilities.

Policies may also exclude coverage for incidents involving payment card data unless the business purchases an additional rider.

8. *Conclusion*

Cyber and privacy risks are increasing and securing a cyber policy that provides responsive coverage is an important part of a business's risk management program. However, comparing and selecting cyber coverage may be challenging given the lack of policy standardization and the complex nature of cyber and privacy risks. The lack of standardization means that companies should take steps to ensure that they purchase cyber policies appropriate for their specific cyber risk profile appetite.

Chapter 3

Potential Overlapping Coverage Between Cyber Policies and Other Business and Crime Policies*

Cybercrime, hacking, system incursion, and other sophisticated schemes dominate the news cycle, affecting not only businesses as a whole, but also individual consumers. Former FBI Director Robert Mueller is credited with a statement that the FBI and other governmental agencies often repeat to describe our world today: "there are only two types of companies: those that have been hacked and those that will be."[1] For that reason, cybercrime, and the potential insurance coverage that may be available to indemnify for loss sustained from cybercrime, are important subjects.

Some traditional commercial insurance policies may provide coverage for some limited cyber-related losses and costs. Additionally, as cyber insurance has increased in popularity, various types of business policies and commercial crime policies have started to include certain specific coverage for defined and limited cyber-related losses. As the cyber insurance market continues to develop, it is important for all businesses to try to learn as much as possible about what types of insurance policies can best serve their individual needs. Cyber coverage can be included in business policies in a number of ways, some unexpected.

Businesses should not rely solely on traditional business insurance policies for primary coverage for extensive cyber losses, however. While some businesses have successfully made claims on traditional business policies, relying on such policies for so-called "silent cyber" or "non-affirmative cyber" coverage, for a cyber or privacy event, the chance of recovery for broad losses is uncertain. This chapter reviews a broad variety

---

* By Toni Scott Reed, Dana Post, and Judy Selby.

1 Robert S. Mueller, III, Director, Federal Bureau of Investigation, RSA Cyber Security Conference in San Francisco (Mar. 1, 2012), http://www.fbi.gov/news/speeches/combating-threats-in-the-cyber-world-outsmarting-terrorists-hackers-and-spies.

of business policies and specialty policies that may include some overlapping coverage for cyber losses with stand-alone cyber policies.

A. Traditional Business Policies

1. General Commercial Liability (CGL) Policies

Most businesses purchase commercial general liability (CGL) insurance to cover potential liability to third parties, and that is the first place businesses historically looked for coverage in the event of a cybercrime.[2] Although CGL policies may differ, most are based on standard policies promulgated by the Insurance Services Office, Inc. ("ISO").[3] CGL policies provide coverage for several areas of risk, but arguably only Coverage A and Coverage B could potentially cover cybercrime losses.[4]

Coverage A addresses liability for "bodily injury" or "property damage" caused by an "occurrence" defined as an "accident."[5] Since "bodily injury" does not typically result from cybercrime, coverage most often depends on how courts interpret "property damage." A discussion of the range of court opinions on "property damage," as well as a discussion on whether loss of electronic or software programs can be "property damage," is included later.

Coverage B in a standard CGL policy provides coverage for "personal and advertising injury."[6] As discussed in other chapters, cybercrime may result in the exposure and publication of personal information, which may lead to litigation involving privacy claims and of claims under breach notification statutes and regulations. Coverage under this provision often

---

2 Lance Bonner, *Note: Cyber Risk: How the 2011 Sony Data Breach and the Need for Cyber Risk Insurance Policies Should Direct the Federal Response to Rising Data Breaches*, 40 Wash. U. J.L. & Pol'y 257, 264 (2012) (quoting Verizon RISK Team, 2011 Data Breach Investigation Report (2011), *available at* http://www.verizonbusiness.com/resources/ reports/rp_data-breach-investigations-report-2011_en_xg.pdf).

3 *Id.* at 270.

4 *Id.*; Paul E.B. Glad et al., *Types of Liability Coverage*, 3 NEW APPLEMAN LAW OF LIABILITY INSURANCE § 16.02 (2014).

5 Glad, *supra* note 4, § 16.02.

6 *Id.*

depends on whether there has been a "publication" that violates the claimant's "right of privacy," since those two terms are not defined in standard-form ISO policies.[7] In 2014, a New York trial court ruled that under the "personal and advertising injury" provision of the CGL policy it issued to Sony Corp. of America and Sony Computer Entertainment America, an insurer had no duty to defend the insured in litigation resulting from the hacking of Sony's PlayStation online services.[8] There, the court ruled that to be covered, the publication of data accessed in the breach should have been performed by the insured and not the hackers.[9] By contrast, in 2013, a federal judge in California ruled that an insurer had a duty to defend under the personal and advertising provision of a CGL policy for a data breach involving hospital records of approximately 20,000 patients.[10] In that case, the publisher of confidential data was a job applicant of a technology consultant who was covered under the policy.[11] These cases clearly illustrate that, as this concept and these claims continue to develop, so too will the approaches to coverage taken by the various courts across the country.

Definitions play a large role in interpretation of these policies in the cyber arena. Coverage A typically defines property damage as a physical injury to or the loss of use of tangible property, and many policies specify that electronic data is not tangible property. Most policies also exclude damage to the insured's own property. Thus, the definitions in traditional commercial policies could potentially exclude losses associated with a cyber incident concerning either or both:

- Electronic data; or

---

7 Roberta D. Anderson, *Viruses, Trojans, and Spyware, Oh My! The Yellow Brick Road to Coverage in the Land of Internet Oz*, 49 TORT & INS. L.J. 529, 545 (Winter 2014) [hereinafter Anderson, *Viruses*].

8 Young Ha, *N.Y. Court: Zurich Not Obligated to Defend Sony Units in Data Breach Litigation*, INS. J. (Mar. 17, 2014), http://www.insurancejournal.com/news/east/2014/03/17/323551.htm.

9 *Id.*

10 *Id.*

11 Judy Selby, *California Court Finds Advertising Injury Coverage is Triggered by Medical Information Data Breach*, LEXOLOGY.COM (Oct. 16, 2013), http://www.lexology.com/library/detail.aspx?g=9caa57e9-7262-45c1- a01a-6706a4fd006a.

- Damage, such as through loss or hacking, to the insured's own property.

Despite these limitations, some businesses have successfully made claims for cyber-related losses under their traditional policies, particularly under Coverage B. However, even if some coverage is available under traditional policies, it may not be broad enough to include both the liability and most of the response costs associated with cyber incidents. In addition, to clarify that a policy excludes coverage for data breaches, insurers have added new endorsements to these policies that specifically exclude liability arising out of the disclosure of confidential or personal information

(a) Non-Cyber Policy Exclusions

Recognizing the potential exposure on cyber losses, insurers have taken action to limit potential cyber coverage under traditional insurance policies. For example, two UK insurance industry associations released new cyber exclusions to eliminate or substantially limit potential coverage for cyber-related claims

In November 2019, the Lloyd's Market Association issued two exclusions for property policies. The first, LMA 5400, excludes coverage for any loss arising out of a cyber act or a cyber incident, but contains a carve out for ensuing fire or explosion from a cyber incident only. All other resultant damage from a cyber act or incident is excluded. However, coverage for the cost of repair or replacement of damaged data processing media and the cost of copying data from backups or from originals of a previous generation exists.

The second exclusion, LMA 5401, is an absolute exclusion that bars coverage for both malicious cyber acts and non-malicious cyber incidents, with no carve out. There is no coverage for repair or replacement of data or for data loss caused by any physical peril.

The International Underwriting Association of London also released two exclusions, an absolute (Cyber Loss Absolute Exclusion Clause, IUA 01-081) and a limited cyber loss exclusion (IUA 09-082).

Individual insurers are also taking steps to address silent cyber exposures. Allianz and AIG, for example, announced initiatives to either affirmatively cover or exclude physical and non-physical cyber exposures across traditional policies.

(b) ISO Endorsements

The Insurance Services Office (ISO) periodically publishes standard insurance policy forms that insurers use widely. Where not used in their entirety, insurers often adopt the forms with substantial standardization.

As insurers started adding exclusions to their traditional commercial policies, ISO has approved new forms for optional endorsements that exclude coverage for personal and advertising injury claims arising from the access to or disclosure of confidential information. Specifically:

- CG 21 08 05 14 (Exclusion: Access Or Disclosure Of Confidential Or Personal Information (Coverage B Only)).
  This endorsement excludes coverage for personal and advertising injury arising out of any access to or disclosure of confidential or personal information even if the insured claims damages for:
  - notification costs;
  - credit monitoring expenses;
  - forensic investigation expenses;
  - public relations expenses; and
  - any other loss, cost, or expense incurred due to the access to or disclosure of personal information.
- CG 21 07 05 14 (Exclusion: Access Or Disclosure Of Confidential Or Personal Information And Data-Related Liability: Limited Bodily Injury Exception Not Included).
  This endorsement is similar to CG 21 08 05 14, but it also excludes coverage for bodily injury and property damage arising out of any access to or disclosure of confidential or personal information or the loss of or damage to electronic data.
- CG 21 06 05 14 (Exclusion: Access Or Disclosure Of Confidential Or Personal Information And Data-Related Liability: With Bodily Injury Exception).
  This endorsement is similar to CG 21 07 05 14, except that bodily injury arising out of the loss of or damage to electronic data is not excluded.

Insurers have widely adopted these endorsements since ISO made them available in 2014.

(c) Typical Cyber-Related Coverage Disputes Under CGL Policies

Courts have issued conflicting decisions when determining whether CGL policies cover data breach losses and other cyber incidents. These cases often turn on variations in or interpretations of policy language or state law, and they highlight the risks that businesses take if they rely solely on CGL policies to cover cybersecurity events.

i. Coverage A Disputes

The standard Coverage A language protects against liability for property damage defined as "physical injury to tangible property . . . or loss of use of tangible property that is not physically injured." Insurers frequently argue against coverage for electronic data loss because data does not constitute tangible property.

In *Eyeblaster, Inc. v. Federal Insurance, Co.*,[12] for example, Eyeblaster sought coverage after a computer user sued Eyeblaster for allegedly infecting the user's computer with a spyware program. The plaintiff alleged that the spyware caused his computer to freeze up and lose data. The insurer denied coverage citing, among other things, policy language excluding "data" from the tangible property definition. The *Eyeblaster* court disagreed with the insurer and found that plaintiff's allegations regarding the loss of his computer, rather than the data, constituted tangible property under the policy.[13]

Other courts have also allowed policyholders to recover for electronic data losses under Coverage A when allegations in the complaint against the policyholder focus on physical damage to the computer.[14] However, most courts have held that lost data itself cannot constitute tangible property.[15]

---

12 613 F.3d 797, 801 (8th Cir. 2010).

13 *Id.* at 800-02.

14 State Auto Prop. & Cas. Ins. Co. v. Midwest Comput. & More, 147 F. Supp. 2d 1113, 1116 (W.D. Okla. 2001) ("Because a computer clearly is tangible property, an alleged loss of use of computers constitutes 'property damage.'").

15 American Online, Inc. v. St. Paul Mercury Ins. Co., 347 F.3d 89, 95 (4th Cir. 2003) (data on a hard drive is "abstract and intangible" and cannot be damage to "tangible property")); *Liberty Corp. Capital Ltd. v. Security Safe Outlet,*

ii. Coverage B Disputes

Standard Coverage B policies define personal and advertising injury as an "oral or written publication, in any manner, of material that violates a person's right to privacy." Insureds relying on Coverage B for cyber insurance may face challenges from insurers about the meaning of "publication" including, for example:

- The number of people able to access the data for publication to have occurred.
- Whether a third party must view the data for it to be published.
- Whether the insured or a third party must do the publishing.

Courts have provided conflicting answers on these questions. In *Recall Total Information Management v. Federal Insurance Co.*, for example, Recall retained a third party that lost 130 IBM data tapes with unencrypted personal information for past and present IBM employees.[16] No third party accessed the personal information on the tapes for an improper purpose. IBM incurred $6 million in costs and expenses resulting from the lost tapes and settled with Recall for the full amount of the loss. Recall pursued CGL coverage but the insurers denied the claim.

The insurance policy in *Recall* defined personal injury as "electronic, oral, written, or other publication of material that . . . violates a person's right to privacy."[17] The *Recall* court found that the policy did not cover the data breach because no third party accessed the information on the tapes and therefore no publication occurred.[18]

By contrast, in *Travelers Indemnity Co. of America v. Portal Healthcare Solutions, LLC*,[19] the United States Court of Appeals for the Fourth Circuit affirmed CGL coverage when a medical records vendor caused confidential information to be released on the internet. The court

---

Inc., 937 F. Supp. 2d 891, 901 (E.D. Ky. 2013) (customer email addresses excluded from definition of tangible property), *aff'd*, 577 F. App'x. 399 (6th Cir. 2014)).

16 83 A.3d 664 (Conn. App. Ct. 2014), *aff'd*, 115 A.3d 458 (Conn. 2015).

17 83 A.3d at 462-63.

18 *Id.*

19 644 F. App'x. 245 (4th Cir. 2016).

stated that the presence of information online constitutes a publication, regardless of whether anyone accesses or views it.[20]

Similarly, in *Brighton Collectibles v. Lloyd's London*,[21] the insured sought coverage to defend a putative class action that alleged that the insured collected and sold customers' personal information in violation of California's Song-Beverly Credit Card Act. The insured argued that the claim triggered its personal injury coverage caused by an offense arising out of Brighton's business, defined to include the "[o]ral or written publication of material that violates a person's right of privacy."[22]

The Ninth Circuit rejected the insurer's assertion that the policies' exclusions for "advertising, publishing, broadcasting or telecasting done by or for" the insured barred coverage. The court stated that the word "publishing" in the coverage exclusion cannot be read to have the same meaning as the word "publication" in the personal injury provision because that reading would exclude coverage for "virtually any publication over which [the insured] might realistically be sued, rendering the policies' express coverage for publications that violate privacy rights practically meaningless."[23]

In a similar line of reasoning in *Zurich American Insurance Co. v. Sony Corp. of America*, a New York judge granted summary judgment in favor of Zurich.[24] In 2011, hackers exposed the personal information of tens of millions of Sony's users through Sony's PlayStation online services.[25] Zurich denied Sony's claim for defense and indemnification under Coverage B of the commercial general liability it issued to Sony.[26] Under Coverage B of Sony's CGL policy, "Zurich committed to 'pay those sums that [Sony] becomes legally obligated to pay as damages because of "personal and advertising injury",' which is defined to include 'injury . . . . arising out of . . . . [o]ral or written publication, in any manner, of material that violates a person's right of privacy."[27]

---

20 *Id.* at 247-48.

21 798 F. App'x 144 (9th Cir. 2020).

22 *Id.* at 145.

23 *Id.*

24 6 N.Y.S.3d 915 (N.Y. App. 2015); 2015 N.Y. Slip Op. 03606 (April 30, 2015).

25 *Id.*

26 *Id.*

27 *Id.*

Zurich argued that under the policy issued to Sony, "coverage is limited to protect against the purposeful and intentional acts committed by the insured or its agents, not by non-insureds or third parties."[28] The court agreed with Zurich and stated that while the data breach resulted in "publication" as required under the policy, there was no evidence that the publication was committed by Sony and not by the hackers. The court further agreed that the policy required an act or conduct by the policyholder in order to find coverage, and thus concluded there was no coverage under the policy.[29]

2. *Commercial Property Insurance*

Another traditional source of potential coverage for businesses is commercial property insurance.[30] Commercial property insurance generally protects commercial property owned by a business. Commercial property insurance began with fire insurance, but has expanded to include many more risks, or "perils."[31] A commercial property policy may either be a "named peril" policy and cover only damages from specific risks, or an "all risks" policy and cover damages from all risks except those excluded by the policy.[32] While these policies were not created with any thought of coverage for cybercrime, the efforts by insureds in the latest large-loss incursions show that insureds may be looking for coverage in even unlikely places today.

Most commercial property policies include some coverage for computers such as an explicit protection for computers, or computer coverage might be folded into broader coverage for electronics. Commercial property policies' computer coverage is typically limited to physical components and may protect computers and related hardware from potential dangers. However, they rarely offer any protection for the

---

28 *Id.*

29 *Id.*

30 Bert Wells et al., *Overview of Risks Related to Cyber-Commerce and Potential Sources of Coverage*, *in* 4 New Appleman Law of Liability Insurance § 29.01 (2014) [hereinafter Wells et al., *Overview*].

31 Eugene Wollan & Arthur N. Brook, *The Basic Policy: Named Perils Versus All-Risk Policies*, BUSINESS INSURANCE LAW AND PRACTICE GUIDE § 5.02 (2013).

32 Wells et al., *Overview*, *supra* note 30, § 29.01.

software or information stored on computers. They also usually don't provide any coverage for data stored in the cloud, or comprised data that is not lost.

(a) Cyber-Related Coverage Disputes Under Property Policies

In January 2020, a federal district court in Maryland did rule that the first-party property coverage in a business owner's insurance policy covered the replacement of the insured's computer system after a 2016 ransomware attack.[33] Following remediation, the system was still functional, but its performance was slowed by new protective software and it was likely that remnants of the virus remained on the system, increasing the risk of reinfection. The court determined that the "loss of reliability, or impaired functionality demonstrate the required damage to a computer system, consistent with the 'physical loss or *damage* to' language in the policy."[34]

While interesting, this decision does not appear to materially advance efforts to secure cyber coverage under first-party property policies for several reasons, including that the 2016 National Ink policy at issue was written on the 1999 ISO form. More recent ISO forms exclude computer-related losses. In addition, the policy contained a specific endorsement covering data-related issues.

3. E&O Insurance

Errors and Omissions (E&O) policies provide coverage for liability arising out of an act, error, or omission of the insured in rendering or failing to render services.[35] The policies are typically sold on a "claims-made" basis and cover only "damages."[36] A sample Technology E&O insuring agreement provides "We'll pay amounts any protected person is legally required to pay as damages for covered loss that . . . results from

---

33 National Ink and Stitch, LLC v. State Auto Property and Cas. Ins. Co., 435 F. Supp.3d 679 (D. Md. 2020) (applying Maryland law).

34 *Id.* at 686.

35 Scott Godes, *Cybersecurity Risks and Insurance Coverage*, 3 New Appleman Law of Liability Insurance § 18.03 (2013).

36 *Id.*

your computer or electronic products or services; and . . . . is caused by an error."[37]

E&O insurance, also referred to as professional liability insurance, provides coverage against losses relating to negligence, preventable mistakes, incompetent work, and other professional errors. However, when dealing with theft or fraud, these policies may not cover cyber-related costs, even if a third party commits the theft.

Insurance companies also provide E&O policies for software, information-technology services, and e-commerce businesses that provide for two basic risks.[38] First, these policies provide coverage for financial losses of third parties arising from failure of the insured's product to perform as intended or expected.[39] Second, these policies provide coverage for financial losses of third parties arising from an act, error, or omission committed in the course of the insured's performance of services for another.[40] These policies require that "wrongful acts" must be committed "in the course of the insured's performance of services for another."[41]

(a) Typical Cyber-Related Coverage Disputes Under E&O Policies

Whether an E&O policy covers cyber losses may depend on whether the covered "act, error, or omission" is required to arise out of performance of professional services, which may be defined narrowly or broadly in the policy. For example, in *FirePond Liquidating Trust v. Vigilant Insurance Co.*, a federal district court in Minnesota held the E&O policy at issue "specifically limited coverage to claims that flowed from the performance of computer related services."[42] The insured, a company that provided sales and marketing solutions through e-commerce systems, sought a

37 *St. Paul Fire & Marine Ins. Co. v. Compaq Computer Corp.*, 530 F.3d 809, 815 (8th Cir. 2008).

38 Bert Wells et al., *Coverage Issues under Third-Party Policies*, 4 NEW APPLEMAN LAW OF LIABILITY INSURANCE § 29.04 (2014) [hereinafter Wells et al., *Third-Party Coverage Issues*].

39 *Id.*

40 *Id.*

41 *Id.*

42 FirePond Liquidating Trust v. Vigilant Ins. Co., Civil No. 06-3050 (DWF/AJB), 2007 U.S. Dist. LEXIS 67210, at *18 (D. Minn. Sept. 11, 2007).

declaration of coverage under an Electronic and Information Technology Errors and Omissions Policy for lawsuits involving breach of agreements, under which the insured agreed to create and maintain an exclusive computerized system.[43] The court determined the claims asserted did not arise out of an act that was done in the performance of or the failure to perform computer-related services, but instead were based on premature termination of the agreement, which flowed from a breach of payment.[44]

Another factor in determining whether an E&O policy applies to cyber losses is whether the policy requires the error, omission, or act resulting in the loss be both intentional and wrongful. In *Eyeblaster, Inc. v. Federal Insurance Co.*, a computer user sued Eyeblaster, alleging that after visiting an Eyeblaster website, his computer was infected with the insured's spyware program, which caused damages to his computer, software, and data.[45] Eyeblaster sought coverage under its Network Technology Errors or Omissions insurance policy, but was denied coverage.[46] On appeal from Eyeblaster's action seeking a declaration that its insurer owed a duty to defend Eyeblaster, the court noted the policy provided coverage for loss for financial injury caused by a wrongful act that results in the failure of Eyeblaster's product to perform its intended function or to serve its intended purpose.[47] The policy defined "wrongful act" as an error, an unintentional omission, or a negligent act.[48] Citing a previous opinion that defined "error" to include "intentional, non-negligent acts but to exclude intentionally wrongful conduct," the court noted that while Eyeblaster may have intentionally installed JavaScript, Flash technology, and cookies on the plaintiff's computer, such actions were not negligent or wrongful as required under the policy.[49] The case illustrates not only that coverage for cybercrime losses may be barred under a policy's exclusions, but also that such losses may never be covered where the policy was only intended to insure against intentional, but not wrongful, acts.

Similarly, in *St. Paul Fire & Marine Ins. Co. v. Compaq Computer Corp.*, the Eighth Circuit held the allegations in a suit against Compaq for

---

43 *Id.* at *2.

44 *Id.* at *18-19.

45 Eyeblaster, Inc. v. Fed. Ins. Co., 613 F.3d 797, 800 (8th Cir. 2010).

46 *Id.*

47 *Id.* at 803.

48 *Id.* at 804.

49 *Id.* (citing St. Paul Fire & Marine Ins. Co. v. Compaq Computer Corp., 539 F.3d 809, 815 (8th Cir. 2008)).

selling defective computers and software claimed wrongful conduct, but did not assert a claim that the conduct was intentionally wrongful.[50] The court noted that there was no allegation that Compaq provided the software knowing that it was defective, and by contrast, the allegations supported an inference that Compaq unintentionally sold defective computers and unintentionally provided a defective product to fix the original defect. As a result, the court held that the allegations fell squarely within the policy's definition of "error"—an unintentionally incorrect act.[51]

Finally, the role of exclusions is very important in cyber-related coverage fights. In 2007, MySpace, Inc. sued Media Breakaway, LLC, an online marketing company, alleging Media Breakaway sent spam e-mails through MySpace users' accounts through phishing.[52] An arbitrator awarded over six million dollars in damages to MySpace.[53] Greenwich Insurance Company filed an action seeking a declaratory judgment regarding its rights and obligations under a directors and liability insurance policy issued by Greenwich to Media Breakaway.[54] When Media Breakaway sued them as a third-party defendant, Indian Harbor Insurance Company filed a counterclaim seeking, inter alia, declaratory judgment as to the application of certain exclusions in an errors and omissions insurance policy issued to Media Breakaway.[55] Greenwich argued the arbitration award against Media Breakaway was excluded from coverage because the arbitrator's findings included that Media Breakaway's actions were intentional acts.[56] Indian Harbor argued the award was excluded under similar exclusions in its policy.[57]

The court agreed with both the insurers, finding that the arbitrator "clearly found that defendants engaged in intentional misconduct and illegal activity."[58] The court also agreed that coverage was precluded

50 St. Paul Fire & Marine Ins. Co. v. Compaq Computer Corp., 539 F.3d 809, 815 (8th Cir. 2008).

51 *Id.* at 816.

52 Greenwich Ins. Co. v. Media Breakaway, LLC, Case No. CV08-937 CAS (CTx), 2009 U.S. Dist. LEXIS 63454, at *3-4 (C.D. Ca. July 22, 2009).

53 *Id.* at *6.

54 *Id.* at *2, 6.

55 *Id.* at *2, 9.

56 *Id.* at *7-9.

57 *Id.* at *9-13.

58 *Id.* at *22, *31.

under exclusions under both policies that provided the policies did not apply to any claim based on the insured gaining profit to which the insured was not legally entitled based on the arbitrator's finding that a substantial damage award was necessary to "prevent Media Breakaway from profiting for its wrongful and illegal past behavior."[59] The case illustrates the importance of exclusions for the insured's intentional conduct, as well as other exclusions for losses brought about by the insured's gain of profit to which it is not legally entitled. Thus, losses from cyber schemes that might otherwise by covered by traditional D&O or E&O policies can be excluded from coverage with similarly traditional exclusions.

(b) Social Engineering Claims Under E&O Policies

Social engineering fraud is one of the most frequently occurring types of cybercrime, and for that reason many types of insurance policies have added limited coverage for such losses by endorsement. Where insureds do not have specific social engineering coverage, they have sought coverage instead under their E&O policies, but often without success. In *Authentic Title Servs. v. Greenwich Ins. Co.*,[60] a New Jersey federal district court ruled that there was no coverage under a title agent's E&O policy for losses resulting from an email phishing scam. In the case, the title agent received emails purporting to be from a mortgage lender, directing the agent to transfer over $480,000 to a specified bank account and to confirm the transfer by email only. The agent followed the directions he received in the spoofed emails, but later realized that the funds had been transferred to a fraudulent account.

The agent then tendered a claim for the loss under its E&O policy. The insurer denied coverage, citing exclusion 14(a) for "the commingling, improper use, theft, stealing, conversion, embezzlement or misappropriation of funds or accounts." The court agreed with the insurer that the exclusion applied regardless of who committed the theft or other prohibited act.[61]

---

59 *Id.* at *24-25, 31-32.
60 2020 WL 6739880 (D.N.J. Nov. 17, 2020).
61 *Id.*

4. *Management Liability Insurance*

Management liability insurance covers exposures faced by directors, officers, managers, and business entities that arise from governance, finance, benefits, and management activities (also called "executive liability insurance"). This category includes (1) directors and officers (D&O) liability insurance, (2) employment practices liability insurance, (3) fiduciary liability insurance, and (4) "special crime" insurance (covering kidnap, ransom, and extortion exposures). These coverages may be written as stand-alone insurance policies or combined into a single "package" policy.

(a) Typical Cyber-Related Coverage Disputes Under Management Liability Policies

The few cases involving disputes about whether management liability policies cover cybersecurity-related costs demonstrate the difficulty of relying on them to cover cyber-related expenses.

For example, in *First Bank of Delaware, Inc. v. Fidelity and Deposit Co. of Maryland*, First Bank subcontracted with DAS to process credit card payments.[62] Hackers caused millions of dollars in unauthorized withdrawals from DAS, for which First Bank was liable. First Bank sought coverage under its D&O policy's "electronic risk liability" coverage, which covered "any unauthorized use of, or unauthorized access to electronic data or software with a computer system."[63]

The insurer in First Bank argued that a fraud exception, which purported to bar claims arising from fraudulent data use in any credit or debit card transaction, excluded coverage. The court refused to enforce the exclusion, reasoning that every unauthorized use or access to the insured's electronic data or software would almost necessarily involve fraud and the exclusion would render the electronic risk coverage illusory.[64]

Spec's Family Partners, Ltd. v. Hanover Insurance Co. is another case involving D&O coverage for cyber-related costs.[65] In that case, Spec's Family Partners, a specialty retail chain, had entered into a merchant

62 2013 WL 5858794 (Del. Super. Ct. Oct. 30, 2013).

63 *Id.* at *2.

64 *Id.* at *2-8.

65 739 F. App'x 233 (5th Cir. 2018).

agreement with a payment processor, First Data Merchant Services, to process credit and debit card transactions. Hackers attacked the credit card network Spec's used, resulting in First Data reimbursing banks for costs associated with fraudulent transactions. First Data demanded reimbursement from Spec's, alleging that it was noncompliant with the Payment Card Industry Data Security Standard (PCIDSS) requirements. Spec's filed suit against First Data alleging a series of contractual breaches.

Spec's sought coverage for the reimbursement claims and the contractual suit under the D&O section of its private company management liability insurance policy with Hanover. The insurer denied coverage based on a provision that excluded coverage for Spec's contractual liabilities. The United States Court of Appeals for the Fifth Circuit held that the district court erred in granting judgment on the pleadings because the exclusion did not unequivocally excuse the insurance company's duty to defend.[66]

On remand, the district court found that Hanover had a duty to defend Spec's against First Data's reimbursement claims and to fund Spec's litigation expenses in its contractual suit against First Data.[67]

5. *Hybrid Business Packages*

Insurers also offer hybrid policies that incorporate provisions from more than one of the insurance products described above.[68] As an example, a hybrid policy may include provisions that cover traditional areas of coverage in a CGL policy as well as provisions that cover liability for errors and omissions.[69] Another example of hybrid coverage would be a financial institution bond with extended coverages for indemnity for injury or death or directors or employees. Because these combined types of coverages can be unique, it is important for each business to analyze the scope of coverage provided, particularly if the business intends to rely on a combination policy for cyber-related coverage.

---

66 *Id.* at 239.

67 2019 WL 3302816, at *7 (S.D. Tex. July 23, 2019).

68 Judy Greenwald, *Bitcoin's Best Insurance Option May Be a Hybrid Policy*, BUSINESS INSURANCE.COM (Mar. 2, 2014, 6:00 AM), http://www.businessinsurance.com/article/20140302/NEWS06/303029997.

69 *Id.*

B. Bonds and Commercial Crime Policies

1. Financial Institution Bonds

The financial institution bond ("FIB"), which is maintained by banks and financial institutions and companies, provides first-party coverage for an insured's direct loss of its own property, or that of others it holds or for which it is legally liable.[70] The FIB standard form does not provide any specific coverage for risks of cybercrime. In fact, in a letter to the Alabama Department of Insurance dated December 24, 2003, the Surety Association of America (now the Surety & Fidelity Association of America, "SFAA") explained that "[e]lectronic transactions present exposures that are not readily compatible with the terms and conditions of" the current form of the financial institution bond.[71] The letter advised banks seeking coverage for losses from electronic transactions that they could obtain such coverage by rider.[72] As the use of electronic transactions has expanded, so too have the types of riders available to potentially expand coverage.

Insureds should be aware that a majority of the standard insuring agreements in the traditional FIB have very limited application to losses from cybercrime overall. For example, coverage under Insuring Agreement A requires involvement of an insured's employee. Studies indicate that most cyber threats originate outside the insured entity, and that as much as ninety-eight percent of data breaches stemmed from external agents.[73] Insuring Agreements B and C cover loss of Property or

---

70 Michael Keeley & Justin Melkus, *Introduction to Fidelity Insurance*, 10 New Appleman Law of Liability Insurance § 111.01 (Michael Keeley et al. eds., 2014).

71 Letter from Robert J. Duke, Director-Underwriting, The Surety Association of America, to Honorable David Parsons, Commissioner of Insurance: Alabama Department of Insurance (Dec. 24, 2003), *reprinted in* FINANCIAL INSTITUTION BONDS 975 (Duncan L. Clore, ed., 3d ed. 2008).

72 *Id.*

73 VERIZON RISK TEAM, 2012 DATA BREACH INVESTIGATIONS REPORT 26 (2012), *AVAILABLE AT* HTTP://WWW.VERIZONENTERPRISE.COM/RESOURCES/REPORTS/RP_DATA-BREACH-INVESTIGATIONS-REPORT-2012-EBK_EN_XG.PDF; Ponemon Institute, 2013 Cost of Cyber Crime Study: United States (2013), *available at* http://media.scmagazine.com/documents/ 54/2013_us_ccc_report_final_6-1_13455.pdf.

loss of or damage to furnishings or equipment in the insured's offices, with the definition of Property clearly indicating intent to include tangible items.[74] Additionally, Insuring Agreement B requires the person committing the covered crime to be "physically present in an office or on the premises of the Insured."[75] Finally, the forgery coverage under Insuring Agreement D requires "reliance on any Written, Original" covered instrument or instruction, again clearly indicating intent to cover traditional risks, rather than newer cyber risks.[76] The limits built into these traditional insuring agreements themselves illustrate how the facts associated with an off-premises electronic incursion or cybercrime would not seem possible to fit within the standard form agreements.

(a) Insuring Agreements Available by Endorsement

Available by rider to the financial institution bond is Insuring Agreement H, which provides coverage for fraudulent transfer instructions sent via e-mail.[77] Coverage for computer systems fraud and extortion are also available by rider for the financial institution bond.[78] The Computer Systems Rider provides coverage for loss resulting directly from a fraudulent entry or fraudulent change of "Electronic Data or Computer Program" into or within any "Computer System" of the Insured as those terms are defined in the rider.[79] However, and very critically, the fraudulent entry or change must actually cause one of the following: the transfer, payment, or delivery of "Property;" an account of the Insured or the Insured's customer to be added, deleted, debited, or credited; or an

---

74 *See* Financial Institution Bond, Standard Form No. 24 (Revised to May, 2011), *reprinted in* ANNOTATED FINANCIAL INSTITUTION BONDS 741 (Michael Keeley ed., 3d ed. 2013) [hereinafter 2011 FIB].

75 *See* 2011 FIB; 2004 FIB.

76 *See* 2011 FIB; 2004 FIB.

77 Form & Rider Filing Letter, *reprinted in* FINANCIAL INSTITUTION BONDS 980 (Duncan L. Clore, ed., 3d ed. 2008).

78 Keeley & Melkus, *supra* note 70, § 111.01.

79 Robert J. Duke, *A Concise History of the Financial Institution Bond, Standard Form No. 24, in* ANNOTATED FINANCIAL INSTITUTION BOND 533, 562-63 (Michael Keeley ed., 3d ed. 2013); Arthur N. Lambert et al., *Description of Current Language of Rider*, 10 NEW APPLEMAN LAW OF LIABILITY INSURANCE § 119.02 (2014) [hereinafter Lambert et al., *Current Language*].

unauthorized account or fictitious account to be debited or credited.[80] Manipulation of the computer system that causes the computer system itself to act, without involvement of the insured's employees, is necessary to trigger coverage.

The most likely source of certain limited coverage under a financial institution bond for losses from cybercrime is therefore that Computer Systems Fraud Rider, which provides coverage for loss resulting directly from fraudulent entry of electronic data or computer program into, or change of electronic data or computer program within, any computer system operated by the insured, provided that the entry causes the transfer of money or property.[81] To be covered under this provision, the loss must arise from fraudulent data entries or changes made on a covered computer system.[82] If the fraudulent changes were made on a system of a vendor of the insured, for example, then that would not be a covered computer system of the insured.[83] Additionally, the cybercrime must involve fraudulent computer activity, in and of itself, not just computer activity that is part of an overall and general fraud scheme.[84]

(b) Coverage Basics Under the FIB

In order to determine coverage under the Computer Systems Fraud Rider, first, the "Computer System" must be one covered by the policy.[85] In *Hudson United Bank v. Progressive Casualty Insurance Co.*, the Third

80 Lambert et al., *Current Language, supra* note 79, § 119.02.

81 Arthur N. Lambert et al., *Electronic Fraud Insuring Agreement Riders, in* ANNOTATED FINANCIAL INSTITUTION BOND 566 (Michael Keeley ed., 3d ed. 2013) [hereinafter Lambert et al., *Riders*].

82 Arthur N. Lambert et al., *Noteworthy Litigated Issues*, 10 New Appleman Law of Liability Insurance § 119.03 (Michael Keeley et al. eds., 2014) [hereinafter Lambert et al., *Noteworthy Litigated Issues*].

83 *Id.*; *see also* Hudson United Bank v. Progressive Cas. Ins. Co., 112 F. App'x 170, 175-76 (3d. Cir. Oct. 14, 2004) (no coverage under computer systems fraud rider where vendor entered fraudulent data into its own system, then provided hard copy documents for insured to enter into its own computer system).

84 Lambert et al., *Noteworthy Litigated Issues, supra* note 82, § 119.03; *see also* Northside Bank v. Am. Cas. Co., 60 Pa. D. & C.4th 95, 96-98 (Pa. Com. Pl. Ct. Allegheny Cnty. 2001).

85 Lambert et al., *Noteworthy Litigated Issues, supra* note 82, § 119.03.

Circuit addressed whether insured's losses were covered when fraudulent data was input into the computer system of a company with whom the insured had a profit-sharing agreement.[86] The court noted the record showed the fraudulent data was not input into the insured's computer system, the other company's system was incapable of electronically transmitting data onto the insured's computers, the other company never had access to the insured's computers, and the other company's reports were supplied to the insured as hard copies only.[87] The court specifically rejected that the insured's actions in inputting data given to it in hard copy form after the fact created coverage, holding that such actions did not fit within the rider's coverage of entries made on instruction from a software contractor.[88]

Another requirement for coverage under a Computer Systems Fraud Rider is that the fraudulent change or entry of electronic data must be part of a fraud and must be fraudulent itself.[89] For example, in *Northside Bank v. American Casualty Co. of Reading*, a bank was insured under a financial institution bond with a computer systems fraud rider that covered "loss resulting from the insured . . . assumed any liability as the direct result of any fraudulent electronic instruction or advice . . ."[90] The court concluded that the electronic instructions submitted to the bank were never modified or altered, much less fraudulent, and therefore the losses the bank incurred as a result of the instructions were not covered.[91] Additionally, exclusions like the commercial crime policy's general exclusion against coverage for "loss resulting from any dishonest or criminal acts committed by any of your 'Employees'" apply to exclude acts of the insured's employees misusing their authorized privileges and system access.[92]

---

86 Hudson United Bank v. Progressive Cas. Ins. Co., 112 F. App'x 170, 171, 175-76 (3d Cir. 2004).

87 *Id.* at 176.

88 *Id.* at 175-76.

89 Lambert et al., *Noteworthy Litigated Issues*, *supra* note 82, § 119.03.

90 Northside Bank v. Am. Cas. Co., 60 Pa. D. & C.4th 95, 96-98 (Pa. Com. Pl. Ct. Allegheny Cnty. 2001).

91 *Id.* at 101.

92 Arthur N. Lambert et al., *Commonly Litigated Issues*, 10 NEW APPLEMAN LAW OF LIABILITY INSURANCE § 125.02 (Michael Keeley et al. eds., 2014) [hereinafter Lambert et al., *Commonly Litigated Issues*]; *see* Universal Am. Corp. v. Nat'l Union Fire Ins. Co. of Pittsburgh, PA, 959 N.Y.S.2d 849, 864 (N.Y. App. Div. 2013) (finding the financial institution bond does not extend

2. *Commercial Crime Policies*

Coverage for first-party losses resulting from cybercrime may also be found in certain provisions of commercial crime policies.[93] Commercial crime policies are written for a broad variety of commercial businesses, and typically protect the insured from first-party losses resulting directly from employee theft and certain other defined criminal activity.

In general, there are many non-standard forms of commercial crime policies that include insuring agreements covering a wide range of risks. In 2000, the SFAA introduced the Crime Protection Policy, which is an all-inclusive policy that contains six basic insuring agreements.[94] During the same year, the ISO introduced four stand-alone policies, including the commercial crime policy (discovery form) and the commercial crime policy (loss sustained form).[95] Since then, the SFAA has issued the Crime Protection Policy, Standard Form No. SP 00 01 04 12 (edition of April 1, 2012) and the Crime Protection Policy For Public Entities, Standard Form No. SP 00 02 04 12 (edition of April 1, 2012).[96] The ISO has also more recently revised over a dozen fidelity policies for use by non-financial commercial and government entities.[97]

These standard forms continue to constantly evolve and to be revised, in response to developments in technology and in response to court cases. Some of the forms have been more widely adopted than others. Many carriers use their own manuscripted language in their own proprietary crime policy forms. When a business is securing its commercial crime policy, it is important for it to consult a knowledgeable broker in order to educate itself on the most appropriate types of forms and coverages for its particular risks.

As cybercrime has continued to grow, the commercial crime policy has addressed those hazards through various types of newer insuring

---

as far as providing coverage for fraudulent claims which were entered into the system by authorized users).

93 Godes, *supra* note 35, § 18.03.

94 Carol A. Pisano & Robert Duke, *Interpretation and Construction of the Commercial Crime Policy*, *in* COMMERCIAL CRIME POLICY 1, 8-9 (Randall I. Marmor & John J. Tomaine, eds., 2d ed. 2005).

95 *Id.*

96 Keeley & Melkus, *supra* note 70, § 111.01.

97 *Id.*

agreements. The SFAA's Insuring Agreement 5 provides coverage for certain specific types of computer fraud committed against the Insured.[98] Various companies issue their own manuscripted versions of coverage for certain types of computer fraud, so it is always important to carefully review the specific language that is being offered and to understand the language and definitions included. As indicated in the context of the FIB, coverage for computer fraud in the commercial crime policy is also targeted and limited.

A 2013 revision of the ISO policy combines the Computer Fraud and Funds Transfer Fraud coverages into one Insuring Agreement that covers loss resulting directly from a fraudulent entry of "electronic data" or "computer program" into, or change of "electronic data" or "computer program" within, any "computer system" owned, leased or operated by the Insured, provided the fraudulent entry or fraudulent change causes "money," "securities" or "other property" to be transferred, paid or delivered, or the Insured's account at a "financial institution" to be debited or deleted. The insuring agreement emphasizes that loss resulting from the incidental use of a computer, for example to generate false documents, is not intended to be covered.[99]

(a) Expansions and Changes to Policy Provisions

In response to market demand, most carriers have offered endorsements to provide limited coverage for loss resulting directly from social engineering, where the insured's employee (who was acting in good faith) was tricked, by means of some electronic commiunication, into transferring the insured's money to a fraudulent actor. So far, carriers are offering this coverage with strict sub-limits and additional deductibles, because of the loss frequency and loss volume, even for single transactions. Many carriers also include call-back requirements and verification requirements in order for social engineering coverage to attach.

Insurance companies have made insuring agreements available under various types of commercial policies that provide additional coverage for

---

98 *Id.* at 8-9.

99 2012 Crime and Fidelity Multistate Forms Revision Advisory Notice to Policyholders, CR P 005 08 13.

"electronic data" and "business interruption losses."[100] The "electronic data" agreement provides coverage for the replacement of "electronic data which has been destroyed or corrupted by a Covered Cause of Loss."[101] The "Covered Cause of Loss" includes "a virus, harmful code or similar instruction introduced into . . . a computer system . . . designed to damage or destroy any part of the system or disrupt its normal operation."[102] Unfortunately for the insured, the standard form policy limits coverage for the loss of Electronic Data to $2,500, which may not even cover the cost of labor to discover and replace the data.[103] The standard ISO business income form transfers coverage for e-commerce related loss to an "Additional Coverages" provision, the covered losses of which are similarly limited to $2,500.[104]

(b) Limitations in Policy Provisions

As for other types of crime coverage under commercial crime policies, various policies may contain exclusions to preclude coverage of losses from cybercrime involving theft of confidential information.[105] The ISO's computer fraud insuring agreement is subject to the policy's general exclusion against losses arising from use or disclosure of confidential information.[106] The policy specifically excludes coverage for losses resulting from the unauthorized use or disclosure of another person or entity's information that is held by the insured.[107] The exclusions applied to Insuring Agreement 6 would likely exclude cybercrime involving losses resulting from theft or disclosure of confidential information held by the

---

100 Bert Wells et al., *Coverage Issues under First-Party Policies*, 4 New Appleman Law of Liability Insurance § 29.03 (2014) [hereinafter Wells et al., *First-Party Coverage Issues*].

101 *Id.*

102 *Id.*

103 *Id.*

104 *Id.*

105 Arthur N. Lambert et al., *Analysis of the "Computer Fraud" Insuring Agreement in the Commercial Crime Policy*, 10 NEW APPLEMAN LAW OF LIABILITY INSURANCE § 125.01 (Michael Keeley et al. eds., 2014) [hereinafter Lambert et al., *Analysis*]; Wells et al., *Overview*, *supra* note 30, § 29.01.

106 Lambert et al., *Analysis*, *supra* note 105, § 125.01.

107 *Id.*

insured.[108] Another exclusion that may apply to a state-sponsored cyber-attacks are the "hostilities and warlike operations" exclusions commonly found in commercial crime policy forms.[109] Finally, commercial crime policies may include an exclusion for "potential income" that would likely operate to exclude any business interruption losses from cybercrime.[110] Even assuming losses from cybercrime were not excluded, similarly to the computer systems fraud rider under the financial institution bond, the insured must demonstrate the requisite "use of any computer" in order to establish coverage.[111]

3. *Examples of New Generation Insuring Agreements*

In addition to the Computer Fraud Insuring Agreement available under the FIB standard form, there are insuring agreements available for data processing service operations, voice initiated transfer fraud, "telefacsimile transfer fraud," destruction of data or programs by hacker, destruction of data or programs by virus, and voice computer systems fraud.[112] Similarly, there are several endorsements available under the commercial crime policy, including data processing service operations, computer hacker insuring agreement, fraudulent instructions insuring agreement, destruction of data or programs by hacker, destruction of data or programs by virus, employee sabotage/destruction of data or computer programs, and business income loss and dependent business income coverage.

Below are examples of first-party insuring agreements from a sample "cyber-risk" policy:

---

108 *Id.*

109 Bert Wells, et al., *Whether Loss of Electronic Data or Software, or Consequent Loss of Use of Hardware, Falls within the Scope of Standard Form First- and Third-Party Policies*, 4 New Appleman Law of Liability Insurance § 29.02 (2014).

110 *See* Diversified Grp., Inc. v. Van Tassel, 806 F.2d 1275, 1277 (5th Cir. 1987) ("We are persuaded that the potential income exclusion is clear and ambiguous. It excludes coverage for the loss of future profits, or future income flow, resulting from the fraudulent or dishonest acts of employees.").

111 Lambert et al., *Commonly Litigated Issues*, *supra* note 92, § 125.02.

112 Arthur N. Lambert et al., *Electronic Fraud Insuring Agreement Riders*, *in* Annotated Financial Institution Bond 566-67 (Michael Keeley ed., 3d ed. 2013) [hereinafter Lambert et al., *Riders*].

- The Company will pay the **Insured Organization** for **Crisis Management Event Expenses** incurred by the **Insured Organization** within 12 months of, and as a result of, any **Network and Information Security Wrongful Act** or **Communications and Media Wrongful Act** taking place prior to the expiration of the **Policy Period** and reported to the Company during the **Policy Period** or, if exercised, during the Extended Reporting Period or Run-Off Extended Reporting Period.
- The Company will pay the **Insured Organization** for **Security Breach Notification Expenses** incurred by the **Insured Organization** within 12 months of, and as a result of, any **Network and Information Security Wrongful Act** taking place prior to the expiration of the **Policy Period** and reported to the Company during the **Policy Period** or, if exercised, during the Extended Reporting Period or Run-Off Extended Reporting Period.
- The Company will pay the **Insured Organization** for **Restoration Expenses** incurred by the **Insured Organization** which are directly caused by a **Computer Violation** taking place prior to the expiration of the **Policy Period** and **Discovered** during the **Policy Period** or the Automatic Extended Period to Discover Loss.
- The Company will pay the **Insured Organization** for **Computer Fraud Loss** incurred by the **Insured Organization** prior to the expiration of the **Policy Period** which is directly caused by **Computer Fraud Discovered** during the **Policy Period** or the Automatic Extended Period to Discover Loss.
- The Company will pay the **Insured Organization** for **Funds Transfer Fraud Loss** incurred by the **Insured Organization** prior to the expiration of the **Policy Period** which is directly caused by **Funds Transfer Fraud Discovered** during the **Policy Period** or the Automatic Extended Period to Discover Loss.
- The Company will pay the **Insured Organization** for **E-Commerce Extortion Expenses** resulting from **E-Commerce Extortion** taking place anywhere in the world during the **Policy Period** or the Automatic Extended Period to Discover Loss.

- The Company will pay the **Insured Organization** for **Business Interruption Loss** incurred by the **Insured Organization** which is directly caused by a **Computer System Disruption** taking place during the Policy Period and Discovered during the Policy Period or the Automatic Extended Period to Discover Loss.

While the older provisions for computer fraud presented challenges for possible application to cyber losses, including the requirement of use of a covered computer system, the newer provisions are designed to cover more expansive cyber losses. These types of policies use specific, rather than general, terms to provide coverage. A cyber loss resulting from an insured's extortion payment would presumably not be covered under an agreement designed to cover business interruption losses. Additionally, the policies often include exclusions for claims based upon or arising out of war, invasion, acts of foreign enemies, etc. The rise of cybercrime from foreign countries, most notably China, means there is an increased likelihood that even specific cyber-risk policies may not cover losses from cybercrime if such losses were traced back to foreign cyber-espionage.[113] However, policies providing specific cybercrime coverage may prove to be worth the premiums, as demonstrated by Target's previous disclosure that their insurance policy covered $44 million of the $61 million in reported losses.[114]

4. *Coverage Disputes for Cybercrime Claims in the FIB and Commercial Crime Arena, and Beyond*

The prevalence of computer schemes, technology losses, and cybercrime has translated directly into a high volume of claim disputes arising out of cyber issues. The cases cover a broad range of subjects and potential insuring agreements, and have resulted in a broad range of outcomes.

---

113 Fernando M. Pinguelo & Bradford W. Muller, *Virtual Crimes, Real Damages: A Prime on Cybercrimes in the United States and Efforts to Combat Cybercriminals*, 16 VA. J.L. & TECH 116, 123-125 (Spring 2011).

114 Target Corporation, Quarterly Report (Form 10-K) (Mar. 14, 2014), *available at* http://www.sec.gov/Archives/edgar/data/27419/000002741914000014/tgt-20140201x10k.htm#sAB82C08697F33781CF8BB8F76D6AE934.

(a) Hacking Schemes

The traditional policy language that provided coverage for computer fraud was drafted with the specific goal of covering computer hacking incidents. The older "use of any computer" phrase that appeared in some insuring agreements, and the overall meaning and intent of the coverage, were focused on covering loss to the insured resulting directly from computer hacking. While some cases have recognized that central purpose, others have expanded coverage to more general computer frauds.

The least controversial of these decisions find coverage where true hacking did occur, and where all the elements of the insuring agreement are met. However, some courts have struggled with interpretation in this technical arena, trying to craft arguments for coverage, even where the facts do not actually fit the written coverage.

One recent case addressed whether a cybercrime scheme was covered under a commercial crime policy. On November 4, 2009, Vonage discovered hackers had fraudulently accessed its servers for the purpose of routing telephone calls to Cuba through one of Vonage's telecommunications carrier partners who then billed Vonage.[115] Vonage claimed losses related to this hacking scheme of over one million dollars and sought coverage under its commercial crime policy with Hartford Fire Insurance Co. After Hartford denied coverage, Vonage sought declaratory judgment against Hartford as to the parties' respective rights under the policy and as to damages for Hartford's alleged breach of contract.[116]

On review of Hartford's motion to dismiss for failure to state a claim, the federal district judge considered Hartford's arguments that Vonage failed to allege that tangible property directly related to the use of a computer was transferred outside of its premises and that Vonage failed to allege that it suffered a "loss of" or "loss from damage to" its tangible property.[117] As for Hartford's first argument, the court quickly decided the servers at issue "unquestionably" met the definition of "other property" under the policy.[118] The court then focused on the reading of the term "transfer of that property" to determine whether Vonage had met the

---

115 Vonage Holdings Corp. v. Hartford Fire Ins. Co., Civ. No. 11-6187, 2012 U.S. Dist. LEXIS 44401, at *2 (D.N.J. Mar. 29, 2012).

116 *Id.* at *1.

117 *Id.* at *6.

118 *Id.* at *8.

required pleading standards.[119] The policy provided that Hartford would insure Vonage against losses "following and directly related to the use of any computer to fraudulently cause a transfer of that property from inside the 'premises' . . . to a person outside those premises, or to a place outside those 'premises'."[120] The court concluded that Hartford's interpretation that the policy required a physical transfer of the property to outside the premises would make the provision "to a person outside those 'premises'" superfluous.[121] Finally, the court concluded Vonage had alleged a sufficient "loss of" or "loss of damage to" its tangible property when Vonage alleged it had lost the ability to use the full capacity of its servers during the time the use of its servers was transferred to the hackers.[122]

The court's decision is clearly results-oriented in favor of finding coverage for a crime not considered by the drafters of the policy. While it is difficult to argue that a server is not "tangible," the reasoning of the court falters where the court states that the policy quoted above "plausibly encompasses insurance against the transfer of use of the servers to a person outside the Plaintiff's premises." The court's analysis then changes from defining "other property" as servers to "use of servers" when the court turns to the insurer's argument that Vonage failed to plead it suffered a "loss of" its property or "loss from damage to" its property.

In an earlier decision, a state appellate court properly declined to stretch the plain language of a "computer fraud" insuring agreement under a general liability policy.[123] In *Royal American Group v. ITT Hartford*, an individual was able to hack into an insured's computer and steal a security code, which the hacker used to gain unauthorized access to the insured's telephone network.[124] The insured sought coverage for the losses resulting from the nearly forty thousand dollars in long distance charges it incurred under a computer fraud provision.[125] The policy provided coverage for loss of "money, securities and property other than money and securities"

---

119 *Id.* at *9.

120 *Id.* at *3.

121 Vonage Holdings Corp. v. Hartford Fire Ins. Co., Civ. No. 11-6187, 2012 U.S. Dist. LEXIS 44401, at *9-10 (D.N.J. Mar. 29, 2012).

122 *Id.* at *10.

123 Royal Am. Grp. v. ITT Hartford, C.A. No. 16246, 1994 Ohio App. LEXIS 104, at *2-3 (Ohio Ct. App. Jan. 12, 1994).

124 *Id.*

125 *Id.*

resulting directly from computer fraud.[126] The court properly rejected the insured's argument that its contracts to use the long distance networks were "contracts representing . . . . other property" as defined under "securities" in the policy.[127] The court based its reasoning on the well-settled rule of insurance policy interpretation that "the words in an insurance policy must be given their plain and ordinary meaning."[128] The court concluded that, even if the insured's contracts with long distance carriers constituted securities under the policy, the insured had failed to show how its contacts or contractual rights were lost or damaged by the unauthorized use of its long distance services.[129] This opinion demonstrates that even policies purporting to cover "computer fraud" may not provide coverage for losses from certain types of cybercrime schemes that may not have been foreseen by the drafters. Further, this case illustrates how the continuously evolving nature of cybercrime schemes can outpace the far slower reaction of the insurance industry to provide coverage.

Similar to that holding, the court in *Universal American Corp. v. National Union Fire Insurance Company of Pittsburgh, Pa.*,[130] recently concluded that the phrase "computer fraud" in a crime policy required an actual hacking or unauthorized entry into a computer system for a scheme to qualify for coverage. In that case, the insured suffered a loss when an authorized user of its computer system submitted Medicare claims for services that were never rendered. The court's conclusion, upheld on appeal, was that coverage applies to loss resulting directly from fraudulent access to the computer system, and not from loss resulting directly from fraudulent content being submitted by authorized users.[131]

---

126 *Id.* at *4.

127 *Id.* at *5.

128 *Id.*

129 Royal Am. Grp. v. ITT Hartford, C.A. No. 16246, 1994 Ohio App. LEXIS 104, at *7 (Ohio Ct. App. Jan. 12, 1994).

130 959 N.Y.S. 2d 849 (N.Y. Sup. Ct. 2013), *aff'd* 972 N.Y.S. 2d 241, *aff'd* 2015 WL 3885816 (N.Y. June 25, 2015).

131 *Id.*

(b) Fraud Schemes Perpetrated Through "Use of a Computer"

One of the more controversial developments in cases involving cybercrime has been the expansion by certain courts of what was intended to be hacking coverage to also cover general fraudulent schemes, which before the rise of computers would have been carried out by paper and/or in person. Initially, certain of these cases improperly expanded the reading of the phrase "use of any computer" and the causation element in order to create coverage for fraudulent schemes. However, in direct contrast, other recent decisions have taken a more conservative approach, rejecting coverage for a fraud scheme that might have happened to be carried out by email or electronic communication.

In *Great American Insurance Co v. AFS/IBEX Financial Services, Inc.*, a federal district court sitting in Texas addressed a scheme in which the insured's agent's son submitted false insurance premium finance applications, causing the insured to issue checks that the perpetrator then endorsed and deposited into his own personal bank account.[132] The insured then submitted a claim to its insurer under its Computer Fraud Insuring Agreement.[133] In the declaratory judgment action, the court granted summary judgment for the insurer because the insured failed to show how use of a computer caused the transfer of funds from the insured's bank account, as opposed to the loss being caused by it simply being duped into issuing checks that the fraudster then deposited into his account, even if a computer may have been used to transmit the false insurance applications.[134] "The language of these provisions indicate that they are designed to cover losses *directly* stemming from fraud perpetrated by use of a computer."[135]

This case demonstrates that courts are able to recognize that computers today often simply serve as a means of transmission for traditional business correspondence, such as insurance applications in this case. For some computer-fraud insuring agreements to apply, the fraudulent use of a computer must directly result in the loss rather than simply serve as a means for a more traditional fraud. In other words, it could be said that for coverage to apply the fraud must have been made possible by the

---

132 Great Am. Ins. Co. v. AFS/IBEX Fin. Servs., Inc., Civil Action No. 3:07-CV-924-O, 2008 U.S. Dist. LEXIS 55532, at *4-5 (N.D. Tex. July 21, 2008).

133 *Id.* at *44.

134 *Id.*

135 *Id.* at *45 (emphasis in original).

fraudulent use of the computer system at issue; the substitution of a computer system for the U.S. mail or the personal delivery of a fraudulent document may not be sufficient to trigger coverage.

In another case, a federal district court in Louisiana addressed a claim arising out of the infamous Bernard Madoff Ponzi scheme.[136] The insured sought recovery under a commercial crime policy for losses suffered in its investment portfolio, arguing coverage because Madoff used a computer to generate false documents that misled investors and gave the appearance of a legitimate investment operation.[137] The court, however, concluded that while the Madoff Ponzi scheme was a contributing factor in the insured's losses, it was not a direct cause of the insured's losses where the insured invested in a mutual fund that in turn invested a portion of its holdings in a hedge fund, which in turn invested a portion of its holdings in one of the funds managed by Madoff.[138] Again, this case illustrates that courts require that not merely the involvement or use of computers in a scheme in order to trigger coverage, but that the fraudulent usage directly cause losses.

In *Brightpoint, Inc. v. Zurich American Insurance Co.*, the insured was the victim of a scam arising out of faxed orders for phone cards.[139] When the insured received faxed copies of purchase orders for phone cards, the insured sent an employee to the company from which the insured purchased its phone cards.[140] That employee would then turn over the phone cards at a third location.[141] The insurer advanced four reasons to deny coverage under a "computer fraud" insuring agreement.[142] First, the insurer argued the phone cards were not owned by the insured when the scheme began.[143] While the court conceded the insured did not own the phone cards at the beginning of the scheme, the court concluded that the phone cards were covered because by the time the phone cards were given

---

136 Methodist Health Sys. Found., Inc. v. Hartford Fire Ins. Co., 834 F. Supp. 2d 493 (E.D. La. 2011).

137 *Id.* at 494-95.

138 *Id.* at 494-96.

139 Brightpoint, Inc. v. Zurich Am. Ins. Co., 1:04-CV-2085-SEB-JPG, 2006 U.S. Dis. LEXIS 26018 (S.D. Ind. Mar. 10, 2006).

140 *Id.* at *5-6.

141 *Id.* at *6.

142 *Id.* at *10.

143 *Id.* at *12.

to a third party, they belonged to the insured.[144] The insurer argued the phone cards were not covered property under the policy because the loss was the purely economic value of the phone cards and not the cards themselves as "tangible" property.[145] The court rejected the first defense, noting that the cards could be sold for value, making them "tangible" property with "intrinsic value" as required by the policy terms.[146] The issue of whether losses result from "tangible" property is another primary recurring legal issue that will be discussed in greater detail further on in this paper.

Despite rejecting the insurer's first defense, the court agreed with the insurer's remaining two defenses to coverage.[147] First, the phone cards were not transferred from inside the "premises" or "banking premises" as required under the policy definition of "computer fraud" since the phone cards were never inside a building the insured occupied or where it conducted its business.[148] Second, the faxed post-dated checks and bank guaranties did not "fraudulently cause[] a transfer" of the phone cards as required under the policy definition of "computer fraud."[149] The court concluded the fraud occurred through the use of unauthorized checks and guaranties, not the manipulation of numbers or events through the use of a computer, facsimile machine or other device, where the faxed documents caused the purchase, but not the transfer of the phone cards.[150] This case also illustrates an approach by a court to show that coverage will not be created under a computer fraud insuring agreement merely by the tangential use of computers as part of an otherwise uncovered fraudulent scheme.

(c) Email and Wire Transfer Schemes—In Policies With No Social Engineering Insuring Agreement

Social Engineering email schemes appear to be the most prevalent form of loss and most frequently occurring type of claim made in recent

144 *Id.* at *12-13.

145 Brightpoint, Inc. v. Zurich Am. Ins. Co., 1:04-CV-2085-SEB-JPG, 2006 U.S. Dis. LEXIS 26018, at *14 (S.D. Ind. Mar. 10, 2006).

146 *Id.* at *13-16.

147 *Id.* at *17-23.

148 *Id.* at *17.

149 *Id.* at *19.

150 *Id.*

years. For a period of time, courts reviewed crime policies that may have had computer fraud types of insuring agreements, but no social engineering insuring agreements, and therefore struggled to try to create coverage for social engineering losses. The often awkward efforts of these courts have left a series of inconsistent decisions that, in some cases, ignore the actual terms of coverage.

In an early example, *Owens, Schein & Nicola, P.C. v. Travelers Casualty & Surety Co. of America*, the insured was a law firm that purchased a crime insurance policy with coverage for computer fraud.[151] The fraud began when the law firm was contacted via e-mail by an individual claiming to be an attorney requiring assistance in a collection matter for a client located in China.[152] The "client" then contacted the law firm, related that a check would be sent to the law firm, and requested the law firm electronically wire the funds to an account in South Korea.[153] After following the "client's" instructions, the law firm discovered the check was fraudulent and submitted a claim to its insurer.[154]

The insurer first argued that the computer fraud policy required the transfer to occur by way of a "'computer hacking' incident, such as the manipulation of numbers or events through the use of a computer."[155] The insurer relied upon the *Brightpoint* decision discussed above to argue "that despite the fact the Chinese business communicated with Owens exclusively by an e-mail and the fraudulent check may have been created by the use of a computer, this does not constitute computer fraud under the policy."[156] The insured law firm countered that the required "use of any computer" under the policy was ambiguous as to the amount of computer usage necessary to constitute computer fraud.[157] The court agreed with the insured that the policy language was ambiguous and held that no "hacking

---

151 Owens, Schein & Nicola, P.C. v. Travelers Cas. & Sur. Co. of Am., CV095024601, 2010 Conn. Super. LEXIS 2386, at *1-2 (Conn. Super. Ct. Sept. 17, 2010).

152 *Id.* at *2.

153 *Id.* at *3.

154 *Id.*

155 *Id.* at *13.

156 *Id.* at *18-19.

157 Owens, Schein & Nicola, P.C. v. Travelers Cas. & Sur. Co. of Am., CV095024601, 2010 Conn. Super. LEXIS 2386, at *19 (Conn. Super. Ct. Sept. 17, 2010).

incident" was required for coverage to apply.[158] The court then addressed the insurer's argument that the loss was not directly caused by the use of a computer and that the fraudulent check was an intervening cause between the e-mails and the transfer of money.[159] The federal court applied Connecticut law in determining "direct cause" was synonymous with "proximate cause" and concluded the e-mails were both the proximate and efficient cause of the law firm's loss "because the e-mails set the chain of events in motion that led to the entire loss."[160]

This case illustrates a very result-oriented approach by a court. It applied the very broadest reading to the insuring agreement and the definition, plus applied an extremely loose and attenuated proximate cause standard, in order to find coverage.

Under the *Owens* court's reasoning, as long as a computer was in some way involved in an otherwise traditional fraud, then a "computer fraud" policy may cover the resulting losses. The ruling leaves unanswered the question of how remotely a computer may be involved in a fraudulent scheme in order for coverage to apply. For example, would the losses have been covered if the e-mails involved had not been from the fraudster but instead e-mails within the firm directing the transfer of funds? Or, alternatively, would there have been coverage if there had been several more intervening events between the e-mail from the "client" and the eventual transfer of funds? This case illustrates how broadly some courts will be willing to read the computer fraud coverage, and is a cautionary tale of how the analysis of a cybercrime loss can be subject to a single court's desire to find coverage for certain losses involving complicated computer-related schemes.

While this case was later resolved and the opinion withdrawn and vacated, the reasoning that was used in the unreported opinion has subsequently been used in other jurisdictions by insureds seeking coverage. When this case is cited in support of such a position, it will be important to note that it was unreported to begin with, and was subsequently withdrawn.

In contrast to the holding in the *Owens* case, the Fifth Circuit Court of Appeals in *Apache Corp. v. Great American Insurance Co.*,[161] concluded that where an insured was tricked into paying invoices to fraudsters who

---

158 *Id.*

159 *Id.* at *18-20.

160 *Id.* at *21-22.

161 662 F. App'x 252 (5th Cir. 2016).

impersonated a legitimate vendor, there was no coverage under the computer fraud insuring agreement. The court properly analyzed the causation and the technical elements of the insurance agreement to reach a proper conclusion. In that case, the insured's employee received a phone call and then an email advising the insured to change the bank account information for one of its vendors. The email included a letter on the vendor's letterhead confirming the change. Based upon that change, the insured paid millions to a fraudulent account. The insured sought coverage under "computer fraud." The claim was denied based upon arguments that the loss did not result directly from usc of a computer, nor did the use of the computer cause the actual transfer of funds. The district court found coverage, but the Fifth Circuit reversed, holding that the email was part of a scheme, but the email was only incidental to the transfer of money.[162] The Fifth Circuit focused on the technical aspects of the coverage and properly interpreted the policy language. Moreover, the Fifth Circuit specifically declined to follow the reasoning from *Owens*.

Similarly, the Ninth Circuit Court of Appeals in *Pestmaster Servs. v. Travelers Cas. & Sur. Company of America,*[163] applied a narrow construction of the computer fraud insuring agreement, and declined to turn a crime policy into a general and unlimited fraud policy. The court's short opinion focused on the language in the insurance agreement that referred to an action to "fraudulently cause a transfer," as requiring an unauthorized transfer of funds. The court agreed with the argument put forward by the insurance company, that computers are ubiquitous to modern business, and as a result, that concluding that computer fraud must cover loss caused by any type of scheme involving any use of a computer would convert the crime policy into a general fraud policy.[164] The force of the Ninth's Circuit's decision is critical, as it too illustrates the proper application of the technical aspects of the actual and intended coverage in the crime policy.

Other courts have also rejected claims under computer fraud policies, finding that the computer use did not relate directly to the loss.[165]

---

162 *Id.* at 258.

163 656 F. App'x 332 (9th Cir. 2016).

164 *Id.* at 333.

165 Interactive Commc'ns Int'l, Inc. v. Great Am. Ins. Co., 731 F. App'x 929, 934 (11th Cir. 2018) (while the fraudster's manipulation of the insured's computers set in motion events that caused loss, court held that the fraudsters'

However, in a case involving fraudulent emails, the Sixth Circuit Court of Appeals concluded that the phrase "resulting directly from" in a commercial crime policy "does not unambiguously limit coverage to loss resulting 'solely' or 'immediately' from the theft itself," despite the fact it also found that direct causation was the relevant standard.[166] Similarly, in *Medidata Solutions, Inc. v. Federal Insurance Co.*, the Court of Appeals for the Second Circuit found coverage under an older form of a computer fraud provision for a spoofing email attack.[167] The court held that the spoofed emails were the proximate cause of Medidata's losses even though Medidata employees made the actual transfer.[168]

The divergence of the court opinions in this area make a few points clear: (1) it is imperative to analyze the actual language of the insuring agreement at issue and to apply that language, not different language or language from other cases; (2) the wording used, including particularly a condition that loss must "directly result from" a defined hazard is important and cannot be ignored in any policy language construction; and (3) the technology and forensic facts of the case—and the way they relate to the coverage language—matter.

(d) Social Engineering Coverage Disputes: The Battle Over Sub-Limits

During 2020 and 2021, the courts finally had an opportunity to address a case where a crime policy specifically included both computer fraud coverage and social engineering coverage in a single policy, and both a United States District Court and the Fifth Circuit Court of Appeals were able to analyze those distinct coverages side-by-side. While the carrier and

---

computer use did not directly cause the loss); G&G Oil Co. of Ind. v. Continental Western Ins. Co., 145 N.E.3d 642 (Ind. App. Ct. 2020) (commercial crime and fidelity coverage did not cover a ransomware payment because the hijacker did not use a computer to fraudulently cause G&G to purchase Bitcoins to pay as ransom).

166 Retail Ventures, Inc. v. Nat'l Union Fire Ins. Co., 691 F.3d 821, 831 (6th Cir. 2010).

167 729 F. App'x 117, 119 (2d Cir. 2018); *see also* American Tooling Ctr., Inc. v. Travelers Cas & Sur. Co., 895 F.3d 455, 462 (6th Cir. 2018) (finding that plaintiff suffered a direct loss where a spoofed email caused plaintiff to transfer funds an imposter).

168 *Id.*

insured agreed that the particular loss was covered under a social engineering coverage agreement, the insured argued it was also covered by a separate computer transfer fraud insuring agreement, because the limit of liability for that coverage was much larger.

The Fifth Circuit Court of Appeals in *Mississippi Silicon Holdings, L.L.C. v. AXIS Insurance Company*[169] focused, in particular, on the technology details and the proper construction of the policy as a whole, where the two separate insuring agreements were both a part of the same policy. By way of context, the Fifth Circuit explained that "both this court and others have ruled that the mere receipt of an email does not constitute computer fraud in the context of similar insurance provisions."[170] The court explained that the "fraudsters apparently gained access to the company's email system, but they did not manipulate those systems through the introduction of data or programs . . . [a]t best, the breach allowed the fraudsters to monitor the computer system and to act based on the information they learned."[171] Recognizing that "contract terms cannot be read in isolation," the Mississippi Silicon court explained that, "[e]ven if we were to assume that the instant scheme constituted Computer Transfer Fraud, other language in the provision clearly suggests that this was not the type of scheme Axis agreed to insure MSH against."[172] That other language included, among others, a social engineering fraud provision that "contemplates situations in which an employee relies in good faith on a fraudulent instruction."[173] As a result, the court affirmed the grant of summary judgment in favor of AXIS, finding that only the social engineering coverage applied to the facts of the case.

(e) Theft of Personal Data

In *Retail Ventures, Inc. v. National Union Fire Insurance Company of Pittsburgh, P.A.*, hackers used the local wireless network at a shoe store to gain unauthorized access to the insured's main computer system and download credit card and checking account information for over a million

---

169 2021 WL 406238, at *3 (5th Cir. Feb. 4, 2021).

170 *Id.*

171 *Id.*

172 *Id. at *8.*

173 *Id.*

customers of over a hundred stores.[174] The insured incurred losses relating to customer communications, public relations, customer claims and lawsuits, and attorney fees in connection with state and federal investigations.[175] The insured sought coverage for its losses under a computer fraud rider to a commercial crime policy and prevailed by summary judgment at the trial court level.[176]

On appeal, the Sixth Circuit's analysis focused on whether the insured's losses "resulted directly from" the theft of insured property by computer fraud.[177] The court rejected the insurer's interpretation that the policy required the theft of property by computer fraud be the sole and immediate cause of the insured's loss.[178] Instead, the court concluded that Ohio courts would apply a proximate cause standard and affirmed the district court's finding of summary judgment in favor of the insured.[179] Despite spending several pages on the different approaches utilized by courts to determine requisite causation, the appellate court did not discuss how the hacker's infiltration of the insured's computer system proximately caused the insured's financial losses sufficient to apply coverage, thus demonstrating that the court could have found any connection to be sufficient in order to apply coverage.[180]

The appellate court further found that an exclusion for "any loss of proprietary information, Trade Secrets, Confidential Processing Methods, or other confidential information of any kind" did not clearly apply to the loss.[181] The court approved of the district court's reasoning that the information accessed by the hackers could not be "proprietary information" since "the information was owned or held by many, including the customer, the financial institution and the merchants to whom the information is provided in the ordinary stream of commerce."[182] The court then agreed with the district court that "trade secrets" and

---

174 Retail Ventures, Inc. v. Nat'l Union Fire Ins. Co. of Pittsburgh, P.A., 691 F.3d 821 (6th Cir. 2012).

175 *Id.* at 824.

176 *Id.*

177 *Id.* at 827-32.

178 *Id.* at 831.

179 *Id.* at 831-32, 835.

180 *See* Retail Ventures, Inc. v. Nat'l Union Fire Ins. Co. of Pittsburgh, P.A., 691 F.3d 821, 831-32, 827-32 (6th Cir. 2012).

181 *Id.* at 831-32, 832-34.

182 *Id.* at 831-32, 832-33.

"confidential processing methods" must belong to the retail stores.[183] Finally, the court briefly addressed "other confidential information of any kind" as similarly information that must belong to the retail stores, and no one else.[184] Under the reasoning of this court, losses resulting from hacked customer information were covered as "theft of any Insured property by Computer Fraud" and yet not excluded as from "confidential information" because the information did not belong to the insured.

(f) Exclusions for Authorized Persons Making Transfers

Insurers may deny coverage for cyber-related claims under commercial crime policy exclusions if an authorized person transfers money in connection with a fraudulent scheme.

For example, in *Midlothian Enters. v. Owners Ins. Co.*,[185] a Virginia federal district court ruled that a crime insurer had no obligation to cover losses resulting of an email phishing scam. In that case, a Midlothian employee had complied with an email request, purportedly from the company president, to wire more than $400,000 from Midlothian's bank account to a bank account in Alabama. Several days later, Midlothian discovered the email was fraudulent and tendered a claim to Owners Insurance Company, which denied coverage.

The crime policy provided coverage for theft of money and securities, but excluded coverage for "[l]oss resulting from your, or anyone acting on your express or implied authority, being induced by a dishonest act to voluntarily part with title to or possession of any property." The court found that the exclusion applied because the employee voluntarily made the transfer.[186]

Similarly, in *Aqua Star (USA) Corp. v. Travelers Casualty & Surety Co.*,[187] a hacker sent fraudulent emails to an Aqua Star employee directing the employee to change bank account information for a vendor for future wire transfers. The Aqua Star employee made the changes as directed and the hacker defrauded the company by $713,890. Aqua Star sought coverage for the loss from its insurer, which denied the claim. The district

183 *Id.* at 831-32, 833-34.
184 *Id.* at 831-32, 834.
185 439 F. Supp. 3d 737 (E.D. Va. 2020).
186 *Id.* at 742.
187 2016 WL 3655265, at *1 (W.D. Wash. July 8, 2016).

court concluded that the policy's exclusion for losses "resulting directly or indirectly from the input of Electronic Data by a natural person having the authority to enter the Insured Computer System" applied because the Aqua Star employee had authority to change the bank account.[188]

C. Conclusion

Cybercrime will remain a primary threat to business in the twenty-first century. Insurers are increasingly developing new products to address cyber-risks, and companies will be well advised to carefully research their risks, and then to seek professional assistance to match their own risks with the best types of products available on the market. Insured businesses need to invest the time necessary to carefully review the terms, definitions, exclusions, and coverages that they purchase, keeping in mind the various risks posed by cybercrime as well as the potential for substantial losses. Organizations that do not purchase more specific insurance products may attempt to continue to seek coverage under traditional CGL and other property policies, as well as commercial crime policies, but may find that as cybercrime continues to evolve, the losses move outside the limited and defined coverages afforded by these policies.

---

188 *Id.*

Chapter 4

Insurance Coverage Developments in Cybersecurity and Data Breach*

This chapter addresses insurance coverage developments in cybersecurity and data breaches. This chapter will particularly look at the development of insurance coverage under standalone cyber insurance policies.

A. Early Standalone Cyber Insurance Policies

Some form of cyber insurance has been available since the 1970s, but policies specifically addressing more sophisticated cyber and internet-related liabilities began to emerge in the late 1990s.[1] As discussed below, growing concern about virus and malware vulnerability, the development of breach notification requirements, and the costs associated with large-scale data breaches led to the creation of the standalone cyber insurance policy.

Cyber insurance as a standalone policy began, in large part, in response to concerns about the dot-com bubble, the "Y2K bug", and also following the 9/11 attacks in the early 2000s.[2] These events raised

---

* By Kyle Black.

1 *See* Andrea Wells, *What Agent Who Wrote First Cyber Policy Thinks About Cyber Insurance Now,* Insurance Journal (Mar. 1, 2018), https://www.insurancejournal.com/news/national/2018/03/01/481886.htm; *see also* Mark Camillo, *Cyber Risk and the Changing Role of Insurance*, 2 J. Cyber Pol'y 53, 53 (2017), available at https://www.tandfonline.com/doi/full/10.1080/23738871.2017.1296878 (discussing the history of cyber insurance). For more information on the history of cyber insurance, *see* Chapter 1: *History/Development of Cyber and Network Security Risk and Insurance*.

2 Camillo, *supra* note 1, at 53; *see also* Paul Kovacs, *Cyber Risks: Implications for the Insurance Industry in Canada,* Insurance Institute of Canada (2015), https://www.insuranceinstitute.ca/en/resources/insights-research/cyber-risks.aspx (discussing the history of cyber insurance and

awareness about cyber vulnerabilities and also raised concerns about the potentially limited coverage available for such risks under traditional insurance policies.[3] Businesses were particularly concerned about the spread of viruses and other types of malware that could create business interruption losses and other potential legal liability unlikely to be covered under traditional insurance policies.[4] However, during the late 1990s and early 2000s, instead of demanding new or better insurance coverage for these potential losses, most businesses focused on loss mitigation measures and other means to boost their network security.[5]

Despite these mitigation measures and boosts in network security, the early to mid-2000s still saw an increase in identity theft cases and major data breaches.[6] As a result, many states began implementing data breach notification statutes which required businesses to immediately notify customers and regulatory authorities of data breaches involving a customer's personal information. California enacted the first data breach notification statute in 2002, and other states followed, enacting their own similar breach notification requirements.[7] In response to these breach notification requirements and the mitigation measures imposed by some

---

assessing cyber security from the perspective of the insurance industry in Canada).

3 *Id.*

4 *Id.*

5 *Id.*

6 *Id.*

7 *Id.; see also* Cal. Civ. Code §§ 1798.80-1798.84, available at http://leginfo.legislature.ca.gov/faces/codes_displaySection.xhtml?lawCode=CIV&sectionNum=1798.80. (California's breach notification statute). By 2012, 46 of the 50 states, the District of Columbia, Puerto Rico and the Virgin Islands enacted breach notification statutes. *See* Peter P. Swire & Kenesa Ahmad, *U.S. Private-sector Privacy: Law and Practice for Information Privacy Professionals*, International Association of Privacy Professionals (2012) (discussing data breach notification laws in the United States). By 2018, all 50 states had breach notification statutes. *See* Jay Kramer & Bryan Thompson, *The United States of Data Breach Notification*, Lewis Brisbois' Data Privacy & Cybersecurity Blog (Apr. 10, 2018), https://lewisbrisbois.com/blog/category/data-privacy-cyber-security/the-united-states-of-data-breach-notification (discussing South Dakota and Alabama being the last two states to enact breach notification laws in 2018).

of these statutes, more cyber insurance policies began indemnifying the costs associated with a data breach.[8]

Major data breaches began to emerge between the late 2000s and early 2010s.[9] For example, in 2007, TJX Companies Inc. announced that over 45 million customers' credit and debit cards were compromised in a data breach.[10] The TJX breach cost the company between $1 billion and $4.5 billion, and was considered at that time the biggest data breach in U.S. history. In 2011, a data breach at Sony PlayStation exposed around 100 million customers' accounts, bringing the network down for nearly a month, and resulting in millions of dollars in losses and fines.[11] In 2013, Target fell victim to a data breach that resulted in the leak of tens of millions of credit and debit card accounts.[12] And in 2014, JP Morgan Chase, Home Depot, and Sony Pictures would each see their own large scale data breach.[13]

B. The Shift in Focus from Seeking Coverage for Data Breaches under Commercial General Liability Policies to Standalone Cyber Insurance Policies

Despite the development of specific cyber insurance policies, policyholders historically have looked to their commercial general liability ("CGL") policies for coverage emerging from data breaches.[14]

---

8 Camillo, *supra* note 1, at 53.

9 *Id.*

10 *Id.* (citing Antony Savvas, *TJX hack the biggest in history*, ComputerWeekly.com (Apr. 2, 2007), http://www.computerweekly.com/news/2240080607/TJX-hack-the-biggest-in-history); *see also* Jaikumar Vijayan, *TJX data breach: At 45.6M card numbers, it's the biggest ever*, ComputerWorld.com (Mar. 29, 2007, 12:00 PM), https://www.computerworld.com/article/2544306/tjx-data-breach--at-45-6m-card-numbers--it-s-the-biggest-ever.html (discussing the TJX data breach).

11 *Id.*

12 *Id.*

13 Gregory Podolak, *Insurance for Cyber Risk: A Comprehensive Analysis of the Evolving Exposure, Today's Litigation, and Tomorrow's Challenges,* 33 Quinnipiac L. Rev, 369, 373-74 (2015).

14 *See* Chapter 2: *Overview of Types of Insurance Coverage Available for Cyber Risks,* and Chapter 3: *Potential Overlapping Coverage Between Cyber*

Policyholders often rely on Coverage A (covering bodily injury or property damage) and Coverage B (covering personal and advertising injury liability) under their CGL policies to cover losses emerging from data breaches.[15] The Insurance Services Office ("ISO") has maintained that their standard CGL policy does not cover, and was not intended to cover, loss due to a data breach.[16] But policyholders and insurers have been litigating coverage for data breaches under CGL policies for several years, with courts providing mixed results on coverage.[17] Starting in 2001, in an effort to clarify that data breaches are not meant to be covered under CGL policies, the ISO began modifying their standard CGL policy forms and issuing new endorsements to explicitly exclude electronic data and liability emerging from electronic publications from coverage.

1. 2001: ISO Redefines "Tangible Property" and "Personal and Advertising Injury"

Under ISO's standard CGL policy, Coverage A states, in pertinent part, that "[w]e will pay those sums that the insured becomes legally obligated to pay as damages because of 'bodily injury' or 'property

---

Policies and Other Business and Crime Policies; *see also* Toni S. Reed, *Cyber Crime: Losses, Claims, and Potential Insurance Coverage for the Technology Hazards of the Twenty-First Century,* XX Fid. L.J. 55 (2014) (discussing different types of cybercrimes and the other insurance policies available).

15 *Id.; see also* Margaret A. Reetz, Lauren B. Prunty, Gregory S. Mantych & David J. Hommel, *Cyber Risks: Evolving Threats, Emerging Coverages, and Ensuing Case Law*, 122 Penn. St. L. Rev. 727, 736 (2018), available at http://www.pennstatelawreview.org/wp-content/uploads/2018/07/Symposium-Reetz-et-al.pdf (discussing the origins and evolution of insurance coverage for cyber losses from traditional CGL, crime, and directors and officers policies to cyber insurance policies).

16 *See* Anthony Mormino & Carol Kreiling, *Is CGL Insurance Coverage Tonic for the Data Breach Blues?*, Swiss Re (2014) available at http://docplayer.net/11592063-Is-cgl-insurance-coverage-tonic-for-the-data-breach-blues.html (explaining that the ISO Circulars for its General Liability Panel meets from 2003 to 2014 "demonstrates that ISO very clearly intends that its CGL form does not provide coverage for data or security breaches.").

17 *See* Chapter 3: *Potential Overlapping Coverage Between Cyber Policies and Other Business and Crime Policies.*

damage' to which this insurance applies."[18] Before 2001, "property damage" meant, in pertinent part, "[p]hysical injury to *tangible property*" and "[l]oss of use of *tangible property* that is not physically injured."[19] But in 2001, "electronic data" was explicitly removed from the definition of "tangible property."[20] ISO's revised CGL policy defined "electronic data" as "information, facts or programs stored as or on, created or used on, or transmitted to or from computer software, including systems and applications software, hard or floppy disks, CD-ROMS, tapes, drives, cells, data processing devices or any other media which are used with electronically controlled equipment."[21]

Since the ISO explicitly excluded electronic data from the definition of tangible property, the ISO introduced the Electronic Data Liability Endorsement, which provided an option to cover electronic data by modifying the definition of property damage to include electronic data, but also clarifying the electronic data is considered intangible property.[22]

Under ISO's standard CGL Policy, Coverage B states, in pertinent part, that "[w]e will pay those sums that the insured becomes legally obligated to pay as damages because of 'personal and advertising injury'

---

18 *See, e.g.,* ISO Form No. CG 00 01 12 07; *see also* Podolak, *supra* note 13, at 382 fn. 66 (discussing the 2001 amendments to the standard CGL policy form).

19 Podolak, *supra* note 13, at 382 fn. 66 (citing to ISO Form No. CG 00 01 10 93, at 12).

20 ISO Form No. CG 00 01 10 01, at 15 ("For the purposes of this insurance, electronic data is not tangible property."); *see also* Ellen M. Farrell and Rachel P. Raphael, *The Internet of Things: Insurance Coverage Considerations*, 10 J. Multidisciplinary Research 61, 74-76 (2018), available at https://www.academia.edu/40093362/Journal_of_Multidisciplinary_Research_Volume_10_Number_3 (discussing ISO endorsements effectively removing coverage for data breaches).

21 ISO Form No. CG 00 01 10 01, at 15; *see also* Jeff Woodard, *The 2001 ISO CGL Revision,* International Risk Management Institute, Inc. (Jan. 2002), https://www.irmi.com/articles/expert-commentary/the-2001-iso-cgl-revision (providing expert commentary on the 2001 ISO CGL Revisions).

22 ISO Form No. CG 04 37 02 02 ("Electronic Data Liability Endorsement"); *see also* Bruce Hicks, *PF&M Companions: Form and Endorsement Changes,* The Rough Notes Company, Inc. (Mar. 2002) http://roughnotes.com/rnmagazine/2002/march02/03p146.htm (discussing ISO forms and endorsement changes in 2001).

to which this insurance applies."[23] Before 2001, coverage for privacy-related offenses under the definition of "personal and advertising injury" was limited to "[o]ral or written publication of material that violates a person's right of privacy . . . ."[24] But in 2001, ISO modified this language to "[o]ral or written publication, *in any manner*, of material that violates a person's right of privacy . . . ."[25] ISO explained they added "in any manner" to the definition of "personal and advertising injury" regarding publications to address internet and electronic publications.[26] Commentators have expressed that this language was "specifically engineered to encompass the type of liability many policyholders now face in our increasingly digital world—liability claims asserting a lack of diligence in keeping such information from falling into the wrong hands."[27]

2. *2004: ISO Introduces Electronic Data Exclusion and also Electronic Data Coverage*

In 2004, the ISO added an "electronic data" exclusion (commonly referred to as "exclusion P") to its standard CGL policy for "[d]amages arising out of the loss of, loss of use of, damage to, corruption of, inability to access, or inability to manipulate electronic data."[28] This Electronic Data Exclusion was added to make clear what was intended when the term "electronic data" was introduced in the 2001 revisions.[29]

But the ISO also introduced a separate claims-made coverage form providing coverage for liability resulting in loss of electronic data caused

---

23 *See, e.g.,* ISO Form No. CG 00 01 12 07.

24 ISO Form No. CG 00 01 07 98, at 12; *see also* Podolak, *supra* note 13, at 380 (discussing ISO modification of the standard form CGL policy to address coverage for electronic-related publications of private information).

25 ISO Form No. CG 00 01 10 01, at 14 (emphasis added); *see also* Podolak, *supra* note 13, at 380.

26 Podolak, *supra* note 13, at 380 (citing Tracey Waller, ISO, 2012 General Liability Multistate Forms Revisions Announced; Proposed 2013 Implementation 14 (2012)).

27 *Id.* at 381 (internal quotations omitted).

28 ISO Form No. CG 00 01 12 04 at 5; *see also* Farrell, *supra* note 20, at 74-76.

29 *See* Donald S. Malecki, *Risk Management—Electronic data exclusions,* The Rough Notes Company, Inc. (Jul. 2004) http://roughnotes.com/rnmagazine/search/commercial_lines/04_07p48.htm (discussing electronic data exclusions).

by an "electronic data incident."[30] An "electronic data incident" is defined as "an accident, or a negligent act, error or omission, or a series of causally related accidents, negligent acts, or errors or omissions, which results in loss of electronic data."[31] This coverage form provided broader coverage than the Electronic Data Liability Endorsement since, unlike the Electronic Data Liability Endorsement, the coverage form does not require the loss of electronic data to result from physical injury to tangible property.[32]

But this coverage form was not designed for policyholders who are providing computer products or services, since losses arising out of such activities are expressly excluded.[33] Additional important exclusions include damage to the insured's own electronic data, liability assumed by contract, failure to perform a contract, infringement of intellectual property rights, and unauthorized use of electronic data.[34]

3. *2013: ISO Endorsements Excluding Claims Involving Access or Disclosure of Confidential Personal Information*

The next major development in cyber insurance coverage emerged in 2013.[35] During this year, the ISO created an endorsement that amended the definition of "personal and advertising injury" coverage. Under Coverage, B, "personal and advertising injury" includes "[o]ral or written publication, in any manner, of material that violates a person's right of

---

30 ISO Form No. CG 00 65 12 04 ("Electronic Data Liability Coverage Form"); *see also* Craig F. Stanovich, *The New ISO Commercial General Liability Policy: A Summary of December 2004 Policy Changes*, International Risk Management Institute, Inc. (Oct. 2004), https://www.irmi.com/articles/expert-commentary/a-summary-of-december- 2004-iso-cgl-policy-changes.

31 *Id.*

32 Stanovich, *supra* note 30.

33 *Id*

34 *Id.*

35 *See* Larry P. Schiffer, Kristin Bryan, Ann Lafrance, and Glenn Brown, *CGL Exclusions for Cyberattacks and Loss of Electronic Data: Is there a Gap in Your Coverage?*, The Brief, Vol 49, No. 4, Summer 2020, https://www.americanbar.org/content/dam/aba/publications/brief/summer20/brf-49-4-summer20-issue.pdf (subscription required) (discussing CGL exclusions for cyberattacks and loss of electronic data).

privacy."[36] But ISO Form No. CG 24 13 04 13 deletes this part from the definition of "personal and advertising injury."[37] Commentators have recognized that this endorsement greatly reduces the potential for coverage of cybersecurity and data breach claims.[38]

In 2013, the ISO updated exclusion P—the electronic data exclusion—to state that "this exclusion does not apply to liability for damages because of 'bodily injury'"[39] In 2013, the ISO also created a series of endorsements broadly excluding claims involving the access or disclosure of confidential personal information.[40] These exclusions and

---

36 ISO Form No. CG 00 01 12 07, at 14 (particularly listed under Paragraph 14.e of the Definitions section in Coverage B Personal and Advertising Injury Liability).

37 The endorsement specifically states that "[w]ith respect to Coverage B Personal And Advertising Injury Liability, Paragraph 14.e. of the Definitions section does not apply."

38 Podolak, *supra* note 13, at 386-87; *see also* Roberta D. Anderson, *Viruses, Trojans, and Spyware, Oh My! The Yellow Brick Road to Coverage in the Land of Internet Oz*, 49 Tort Trial & Ins. Prac. L.J. 529, 566 (2014) (explaining the endorsement "entirely eliminates in the first instance the key definition that is the 'hook' for the data breach coverage under the CGL Coverage B . . . ."); Harvey Nosowitz, *In the Age of Facebook, CGL Policy Privacy Coverage is Shrinking Fast,* Anderson & Kreiger, LLP (Mar. 14, 2013), https://www.andersonkreiger.com/insurance-law/2013/03/14/shrinkingprivacy coverage/ (explaining the endorsement "gives insurers the option to eliminate coverage that has become increasingly contentious as insurers grapple with the potential expansion of Coverage B to include liability for 21st Century conduct—spam, tweets, Facebook posts, computer hacking and the like."); *see also* Chad Milton and Michelle Worrall Tilton, *ISO Broadens Personal and Advertising Injury Coverage Gaps,* Media Risk Consultants, LLC (2014), http://mediarisk consultants.com/wp-content/uploads/2014/11/MRC_New_Revisions_to_ CGL.pdf; and Kevin DiGrazia, *Cyber Insurance, Data Security, and Blockchain in the Wake of the Equifax Breach*, 13 J. Bus. & Tech. L. 255 (2018), available at http://digitalcommons.law.umaryland.edu/jbtl/vol13/ iss2/5 ("Although many of these changes were aimed at tightening cyber related exposure to third-party claims, the ISO's actions further reinforce the notion that barring specific endorsements or an independent insurance policy, an insured is not likely to find cyber related coverage under their CGL policies.").

39 ISO Form No. CG 00 01 04 13; *see also* DiGrazia, *supra* note 38, at 266.

40 Podolak, *supra* note 13, at 398.

endorsements went into effect around 2014.[41] ISO Endorsement CG 21 06 05 14 (*Exclusion—Access Or Disclosure Of Confidential Or Personal Information And Data-Related Liability—With Bodily Injury Exception*) excludes under Coverage A and Coverage B, coverage for damage arising out of "[a]ny access to or disclosure of any person's or organization's confidential or personal information, including patents, trade secrets, processing methods, customer lists, financial information, credit card information, health information or any other type of nonpublic information[.]"[42] ISO Endorsement CG 21 07 05 14 (*Exclusion—Access Or Disclosure Of Confidential Or Personal Information And Data-Related Liability—Limited Bodily Injury Exception Not Included*) is similar to CG 21 06 but does not include the bodily injury exception.[43] ISO Endorsement CG 21 08 05 14 (*Exclusion—Access Or Disclosure Of Confidential Or Personal Information (Coverage B Only)*) excludes from coverage any access to or disclosure of any person's or organization's confidential or personal information limited to personal and advertising injury.[44] These endorsements essentially eliminated a policyholder's coverage for cybersecurity and data breaches.[45]

---

41 *ISO Comments on CGL Endorsements for Data Breach Liability Exclusions,* Insurance Journal (Jul. 18, 2014) https://www.insurancejournal.com/news/east/2014/07/18/332655.htm.

42 ISO Form No. CG 21 06 05 14.

43 ISO Form No. CG 21 07 05 14.

44 ISO Form No. CG 21 08 05 14.

45 DiGrazia, *supra* note 38, at 266; *see also* Rina Carmel & Sherilyn Pastor, *Insurance 101: Understanding ISO's New 2014 Cyber Insurance Endorsements*, American Bar Association (Jan 4, 2015), https://www.americanbar.org/groups/litigation/committees/insurance-coverage/articles/2015/novdec2014-changing-cyberinsurance-landscape/. The ISO has also sought to make clear that its commercial property and business owner policies were also not intended to cover cyber-related events; as of December 2020, a number of jurisdictions that are part of ISO's commercial property and business owner programs rules will require the attachment of cyber incident exclusions to all commercial property and business owner policies. *See* ISO Form Nos. CP 10 75 12 20 and BP 15 60 02 21 (Cyber Incident Exclusion) and ISO Form Nos. CP 10 76 12 20 and BP 15 61 02 21 (Cyber Incident Exclusion with Ensuing Cause(s) of Loss Exceptions); *see also Cyber Incident Exclusion Endorsements and Cyber-Attack Coverage Discussed in Commercial Property Insurance,* International Risk

C. Standardized Cyber Insurance Policies Are on the Horizon

In promulgating the new exclusions, the ISO commented that coverage for cybersecurity and data breaches was available under specific cyber insurance policies.[46] In fact, in 2005, the ISO introduced its E-Commerce Program which provided standalone cyber insurance policies.[47] And while the ISO introduced endorsements essentially excluding cyber liability from CGL policies in 2014,[48] the ISO also began introducing new cyber insurance policies on standard forms and also began offering endorsements for business owner policies.

For example, in 2014, the ISO introduced its Information Security Protection Endorsement.[49] This endorsement for business owner policies provides first-party coverage expenses resulting from a data breach.[50] This endorsement can also extend to cover third-party expenses for claims brought by customers whose personal information was compromised.[51]

The ISO also introduced its Information Security Protection Policy in 2014.[52] This standalone cyber insurance policy provides policyholders with eight separate insuring categories: (1) security breach expense; (2) security breach liability; (3) replacement or restoration of electronic data; (4) business income and extra expense; (5) extortion threats;

Management Institute, Inc. (Aug. 2020) https://www.irmi.com/whats-new/product-update/cyber-incident-exclusion-endorsements-and-cyber-attack-coverage-discussed-in-cpi and *ISO Commercial Property and Businessowners Mandatory Cyber Incident Exclusion Endorsements Analysis*, NUCO.com (Jun. 22, 2020) https://www.nuco.com/fcs/2020/06/22/iso-commercial-property-and-businessowners-mandatory-cyber-incident-exclusion-endorsements-analysis/ (subscription required).

46 Carmel, *supra* note 45.

47 *ISO Introduces Cyber Risk Program to Help Cover $7 Trillion E-Commerce Market,* Verisk Analytics, Inc., (Jan. 11, 2005), https://www.verisk.com/archived/2005/iso-introduces-cyber-risk-program-to-help-cover-7-trillion-e-commerce-market/.

48 *See supra* note 41.

49 Carmel, *supra* note 45 (citing ISO Form No. BP 15 07 03 15).

50 *Id.*

51 *Id.; see also* Mindy Pollack, *New Cyber Option for BOP Writers—ISO Has Endorsements,* General Re Corporation (Sept. 15, 2014), https://www.genre.com/knowledge/blog/new-cyber-option-for-bop-writers-iso-has-endorsements. html.

52 ISO Form No. EC 00 10 01 14.

(6) public relations expense; (7) website publishing liability; and (8) programming errors and omissions liability.[53]

But several insurers throughout the 2000s and 2010s were still offering standalone cyber insurance on nonstandard forms.[54] In an effort to make cyber insurance more standardized, in July 2017, the ISO announced a revised and more expansive cyber insurance program, renaming its E-Commerce Program to the ISO Cyber Program.[55] ISO's new cyber insurance program offers cyber insurance particularly for small, medium and large commercial enterprises.[56] The United States may see these ISO cyber insurance policies become standardized. In March 2018, the ISO announced that 42 states and U.S. territories have implemented the ISO's cyber insurance program.[57]

---

53 *See* DiGrazia, *supra* note 38, at 267 (discussing Form No. EC 00 10 01 14); *see also* David Thamann, *Reducing Cyber Risk Exposures: 8 Category Coverages to Consider*, PropertyCasualty360.com (Feb. 19, 2015), https://www.propertycasualty360.com/2015/02/19/reducing-cyber-risk-exposures-8-category-coverages-to-consider/ (same); and *ISO Comments on CGL Endorsements for Data Breach Liability Exclusions,* Insurance Journal (Jul. 18, 2014) https://www.insurancejournal.com/news/east/ 2014/07/18/ 332655.htm (same).

54 *See, e.g.,* Travelers Indemn Co., Form CYB-3001 (Ed 07-10), available at https://www.travelers.com/iw-documents/apps-forms/cyberrisk/cyb-3001. pdf; Chubb Group of Ins. Cos., Form Chubb Form 14-02-17276 (12/2010), available at http://www.eperils.com/pol/14-02-17276.pdf; and Beazley, Form F00106SL (082011 ed.) available at https://www.beazley.com/documents/Private%20Enterprise/Wordings/NEW%202011%20Info%20Sec%20Form%20F00106SL%2008201l%20ed.pdf.

55 *See ISO Launches Cyber Insurance Program with Enhanced Rating and Coverage Options*, Verisk Analytics, Inc. (July 11, 2017) https://www.verisk.com/press-releases/2017/july/iso-launches-cyber-insurance-program-with-enhanced-rating-and-coverage-options/#; *see also Cyber Insurance Policy,* Law.com (Mar, 20, 2018 at 5:00 AM), https://www.law.com/insurance-coverage-law-center/2018/03/20/iso-commercial-cyber-insurance-policy-423-1925/ (subscription required).

56 *Id., see also* ISO Form Nos. CY 00 01 (Commercial Cyber Insurance Policy), CY 00 10 (Information Security Protection cyber Policy); CY 00 11 (Financial Institutions Information Security Protection Cyber Policy CY 00 12 and CY 00 13 (Media and Information Security Protection Policy).

57 *ISO's New Cyber Insurance Program Implemented in 42 States and U.S. Territories*, Verisk Analytics, Inc., (March 19, 2018) https://www.verisk.

ISO's cyber insurance policies, as well as the nonstandard cyber insurance policies offered by various insurers, provide first- and third-party coverage for various cyber liabilities that have been excluded from CGL policies.[58] Coverage under today's standalone cyber insurance policies typically include coverage for breach responses expenses (*i.e.*, forensic services, notification costs, call centers, credit or identity monitoring); cyber extortion/ransomware loss; data recovery and computer program costs; business interruption loss; public relations expense; and legal defense expenses.[59]

D. Case Law Interpreting Standalone Cyber Insurance Policies

To date, there are not many cases interpreting standalone cyber insurance policies, particularly in comparison to the volume of cases addressing other types of policies.[60] One of the few cases to specifically deal with a standalone cyber insurance policy was *P.F. Chang's China Bistro, Inc. v. Fed. Ins. Co.*[61] In that case, P.F. Chang purchased a standalone cyber insurance policy from Federal Insurance Company.[62]

---

com/press-releases/2018/march/isos-new-cyber-insurance-program-implemented-in-42-states-and-us-territories/.

58 *See* Chapter 2: *Overview of Types of Insurance Coverage Available for Cyber Risks*; *see also* OECD (2020), *Encouraging Clarity in Cyber Insurance Coverage: The Role of Public Policy and Regulation,* www.oecd.org/finance/insurance/Encouraging-Clarity-in-Cyber-Insurance-Coverage.pdf.

59 *Id.; see also* ISO Form No. CY 01 01 01 18 (ISO Form Commercial Cyber Insurance Policy); Travelers Indemn Co., Form CYB-3001 (Ed 07-10), available at https://www.travelers.com/iw-documents/apps-forms/cyberrisk/cyb-3001.pdf; Chubb Group of Ins. Cos., Form Chubb Form 14-02-17276 (12/2010), available at http://www.eperils.com/pol/14-02-17276.pdf; and Beazley, Form F00106SL (082011 ed.) available at https://www.beazley.com/documents/Private%20Enterprise/Wordings/NEW%202011%20Info%20Sec%20Form%20F00106SL%2008201l%20ed.pdf.

60 *See P.F. Chang's China Bistro, Inc. v. Fed. Ins. Co.*, No. CV-15-01322-PHX-SMM, 2016 U.S. Dist. LEXIS 70749 (D. Ariz. May 31, 2016) (relying on "cases analyzing commercial general liability insurance policies for guidance, because cybersecurity insurance policies are relatively new to the market but the fundamental principles are the same.").

61 2016 U.S. Dist. LEXIS 70749 (D. Ariz. May 31, 2016).

62 *Id.* at *2.

The policy was marketed on Federal's website as "a flexible insurance solution designed by cyber risk experts to address the full breadth of risks associated with doing business in today's technology-dependent world" that "[c]overs direct loss, legal liability, and consequential loss resulting from cyber security breaches."[63]

In order to facilitate the processing of credit card transactions, P.F. Chang, like most similarly situated merchants, entered into a master service agreement with a third-party service provider who can process the credit card transactions.[64] The third-party service provider in turn contracted with MasterCard to process these transactions.[65] As part of the service provider's contract with MasterCard, the service provider was required to pay certain fees and assessments in the event of a data breach.[66] Under the master service agreement between the service provider and P.F. Chang, P.F. Chang agreed to reimbursement the service provider for any fees and assessments charged by MasterCard.[67]

In June 2014, P.F. Chang learned that a computer hacker obtained and posted thousands of customers' credit card information online.[68] This data breach resulted in a forensics investigation and litigation costs to defend class action lawsuits.[69] Federal did provide coverage for these costs, totaling approximately $1.7 million.[70]

In March 2015, MasterCard charged approximately $2 million in fees and assessments on the third-party service provider.[71] Pursuant to their master service agreement, P.F. Chang reimbursed the third-party service provider for the fees and assessment.[72]

P.F. Chang notified Federal and sought coverage for the assessment, but Federal denied coverage.[73] P.F. Chang eventually sued Federal for breach of contract and also sought a declaratory judgment that Federal's

---

63 *Id.*

64 *Id.* at *3-4.

65 *Id.*

66 *Id.*

67 *Id.*

68 *Id.* at *4.

69 *Id.* at *5.

70 *Id.*

71 *Id.* at *6.

72 *Id.*

73 *Id.* at *6-7.

cyber insurance policy covered the MasterCard assessment.[74] Federal filed a motion for summary judgment, arguing that the MasterCard assessment was excluded from coverage.[75]

The court ultimately granted Federal's motion for summary judgment.[76] First, the court looked at the policy language and concluded that the policy's exclusion of liability for contractual obligations P.F. Chang assumed with a third-party outside of the policy excluded coverage of the assessment.[77] Next, the court rejected P.F. Chang's argument that coverage existed pursuant to the reasonable expectation doctrine.[78] The court ultimately held that no evidence was presented showing that Federal expected coverage would exist for assessments or that P.F. Change asked for such insurance coverage.[79]

---

74 *Id.*

75 *Id.*

76 *Id.* at *29.

77 *Id.* at *21-25. The court looked at the policy's Exclusion D.3.b, which stated that "[Federal] shall not be liable for any Loss on account of any Claim, or for any Expense . . . based upon, arising from or in consequence of any . . . liability assumed by any Insured under any contract or agreement." The court next looked at the policy's Exclusion B.2, which stated that "[Federal] shall not be liable for . . . any costs or expenses incurred to perform any obligation assumed by, on behalf of, or with the consent of any Insured." Lastly, the court looked at the policy's definition of "Loss," which expressly excluded "any costs or expenses incurred to perform any obligation assumed by, on behalf of, or with the consent of any Insured." The court explained that "[f]unctionally, these exclusions are the same in that they bar coverage for contractual obligations an insured assumes with a third-party outside of the Policy."

78 *Id.* at *25-29. The reasonable expectation doctrine applies if (1) the insured's expectation of coverage is objectively reasonable; and (2) the insurer "must have had reason to believe that the [insured] would not have purchased the . . . policy if they had known that it included" the complained of provision. *Id.*

79 *Id.* A case currently pending in California deals with a standalone cyber insurance policies and is worth keeping a close eye on. *See Cottage Health v. Columbia Cas. Co.,* No. 16CV02310 (Cal. App. Dep't Super. Ct. filed May 31, 2016). In this case, Cottage Health System suffered a data breach in 2013 where over 32,000 confidential medical records were exposed. Columbia filed a declaratory judgment action seeking a declaration that Columbia is not obligated to defend or indemnity Cottage because Cottage did not maintain certain minimum risk controls as required under its cyber insurance policy.

E. Recent Statistics Regarding Cyber Insurance Policies

The cyber insurance market continues to grow every single year. Back in 2016, the ISO estimated that standalone commercial cyber insurance amounted to almost $1.5 billion of written premiums, and standalone plus packaged policies was an estimated $2.5 million.[80] By 2020, the cyber liability market is expected to grow by 20-30%—standalone commercial cyber insurance is forecasted to reach $4.1 million, and standalone plus packaged policies is forecasted to be $6.2 million.[81]

The demand for cyber insurance is matched with—if not outpaced by—the number of data breaches and cybersecurity incidents and their associated costs. A NetDiligence® study reported that average incident cost grew from $103,000 in 2016 to $275,000.[82]

The COVID-19 pandemic has further accelerated the demand for cyber insurance. A Coalition® study observed a 67% increase in the number of business email compromises during the pandemic.[83] This study also noted a dramatic increase in the severity of ransomware attacks, with the ransom demand being higher and the complexity and cost of remediation growing.[84]

F. Conclusion

The emergence of standalone cyber insurance as a central focus for businesses, and the corresponding growth in that market, will continue as the cyber risks to businesses grow. Cyber insurance as in independent

---

Columbia also alleges that Cottage provided false responses to its Risk control Self-Assessment questionnaire. As of this publication, a decision in this case has yet to be reached.

80 *Sizing the Standalone Commercial Cyber Insurance Market*, Verisk Analytics, Inc. (2018), available at https://cyber-liability.org/reports/cyber-risk-white-paper.pdf.

81 *Id.*

82 NetDiligence® Claims Study 2020 Report, available for download at https://netdiligence.com/cyber-claims-study-2020-report/.

83 Coalition® H1 2020 Cyber Insurance Claims Report, available at https://info.coalitioninc.com/rs/566-KWJ-784/images/DLC-2020-09-Coalition-Cyber-Insurance-Claims-Report-2020.pdf.

84 *Id.*

product is still in its relative infancy, particularly compared to other types of policies. For that reason, the developments in scope and in coverage disputes will be fast evolving. Coverage disputes may increase in frequency as more complex coverages are added to standalone policies.

Chapter 5

Basic Requirements for any Cyber Insurance Policy*

As the risks and regulations of cyber security and privacy liability have expanded, so has the scope of cyber insurance available. With the burgeoning statutory, regulatory, and contractual requirements for keeping networks secure and personal data of individuals private, has come an expansion of the obligations and associated liability of companies for compliance with those requirements. That has led to associated expansion in cyber insurance products and the coverages they offer. As exposures change, along with statutes and regulations, so does the scope of available cyber insurance products. While cyber insurance policies over the past two decades have mostly been expanding the scope of coverages offered, at times coverages may contract, or at least certain ones may be subject to lowered limits. Overall, cyber insurance policies have developed to take into account the additional risks and exposure companies face by offering additional coverages.

Affecting the scope of coverage available is the fact that cyber insurers and the insurance products they offer are also increasingly the subject of scrutiny by insurance regulators. Regulators recognize the important role of cyber insurance in assisting businesses to address cyber risks and the exposures they present. Insurance regulators want the cyber insurance market to remain robust so that they remain able to offer cyber insurance to businesses. Thus, there are increasing efforts to encourage cyber insurers to effectively identify and manage not only the cyber risks of their policyholders, but also their own exposures to loss that they assume under the cyber insurance policies they issue.[1]

---

* By Laurie Kamaiko.

1 On February 4, 2021, the New York Department of Financial Services issued a guidance for property/casualty insurers writing cyber insurance, and was the first state insurance regulator in the U.S. to do so. It set forth best practices for New York regulated property/casualty insurers that write cyber insurance. Those included having cyber insurance policies require that victims of cyber incidents notify law enforcement. The guidance also included recommending against ransom payments. Such guidelines and law enforcement concerns

As the cyber risk landscape is constantly evolving, and as cyber insurance itself is a relatively new specialty insurance product, there currently is no standard policy form. There are, however, some basic coverages typically provided by most cyber insurers, as discussed in this chapter.

A. Cyber Insurance Coverages Vary

Key to understanding cyber insurance policies is to accept that there is no standard product or scope of coverage. Coverages offered by insurers vary in scope and in wording. Categories of coverages offered, definitions used, and exclusions included in policies can lead to very different scopes of coverage, and thus at times different coverage results in the event of a claim.

Some of these variances are driven not just by the risk and regulatory environment, but by the different needs of different policyholders in different industries. A retailer and or medical facility may be more concerned with the scope of coverage afforded for data breaches involving unauthorized access to personally identifiable information of customers or patients, and related notification and monitoring costs. A manufacturer may be more concerned with coverage of failures in the security of the networks running the machinery of its manufacturing facilities and those in its supply chain and coverage of resulting business interruption losses. Companies in all industries these days are increasingly interested in coverage of cyber extortion events, with the exponential increase in ransomware attacks and associated ransomware payments demands, often with resulting data replacement costs and business interruption losses.

To keep in mind is that cyber insurance is not an all-risk policy, such as a general liability policy or many property policies with which companies are more familiar. Rather, there is typically a list of coverages available, and insureds can often request and choose specific types of coverages, with the cost of their cyber Insruance varying depending on the scope of coverage they purchase as well as the policyholder's own risk profile.

---

about payment of ransom may soon have an effect on the scope of insurance coverage offerings for reimbursement of ransom payments. NYDFS Insurance Circular Letter No. 2 (2021).

Stand-alone cyber policies are available, as well as cyber insurance endorsements to other types of insurance policies, such as professional liability or sometime general liability policies. While some endorsements can offer fairly extensive coverage, most are more limited in scope and in available limits of liability than stand-alone cyber insurance policies.

B. Basic Coverages

Most stand-alone cyber insurance policies offer both first party and third party coverages. Cyber endorsements added to policies in other lines of insurance often focus more on the first party coverages than third party claims.

The categories of costs and loss for which coverage is provided are often evident from the list of Insuring Agreements on the Declarations page and in the policy, with titles such as Breach Response Costs, Extortion, Data Replacement, Security Liability, Privacy Liability, Regulatory Proceedings, and Funds Transfer Fraud or Social Engineering, although there are variations in the terminology used, and not all policies provide all coverages.

Important to understanding the scope of cyber coverage provided by a policy is not only identifying whether a particular coverage is provided, but also reviewing the definitions of the terms used and the exclusions that may apply. The scope of coverage of a policy that provides for coverage of violation of a "privacy law" may not be as broad as initially apparent if "privacy law" is defined narrowly to be, for example, just U.S. laws governing breached of Personally Identifiable Information versus a policy that provides coverage for violations of privacy laws worldwide and for other obligations imposed by privacy laws such as those restricting collection or mandating disclosure of collection of Personally Identifiable Information, appointment of data security officers, and other obligations. Similarly, the scope of coverage for failure of security of a "computer system" can depend on the definition of a "computer system," and whether it requires that it be owned or controlled by the insured or also includes computer systems operated by third parties.

1. *First Party Coverages*

First party coverages are those that reimburse the policyholder for its own costs in responding to a cyber incident.

The initial driver behind much of the development of modern day cyber insurance policies is providing an insurance product to cover the typical costs of responding to data breaches involving unauthorized access to Personally Identifiable Information. With the expansion of cyber events, such as those involving ransomware attacks and associated extortion demands for payment of ransoms, denial of service attacks, and funds transfer frauds, there has also been an expansion in the first party coverages generally offered. Those first party coverages more commonly offered are discussed below.

(a) Incident Response Costs

The fundamental coverage of modern day cyber insurance is incident response costs, sometimes referred to as crisis management or crisis response costs (or similar titles), typically triggered when there is a unauthorized access or acquisition of Personally Identifiable Information, which is most commonly what is referred to as a data breach.

A significant part of the benefits of cyber insurance is that it provides for services of specialized vendors that can assist the insured in its investigation and response to a cyber incident. However, it is important for an insured to check whether the policy they purchase requires use of vendors pre-approved by the insurer, as an insurer that does have such a requirement may not reimburse its insured for costs of vendors not on such a list, at least not without prior consultation and consent of the insurer.

Almost all cyber insurance policies (and endorsements) will provide coverage at least to some extent for the associated costs incurred in responding to a reasonably suspected data breach that are for:

- Forensic investigation: costs for investigating the breach and identifying what, if any, information was accessed or acquired by the attacker or other unauthorized person.
- Legal advice: retention of a lawyer, often referred to as a breach coach in this context, to advise on whether the incident triggered statutory or regulatory obligations to notify affected consumers or regulators.

- Notification: costs such as printing and mailing of notice of breach to affected individuals.
- Call Centers: Notifications to affected individuals usually include a telephone number that the recipient of a notice can call for any questions about the incident and any remediation they may be offered; thus, a call center with experience in such incidents is often used, and these costs are included within the scope of notification costs or as a separate item.
- Monitoring for identity theft: costs of credit and/or identity theft monitoring if offered to affected individuals, as required or encouraged by many states and other regulators in event of a data breach involving Personally Identifiable Information of individuals. The coverage of such costs is usually limited in time, *e.g.* to one year of such costs.
- Public Relations: costs of a public relations specialists, often subject to sublimits, to assist in the public facing statements about the incident, to help minimize damage to the insured's brand.

Policies may also include catch-all clauses that provide for coverage of other reasonable and necessary expenses, if incurred with the prior consent of the insurer. These clauses allow for some leeway in addressing the costs incurred in responding to specific incidents, if done in consultation with the insurer as to what and why costs are being incurred. Key is obtaining the prior written consent of the insurer to incurring costs that are not specifically identified in the policy as covered ones.

(b) Extortion Threats and Costs (Ransomware Attacks)

An increasingly common type of cyber attack is the ransomware attack, in which the attacker inserts malware into an insured's computer system that encrypts the electronic data on that computer system, with an associated demand for a ransom payment—usually a payment in crypto currency sent to an anonymous crypto currency wallet—in exchange for the decryption key. There are variations on such extortion, including threats to destroy the data or to release into the public the information it obtained when it infiltrated the insured's network, which can be confidential or sensitive information about individuals or the insured's business.

Thus, cyber insurance policies often provide coverage for the costs of such extortion, including reimbursement not only of the ransom itself, but also of the cost to retain specialized vendors that are often (and should be) used to contact, negotiate with and remit payment to the attacker (if the insured decides to make payment).

Vendors who specialize in assessing and negotiating with such attackers can be an important part of the process of responding to a ransomware attack. They often have specialized capabilities and knowledge of such attacks and the malware used that can assist the insured in determining whether the attacker is one likely to provide decryption keys if a ransom is paid or likely to repeat the attack. It may also be able to assist the insured in determining if the attacker is on a U.S. sanctions lists such that payment of a ransom would be prohibited by applicable U.S. trade sanctions laws or regulations.

However, as ransomware attacks now are increasing in the size of ransoms, and regulators are increasingly scrutinizing whether both insureds and insurers are applying appropriate due diligence in assessing if payment of the ransom would violate sanctions laws, cyber insurers are now tending to consider limitations on the scope of coverage for ransom payments.[2] Thus, when considering a cyber insurance policy and its application to ransomware attacks/extortion events, it is also important to consider whether the policy provides coverage for the other effects of a ransomware attack, particularly if the ransom is not paid, which include the cost of replacing data if it cannot be decrypted and the business interruption losses that an insured can sustain while its computer systems are not fully operational.

---

2 The U.S. Department of Treasury, Office of Foreign Asset Control ("OFAC") administers and enforces U.S. economic and trade sanction programs against specified foreign governments, individuals, groups and entities in accordance with U.S. national security and foreign policy. It governs not only those making direct payments to those on sanctions lists, but also those facilitating payments, which can include insurers. OFAC has recently issued advisories to alert companies that engage with victims of ransomware attacks of the potential sanctions risks for facilitating ransomware payments. https://home.treasury.gov/system/files/126/ofac_ ransomware_ advisory.pdf.

(c) Data Replacement Costs

As so many cyber attacks involve damage to or loss of electronic data stored in an insured's computer system, often cyber policies include coverage for data restoration and replacement costs.

Usually, such coverage is limited to the actual cost of date re-creation, such as the cost of data re-entry. However, there are also usually limitations, such as not paying for the costs to duplicate research that led to the development of that data. Thus, for example, if the data lost is a formula that was the result of scientific research, the time and effort to re-create the formula by duplicating the research that led to the formula is not covered. If the data cannot be replaced or restored, covered costs may include the cost to replace the media on which the electronic data was stored (*e.g.*, the hard drive), even if the data itself cannot be restored. Some may explicitly provide for coverage for the cost of an expert to determine if the data can be restored, even if it ultimately cannot be.

(d) Business Income Loss

Increasingly, but not always, cyber insurance policies provide coverage for the business income losses that an insured can sustain while its computer systems are not operational due to a ransomware or denial of service attack.

Variations among policies include whether the policy also provides coverage for "extra expense" incurred in an effort to reduce business interruption losses, or differences in the duration of the period of indemnity.

However, as claims for business interruption losses increase in frequency and severity, coverage is likely to become more limited and subject to higher premium.

(e) Other First Party Coverages

As risks develop, so do offerings of new coverages to address many of them. However, not all cyber policies may include coverage of all emerging risks. As of now, some of the additional coverages, sometimes referred to as coverage enhancements or extensions, that many cyber insurers offer include the following:

i. Fraudulent Funds Transfer/Businesses Email Compromise (BEC)/Social Engineering

This coverage was developed to respond to situations in which an insured receives fraudulent instructions from a third party falsely representing themselves to be authorized to direct that funds be paid to an account they designate. The impersonator may pretend to be a vendor, or a superior of the person contacted to direct payment to a purported vendor, with the result that an employee transfers money from the insured business' account to one set up by the impersonator (there are a wide variety of such scenarios). While not historically a coverage under cyber insurance policies, now because the bad actors often communicate through use of a computer, or use information about the company or its employees that were obtained through hacking the insured's computer system, some cyber insurers affirmatively grant coverage. Moreover, as often information about the company and its employees authorized to make money transfers is gained through scrutiny of social media about the company and its employees, this has been at times referred to as "social engineering" coverage.

Such coverages are often limited in scope, sometimes to just the forensic investigation costs and not including the funds lost, and are often subject to lower limits. A debate in the insurance industry continues as to whether these risks are best addressed under a crime policy or a cyber insurance policy, and cyber insurance policies vary as to whether they offer such coverage and to what extent.

ii. Bricking

Some cyber attacks use malware that renders computer hardware unusable, effectively making it like a brick. Thus, coverage for the replacement costs of such unusable hardware is sometimes referred to as "bricking" coverage. It is not included in many cyber insurance policies; some insurers consider such coverage to be more in the domain of property insurance.

2. *Third Party Coverages*

Cyber incidents that are the basis for the first party coverages in a cyber insurance policy can also give rise to claims against the policyholder by third parties who were, or allege to be, damaged by those events.

Thus, cyber insurance policies generally include not only first party coverages for the policyholder's own costs resulting from a cyber incident, but also third party liability coverages for defense and indemnity of liability claims brought by others who alleged they were damaged as a result of the cyber incidents that affected the insured's computer systems and were due to the insured's acts, errors or omissions.

Third party coverages in cyber policies generally include coverage of claims arising from cyber security incidents that result in unauthorized acquisition of individuals' Personally Identifiable Information. They increasingly also include coverage of privacy based claims arising from purported violations of laws imposing obligations on companies to protect the privacy of consumers, such as failure to post privacy policies identifying how an insured company uses the information it has of consumers or other violations of the expanding scope of state, federal and foreign privacy laws.

For covered claims, these liability coverages provide for payment of claim expenses incurred by the insured in its defense of such claims, and for payment of settlements and judgments awarded against the insured. As with any liability insurance, these coverages are subject to the policy's other terms, conditions and exclusions.

(a) Network Security Liability

Insurance for claims by those injured by the failure of the security of the insured's computer systems and network is generally found under a coverage referred to as Network Security Liability, or similar terminology. This includes claims by individuals whose Personally Identifiable Information was accessed without authorization, or customers of the insured who were harmed by malware that was inadvertently transmitted by the insured.

The scope of this third party liability coverage, just as the scope of first party breach costs or business interruption loss, can be limited by how the policy defines the computer systems to which coverage applies. For example, does the policy limit the coverage to computer systems owned or operated by the named insured company, or does it also cover computer systems operated by others on the insured's behalf? Are there exclusions that would apply, such as those for network failure due to a utility failure or interruption? As with any insurance, definitions and exclusions must be examined as well as the insuring agreements.

(b) Privacy Liability

There is an expanding array of statutes and government regulations that require businesses that collect information about individuals to post privacy policies, adopt security and privacy controls, and otherwise regulate how businesses use Personally Identifiable Information they collect, and how they disclose those usages. These are often generically referred to as "privacy laws," and are issued by countries all over the world as well as in the U.S. on a federal, state and local level. Such privacy laws of other countries may also apply to U. S. businesses, not only if they have facilities or employees in other countries, but also if they are only in the U.S. but solicit business from individuals in other countries. Privacy liability coverages are directed at providing coverage for violations of privacy laws, although again the scope of that coverage may be limited in the policy to only certain aspects of such privacy laws, such as failure to post privacy policy or secure Personally Identifiable Information. Moreover, exclusions may apply to limit coverage when a company engages in the collection of consumer information as a business practice, or violates specified consumer protection statutes limiting the collection or usage of information. Thus, the definition of privacy laws, and the scope of exclusions, are an important factor in determining the scope of insurance coverage provided under a cyber insurance policy.

(c) Regulatory Proceedings

Cyber incidents and violations of privacy law often result in scrutiny from regulators. This can range from inquiries and requests for information by states attorneys general about a data breach involving consumers' personally identifiable information, to full scale lawsuits by a government agency that has oversight of an insured's business.

When the regulatory proceeding is based on an cyber incident or privacy event that is otherwise covered by the cyber insurance policy, that policy will generally provide coverage for the legal fees for responding to that regulatory inquiry or proceedings.

Coverage for resulting fines, penalties, or costs of injunctive relief is less common.

(d) PCI Proceedings and Assessments

Often attackers target consumer credit, debit and gift card (payment card) information, and unauthorized access to payment care information; while less common these days than ransomware attacks, it is still a major risk. Unauthorized disclosures can also be due to employee errors. The Payment Card Industry (PCI) imposes its own industry data security standards on businesses that process payment cards, with which businesses in the chain of payment card processing are contractually obligated to comply. A data breach involving such payment cards can reveal violations by an insured business of those Payment Card Industry Data Security Standards, and result in investigations by the Payment Card Brands and contractually imposed fines, penalties and other assessments such as for the costs of replacement credit cards.[3]

Cyber insurance policies often include some coverage for PCI proceedings, but again the extent can vary greatly among policies, particularly with regard to coverage of the contractual fines and penalties that can be imposed by the card brands.

3. *Other Coverages May Be Available, Depending on Insurer and Insured*

Cyber insurance policies can also include other coverages than those discussed above. Some policies, for example, include media liability coverage, which is discussed separately in this book. In this day and age, many businesses conduct some form of media activity, such as maintaining websites with postings, blogs, and social media sites.

---

3 The Payment Card Industry Security Standards Counsel establishes the Payment Card Industry Data Security Standards (PCI DSS). See https://www.pcisecuritystandards.org. Each card brand (Visa, Mastercard, American Express, Discover) conducts its own investigation in the event of a data breach involving its cards and imposes its own contractual fines, penalties and assessments.

Increasingly, cyber insurance policies are being offered that are designed to apply to specific industries and the particular cyber and privacy risks they face, such as healthcare, construction, or retail enterprises.

Important to understanding cyber insurance is not to assume that all policies are the same, or coverages uniformly offered. Some coverages may be built into others and not listed as a separate coverage; others are set forth as separate coverages. Some coverages such as PCI may be listed as a first party coverage in some policies and listed under third party coverage in other policies. A knowledgeable broker is particularly important for this line of insurance.

Moreover, as new risks develop, so do new coverages to address many of them, and modifications of coverages previously offered.

Most important is to remember that cyber insurance can be a substantial part of a business' arsenal in preparing for and responding to cyber incidents. Cyber insurance often provides access to services of experienced lawyers and vendors who can assist an insured in responding to a cyber incident, as well as provides coverage for at least some of the costs incurred in responding to incidents and resulting claims.

Chapter 6

Obtaining Cyber Insurance—the Application Process and Pre-Underwriting Audits*

Few businesses in 2020 were not directly impacted by the COVID-19 pandemic, whether they were closed completely or partially shut, often with modified schedules, new supply chain arrangements, and employees working from home. New forms of operating and communicating became commonplace and are here to stay. Moreover, as the shutdowns from the pandemic were getting underway, unbeknownst except to the perpetrators, Russia's hack of IT management company SolarWinds had commenced—having begun in March 2020, or earlier. The breach was not disclosed by cybersecurity firm FireEye until December 9, 2020, after it was discovered. As has been reported, the SolarWinds hackers created a malicious software update that was shipped to customers and used to compromise the systems of potentially hundreds of other customers. In all, about 18,000 Solar Winds customers downloaded the malicious software update.

As we approached the January 2021 renewal season, cyber insurance underwriters were already facing increased risk as a result of the proliferation of ransomware attacks, so the pandemic and SolarWinds only added increased risk and complexity. Prior to SolarWinds, insureds and insurers were reacting to the aftermath of the NotPetya attack and there will surely be new risks this year and the years to come. As a result, the underwriting process for cyber insurance will continue to evolve in reaction to these events and how businesses are changing their operations.

---

* By Kristi W. Richard, Ross H. Benson, and Joseph P. Gunset.

A. The Application Process Starts Before Submitting the Application

Whether a company is purchasing cyber insurance for the first time or is at renewal of an in-force policy, there are considerations prior to the application being submitted.

For Matthew Webb, cyber line underwriter at Hiscox, the first step for the insured—before underwriters are even approached to write a policy—is understanding its own risk, then quantifying that risk and having an appropriate set of controls.[1] Webb, who heads the London Market Association Cyber Business Panel, has a team of five underwriters who write cyber risk, mostly for Fortune 500 global businesses with revenue greater than $1 billion.

According to Webb, backup systems, data encryption, and segregated systems are all vital defenses to a cyber attack. A company should understand its risk profile and implement these systems accordingly. For example, a retailer's most important defense may be data encryption designed to protect customers' personally identifiable information whereas backup systems may be a key factor for another industry. Likewise, a conglomerate with different lines of business or a manufacturer with heavy machinery may benefit from insulating various departments' systems. In this regard, Webb's team looks critically at the segmentation that the insured has in place, particularly between the IT department and other networks. Because companies have unique risk profiles, Webb says a "road map of risk improvement" is important when an insured may be looking to transfer a challenging risk to underwriters. Webb notes that his team can put together a policy in such situations where an insured can show a viable plan to improve data security. The result can be broader coverage, at a lower cost.

Webb noted that the two predominant cybersecurity frameworks, one promulgated by the National Institute of Standards and Technology ("NIST framework"), and the other by the International Electrotechnical Commission and the International Organization for Standardization ("ISO/IEC 27001") are both helpful. Also, Webb observed that insureds may also gain significant assistance from in-house expertise at some of the major insurance brokers. In any event, Webb emphasized that the starting

---

1 Telephone Interview with Matthew Webb, Global Head of Cyber, Hiscox London Market (Jan. 7, 2021).

point is having the right team—getting the necessary cohort of people together and getting them to work in unison.

Andrew Wagley, Commercial Lines Account Executive at Dupre Carrier Godchaux, agrees that potential insureds benefit from third party expertise.[2] "In certain cases, particularly for large coverage limits, a company's IP provider is required to provide certain data." Therefore, it is important for a company to notify relevant vendors and providers in the event their assistance is required during the application process.

B. Inquiries the Applicant Should Expect in the Application and the Data It Should Be Prepared to Share

First time buyers shopping for cyber insurance coverage will quickly find that applications vary greatly between insurance providers. "Different underwriters look for different things," says Delvan Irwin, Senior Vice President of FNBB Insurance Agency.[3] "The applications for two competing brokers could be completely different, even if the product may be similar." Irwin states the amount of variance between applications and lack of concrete industry standards creates a lack of clarity for brokers shopping for policies. However, there are a few requirements that are common to most applications.

As a general rule, applications will require detailed information about a prospective insured's processes and procedures for software updates, employee controls, and company-issued electronics that have access its systems. A company should also expect to provide business information relevant to its specific industry. For example, a financial institution may be required to disclose its number of credit cards or customer accounts, while a healthcare provider may need to state the number of patient files within its system. Similarly, an applicant must provide its roadmap for complying with applicable federal law. This is particularly important when operating within a highly regulated industry, such as healthcare, where failure to safeguard patient data could create high levels of exposure.

In addition to the technical details above, underwriters will also request contracts and agreements between an applicant and its customers

---

2 Telephone Interview with Andrew Wagley, Commercial Lines Account Executive, Dupre Carrier Godchaux (April 30, 2021).

3 Telephone Interview with Delvan Irwin, Senior Vice President, FNBB Insurance Agency (April 21, 2021).

and vendors. "Reviewing these agreements is an important step in determining who may be responsible for a breach," says Wagley. "Where third parties are involved, policies need to be tailored to account for various responsibilities."

Both Irwin and Wagley agree that the complexity of an application is often directly correlated to the size of the policy. Companies seeking lower limits may look to add cyber coverage by endorsement on the BOP or commercial property policy. In these instances, applications will be more simplistic and may be offered as a way to round out existing policies. However, Wagley advises prospective insureds seeking limits of $10 million or more or that have definite risk exposure to obtain standalone policies. "It would be foolish not to get standalone coverage if you have true exposure." While the type of information requested may focus on the same areas and concepts regardless of size, larger companies seeking higher policy limits are expected to provide additional details that correspond to the risk level they are seeking to insure.

C. Underwriters' Considerations for New Risks and Policy Renewals, Including under Writing Audits and Evaluations

Geoff White, CEO of Tarian Underwriting Ltd., part of the Lloyd's market, described ransomware as once a "minimal threat" that has now evolved into a great concern for underwriters. Whereas there once were a range of possible motives behind an attack, the ransomware cyber-criminal is looking for immediate financial gain—and often the criminals look for easy targets such as poorly protected local governments and school administrations with inadequate systems.

As a result, White's firm maintains strict controls and procedures concerning risk selection and continues to monitor its insured after the policy is underwritten. To this end, Tarian uses of a variety of tools to confirm that the insured understands its own risk and vulnerabilities. White's initial approach involves performing an "exterior perimeter scan" or a "friendly hack" of the company that will identify the types of vulnerabilities that would be visible to a wrongdoer. In the same way a prospective homebuyer might drive by a property to see if the seller has maintained the home, cyber-insurers will actively scan a prospective insured's systems to determine whether it has a steady foundation in place. If the scan reveals that the company is susceptible to a breach, the problem must be remedied prior to obtaining insurance. However, White says insureds are in the best position to conduct a "deep dive," which is often completed with the aid of consultants. Tarian does not have specific protocols requiring that insureds conduct risk surveys on a particular schedule; however, the firm makes an effort to regularly check in with and monitor clients. White notes that when the SolarWinds breach occurred, his firm was able to reach out to its affected insureds and make certain that they were aware of the software patch which was available to rectify the problem. Both the insurer and the insured stand to gain by working together to address potential vulnerabilities during and after the underwriting process.

Likewise, Irwin recommends that his clients engage a third-party provider to perform audits of their system and implement patches and procedures prior to renewing their policies. Irwin notes that due to an increase in cyber incidents there has been a tightening of additional applications and standards over the last six months. Insureds that do not have the appropriate protocols in place will be declined coverage, and, at a minimum, must fix any issues before they will be given a renewal quote or policy.

D. Applicants May Not Be Able to Obtain Their Current Limits Without Higher Premiums and That Terms May Change

In addition to tightening of applications, Irwin and Wagley have found that prices are going up across all markets. The increasingly difficult market conditions for cyber have led some insurers to reevaluate cover in cyber policies, states Jeremy Cottle, underwriting manager for the Corporation of Lloyd's, which runs and oversees the Lloyd's market. Cottle states that a 50% coinsurance clause or sublimits are beginning to be seen in the context of cover against ransomware attacks.

All of the underwriters we spoke to for this article agreed that underwriting for cyber risks had become more difficult and agreed also that sublimits and coinsurance clauses were becoming standard. Sublimits and coinsurance may serve as a "carrot and stick" to encourage diligence or punish negligence. On one hand, implementing stricter controls, such as multi-factor authentication and phishing training, may result in higher sublimits and lower coinsurance rates. On the other, the failure to properly maintain systems and standards will cause an inverse effect.

At the same time, despite recent attacks and uncertainties surrounding the current risk environment, the market for cyber remains competitive, and while limits are constrained, there is substantial capacity in the market.

Finally, in responding to greater frequency and quantum of claims, insurers are looking to put in place clearer policy language. As an example, the London market has been working for some time on a revised war risk exclusion.

Insureds who are in a position to negotiate policy language or endorsements to address specific coverage concerns should do so. Underwriters want to provide protection that's needed, and disputes don't serve either party.

E. Summary

In summary, the key components of brokers' and underwriters' recommendations for those seeking cyber coverage are:

1. Get the right team together, including risk management, legal, compliance, IT and data security before obtaining cyber-insurance. Make sure your legal/compliance teams can demonstrate how they are addressing privacy regulations, such as the General Data Privacy Regulations (GDPR) and the California Consumer Privacy Act (CCPA). Insurers are particularly concerned with steps being taken to implement data protection policies, controls, and procedures, as this is a growing area for claims. This will pay immediate dividends in the form of better rates and terms.
2. Understand your company's vulnerabilities: keep patching up to date; do regular phishing training with staff and maintain good back-up procedures. The 2017 WannaCry cyber attack, attributed to North Korea, is an example of both the importance of keeping software patches current, but also the significance of back-up systems.
3. Ensure multi-factor authentication and/or another type of endpoint protection is in place.
4. Review data controls and policies, and address deficiencies and vulnerabilities on a regular basis.

5. Make sure the underwriters are aware of the improvements that the company has made to its systems and protocols and stress the company's continuing commitment to high data protection and cybersecurity standards, with reference to the NIST framework or ISO 21007, as appropriate.

When deciding if obtaining a cyber insurance policy is an appropriate step, companies should not view the policy as an absolute safety net. The fact that a company is insured does not relieve it of the continuous responsibility to be vigilant against ever-changing and evolving threats. With appropriate planning, teamwork, and where appropriate, use of a recognized data protection framework, perhaps guided by strategic advisors, insureds can maximize their insurance protection from leading cyber insurers.

Chapter 7

Preparing a Cyber Claim*

This Chapter addresses what happens in the event of a cyber incident or cybercrime and the process of preparing a claim for insurance coverage. Although the trigger of coverage and the specific steps to be taken may differ from policy to policy, what follows is a general overview to help those confronting a cyber incident.

At its heart, the submission of a claim is a process—an insured or an insurance broker needs to give an insurer details regarding the claim so that the insurer can investigate coverage and pay the claim.

Preparing and submitting the notice of loss, by-and-large, requires analyzing the policies to see what and how much coverage is available, including reviewing any exclusions or limitations that could impact coverage. Insureds should be mindful of conditions, particularly those pertaining to giving notice, mitigating damages, claim preparation, dispute resolution, and any time limitations, including contractual suit limitations. After careful review of the policy terms, an insured should have the contours of what notice of the event or, perhaps just circumstances at an early stage, will entail.

In addition to providing notice of their claim, insureds should work closely with those who can prepare claims and tabulate losses to determine the operational impacts and scope of damages. Insureds should establish loss tracking mechanisms and preserve records. With an understanding of the operational impacts, insureds should carefully review revenue and expense considerations. Working through these issues, insureds will be able to put together an estimate of their losses.

But, of course, it takes two to tango. Simply put, even proper notice and a fully supported and documented loss does not mean that a check is soon to follow. The insurer will appoint a claims adjuster to work through the materials. It may also appoint defense or privacy counsel, cyber forensic teams, and accountants. The insurer might also retain outside lawyers to represent it in relation to the claim. This is not to say that the appointment of defense or privacy counsel, a request for the input of a cyber forensic team, or even bringing in accountants is necessarily

---

* By Peter Halprin and Stan Johnson. The authors acknowledge and thank Nick Pappas for contributions to the chapter.

adversarial. After all, having insurer-appointed counsel representing an insured in the immediate aftermath of a cyber breach could be critical to helping the insured navigate the situation. Likewise, insurer-appointed forensic teams may even assist insureds in finding the source of a breach or negotiating ransom amounts with cyber criminals. Unless there is a coverage dispute, the interests of the insured and insurer should be aligned.

Things get more complicated when an insurer, following an investigation, issues a reservation of rights or denies coverage. At that point, an insured may now face an insurer who is unwilling to pay the insured's claim. Negotiation, mediation, litigation or arbitration, or some other process may then ensue. It is the authors' hope that with this Chapter, insureds and insurers alike will find common ground and work together through even the most challenging, high-stakes claim.

A. Pre- and Post-Breach Action Plan

1. Have An Incident Response Plan

Having a predetermined incident response plan is crucial for any organization and can help victims of cyberattacks recover faster and with less downtime. An incident response plan should include, at the very least, plans, procedures, and policies for handling and responding to various types of anticipated and unanticipated cyberattacks. These plans should include contact information for all stakeholders and secondary and tertiary methods of contact so that the stakeholders can contact one another in the event that internal communications are compromised. The incident response plan should also clearly divide responsibilities between the stakeholders so that the response is as streamlined as possible. Additionally, the incident response plan should have predetermined outside counsel, incident response services, and law enforcement agencies who can be contacted during the incident response. Additionally, any incident response plan should include a section devoted to insurance, such as contact information, policy documents, and other information necessary to coordinate the response with the insurer in the event of a cyber incident. To the extent possible, insureds should keep valuable data backed up and in secure servers or storage facilities. This will serve to not only protect that data from outside intrusions, but also enable the insured to be in a better position to prepare and submit its claim to the insurer and provide the necessary documentation. If possible, the company should practice executing the incident response plan. As the maxim goes, "an ounce of prevention is worth a pound of cure." This is sound advice in the cyber insurance context.

(a) Assemble a Claim Team

Prior to any event and submitting a claim, it is important to identify the individuals who will perform certain functions within the group which will be responsible for carrying the claim to completion. The claim adjustment process can be long, burdensome, and time-consuming. Inevitably, it demands the attention of high-level management, who will not get a break from their other day to day duties. To ensure that there is no drop-off in normal business operations during the claim (to the extent possible), the insured should establish clear roles and assign players to finite roles of either operating the business in the wake of the incident or focusing primarily on assisting the insurer in the claim process. This might include individuals in the following roles:

- Risk Management—Central point of contact for the organization's claim.
- Facilities/IT—To document sequence of events and operational impacts resulting from system shutdowns and direct physical asset impacts, and support the nature and cost of recovery efforts.
- Finance/Accounting—To provide the necessary records and information supporting the claim from a financial standpoint.
- Sales/Operations—To determine the impact to operations and ensuing production and sales losses.
- Broker—To advise on policy concerns and leverage relationship with the insurer.
- Legal—Both internal and external to manage issues surrounding coverage and legal ramifications of the attack with customers, vendors, and other parties.
- Claims Accountant—Forensic accountants with specialized experience with commercial insurance claims to prepare and submit the claim measurement. Most policies provide coverage to engage such services, with the cost covered in the claim.

In the absence of an incident response plan and a predetermined team with defined, finite roles, insureds may be left scrambling to determine their losses, coordinate with the insurer, coordinate with breach counsel, coordinate with coverage counsel, manage forensic teams and tech support, and while still managing their day-to-day regular tasks. This can put the insured in a position where the claim is still ongoing after years simply because the point of contact at the insured is juggling too many tasks. This compromises the claim process and the business function.

(b) Determine Operational Impacts

Cyberattack losses can impact organizations in profoundly different ways. Sometimes, these effects are latent and not discovered until the recovery efforts are well underway. It is important to identify those impacts and establish the causal relationship to the circumstances of the attack itself. This can include outages in e-mail, internet access, server/data center access, point of sale systems, inventory management, production controls, website access, accounting/general ledger access, and a wide variety of other mission critical system interruptions.

Cyberattack business interruptions are often different from business interruption caused by property losses. Cyberattacks can affect a much wider scope across the enterprise, due to the interconnectivity of the insured's operations and systems. This differs from property losses, which can be limited to a single location or a concentration of locations in a geographic area affected by a natural disaster.

The graphic below illustrates a comparison between the operational impacts of a cyberattack, compared to that of a property loss event:

Property Loss Scenario	HQ/Admin Locations	Distribution	Plant 1	Plants 2 - 50
Operations			X	
Sales				
Marketing				
Finance				
Administrative				
Other				

[shaded box] = Unaffected   X = Potentially affected

Cyber Loss Scenario	HQ/Admin Locations	Distribution	Plant 1	Plants 2 - 50
Operations	X	X	X	X
Sales	X	X	X	X
Marketing	X	X	X	X
Finance	X	X	X	X
Administrative	X	X	X	X
Other	X	X	X	X

= Unaffected   X = Potentially affected

(c) Preserve Documentation

As in any insurance claim, it is critical to maintain all documentation in support of loss elements, causation, and quantification. While some of this information is easily accessible within the company's books and records, it may be necessary to take measures to preserve certain relevant claim information which may not be preserved in the normal course of business. This may include information such as production planning, daily inventories, appointment schedules, reservation logs, order backlogs, etc. (depending on the relevant industry), to name a few examples.

(d) Understand Policy Terms & Conditions

A key step in the claim submission process is analyzing coverage. Although there is significant competition amongst insurers for business and no standard form cyber policy language, insured are unlikely to have obtained, let alone contemplated, every possible cyber threat or claim. How could they? Threats change by the minute. And, after all, this is not their business. Insurers, on the other hand, are in the business of constantly analyzing and assessing the risks that the underwrite. As Lord Mansfield famously proclaimed in the case of *Noble v. Kennaway*, 2 Doug. 511 (K.B. 1780), "Every under-writer is presumed to be acquainted with the practice of the trade he insures, and that whether it is recently established, or not."

As such, any given loss scenario/claim may require a deep dive into the terms of the policy to understand coverage. Risk professionals should review coverage grants, exclusions and limitations, and conditions. This review should, obviously, include the definitions that control those provisions and endorsements that alter them. Further, conditions of coverage often set forth the timing of submission of the claims, timing of proof of loss submissions, and time to bring legal action against the insurer. Failure to comply with the notice and reporting provisions of the policy are raised by insurers as defenses to coverage.

i. Claims Process for First-Party Coverage

As discussed in earlier chapters, many cyber policies provide coverage for first-party losses. Cyber first-party coverage varies by policy and is highly dependent on how each policy defines the coverages and terms it contains.

First, reporting the claim is of the utmost importance. Many policies require claims or losses to be reported within a specified time frame. Cyber policies, however, often contain breach response services that lose their efficacy with the passage of time. To take advantage of these types of coverage, the insured will need to report the claim as soon as possible. In its notice to the insurer, the insured should provide as much detail about the loss as it has available. Often, insureds will be scrambling and do not have a complete picture of the events and circumstances surrounding the loss. In that case, the insured should provide information about what it knows and describe what is happening.

Second, insurers often request copious amounts of information. This ranges from information regarding the incident to financial information going back many years. While directly supplying the insurer with available information can be helpful, it is usually in the insured's interest to enlist the assistance of a claim preparation team to help prepare the responses to the insurer's requests for information and the proof of loss. Many policies provide coverage for claim preparation fees.

Third, many policies require the submission of a proof of loss and impose a deadline for its submission. Insureds should be mindful of these requirements and deadlines and comply with them whenever possible. In the event an insured is concerned about the ability to comply with timing requirements, it should communicate its difficulties to the insurer and ask for an extension. If the insurer provides the insured with a form proof of loss, the insured should complete the form the extent possible, supplementing with additional information where necessary. If the insurer does not provide a form, the insured should follow the proof of loss requirements listed in the policy and draft a proof of loss narrative with supporting data and exhibits.

Supporting data can include, among other things, the costs to repair the damage or replace the damaged property, accounting data to support business interruption claims, invoices for vendors who assisted in responding to the loss, costs to prevent further damage, costs associated with responding to the damage. Insureds may want to consider enlisting the assistance of a claim preparation team to assist with the proof of loss given these complexities.

Once the proof is completed, insurers may have follow-up questions often regarding the causal links between incident and the claimed loss. It is important to remember that insurers often do not understand the insured's property or business the way the insured does. Often, insurers ask about how certain revenues streams may be interrupted by a network outage or may evaluate profits and losses on a year over year basis and discount a seasonal surge in profits that would have occurred but for a network disruption. Insurers also may ask why the insured purchased a different operating system for the hardware that was bricked and may claim that the purchase was an upgrade, not a replacement. These are things that insurers cannot easily on their own and insureds must explain and demonstrate how their losses fall into their policy's coverage.

Insureds should also keep in the that their submission of a proof of loss may trigger certain legal requirements that the insurer must comply with, such as responding to the proof of loss within a certain amount of time or accepting or denying coverage. If the insurer does not comply with those requirements, they may be in violation of applicable insurance law.

ii. Claims Process for Third Party Coverage

As discussed in earlier chapters, third-party coverages typically focus on defense and indemnity, i.e. attorneys' fees and costs and settlement costs incurred as the result of a third-party claim. For example, a cyber-specific liability coverage may provide coverage for replacement of credit cards after the insured suffers a breach that compromised its customers credit card data. Banks that must issue new credit cards may seek reimbursement from the insured for those costs and a cyber policy may provide third-party coverage for such a claim. Defending and resolving regulatory claims can also arise under third-party coverage.

Generally, the claims adjustment process is different as, with third-party claims, questions tend to revolve more around the facts of the underlying actions and how they fit within the coverage. And, to the extent the carrier provides defense counsel to defend the insured, the facts of the underlying claim will reveal themselves through the normal course of litigation or a regulatory proceeding.

iii. Claim Process for Crime Coverage

Crime policies that are not cyber specific may, nevertheless, provide coverage for certain cyber losses. In fact, as discussed in more detail in an earlier chapter, various crime policies have been found to provide coverage for phishing attacks[1] and ransomware attacks.[2] Crime policies

---

1 *See Medidata Sols., Inc. v. Federal Ins. Co.*, 729 F. App'x 117 (2d Cir. 2018) (crime policy covered phishing losses); *Am. Tooling Ctr., Inc v. Travelers Cas. & Sur. Co. of Am.*, 895 F.3d 455 (6th Cir. 2018) (crime policy coverage phishing losses); *Owens, Schine & Nicola, P.C. v. Travelers Cas. & Sur. Co. of Am.*, No. CV095024601, 2010 Conn. Super. LEXIS 2386 (Conn. Super. Ct. Sept. 17, 2010) (trial court held that losses related to fraudulent e-mail and check scheme covered under crime policy); *but see Miss. Silicon Holdings, LLC v. AXIS Ins. Co.*, 2021 WL 406238 (5th Cir. Feb. 4, 2021) (holding no coverage for business e-mail compromise scheme under crime policy); *Interactive Comms. Int'l Inc. v. Great Am. Ins. Co.*, 723 Fed. App'x 929 (11th Cir. 2018) (holding that there was no coverage under a "Computer Fraud" policy because policyholder's loss did not "result[] directly" from the fraud); *Apache Corp. v. Great Am. Ins. Co.,* 662 F. App'x 252 (5th Cir. 2016) (holding that there was no coverage under a crime policy because the email that caused the loss was "merely incidental" to the loss and did not directly cause the loss); *Midlothian Enters. v. Owners Ins. Co.*, 439 F. Supp. 3d 737 (E.D. Va. 2020) (court held crime policy not responsive to phishing losses); *Crown Bank JJR Holding Co., Inc. v. Great Am. Ins. Co.*, 2020 WL 634147 (D.N.J. Feb. 11, 2020) (holding that under the terms of the policy, an emailed PDF with the client's signature did not constitute a "Written" "Original" document under the policy and, therefore, did not trigger the Financial Institution Bond policy's forgery coverage.).

2 *G&G Oil of Ind., Inc. v. Continental W. Ins. Co.*, 165 N.E.3d 82 (Sup. Ct. Ind. 2021) (The Indiana Supreme Court held that an Indiana trial court improperly granted an insurer's motion for summary judgment because fact issues existed as to whether the cyber criminals' intrusion into the insured's computer system were obtained by trickery, whether the loss was direct, and other issues about the application of the policy language to the facts).

contain their own specific coverages, exclusions, and conditions. Although the claim submission process is largely similar to the first-party processes described above, there may be certain nuanced differences in relation to the facts sought by the insurer, particularly as relates to causation.

(e) Be Aware of Exclusions

Insurers may assert various exclusions to avoid coverage for cyber claims. Exclusions must be carefully reviewed to determine whether they apply. The rules governing the interpretation of exclusions are favorable to coverage. Although they are determined by applicable state law, the general contours follow below.

(1) Exclusions must be conspicuous, plain, clear, and understandable in order to be given effect.[3]

(2) Exclusions will be strictly construed against the insurer.[4]

---

3 *Ponder v. Blue Cross*, 145 Cal. App. 3d 709, 719 (1983); *Travelers Prop. Cas. Co. v. Super. Ct.*, 215 Cal. App. 4th 561, 575 (2013); *see also State Farm Fire & Cas. Ins. Co. v. Deni Assoc. of Fla., Inc.*, 678 So. 2d 397, 401 (Fla. Dist. Ct. App. 1996) ("strict construction is required of exclusionary clauses in insurance contracts only in the sense that the insurer is required to make clear precisely what is excluded from coverage"); *Seaboard Sur. Co. v. Gillette Co.*, 64 N.Y.2d 304, 311 (1984) ("whenever an insurer wishes to exclude certain coverage from its policy obligations, it must do so 'in clear and unmistakable' language").

4 *Meraz v. Farmers Ins. Exch.*, 92 Cal. App. 4th 321, 324 (2001); *see also Manzarek v. St. Paul Fire & Marine Ins. Co.*, 519 F.3d 1025, 1032 (9th Cir. 2008) ("California law requires us to adopt a narrow construction" of an exclusion; holding that field of entertainment exclusion does not excuse insurer from duty to defend suit brought against two members of The Doors by another member for infringing trademark, name, and logo); *Pioneer Tower Owners Ass'n v. State Farm Fire & Cas. Co.*, 12 N.Y.3d 302, 306 (2009); *Demshar v. AAA Con Auto Transport, Inc.*, 337 So.2d 963, 965 (Fla. 1976) ("Exclusionary clauses in liability insurance policies are always strictly construed."); *Pekin Ins. Co. v. Miller*, 367 Ill. App. 3d 263, 267 (2006) ("Exclusion provisions that limit or exclude coverage must be construed liberally in favor of the insured and against the insurer.").

(3) Even if the insurer's interpretation of an exclusion is the most reasonable interpretation, it should not be adopted if the insured has a reasonable interpretation.[5]

(f) Be Aware of Conditions

In general, the "Conditions" section of an insurance policy "identifies general requirements of an insured and the insurer or matters such as loss reporting and settlement, property valuation, other insurance, subrogation rights, and cancellation and nonrenewal."[6] In this section, we focus on five conditions—notice of loss or circumstance, mitigation of damages (sometimes part of the same section as the notice of loss), other insurance, dispute resolution, and suit limitation. Insureds must take note of the conditions because if they do not comply with the conditions, the insurer will use that non-compliance as a defense to its coverage obligations. In other words, if the insured is not mindful of the conditions in its policy, it may be obstructing its recovery efforts or shutting it off completely.

i. Notice

Given the rapid pace cyber breaches take, it will likely benefit an insured to inform their insurer of what happened when the insured believes it has suffered a security or data breach. As noted above, some insurers help to provide services to insureds to assist with such breaches and early intervention can be critical to reducing the impact of a breach. In many cases, however, threat actors burrow themselves in systems and may not be discovered for some time after the initial intrusion, even years later.

The manner and timing of notice is typically provided for in the policy. Insureds should to pay close attention to this language because it can differ from policy-to-policy and, within policies, from coverage-to-coverage. First-party and third-party loss, for example, will have different triggers and notice requirements.

Policies may also provide for notice in the event of the awareness of a circumstance which could result in the defined term "Claim." The import of a notice of circumstance is that notice will be deemed to have been

---

5 MacKinnon v. Truck Ins. Exch., 31 Cal. 4th 635 (2003).

6 *Policy Conditions*, *IRMI*, https://www.irmi.com/term/insurance-definitions/policy-conditions (last visited Dec. 10, 2020).

given in the policy period in which the notice of circumstance was given, even if the eventual claim does not arise until years later.

ii. Mitigation

Insurers typically are obligated to pay for the expenses their insureds incur in trying to reduce or mitigate loss that might be covered by a policy. The reasonable costs of mitigation efforts are covered, even if it turns out that those expenses exceeded what the loss otherwise might have been. This coverage commonly applies when, for example in the property context, an insured boards up its windows to prevent storm damage.

In the cyber context, policies may require an insured to "take all reasonable steps to protect the computer system from further loss or damage" or take "such actions that such Insured and Insurer agree are necessary and practicable to prevent or limit Loss . . ." or other variants of this provision. There may be, however, implications for the insured's retention or deductible as well as coverage. Particular attention should be paid to such provisions following a loss.

When including these costs in a claim, the insured will need to demonstrate the ways that its mitigation efforts were connected to reducing or mitigating the covered or potentially covered loss. In the cyber context, this could be preemptively taking steps to secure the insured network when the insured discovers a malicious code in it. Ostensibly, the insured would need to take such action to prevent the code from spreading throughout the network or its system. Such action would prevent the code from spreading but may hamper the functionality of the insured's operation to some extent, causing the insured loss. When submitting this type of claim, the insured will need to be able to tell the story in a narrative form and quantify its losses with the appropriate proof. Such proof can be statements showing daily revenues and the interruption of those revenues during the outage or vendors invoices for work performed in mitigation of the harm. Such proof will differ with each loss.

iii. Other insurance

"Other Insurance" provisions typically provide that the policy's coverage shall apply as excess over any other valid and collectible insurance, unless as expressly written.

As discussed above, as there may be overlap between coverages under traditional cyber policies and other policies, which insurance is primary may be important, particularly in relation to different limits and retentions or deductibles.

In addition, where an insured has entered into a contractual relationship with a party that requires that insured to be an additional insured under a traditional cyber policy, there may be issues in relation to the interplay between the insured's cyber policy and that to which it is an additional insured.

iv. Dispute Resolution

Many cyber insurance policies contain alternative dispute resolution provisions. Such provisions require arbitration, mediation, negotiation, or some combination of the three.[7] They may also permit litigation if, for example, mediation has taken place and failed.[8]

Arbitration is "a creature of contract; it involves one or more impartial persons to adjudicate the dispute; it is generally binding, and; it is generally private and confidential."[9] Insureds should understand the advantages and disadvantages of proceeding with arbitration or some other form of dispute resolution.[10]

---

7 See, e.g., *New Hotel Monteleone, LLC v. Certain Underwriters at Lloyd's of London, Subscribing to Ascent Policy No. ASC14C000944*, Case No. 2:15-cv-00061, 2016 WL 3382630 (E.D. La.). Underwriters' Motion to Dismiss or, in the Alternative, Motion to Compel Arbitration and Stay.

8 *See Columbia Cas. Co. v. Cottage Health Sys.*, Case No. CV 15-03432, 2015 WL 4497730 (C.D. Cal. Jul. 17, 2015).

9 For more details on the differences between forms of dispute resolution, *see* Peter A. Halprin, *Arbitrating Insurance Coverage Disputes and the New ARIAS Rules*, *Risk Management Magazine* (Feb. 20, 2020), http://www.rmmagazine.com/2020/02/20/arbitrating-insurance-coverage-disputes-and-the-new-arias-rules/.

10 Peter A. Halprin and Joshua Gold, *Cyber Insurance Disputes: Will Arbitration Clauses Be A Battleground?*, AGENTS OF AMERICA (May 2016), http://www.agentsofamerica.org/eo-prevention/cyber-insurance-disputes-will-arbitration-clauses-be-a-battleground/; Peter A. Halprin and Daniel Garrie, *Arbitrating Cyber Coverage Disputes*, COVERAGE MAGAZINE (Mar. 21, 2019).

v. Suit Limitation

As with all policies, a cyber policy may contain a suit limitation provision. These provisions establish the amount of time in which an insured can bring a suit against the insurer. Given that these provisions contractually, and generally, reduce the available time in which suit can be brought, insureds should be attentive to them.

B. Claim Development

Cyber events, like property claims, typically involve loss and claim components that fall into two major categories: direct damages and business interruption (or time element).

1. Direct Damages

Direct damages include those that are typically documented through direct out-of-pocket costs, physical damages or other costs that are relatively straightforward to quantify and document. These normally involve minimal subjectivity to quantify, and are usually documented through invoices, receipts or other purchase cost documentation. Examples of such claim components may be legal fees, cyber incident response, breach response and notification services, computer forensic investigative costs, ransom payments, data recovery services, equipment replacement, privacy & security, and claim preparation costs.

While these costs are conceptually simple to document and include in a claim, there are complexities which come into play in the realities of loss scenarios, *e.g.* periods of interruptions, periods of restoration, exclusions, etc. Other complexities relate to the cost of transactions themselves, including causation for the cost/loss and proper valuation. Each claimed cost is scrutinized by the adjuster to assure that the cost is directly associated with the loss event and covered by the policy. There are sometimes costs that may relate indirectly to a loss occurrence yet may not represent a cost incurred to recover from that particular event, but rather to protect against future events, as an example. Other costs may be recoverable from another party, such as intangible products such as software licenses or remaining lease obligations associated with damaged computer equipment. In the event of physical damage to computer and other equipment in a cyber event, some complexities may come into play for properly establishing the insured value for such assets. Some policies may provide for replacement cost, while others may insure on an actual cash value basis.

Ultimately, the direct damages claim would consist of detailed listings of all transactions including vendor/supplier names, dates of transactions, amounts incurred, description of charges, supported by invoices, receipts and other external or object supporting evidence, and referenced in the claim's source/supporting documents. As the adjustment of the claim progresses, the insured should ensure that each item is addressed and paid, or that the insurer provides a proper explanation of any items for which it denies coverage. The level of detail to such documentation and proof of payment required may vary by insurer or adjuster, but the nature of the claim packages is essentially the same on most claims.

2. *Time Element*

Time element coverages generally addresses two primary types of coverage: business interruption, which is associated with lost earnings, and extra expense, which represents increased costs to maintain operations. Time element insurance coverage and claims are considered one of the most complex challenges for risk managers with large, multifaceted and/or global programs. This is true whether the event is associated with a cyberattack, or an interruption due to a property event such as a natural disaster. Disaster, in any form, can strike at any time and insureds should prepare by having a comprehensive plan for recovery, including a preordained team, to best manage the claims process.

3. *Extra Expense*

Extra expense coverage is a very important resource for many companies facing an interruption and recovery situation. Generally, extra expense claims are similar to direct damages claims, in that much of their claim presentation includes listings and documentation associated with direct out of pocket costs. Some examples of extra expenses would include excess freight, overtime, outsourcing, travel expenses, and other items which one would consider normal operating expenses. In certain cases, these claims do involve calculations to determine the impact on affected categories of expenses incurred during an insured's response to a cyberattack. In a loss scenario, those operating expenses increase to deal with achieving a return to normal operations. Thus, it is important to establish what is the "normal" level of those expenses, in order to understand and quantify the portion which is "extra" and warrants inclusion in the extra expense claim. Otherwise, the insured must demonstrate that the expenses were reasonable, necessary and associated with the loss event.

4. *Business Interruption*

Business interruption ("BI") coverage is complex and a submitting a claim for BI often presents substantial challenges to the insured. Here, we outline some practical guidance for loss determination and claim submittal, which should help minimize issues and facilitate a smooth and successful claim.

The general structure for BI coverage forms commonly fall into 2 categories:

1—"Gross Earnings"—Revenue less "non-continuing" expenses
2—"Gross Profits"—Net profit plus "continuing" expenses

While the formulation of a claim under these forms do differ, they yield the same answer, as illustrated in the graphic below:

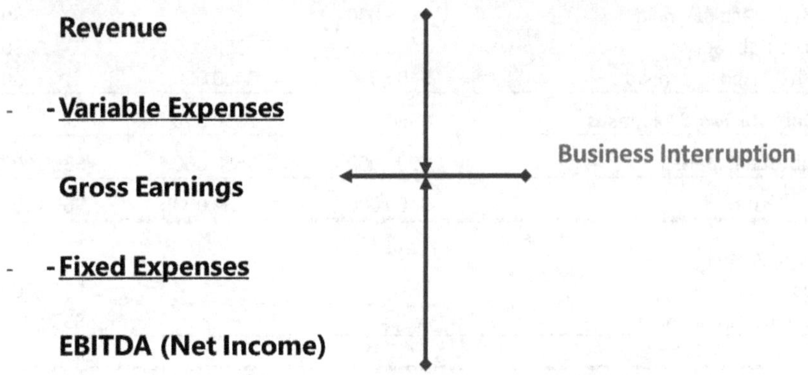

Essentially, under the Gross Earnings form, the policy requires the insured to calculate the revenue lost due to the covered event for the period of interruption. Then, any variable expenses which are saved ("non-continuing expenses") are deducted to yield the "Gross Earnings" figure which is the BI claim amount. This is commonly referred to as a "Top-down" approach. Under the Gross Profits form, the starting point is determining lost net income, then adding back any unearned fixed expenses to arrive at the BI claim amount. This is commonly referred to as a "Bottom-Up" approach. Under both approaches, the answer is the same, as denoted by the horizonal mid-line, labeled "Gross Earnings" and "Business Interruption".

To determine these amounts, the insured can follow a framework that is commonly referred to as a "3-column measure", illustrated in the graphic below using hypothetical claim figures. The figures at the bottom indicate the primary parts of the Gross Profits equation, and the primary parts of the Gross Earnings equation.

<u>3 Column Graphic:</u>

Description	Projected	Actual	Difference
Revenues	$1,000,000		($1,000,000)
Less Expenses:			
Direct Material	$250,000		($250,000)
Other Variable Overhead	$100,000		($100,000)
Subtotal Variable Expenses	$350,000	$0	($350,000)
Fixed Labor	$75,000	$75,000	$0
Fixed Lease Payments	$25,000	$25,000	$0
Fixed Debt Service	$50,000	$50,000	$0
Other Fixed Overhead	$400,000	$400,000	$0
Subtotal Fixed Expenses	$550,000	$550,000	$0
Subtotal Expenses	$900,000	$550,000	($350,000)
Net Profit	$100,000	($550,000)	($650,000)
<u>Gross Profits</u>			
Lost Net Profit			$100,000
Continuing Expenses			$550,000
Total			$650,000
<u>Gross Earnings</u>			
Lost Revenue			$1,000,000
Less: Saved (Non-continuing) Expenses			($350,000)
Total			$650,000

While the above graphic illustrates a simplistic general framework for a BI claim equation, the reality is that such claims involve quite a bit more complexity. Underlying this simple overview are granular details that much be assembled to develop an adequate claim which demonstrates the loss in compliance with the policy coverage and industry standards. Some of these details include:

- Establishing the period of interruption and determining losses during that period—This a function of the nature, duration, and scope of the event's impact on operations and earnings. Some losses may extend beyond the covered policy period.

  Example: A retail operation suffers an outage which affects multiple systems for 2 weeks, causing it to close all locations completely for 10 days and partially for the next 5 days, forcing customers to go to competitors for their needs. As a result, the business loses customers and suffers sales losses over the next 6 months as it recovers its customer base and regains its reputation. If the business interruption or extra expense coverage has a period of restoration less than the total period of loss i.e., less than 6 months in this example, the insured will have to look to other provisions for coverage for those losses incurred outside the period of restoration.

- Building loss values across multiple locations, divisions, product lines or other operational categories. Ultimately, these combine into a single loss figure, but there is typically a unique story as to the impact to each category, and potentially a unique approach to measuring the associated losses.

  Example: A multinational manufacturing company operates multiple separate and distinct production divisions which produce various, unrelated products. However, all divisions utilize the same shared accounting systems, e-mail, sales and CRM systems, and other resources, all of which are taken down by a ransomware attack, forcing a shutdown at all locations. Each of the divisions may be affected to varying degrees and have their own logical way of quantifying damages and formulating their respective claims. However, the policy covers the single incident affecting all divisions, thus the claim itself must encapsulate the impacts to all divisions under a single, consolidated claim submittal.

- Demonstrate causation of losses associated with cyber event. This is qualitative aspect that is critical to establishing coverage for whatever loss figure is determined. This is a consideration relevant across all categories of revenue and expenses impacted by the event, and one must constantly ask the question of "How is the impact to this account related to the covered cyber-attack loss event?".

Once the proof is completed, the insurer will likely have follow-up questions, often regarding the causal links between incident and the claimed loss. It is important to remember that insurers often do not understand the insured's property or business the way the insured does. There are things that insurers cannot easily ascertain on their own and insureds must explain and demonstrate how their losses fall into their policy's coverage.

5. Dependent or Contingent Business Interruption

Some policies will provide coverage for instances in which an insured suffers a business interruption or loss when a business that supplies the insured with products or services or purchases products or services from the insured suffers a security breach or system failure. To anticipate and prepare for such a claim, insureds must know who their service providers and customers are, what services or products they provide, and how they rely on those companies. Having this type of information readily available will enable insureds to submit this information to the insurer in a timelier and more cost-effective manner which in turn leads to faster payment of claims. The insured will need to demonstrate in its claim submission the way that the interruption affected its business. With the interconnectedness of vendors, services, and clients, this type of loss could be extremely complex and will require outside experts to assist assessing the extent of the interruption and preparing the claim.

C. Additional Claim Measure Topics

1. Calculating Lost Revenues/Saved Expenses

To calculate the loss of revenues and expenses, one must develop a projection of what those figures would have been, but-for the loss event. What is the appropriate way to project those revenues and expenses? This is debated in virtually every business interruption claim.

Some of the methods commonly used include:

- Pre or post-event monthly, weekly or daily averages
- Year-over-year growth trends
- Budget/Adjusted Budgets
- Market performance indices
- Comparable/proxy group

Factors that affect whether an approach is appropriate depend on the circumstances of the business and the loss event itself. In an industry that experiences seasonal fluctuations in business throughout the year, a YOY trend may be more appropriate. When the historical performance is not a valid indicator, then one of the other approaches is more suitable. Naturally, every industry has their own metrics which feed into the equation as well. For example, production volumes are important in a manufacturing setting; room occupancy and rates are the primary drivers for a hotel business; while a hospital measure will involve admissions, patient days, and census data. The claim preparer must determine what set of data best represents a proper basis for quantifying the loss and apply a reasonable method of projecting those metrics to reflect what results should have been, absent the covered loss.

Other considerations in developing a projection include defining the appropriate historical period ("base period") to consider when developing averages and trends. Changes in the business during that base period can make a difference—exceptional events like new products, expansion/reductions, prior business interruptions, and market changes, among others, can have a significant impact on the business.

2. *Claim Preparation Expenses*

As noted above, claim preparation is a crucial component of submitting a claim for coverage for a cyber incident. Claim preparation often involves forensic accountants, computer forensic specialists, and other specialists who assist the insured in understanding the scope of the damage and presenting it to the insurer for coverage and reimbursement. Given the complexity of business interruption losses and calculating business income, these costs can be quite expensive. Additionally, in many cases, the calculation of property damage can also be multi-faceted and complex. Many policies, however, cover these costs, and insured should not overlook this coverage if their policy includes it.

3. *Other Topics to Consider*

Some more advanced topics/issues which commonly arise in the settlement of a business interruption claim include:

- Ordinary payroll—Optional coverage for hourly/non-managerial employees during an interruption.
- Depreciation and other non-operating expenses—How these should be treated in the calculation of net profit or continuing expenses.
- Value based deductibles—How to develop the basis value in terms of time frame and breadth of operations to include.
- Actual loss sustained provisions—How to demonstrate the resultant financial losses suffered due to a demonstrable loss event.

D. Summary and Checklist of the Claims Process

As important as the quantitative aspects are for the success of a BI claim, familiarity with and attention to the claim adjustment process will help assure a smooth progression to settlement and payment of a cyber claim. Insureds should keep in mind:

- Proactive claim preparation
  - To effectively prepare a claim for submission, the insured must understand their policy and comply with the applicable provisions to the extent possible. Often, insurance recovery counsel are useful in the achieving that end. Further, computer forensic specialists are useful in understanding the scope of the damage and forensic accountants are useful in quantifying the financial impact of the damage.
- Comprehensive documentation/support
  - It is vital to have necessary documentation to support the claim submission. Such documentation may include a timeline of events, reports detailing the losses, and other sources of information that could bear on the claim submission. An insured may, however, want to consider engaging counsel to navigate privilege issues that may arise when preparing a claim for submission.[11]

---

11 For a discussion of these issues *see, e.g., In re Arby's Restaurant Group, Inc. Data Sec. Litig.*, No. 1:17mi55555-WMR (N.D. Ga. March 25, 2019) (a report created after an internal investigation by Mandiant Services Inc. was protected work product); *In re Experian Data Breach Litig.*, 2017 WL 4325583 (C.D. Cal., May 18, 2017) (third party forensics report was protected work product); *In re Target Corporation Customer Data Sec. Breach Litig.*, 2015 WL 6777384 (D. Minn. Oct. 23, 2015) (finding that attorney-client privilege and work product doctrine applied to emails relating to the work of Target's Data Breach Task Force, which focused on informing Target's in-house and outside counsel about the breach so that Target's attorneys could provide the company with legal advice and prepare to defend the company in litigation); *but see In re Capital One Consumer Data Sec. Breach Litig.*, 2020 WL 3470261 (E.D. Va. June 25, 2020) (Capital One ordered produce a forensic report prepared by cybersecurity consultant after July 2019 data breach. The court found that the report fell under the scope of an engagement that predated the data breach and was not protected attorney work product.); *Wengui v. Clark Hill, PLC*, 2021 WL 106417 (D.D.C Jan. 12, 2021) (Consultant's breach report was not significantly different than an unprivileged report prepared in the ordinary course of business i.e., not prepared in anticipation of litigation, and was discoverable. There was also nothing in the record to support the defendant's claim of a "two-track" investigation).

- Establish timelines for adjustment progression—internal and external
  - The insured should establish a timeframe for progress on the claim submittal and adjustment, which suitably meets their timing requirements during which it needs to recover proceeds of an insurance policy under which it is submitting its claim. As the old adage goes, "the squeaky wheel gets the grease."
- Identify specific issues/differences to tackle and resolve
  - It is important for insureds to work with their counsel and consultants to identify issues that may arise in the preparation of their claim. This can help insureds anticipate an insurer's questions or reservations and address them peremptorily, thus speeding up the timeline to recovery.
- Understanding insurer team's roles and responsibilities
  - The more an insured understands how the insurer's team's functions, and the purpose of their information needs and requests, the easier it will be for the insured to figure out what useful information exists, and where that information needs to go to facilitate rapid claim resolution.

Submitting a claim for cyber insurance coverage can be a complex, drawn-out process. It is helpful for the insured to understand their coverage as well as the proactive steps they can take to try to streamline the process. If the insured understands the process and the challenges confronting it and assembles the right team to assist it in its claim submission, the insured will be well positioned for claim resolution.

Chapter 8

The Interaction Between Cyber Insurance, Data Breach Response Plans, and Cybersecurity Governance*

Data breach incidents and their associated costs are continuing to rise,[1] despite significant investments in security. Even the largest organizations cannot completely avoid the risk of a data breach. Security breaches like Target,[2] Equifax,[3] and most recently SolarWinds,[4] are examples of attacks that bypassed best-in-class security mechanisms and exposed the limit of security hygiene alone in avoiding data breaches. To adequately protect their bottom line, organizations must increase investment in mechanisms to mitigate the risk of loss when security measures to prevent or detect a breach fail.[5]

---

* By Rafae Bhatti.

1 Anastasios Arampatzis, *IBM Study Shows Data Breach Costs on the Rise*, The State of Security, Aug 25, 2019, *available at* https://www.tripwire.com/state-of-security/security-data-protection/data-breach-costs-rise/.

2 Tracy Kitten, *Target Breach: What Happened?*, Bank Info Security, Dec 20, 2013, *available at* https://www.bankinfosecurity.com/target-breach-what-happened-a-6312.

3 Josh Fruhlinger, *Equifax data breach FAQ: What happened, who was affected, what was the impact?*, CSO Online, Feb 12, 2020, *available at* https://www.csoonline.com/article/3444488/equifax-data-breach-faq-what-happened-who-was-affected-what-was-the-impact.html.

4 Lawrence Abrams, *The SolarWinds cyberattack: The hack, the victims, and what we know,* Bleeping Computer, Dec 19, 2020, *available at* https://www.bleepingcomputer.com/news/security/the-solarwinds-cyberattack-the-hack-the-victims-and-what-we-know/

5 Rafae Bhatti, *What SolarWinds teaches us about managing risk of cyber loss,* The Privacy Advisor, Jan 6, 2021 [hereinafter SolarWinds], *available at* https://iapp.org/news/a/what-solarwinds-teaches-us-about-managing-risk-of-cyber-loss/.

An organization's ability to recover financially from a data breach incident can be vastly improved by the selection of an appropriate cybersecurity insurance that is consistent with its data loss exposure. The important question is to identify the factors that determine the level of coverage appropriate for an organization. Cyber insurance should not be purchased or sold as a one-size fits all service. Proper selection should, and often does. account for the size of the organization. But, the business' cybersecurity maturity is a critical piece of the insurance assessment because, the probability of a cyber loss event for an organization is correlated with its cybersecurity maturity. In addition to the insurance a company purchases, the other crucial factor of how well a company responds after a cyber incident is the data breach response plan and the corporate governance priorities that the company implemented prior to the breach. Indeed, the risk management and governance practices of an organization can help improve its relative cybersecurity maturity and resiliency and decrease its risk of data loss.

This chapter explores the interactions between cyber insurance, data breach response plans, and cybersecurity governance. The goal is to help organizations understand their cybersecurity maturity and estimate their cyber insurance.

A. Data Breach Trends

1. *Business Impact of Data Breaches*

(a) Types and impact of data breaches

The scope of a data breach response plan, and consequently the resulting cyber insurance coverage, needs to be broad enough to recognize various types of breach scenarios. The only way to develop a plan with the necessary scope is to understand the current trends and incident scenarios. While no one can know the next development in malicious cyber-attacks, understanding the current state of the risks can and should be a priority. These current scenarios include malicious data breach events, non-malicious exposure of personal data, and social engineering and ransomware attacks. Business must be prepared to respond to each.

i. Malicious breach by third parties

The most common data breach scenario is unauthorized access to a company's systems by malicious third parties. All companies, no matter how large or small, are at a risk of becoming victim of a malicious data breach. The Target incident was a result of hackers breaking into the company's systems.[6] So was Equifax.[7] These breaches resulted in major financial losses for the company in addition to resignation by the senior management. This included the CEO of Target,[8] and Equifax.[9] The total losses for Target in the aftermath of the breach that affected about 41 million of its customers are reported to be about $300 million,[10] including costs for class action settlements and settlements with various states and financial institutions that had issued Visa and Mastercard cards to affected customers. The Equifax breach, which affected half of all Americans, has reportedly cost the company at least about $1.4 billion.[11] This includes costs related to incident response, legal fees, and investments in new technology. The company received a $651,000 fine from UK regulators and became a target of numerous lawsuits by individuals and US states.[12]

---

6 Brian Krebs, *Target Hackers Broke in Via HVAC Company*, Krebs on Security, Feb 05, 2014, *available at* https://krebsonsecurity.com/2014/02/target-hackers-broke-in-via-hvac-company/.

7 Thomas Brewster, *How Hackers Broke Equifax: Exploiting A Patchable Vulnerability*, Forbes, Sep 14, 2017, *available at* https://www.forbes.com/sites/thomasbrewster/2017/09/14/equifax-hack-the-result-of-patched-vulnerability/?sh=20206ea35cda.

8 Danielle Douglas, *Target CEO resigns after massive data breach*, The Washington Post, May 5, 2014, *available at* https://www.washingtonpost.com/business/economy/target-ceo-resigns-after-massive-data-breach/2014/05/05/ef6cbee2-d457-11e3-8a78-8fe50322a72c_story.html.

9 Brewster, *supra*.

10 Vincent Lynch, *Cost of 2013 Target Data Breach Nears $300 Million*, The SSL Store: Hashed Out, May 26, 2017, *available at* https://www.thesslstore.com/blog/2013-target-data-breach-settled/.

11 Mathew J. Schwartz, *Equifax's Data Breach Costs Hit $1.4 Billion*, Bank Info Security, May 13, 2019, *available at* https://www.bankinfosecurity.com/equifaxs-data-breach-costs-hit-14-billion-a-12473.

12 *Id.*

ii. Non-malicious breach by third parties

While not the most frequent or costly, data breaches caused by non-malicious third-parties requires attention. It is particularly important within the context of emerging data protection regulations that place emphasis on avoiding unreasonable exposure of personal data.[13] The recent high profile data breaches, such as Cambridge Analytica and Clearview AI, were not the result of the companies' systems being infiltrated by malicious users. The Clearview AI breach disclosed data about its customers despite no compromise of its systems or network.[14] Similarly, no Facebook systems were infiltrated in the Cambridge Analytica data scandal that involved the use of Facebook profile data to target users in political campaigns.[15] These examples suggest that modern data breaches are no longer limited to unauthorized access by malicious third-parties, but also can be caused by inappropriate sharing of personal data with third parties.

And they have legal and financial consequences for the business. The Facebook data breach cost the company 500,000 GBP, and the maximum fine if that incident happened today could be up to 1.4 billion GBP.[16] In the case of Clearview AI, the breach is about sharing consumer personal data with undeclared third parties without explicit consumer consent. The timing of the breach makes Clearview AI potentially worse than Cambridge Analytica because data privacy laws had been passed prior to this misuse of data.[17] Prior to the breach, litigation had already been filed Clearview AI's potential misuse of data under Illinois' Biometric

---

13 Rafae Bhatti, *Breaches at our front door: What we can learn from Clearview AI,* Privacy Perspectives, Mar 19, 2020 [hereinafter Clearview AI], *available at* https://iapp.org/news/a/breaches-at-our-front-door-what-we-can-learn-from-clearview-ai/.

14 Betsy Swan, *Facial-Recognition Company That Works With Law Enforcement Says Entire Client List Was Stolen*, The Daily Beast, Feb 26, 2020, *available at* https://www.thedailybeast.com/clearview-ai-facial-recognition-company-that-works-with-law-enforcement-says-entire-client-list-was-stolen.

15 Julia Carrie Wong, *The Cambridge Analytica scandal changed the world—but it didn't change Facebook*, The Guardian, Mar 18, 2019, *available at* https://www.theguardian.com/technology/2019/mar/17/the-cambridge-analytica-scandal-changed-the-world-but-it-didnt-change-facebook

16 Clearview AI, *supra*.

17 *See* Section 2(b) *infra*.

Information Protection Act. Since the breach, additional actions were filed alleging violations of the California Consumer Privacy Act and Vermont's data privacy laws.[18]

iii. Social engineering and ransomware

Other prominent categories of breach scenarios include social engineering and ransomware attacks. The massive Twitter hack,[19] that resulted in the compromise of various high profile Twitter user accounts, was caused by a social engineering (spear phishing) attack that targeted highly privileged Twitter employees. The hackers then used compromised credentials of those employees to gain access to the company's user administration panel.[20]

Ransomware infects an affected computer and encrypts the data to make it inaccessible without the encryption key.[21] The hackers then demand payment of a ransom to make the data accessible again to the affected organization. The malware responsible for a ransomware attack typically spreads via social engineering attacks, such as spear phishing or via untrusted sites on the internet. "WannaCry" is one of the most famous ransomware attacks, which hit the NHS in the UK particularly hard, and reportedly cost them £92 million.[22] Ransomware attacks on healthcare institutions have been on the rise during the COVID-19 pandemic around the globe, including the Ryuk ransomware affecting many US hospitals, which saw ransom demands spike to $200,000.[23] Because both social engineering and ransomware attacks rely on actions by internal authorized

18 *Id.*

19 Twitter Inc., *An update on our security incident,* Twitter, Jul 18, 2020, *available at* https://blog.twitter.com/en_us/topics/company/2020/an-update-on-our-security-incident.html

20 *Id.*

21 Armstrong, et al, *Ransomware: What COVID-19 Means for Upgrading Your Defenses*, Law.com, Sep 22, 2020, *available at* https://www.law.com/legaltechnews/2020/09/22/ransomware-what-covid-19-means-for-upgrading-your-defenses/?slreturn=20210019200158.

22 *Id.*

23 Lily Hay Newman, *Ransomware Hits Dozens of Hospitals in an Unprecedented Wave*, Wired, Oct 29, 2020, *available at* https://www.wired.com/story/ransomware-hospitals-ryuk-trickbot/.

users to be successful, they are viewed as distinct from other data breaches for purposes of cyber liability.

(b) Analysis of recent cyber loss events

In order to understand how an organization can be prepared to protect itself from risk of cyber loss, it is important to discuss data breach readiness within the context of cyber insurance and analyze empirical data on what kinds of cyber loss events are the most frequent and expensive.

i. Data breach breakdown by type:

According to the Willis Towers Watson global cyber claims report based on data from 2013 to December 2019, malicious data breaches are the most frequently reported losses and have the largest total amount of costs associated with them.[24] This comes as no surprise given the importance of personal data to modern business on one hand, which has resulted in rapid proliferation of it, and the rising cost of fines when the data is compromised. The 2020 Verizon Data Breach Investigations Report reaffirms that nearly 45% of all reported data breaches involved hacking and reminds us that personal data of victims is compromised in about 58% of data breaches.[25] Given the increasing regulatory focus on avoiding unreasonable exposure of personal data,[26] businesses should expect that personal data losses, even from accidental breaches, will become increasingly costly. Therefore, for both malicious and accidental breaches, businesses must try to mitigate the risk of such compromises and prepare for their occurrence.

ii. Data breaches and insurance claims

How do insurance claims correlate with the various types of attacks? Human error (such as employees clicking on phishing emails or replying

---

24 Willis Towers Watson, Cyber claims analysis report (Jul 31, 2020), *available at* https://www.willistowerswatson.com/en-GB/Insights/2020/ 07/cyber-claims-analysis-report

25 Verizon, 2020 Data Breach Investigations Report—Executive Summary, *available at* https://enterprise.verizon.com/resources/executivebriefs/2020-dbir-executive-brief.pdf.

26 *See* Section 2(b) *infra.*

to spoofed messages), third party breaches (as opposed to accidental compromise by third parties), and lack of adequate IT controls (such as failure to install patches or lack of password protocols) are among the most frequent root causes for data breach costs.[27] Overall, they account for 29%, 24%, and 10% respectively of all reported data breaches.[28] Claims arising out of accidental compromises by third parties account for about 11% of all reported data breaches,[29] a number that is expected to increase with increased obligations on third party providers to safeguard personal data. In terms of claims coverage, 71% of the average data breach financial cost falls within the coverage and limits of cyber insurance policies.[30] The largest share of the covered costs, about 18-21% each, is for incident forensics and legal defense costs.[31] The rest includes advice of legal and cyber security experts, breach notification, credit monitoring, identity theft protection, and penalties, each of which accounts for between 5-8% share of the costs.[32] 1 in 10 settled data breach claims reach a total cost (including defense costs and other expenses) exceeding $2.5m.[33]

iii. First-party losses and insurance claims

When it comes to first party cyber losses, human error, third party breaches, and lack of adequate IT controls are still among the most frequent root causes.[34] However, their share of losses in first party loss events is different. Overall, they account for 25%, 17%, and 24% respectively of all reported first party losses.[35] Claims arising out of accidental compromise by a third party account for only 3% of all reported first party losses.[36] In terms of claims coverage, 75% of the average first party cyber loss falls within the coverage provided by cyber policies.[37] Based on the report, the largest share of the covered costs, about 45%, is

---

27 Watson, *supra,* at 7.
28 *Id.*
29 *Id.*
30 *Id.*, at 8.
31 *Id.*
32 *Id.*
33 *Id.*
34 *Id.*, at 10.
35 *Id.*
36 *Id.*
37 *Id.*, at 11.

for operational/trading costs in first party loss events. These costs primarily comprise loss of profits/revenue and increased costs of working, about 63% and 36% respectively of the total operational/trading costs.[38] The next biggest share, about 23%, in case of first party loss events is settlement costs.[39] That is followed by forensics, ransom payments, and system restoration costs, each of which accounts for between 5-11% share of the costs.[40]

(c) Important insurance coverage issues

Another important issue in preparing for a cyber incident, is for a business to choose appropriate retention levels in its cyber insurance program, under the limits, i.e. exclusions to its coverage, and the possible timelines between when a company is compromised and when the incident is fully resolved. This is another example of how the company's insurance coverage and the pre-breach planning interact.

i. Retention levels

It is worth highlighting that the funding for a covered claim in the case of a loss event, whether data breach or first party loss, is determined based on a combination of insurer payments and insured payments within the selected retention level.[41] This underscores the significance of selecting retention/excess levels that correlate with the insured's risk appetite. Understanding an organization's cybersecurity maturity can help estimate the amount of cyber insurance it needs and assist with this task, a topic we will discuss in Section 4.

ii. Exclusions

It is also worth noting that, for both data breach and first party losses, certain elements of the reported insurance claims were excluded from coverage.[42] The two most frequently observed coverage issues relate to the

38 *Id.*
39 *Id.*
40 *Id.*
41 *Id.*
42 *Id.*, at 13.

use of unapproved vendors or acting without insurers' consent.[43] On the other hand, coverage was almost always confirmed by insurers under certain insuring clauses for all reported cyber claims.[44] The highest among the triggered clauses are the breach/incident response & crisis management clauses,[45] which highlights the insurer's proactive and cooperative approach to having breaches investigated and remediated.

iii. Timeline

Finally, an organization's ability to respond to a breach in a timely manner correlates directly with its ability to recover on an insurance claim. Based on data from the global cyber claims, the recovery is reduced up to 60% if a loss remains undiscovered for over two weeks.[46] This is significant, because on average the breach/loss lasts about 61 days and it then takes a further 17 days to discover the loss/ breach.[47] The duration and discovery times are increased for malicious data breaches and those caused by rogue employees.

These issues highlight the significance of having a breach response plan that improves the ability of an organization to be prepared to detect and remediate breaches at an early stage. It also underscores the importance of cybersecurity risk management and governance to help an organization better understand its cybersecurity maturity, and allow it to select appropriate coverages and retention levels consistent with its cyber risk appetite.

2. *Regulatory Compliance and Risk of Loss*

In recent years, there has been a tide of emerging data protection regulations sweeping the globe, such as the General Data Protection Regulation (GDPR) and the California Consumer Privacy Act (CCPA).[48] These regulations require organizations to put in place reasonable cybersecurity safeguards to protect personal data of their users, and at the

---

43 *Id.*

44 *Id.*

45 *Id.*

46 *Id.*, at 12.

47 *Id.*, at 16.

48 Clearview AI, *supra*.

same time impose stiff penalties for data breach events that result in a compromise of personal data. In fact, scrutiny of security and privacy practices, particularly of technology companies, has been on the rise in a post-GDPR and post-CCPA world.[49] Notably, CCPA provides a private right of action, which allows California residents to sue a company for failure to protect their personal information.[50] The Federal Trade Commission (FTC) can also bring actions for unfair or deceptive security practices under the FTC Act.[51] Given the high stakes, it is important for organizations to analyze how these regulatory compliance obligations impact the risk of loss from data breach events and reduce their liability exposure. Indeed, some of the regulatory risks, i.e. fines, may not be insurable, which provides for a different dynamic between insurance and response than when cyber losses are fully insured.

(a) Reasonable security standards

The fundamental question to answer when determining the liability of a company in case of a cyber loss event is whether or not it satisfied the legal standard used by the courts to hold companies accountable. That legal standard under most regulations is that of "reasonable security".[52] However, it's not always clear what reasonable security means. The FTC has stated that there is no one-size-fits-all data security program.[53] The mere fact that a breach occurred does not mean that a company has violated the law or will be subject to FTC action. However, repeated occurrences of failing to meet security obligations will be seen as an indicator of lack of reasonable security.

---

49 Rafae Bhatti, *The road to reasonable security: What CISOs should know*, Privacy Perspectives, Sep 3, 2020 [hereinafter Reasonable Security], *available at* https://iapp.org/news/a/the-road-to-reasonable-security-what-cisos-should-know/

50 *Id.*

51 *Id.*

52 Paige M. Boshell, *The LabMD Case and the Evolving Concept of "Reasonable Security"*, American Bar Association: Business Law Today, Jul 16, 2018, *available at* https://www.americanbar.org/groups/business_law/publications/blt/2018/07/labmd/.

53 Andrew Smith, Prepared Statement of the Federal Trade Commission in United States Senate (Mar 7, 2019), *available at* https://www.ftc.gov/system/files/documents/public_statements/1466607/commission_testimony_re_data_security_senate_03072019.pdf

So, what would reasonable security look like?

This question can be answered by looking at what reasonable security is not, based on the case history of FTC decisions against organizations which were found to be lacking reasonable security,[54] and the allegations of unreasonable security in class action lawsuits.

i. Appropriate Safeguards

The most basic form of reasonable security comprises security mechanisms that provide appropriate safeguards to protect personal data. The FTC recognizes a company's failure to perform security scanning or testing to identify vulnerabilities, or its failure to take steps to protect personal data stored on its network using means such as encryption, as lack of reasonable security.[55]

The bulk of CCPA class action lawsuits brought on behalf of consumers under the private right of action tends to focus on a company's failure to put in place appropriate safeguards to protect personal information when it knows or should know that the risk of unauthorized access or disclosure is likely.[56] For example, failure to protect "non-encrypted and non-redacted personal information from unauthorized disclosure" was one of the allegations in a CCPA lawsuit brought against a popular video conferring application.[57]

Recommendations from FTC as well as other regulatory authorities that can help organizations implement reasonable security will be reviewed in Section 4(b).

ii. Third-Party Sharing

An important concern under the data protection laws is the data sharing with third parties. This is where the organizations need to obtain guidance specific to their unique footprint to navigate the data protection

---

54 FTC, Stick with Security: FTC resources for your business (June 2015), *available at* https://www.ftc.gov/system/files/documents/plain-language/pdf0205-startwithsecurity.pdf

55 Reasonable Security, *supra.*

56 *Id.* (citing Cal. Civ. Code § 1798.150(a) and Cal. Civ. Code § 1798.81.5(b))

57 Reasonable Security, *supra.*

risks and connect them to the security agenda.[58] Personal data may be shared with third parties for no other purpose than reasonably related to providing the service. In particular, CCPA requires businesses to secure this assurance from the third parties that process personal data, called "service-providers" under the law. Non-compliance with this requirement could result in legal liability for the organization if the personal data is used for purposes that exceed reasonable expectations of the users.

The Clearview class action complaint is the most notable recent example of this violation, resulting from sharing of personal data with third parties that goes beyond the user expectation.[59] Other examples include FTC action for "unfair public disclosure of consumers' sensitive personal and financial information" by posting on its website "unencrypted, unprotected Excel spreadsheets". Such action not only goes beyond reasonable user expectations but also demonstrates a lack of reasonable security.[60]

iii. Misrepresentation

Misrepresentation as applied to an organization's security practices is commonly used as the underlying theory of liability when pursuing a claim for deceptive practices under the FTC Act. An FTC complaint against a dating website cited no less than four different counts of misrepresentation, regarding areas such as network security, user profiles, terms and conditions for deleting profiles, and data security attestations.[61] The FTC complaint against Uber, in the wake of two consecutive data breaches, also stemmed from charges that the organization failed to live up to its data security claims, including misrepresenting the level of monitoring and protection that it provided to consumer and driver data. Implicit in the concept of misrepresentation is concealing a data breach, and the FBI charges filed against Uber CISO subsequent to the FTC action suggest that organizations are going to be held accountable for it.[62]

---

58 Clearview AI, *supra*.

59 Reasonable Security, *supra*.

60 *Id.*

61 *Id.*

62 *Id.*

iv. Statutory requirements

Organizations in heavily regulated industries such as healthcare and finance should always pay attention to their existing security compliance obligations. A case in point is FTC's action against a financial institution that was subject to the Gramm-Leach-Bliley Act, citing the organization's failure to comply with the statute as contributing to a security vulnerability on its site that was exploited in a data breach.[63]

(b) Data breach notification

Just as the lack of reasonable security can result in legal liability, so does the failure to provide timely notification of a data breach. Under both GDPR and CCPA, an organization is under an obligation to provide data breach notification to affected parties and regulatory authorities. GDPR imposes a 72-hour timeframe for breach notification, whereas CCPA follows the "reasonable timeframe" required under CA law.[64] It is recommended that organizations trying to streamline their breach response efforts across multiple jurisdictions choose the strictest standard, in this case GDPR, as the baseline. Lack of notification may not only be a violation of these laws but can even be considered as misrepresentation under the FTC Act, as suggested by the FBI charges filed against Uber CISO for concealing a data breach mentioned in Section 2(a)(i).

B. Cyber Insurance and Breach Response Plans

1. *Importance of a Data Breach Response Plan*

(a) What It Takes to Respond to a Data Breach

A well-designed breach response plan is a tool that can help mitigate both the technical and financial impact to an organization in case of a data

---

63 *Id.*

64 Maria Korolov, *California Consumer Privacy Act (CCPA): What you need to know to be compliant*, CSO, Jul 7, 2020, *available at* https://www.csoonline.com/article/3292578/california-consumer-privacy-act-what-you-need-to-know-to-be-compliant.html.

breach event. An incident response plan that provides a clear protocol for recovery and remediation, and incident notifications, can save valuable time when time is of essence, not only as a matter of site availability efforts to bring the business back up but also downstream financial and legal consequences.

Technical recovery from a breach to bring the business back up as quickly as possible is necessary to reduce lost revenue and prevent adverse affect on customer satisfaction.[65] However, it is also important to plan for financial recovery, as significant costs can arise after a breach. These range from forensic investigations, to data breach notifications, as well as credit monitoring and other remedial measures.

Besides these known costs, a company is exposed to intangible costs as well, including brand reputation and damage, loss of productivity, and a negative impact on business performance, in addition to other liabilities, such as lawsuits by third parties.[66] Further, as discussed in Section 2(b)(i), there is an increasing trend of lawsuits against organizations alleging that they failed to adhere to the "reasonable security" standard required under the applicable laws. Overall costs can be in several millions of dollars after a reported cyber breach.

(b) Types of Data Breach Response Scenarios

For a breach response plan to be effective, it should anticipate various types of scenarios that the company is likely to encounter, and provide detailed guidance on how to respond to them.

i. Recovery and Remediation

A. Importance of Backup and Restoration

The most immediate priority for a business after a data breach is to restore its mission critical applications as fast as possible. An organization must maintain complete and readily accessible data backups at all times. One of the main benefits of doing so is the ability to recover from breach

65 Paul Ferrillo, et al., Cyber Security, Cyber Governance, and Cyber Insurance, Harvard Law School Forum on Corporate Governance, Nov 13, 2014, available at https://corpgov.law.harvard.edu/2014/11/13/cyber-security-cyber-governance-and-cyber-insurance/

66 *Id.*

events, especially ransomware attacks, in the fastest and most cost-effective way possible.[67] In the absence of working backups, organizations may risk losing valuable data, or pay a hefty ransom for access to critical data to be restored.

Some common scenarios may result in an organization's inability to rely on backups to recover from. They may realize that their service provider never actually set up data backups in the first place or didn't set them up correctly, leaving the organization entirely without any backup option.[68] In other cases where data backups are available following an attack, critical data may not have been backed up for weeks or even months either because the backups do not go back far enough in time, or the backup process may have stopped at some point.[69] In either case, such data may not be seen as a viable recovery option.

A more recent and growing trend in which data backups are not an option for recovery occurs when a ransomware attack itself is able to propagate across the organization's network and ultimately access, and thereafter encrypt, the organization's data backups.[70] Therefore, it's important an organization is able to adequately map the critical data and dependencies, and appropriately segregate the backups from the rest of the network to prevent them from being accessed by an attacker.

B. Data Backups and Preparedness

There are several steps that an organization can take to help ensure that critical data backups are available after a breach so that business operations can be quickly restored. This is especially important in wake of the prevalence of data breaches that propagate across networks, access sensitive data, and in case of ransomware attacks make critical data inaccessible and demand increasingly higher ransoms.

---

67 Jacob Ingerslev, *Best Practices for Data Backup and Recovery in the Age of Ransomware, Global Cyber Risks Uncovered*, Dec 20, 2020, available at https://www.linkedin.com/pulse/best-practices-data-backup-recovery-age-ransomware-jacob-ingerslev/

68 *Id.*

69 *Id.*

70 *Id.*

Below are some of the important considerations for proactive data backup preparedness:[71]

- A business impact analysis (BIA) should be conducted to determine what critical data needs to be backed up, the frequency and duration of backups, how long backups need to be retained, and how they will be stored and protected.
- The retention periods of backups for different types of systems should be determined based on the applicable laws. For examples, the retention of HR data is determined by employment laws, the retention of personal data is determined by privacy laws, and so on.
- Formal policies and procedures should be established to validate that data backups are configured correctly, and monitored to ensure that they are being done at correct intervals.
- Internal or external IT resources should be consulted to ensure that the organization's data backups are appropriately segregated from the rest of the network or otherwise protected.
- Periodic "fail-over" testing should be conducted in which the organization tests whether or not it can actually access critical data stored via backups, if ever needed. Quarterly tests are recommended but at the minimum should be performed at least annually.

ii. Forensics Investigations

A forensics investigation is used to determine the extent of the breach, the cause and what types of data were stolen. A forensic report that analyzes the causes and effects of data breaches has long been a staple of incident response.[72] A typical incident response protocol involves a team of legal and forensics experts to guide the company in conducting the investigation. As mentioned in Section 2(a)(ii), the largest share of the covered costs, about 21%, goes toward incident forensics, while it comprises about 11% of the covered costs in first party loss events.

---

71 *Id.*

72 Thompson Coburn LLP, Maintaining privilege over forensic data-breach reports (Dec 2020), *available at* https://www.jdsupra.com/legalnews/maintaining-privilege-over-forensic-47708/

While producing a forensics report may appear to be a purely technical matter, it involves dealing with information that could serve as important evidence for any future legal proceedings. Therefore, dealing with incident forensics is a sensitive part of the breach response protocol where care must be exercised by the organization to avoid any costly missteps. Two important issues in this regard relate to privilege and disclosure.

A. Privilege

Reports prepared by third-party forensics consultants at the request of an organization's legal counsel (or representative) are privileged. However, the recent increase in data breaches affecting consumer information has resulted in increasing scrutiny of the assertions of privilege.[73] Because breach reports contain key information about how the breach was caused and what steps were taken to fix it, it is likely to get more judicial scrutiny as more breaches occur. Privilege claims are at their weakest when an organization has already engaged with a forensics team prior to the breach to audit its systems. That is what happened in the case of Capital One, where the privilege claim was rejected by the court on the grounds that the report was not prepared in anticipation of litigation, rather under a pre-existing agreement.[74] In light of this, organizations are advised to retain a new forensics firm (or team) under a new engagement agreement that differentiates the services specific to the breach.[75]

B. Disclosure

Organizations may ultimately be forced to strike a careful balance between protecting results of forensics investigation and complying with various laws requiring disclosure to consumers.[76] Regulations like GDPR and CCPA place a strong emphasis on transparent data collection, use, and security of personal information. The organization should consider if disclosing a report would provide benefits that outweigh the risks. For example, a report may provide invaluable information about the nature of an incident, the effectiveness or ineffectiveness of controls, how the entity

---

73 *Id.*

74 *Id.*

75 *Id.*

76 *Id.*

responded to the incident, and possible future issues.[77] In other situations, disclosing this information may be helpful to fulfill other legal obligations, such as notification or "cure" provisions under CCPA, and may be done in a way that does not pose an unnecessary risk to the entity.[78]

iii. Remedial Measures

Once the organization is informed about the effectiveness or ineffectiveness of controls that led to the breach, it is expected to implement remedial measures to "cure" the breach. "Cure" may include both system changes to address the deficiencies in controls, as well as services necessary to help mitigate the risk exposure from the breach.

The cost of system changes depends on the extent of changes that are required in the underlying controls to remove the deficiency that led to the breach. As mentioned in Section 2(a)(ii), about 5% of the covered costs in first party loss events goes toward system restoration and remediation.

Services like credit monitoring and identity theft protection can help mitigate risk exposure for customers that are more susceptible to identity fraud. After a breach, it's typical for organizations to offer customers a one-year credit monitoring and/or identity theft protection services that helps decrease this exposure. As mentioned in Section 2(a)(ii), about 7% of the covered costs in data breach claims goes toward each of these services.

iv. Notification and Reputation

A. Data Breach Notification

Under most regulations, including GDPR and CCPA, there are strict requirements to provide notification for a data breach to affected consumers and regulatory authorities. As mentioned in Section 2(a)(ii), about 7% of the covered costs in data breach claims goes toward privacy notification.

Data breach notifications are typically due in specific format within a specific timeline, which varies slightly based on jurisdiction. In most

---

77 *Id.*

78 *Id.*

cases, the breach notification is expected to include at least the following information:[79]

- Organization name
- Date of breach
- Date of discovery
- Breach description
- Types of personal data affected
- Number of personal records affected
- Likely consequences of the breach
- Steps the organization can take to mitigate risk of harm
- Remedial action taken, or to be taken

In terms of when a notification is due, some jurisdictions like CA require notification "without unreasonable delay" whereas GDPR requires notification within 72-hours of discovering a breach, as mentioned in Section 2(b)(ii). Delayed or otherwise inappropriate notifications have increasingly become the cause of stiff penalties from regulators, and can lead to additional liabilities if deemed in violation of an organization's contractual obligations.[80]

B. Legal, Cybersecurity and PR Services

During the process of responding to a data breach, an organization needs to engage with legal and cybersecurity experts to address the technical and legal consequences of the breach. As mentioned in Section 2(a)(ii), about 8% and 5% of the covered costs in data breach claims goes toward advice of legal and cyber security experts, respectively.

---

79 Information Commissioner's Office, Guide to the GDPR: Personal data breaches, *available at* https://ico.org.uk/for-organisations/guide-to-data-protection/guide-to-the-general-data-protection-regulation-gdpr/personal-data-breaches/.

80 Joseph Duball, *Irish DPC finalizes 450K euro GDPR fine against Twitter*, The Privacy Advisor, Dec 15, 2020, *available at* https://iapp.org/news/a/irish-dpc-finalizes-450k-euro-gdpr-fine-against-twitter/

In addition, an organization also needs the services of PR professionals to help minimize reputational damage after a breach.[81] It is essential to monitor the brand perception of the company and have a communication plan to respond to adverse publicity on social media and other channels.

C. Lawsuits and Investigations

As mentioned in Section 2(a)(i), modern data breaches have legal consequences for the business. There has been a rise in lawsuits and fines resulting from compromise of personal data, which creates a significant financial burden for an organization when responding to a data breach. In fact, as mentioned in Section 2(a)(ii), legal defense from lawsuits comprises the second largest share, about 18%, of the covered costs in data breach claims, with about 5% going towards fines and penalties.

2. Data breach response and cyber insurance

Purchasing appropriate amounts of cyber insurance can play a significant role in protecting an organization's bottom line, as suggested by the analysis of data breach loss and insurance claims data presented in the previous sections. A stand-alone cyber insurance policy offers organizations an immediate solution to transfer the associated first- and third-party costs of a data breach, and often offers the crisis management expertise and assistance that is crucial when responding to a data breach.[82]

(a) Important Coverages for Cyber Risk Exposure

Below is a checklist of first- and third-party risk exposures that can be covered through cyber insurance, depending upon the carrier and cyber insurance policy purchased.[83]

- First-party Cyber Risk Exposures
  - ***Loss or damage to digital assets:*** Loss or damage to data or software programs, resulting in costs incurred through

---

81 Ferrillo, et al., *supra.*

82 *Id.*

83 *Id.*

restoring, updating, recreating or replacing these assets to the same condition they were in prior to the loss or damage.

- ***Business interruption:*** Interruption, degradation in service, or failure of the network, resulting in loss of income incurred as the direct result of a cyber peril or a cloud computing provider's systems failure or impairment due to a cyber peril first discovered during the period of the policy. May additionally cover increased cost of operation and/or costs incurred by mitigating and investigating the loss.
- ***Cyber extortion:*** Attempts to extort money, such as if a hacker demands ransom as a condition of not carrying out a cyber threat. Given the rise in ransomware attacks, this coverage is becoming a valuable component. Some examples of extortion threats may include threatening to infect the organization's computer systems with malware, threatening to disseminate, divulge or utilize information contained or once contained in the organization's computer systems, or threatening to damage, destroy or alter the organization's computer systems; or threatening to communicate with the customer base under false pretenses to obtain personal information.

- ***Theft of money and digital assets:*** Direct monetary losses from electronic theft of funds/money from the organization by hacking or other types of cyber crime.
  - ***Computer forensics investigation:*** Engaging a forensics investigator to determine the extent of the breach, the cause and what types of data were stolen.
  - ***Data Breach Coach (or a Privacy attorney):*** Engaging a data breach counsel or attorney to obtain assistance with navigating the various applicable data protection laws, including drafting the breach communication documents and notification letters.
- Third-party Cyber Liability Exposures
  - ***Security and privacy breaches:*** Investigations, defense costs, and civil damages associated with security breaches, transmissions of malicious code, or breaches of third-party or employee privacy rights or confidentiality, including failures by outsourced service providers. Some examples of liability coverage may include negligence by the company for failure

to follow "reasonable security" safeguards as discussed in Section 2(b) (i), or a violation of an applicable data protection law or a contractual obligation.

- ***Investigation of data breach:*** Forensics investigations, defense costs, regulatory penalties and fines (may not be insurable in certain states) resulting from an investigation or enforcement action by a regulator as a result of security and privacy liability.
- ***Customer notification/credit monitoring and Public Relations expenses:*** Legal, postage, and advertising expenses where there is a legal or regulatory requirement to notify individuals of a security or privacy breach, including credit monitoring program costs and PR media assistance. While a company may not be able to insure its reputation with a specific coverage limit, cyber insurance helps guard and minimize reputational damage by offering a communications team that helps assist a company after a crisis happens. Cyber insurance also helps with the coverage costs of communications in response to adverse publicity on social media and other forums, along with the costs associated with helping to monitor the brand perception of the company.
- ***Multi-media liability:*** Investigations, defense costs and civil damages arising from defamation, breach of privacy, negligence in publication of any content in electronic or print media, and infringement of the intellectual property of a third-party.
- ***Loss of third-party data:*** Liability for damage to, or corruption/loss of, third-party data or information, including payment of compensation to customers for denial of access, failure of software, data errors and system security failure.
- ***Third-party contractual indemnification:*** Financial obligations to third-parties due to a security or data breach incident.

C. Cybersecurity Governance

Cyber insurance helps offer an extra layer of defense in a company's cyber security program, but it is not a substitute for good cyber hygiene and governance. As noted in Section 1, while cyber insurance is usually sold as a one-size fits all service, the probability of a cyber loss event for an organization in practice is correlated with its cybersecurity maturity. Therefore, focusing on governance and risk management practices can play an important role in improving the cybersecurity maturity of an organization, and consequently reducing its risk of data loss.

1. Reducing the Risk of Cyber Loss

The exposure to risk of cyber loss can be minimized through risk assurance mechanisms. Security and data protection assessments should be conducted to identify the cyber risk exposures, the level of scrutiny that those risks warrant, and whether they can be addressed by putting appropriate controls in place. Based on this information, the organization should determine which risks to avoid, accept, mitigate, or transfer through insurance, and align its cyber insurance policy with the risk management strategy.[84]

(a) Risk Avoidance

As noted in Section 2(b)(i), organizations have the duty to ensure reasonable security safeguards to protect personal data under applicable data protection laws such as the GDPR and CCPA. The proper selection of these safeguards can help avoid the cyber risk exposures for the organization. This will be discussed further in Section 4(b).

(b) Risk Acceptance

It can sometimes be the case that an organization considers a risk exposure as part of the cost of doing business, and deems it acceptable. Examples include the risk of a catastrophic event or a pandemic affecting the business location of an organization. Not all organizations are prepared to handle an event of this magnitude, and they might designate this risk as acceptable after weighing the likelihood of its occurrence and the investment required to prepare for it. It should be noted that accepting a risk only means that the organization defers taking any action on it until the associated event happens. It does not take away its responsibility for

84 SolarWinds, *supra.*

dealing with the event, and it remains liable for any associated consequences. Therefore, organizations should not accept or ignore risk exposures from events that are very highly likely to occur.

(c) Risk Mitigation

Certain types of risks are not within direct control of an organization. Examples include security risks introduced by third parties in your supply chain, which has become a major cause of multiple recent data breach events.[85] When a third party risk cannot be avoided by technical controls, and exceeds the threshold at which it can be accepted by the organization, it should be mitigated by means of contractual obligations. Under both GDPR and CCPA, organizations have the liability for a data breach, even if caused by third parties. Therefore, they should mitigate the risk of loss by making sure that contractual commitments commensurate with the risk exposure are put in place with the third parties.

(d) Risk Transfer

Despite the best efforts of organizations to mitigate cyber risk, the risk will never be zero. Therefore, purchasing cyber insurance helps transfer the residual risk, and assist with recovery after a data breach event. It must be emphasized that organizations should not solely rely on risk transfer, rather use it in conjunction with risk management mechanisms. To ensure adequate coverage, the contractual commitments negotiated with third parties should align with the liability protection cap in the insurance policy. Further, an organization's ability to recover on a cyber claim is tied to a robust incident response plan, and delayed response may limit full recovery.

2. *Improving Cybersecurity Maturity*

The overall data breach risk for an organization can be lowered by improving its cybersecurity maturity. This is done through proper selection of reasonable security safeguards that address cyber risk exposures.[86]

---

85 *Id.*

86 Reasonable Security, *supra.*

As noted in Section 2(b)(i), there is no one-size-fits-all set of "reasonable security" safeguards. However, organizations can often meet the requirements for reasonable security by aligning their security practices with the recommendations from regulatory authorities and industry-accepted standards, such as the NIST Cybersecurity Framework.[87] These controls are typically grouped into the following areas:

(a) Policies and Training

A written information security policy and training employees on that policy is among the most important pillars of any information security program. This makes sure that security policies and procedures for an organization are clearly communicated to all employees, who in turn understand their obligations to meet those requirements. More often than not, the root cause of data breaches can be linked to a human error or an employee mistake, such as clicking on a phishing email or sharing of sensitive information with an unauthorized third party. Providing security awareness training to employees on proper policies and procedures, for e.g., about securing their identity and accounts or dealing with sensitive information, can help prevent these costly mistakes. For organizations looking for guidance in the area of policies and training, SANS Institute is a good source.[88]

(b) Access Control and Data Protection

The risk of information disclosure for an organization can be controlled by imposing access controls on data appropriate for its sensitivity. As noted in Section 2(a)(i), under modern data protection laws, such as GDPR and CCPA, organizations have an obligation to protect sensitive data not only from unauthorized access but also from being shared inappropriately with third parties without a legitimate purpose.[89] Making sure that information can be accessed or shared based only on a need to know and for a reasonable purpose comprises an important risk mitigation mechanism. This policy should take into account the sensitivity

87 *Id.*

88 SANS Institute, Cyber Security Training. https://www.sans.org/.

89 Clearview AI, *supra*.

of the information being protected as well as the reasonable expectations of the user to whom the information belongs. For example, healthcare information is both sensitive and reasonably expected to be kept private, and can only be shared with a third party when the disclosure is minimum and necessary under the law to serve a valid medical purpose.

(c) Vulnerability and Patch Management

Protecting an organization's systems from vulnerabilities is among the most important safeguards when it comes to reasonable security. Data breach incidents related to unauthorized access to information typically arise as a result of hackers exploiting vulnerabilities in an application. Whether the vulnerability is in the organization's own systems, or those of its third party provider, it remains liable for any information that gets compromised due to unpatched vulnerabilities. An organization should put in place a vulnerability management program that helps detect, track and patch security vulnerabilities in its systems, and require its third party vendors to also provide evidence of putting in place a similar program. The recent rise in supply chain attacks has emphasized the importance of requiring these assurances from third party vendors.[90]

(d) Authentication and Passwords

A large number of data breaches each year are caused by hackers being able to crack weak passwords. Applying a strong password policy for authentication to its systems is the easiest way for an organization to avoid such data breaches. Most industry standards, such as NIST, recommend that passwords should not contain dictionary words, repetitive or sequential characters, or otherwise context-specific words such as username or date of birth.[91] NIST guidance further emphasizes the length of the password as more important than its complexity, with eight characters being the minimum recommended length.[92] Therefore, an organization's authentication policy should forbid any passwords that are not at least eight characters long, or otherwise contain forbidden words.

---

90 SolarWinds, *supra*.

91 NIST, Special Publication 800-63B: Digital Identity Guidelines (Jan 2021), *available at https://pages.nist.gov/800-63-3/sp800-63b.html*.

92 *Id.*

Further, organizations should consider requiring Two-Factor authentication ("2FA") for sensitive systems, which strengthens login security by requiring a second piece of information along with username and password.[93] This second factor of authentication makes an account more secure since a password alone, even if cracked by a hacker, is no longer sufficient to compromise an account.

(e) Encryption

Encryption as a security safeguard is arguably one of the most effective ways to manage risk of loss in a data breach event. This is because it converts information into a code to prevent unauthorized access. Unless the person in possession of the encrypted data has a key to unlock the code, the information is effectively rendered inaccessible. Therefore, under most data protection laws, an organization can avoid significant liabilities if the compromised information was, in fact, encrypted. The industry standard in this regard is AES encryption for data in storage and TLS encryption for data in transit, as recommended by NIST.[94]

(f) Monitoring and Audit

To defend an organization's systems from attacks, it should implement security measures to monitor its systems and assets so that it can detect and respond to them in a timely manner. These include mechanisms such as network and application firewalls to block malicious traffic, and intrusion detection systems to alert the organization when suspicious activity occurs. Additionally, organizations should put in place mechanisms to audit their system configurations on a regular basis and correct any deviations from the recommended baseline, such as 2FA being enabled for sensitive accounts, AES encryption turned on for cloud storage, firewall rules set to deny-by-default, and to restrict incoming traffic to SSH ports. Such recommendations can be found in industry

---

93 *Id.*

94 NIST, Cyber Security Framework. https://www.nist.gov/cyberframework/protect.

standard frameworks, such as Center for Information Security (CIS) Benchmarks, which the organizations can turn to for additional guidance.[95]

The amount of cyber insurance that a company should purchase depends on its risk exposures. Being able to measure the effectiveness of governance and risk management practices can help quantify the cybersecurity maturity and consequently help estimate an organization's cybersecurity needs.[96]

D. Conclusion

The rise in data breach events has exposed the limit of security hygiene alone in avoiding data breaches, and organizations must increase investment in mechanisms to recover from data breaches and mitigate the risk of loss. The ability of an organization to do so can be vastly improved by the selection of an appropriate cybersecurity insurance that is consistent with its risk exposure. This exposure is correlated with its cybersecurity maturity, which in turn can be improved by proper risk management and governance practices that may help organizations lower their risk of loss.

95 Center for Information Security, The 20 CIS Controls and Resources, *available at* https://www.cisecurity.org/controls/cis-controls-list/.

96 Ferrillo, et al., *supra.*

Chapter 9

Risk Management For Private and Publicly Traded Companies*

As the number and scope of cyber attacks and data breaches continues to rise, private and publicly traded companies are increasingly focusing on management and mitigation of cybersecurity risks. This is in no small part due to the vast amounts of personal information collected by companies—about employees, customers, consumers—which raises the stakes in the event of a disclosure of personal information in the wake of a data breach or data event. The significance of this issue is illustrated by several data breaches in 2020 involving publicly traded and private companies. This includes, among others:

- **The Estée Lauder Companies Inc.**: In February 2020, it was revealed that a non-password protected cloud database containing hundreds of millions of customer records (over 440 individual data pieces) and internal logs for the publicly traded cosmetics company giant Estée Lauder was leaked online.[1]
- **General Electric**: In March 2020, the publicly traded technology company General Electric disclosed a third-party vendor data breach that exposed the personally identifiable information of nearly 300,000 current and former employees. Information disclosed in the breach included names, addresses, Social Security numbers, driver's license numbers, bank account numbers, passport numbers, and dates of birth.[2]
- **Virgin Media**: In March 2020, the publicly traded telephone, television and internet provider Virgin Media disclosed a data

---

* Kristin L. Bryan and Aaron C. Garavaglia.

1 Tara Seals, *Estée Lauder Exposes 440M Records, with Email Addresses, Network Info* (Feb. 11, 2020), https://threatpost.com/estee-lauder-440m-records-email-network-info/152789/.

2 Sergiu Gatlan, *Tech Giant GE Discloses Data Breach After Service Provider Hack* (Mar. 23, 2020), https://www.bleepingcomputer.com/news/security/tech-giant-ge-discloses-data-breach-after-service-provider-hack/.

breach as a result of an unencrypted data base. This resulted in the exposure of the personal information of approximately 900,000 customers including names, addresses, emails, phone numbers and other information.[3]

Cyber liabilities in the wake of a data breach are not limited to civil liability—the SEC and other regulators are taking a closer look at cyber issues and shareholders are also seeking to hold publicly traded companies accountable for deficiencies in their data privacy and cybersecurity practices.

With the transition from the office to remote work increasing, especially as exacerbated by changes to the workplace from the COVID-19 pandemic, offices are becoming more decentralized and cybersecurity issues for publicly traded and private companies remain fundamentally important, especially due to the increase in attacks from cyber criminals. Companies are concerned about the cyber risks facing their organizations, due in no small part to the staggering losses that can result from a major cybersecurity incident. These losses can encompass harm from the loss of data, reputational damage as a result of customer impacts and subsequent media attention, and earnings due to the theft of trade secrets or intellectual property. For instance, in 2020, the graphics source code for a gaming system was allegedly stolen by cyber criminals that demanded a $100 million ransom.[4] Technical cybersecurity safeguards and organizational preparedness for a cyber incident remain critical for an effective cybersecurity program. Adequate insurance for cyberattacks and loss of data is just as essential, however, although often overlooked.

In 2019, one of the world's largest commercial property insurers conducted a survey of chief financial officers ("CFOs") at companies with over $1 billion in revenue.[5] Of the CFOs surveyed, 71 percent believed

---

3 Mike Bedigan, *Virgin Media data breach that exposes personal details of 900,000 customers* (Mar. 6, 2020), Virgin Media data breach that exposes personal details of 900,000 customers | The Independent | The Independent.

4 Jordan Oloman, IGN, *Xbox Series X Graphics Source Code Reportedly Stolen, Being Held for $100 Million Ransom* (Mar. 27, 2020), https://www.ign.com/articles/xbox-series-x-graphics-source-code-reportedly-being-held-to-100-million-ransom-by-hacker.

5 Press Release, FM Glob., *Cyber Insurance May Create False Sense of Security among Senior Financial Executives at World's Top Companies, Suggests FM Global Survey* (July 30, 2019), https://newsroom.

that their insurer would cover "most" or "all" of the damages their company would incur in a cyberattack. Unfortunately, however, the vast majority of the effects the CFOs expected to experience in a material cybersecurity event (such as issues arising from increased investor scrutiny), are not typically covered by cyber insurance policies. With the risks posed by cyber threats and data breaches expected to increase, particularly as public and private companies' reliance on online and cloud-based services increases, attention to potential coverage issues arising out of these incidents is critical.

A. Cybersecurity Best Practices for Publicly Traded and Private Companies

The number of data breaches has increased, and trends suggest that this number will only continue to rise. According to experts, there were approximately 3,950 data breaches in 2020,[6] a 78% increase from 2018.[7] Breaches have become sophisticated, well-funded operations.[8] External actors targeting large businesses for money perpetrated the majority of breaches.[9] Some breaches incorporate the use of malware, which, when used, has generally meant ransomware attacks.[10] Although breaches affect

---

fmglobal.com/releases/cyber-insurance-may-create-false-sense-of-security-among-senior-financial-executives-at-worlds-top-companies-suggests-fm-global-survey.

6 Verizon, 2020 Data Breach Investigations Report 4, https://enterprise.verizon.com/resources/executivebriefs/2020-dbir-executive-brief.pdf.

7 Verizon, 2018 Data Breach Investigations Report 4 https://enterprise.verizon.com/resources/reports/2018/DBIR_2018_Report.pdf.

8 For instance, a grand jury recently indicted six Russian intelligence officers for computer crimes related to the French 2017 elections and the 2018 Winter Olympic Games. The defendants, allegedly belonging to Russian military intelligence, allegedly caused over $1 billion in damages. *See* Press Release, U.S. Dep't of Justice, Six Russian GRU Officers Charged in Connection with Disruptive Actions in Cyberspace (Oct. 19, 2020), https://www.justice.gov/opa/pr/six-russian-gru-officers-charged-connection-worldwide-deployment-destructive-malware-and.

9 2020 Report, *supra* note 1, at 5.

10 2018 Report, *supra* note 2, at 23.

companies across all industries, health care, financial, and insurance industries have been the hardest hit.[11]

The evidence confirms it is past time to do away with any remaining vestiges of the idea that only small, unsophisticated companies are vulnerable to data breaches. The past decade has shown us that "too big to fail" is not applicable to data breaches. In fact, a compilation of the preceding decade's most prominent data breaches lists many household names.[12] To date, the largest data breach experienced so far involved Yahoo and affected over 3 billion user accounts, resulting in extensive fines and enforcement actions.[13]

1. General Approach

Organizations should invest the time necessary to respond effectively and efficiently to a cyber event. There are many components to an effective and efficient response, including preparing and practicing incident response plans and requiring business leaders to develop the requisite knowledge of data breaches. Any industry plan would be remiss, however, without insurance policies as a cornerstone.

A standalone cyber insurance policy may provide first and third party coverage for a cyber incident. Due in part to its relative newness and small market share, there is very little case law interpreting cyber insurance policies and standardized policy language has not been developed.[14] Some common areas of coverage include costs for notifying consumers about a breach, recovering compromised data, and repairing damaged systems.[15]

---

11 2020 Report, *supra* note 1, at 10. In 2020, the healthcare industry suffered 798 incidents and 521 confirmed disclosures of data. The financial and insurance industry fared worse: it suffered 1,509 incidents and 448 confirmed disclosures of data.

12 Dan Swinhoe, *The 15 Biggest Data Breaches of the 21st Century*, CIO (Jan. 8, 2021), https://www.csoonline.com/article/2130877/the-biggest-data-breaches-of-the-21st-century.html.

13 Kenneth Kiesnoski, *5 of the Biggest Data Breaches Ever*, CNBC (July 30, 2019), https://www.cnbc.com/2019/07/30/five-of-the-biggest-data-breaches-ever.html.

14 Jones Day, COVID-19 Crisis May Warrant Changes to Your Cyber Insurance Coverage, https://www.jonesday.com/en/insights/2020/07/covid 19-crisis-may-warrant-changes-to-your-cyber-insurance-coverage.

15 Nationwide, What is Cyber Insurance?, https://www.nationwide.com/lc/resources/small-business/articles/what-is-cyber-insurance#:~:text=Cyber

Coverage may also include business and network disruption costs incurred as a cyber incident disables an organization's systems.[16] Finally, cyber insurance may also cover regulatory claims, which can include civil fines, penalties, or settlements, and legal fees for responding to government investigations.

Cyber insurance, however, should not be an organization's only line of available potential coverage to a cyber incident. A cyber incident can easily turn into a claim for coverage under an organization's D&O policy. Publicly traded corporations especially should take note of this development. As explained in more detail later in this chapter,[17] a tide has turned and some shareholders of publicly held corporations have been succeeding in their lawsuits against individual directors or officers for their alleged role in cyber incidents. These shareholder claims include breaches of fiduciary duty for failing to adequately prepare for incidents and unjust enrichment for collecting a salary while breaching fiduciary duties in connection with cyber incidents.[18] The nature of these claims often places them under a D&O policy rather than a cyber policy.[19]

Accordingly, organizations, especially those that are publicly held, should ensure that their D&O policies do not expressly exclude coverage

---

%20insurance%20generally%20covers%20your,license%20numbers%20and%20health%20records.

16 Jaclyn Jaeger, *Cyber-insurance: Why you need it and how to choose the right plan*, Compliance Week (Feb. 22, 2021), https://www.complianceweek.com/cyber-security/cyber-insurance-why-you-need-it-and-how-to-choose-the-right-plan/30067.article.

17 *Infra* section VIII.

18 *See generally Palkon v. Holmes, et al.*, No. 2:14-cv-01234, 2014 U.S. Dist. LEXIS 148799 (D.N.J. Oct. 20, 2014). In *Palkon*, a derivative shareholder suit, the plaintiff filed a complaint against various corporate officers and directors at Wyndham Worldwide, a hospitality corporation, regarding three alleged data breaches. The plaintiff alleged that the defendant "breached their duties of care and loyalty" by "failing to implement a system of internal controls to protect customers" personal and financial information" and were unjustly enriched "at the expense of and to the detriment of [the corporation]" by "a result of the compensation they received while breaching fiduciary duties".

19 Marsh, A New Guide on Directors and Officers Liability—Understanding Cyber Directors & Officers Liability Risks and Buying Insurance, https://www.marsh.com/uk/insights/research/understanding-cyber-directors-officers-liability-risks-buying-insurance.html.

for cyber incidents. These exclusions may come in many forms. They may be explicit, such as precluding coverage for "privacy incidents," or not as immediately obvious. For instance, many policies—both D&O and cyber—exclude coverage for incidents tied to terrorisms or acts of war,[20] which may be implicated should an organization suffer a cyber incident due to a nation state threat actor.[21] This is not a hypothetical scenario: in 2017, a pharmaceutical company faced a setback when most of its property insurers denied coverage for nearly $1 billion in damages arising under the infamous NotPetya cyber attack, which was allegedly attributed to a state actor.[22] A primary reason cited for declining coverage was the presence of act of war exclusions in the relevant policies.[23]

Besides illustrating the impact that an act of war or terrorism exclusion can have when seeking coverage for a cyber incident, the case study of NotPetya saliently illustrates the importance of a standalone cyber insurance policy. NotPetya allegedly caused $10 billion in damages worldwide, only 3% of which was paid to policyholders under cyber insurance policies.[24]

Aside from cyber insurance, organizations should develop and implement robust incident response plans, or IRPs, that cover how incidents are detected and reported internally, triaging, escalation, remediation and external notification if necessary. IRPs have an additional pragmatic benefit: developing a formal plan may also favorably influence the amount in premium that an organization may pay for cyber insurance

20 Evan Bundschuh, *The Many Cyber Exclusions in D&O Policies*, Fordham Journal of Corp. & Fin. Law (Apr. 28, 2017), https://news.law.fordham.edu/jcfl/2017/04/28/the-many-cyber-exclusions-in-do-policies/.

21 Report, U.S. Dep't of Homeland Sec., Commodification of Cyber Capabilities: A Grand Cyber Arms Bazaar, at 16-18, https://www.dhs.gov/sites/default/files/publications/ia/ia_geopolitical-impact-cyber-threats-nation-state-actors.pdf.

22 Elizabeth Blosfield, *Cyber Lessons for the Insurance Industry Continue Three Years After NotPetya*, Ins. Journal (Aug. 12, 2020), https://www.insurancejournal.com/news/national/2020/08/12/578788.htm; Dustin Volz & Sarah Young, *White House blames Russia for 'reckless' NotPetya cyber attack*, Reuters (Feb. 15, 2018), https://www.reuters.com/article/us-britain-russia-cyber-usa/white-house-blames-russia-for-reckless-notpetya-cyber-attack-idUSKCN1FZ2UJ.

23 https://www.insurancejournal.com/news/national/2020/08/12/578788.htm.

24 https://hbr.org/2020/10/does-your-cyber-insurance-cover-a-state-sponsored-attack.

coverage.[25] Companies should prepare for breaches and test their IRPs by engaging counsel to conduct a privileged tabletop exercise that simulates an actual data breach. As part of a comprehensive cybersecurity plan, companies should also document customized policies and procedures to reduce risk. Although writing down policies might not seem like the most important thing in the world, it helps formalize requirements, provide a yardstick to measure against, and foster a culture of compliance. Key documents, beyond an IRP, include an acceptable use policy that provides guidance to employees about permissible use of data, networks, systems and other resources; VPN usage policies—particularly given the significant move to remote work—data backup and business continuity plans; and many others.

Importantly, however, given the recent increase in cybersecurity incidents, and with the expectation that the trend will only continue to rise, it is important for business leaders to understand common types of data breaches that may affect their organizations. Ransomware is one type of data breach. The U.S. Department of Justice defines ransomware as a "type of malicious software cyber actors use to deny access to systems or data."[26] The U.S. Department of Homeland Security's Cybersecurity & Infrastructure Agency ("CISA") states that ransomware has "rapidly emerged as the most visible cybersecurity risk playing out across our nation's networks, locking up private sector organizations and government agencies alike."[27] During a typical ransomware attack, the threat actor will use malware to gain control of a system and demand payment for the restoration of files that it is holding hostage.

When an organization is in the throes of a ransomware attack and its important systems and files are in jeopardy, payment may become a tempting response. Many cyber insurance policies, however, cover ransom payments, and some insurers have argued that payment may be the cheapest and most direct way to conclude a ransomware attack.[28] Despite

---

25 https://www.propertycasualty360.com/2021/04/08/can-a-business-forgo-a-cyber-insurance-policy/?slreturn=20210314152919

26 Memorandum, U.S. Dep't of Justice, Ransomware: What It Is and What To Do About It, justice.gov/criminal-ccips/file/872766/download.

27 Memorandum, U.S. Dep't of Homeland Sec., Insights: Ransomware Outbreak, https://us-cert.cisa.gov/sites/default/files/2019-08/CISA_Insights-Ransomware_Outbreak_S508C.pdf.

28 Renee Dudley, *The Extortion Economy: How Insurance Companies Are Fueling a Rise in Ransomware Attacks*, ProPublica (Aug. 27, 2019),

the insurance position, however, paying ransom to a threat actor introduces at least two issues. First, law enforcement does not recommend paying ransom. Generally, law enforcement has expressed concern that paying ransom will incentivize future ransomware attacks without necessarily guaranteeing the return of the files or systems held hostage.[29] In fact, insurers recently stated that almost $400 million was paid for cyber insurance claims,[30] and experts have opined that ransomware payments now constitute a majority of cyber insurance claims.[31] Second, public companies have additional issues to consider when faced with a ransomware attack. Under U.S. federal law, public companies must satisfy certain reporting and disclosure requirements.[32] Companies that fail to meet their reporting requirements run the risk of civil penalties and adverse business consequences.

2. *Recent Developments*

Public companies were recently reminded of reporting requirements as they pertain to cybersecurity incidents, such as ransomware attacks. On February 21, 2018, the U.S. Securities & Exchange Commission ("SEC") issued cybersecurity interpretive guidance.[33] This guidance addressed some of the issues that public companies may encounter, such as disclosure. The SEC advised public companies to "consider the materiality of cybersecurity risks and incidents when preparing the disclosure that is

---

https://www.propublica.org/article/the-extortion-economy-how-insurance-companies-are-fueling-a-rise-in-ransomware-attacks.

29 Fed. Bureau of Investigation, Ransomware, https://www.fbi.gov/scams-and-safety/common-scams-and-crimes/ransomware.

30 Matthew McCabe, *How Cyber Insurance Supports the Fight AGAINST Ransomware: Marsh*, Ins. Journal (Oct. 9, 2019), https://www.insurancejournal.com/news/national/2019/10/09/544884.htm.

31 Catalin Cimpanu, *Ransomware accounted For 41% Of All Cyber Insurance* Claims In H1 2020, ZDNet (Sept. 10, 2020), https://www.zdnet.com/article/ransomware-accounts-to-41-of-all-cyber-insurance-claims/.

32 *See generally* Securities Act of 1933, 15 U.S.C. § 77a et seq.; Securities Exchange Act of 1934, 15 U.S.C. § 78a *et seq.*

33 Memorandum, Securities and Exch. Comm'n, Commission Statement and Guidance on Public Company Cybersecurity Disclosures, https://www.sec.gov/rules/interp/2018/33-10459.pdf.

required" for various registration statements and periodic reports under either the Securities Act of 1933 or the Securities Exchange Act of 1934.[34]

The timing of the SEC's guidance is no coincidence. On April 24, 2018, the SEC announced a settlement related to the one of the largest data breaches reported thus far.[35] Although not explicitly a ransomware incident, the case provides a valuable look at what a public company may find itself facing. In 2014, Yahoo experienced a data breach that affected more than 500 million user accounts. By the time Yahoo reported the breach more than two years later, the costs of its delayed disclosure became clear, in both civil penalties and adverse business consequences. The SEC imposed a $35 million civil penalty. The day after its disclosure, Yahoo experienced a 3% decline in its market capitalization, which was equivalent to $1.3 billion. Additionally, a stock purchase agreement with Verizon for stock worth approximately $4.825 billion was renegotiated and reduced by $350 million.

Although federal agencies have consistently maintained the position that paying ransom may empower threat actors to continue their attacks and does not guarantee the release of systems or files held hostage, victims of ransomware that opt to pay ransom may soon face consequences other than federal disapproval, such as sanctions.

In October 2020, the U.S. Treasury's Office of Foreign Assets Control ("OFAC") issued a bulletin to "highlight the sanctions risks associated with ransomware payments related to malicious cyber-enabled activities."[36] OFAC is an agency tasked with supervising the enforcement of sanctions laws. U.S. federal law generally prohibits U.S. persons from engaging in transactions, directly or indirectly, with certain individuals or entities.[37] Some of these individuals or entities are identified on OFAC's Specially Designated Nationals and Blocked Persons List ("SDN"), or may otherwise be covered by comprehensive country or region embargoes, such as those involving Cuba, the Crimea region of Ukraine, Iran, North Korea, and Syria.

---

34 *Id.*, at 7.

35 Altaba Inc., f/d/b/a Yahoo! Inc., S.E.C. 3-18448 (Apr. 24, 2018), https://www.sec.gov/litigation/admin/2018/33-10485.pdf.

36 Memorandum, U.S. Dep't of Treasury, Advisory on Potential Sanctions Risks for Facilitating Ransomware Payments, https://home.treasury.gov/system/files/126/ofac_ransomware_advisory_10012020_1.pdf.

37 *See generally* International Emergency Economic Powers Act, 50 U.S.C. § 1701 et seq.; Trading with the Enemy Act; 50 U.S.C. § 4301 et seq.

OFAC's bulletin is significant for several reasons. OFAC stated it may impose civil penalties for transacting with a person or entity where the transaction is prohibited under federal law. This highlights that payment a ransom may run the risk of violating federal law if the threat actor falls within a restricted category, such as the SDN. Although threat actors are typically anonymous and their victims have few (if any) means to learn their identity, OFAC confirmed that violations might be determined by strict liability. In other words, the bulletin is a de facto warning that insureds and insurers may face sanctions for paying ransom, even when they did not know or did not have any reason to know that the threat actor was a restricted person or entity.

Publicly traded companies have also received additional attention. On July 10, 2020, the SEC's Office of Compliance Inspections and Examinations issued a ransomware alert.[38] In this alert, the SEC encouraged public companies to monitor CISA warnings and listed "observations" concerning "how to enhance cybersecurity preparedness and operational resiliency to address ransomware attacks."[39] Many of the "observations" have been previously mentioned, but a few are worth restating, such as: developing procedures to addressing compliance with federal and state reporting requirements for cyber incidents or events; auditing networks of systems that use Remote Desktop Protocol; and ensuring all firmware and software have the most current updates.[40]

These alerts highlight the possibility of civil or financial liability by various government agencies for failure to comply with certain guidance. It would serve private and public companies well to ensure that any acquired cyber insurance policies provide coverage for costs accrued due to regulatory fines and investigations. The OFAC bulletin does not distinguish between public and private companies, and the SEC's guidance for public companies is, for now, limited to only "observations."

B. Disclosure and Regulatory Issues

The interest of regulators in cybersecurity issues uniquely faced by publicly traded companies has been building for some time. In 2011, the

---

38 Memorandum, Securities and Exch. Comm'n, Cybersecurity: Risk Alert, https://www.sec.gov/files/Risk%20Alert%20-%20Ransomware.pdf.

39 *Id.*

40 *Id.*

SEC provided a statement on the Division of Corporation Finance's views regarding disclosure obligations relating to cybersecurity risks and cyber incidents.[41]

In February 2018 the SEC Issued a "Commission Statement and Guidance on Public Company Cybersecurity Disclosures."[42] The Statement acknowledged that "[i]n a digitally connected world, cybersecurity presents ongoing risks and threats to our capital markets and to companies operating in all industries, including public companies regulated by the Commission.[43] As such, "[g]iven the frequency, magnitude and cost of cybersecurity incidents, the Commission believes that it is critical that public companies take all required actions to inform investors about material cybersecurity risks and incidents in a timely fashion, including those companies that are subject to material cybersecurity risks but may not yet have been the target of a cyber-attack."[44] The Statement outlined that:

- Listed companies should consider the materiality of cybersecurity risks and incidents when preparing the disclosure that is required in registration statements under the Securities Act of 1933 ("Securities Act") and the Securities Exchange Act of 1934 ("Exchange Act"), and periodic and current reports under the Exchange Act.[45]
- Notwithstanding that these disclosure forms do not specifically address cybersecurity risks and incidents, a number of the requirements impose obligations to disclose such risks and incidents, contingent on a company's specific circumstances (e.g., periodic reports, etc.).[46]
- Moreover, Item 503(c) of Regulation S-K and Item 3.D of Form 20-F require companies to disclose "the most significant factors

41 Division of Corporation Finance Securities and Exchange Commission CF Disclosure Guidance: Topic No. 2 Cybersecurity (Oct. 13, 2011), https://www.sec.gov/divisions/corpfin/guidance/cfguidance-topic2.htm.

42 SEC, Commission Statement and Guidance on Public Company Cybersecurity Disclosures (Feb. 26, 2018), https://www.sec.gov/rules/interp/2018/33-10459.pdf.

43 *Id.*

44 *Id.*

45 *Id.*

46 *Id.*

that make investments in the company's securities speculative or risky." Accordingly, companies should disclose the risks associated with cybersecurity and cybersecurity incidents ***if these risks are among such factors***. This would notably include risks that arise in connection with acquisitions.[47]

- Disclosures could additionally be required concerning: (i) legal proceedings related to cybersecurity issues; (ii) if cybersecurity incidents or risks materially affect a company's products, services, relationships with customers or suppliers, or competitive conditions; or (iii) the cost of ongoing cybersecurity efforts (including enhancements to existing efforts), the costs and other consequences of cybersecurity incidents, and the risks of potential cybersecurity incidents, among other matters.

At bottom, cybersecurity disclosure review is among the SEC's current key priorities, with increasing pressure on publicly traded companies towards increased disclosure. Recent comments provided by the SEC to disclosures illustrate this trend:

- **Luckin Coffee Inc.**: In a March 20, 2019 correspondence regarding Luckin Coffee Inc.'s draft registration statement, the SEC commented that "[s]ince it appears that cybersecurity risks are material to your business, please disclose the nature of the board's role in overseeing your cybersecurity risk management, the manner in which the board administers this oversight function and any effect this has on the board's leadership structure."[48]

Similarly, the SEC also recently requested additional information regarding the cybersecurity disclosures of Tectonic Financial, Inc. and other companies.[49]

---

47 *Id.*

48 SEC Correspondence Re: Luckin Coffee Inc. Draft Registration Statement on Form F-1 Submitted February 22, 2019CIK No: 0001767582 (Mar. 20, 2019), https://sec.report/Document/0000000000-19-005368/.

49 April 3, 2019 Correspondence Re: T Acquisition, Inc. Draft Registration Statement on Form S-1 Submitted February 13, 2019 CIK No. 0001766526, https://sec.report/Document/0001140361-19-006372/. ("The occurrence of fraudulent activity, breaches of our information security, and cybersecurity attacks, page 50. Please clarify whether you have experienced any of the

C. Audits

Although an organization's information technology unit often serves as the first line of defense against cyber incidents, preparation is also an important factor to consider. Auditing can be a crucial component of preparation. The question remains: where to begin? As an initial step, experts recommend internal auditors conduct a forward-looking cyber risk assessment.[50] In lieu of targeting specific parts of an organization, the assessment should be broad. A broad audit is important because targeted audits run the risk of missing an important part of an organization's response system.

The initial assessment should not be exhaustive. As a starting point to preparing multi-year plans, an initial assessment may be considered successful if it identifies areas for additional, deeper-level subsequent reviews. Its findings should be distilled into a concise summary for the organization's audit committee and/or relevant board for evaluation and planning.

Besides providing a means-tested way to prepare for cyber incidents, auditing may also reduce an organization's liability. Companies should be aware of OFAC's Economic Sanctions Enforcement Guidelines (the "Guidelines"), which guide OFAC when "determining an appropriate enforcement response to apparent violations of U.S. economic sanctions programs that OFAC enforces."[51] The Guidelines allow OFAC to consider "the existence, nature and adequacy of a[n] [entity's] risk-based OFAC compliance program at the time of the apparent violation" when determining whether to initiate an enforcement proceeding. In other words, an audit, as part of a vigorous compliance program, may mitigate the effects of an enforcement proceeding.

Large, publicly traded companies should pay exceptional attention to the benefits of auditing their systems. Public companies may face a higher risk of being the subject of an OFAC enforcement proceeding than a smaller, private company. Under the Guidelines, OFAC may consider an

---

referenced types of breaches. Refer to CF Disclosure Guidance: Topic No. 2.").

50 Deloitte, Cybersecurity and the Role of Internal Audit, https://www2.deloitte.com/content/dam/Deloitte/us/Documents/risk/us-risk-cyber-ia-urgent-call-to-action.pdf.

51 Office of Foreign Assets Control, 31 C.F.R. § 57593 (2009).

entity's size and commercial sophistication as part of its evaluation.[52] As public companies tend to be larger, especially in terms of revenue and headcount, than private companies, they may find enforcement proceedings against themselves assuming a higher priority.

D. COVID-19 Considerations

As it has with so many other things, COVID-19 has and will continue to significantly affect cybersecurity. The pandemic has placed organizations under immense pressure, especially from suddenly transitioning to a remote workforce and the increased vulnerabilities that have developed.[53] Threat actors, unfortunately, have noticed these vulnerabilities. The number of reported ransomware attacks has increased during the pandemic.[54] Due to the pandemic, CISA has issued several alerts. In one alert, CISA identified a vulnerability in virtual private networks that threat actors were exploiting.[55] In another alert, it reported an increase in ransomware attacks against K-12 educational institutions.[56] CISA reported that over half of ransomware incidents reported to it involved K-12 educational institutions, an increase from only 28% of reported incidents. Finally, the U.S. Department of Homeland Security and the U.K. National Cybersecurity Centre took an unusual step by

---

52 *Id.* at § 57603.

53 As an example, this has resulted in a 127% increase in the number of exposed remote desktop protocols. Asaf Aprozper, *127% Increase in Exposed RDPs Due to Surge in Remote Work*, Reposify (Mar. 30, 2020), https://blog.reposify.com/127-increase-in-exposed-rdps-due-to-surge-in-remote-work.

54 Danny Palmer, *Ransomware: Surge In Attacks As Hackers Take Advantage Of Organisations Under Pressure*, ZDNet (Oct. 7, 2020), https://www.zdnet.com/article/ransomware-surge-in-attacks-as-hackers-take-advantage-of-organisations-under-pressure/.

55 Alert AA20-107A, U.S. Dep't of Homeland Sec., Continued Threat Actor Exploitation Post Pulse Secure VPN Patching, https://us-cert.cisa.gov/ncas/alerts/aa20-107a.

56 Alert AA20-345A, U.S. Dep't of Homeland Sec., Cyber Actors Target K-12 Distance Learning Education to Cause Disruptions and Steal Data, https://us-cert.cisa.gov/ncas/alerts/aa20-345a.

issuing a joint alert concerning increased cyber threats due to changes made in workplaces in response to the pandemic.[57]

As organizations face these challenges, it is important for them to be aware of the implications they may have in any available cyber insurance policies. For instance, because cyber insurance policies have not yet widely adopted standardized language, policyholders and organizations researching cyber insurance may find themselves with policies that do not necessarily cover some cyber incidents. For instance, some cyber policies exclude coverage for cyber incidents that are the result of negligent network practices.[58]

E. The Board's Role

As the head of an organization, a board of directors plays an important part in managing risks related to cybersecurity. A recent survey of public companies provides guidance and a starting place for boards looking to manage cybersecurity vulnerabilities.

According to a review of 76 of the Fortune 100 companies, most boards have taken significant steps towards managing cybersecurity risks. For instance, the vast majority of surveyed boards now designate a board member with oversight of cybersecurity matters and use an audit committee to review cybersecurity matters.[59] One of the biggest changes was the number of boards that identified at least one director with cybersecurity expertise: between 2018 to 2020, that number rose almost 20 points, to 58%. The report, however, still identifies numerous areas for improvement. According to the study, only 7% of reviewed boards disclosed that their cyber preparations included simulations or readiness

---

57 Alert AA20-099A, U.S. Dep't of Homeland Sec., COVID-19 Exploited by Malicious Cyber Actors, https://us-cert.cisa.gov/ncas/alerts/aa20-099a.

58 Jones Day, COVID-19 Crisis May Warrant Changes to Your Cyber Insurance Coverage, https://www.jonesday.com/en/insights/2020/07/ covid19-crisis-may-warrant-changes-to-your-cyber-insurance-coverage.

59 Steve W. Klemash, Jamie C. Smith, and Chuck Seets, *What Companies are Disclosing About Cybersecurity Risk and Oversight*, Harvard Law School Forum on Corporate Governance (Aug. 25, 2020), https://corpgov.law.harvard.edu/2020/08/25/what-companies-are-disclosing-about-cybersecurity-risk-and-oversight/.

tests. Additionally, only 16% of boards use an external independent advisor.

Cybersecurity is a relatively new concern for most organizations, and the expertise is still developing. Becoming literate in cybersecurity does not necessarily require technical expertise. Instead, directors, as the leaders of their organizations, are responsible for establishing a risk tolerance and developing a culture of cybersecurity vigilance.[60]

Public company boards should also be aware of recent direction from the SEC. In its February 2018 "Commission Statement and Guidance on Public Company Cybersecurity Disclosures," the SEC cautioned that reporting requirements may require public companies to disclose their boards' cybersecurity-related roles.[61] Specifically, if "cybersecurity risks are material to a company's business," then the Commission stated companies "should include the nature of the board's role in overseeing the management of that risk."[62]

F. Other Issues

Insider trading has always been an issue for public companies, but, in the cybersecurity context, boards should be aware of actions taken after a data breach but prior to an announcement.

Under U.S. federal law, it is illegal to trade a security based on material nonpublic information. This has important ramifications when a company is aware of a data breach but has not yet made a public disclosure. In its cybersecurity interpretive guidance, the SEC recommended that while companies investigate cybersecurity incidents, "they should consider whether and when it may be appropriate to implement restrictions on insider trading in their securities."[63]

---

60 Daniel Dobrygowski and Derek Vadala, *Does Your Board Really Understand Your Cyber Risks?*, Harvard Business Review (Sept. 1, 2020), https://hbr.org/2020/09/does-your-board-really-understand-your-cyber-risks.

61 SEC, Commission Statement and Guidance on Public Company Cybersecurity Disclosures (Feb. 26, 2018), https://www.sec.gov/rules/interp/2018/33-10459.pdf.

62 *Id.*

63 Memorandum, *supra* note 17.

This warning was not just for show. In 2018, both the SEC and U.S. Department of Justice charged a former chief information officer for allegedly selling $950,000 worth of stock for a profit after he became aware of a data breach but prior to the company's announcement.[64] He was eventually sentenced to four months in prison.[65]

G. Area of Recent Activity for Board Failing to Act in Area of Cybersecurity

Cybersecurity has the attention of regulators and plaintiffs. Directors and officers should be specifically aware of increasingly aggressive enforcement activity and a newfound danger of personal liability for cybersecurity incidents.

Recently, U.S. federal agencies, such as the SEC, Federal Trade Commission ("FTC"), and Consumer Financial Protection Bureau ("CFPB"), have become more aggressive in cybersecurity enforcement. As an example, in the first action of its kind, the SEC fined Yahoo a $35 million civil penalty for its alleged actions related to the series of data breaches.[66]

Yet writing a check will not necessarily resolve the issue by itself. The FTC also announced that it would be pursuing "strong injunctive provisions" pertaining to cybersecurity measures.[67] As a preview of what enforcement proceedings may be to come, companies should review the

---

64 Peter J. Henning, *Insider Trading Remains a Fixture for Securities Enforcement*, N.Y. Times (Jan. 1, 2019), https://www.nytimes.com/2019/01/01/business/dealbook/insider-trading-enforcement-prosecution.html.

65 Dave Simpson, *U.S. Att'y in Georgia Resigns Citing "Unforeseen Circumstances,"* Law360 (Jan. 4, 2021), https://www.law360.com/articles/1341541.

66 Press Release, Securities and Exch. Comm'n, Altaba, Formerly Known as Yahoo!, Charged With Failing to Disclose Massive Cybersecurity Breach; Agrees To Pay $35 Million (Apr. 24, 2018), https://www.sec.gov/news/press-release/2018-71.

67 Statement, Fed. Trade Comm'n, Regarding Unixiz, Inc. d/b/a i-Dressup.com and Zhijun Liu and Xichen Zhang individually & James V. Grago, Jr. d/b/a ClixSense.com (Apr. 24, 2019), https://www.ftc.gov/system/files/documents/cases/2019-03-19_idressupclixsense_statement_final.pdf.

2017 data breach of a leading consumer reporting agency. As part of the resolution, the FTC, CFPB, and various state enforcement agencies agreed to settle claims for $575 million.[68] Echoing the FTC's priority of "strong injunctive provisions," however, the terms of the settlement include the following noteworthy mentions:[69]

- The agency must designate an employee to oversee its information security program;
- Every two years, obtain a third-party assessment of its information security programs;
- The agency's board or relevant subcommittee must annually certify and attest that the corporation is complying with the settlement's information security requirements; and
- Ensure that service providers that access personal information stored by the agency also implement adequate safeguards to protect such data.

Due to the newness and apparent unpredictability of cybersecurity threats, corporate directors and officers have generally enjoyed a respite from personal liability for cybersecurity incidents. In the wake of several data breaches that captured significant media attention, shareholders filed derivative lawsuits against corporate directors and officers. Notable lawsuits have included claims against directors and officers of Wyndham[70] and Target.[71] In each lawsuit, shareholders generally alleged that actions (or lack thereof) by officers and directors enabled the alleged data breaches. Each lawsuit, however, was dismissed in favor of the directors and officers.

---

68 Press Release, Fed. Trade Comm'n, Equifax Data Breach Settlement (Jan. 2020), https://www.ftc.gov/enforcement/cases-proceedings/refunds/equifax-data-breach-settlement.

69 Press Release, Fed. Trade Comm'n, Equifax to Pay $575 Million as Part of Settlement with FTC, CFPB, and States Related to 2017 Data Breach (July 22, 2019), https://www.ftc.gov/news-events/press-releases/2019/07/equifax-pay-575-million-part-settlement-ftc-cfpb-states-related.

70 *Palkon v. Holmes, et al.*, No. 2:14-cv-01234, 2014 U.S. Dist. LEXIS 148799 (D.N.J. Oct. 20, 2014).

71 *Davis v. Steinhafel*, No. 14-cv-00213, 2016 U.S. Dist. LEXIS 195486 (D. Minn. July 7, 2016).

The honeymoon period, however, has ended. The growing frequency of cybersecurity incidents has made the argument that directors and officers were not aware of cybersecurity threats or otherwise could not have known less tenable. We now find ourselves with the looming prospect of personal liability for corporate officers regarding cybersecurity incidents. Situations like this may be ripe for filing claims under D&O policies, which should motivate organizations to verify that their policies do not exclude coverage for cyber incidents.

As a sign of a changing tide, we return to the case study of Yahoo. In one of the first actions of its kind, a court approved a $29 million settlement in a derivative lawsuit against 15 directors and officers related to the series of data breaches that shook the company a few years earlier.[72]

This trend may, however, affect certain corporate officers more than others. Recently, a court dismissed claims against several senior vice presidents and a CFO, but declined to dismiss claims made as to the former CEO.[73] The court's reasoning for distinguishing the former CEO from other corporate officials individually named as defendants was that only the CEO "had the power to control the general affairs" of the corporation, such "the power to control [the corporation's] cybersecurity policy and the statements made by [the corporation] and the other Individual Defendants as to these cybersecurity policies."[74]

H. Needed Coverage Grants Specific to the Industry

1. Discussion of ISO Endorsement CG 21 06 05 14, ISO Endorsement CG 21 08 05 14

A commercial general liability ("CGL") insurance policy is the foundation of most risk management plans. Standard CGL policies provide coverage for several categories of incidents. The two most relevant, for our purposes, are "Coverage A" and "Coverage B." "Coverage A" may provide coverage against third-party claims for bodily injury and property damage, while "Coverage B" may provide coverage

72 *In re Yahoo! Inc. Shareholder Litig.*, No. 17-cv-307054, (Cal. Supp. Ct Jan. 4, 2019).

73 *In re Equifax Inc. Securities Litigation*, 357 F. Supp. 3d 1189 (N.D. Ga. 2019).

74 *Id.* at 1252 (internal quotations omitted).

for personal and advertising injuries, such as libel or slander.[75] CGL policies incorporate broad coverage language, such as "physical damage" or "bodily injury," and it was not foreseeable that the rise of cyber incidents would create ambiguities in interpreting either term when the policies were drafted years earlier, when cyber incidents were almost unheard of.

In response to differing court interpretations of whether a cyber incident was "property damage,"[76] in 2013, the Insurance Services Office ("ISO"), a company that develops policy and endorsement language for insurers, introduced at least two endorsements regarding data breaches. One endorsement, CG 21 06 05 14, is an exclusion to Coverage A or Coverage B that is entitled, "Access Or Disclosure Of Confidential Or Personal Information And Data-Related Liability—With Bodily Injury Exception." It excludes coverage for injury or damage arising out of any access to or disclosure of any person's or organization's confidential or personal information, including patents, trade secrets, processing methods, customer lists, financial information, credit card information, health information or any other type of nonpublic information.

Another endorsement, CG 21 08 05 14, is an exclusion to Coverage B that is entitled, "Access Or Disclosure Of Confidential Or Personal Information." It largely mirrors the first endorsement.

Given the prevalence of these exclusions, it is important for private and public companies to realize their CGL policies will probably not provide coverage for cybersecurity incidents and plan accordingly,[77] including by assessing the scope of cyber insurance coverage.

2. *Assess Scope of Cyber Insurance Coverage*

Prior to purchasing a cyber insurance policy, an organization should determine its vulnerabilities and understand what type of loss cyber

---

75 Insurance Information Institute, Commercial General Liability Insurance, https://www.iii.org/article/commercial-general-liability-insurance.

76 In *Am. Online, Inc. v. St. Paul Mercury Ins. Co.*, 347 F.3d 89, 93 (4th Cir. 2003), the court found that software damage was not "property damage"

77 U.S. Dept' of Homeland Sec., Cybersecurity Insurance, https://www.cisa.gov/cybersecurity-insurance ("Traditional commercial general liability and property insurance policies typically exclude cyber risks from their terms, leading to the emergence of cybersecurity insurance as a 'stand alone' line of coverage.").

insurance may cover. The first query may be resolved by an audit, while the second inquiry requires research into what cyber insurance policies may pay for.

The potential for coverage should always be evaluated by examining the exact language of an organization's specific policy. In general, however, cyber insurance generally provides coverage for loss stemming from data breach and event responses; the costs of defending against a regulatory action brought by the authorities; liability coverage; loss of income or extra expenses due to security breaches or system failures; and cyber extortion (e.g., payments made in response to ransomware attacks).[78]

3. *Purchasing Cyber or Network Security Insurance to Cover Gaps in an Organization's CGL Policy*

A CGL policy does not necessarily cover all of the risks that policyholders may assume would be covered. As endorsements CG 21 06 05 14 and CG 21 08 05 14 demonstrate, CGL policies should not be presumed to cover damages related to cyber incidents. Instead, purchasing a cyber insurance policy is an important investment for an organization, especially to address coverage gaps left behind by a CGL policy.

Although beneficial to many organizations, cyber insurance is not a panacea for all cyber woes. When selecting and purchasing a cyber insurance policy, industries should be mindful of the likelihood that a cyber insurance policy will probably not provide coverage for physical damage or bodily harm that may result from a cyber attack against critical infrastructure.[79]

To ensure there is adequate liability coverage, policyholders should review their CGL and standalone cyber insurance policies with seasoned counsel to determine whether there are any gaps in coverage. If a gap is uncovered, then policyholders should explore available coverage options. With cyber incidents like NotPetya and its $10 billion in damages still fresh in our minds, the costs of inaction have never been higher.

---

78 University Risk Management and Insurance Association and Educause, Frequently Asked Questions About Cyber Insurance (Nov. 2017), https://library.educause.edu/~/media/files/library/2017/10/urmiafaq.pdf; Frequently.

79 U.S. Dep't of Homeland Sec., *supra* note 49.

Chapter 10

Media Liability and the Cyber Policy*

Media companies directly or indirectly own, control, or operate, or have an attributable interest in (a) a U.S. broadcast radio or television station or a U.S. cable televisions system, (b) a "daily newspaper," (as such term is defined in Section 73.3555 of the rules and regulations of the Federal Communication Commission ("FCC")), (c) any U.S. communications facility operated pursuant to a license granted by the FCC and subject to the provisions of Section 310(b) of the Communications Act of 1934, as amended, or (d) any other business that is subject to FCC regulations. Media companies have a number of unique exposures in the cyber arena, and therefore a number of considerations in the context of cyber policies. Those details are discussed in this chapter.

A. Description of Non-Media Companies with Media Exposure

A common position amongst social media platforms and online content aggregators is their resistance to being characterized as media companies. Companies such as Google, Facebook, and Twitter have regularly insisted that they should be thought of purely as technology companies. Many critique this position that these platforms are technology companies rather than media companies. This is an ongoing controversy which explores the underlying rationales, and considers the political, legal, and policy implications associated with accepting or rejecting this position. This is no mere semantic distinction, given the history of the precise classification of communications technologies and services having profound ramifications for how these technologies and services are considered by policy-makers and the courts.[1]

Many companies that advertise or communicate with the public through a variety of platforms, such as social media, print/broadcast

---

* By John Stephens and Michelle Worrall Tilton (authored while Ms. Tilton was a Consultant with Media Risk Consultants, LLC).

1 Napoli, P., & Caplan, R. (2017). Why media companies insist they're not media companies, why they're wrong, and why it matters. *First Monday*, *22*(5). https://doi.org/10.5210/fm.v22i5.7051.

advertising, and websites, also have a media exposure. Advertising communications are particularly exposed to intellectual property exposures, as well as right of publicity. Companies that engage in comparative advertising as exposed to trade libel, product disparagement and related unfair competition claims.

B. Media Liability Cyber Exposures

The past few years have seen a series of controversies emerge in the realm of social media. These controversies have erupted around issues such as accusations of bias in the construction of Facebook's and Twitter's trending topics lists;[2] criticisms of social media platforms for censoring photos of historical/journalistic significance;[3] evidence of increased prominence of false news reports in social media feeds; and concerns about the possible impact of social media-disseminated false news reports on election outcomes in the U.S. and Europe.[4]

This sequence of events has focused public attention on the question of if and how social media platforms are functioning as news organizations; along with the related question of whether these platforms should behave as news organizations. These discussions are taking place as data indicate that social media platforms have established themselves as one of the primary mechanisms via which individuals access and consume news. The potentially troubling irony of this situation is that these social media companies that are playing an increasingly important and influential role in the news and information ecosystem have a long history of insisting that they are not news organizations, or even media companies, at all. Rather these companies have insisted that they should

2 Michael Nunez, 2016, May 9. "Former Facebook workers: We routinely suppressed conservative news," *Gizmodo* (9 May), at http://gizmodo.com/former-facebook-workers-we-routinely-suppressed-conser-1775461006.

3 Marc Scott and Mike Isaac, 2016. "Facebook restores iconic Vietnam War photo it censored for nudity," *New York Times* (9 September), at http://www.nytimes.com/2016/09/10/technology/facebook-vietnam-war-photo-nudity.html.

4 Emily Bell, 2016. "Facebook is eating the world," *Columbia Journalism Review* (7 March), at http://www.cjr.org/analysis/facebook_and_media.php.

be thought of only as technology companies.[5] In this regard, these social media companies are following a pattern established and maintained by other digital media companies, such as Google and Apple, in insisting that they not be thought of as media companies.

A number of analysts have pointed out this growing disconnect between how these companies have perceived themselves—and want to be perceived by others—and how they actually function in the contemporary news and information ecosystem.[6] The goal here is to take this observation a few steps further, by critically examining the articulated rationales and underlying motivations of this position, and by considering the broader implications of accepting this argument. A key goal of this chapter is to show how this argument fits within broader, ongoing efforts by these companies to "discursively . . . frame their services and technologies".[7] As many digital media companies use terms like "platform" strategically, "to position themselves both to pursue current and future profits, to strike a regulatory sweet spot between legislative protections that benefit them and obligations that do not, and to lay out a cultural imaginary within which their service makes sense".[8] We see the self-definition as technology companies and the strong resistance to any classification as media companies as a key dimension of this discursive framing, which has important implications for the legal and regulatory frameworks that are applied to these platforms.

This critique of the argument that social media platforms (and digital content curators more broadly) should be considered purely as technology companies, and not as media companies will be grounded in economic, historical, and policy perspectives on media, in an effort to illustrate the

---

5 Chris Dixon, 2014. "BuzzFeed," *CDixon Blog* (10 August), at http://cdixon.org/2014/08/10/buzzfeed/.

6 Robyn Caplan, 2016. "Like it or not, Facebook is now a media company," *New York Times* (17 May), at http://www.nytimes.com/roomfordebate/2016/05/17/is-facebook-saving-journalism-or-ruining-it/like-it-or-not-facebook-is-now-a-media-company.

7 Tarleton Gillespie, in press. "Regulation of and by platforms," In: Jean Burgess, Thomas Poell, and Alice Marwick (editors). *Sage handbook of social media*. Thousand Oaks, Calif.: Sage; version at https://www.microsoft.com/en-us/research/wp-content/uploads/2016/12/Gillespie-Regulation-ofby-Platforms-PREPRINT.pdf.

8 Ibid.

significant points of continuity, rather than distinction, between traditional and new platforms for news and information.

C. Media Companies Insisting They Are Not Media Companies and Why

It seems that in today's technology-driven business environment, firms increasingly see their identity in terms of the technological approaches they take to their business, rather than in terms of the particular business in which they operate. One of the most prominent—and controversial—current examples involves Uber. Uber has steadfastly maintained that it is a technology company rather than a transportation company because, according to one Uber representative, "we don't transport goods or people—our partners do. We just facilitate that".[9] The ramifications of accepting or rejecting this argument are profound, because if Uber is perceived as a transportation company, then it is subject to the regulations under which the transportation industry operates. If, on the other hand, Uber is perceived as a technology company, then these transportation industry regulations simply don't apply; which, could represent an important source of competitive advantage for Uber.[10] Uber is certainly not alone in maintaining such a position. Automotive, finance, and telecommunications companies have similarly argued that they should be seen purely as technology companies.[11]

Similarly, it seems that a defining characteristic of social media platforms and digital content curators is the consistency with which they have resisted being characterized as media companies and instead have

---

9 Jerome Cukier, 2016. "Why is Uber considered a technology company and a lot of people place it among tech giants like Google, Facebook, etc?" *Quora* (1 March), at https://www.quora.com/Why-is-Uber-considered-a-technology-company-and-a-lot-of-people-place-it-among-tech-giants-like-Google-Facebook-etc.

10 Michael Carney, 2015. "As Uber fights to maintain its technology company classification in India, the rest of the world watches," *Pando* (20 February), at https://pando.com/2015/02/20/as-uber-fights-to-maintain-its-technology-company-classification-in-india-the-rest-of-the-world-watches/.

11 Robyn Caplan, 2016. "Like it or not, Facebook is now a media company," *New York Times* (17 May), at http://www.nytimes.com/roomfordebate/2016/05/17/is-facebook-saving-journalism-or-ruining-it/like-it-or-not-facebook-is-now-a-media-company.

insisted that they be thought of purely as technology companies.[12] Even companies that are unequivocally in the business of producing media content, like Gawker and Vox, have had their CEOs maintain that they are technology companies rather than media companies.[13]

We turn now to the primary arguments put forth in support of the position that social media platforms and digital content curators are technology companies rather than media companies.

1. No Content Produced

The most prominent argument digital media companies make to support the position that they are not media companies is that many of these companies do not produce original content; rather they merely facilitate the distribution of content created by their users. Some of the companies that have made this argument have subsequently vertically integrated into content creation, following a fairly predictable pattern in media history, in which content distributors inevitably pursue the strategic and economic advantages of also being content creators.[14] So, for instance, in 2016 YouTube began producing original series on its subscription service; while Facebook has recently initiated a foray into original video content creation. Nonetheless, given the past—and likely future—persistence of this argument amongst content distributors, it is important that it receive detailed scrutiny.

This argument obviously invites discussion of the types of activities that are central to our understanding of what media companies do. Traditionally, the industrial organization of media has been described in terms of three fundamental—but seldom mutually-exclusive—activities:

a. production (exemplified by content creators such as news outlets and television studios);

---

12 Miguel Helft, 2008. "Is Google a media company?" *New York Times* (10 August), at http://www.nytimes.com/2008/08/11/technology/11google.html.

13 Choire Sicha, 2011. "Inside Gawker Media's first company-wide meeting," *The Awl* (8 September), at https://theawl.com/inside-gawker-medias-first-company-wide-meeting-8abf673bf61#.umax6qp27.

14 Philip M. Napoli, 2016. "Requiem for the long tail: Towards a political economy of content aggregation and fragmentation," *International Journal of Media & Cultural Politics*, volume 12, number 3, pp. 341–356.doi: http://dx.doi.org/10.1386/macp.12.3.341_1.

b. distribution (the process of moving content from producers towards consumers); and,
c. exhibition (the process of providing content directly to audiences).[15]

Digitization and media convergence have meant that these processes have, in some cases, merged, as content can now be distributed directly to the end user. The decline of traditional exhibitors such as book and music retailers in the face of content digitization and digital distribution represents a case in point. One would be hard pressed to argue that traditional exhibitors such as movie theaters, book stores, or record stores should be thought of as media companies. However, the replacements for these entities, such as Amazon, iTunes, and Netflix, are fundamentally different, utilizing an electronic media infrastructure to distribute content to audiences in a pure public good form in a manner that more closely parallels traditional content curators and distributors such as cable systems and broadcast networks. This is in many ways also the case with social media platforms such as Twitter, Snapchat, and Facebook, which now serve as central means of content distribution for many content creators (ranging from news outlets, to individuals, to the NFL), while also serving as the exhibition endpoint for users, who access the content through these platforms via a variety of devices. And, with services like Facebook Live (which allows direct and immediate broadcasting over the Facebook platform) and Facebook Instant Articles (through which Facebook directly hosts the content produced by news organizations;[16] the processes of production, distribution, and exhibition are even more integrated.

Content creation/ownership has never served as a point of distinction in defining a media company from the perspectives of those charged with regulating the media sector. Consider, for instance, that both the cable television and satellite industries were built entirely on a foundation of serving exclusively (at least initially) as distributors of media content. This fact never served as a mechanism for keeping these companies beyond the bounds of the U.S. Federal Communications Commission's (FCC) regulatory authority. In the case of cable television, the FCC extended its

15 Robert Picard, 2011. *The economics and financing of media companies*. Second edition. New York: Fordham University Press.

16 Josh Constine, 2015. "Facebook starts hosting publishers' 'instant articles'," *TechCrunch* (12 May), at https://techcrunch.com/2015/05/12/facebook-instant-articles/.

regulatory authority to cable in part by classifying cable as ancillary to broadcasting (*United States v. Southwestern Cable Co.*, 1968). That is, the fact that cable systems served as a central means of distributing and accessing content (broadcast television) that did fall under the FCC's regulatory authority acted as a mechanism for the expansion of that regulatory authority to cable.

2. *Algorithms Run Everything*

The second prominent line of argument put forth by social media platforms and digital content curators focuses on the nature of their personnel. Specifically, representatives of these companies frequently point to the professional training and backgrounds of themselves and their employees in support of the argument that they are technology companies rather than media companies. Google's Eric Schmidt emphasized that Google is a technology company "because it is run by three computer scientists".[17] Similarly, Cheezburger CEO Ben Huh has emphasized the proportion of the company's employees that are developers on behalf of his assertion that the company is a technology company rather than a media company.[18]

Here too we see an argument lacking in logical or historical grounding. Consider, for instance, that at the time of its introduction there was no greater technological marvel than over-the-air broadcasting. It represented a technological leap forward in the means of communication of a magnitude that can probably only be approached by the introduction of the Internet. Consequently, broadcasting was the province of the technologists and engineers of the time, given its relative technical complexity compared to other available means of communication, such as print newspapers. Technological expertise was at the core of early radio broadcasting companies such as RCA and the Marconi Company.[19] Satellite technology

---

17 Staci D. Kramer, 2006. P. 1. "Google is still a tech company. Really," *Gigaom* (12 June), at https://gigaom.com/2006/06/12/google-is-still-a-tech-company-really/.

18 John Koetsier, 2012. "Exclusive: Cheezburger will take page out of Reddit's playbook, allow users to create own subsites," *Venturebeat* (22 August), at http://venturebeat.com/2012/08/22/exclusive-cheezburger-will-take-page-out-of-reddits-playbook-allow-users-to-create-own-subsites/.

19 Scott Woolley, 2016. The network: The battle for the airwaves and the birth of the communication age. New York: Ecco.

represented another dramatic advancement; once again requiring professionals with a high level of technical expertise.

Technological advancements—and the associated technical expertise—have been fundamental to the media sector since at least the advent of the printing press. It is important that we recognize "the pivotal role technologies play in media work".[20] To argue that the technical orientation of the personnel or leadership of a company represents a logical grounding for precluding it from being thought of as a media company reflects either an ill-informed understanding of the history and evolution of media, or a strategic effort to narrow the definition of media relative to its traditional parameters.

3. *"No Human Editorial Intervention"*

A less explicit argument that these digital media platforms put forth, but one that certainly ties into the previous argument, is the frequent contention that the content that is "surfaced" is not done by human judgment, but by algorithms and data-driven technologies that filter, categorize and classify information that is already present in the system, and reflect what users want back to them. Platforms such as Google and Facebook have frequently emphasized the lack of human intervention in their content curation processes, and have been hesitant to acknowledge such human intervention when it does take place.[21] Facebook, in the wake of the Trending News controversy, in which a report contended that human editors employed by Facebook were suppressing conservative news stories in the platform's Trending list, focused on downplaying as much as possible the role that direct human editorial intervention played in the platform's operation, even going so far as to eliminate the positions of the journalists and editors overseeing its Trending module in the aftermath of the controversy.[22]

---

20 Mark Deuze. 2007. *Media work*. Cambridge: Polity Press.

21 Daniel Trielli, Sean Mussenden, Jennifer Stark, and Nicholas Diakopoulos, 2016. "Googling politics: How the Google issue guide on candidates is biased," *Slate* (7 June), at http://www.slate.com/articles/technology/future_tense/2016/06/how_the_google_issue_guide_on_candidates.

22 Sam Thielman, 2016. "Facebook fires trending team, and algorithm without humans goes crazy," *Guardian* (29 August), at https://www.theguardian.com/technology/2016/aug/29/facebook-fires-trending-topics-team-algorithm.

This asserted/perceived lack of direct human editorial involvement is, in many ways, fundamental to the logic of perceiving these platforms as technology companies rather than media companies. Indeed, the term platform itself has been strategically deployed as a means of casting these services strictly as neutral, technology-driven facilitators of content creation and dissemination. Facebook's Mark Zuckerberg has favored emphasizing that the platform simply provides tools to users, to help them to engage in their own content creation and curation,[23] a position that seems to ignore—or at least mischaracterize—the role that the platform's algorithms play in prioritizing and filtering content for users. The asserted absence of direct human editorial involvement helps to further this perception of distance from, and/or neutrality in, the content selection process—a model that is presumably fundamentally different from the kind of direct (and human) editorial discretion that has been a defining characteristic of traditional media companies.

However, simply because the mechanisms for exercising editorial discretion—for gatekeeping—have changed doesn't mean that the fundamental institutional identity of the gatekeepers should be recast. Representatives of these platforms would likely argue that the nature of their interaction with users is fundamentally different from traditional media, in that social media users play a much more autonomous role in determining the content that they receive. That is, the users, in collaboration with their social networks, ultimately dictate the content that they consume, with the platform serving as neutral facilitator. Whether a reflection of naivete or disingenuousness, this position is simply no longer tenable.[24]

We can look to recent developments, like the much-maligned rebranding of struggling traditional media company Tribune Publishing as

---

23 Kelly Fiveash, 2016. "'We're a tech company not a media company,' says Facebook founder," *Ars Technica* (20 August), at https://arstechnica.com/tech-policy/2016/08/germany-facebook-edit-hateful-posts-zuckerberg-says-not-media-empire/.

24 Tarleton Gillespie, in press. "Regulation of and by platforms," In: Jean Burgess, Thomas Poell, and Alice Marwick (editors). *Sage handbook of social media*. Thousand Oaks, Calif.: Sage; version at https://www.microsoft.com/en-us/research/wp-content/uploads/2016/12/Gillespie-Regulation-ofby-Platforms-PREPRINT.pdf.

technology company,[25] as an indicator of how permeable the boundary is separating a technology company from a media company. Tribune's metamorphosis into technology company appears to rest almost entirely on a stated greater reliance on machine learning and algorithms to better serve audience interests and to facilitate the use of automation in content production. The widespread skepticism (and even derision) that has met this rebranding, in terms of whether it represents anything truly transformative, helps to illustrate that an increased reliance on technology to serve audience interests doesn't serve as a meaningful distinction between technology companies and media companies.

In addition, regardless of the gatekeeping mechanisms employed, platforms such as Facebook, Google, and Twitter find themselves having to navigate a range of editorial policy issues that place them firmly in line with traditional media organizations such as newspapers and broadcasters.[26] Issues related to protecting users from offensive, inflammatory, or adult content are central to the operation of these platforms.[27] This tension was well-illustrated by the controversy that arose around Facebook's decision to censor a posting by a Norwegian journalist, which featured the well-known Vietnam War photo of a nude young Vietnamese girl fleeing a napalm attack. Amid the outcry, Facebook quickly reversed its decision on the basis of the photograph's historical importance.[28] Nonetheless, the controversy that arose highlighted the reality of the extent to which editorial policy decisions not unlike those associated with traditional news publishers are essentially part and parcel of what it means to be a social media platform, even when the editorial

---

25 Greg Satell, 2016. "Tronc's data delusion," *Harvard Business Review* (23 June), at https://hbr.org/2016/06/troncs-data-delusion.

26 Tarleton Gillespie, in press. "Regulation of and by platforms," In: Jean Burgess, Thomas Poell, and Alice Marwick (editors). *Sage handbook of social media.* Thousand Oaks, Calif.: Sage; version at https://www.microsoft.com/en-us/research/wp-content/uploads/2016/12/Gillespie-Regulation-ofby-Platforms-PREPRINT.pdf.

27 David Pierson and Paresh Dave, 2016. "If Facebook promotes propaganda, can it be a neutral news platform?" *Los Angeles Times* (31 May), at http://www.latimes.com/business/la-fi-tn-eu-tech-20160531-snap-story. html.

28 Mike Isaac, 2016. "Facebook, facing bias claims, shows how editors and algorithms guide news," *New York Times* (12 May), at http://www.nytimes.com/2016/05/13/technology/facebook-guidelines-trending-topics.html.

decision-making is initially being handled by algorithms, as was the case with the Vietnam photo.

As should be clear, this scenario points toward these companies operating not only as media organizations in the broadest sense, but more specifically as news organizations, given the extent to which they are engaged in editorial and gatekeeping decisions related to the flow of news and information.

4. *The Centrality of Advertising*

Finally, it is worth noting that all of the arguments put forth by these platforms collapse under the fact that the primary revenue stream for the bulk of these platforms is advertising. Being in the business of providing content to audiences, while selling those audiences to advertisers is a defining characteristic of the media sector[29] (Ingram, 2012; Wolff, 2012). When advertisers are exploring how best to reach potential consumers, the strengths and weaknesses of digital media platforms such a Facebook, Twitter, and Google are being evaluated right alongside those of more traditional media options such as broadcast and cable television, and print and online publications. Moreover, these digital media platforms are proving increasingly effective at siphoning off advertising revenues from these other media sectors (Bhattacharyya, 2016). From this perspective, it is hard to dispute that these firms are all operating in the same business sector. And it is a business that, as history has shown (see above), firms can enter without owning or producing their own content.

D. Underlying Motivations

The discussion thus far has focused on the expressed rationales put forth by these digital media companies for being considered technology companies rather than media companies. The next step is to look beyond these expressed rationales and consider some of the underlying reasons why this argument is so consistently put forth.

---

29 Matthew Ingram, 2012. "Facebook's biggest problem is that it's a media company," *Gigaom* (16 May), at https://gigaom.com/2012/05/16/facebooks-biggest-problem-is-that-its-a-media-company/.

1. Legal and Policy Motivations

It is also important to consider the legal and policy motivations for being thought of as a technology company rather than a media company. As was illustrated in the Uber example above, the way in which a company is classified can have significant legal and policy implications. This has certainly long been the case in the media sector as well.

For instance, in deciding the constitutionality of the Communications Decency Act (which applied a broadcast regulatory model to the Internet), the U.S. Supreme Court struggled with whether to treat the Internet as akin to the telephone, a print newspaper, or television/radio[30] (Stein, 1997). Given the long tradition in the U.S. of applying completely different regulatory regimes to different communication technologies based upon their technological characteristics, the argument of which—if any—analogy to embrace for the Internet had far-reaching legal and policy implications. More recently, the FCC's decision to impose network neutrality regulations on Internet service providers (ISPs) hinged on the re-classification of Internet service providers as telecommunications service providers (akin to phone companies) rather than information service providers (akin to Web hosting services)[31] The FCC's regulatory authority over telecommunications service providers is much greater than its authority over information service providers (again, different technologies and services frequently operate under different regulatory models); so much so that the net neutrality regime imposed by the FCC would be impermissible if ISPs were classified as information service providers.[32] The Trump FCC's impending reversal of the network neutrality regulations will likely involve another round of re-classification.

---

30 Bradley J. Stein, 1997. "Why wait? A discussion of analogy and judicial standards for the Internet in light of the Supreme Court's *Reno v. ACLU* opinion," *St. Louis University Law Journal*, volume 42, pp. 1,471-1,497.

31 William Rinehart, 2015. "A semantic network analysis of the network neutrality debate," paper presented at the Research Conference on Communication, Information and internet Policy, at https://tprc2015.sched.com/event/3v9Q/a-semantic-network-analysis-of-the-network-neutrality-debate.

32 Nilay Patel, 2014. "The wrong words: How the FCC lost net neutrality and could kill the Internet," *The Verge* (15 January), at http://www.theverge.com/2014/1/15/5311948/net-neutrality-and-the-death-of-the-internet.

Similar issues of classification are beginning to confront digital content curators such as social media platforms. This is well-illustrated by some of the legal challenges that have confronted Twitter. In a case involving a government subpoena for information (including tweets) about an individual Twitter user, the court suggested that Twitter was analogous to "scream[ing] out the window"[33] In another subpoena made to Twitter for the IP information for some of its users (who were associated with the organization Wikileaks), the court used a different classification, comparing Twitter, and the IP addresses used to connect to the site, to using a telephone.[34]

A fundamental question underlying these classification efforts involves if, or to what extent, Twitter holds ownership and editorial authority over the content that circulates on its platform. In navigating these issues of classification, industry observers have noted, "It has . . . suited Twitter to pose as a tech company when it comes to potential regulatory and legal burdens."[35] For instance, in a response to a court order for information about a user who was arrested during an Occupy Wall Street protest, Twitter adopted the legal position that it has no ownership of individual tweets, a position that would seem to operate in conflict with the various forms of editorial discretion that Twitter has engaged in in relation to the content on its platform.

The reality is that platforms such as Twitter have substantial leeway to engage in editorial discretion over the content they host without triggering categorization as a publisher, and thus contracting the wide-ranging legal liabilities that come with being a publisher. This is the essence of Section 230 of the Telecommunications Act of 1996. Section 230 provides platforms such as search engines, Internet service providers, and social media sites with broad protection from legal liability for any of the third-party speech that they host, curate, or distribute. From this

33 *New York v. Harris*, 2012. 36 Misc. 3d 868; 949 N.Y.S.2d 590; 2012 N.Y. Misc. LEXIS 3076; 2012 NY Slip Op 22175; see also https://www.eff.org/cases/new-york-v-harris.

34 *New York v. Harris*, 2012. 36 Misc. 3d 868; 949 N.Y.S.2d 590; 2012 N.Y. Misc. LEXIS 3076; 2012 NY Slip Op 22175; see also https://www.eff.org/cases/new-york-v-harris.

35 Shayne Rana, 2012. P. 1. "Is Twitter a technology platform, a media company—or both?" *Tech2* (12 July), at http://tech.firstpost.com/news-analysis/is-twitter-a-technology-platform-a-media-company-or-both-29998.html.

standpoint, social media platforms and digital content curators are sheltered from many of the negative obligations (*i.e.*, obligations to police/protect against the circulation of various types of speech) associated with media companies; or, in the words of Section 230, "information content providers." Much of the policing of their content that these platforms do engage in, it should be emphasized, is actually voluntary (under what is referred to as the "Good Samaritan Provision"), not unlike the way that the cable television industry has long restricted foul language and nudity in the programming they provide, despite being outside the bounds of the FCC's indecency regulations.

The key point in reviewing how the notion of the public interest is applied within the context of electronic media regulation is to illustrate that classification as a media company—at least in the realm of electronic media—has historically meant more intensive government oversight, in the form of affirmative obligations to serve the public interest and more stringent regulation in areas such as concentration of ownership. Given these greater regulatory burdens that fall upon the electronic media sector, one can see why digital media platforms would work to establish an organizational identity that places them well outside of this regulatory model.

2. *Background on Publisher and Distributor Liability Defamation*

Under standard common-law principles, a person who publishes a defamatory statement by another bears the same liability for the statement as if he or she had initially created it. Thus, a book publisher or a newspaper publisher can be held liable for anything that appears within its pages. The theory behind this "publisher" liability is that a publisher has the knowledge, opportunity, and ability to exercise editorial control over the content of its publications.[36]

Distributor liability is much more limited. Newsstands, bookstores, and libraries are generally not held liable for the content of the material that they distribute. The concern is that it would be impossible for distributors to read every publication before they sell or distribute it, and that as a result, distributors would engage in excessive self-censorship. In

36 Digital Media Law Project, Immunity for Online Publishers Under the Communications Decency Act, January 21, 2021.

addition, it would be very hard for distributors to know whether something is actionable defamation; after all, speech must be false to be defamatory.[37]

Not surprisingly, the first websites to be sued for defamation based on the statements of others argued that they were merely distributors, and not publishers, of the content on their sites. One of the first such cases was *Cubby v. CompuServe, Inc.*[38] CompuServe provided subscribers with access to over 150 specialty electronic "forums" that were run by third parties. When CompuServe was sued over allegedly defamatory statements that appeared in the "Rumorville" forum, it argued that it should be treated like a distributor because it did not review the contents of the bulletin board before it appeared on CompuServe's site. The court agreed and dismissed the case against CompuServe.

Four years later, a New York state court came to the opposite conclusion when faced with a website that held itself out as a "family friendly" computer network. In *Stratton Oakmont v. Prodigy*[39] the court held that because Prodigy was exercising editorial control over the messages that appeared on its bulletin boards through its content guidelines and software screening program, Prodigy was more like a "publisher" than a "distributor" and therefore fully liable for all of the content on its site.

The perverse upshot of the *CompuServe* and *Stratton* decisions was that any effort by an online information provider to restrict or edit user-submitted content on its site faced a much higher risk of liability if it failed to eliminate all defamatory material than if it simply didn't try to control or edit the content of third parties at all.

3. *The Communications Decency Act*

This prompted Congress to pass the Communications Decency Act in 1996. The Act contains deceptively simple language under the heading "Protection for Good Samaritan blocking and screening of offensive material":

---

37 Ibid.

38 Cubby v. CompuServe, Inc., 776 F.Supp. 135 (S.D.N.Y. 1991).

39 In Stratton Oakmont v. Prodigy, 23 Media L. Rep. 1794 (N.Y. Sup. Ct. 1995).

> *No provider or user of an interactive computer service shall be treated as the publisher or speaker of any information provided by another information content provider.*

Section 230 further provides that "[n]o cause of action may be brought and no liability may be imposed under any State or local law that is inconsistent with this section."

Section 230 of the Communications Decency Act grants interactive online services of all types, including blogs, forums, and listservs, broad immunity from tort liability so long as the information at issue is provided by a third party. Relatively few court decisions, however, have analyzed the scope of this immunity in the context of "mixed content" that is created jointly by the operator of the interactive service and a third party through significant editing of content or the shaping of content by submission forms and drop-downs.

4. Internet Websites and Applicability of Section 230

Is an "interactive computer service" some special type of website? No. For purposes of Section 230, an

> *"interactive computer service" means any information service, system, or access software provider that provides or enables computer access by multiple users to a computer server.*

Most courts have held that through these provisions, Congress granted interactive services of all types, including blogs, forums, and listservs, immunity from tort liability so long as the information is provided by a third party.

As a result of Section 230, Internet publishers are treated differently from publishers in print, television, and radio. Let's look at these differences in more detail.

5. Legitimate Claims Based Upon Section 230

Section 230 has most frequently been applied to bar defamation-based claims. In the typical case, a plaintiff who believes she has been defamed sues both the author of the statement and the website that provided a forum or otherwise passively hosted the material. Courts have held with virtual unanimity that such claims against a website are barred by Section 230.

But immunity under Section 230 is not limited to defamation or speech-based torts. Courts have applied Section 230 immunity to bar claims such as invasion of privacy, misappropriation, and most recently in a case brought against MySpace[40] a claim asserting that MySpace was negligent for failing to implement age verification procedures and to protect a fourteen-year old from sexual predators.

However, Section 230 explicitly exempts from its coverage criminal law, communications privacy law, and "intellectual property claims." In interpreting these exclusions, courts agree that Congress meant to exclude federal intellectual property claims, such as copyright and trademark, but they disagree whether state-law intellectual property claims (or claims that arguably could be classified as intellectual property claims, such as the right of publicity) are also exempted from the broad immunity protection Section 230 provides.

Finally, Section 230 does not immunize the actual creator of content. The author of a defamatory statement, whether he is a blogger, commenter, or anything else, remains just as responsible for his online statements as he would be for his offline statements.

6. *Online Activities Covered by Section 230*

Courts have consistently held that exercising traditional editorial functions over user-submitted content, such as deciding whether to publish, remove, or edit material, is immunized under Section 230.[41] As one moves farther away from these basic functions, immunity may still exist, but the analysis becomes more fact-specific.

7. *Summary*

So what are the practical things you can take away from this guide? Here are five:

1. If you passively host third-party content, you will be fully protected under Section 230.
2. If you exercise traditional editorial functions over user submitted content, such as deciding whether to publish, remove, or edit

40 Doe v. MySpace, 474 F.Supp.2d 843 (W.D. Tex. 2007).

41 Digital Media Law Project, Immunity for Online Publishers Under the Communications Decency Act, January 21, 2021.

material, you will not lose your immunity unless your edits materially alter the meaning of the content.

3. If you pre-screen objectionable content or correct, edit, or remove content, you will not lose your immunity.
4. If you encourage or pay third-parties to create or submit content, you will not lose your immunity.
5. If you use drop-down forms or multiple-choice questionnaires, you should be cautious of allowing users to submit information through these forms that might be deemed illegal. Source: http://www.dmlp.org/legal-guide/immunity-online-publishers-under-communications-decency-act.

E. Media Liability Risk Management

Internal risk management policies that are formally implemented, practiced, and reinforced are important for mitigating media liability exposure. This is true for all types of media content whether in digital or hard copy formats. Media liability can give rise to significant judgments, settlements, and defense costs. In its most recent biannual damages survey, The Media Law Resource Center, which reports on jury awards in defamation cases against the media, stated that the average of all defamation and invasion of privacy-related awards from 2010-17 was $7.7 million.[42] This doesn't include defense costs through trial and appeal, which can well exceed $1.5 million. Because most companies have a relatively low tolerance for risk, insurance is a key component of risk mitigation. To apply for media insurance, there must be underlying risk management in place with respect to the manner in which content is gathered, created and/or distributed.

1. Nature of Content and Risk Mitigation

The more provocative the content, the greater the risk for litigation and the need for sound risk mitigation. Investigative reporting, for example, has the highest risk for exposure to defamation. Claimants are often wealthy business people or public officials. They have access to

42 Media Law Resource Center *2018 Report on Trials and Damages*, MLRC Bulletin, (April 2018), https://www.medialaw.org/publications/mlrc-bulletin.

defense counsel and are often successful libel plaintiffs. Investigative reporting often relies upon complex business records, legal pleadings, and/or confidential or anonymous sources. It is important to have experienced staff and review from counsel, prior to publication, as to the manner in which the information was collected and its accuracy. If content is likely to damage the reputation of a person or a business, the more critical it is to have review by counsel prior to its dissemination. Creators of content generally have more exposure than companies that distribute the third party content of others. Certainly, insurers will likely charge increased premium for content creators.

There is also significant risk if a media companies rely on third party content in the creation of content that is distributed as its own. Third party content—music, photographs, art, prose—is used in a variety of ways in other content. In the 1980's hip-hop music would frequently use a sample of a sound recording and loop or mix it with original music. The 1994 Supreme Court decision in *Campbell v. Acuff Rose Music., Inc.* arose from 2 Live Crew's sampling of Roy Orbison's, "Pretty Woman." The Court ultimately found in favor of 2 Live Crew, ruling that the rap was a parody and not a copyright infringement because of the new lyrics. Parody is protected as a fair use and a defense to copyright infringement. Most risk managers and copyright counsel recommend licensing the underlying music and avoiding the time, expense, and risk of copyright litigation.

(a) Licensing Unoriginal Content Mitigates Risk

It is important to have risk management in place as to licensing unoriginal content and compliance with attendant licensing agreements. License agreements are generally limited in scope and duration of use. Most licenses do not allow third party content to be used in perpetuity. Likewise, there may be other restrictions with respect to the licensed use. For example, if third-party content is licensed for a billboard campaign, it may not be permissible to use the content in a different medium, such as its use on a website. Ideally, counsel is consulted with respect to the execution of all licensing agreements. As a rule of thumb, all third-party content must be licensed if used for a commercial purpose. This is even true of ubiquitous memes and viral videos that are circulated on social media. Lawsuits are frequently filed by the photographers, who capture the popular images. There are also companies that specialize in monetizing such content for third party creators and use algorithms to track and identify unauthorized commercial use.[43] Litigation is threatened if the offender does not pay a grossed up amount for the unauthorized use.

Third-party content that is used to inform or educate may fall within the "fair use" exemption to copyright. A fair use is the copying of third-party content without permission from its owner that is used in a limited and "transformative" way.[44] Relying upon a fair use defense is not without risk as it is expensive to defend. Again, it's important to retain experienced copyright counsel to conduct a fair use analysis before using third-party content. Creative works that are deemed to be in the public domain are free of copyright protection. In many cases, the ownership rights have expired. This would be true, for example, of works by William Shakespeare. For works created after 1977, copyright lasts for the life of the author plus 70 years. There are some exceptions to this. All works published in the United States before 1924 are in the public domain. Works published after 1923, but before 1978 are protected for 95 years from the date of publication. Determining whether something is in the public domain is fraught with peril because there is not one hard and fast rule. Copyright law varies from country to country, which can create complications when the copyright owner is from another country. There is not a standard international copyright law. It is sound risk management to use experienced copyright counsel to confirm whether a work is in the public domain and free from copyright.

(b) Contracts with Third Party Content Creators—Advertising Agencies, Freelancers, Authors

If media-related content is created by a third party, such as an advertising agency or freelance writer, it is important to have contracts with such parties to help manage expectations with respect to claims that may arise from the services they provide. The agreements often include warranties that the material provided is not defamatory, infringing, or invade privacy rights. Content creators should also agree to defend and indemnify their clients should a claim arise from the content they created. Such indemnity agreements should be backed by appropriate insurance

43 Brian Brian Koerber, *How one company reshaped - and kind of ruined - the viral video landscape*, Mashable, (Aug. 6, 2018), https://mashable.com/article/jukin-media-viral-videos/.

44 Stanford University Libraries, Copyright & Fair Use, https://fairuse.stanford.edu/overview/fair-use/four-factors/.

with adequate limits of liability. Some advertising clients, for example, ask for a certificate of insurance, to ascertain the type of insurance that is in place, as well as the limits of insurance. In some instances, larger clients ask to be added to the content creator's insurance policy as an additional insured.[45]

F. The Insurance Application Process

The application process is the first key step towards procuring media insurance. It is helpful to work with a knowledgeable insurance broker or consultant to know which insurance markets to approach for media insurance. Only a dozen or so insurers write stand-alone media liability coverage. A number of insurers, however, will include a media liability coverage agreement with cyber and/or professional liability insurance offerings. These policies vary greatly with respect to coverage. It's important for the insurance broker to solicit quotes from several markets so that the client can compare coverages and premium.

The application should be executed fully and completely. In some instances, it may be helpful to include an addendum so that responses can be fully set forth. Insurers will want to know how media-related exposures, including advertising risk, are mitigated. In particular, they will want to know if third party content is licensed. They will also inquire if in-house or outside counsel is retained for the purposes of reviewing content that may be considered provocative. For companies that post user generated content, the underwriter will want to know if there are terms of use agreements that help identify the type of content that can be shared, as well as compliance with the Digital Millennium Copyright Act and the applicant's ability to promptly respond to content that has been identified as potentially infringing or defamatory.

Underwriters will also want to know about the applicant's loss history with respect to any media-related claims. If there has been a loss, it is important to provide detailed information regarding the underlying matter and how much was incurred in defense costs, as well as any settlement or judgment. If additional risk mitigation protocols were implemented by the media company after the claim, it is helpful to include this information.

45 The additional insured endorsement should address insured v. insured exclusions. Ideally, there is an exception to the exclusion with respect to claims brought by clients of the insured.

Likewise, if the operations that gave rise to the claim were changed on a going forward basis to mitigate future risk, it is helpful to provide this information. A problematic loss history will be a red flag to most insurers and will impact premium and self-insured retention levels for insurers that are willing to quote.

Companies that integrate media content with services and technology will require a more robust insurance offering that includes media liability, professional services errors and omissions, and technology errors and omissions. Of course, cyber liability is also a necessary coverage to protect insureds for first and third party loss arising from network security and data privacy risks. Many media liability insurers will agree to endorse professional services and technology errors and omissions to the media liability policy. However, if the technology services exposure is significant - and if there is exposure to software infringement - a stand-alone technology services policy may be required. Media insurers often sublimit these ancillary exposures. Most cyber insurers, however, will also offer insuring agreements for technology and media along with the other cyber-related first and third party coverages. The decision whether to combine coverages and share limits of liability with a number of coverages is a difficult one and must be determined with the assistance of a knowledgeable insurance broker. An experienced broker or consultant can provide benchmarking data regarding large losses in cyber, media and professional services, which will be helpful in identifying proper limits of liability. There may be a premium savings with a combined policy, but the limits will be shared and there may be coverage shortcomings in a "one size fits all" policy. Depending on the unique risk profile of the media company, it may also be necessary to procure relevant excess coverage.

G. Insurance Coverages Available for Media Risks

Media liability coverage is a specialty niche of insurance and is a standard coverage for media companies and other content creators and distributors, such as radio/television/cable broadcasters, advertising agencies, freelance writers/authors, social media influencers, digital content companies, multimedia companies, book/magazine/newspaper publishers, digital companies, and film and program producers/distributors. Companies that engage in prolific advertising also buy media liability coverage. Media liability is generally available through professional liability insurance markets and placed by specialty retail and wholesale brokers. Media policies provide coverage on either a claims-made or occurrence basis for newsgathering, publishing, broadcasting, public speaking, social media, and advertising exposures. It is a key part of risk mitigation for companies seeking to shift exposure arising from their media content to insurance.

Coverage for media-related exposures, such as defamation and copyright infringement, is available through the following types of insurance policies:

1) Media Liability Policy;
2) Specialty Errors and Omissions Policy;
3) Commercial General Liability Policy; and
4) Cyber Liability Policy

1. The Media Liability Policy

The most robust coverage available for a media company is a stand-alone policy that is available through specialty media insurers.[46] While this book is geared toward cyber, it is helpful to understand the breadth of other policies that cover media to better understand the depth and adequacy of a cyber policy's coverage. It's also helpful for insurers to have a broad understanding of media coverage under other policies to better identify and monitor accumulation issues in the event a media claim implicates more than one policy.

There are approximately ten markets that provide stand-alone media coverage for media companies, public figures who engage in public speaking or product endorsements, and non-media companies with robust public communications, including advertising. A key benefit of a media liability policy is that there are dedicated liability limits for a covered media liability claim. Additionally, media liability policies contain a number of nuanced coverages because of the First Amendment protections available to news media companies, in particular. As an example, Mutual Insurance Company, Ltd, which is a Bermudian-based media insurer, identifies the following named media perils in its media liability insuring agreement:

---

46 Media insurers that offer stand-alone policies include AIG, Axis, Beazley, CapSpecialty, Chubb-ACE, CNA, Hiscox, Mutual Insurance Company, LTD., OneBeacon, Philadelphia Insurance Company, QBE and XL.

* * *

1. *libel, criminal libel, slander, product or personal disparagement, trade libel or other forms of defamation or tort relating thereto;*
2. *intentional or negligent infliction of emotional distress or outrageous conduct;*
3. *invasion or infringement of, or interference with, the right of privacy or publicity, including but not limited to intrusion upon seclusion, public disclosure of private facts, unwarranted or wrongful publicity, false light invasion of privacy or commercial appropriation of name, likeness or persona;*
4. *infringement of copyright or any plagiarism; violation of moral rights (droit moral), artist's rights or neighboring rights; failure to provide or give appropriate credit, acknowledgment or attribution for third party* ***Material****; passing off,* ***Piracy****, misappropriation of ideas under implied contract or other misappropriation of intellectual property rights, ideas or information;*
5. *infringement of title, slogan, logo, trademark, trade name, trade dress, service mark or service name, including infringement arising from domain names and the use of meta tags;*
6. ***Unfair Competition****, deceptive trade or unfair business practices, consumer protection act violations, civil actions for fraud, or false and deceptive* ***Advertising****, but only when such perils are alleged with and arise from the same factual basis as a* ***Claim*** *asserted in one or more of subparts 1.—5. above;*
7. *inadvertent breach of a license agreement with respect to* ***Material*** *in* ***Covered Media****, but only when alleged with and arising from the same factual basis as a* ***Claim*** *asserted in one or more of subparts* ***4.*** *or* ***5.*** *above;*
8. *breach of contract, promissory estoppel or misrepresentation arising from:*
   a. *an alleged breach of promise to maintain the anonymity of a confidential or private source or the* ***Material*** *provided by such source or from the failure to portray the source in a particular manner; or*

b. *an alleged breach of promise, commitment or undertaking to a third party regarding* ***Material*** *or contemplated* ***Material****, including an agreement to publish or refrain from publishing certain* ***Material*** *or the failure to portray a subject in a particular manner, but excluding any* ***Claim*** *to the extent alleging that money would be paid to the third party in consideration for a commitment or undertaking;*

9. *false arrest, detention, imprisonment, abuse of process or malicious prosecution;*
10. *invasion of the right of private occupancy, including wrongful entry or eviction, trespass by any individual or any manned or unmanned aircraft, eavesdropping or violation of state consent statutes or similar law, act or regulation relating to the recording of communications wherein the* ***Insured*** *is a party; provided, any nonconsensual or surreptitious recording of telephone or mobile communications by or on behalf of the* ***Insured*** *is subject to coverage, but only if such recording is supported by advice or opinion from legal counsel that such conduct is lawful;*
11 *harassment or stalking relating to the gathering of* ***Material****;*
12. *negligence, including any actual or alleged error, omission, misstatement, or misleading statement of the* ***Insured****, but only in* ***Material*** *disseminated by or which should have been disseminated by the* ***Insured****, including but not limited to any* ***Claim*** *alleging harm to any person or entity who has acted or failed to act in reliance upon the content of such* ***Material****;*
13. *public disclosure of trade secrets or any other confidential, third-party business or commercial matter, but only when disclosed in* ***Material****;*
14. *discrimination or other civil rights violations, including but not limited to violation of a claimant's Fourth Amendment rights against unreasonable searches and seizures arising out of the gathering of* ***Material****;*
15. *prima facie tort, but only when alleged with and arising out of the same factual basis as a* ***Claim*** *asserted in one or more of subparts* ***1.—14.*** *above;*

16. *conspiracy, but only when alleged with and arising out of the same factual basis as a* ***Claim*** *asserted in one or more of subparts* ***1.—15.*** *above;*
17. *breach of any indemnification or hold harmless agreement, but only when alleged with and arising out of the same factual basis as a* ***Claim*** *asserted in one or more of subparts* ***1.—16.*** *above;*
18. *negligent or intentional interference with any contractual, economic or business relationships, but only when alleged with and arising out of the same factual basis as a* ***Claim*** *asserted in one or more of subparts* ***1.—17.*** *above;*
19. *negligent supervision or training of an employee, but only when alleged with and arising out of the same factual basis as a* ***Claim*** *asserted in one or more of subparts* ***1.—18.*** *above;*

and which shall have been committed or alleged to have been committed during the ***Period of Insurance****.*[47]

* * *

The above list of perils is quite comprehensive. Most media insurers include a similarly robust list of causes of action that are subject to coverage. Some media insurers offer "open peril" or "all-risk" policies, which means that all perils arising from media activities are covered—unless specifically excluded. An all-risk media policy will include language such as, "including, but not limited to," prior to identifying examples of media-related perils (causes of action) that are subject to coverage. An all-risk media policy is generally offered to smaller, lower risk media companies, such as those that do not publish provocative content. Additionally, such coverage is generally offered with a low limit of liability, such as $1M to $2M per claim and in the aggregate. An all-risk policy will have a number of exclusions, as well as carve-outs to defined terms that may also impact coverage. Whether the coverage offered is named peril or open peril, it is important for the broker and the risk manager for the insurance applicant to closely review policy language in its entirety.

47 Mutual Insurance Company, LTD, Global Media Liability Policy 2.0 (Occurrence).

(a) Policy Benefits

Specialty media insurers offer a number of other coverage benefits include the following:

1) Occurrence coverage trigger for many lower risk media classes. Large insureds, authors, and film and program producers, and music entities are often underwritten on claims-made policies to limit the long-tail exposure associated with occurrence trigger policies;
2) Defense costs written "in addition to the limits of liability" for smaller media risks meaning that the limits of liability are not eroded by defense costs. The trade-off is that when the limits are not eroded by defense costs, the insurer usually retains the right to select defense counsel;
3) Broad named peril or open peril coverage as referenced above;[48]
4) Definition of "Claim," includes equitable actions;;
5) Definition of "Insured" includes coverage for freelance writers and other independent contractors providing content or other media-related services to the "Insured" at the sole discretion of the "Named Insured";
6) Definition of "Loss," includes coverage for punitive damages based upon "most favorable jurisdiction" language;
   (a) Some policies may even state that the insurer will not question a determination of insurability made by the insured.
7) Definition of "Loss" includes coverage for multiplied or treble damages arising from covered perils;
8) The Named Insured may have the right to select counsel or agree in advance on the selection of counsel, who will be endorsed to the policy;
9) The Definition of "Occurrence" or other term, such as "Wrongful Act" or "Covered Activity" identifies the media-related conduct that is subject to coverage, including the gathering or other acquisition of content, dissemination of content, advertising of the Insured's own products or services, public speaking, merchandising, licensing, and the use of third party social media platforms;

---

48 With an open peril policy, all perils are covered unless excluded.

10) Usually, there is a definition for "Scheduled Media" or "Covered Media." This allows the underwriter to specifically schedule the names or titles of the Named Insured's covered media entities, such as publications, film and program titles, radio/television station call letters, and websites. Rarely will media insurers provide coverage on a blanket basis;
11) The Settlement Condition often has favorable terms wherein the insurer is prohibited from settling excess the self-insured retention without the Named Insured's permission. When important First Amendment considerations are at stake, media companies often resist settlement advances;
12) A number of exclusions are softened with coverage carve-backs—in other words, language that gives back coverage from a policy exclusion. Below are common carve-backs that appear in media liability policies:
    a. Malicious and intentional actions are typical exclusions. Such conduct should not be excluded under media policies because "actual malice" is a pleading requirement in defamation and false light invasion of privacy actions when a plaintiff is seeking punitive damages and/or legally required to meet First Amendment standards of proof to recover actual damages.[49] Likewise exclusions for intentional wrongful conduct should likewise be tempered because defamation, invasion of privacy and trespass, for example, are intentional torts. Ideally, exclusions for intentional, dishonest and fraudulent content includes control group and severability language wherein only the wrongful conduct of an executive officer or other high ranking corporate individual, i.e. a member of the "control group," can be imputed to the insured entity. Likewise, there should be a duty to defend such allegations of wrongful conduct (if subject to coverage through the insuring agreement) through final adjudication.
    b. The exclusion for breach of contract should include a carve-back for liability assumed under contract for the types of media claims covered under the policy. If the policy provides an affirmative coverage grant for breach of a license agreement or for breach of an agreement to protect the identity

49 New York Times v. Sullivan, 376 U.S. 254 (1964).

of a source or materials provided by a source, which are typical perils, there should be an appropriate carve-back.

c. Most media liability policies exclude coverage for bodily injury and property damage. There should be a carve-back to coverage for bodily injury arising exclusively from emotional distress, which is a covered peril under media policies.

d. Most media policies specifically exclude cyber-related exposures relating to network security and data privacy. Because media policies provide coverage for privacy-related causes of action arising from newsgathering and content, this can be a gray area at times. There should be a carve-back for editorial decisions to publish or disclose information about an individual or business entity that is private, but newsworthy under the circumstances. This still allows the insurer to specifically exclude coverage for an unintentional data breach caused by a negligent employee or malicious actor.

13) The subrogation condition may be more relaxed in that the insurer will not seek subrogation against a third party absent written permission from the insured;

14) World-wide coverage territory condition provides coverage for claims and occurrences that take place anywhere in the world;[50]

15) The Insured may issue a retraction or other apology without running afoul of any policy condition prohibiting the insured from making an admission of liability;

(b) Policy Exclusions

Typical Policy Exclusions in media liability policies include the following:

1) Alleged wrongful acts that precede the inception date of the policy.
2) Claims, demands, or other proceedings against any Insured prior to the inception date of the policy.
3) Bodily injury and property damage claims.

---

50 Note that Sanctions Endorsements may apply wherein the Insurer will not provide coverage or make any payments to an Insured or claimant in violation of any applicable trade or economic sanctions law or regulation.

4) Breach of any express or implied contract, agreement, or warranty.
5) Employment practices liability - some insurers may allow a carve-out to this exclusion for defamation actions against former employees that are broadcast or published through a scheduled entity, such as a publication or broadcast station, which is often defined as "Scheduled Media" or "Covered Media."
6) Patent infringement and theft of trade secrets are excluded. There may be a coverage carve-out for an editorial decision to publish a trade secret in "Scheduled Media."
7) Network security and privacy claims arising from access or disruption to a computer network (including hardware, firmware, software and other components) and/or the compromise of personal identifiable information or other sensitive data in the care, custody, or control of the insured. If a media company wants coverage for first and third party liability for its network and data, it is important to purchase a cyber liability policy. Unless specifically endorsed, it is not the intent of media policies to cover cyber-related events.
8) Clams brought by music licensing entities, such as ASCAP and BMI are excluded. Some insurers may be broader and reference "licensing entities." This may be interpreted to include companies that license third party videos in addition to the music licensing entities.
9) Claims brought by independent contractors supplying matter, material, or services to the Insured are excluded.
10) Intentional false advertising of the products and/or services of the Insured is excluded.
11) Claims relating to the purchase or sale of securities are excluded.
12) Claims for deliberately criminal, fraudulent or dishonest acts or omissions are exclusion. As a general rule, there should be severability for innocent insureds, as well as control group language wherein only conduct of the defined control group is imputed to the Insured.
13) Violation of the United State of America Telephone Consumer Protection Act (TCPA) of 1991, the CAN-SPAM Act of 2003 and any other law or ordinance regarding the distribution of content to any third-party telephone, fax, computer or other electronic device are excluded.

14) Administrative and regulatory actions, including those commenced by the FCC or FTC, are excluded.
15) Contests, lotteries, gambling, or games of chance, including the over or under redemption of prizes with respect to any of the following are excluded. Some insurers may allow the Named Insured to buy back this coverage subject to a sub-limit of liability.
16) Professional services, unless specifically scheduled to the policy, are specifically excluded. Many media companies engage in professional services that are ancillary to media activities, such as advertising professional services, website hosting, and digital analytics. If a media company is providing any services for others, such activities should be covered.
17) Usual and ordinary business operations, including media perils arising from defamation set forth in non-scheduled communications, such as email and correspondence, are generally excluded. The content is generally created for and disseminated to the public or subscribers. It is not the intent of the insurer to provide coverage for non-public or one-on-one communications.
18) Pollution exclusionary language. This may seem like an unusual exclusion to include in a media policy. However, before digital copies, publications required the transfer of ink onto paper. The improper handling and disposal of ink and other chemicals used in the printing process could give rise to a pollution claim.

The above are standard media liability endorsements. It is always possible to attempt to negotiate coverage from an exclusion, but expect the insurer to limit its exposure through sublimited coverage, coinsurance, and a higher self-insured retention.

(c) Media Coverage Endorsements

There are a number of coverage enhancements available by endorsement to extend coverage under a media policy even further. Some of these endorsements may be available depending upon the loss experience of the media company and its unique risk profile. Some endorsements may be added to the policy without additional premium while others may be premium bearing. Typical endorsements include the following:

1) Subpoena Defense—provides coverage for the attorney expense necessary to respond to a subpoena seeking testimony or materials from the media company. As a general rule, the Insured must not be a party to the legal proceeding. Broadcasting companies, for example, may have news footage that a plaintiff attorney wants to review because s/he believes it may be helpful to the client. This coverage is unusually sublimited and subject to a self-insured retention. Unless there are mitigating circumstances, most insurers will add this coverage without additional premium.
2) First Amendment Defense—this coverage provides a sublimit of coverage for the Insured to defend itself following interference by a governmental entity that violates First Amendment rights. Government conduct may include prior restraint of the media company's ability to gather or disseminate content—or a judicially imposed gag order.
3) Prior Acts—this coverage provides coverage for media acts taking place prior to the inception date of an occurrence policy. It is purchased by media companies that have engaged in media operations without coverage in place. There is always additional premium for prior acts coverage.
4) Professional Services—this endorsement provides coverage for professional services performed by the media company for third parties for a fee. Such services typically include advertising professional services, web hosting, application development, digital analytics and the like. Some media companies with iconic buildings host special events for third parties, such as weddings. Musical artists may also choreograph for others. For a media insurer to consider such coverage, the professional services risk must generally be ancillary to the media content exposure. Media companies that provide internet service, for example, may be required to insure this exposure with a stand-alone technology errors and omissions policy depending on the number of subscribers and gross revenues from such business operations. If the insurer is willing to endorse technology services, the coverage will generally be for additional premium and sublimited.
5) Broad Form Errors and Omissions—this endorsement broadens the policy to provide coverage for bodily injury and property damage arising directly from media content, and possibly newsgathering. Media risks with this type of exposure include

"how-to" books, work-out videos, financial publications, and medical journals. This endorsement is premium bearing. Media companies with significant risk may have a higher self-insured retention for broad form exposures, as well as sublimited limits of liability.

2. *The Miscellaneous Errors and Omissions Policy*

Insurers that offer errors and omission policies for non-high duty professionals, such as insurance and real estate agents, business consultants, and bookkeepers, may also include coverage agreements for media companies. These policies, which are also known as specialty E&O, offer flexible coverage for a variety of small businesses and offer specialized coverage based upon the unique exposures of the applicant's business. These policies may have common definitions, exclusions and conditions to which the insuring agreement is added. The media coverage part, for example, will include its own definitions and exclusions that apply to the coverage grant. Because professional liability policies provide coverage on a claims-made basis, the media liability coverage will also be claims-made. As a general rule a specialty errors and omissions policy provides significantly less nuanced coverage than a media liability policy.

3. *The Commercial General Liability Policy—Coverage B*

The specialty media liability market exists because of exclusions and shortcomings in the commercial general liability (CGL) policy, which is the go-to liability policy for most businesses. The CGL policy provides coverage for third-party liability arising from a number of exposures, including "personal injury" and "advertising injury" under Coverage B. The Institute of Risk Management and Insurance (IRMI) defines *advertising injury* and *personal injury* as "categories of insurable offenses that produce harm other than bodily injury."[51] The perils covered under Coverage B of the CGL policy include false arrest, detention or imprisonment, malicious prosecution, wrongful eviction, slander, libel, invasion of privacy, copyright infringement, and misappropriation of advertising ideas.

---

51 IRMI Definitions, https://www.irmi.com/term/insurance-definitions/personal-and-advertising-injury.

While the list of enumerated perils is quite broad, there are approximately 16 exclusions that whittle away coverage. Coverage for communications companies, such as broadcasters, publishers, and advertising agencies, is specifically excluded because of a sweeping exclusion in Coverage B that restricts coverage for companies involved in media and internet-related business. This exclusion, in particular, creates the need for niche media liability coverage for media and internet companies.

This "professional liability" exclusion as set forth in the most current Insurance Services Offices (ISO) CGL form is as follows:

> **2. Exclusions**
> This insurance does not apply to: . . .
> **j. Insureds in Media and Internet Type Businesses**
> "Personal and advertising injury" committed by an insured whose business is:
> **(1)** Advertising, broadcasting, publishing or telecasting;
> **(2)** Designing or determining content of web sites for others; or
> **(3)** An Internet search, access, content or service provider.[52]

ISO published this CGL form in 2012 along with an amendatory endorsement that eliminates coverage for invasion of privacy relating to advertising and personal injury coverages. The endorsement states as follows:

> With respect to **Coverage B Personal And Advertising Injury Liability**, Paragraph **14.e.** of the **Definitions** section does not apply.[53]

The relevant paragraph of the CGL form deleted by this endorsement is as follows:

> **SECTION V—DEFINITIONS . . .**
> **14.** "Personal and advertising injury" means injury, including consequential "bodily injury" arising out of one or more of the following offenses: . . .

---

52 Ins. Servs. Office, Inc., Form CG 00 01 04 13 (2012).

53 Ins. Servs. Office, Inc., Endorsement CG 24 13 04 13 (2012).

e. Oral or written publication, in any manner, of material that violates a person's right of privacy.[54]

Invasion of privacy is a key publishing and advertising peril and is often plead in combination with defamation. Likewise, right of publicity, which is a privacy-related tort, is a common advertising exposure. Clearly, it is not the intent of CGL insurers to provide coverage for media companies under Coverage B. However, the cited endorsement reflects that personal and advertising injury coverage for non-media insureds has been eroded under the insuring agreement, which is already quite narrow. This is problematic for policyholders who rely on their CGL policies for media-related exposures, such as advertising. While the latest coverage-narrowing amendatory endorsement is intended to insulate CGL insurers from the risk of a data breach in the context of network security and privacy, it also eliminates coverage for the four distinct invasion of privacy torts enumerated by William L. Prosser, which include false light, intrusion upon seclusion, publication of private facts, and right of publicity arising from content and the manner in which it was gathered.[55]

There are a number of other policy limitations in the CGL policy that undercut coverage for media exposures for non-media companies:

- The coverage territory is not worldwide. With the global reach of digital content, claims can arise anywhere in the world.
- The insurance company has the right to select counsel and supervise the defense. Does counsel retained by the CGL insurer have the requisite expertise to manage intellectual property litigation and other media exposures?
- The insurance company has the sole power regarding whether to settle. This may be an issue of contention if the insured's reputation or intellectual property is at stake.
- Punitive damages may be covered by the policy depending on the jurisdiction, unless specifically against public policy. In some states, such as New York, California, and Illinois, it is against public policy to insure punitive damages. This is because the

54 Ins. Servs. Office, Inc., Form CG 00 01 04 13 (2012).

55 William L. Prosser, *Privacy*, 48 Cal. L. Rev. (Aug. 1960), https://scholarship.law.berkeley.edu/cgi/viewcontent.cgi?article=3157&context=californialawreview.

intent of punitive damages is to punish and deter future conduct; if the damages are paid by a third party, such as an insurer, the punishment has been circumvented.[ix] Most media policies, on the other hand, provide unequivocal coverage for punitive damages, or include most favorable venue language.[56]

- Copyright infringement is specifically excluded except with respect to claims arising from "infringement in your advertisement" of copyright, trade dress, or slogan. There would not be coverage for copyright infringement, for example, arising from the publication of a white paper, newsletter, blog, or other noncommercial content.
- Trademark infringement is specifically excluded under the most recent ISO form and is arguably one of the most important coverages for any insured who advertises products or services.

Media liability claims are not predictable. The damages and defense costs can be high, and specialized underwriting and claims handing are required. As such, it is understandable for CGL insurers to limit personal and advertising injury coverage for media-related companies, essentially excluding professional liability coverage for such companies and requiring them to seek coverage from a specialty market. In fact, the media and internet blanket exclusion is nothing new—it has been around for many years. What is new, however, is that most businesses and organizations are robust creators of content—much like a media company—because the internet has changed the way that firms and organizations communicate. Therefore, non-media companies that rely on the CGL policy for advertising and publishing exposures should assess their specific media-related exposures and weigh the policy's numerous shortcomings against individual tolerance for risk.

4. *Media Coverage under Cyber Policies*

Network security and data privacy insurance policies (cyber policies) typically provide first- and third-party coverage for claims arising from the unauthorized disclosure of personally identifiable information and

---

56 Craig F. Stanovich, *Punitive Damages—Setting an Example*, IRMI (June 2012), www.irmi.com/articles/expert-commentary/punitive-damages-setting-an-example.

other sensitive third-party information in the care, custody, or control of the named insured, as well as security breaches of the insured's computer network. Many cyber policies include elective insuring agreements for electronic media, which provide third-party liability coverage for claims arising from the insured's website (relating to, for example, blogs and other online content, perhaps even social media posts on third party platforms. Broader cyber policies provide elective insuring agreements for the named insured's comprehensive media liability, which includes both online and offline media communications.[57]

A digital copy of the Beazley BBR policy, for example, provides a coverage agreement for media liability as follows:

> ***Media liability***
>
> *To pay **damages** and **claims expenses**, which the **insured** is legally obligated to pay because of any **claim** first made against any **insured** during the **policy period** for media liability.*[58]
>
> *The BBR policy defines media liability in the following way:*
>
> *[M]edia liability means one or more of the following acts committed by, or on behalf of, the **insured organization** in the course of creating, displaying, broadcasting, disseminating or releasing **media material** to the public:*
>
> 1. *defamation, libel, slander, product disparagement, trade libel, infliction of emotional distress, outrage, outrageous conduct, or other tort related to disparagement or harm to the reputation or character of any person or organization;*
> 2. *a violation of the rights of privacy of an individual, including false light, intrusion upon seclusion and public disclosure of private facts;*
> 3. *invasion or interference with an individual's right of publicity, including commercial appropriation of name, persona, voice or likeness;*

57 Beazley Breach Response Policy, https://policies.dppl.com/policy.php?policy_number=BBR-5A8ED7A3-8OEF#pagenav-ag-3.

58 *Id.* (emphasis in original).

4. *plagiarism, piracy, or misappropriation of ideas under implied contract;*
5. *infringement of copyright;*
6. *infringement of domain name, trademark, trade name, trade dress, logo, title, metatag, or slogan, service mark or service name;*
7. *improper deep-linking or framing;*
8. *false arrest, detention or imprisonment;*
9. *invasion of or interference with any right to private occupancy, including trespass, wrongful entry or eviction; or*
10. *unfair competition, if alleged in conjunction with any of the acts listed in parts 5. or 6. above.*[59]

While it is always important to review an insurance policy in its entirety, including definitions, exclusions, conditions, and amendatory endorsements that may limit or exclude coverage, the BBR "media liability" coverage agreement creates the potential for broad media coverage.

Cyber policies differ with respect to breadth of coverage and are not standardized. At the time of this writing, it is estimated that there are more than 500 insurance markets that write cyber insurance either as part of a package, a stand-alone product, or by endorsement.[60] A small percentage of these markets have admitted products; meaning that the forms have been filed and approved by state department of insurance. Because there are so many forms available and a lack of standardization, it is important to read the policy wording carefully and discuss breadth of coverage with respect to online and off-line media content, as well as professional and technology services exposures, with an experienced insurance professional.

(a) Key Coverage Provisions

A cyber policy will not include all of the nuanced "bells and whistles" coverages for a media company that media specialty insurers provide.

---

59 *Id.* (emphasis in original).

60 Geraldine Grimes, Top 10 cyber insurance markets in the US, Insurance Business America, (Dec. 20, 2019), https://www.insurancebusinessmag.com/us/news/cyber/top-10-cyber-insurance-companies-in-the-us-195463.aspx.

However, a cyber policy's media insuring coverage may provide adequate coverage for a non-media company that regularly communicates to the public through advertising, its website, and social media. With a cyber policy, there may not be a dedicated limit for media liability. Unless the coverage is sub-limited, the media liability insuring agreement will share the "per claim" and annual aggregate limits of liability with first and third party cyber coverages. In the event a loss relating to a data breach erodes the annual aggregate limit of liability, there may not be adequate coverage for a media liability claim made during the same period of insurance. Because of the shared limit of liability issue, if a company has significant risk arising from media communications, its risk manager may want to consider insuring the media risk under a separate policy—especially if there is concern about eroding primary limits. Of course, this concern can be mitigated by building adequate excess coverage over the primary limits to better ensure limits adequacy.

(b) The Media Insuring Agreement

The insuring agreement will identify if the coverage is claims-made or an occurrence trigger. The majority of cyber policies insure media liability on a claims-made and reported basis meaning that the claim must be reported during the policy period or any optional extended reporting period following expiration of the policy period.[61] Likewise, the conduct giving rise to the claim must take place after any retroactive period, which will be identified in the policy's declarations. The retroactive date, which is typically a defined term, is the date after which a qualifying event or act may take place and to be subject to coverage under the policy. If the applicant for insurance hasn't had previous media insurance, for example, the retroactive period will likely align with the policy's inception date. Ideally, however, it is in the best interest of the applicant to negotiate a retroactive date that can capture media conduct going back at least three years because of the applicable statute of limitations for defamation, invasion of property relating to content (as opposed to data) and intellectual property. As a general rule, a media liability insuring agreement will need to be specifically elected by the applicant for insurance and will generally require the payment of additional premium.

---

61 At the time of this writing, the authors are not aware of any media liability insuring agreements offered under cyber forms on an occurrence basis.

(c) Media-Related Policy Definitions

There are a number of key definitions under cyber insurance policies with respect to the media insuring agreement.

Content/Material/Matter—There will be a definition for the information created and/or disseminated by the media company. The Beazley policy describes "Media Material," as follows:

> ***Media Material*** *means any information in electronic form, including words sounds, numbers, images, or graphics and shall include, advertising, video, streaming content, web-casting, online forum, bulletin board and chat room content, but does not mean computer software or the actual goods, products or services described, illustrated or displayed in such* ***Media Material****.*[62]

Most cyber forms include robust descriptions of the type of communications that are subject to coverage. Ideally, the definition that defines covered acts will also include public speaking on third party platforms by those acting within the course and scope of employment. This would cover claims arising from presentations made by insureds. A robust definition will also include corporate communications or public speaking by those in the course and scope of employment on third party social media platforms, as well as third party media outlets.

It is common to carve software infringement from the media coverage. Media insuring agreements do not intend to extend to the technology that creates the communication functionality or helps to distribute it to the public. If the insurance applicant develops software, applications or other technology for themselves or for others, many cyber insurers will also provide coverage for technology errors and omissions, as well as for software infringement, as a separate insuring agreement or by endorsement. Such exposures should be identified during the application process and discussed with the broker and the various insurance markets.

Likewise, it is not the intent of cyber insurers to extend coverage to the insured's products, goods, or services, which may be depicted in advertising or other communications. This is often called merchandising and specifically excluded. Most cyber insurers also specifically exclude coverage for claims for false advertising or other false representations

---

62 Beazley F00403 092916 ed.

about the insured's own products or services. Some stand-alone media insurers may specifically endorse policies to specifically insure intellectual property claims arising from products, such as design elements in jewelry, tennis shoes, greeting cards, or fabrics, but such merchandising coverage must be specifically negotiated and endorsed.

As a general rule, cyber policies cover communications made to the public and not one-on-one communications in email, text messages, correspondence or other private communications. Some forms may be silent on the subject. A cyber insurer may be willing to add this coverage to the policy with a "business operations endorsement," which provides coverage for communications made in the course and scope of business, but not to the public.

i. Loss/Damages

Ideally, the definition of "loss" or "damages" should reference coverage for punitive damages as determined by the jurisdiction most favorable to the insured.[63] With this language, the insurer and insured will look to the law in a variety of jurisdictions that most favors coverage, such as the state where the damages were awarded, where the conduct giving rise to the claim took place, the state where the policy was issued, or the insured's principal place of business. Larger insureds with a number of locations may have their insurance policies issued in states that most favors insurability. In New York and Illinois, for example, punitive damages are not insurable.[64] If an insured has exposure to defamation, for example, where punitive damages are always a risk, insurability is an important insurance consideration that should be discussed with the broker.

---

63 Mark Rosenberg, *Survey of U.S. State Laws on Insurability of Punitive Damages*, Seasonal Meting of the International Section of the New York Bar Association, (October 2018), https://nysba.org/NYSBA/Sections/International/Seasonal%20Meetings/Montreal%202018/Coursebook/Panel%209/Rosenberg%20paper%20Combined_50_State_Survey_on_Insurance Coverage_for_Punitives_Damages.pdf.

64 Richard Porter, *A Review of the U.S. Punitive Damages Liability Landscape*, Chubb Bermuda, (Feb. 2, 2017), http://filecache.mediaroom.com/mr5mr_chubbus/177911/punitive-damages-white-paper-21feb17-final.pdf.

ii. Wrongful Act

The definition of “wrongful act” will typically identify the various causes of action that are subject to coverage. It may be embedded in the definitions section or the insuring agreement. Under cyber policies, the covered torts typically include the following:

1) Defamation, libel, slander, trade libel, product disparagement;
2) Invasion of privacy, including the torts of false light, public disclosure of private facts, misappropriation of name or likeness, and intrusion upon seclusion;
3) Emotional distress arising from the defamation and privacy perils;
4) Infringement of copyright, title, plagiarism, misappropriation of ideas under implied contract;
5) Infringement of trademark, trade name, trade dress, slogan, service mark or name;
6) Deep-linking or framing;
7) Unfair competition, but only when arising from a covered intellectual property claim or trade libel.

Some cyber forms also include within the media insuring agreement the following personal injury perils, which are newsgathering exposures for media companies:

1) False arrest, detention, imprisonment, abuse of process or malicious prosecution; and
2) Invasion of the right to private occupancy, including wrongful entry or eviction, trespass, and eavesdropping.

It should be noted that non-media companies that do not engage in newsgathering do not generally have newsgathering exposures relating to their communications activities. They shouldn’t be committing trespass in the normal course of employment to gather information. Likewise, a non-media company is probably not going to follow a story subject. Additionally, non-media companies with a comprehensive general liability policy may also have coverage for advertising injury and personal injury perils under the Personal and Advertising Injury Coverage of their commercial general liability policy as discussed previously. Whether or not the CGL policy provides adequate coverage for advertising and personal injury risks is another area for discussion with the insurance broker. If the same insurer is writing a company's cyber (with media coverage) and Commercial General Liability, there may be some overlap in coverage as to personal and advertising injury exposures. The insurer may issue a coverage limiting endorsement that addresses the accumulation of coverage issue should a claim implicate the two policies and two separate limits of liability.

The definition of "wrongful act," will generally indicate that the conduct must be committed by the insured or by a third party acting on behalf of the insured, such as an advertising agency. Furthermore the wordings will state that the alleged wrongful act(s) or conduct must take place after the retroactive period of the policy, and the resulting claim against the insured must be made during the policy period or optional extension period (if applicable).

(d) Exclusions

Cyber policies contain a number of exclusions that limit coverage. It is important to read them and understand how such exclusions may limit media liability exposure. While most of the exclusions referenced below are standard, there are some important nuances with respect to media liability coverage as follows:

1) Bodily Injury and Property Damage Exclusion—this is a standard exclusion that excludes coverage for bodily injury and property damage. If the policy covers emotional distress arising from media content, there should be a carve-back to the exclusion with respect to emotional distress arising exclusively from a media wrongful act.
2) Breach of Contract—this is a standard exclusion in all policies, including cyber. Most insurance policies exclude coverage for claims that arise from contractual liability. This is nothing new as it is not the intent of insurers to cover non-fortuitous conduct, such as a business decision to terminate a contract. That being said, the breach of contract exclusion will generally include a number of carve-backs to the exclusion. With respect to media liability, the following are of particular importance:

a) There should be carve-out for claims for misappropriation of ideas under implied contract if it is a covered peril under the media insuring agreement;
b) There should be a carve-out for liability assumed under contract for the types of media perils covered under the media insuring agreement.

3) False, deceptive or unfair trade practices—this is a standard exclusion under most insurance policies, including cyber. If the media insuring agreement covers unfair competition arising from intellectual property and trade libel/product disparagement, there should be an attendant carve-back in the exclusion.
4) Criminal, dishonest, fraudulent, or malicious acts, errors, or omissions—this is a standard exclusion. However, the reference to "malicious acts" can create issues with respect to libel and false light actions. Actual malice is the legal standard established by the U.S. Supreme Court for libel cases when public officials or public figures are seeking damages in lawsuits against the news media. Likewise, it is the legal standard when all libel plaintiffs seek punitive damages. The reference to actual malice in a libel pleading may result in a reservation of rights or a coverage denial from the insurer. As a result, it is important to address this wording when negotiating the placement of the coverage.
Ideally, this exclusion will include severability as to insureds who did not participate in the alleged intentional wrongful conduct giving rise to the claim and that only wrongful conduct of executive members of a defined "control group" will be imputed to the insured organization. Look, too, for language that the insurer will pay for defense costs incurred in the defense of the claim until there is an admission of the alleged wrongful conduct or final non-appealable adjudication of the matter.
5) Claims brought by state, federal, or local governments or regulatory bodies—this exclusion will exclude criminal or regulatory actions commenced by governmental entities. From a media liability context, this will also exclude actions commenced by the Federal Trade Commission or the Federal Communications

Commission.[65] These types of claims are universally excluded by cyber, as well as stand-alone media liability policies. It may be possible, however, to negotiate a sub-limit of coverage by endorsement for FTC matters arising from advertising. Any negotiated coverage, however, will be quite narrow.

6) Infringement of software code or products—cyber policies do not cover software-related claims, unless specifically covered under a technology errors and omissions insuring agreement or endorsement. There is not coverage for such claims under the media insuring agreement.
7) Patent infringement is universally excluded under cyber and media policies without exception.
8) Misappropriation of ideas and trade secrets are universally excluded under cyber policies. Media policies, in comparison, may clarify in an exception to the exclusion that the exclusion does not apply to an editorial decision to publish a trade secret because of a newsworthy consideration.
9) Insured v. Insured claims—this is a typical exclusion. For insureds in service industries, larger clients of the insured often request to be added to the policy as "additional insureds." While there are certainly benefits of being identified as an additional insured, an unintended consequence is falling within the crosshairs of this exclusion. It is important that there be a coverage carve-back indicating that it does not apply to clients, who are additional insureds under the policy, and have brought a claim against the insured without collusion.
10) Licensing fees and the payment of royalties—this is a typical exclusion in cyber and media liability policies. In some policies, this exclusion appears as an exception to the definition of "Loss." While media liability policies typically cover infringement of copyright, for example, it is not the intent of the policy to pay for a license agreement with the intellectual property owner in

65 Most cyber policies will include a carve-out for regulatory proceedings if an insuring agreement for regulatory actions has been purchased. This is a standard offering, as well as payment of related fines and penalties. The policies will define the types of regulatory actions that are subject to coverage, as well as the coverage trigger, i.e. violations related to privacy laws.

settlement of an infringement dispute for the continued use of the work at issue.

11) Over or under redemption of coupons or other games of chance—it is not the intent of cyber or media insurers to pay for printing errors on coupons or for an over-redemption of coupons from a successful marketing campaign that exceeds what was expected. There is a potential financial risk with respect to the public redemption of coupons or rebates when the response rate exceeds the fulfillment costs. While there is insurance available for this risk, it is not standard under cyber or media liability policies.
12) Claims brought by music licensing groups, such as ASCAP and BMI are typically excluded. This is a standard exclusion in both cyber and media policies. This exclusion first appeared in media policies because music library licenses are required by broadcast entities as part of a cost of doing business. Media insurers determined that this was not an appropriate insurable risk and specifically excluded the exposure. This exclusion was carried over to cyber policies because of the media insuring agreement. Some licensing exclusions in cyber policies are drafted more broadly and omit the reference to "music-licensing" organizations. As a result, the exclusion would also extend to licensing entities that monetize videos and images that are shared on social media and more traditional media platforms. Claims brought by owners of viral videos and those who license them and track unauthorized use by companies have proliferated, which has led to the broadening of this exclusion.

(e) Conditions

There are a number of conditions that are important with respect to the media insuring agreement.

<u>Selection of Counsel</u>—This is an important issue when intellectual property rights, in particular, are at stake. The interests of the insurer and the insured may diverge in that the insured is interested in protecting its property rights at any cost and the insurer is interested in resolving the litigation expeditiously. Cyber policies vary with respect to the right to select counsel. Some insurers will negotiate with the insured and select counsel with agreed upon hourly rates in advance by manuscript

endorsement. Other insurers retain the right to select defense counsel and will not negotiate with the insured.

Territory Condition—Because media communications are potentially global in reach, it is important to have a global or world-wide coverage territory instead of one limited to claims made in North America and its territories.

Settlement Clause Condition—Some settlement conditions give the right to settle any claim excess the self-insured retention to the insurer. The policy may also allow the insurer to "buy out" of the claim by tendering to the insured the amount excess the self-insured retention demanded by the claimant. Some buy-outs allow the insurer to completely limit its exposure while others allow the insurer to cap its exposure to loss and/or defense costs at a certain percentage. It is important to be familiar with this coverage term because it may have a profound impact in respect to the resolution of any litigation. An insured seeking to litigate through trial may be precluded from doing so if the insurance company is contractually able to settle with the claimant without the insured's approval.

H. Conclusion

All companies that communicate with the public have media exposures. There are a number of insurance options available that address the risks attendant to the creation and distribution of the applicant's content to the public, as well as extending coverage to media-related services provided to third parties. Fortunately, there are a number of insurance options available depending on the unique exposures of the applicant and its budgetary considerations. Because media liability is addressed through so many different types of insurance, it is critically important to understand the applicant's unique set of exposures and the various nuances in coverage.

Chapter 11

Health Care Industry*

Before COVID-19, the health care industry was already one of the most targeted sectors by cyber threat actors. The scramble to develop vaccines and treatments while protecting critical data only increased the threats by bad actors.

In this chapter, we address the different types of industry participants, the types of data to be protected, the risks to account for when protecting that data, the types of coverage to address the risks, the exclusions to consider, and the potential other ways to mitigate the risk.

A. Entities That Comprise the Health Care Industry

1. Section Introduction

While the public may primarily think of health care providers, a myriad of other companies exist to support the medical care provided in this country. This chapter will explore the cyber insurance risks prevalent to all types of businesses working in the industry. First, we examine the industry participants and the unique role each plays in the industry.

This chapter breaks health care industry participants into two major groups: providers and other companies. Like the name suggests, providers are entities whose primary function is to provide health care services to patients. These entities either bill the patients or the patients' insurance companies for the health care provided.

The other companies are businesses that do not provide health care, but provide services, equipment, or materials to the health care providers. In addition, these companies consist of companies that are subcontractors to other businesses that provide services, equipment, or materials to the providers.

---

* By Michael Nitardy and Chad Eckhardt.

2. *Providers*

(a) Medical Practices and Ambulatory Care

Medical practices are the primary mechanism through which licensed medical practitioners, either individually, or through groups with other individual practitioners, provide medical care to patients. Medical practices focus on seeing patients and providing care. They typically consist of multiple licensed individuals who form a business in order to provide care to patients. The medical practices will need to contract with insurance companies and bill for their services. As a result, in addition to employing licensed practitioners, like physicians, nurses, and phlebotomists, medical practices will also need to employ staff to take care of the facilities, billing, scheduling, and medical records. In addition, the medical practices may also own the facilities in which they see patients, but typically only provide care at these facilities on an outpatient basis.

The individuals who make up the medical practices generally obtain privileges to admit and treat patients at a hospital. Medical practices can be affiliated with hospitals or insurance providers/health plans.[1] In addition, medical practices can be organized by medical specialty.

Medical practices can range in size and specialty. They can consist of one type of medical specialty or can run the gamut. Medical practices as an organization can even contract with other medical providers, like hospitals, ambulatory care facilities, or laboratories to provide medical care at those other facilities. For example, a medical practice consisting of radiology physicians may contract to provide radiology services at specific hospitals.

Medical practices may own their own ambulatory care facilities. Ambulatory care facilities are facilities that provide some specialized medical care to patients but on an out-patient basis. For example, an orthopedic surgery group may own its own outpatient ambulatory surgery center where it performs surgeries that do not require hospitalization.

(b) Pharmacies, Laboratories, and Other Ancillary Providers

Pharmacies, laboratories, and other ancillary providers are individuals and entities that provide important services that assist the hospitals,

---

1 For information on insurance companies, please see the chapter on Financial Services.

medical practices, and ambulatory facilities. A pharmacy can be a free-standing organization, or it can be a part of another business, such as a grocery chain. The pharmacy will need to employ licensed pharmacists, pharmacy techs, cashiers, and individuals who are responsible for inventory management and billing. Pharmacies may also own their own facilities or lease space from another entity.

Laboratories, like pharmacies, may either be independently owned or be part of another medical practice or medical provider. Laboratories will need to employ licensed staff who are able to perform the tests that will be performed at the laboratory or testing facility. In addition, the laboratories will need to provide for inventory needs.

These entities provide health care that is dependent upon the relationship between the medical practice and the patient or the hospital and the patient. For example, a medical practice's physician might prescribe a medication to a patient. The patient takes the prescription to the pharmacy to be filled. An ambulatory care facility might issue an order for a patient to have blood work done at a private laboratory. The pharmacy and the private laboratory get the business with the patient after the order is first initiated by the physician at the medical practice or the ambulatory care center. The pharmacy and private laboratory are still considered providers because they have a direct relationship with the patient (i.e., providing the medication or laboratory test). The pharmacy and the laboratory will bill the patient or the patient's insurance company directly.

(c) Hospitals and Other Facilities

Hospitals are generally understood to be facilities that provide, "by or under the supervision of physicians, to inpatients . . . diagnostic services and therapeutic services for medical diagnosis, treatment, and care of injured, disabled, or sick persons" with "24-hour nursing service rendered or supervised by a registered professional nurse[.]"[2]

According to the American Hospital Association latest statistics, there are 6,090 hospitals in the United States.[3] Of those, 5,141 are considered "community hospitals", defined as "all nonfederal, short-term general, and other special hospitals. Other special hospitals include obstetrics and

2 42 U.S.C. § 1395x(3).

3 *Fast Facts on U.S. Hospitals, 2021*, https://www.aha.org/statistics/fast-facts-us-hospitals (last updated January 2021).

gynecology; eye, ear, nose and throat; long term acute-care; rehabilitation; orthopedic; and other individually described specialty services. Community hospitals include academic medical centers or other teaching hospitals if they are nonfederal short-term hospitals. Excluded are hospitals not accessible by the general public, such as prison hospitals or college infirmaries."[4] Three thousand four hundred fifty-three of these community hospitals are considered to be in a "health system."[5]

The AHA defines a "system" as "either a multihospital or a diversified single hospital system. A multihospital system is two or more hospitals owned, leased, sponsored, or contract managed by a central organization. Single, freestanding hospitals may be categorized as a system by bringing into membership three or more, and at least 25 percent, of their owned or leased non-hospital pre-acute or post-acute health care organizations."[6]

Hospitals are generally the focus of health care provision in a particular community. Due to their size, they can provide an array of services in one place. As hospitals have combined for economies of scale, health systems have grown. In the past, hospitals generally employed nursing staff, laboratory staff, pharmacy staff, janitorial staff, billing staff, etc. But in the past, hospitals did not primarily employ physicians. Physicians were employed by medical practices and worked through hospitals via obtaining "privileges" to admit and treat patients at the hospital. Physicians who were admitted to the hospital would form a medical staff and would follow certain bylaws and rules. Today, hospitals (either stand alone or through health systems) are employing more and more physicians.

A good way to consider how all of the different providers might interact is through a hypothetical patient surgery. A patient goes to her orthopedic surgeon and schedules a shoulder surgery. The orthopedic surgeon is employed by a medical practice. The medical practice also owns an ambulatory surgical facility. The orthopedic surgeon could have the surgery scheduled at the ambulatory facility, but she is concerned that the surgery might necessitate an overnight stay, so she has the surgery scheduled to take place at the local hospital where the physician also has admitting and surgical privileges. The patient arrives at the hospital and is checked in by staff and prepared for the surgery by nurses who are employed by the hospital. An anesthesiologist that works for an

---

4 *Id.*

5 *Id.*

6 *Id.*

anesthesiology practice that contracts with the hospital meets with the patient before the surgery and orders the anesthesia from the hospital's pharmacy. The surgery takes place in one of the hospital's operating rooms ("OR"). In the room for the surgery are the surgeon, the anesthesiologist, and two OR nurses. The anesthesia that is provided through the hospital pharmacy is administered and the surgery goes smoothly. No overnight stay is warranted, so the patient is discharged with prescriptions to get filled at her own local pharmacy.

In this scenario, the hospital owns the building and the pharmacy and employs the staff and the nurses. Both physicians are employed by their own medical practices and just have "privileges" to provide care at the hospital. As a result of the surgery, the patient or the patient's insurance company will receive a bill from the orthopedic surgeon's medical practice, the anesthesiologist's medical practice, the hospital (for the anesthesia and other medicines provided by the pharmacy and for the operating room and other charges), and the outside pharmacy (for the prescription the patient obtains from there).

In addition to hospitals, there are other facilities that provide health care, including rehabilitation care centers, mental health care centers, and long-term care centers. These facilities have similar staffing needs to hospitals. In addition, these facilities may also be part of larger health systems.

3. *Other Companies*

(a) Management Companies

As health care has grown and changed, hospitals have combined with medical practices, ambulatory centers, laboratories, and pharmacies to form large health systems.[7] Each of the component parts may keep its own identity while obtaining certain benefits from a unified administrative arm. These roles may be performed by a management services company or "MSO". An MSO is an "[e]ntity that renders health care-related business, managerial, and/or ministerial services to a health care delivery organization or a physician group."[8] The tasks performed by the MSO could include central billing, accounts payable, inventory, insurance

---

7 See Section I.B.3. *supra*.

8 DOUGLAS DENNER, 5 MED. MALPRAC. CHKLSTS. & DISC. § 36:9 (Sept. 2020 update).

credentialing, scheduling, human resources, and information technology ("IT") services.

In addition, health systems or hospitals could contract with MSOs to provide more discrete functions. For example, while certain MSOs could provide all of the "back office" work for a certain medical practice or hospital, another MSO may be retained to only perform billing work or marketing. As a result, the MSOs can be as varied as the providers themselves.

Though not strictly an MSO, a health information exchange ("HIE") provides another critical role in the coordination and movement of electronic data through the health community. Technically speaking, an HIE "enables and supports the electronic movement of health-related information among organizations according to nationally recognized standards, while maintaining the meaning of the information exchanged. Such movement may be within a region, community, or hospital system."[9] The term "HIE" can either describe the system that moves the data, or the term can be used to refer to the actual organization that has set up the system to move the data.

Like the providers, management companies must employ people to perform their work. Unlike providers, management companies generally do not employ licensed practitioners, i.e., physicians, nurses, technicians, etc. Instead, management companies employ the administrative and IT staff that enable the organizations to run.

(b) Medical Device and Innovation Companies

Innovation is at the heart of medical care. The companies working in this field strive to discover and bring to market innovative devices, products, and equipment that improve health outcomes in efficient and safe ways. The companies in this area include Medical product companies, medical equipment companies, pharmaceutical companies, electronic health record (EHR) vendors, software companies, and medical analysis companies.

Each new technological advancement in health care spurs the creativity of the entire industry. Each new successful innovation spurs more competition and more entrants into the field. All of this provides more room and demand for innovation to stretch current technologies as far as they can go to provide the best health care possible. Many companies

---

9 BERNADETTE BROCCOLO, ET AL., 1 HEALTH L. PRAC. GUIDE § 4A:4 (2020).

are fighting to enter this space. For example, many companies are working on software or applications that can work with EHRs and patients to improve clinical outcomes. For example, "[c]linical decision support software ("CDS Software") is technology that 'provides health care providers and patients with knowledge and person-specific information, intelligently filtered or presented at appropriate times, to enhance health and health care[.]'"[10]

Another area of growth and innovation is in the delivery of medical care via telephone or live streaming. Telemedicine, the "remote delivery of health care services and clinical information using telecommunications technology . . . encompasses three broad categories of technologies for the provision of patient care: interactive services, remote patient monitoring, and store-and-forward."[11]

The companies working in the medical innovation field range from the lions of Wall Street to start-ups working in the basement. As a result, these companies could utilize vast and complicated IT infrastructures or could be relying on the free wifi at Starbucks.

Necessary assets include information technology and intellectual property talent and the ability to utilize innovative ideas and apply them to old concepts and technologies. As a result, these businesses may employ programmers, developers, and researchers. Usually, at some level, the innovation companies also employ licensed practitioners. These licensed practitioners contribute keen insight into the areas of medicine that are being researched, the treatments that are being refined, or the products that are being developed. As a result, these companies are constantly testing and re-testing potential innovations. These companies want access to patients and to patient data to prove that their innovations work. As a result, these companies are constantly looking for ways to partner with health care providers.

(c) Non-Management Companies That Work as Business Associates

Many organizations are considered to be in the health care field not because of the work that they do but because of who they do their work for. These companies, known as "business associates" (or contractors to business associates) may provide services and activities such as claims

---

10 *Id.* § 4A:5.

11 *Id.* § 4A:9.

processing, data analysis, utilization review and billing, as well as legal, actuarial, accounting, consulting, data aggregation, management, administration, accreditation, and/or financial services."[12]

Business associates can include billing companies, marketing companies, law firms, accounting firms, and consulting firms. The test of whether these entities are "business associates" and thus brought under the rubric of U.S. health law, is whether these companies receive a certain type of information from the providers, health plans, or health care clearing houses to whom they are providing services (known as protected health information, or "PHI"). If they do receive such health information, these companies are subject to federal regulations that put them within the ambit of the health care industry.

Accordingly, although these entities may not specifically think of themselves as being in the health care industry, by virtue of the work they do for health care companies, they are brought under the U.S. health care regulatory regime called "HIPAA" and are subject to potential exposure because of it.

B. Brief Primer on the Regulation of Protected Health Information

As varied as the organizations that make up the health care industry may be, there is a unifying element that connects them all: the patient. The health care industry exists to provide care to individual patients. The patient's information is thus critical to health care. In the health care industry, participants face the ever-present risk that the health care information will either not be available when needed or that it will be improperly disclosed.

Although not a treatise on HIPAA, a basic understanding is necessary to understand the regulatory framework in which industry participants find themselves as they consider insurance coverage options. Below, we quickly discuss the Health Insurance Portability and Accountability Act of 1996 ("HIPAA"), as updated by the Health Information Technology for Economic and Clinical Health Act of 2009 ("HITECH").

---

12 PETER P. SWIRE & KENES AHMAD, U.S. PRIVATE-SECTOR PRIVACY: LAW AND PRACTICE FOR INFORMATION PRIVACY PROFESSIONALS, 47 (2012). *See also* 45 CFR § 103(3) and 42 U.S.C. § 17921(2).

1. HIPAA Privacy Rule

The HIPAA Privacy Rule issued by the U.S. Department of Health and Human Services ("HHS") placed certain limitations on when and how health plans, health insurers and health care providers, known as "covered entities,"[13] may use and disclose protected health information ("PHI"). Subject to certain limited exceptions, PHI is defined as individually identifiable health information held or transmitted in any form or medium by HIPAA covered entities or business associates.[14] The definition of individually identifiable health information ("IIHI") demonstrates the breadth of information included in PHI.

IIHI is "information . . . including demographic information collected from an individual," that:

> (1) Is created or received by a health care provider, health plan, employer, or health care clearinghouse; and
> (2) Relates to the past, present, or future physical or mental health or condition of an individual; the provision of health care to an individual; or the past, present, or future payment for the provision of health care to an individual; and
> (i) That identifies the individual; or
> (ii) With respect to which there is a reasonable basis to believe the information can be used to identify the individual.[15]

Accordingly, PHI covers a lot of important information that is necessary for the daily operation of the health care industry. At a very high-level, HIPAA mandates how entities must collect, use, secure, and disclose that PHI. Accordingly, HIPAA imposes obligations not just on the entities providing the care to the patients, but also to the businesses who provide various services to the providers that in some way involve the collection, use, disclosure, and security of PHI (for our purposes, both Providers AND the Other Companies referenced in Section 1 above). HIPAA imposes regulatory risk and potential fines and penalties on organizations that fail to comply with the regulations. Part of the regulations deal with unauthorized disclosures or "breaches" of PHI.

---

13 45 C.F.R. § 160.103.

14 45 C.F.R. § 160.103.

15 45 C.F.R. § 160.103.

Under HIPAA, a breach is defined as "the acquisition, access, use, or disclosure of protected health information in a manner not [otherwise] permitted . . . which compromises the security or privacy of the protected health information."[16]

As referenced in the prior section, like covered entities, business associates also must comply with HIPAA. As referenced above, a "business associate" is a person (or entity) who performs functions or activities on behalf of, or certain services for, a covered entity that involve the use or disclosure of PHI. Before the HITECH update, the HIPAA Privacy and Security Rules permitted covered entities to disclose PHI (and ePHI) to their business associates provided the covered entity received satisfactory assurance in the form of a written contract (typically referred to as a "Business Associate Agreement") that the business associate would appropriately safeguard the PHI (and ePHI).[17] "Under HITECH, however, HIPAA privacy and security rules are codified and apply to directly to business associates."[18]

2. *HIPAA Security Rule*

HHS issued the HIPAA Security Rule to require that PHI in electronic form (ePHI) be safeguarded against unauthorized access, use and disclosure.[19] The Security Rule "establishes minimum security requirements for PHI that a covered entity receives, creates, maintains or transmits in electronic form (ePHI)."[20]

The Security Rule is comprised of "standards and 'implementation specifications,' which, depending upon the size of the entity, either encourages or requires entities to adopt certain administrative, technical and physical safeguards that are designed to keep the ePHI secure and not improperly disclosed."[21] Each entity has some latitude in determining a specific safeguard to utilize, but if it decides not to use one at all, "it must

---

16 *See* 45 C.F.R. § 164.402.

17 *See* Swire & Ahmad, *supra* note 12, at 47 ("This contract must include provisions that pass the privacy and security standard down to the contracting entity.") *Id.*

18 *Id.*

19 *Id.* at 50.

20 *Id.*

21 *Id.*

document why it is not reasonable, and if appropriate, adopt an alternative measure."[22]

3. *Penalties for Failure to Comply with HIPAA*

HHS's Office for Civil Rights ("OCR") is tasked with enforcing both the HIPAA Privacy and Security Rules.[23] The OCR investigates complaints filed with it and also conducts compliance reviews on entities.[24] In investigating complaints, the OCR may find no violation of the Rules. In others, the OCR may seek to obtain the entity's voluntary compliance, bring a correction action against the entity, and/or enter a resolution agreement with the entity.[25] If no action is taken by the entity to resolve the violation(s), the OCR may impose civil money penalties.[26]

Under HIPAA, business associates must report all breaches to their respective covered entities and covered entities must report all breaches to the HHS.[27] The reported breaches may lead to investigations by the OCR. The investigations may lead to correction actions or resolution agreements being sought by the OCR against either the covered entity or the business associate which may include the imposition of a monetary penalty or payment of money as part of a settlement agreement.[28] These are some of the risks faced by entities working in the health care industry.

---

22 *Id.*

23 *See HIPAA Enforcement*, https://www.hhs.gov/hipaa/for-professionals/compliance-enforcement/index.html. *See also* Broccolo, et al., *supra* note 9, § 5B:15.

24 *See How OCR Enforces the HIPAA Privacy & Security Rules*, https://www.hhs.gov/hipaa/for-professionals/compliance-enforcement/examples/how-ocr-enforces-the-hipaa-privacy-and-security-rules/index.html. *See also* Broccolo, et al., *supra* note 9, § 5B:15.

25 *See id.*

26 *Id.*

27 45 CFR § 164.408.

28 For example, one business associate agreed to pay the OCR $2,300,000 and to adopt a corrective action plan in settlement of potential violations of the Privacy and Security Rules arising out of a breach that occurred to the business associate that resulted in the PHI belonging to over six million individuals being disclosed. *See* https://www.hhs.gov/about/news/2020/09/23/hipaa-business-associate-pays-2.3-million-settle-breach.html.

C. Exposures Unique to the Health Care Industry (Types of Data Used and Collected)

1. Section Introduction

In assessing cyber insurance needs, all organizations must first identify the information being protected, its value, and the risks of exposure.[29] The health care industry is no different.[30] In assessing these needs, businesses in the health care industry should "consider how technology affects every issue of business operations including, but not limited to, government regulation; privacy and data security; enterprise cyber networking; electronic communications; data management and network penetration."[31]

For the health care industry, the analysis above takes place with the increased burden of having to protect the type of information most highly sought after by cyber criminals: PHI. In addition, because the health care industry is part of the nation's critical infrastructure, industry participants must guard against criminals and intruders gaining operational information/system access. Below, we first explore the specific types of data providers must protect. Next, we examine the data to be protected from the other company perspective.

2. Data to Protect

(a) Providers.

As has become clear, providers are targets of multiple cyber threats because they are collectors and users of large amounts of sensitive data

---

29 RICHARD J. BORTNICK, ET AL., 2 DATA SEC. & PRIVACY LAW § 14:17 (Sept. 2020 Update). ("In evaluating whether it should buy dedicated cyber insurance coverage in what quantum, a business must examine itself and candidly analyze both the types of data it is obligated to protect (privacy) as well as the steps it has taken (or not taken) to, in fact, protect that data (security).") *Id.*

30 *Id.* § 14:1. ("In this regard, businesses typically assess common cyber risks as including, but not limited to the following: electronic data security, (the amount and type of data) professional technology services; information publication; technology failures, and internal malfeasance.") *Id.*

31 *Id.*

(i.e., PHI). In addition, industry participants can provide bad actors access points to critical infrastructure and to large amounts of sensitive data.

The information contained in PHI and ePHI represent treasure troves for criminals. In one place, criminals can access not just social security numbers and other personal information such as addresses and phone numbers, but they can also access health histories, insurance information, payment information, and potentially employment information.[32] As such, the value presented for a criminal in obtaining a health record eclipses that found in financial records alone. "While stolen bank data and certain retail data becomes useless if passwords are changed or account numbers are modified, health data may have a longer lifespan of value to cyber attackers and those who purchase such data from the cyber attackers."[33]

Since October 2009, over 78 million health care records have been breached.[34] Headlines every day seem to report another medical record breach. In fact, according to www.HIPAAJournal.com, "[m]ore large health care data breaches were reported in 2020 than in any other year since the HITECH ACT called for the U.S. Department of Health and Human Services' Office for Civil Rights to start publishing health care data breach figures on its website."[35]

According to www.HIPAAJournal, hacking and other IT incidents were the primary culprits in data breaches in 2020.[36] "These incidents include exploitation of vulnerabilities and phishing, malware, and ransomware attacks, with the latter [having] increased considerably in recent months."[37]

Like other organizations, health care providers must protect their data and their systems. The data to protect includes PHI, ePHI, trade secret information, financial information, and intellectual property information. The loss or improper disclosure of data can have multiple ramifications, including governmental, financial, and reputational.

---

32 Katie Kenney & Valerie Breslin Montague, *Cybersecurity Threats, Enforcement Trends, and Practical Challenges*, 20170201 AHLA SEMINAR PAPERS 40 (2017).

33 *Id.*

34 *See 2020 Healthcare Data Breach Report: 25% Increase in Breaches in 2020*, https://www.hipaajournal.com/2020-healthcare-data-breach-report-us/.

35 *Id.*

36 *Id.*

37 *Id.*

Providers must likewise protect the integrity and availability of its systems and IT infrastructure. The infiltration of an organization's system can impact not only the integrity and availability of data needed to deliver health care or run the organization, but also can give bad actors access to other entities throughout the industry. If an organization is infected with ransomware, an entire enterprise can be impacted and the ability to see patients or do business can be ground to a halt. In other industries, where the provision of life-saving care is not at stake, businesses may have the luxury of responding to attacks or intrusions at a reasoned speed. But the "health care industry provides the perfect storm for cyber attackers."[38] Attackers know that an urgent response to restore functionality must often greet cyber intrusions and ransom attacks in the health care field.[39] In the health care industry, there "literally may be a life on the line."[40]

(b) Other Companies

Many of the companies in this group are business associates to providers and thus have PHI and ePHI to protect as well. As a result, these entities must comply with the HIPPA Privacy and Security Rules and all PHI and ePHI must be appropriately collected, used, and disclosed. But even the companies that may not have PHI to deal with (pharmaceutical companies or medical equipment and innovation companies) still have employee information, financial information, proprietary and trade-secret information to protect, as well as critical network systems that keep their businesses running. Finally, companies in the health care industry that provide IT services or innovative software to providers will have the added exposure of legal claims surrounding the negligent provision of those services.

D. Needed Coverage Grants Specific to the Health Care Industry

1. Section Introduction and Brief Cyber Insurance Refresher

Cyber events in the health care industry can lead to data breaches and the destruction of computer networks. Accordingly, organizations must be

---

38 Kenney & Montague, *supra* note 32.

39 *Id.*

40 *Id.*

prepared to address such breaches, including the financial and regulatory fallout. Likewise, if a cyber event cripples the organizations' ability to provide care or do business, the cyber insurance should also prepare the organization for business interruption and lost income or profits.

Most organizations are accustomed to the differences between first-party and third-party policies. Cyber policies provide "a hybrid" of the two.[41] In cyber policies,

> [T]he first-party coverage is designed to protect against damage or loss arising from e-commerce, networking, technology, and other cyber-risks. For example, first party coverage pays for such things as: (1) crisis management expenses, (2) business interruption loss and extra expense, (3) reputational loss, (4) denial-of-service attacks, (5) lost income, (6) cyber extortion, and (7) media and web content liability. In turn, third party coverage typically extends to: (1) privacy and security—related Claims, (2) Regulatory Claims, (3) Media Content Claims, and (4) PCI (i.e., credit card—related) Claims.[42]

In addition, as we will see below, "[a] cyber policy's third party coverage is designed to extend to an insured's failure to prevent intruders from gaining access to and, in some cases, disclosing a natural person's Personally Identifiable Information ("PII") and Protected Health Information ("PHI")[.][43]

2. *Coverage Needed*

(a) Providers

Due to the nature of the provider's business, most of the risk surrounding cyber incidents will flow from the fallout of breaches of PHI or ransomware events that lock-down their systems. As a result, when assessing the needed coverage for health care providers, organizations should analyze whether the coverage they are considering provides breach notification costs, crisis management costs, payment of ransoms, regulatory defense costs, costs for data and systems recovery, and loss of

---

41 Bortnick, et al., *supra* note 29, § 14:16.

42 *Id.*

43 *Id.* § 14:18.

business income.[44] We consider the types of policies that provide this coverage below.

(b) Breach Expense Coverage

Each industry participant is concerned about data breaches. This type of coverage, "affords first party coverage for costs incurred by the policy holder directly as a result of a cyber occurrence[.]"[45] Due to the potentially large costs, "insurers will often specifically define what is included with the policy's definition of "privacy breach expenses" or "privacy breach costs."[46]

These costs usually include "the reasonable and necessary expenses . . . to provide

1. crisis management costs;[47]
2. notification to patients and/or employees of a privacy breach, including the costs of preparing and mailing such notifications, or if a notification must be made through the media, costs for such notification;[48]
3. credit monitoring, credit counseling, or identity theft mitigation services costs to be supplied to patients and/or employees;[49]
4. if the breach is a large one, costs to implement and man a third-party call center to receive inquiries from patients and/or employees;[50]
6. if necessary, the costs to engage a forensic investigator to analyze how the breach occurred or the extent of the breach;[51]
7. and potential legal costs to determine any indemnification rights or the potential claims against third-parties arising from the breach."[52]

---

44 Sheila Limmroth, *Cyber Insurance: An Insider's Guide to Why You Should Have Coverage*, 22 No. 3 J. HEALTH CARE COMPLIANCE 51 (2020).

45 Bortnick, et al., *supra* note 29, § 14:20.

46 *Id.*

47 *Id.*

48 *Id.*

49 *Id.*

50 *Id.*

51 Bortnick, et al., *supra* note 29, § 14:20.

52 *Id.*

(c) Regulatory Investigation Coverage

As referenced in sections above, the collection, use, and disclosure of PHI and ePHI in the United States is highly regulated. An entity in the health care industry does not only have to be concerned about a potential security incident that results in the disclosure of PHI or ePHI, but must also be concerned that the disclosure will give rise to governmental investigations into the incident, and ultimately into the organization's privacy and security practices. Accordingly, many cyber policies are now including provisions that cover "the attorneys' fees associated with formal regulatory investigations as well as regulatory proceedings."[53]

(d) Data and Digital Asset and Electronic Business Interruption Coverage

This type of coverage deals with "[f]irst party computer network security failures" that could be attributed to various causes.[54] Accordingly, companies wishing to cover the potential network security failure would want to be covered for the "transmission of malicious computer code, denial of service attacks, the actions of 'rogue employees,' the actions of third party vendors and, on occasion, cloud service providers."[55]

But in addition to experiencing their own network security failures, for providers, the very real threat of losing critical information needed to provide care to patients looms over any network intrusion scenario. This has become more acute as the prevalence of ransomware events have increased.

Accordingly, data and digital assets coverage should be investigated to provide coverage for the costs associated with restoring computer systems, including networks, and the critical data, including patient data, that may have been corrupted during the network intrusion.[56] This type of coverage stands in contrast to a privacy breach, because digital asset coverage only requires, "(1) unauthorized access to a 'data asset,' and (2) resulting Loss that are caused by the failure of an insured's cybersecurity."[57]

---

53 *Id.* § 14:25.

54 *Id.* § 14:18.

55 *Id.*

56 *Id.* § 14:21.

57 Bortnick, et al., *supra* note 29, § 14:21.

Coupled with digital asset coverage can be electronic business interruption coverage. These policies are "designed to cover expenses incurred by the policyholder during a period of restoration and/or remediation, i.e., returning the policyholder's network to normal following a partial or complete interruption or reduction in the computer or network's performance."[58]

In the health care provider world, electronic business interruption coverage would likely be crucial given the numerous instances of system outages that have occurred due to ransomware events.[59] Such incidents include the one experienced by Erie County Medical Center where a ransomware attack rendered over 6,000 computers in the system useless and forced the medical center to use pen and paper for some time.[60] Of course, entities are creatively asserting such claims based on cyber events and insurance companies have responded with narrowly defining the scope of coverage in this area.[61]

(e) Privacy Liability Coverage

This type of coverage provides third-party liability coverage for losses occurring due to the insured's alleged failure to protect sensitive, personal or confidential corporate information, or violation of specified privacy regulations or the insured's own privacy policies."[62]

---

58 *Id.* § 14:23. ("Given the primacy of business interruption risk to policyholders that utilize computers and computer networks to conduct normal business activities, appropriate cyber insurance is a significant aspect to risk management.") *Id.*

59 Jessica Davis, *What Is Cyber Insurance for Healthcare Organizations?*, https://healthitsecurity.com/features/what-is-cyber-insurance-for-healthcare-organizations.

60 *Id.*

61 *Id.* ("As hackers look to medical devices and new ways to break into a network, malpractice and other legal issues can arise from cyberattacks. The new reality for health care is that the risk of security incidents has expanded past the possibility of data loss: it is now a matter of patient safety.") *Id.*

62 Bortnick, et al., *supra* note 29, § 14:19. ("The factual trigger for coverage under privacy liability insuring agreements include claims for damages by third parties purportedly arising out of the unauthorized disclosure or loss of personally identifiable information or confidential corporate information. Theories of liability that have constituted such a trigger include claims that the company did not comply with its own privacy policy, failure to implement

HIPAA does not currently provide a private right of action to individuals that have been harmed due to the disclosure of their PHI or ePHI.[63] But the absence of such a provision has not stopped litigation over privacy liability. Entities in the health care industry also maintain a vast amount of confidential employee information, as well as other confidential information belonging to business partners. In addition, some of the participants in this industry may also have consumer information that may be the subject of a cyber incident. Accordingly, obtaining Privacy Liability coverage might make sense for many industry participants.

(f) PCI Compliance Coverage

Health care providers may accept payment (whether co-payments or deductible amounts) from patients on site, through the internet, or via call centers. If they do, they are usually accepting payment from patients via credit or debit card. As such, Payment Card Industry Data Security Standards ("PCI DSS") may apply. Incidents involving the payment card industry will likely involve third-party claims for failure to follow the PCI DSS. Coverage in this area may include amounts the entity is obligated to pay for its failure to conform to the PCI DSS.[64] Accordingly, these entities may desire to seek additional coverage for potential failure to follow the PCI DSS guidelines.

(g) Cyber Extortion Coverage

This type of coverage is "triggered when the policyholder receives an extortionist's threat to either attack its computer system or to either destroy or disclose the policyholder's data for the purpose of demanding money[.]"[65] This coverage would then be suited for potential ransomware

---

an identity theft prevention program or anti-phishing/social engineering training as well as failure to appropriately disclose a data breach.") *Id.*

63 Davis, *supra* note 59. Of course, "[a]s hackers continue to pummel the health care sector with cyberattacks, litigation stemming from a breach has increased in equal measure. Even when data isn't breached, an organization can still be sued when a cyberattack impacts the ability to deliver patient care." *Id.*

64 Bortnick, et al., *supra* note 29, § 14:27 (2020-2021).

65 *Id.*§ 14:22.

events, where the provider is threatened with either the inability to treat patients or with the revelation of PHI by the extortionist, or both.

In 2016, the HHS issued its ransomware guidance: "FACT SHEET: Ransomware and HIPAA."[66] The guidance was the result of an alarming increase in ransomware events being experienced by health care entities across the United States. The incidences have only increased since that time. As referenced above, health care providers do not have the luxury to methodically bring systems back on line to care for patients. As such, the paying of ransoms in response to ransomware is something that many health care providers are forced to prepare for. Health care systems have repeatedly had to make the excruciating decision to either turn patients away while their systems were down, or endure the lesser of the bad alternatives and pay the ransom.[67] Obtaining this type of coverage will help in making that critical and difficult decision.

3. *Other Companies*

(a) Similarities/Differences to Coverage Needed by Providers

The "other companies", likewise should at a minimum, have cyber insurance coverage that accounts for the following eventualities: unauthorized access to systems; damage to network assets; business interruption; data breach response costs (investigation, notification, credit monitoring); litigation and fines associated with a data breach; cyber extortion; cyber terrorism attack; and employee error. As a result, depending on the cost for coverage, many companies in this category should consider retaining the coverage discussed in the section above for providers. This certainly applies to breach expense coverage, data/digital asset and electronic business interruption coverage, privacy liability coverage, and cyber extortion coverage.

What might not be as evident is the fact that other companies, like providers, also should consider regulatory investigation coverage. As discussed, business associates are just as susceptible to be investigated for

66 *See FACT SHEET: Ransomware and HIPAA*, https://www.hhs.gov/sites/default/files/RansomwareFactSheet.pdf.

67 Patricia A. Markus, *Health Data is More Precious than Gold: HIPAA Enforcement and Biosecurity Concerns*, 20180625 AHLA SEMINAR PAPERS 45 (2018). This situation was faced by the Kansas Heart Hospital when it paid a ransom for access to its system.

their failure to conform to the HIPAA Privacy and Security Rules. In addition, each of the states impose on organizations requirements to notify various state agencies in the event certain breach thresholds are met. As a result, "[l]ike their federal counterparts, state regulators have imposed millions of dollars of fines and penalties on entities that fail to comply with their state's breach notification laws."[68] Regulatory investigations arising out of breaches are becoming the norm.

Depending upon the business operations of the "other companies," the one area that they may not need coverage is for PCI DSS Compliance. If the entity does not deal in electronic payments, this would not be a risk to prepare for.

(b) Technology E&O Insurance

One area that providers may not need coverage in that many "other companies" will likely need is for Technology Errors and Omissions. This insurance (E&O insurance) is designed to cover "third-party damages arising from a product's failure to perform as intended or expected" and is also designed to protect "from acts, errors, or omissions committed in the course of the performance of technology services."[69] Accordingly, this type of coverage can address potential "programming errors, problems with large integration/installation projects, development problems, problems with integrating software or hardware[.]"[70]

This type of coverage can be necessary for several participants in the health care industry. Each of the companies in the health care innovation space should consider this type of coverage. For example, in 2018, Allscripts suffered a ransomware attack that led to litigation being initiated by several of its clients.[71] Although the incident did not allegedly involve the breach of any data, the clients sued Allscripts based on their inability to access their EHRs as a result of the attack.[72]

In addition, business associates providing services that entail programming or network integration should consider this coverage as well as any entity that might face claims of "negligent IT consultation,

---

68 Bortnick, et al., *supra* note 29, § 14:25.

69 *Id.* § 14:24.

70 *Id.*

71 Davis, *supra* note 59.

72 *Id.*

incomplete work and ineffective project management or simply deficiently provided services."[73]

E. The Exclusions That Should Be Included or Excluded

As the trite saying goes, if you've seen one insurance policy . . . you've seen one insurance policy. Knowing the ins and outs of one policy's provisions will provide you with no assurances for the next policy. As such, the exclusions contained in each cyber policy should be highly scrutinized. In this section, we will briefly discuss some of the exclusions to be mindful of in the health care industry.

1. Exclusions

When reviewing a policy, it is important to identify the elements that you want to have covered in the event of an incident. Some areas that are not always clearly spelled out include whether the policy covers losses due to e-mail compromise; mobile device compromise; or due to an insider threat.[74]

It is also important to remember that when purchasing breach expense coverage, it is usually very explicit in the types of costs it will provide payment for.[75] Accordingly, breach expense coverage does not typically include the costs to retrieve/recover data assets, improve the security system, or compensate for lost profits or wages to the insured or another third-party.[76]

As it relates to exclusions for cyber coverage, one particular exclusion to look out for is the exclusion for breach of contract claims.[77] For example, some policies include exclusions from coverage for incidents involving the insured's alleged breach of contractual duty to prevent a data breach from occurring.[78]

Perhaps the exclusion that at times has received the most notoriety, especially as it relates to the ongoing increase in ransomware attacks (that

---

73 Bortnick, et al., *supra* note 29, § 14:24.
74 Limmroth, *supra* note 44.
75 See section IV.B.1.a. *supra*.
76 Bortnick, et al., *supra* note 29, § 14:20.
77 *Id.*
78 *Id.*

may be initiated by advanced persistent threat actors linked to nation-states), is the War Risk Exclusion. We discussed above the cyber extortion coverage. But this exclusion

> typically bars coverage for: 'Bodily injury' or 'property damage', however caused, arising, directly or indirectly, out of:
> (1) War, including undeclared or civil war;
> (2) Warlike action by a military force, including action in hindering or defending against an actual or expected attack by any government, sovereign or other authority using military personnel or other agents; or
> (3) Insurrection, rebellion, revolution, usurped power, or action taken by governmental authority in hindering or defending against any of these.[79]

In addition to these specific exclusions from coverage, participants in the health care industry need to recognize that some policies also reduce the amount of indemnification coverage based on the amount of defense costs spent defending the claim. Insureds must be wary that, "[o]n the whole, stand-alone cyber policies are 'cost inclusive[.]'"[80] and expenses paid in defense of claims will erode the amounts left to pay for any incurred liability.[81]

F. Other Risk Transfer or Risk Mitigation Strategies

1. Section Introduction

In addition to obtaining cyber insurance, there are other ways for entities in the health care industry to mitigate or transfer their risk. Below, we consider the benefits of implementing strong a HIPAA Security program as well as other forms of insurance that might provide needed coverage.

---

79 *Id.*
80 *Id.*
81 *Id.*

2. *Compliance with HIPAA*

Most industry participants already have HIPAA Privacy Rule and HIPAA Security Rule compliance requirements. Although proper preparation and diligence is not a guarantee an organization will never experience a cyber event or a data breach, it can help in terms of governmental investigations actions and with any potential reputational fallout that might accrue.

As referenced above, the HIPAA Security Rule requires Covered Entities and business associates to protect the ePHI under their care. The Security Rule imposes obligations on these entities to do so by ensuring the confidentiality, integrity, and availability of all ePHI the covered entity creates, receives, maintains, or transmits;[82] protecting against any reasonably anticipated threat against the ePHI's security;[83] protecting against reasonably anticipated disclosures of the ePHI that are proscribed by the Privacy Rule;[84] and ensuring compliance with HIPAA by its workforce.[85]

Further, the HIPAA Security Rule mandates that each entity subject to it have an individual responsible for its implementation and oversight;[86] perform ongoing risk assessments;[87] and perform ongoing workforce security awareness and training.[88]

These steps, already required by the Rule, if internalized by the entity, may lessen the number of incidents experienced. In addition, following the Security Rule, and implementing its requirements, may mitigate any potential regulatory fines in the event of a breach.

---

82 Swire & Ahmad, *supra*, at 50.

83 *Id.*

84 *Id.*

85 *Id.*

86 *Id.*

87 *Id. See also* Broccolo, et al., *supra* note 9, § 4A:24. ("Given the sensitivity of health information stored on Health IT systems and the rise in malicious intrusions and attacks on Health IT systems, however, organizations implementing Health IT solutions should consider conducting a security risk assessment on at least an annual basis.") *Id.*

88 Swire & Ahmad, *supra* note 12, at 50.

3. *Other Insurance*

Even if cyber insurance is not obtained, some type of insurance is critical for the entities working in this industry.

At one time, traditional insurance policies potentially provided some coverage for cyber incidents.[89] These policies included third-party policies such as Comprehensive General Liability,[90] Errors-and-Omissions; and Directors and Officers ("D&O") coverage.[91]

The D&O coverage might be particularly important as plaintiffs' lawyers become more creative in the claims they assert against entities that have experienced a data breach. Directors and officers are responsible for setting the priorities of an organization, including the budget and support given to information technology and cybersecurity.[92] "[A]s the United States' and other countries' cybersecurity laws continue to evolve, cybersecurity and privacy are critical aspects of a D&O's oversight."[93] As a result, Plaintiffs may allege that the leaders of an organization failed to meet the standard of care by not prioritizing protection against cyber related events.

G. Conclusion

The importance of the health care industry cannot be overstated. As covered in this chapter, the participants in this industry vary from the actual providers that care for patients to the multiple organizations that make the providers' work possible. Due to the valuable types of information held by the industry participants, including PHI and cutting

---

89 Bortnick, et al., *supra* note 9, § 14:4.

90 *Id.* ("Comprehensive General Liability ("CGL") insurance is the most common type of third-party coverage available for businesses. As such, most businesses will look to their CGL policies for defense and indemnification in the event of lawsuits by third parties.") *Id.*

91 *Id.* § 14:11. For the most part, D&O coverage provides coverage for the failure to "exercise proper care and diligence in managing the corporate business. This in turn, may include an act, error, omission, misstatement, or misleading statement. D&O policies cover negligent business decisions, but they exclude gross negligence, which may consist of doing nothing to defend against well-known cyber loss problems." *Id.*

92 *Id.*

93 *Id.*

edge proprietary information, each of these organizations presents an enticing target to cyber criminals. In addition, each of the industry participants could pose an entry-way into the critical infrastructure that comprises the health care industry as a whole. As a result, identifying the assets and systems to be protected, and providing for the appropriate insurance coverage in case of an incident, is vital.

The risks and threats are not static, however. Continuing to monitor the risks present in the industry, while also re-assessing whether an organization's current insurance coverage is sufficient to manage the risks, will be an ongoing task for entities in the health care industry. As a result, keeping up with the pace of the changing threats, while assuring an organization's risk is appropriately managed, will continue to be a challenge for all industry participants.

Chapter 12

Cyber Insurance for Defense Contractors*

The defense industry is more focused than ever on cybersecurity. The Department of Defense has introduced new programs—like CMMC and the Basic Assessment—to both require and incentivize hardened systems. As cyber attacks continue to cause economic damage throughout the supply chain, defense contractors need to maintain (and understand) robust cyber insurance coverage.

This chapter introduces concepts related to cyber insurance that may be particularly relevant to defense contractors. Section A. outlines important new cybersecurity requirements. Section B. then describes our current understanding of the allowability of cyber insurance costs under these new programs. Section C.—a major focus of this chapter—explains current litigation and commentary about the interpretation of "war exclusions" in the context of cyber attacks. The operation of war exclusions has particular relevance to and impact on the defense industry.

The rules, guidance, and narratives about cyber insurance for defense contractors continues to evolve rapidly. Thus, it is likely that some of the information in this chapter may be out of date by the time it is printed or read. In particular, the litigation reported herein is as yet unresolved and ongoing. Nonetheless, the general guidance and the trends identified will have continuing general relevance irrespective of rapidly changing details and of future outcomes.

A. DFARS Clauses and Requirements

The Defense Federal Acquisition Regulation Supplement ("DFARS") contains two clauses that impose cybersecurity requirements on defense contractors. Many contractors are already familiar with DFARS 252.204-7012, Safeguarding Covered Defense Information and Cyber Incident Reporting (the "7012 Clause"). In addition, the phased roll-out of DFARS

---

* By Heather Howell Wright, Elizabeth R. Brusa and Andrew Tuggle.

252.204-7021, Cybersecurity Maturity Model Certification Requirement (the "CMMC Clause") has begun. Contractors, brokers, and cyber insurers should focus on compliance with these standards.

1. The 7012 Clause

The 7012 Clause, which is included in all solicitations and contracts from the Department of Defense ("DoD"), requires contractors to "provide adequate security on all covered contractor information systems."[1] While the 7012 Clause is included in all contracts, it does not require security on all systems, but only on "covered" systems. Covered systems include those with controlled unclassified information ("CUI").[2,3]

Exactly what constitutes "adequate security" is for most CUI defined by the National Institute of Standards and Technology Special Publication 800-171, Protecting Controlled Unclassified Information in Nonfederal Systems and Organizations (the "NIST Standard").[4] For years, the NIST

---

1 DFARS 252.204-7012(b).

2 DFARS 252.204-7012(a).

3 As used in NIST SP 800-171, CUI includes "any information that law, regulation, or governmentwide policy requires to have safeguarding or disseminating controls" (with some exceptions). Ron Ross *et al.*, *Protecting Controlled Unclassified Information in Nonfederal Systems and Organizations*, at 1 n.3 (Nat'l Inst. of Standards & Tech. Special Publ'n 800-171 rev. 2, Feb. 21, 2020). The CUI definition was created to harmonize the "inefficient, confusing patchwork" of control markings. Exec. Order No. 13,556 (Nov. 4, 2010), 3 C.F.R. 267 (2011). Some agencies (*e.g.*, FAA), however, still use legacy markings such as "sensitive but unclassified (SBU)" and "sensitive unclassified information (SUI)." The National Archives notes that "[e]xisting agency policy for all sensitive but unclassified information remains in effect until your agency implements the CUI program." Nat'l Archives, *CUI Categories*, CONTROLLED UNCLASSIFIED INFORMATION (Apr. 13, 2020), https://www.archives.gov/ cui/registry/category-list[https://web.archive.org/web/20210124014053/ https://www.archives.gov/cui/registry/category-list].
Information that is merely federal contract information ("FCI") is *not* CUI. The basic safeguarding requirements for FCI are specified at FAR 52.204-21. Because FCI is common to all government contractors, and not just Department of Defense contractors, this chapter does not cover the cybersecurity of FCI, except to the extent that such is protected under CMMC Level 1 (discussed *infra*, section I.B).

4 DFARS 252.204-7012(b)(2).

Standard has been a gold standard for cybersecurity practices in the defense industry. Historically, it was largely aspirational, and contractors have been allowed to self-certify that they either comply or have a plan to comply in the future. The vagueness of self-certification led to varying degrees of—and endlessly delayed plans for—compliance.

2. *The CMMC Clause*

To address the shortcomings of self-certification of compliance, the Cybersecurity Maturity Model Certification ("CMMC") Framework will end the self-certification option. Instead, contractors must obtain certification from a CMMC Third-Party Assessment Organization ("C3PAO"). C3PAOs must themselves be accredited by an Accreditation Body. The rollout began on November 30, 2020 and will continue through 2025.[5] As of this publication date, no C3PAOs have yet been accredited, so it will be a while longer before contractors can be CMMC-certified.[6]

CMMC has five levels of compliance, and the required compliance level will be defined in each contract based on the associated risks. Every contractor will need to meet CMMC Level 1, if only for FCI. And any

---

5 Defense Federal Acquisition Regulation Supplement: Assessing Contractor Implementation of Cybersecurity Requirements (DFARS Case 2019-D041), 85 Fed. Reg. 61505, 61505-06 (Sep. 29, 2020).

6 As of April 15, 2021, more than one hundred entities were listed on the Accreditation Body's website as in the process of obtaining certification as C3PAOs, but none have yet passed their own Level 3 assessment. *See* CMMC Accreditation Body, *CMMC-AB Marketplace Listings*, https://portal.cmmcab.org/marketplace/ (last visited Jan. 24, 2021). As a result, there are not yet any C3PAOs that can perform assessments for certification. *Id.* ("Before a C3PAO can conduct an assessment, they must successfully complete a CMMC ML3 Assessment conducted by DCMA DIBCAC."). Katie Arrington, the Chief Information Security Officer to the Assistant Secretary of Defense for Acquisition and Sustainment, has predicted that at least some C3PAOs should be fully accredited before Summer 2021. Mariam Baksh, *DOD's Cybersecurity Certification Requirements to Appear in DHS Contracts*, NEXTGOV (Jan. 21, 2021), https://www.nextgov.com/cybersecurity/2021/01/dods-cybersecurity-certification-requirements-appear-dhs-contracts/171551/[https://web.archive.org/web/20210125145544if_/ https://www.nextgov.com/cybersecurity/2021/01/dods-cybersecurity-certification-requirements-appear-dhs-contracts/171551/].

contractor handling CUI will likely need to meet at least CMMC Level 3. The Level 3 requirements remain very similar to the NIST Standard. For many contractors, then, their CMMC efforts will help improve their Basic Assessment score (*see infra*, section I.C).

The defense industry has been preparing for CMMC since 2019, so its entry into the DFARS comes as no surprise. As discussed above, though, no C3PAOs have yet been accredited. Nonetheless, efforts to comply with the CMMC standards will not be wasted.

3. *The NIST Assessment Methodology*

In the meantime, as a bridge to CMMC, contracts and solicitations are requiring a more robust assessment framework for the NIST Standard.[7] Rather than simply self-certifying their compliance, contractors must specifically score their cyber hygiene according to a detailed list of controls, on a scale from –203 to +110.[8] This "Basic Assessment" score will be posted to the Supplier Performance Risk System (SPRS), where it can affect procurement decisions.[9] Posting of that score creates additional incentive to comply with the NIST Standard sooner, rather than later. Because of substantial overlap between the NIST Standard and the CMMC controls, the scoring could also smooth the eventual transition to the CMMC Framework.[10]

4. *Cyber Insurance Policies Will Focus on Compliance with DoD Standards*

Contractors should expect that cyber insurance policies will require businesses to comply with the appropriate regulations as a condition

7 *See* DFARS 252.204-7019 and -7020.

8 A template for scoring an organization's practices is available from Defense Pricing and Contracting. *See* Def. Pricing & Contracting, *NIST SP 800-171 DoD Assessment Methodology*, at 12-20 (Annex A) (version 1.2.1 June 24, 2020), https://www.acq.osd.mil/dpap/pdi/cyber/strategically_assessing_contractor_implementation_of_NIST_SP_800-171.html[https://web.archive.org/web/20201201085107/https://www.acq.osd.mil/dpap/pdi/cyber/docs/NIST%20SP%20800-171%20Assessment%20Methodology%20Version 1.2.1%20%206.24.2020.pdf].

9 *See* DFARS 252.204-7019(d).

10 So-called "Medium" and "High Assessments" are also provided but are conducted by the government. *Id.*

precedent to coverage. Both the CMMC Clause and the NIST Assessment Methodology require that certifications be kept current, *viz.* less than three years old.[11] We anticipate that insurers will ask to receive copies of certificates as part of the application and renewal process. In addition, as the CMMC certification process becomes fully implemented, it is likely that insurers could prepare "protective safeguards"-type endorsements that could require CMMC certification (or a minimum Basic Assessment score) as a condition precedent to coverage.

Further, insurers could also ask to see proof of compliance by an insured's subcontractors. All three of the 7012 Clause, the CMMC Clause, and the NIST Assessment Methodology must be flowed down to subcontractors.[12] The flow-down requirement includes that certificates must be not older than three years.[13]

Even if insurers do not specifically require compliance or expressly ask for the certificates, companies and brokers should still consider providing proof anyway as they could assist in obtaining favorable risk ratings. In this way, the company may be able to negotiate for more favorable coverage terms or premiums. Providing favorable terms to compliant insureds appropriately incentivizes insureds to comply, helping to protect not only the defense-industrial supply chain but also its insurance ecosystem (*e.g.*, against unpredictable aggregation).

5. *Cyber Insurance Not Required*

The DFARS references FAR 52.228-7000, Insurance—Liability to Third Persons,[14] but the FAR (at least for now) does not specifically require cyber insurance.[15] It does, however, leave room for "such other insurance as the Contracting Officer may require under th[e] contract."[16] As the DoD works to harden its supply chain, we anticipate the procurement of cyber insurance as a condition to DoD contracting will be more common.

---

11 DFARS 252.204-7020(g)(2) and -7021(b).

12 DFARS 252.204-7012(m), -7020(g), and -7021(c).

13 *Id.*

14 DFARS 228.311-1.

15 *See* FAR 52.228-7(a)(1) (requiring "workers' compensation, employer's liability, comprehensive general liability (bodily injury), [and] comprehensive automobile liability (bodily injury and property damage)").

16 *Id.*

For instance, the most recent authorization bill for the DoD instructs the Government Accountability Office to "conduct a study to assess and analyze the state and availability of insurance coverage in the United States for cybersecurity risks."[17] The Cyberspace Solarium Commission—formed by Congress in 2019—had pushed for such a study and had even recommended that Congress establish a program to develop certifications for cybersecurity insurance products.[18] Both insurers and contractors should look closely at the eventual report and the signals it sends to Congress and to the DoD regarding the mandatory purchase of cyber insurance.

B. Cyber Insurance as an Allowable Cost

Generally, the cost of insurance for liabilities arising from acts or incidents that are beyond the control of the contractor is an allowable cost as part of a DoD contract.[19] Notwithstanding the foregoing, guidance is sparse as to whether such allowable costs include the cost of cyber insurance coverage. Even if cyber insurance is ultimately deemed an unallowable cost, contractors may nonetheless elect to purchase cyber insurance policies to ensure compliance with other cybersecurity requirements as well as to protect themselves against cyber liability.[20]

---

17 William M. (Mac) Thornberry National Defense Authorization Act for Fiscal Year 2021, Pub. L. No. 116-283, § 9005(a), --- Stat. ---, --- (Jan. 1, 2021).

18 *See* Cyberspace Solarium Comm'n, *Legislative Proposals* § 4.4 (July 15, 2020), https://www.solarium.gov/report/legislative-proposals [https://web.archive.org/web/20201020180129/https://drive.google.com/file/d/1S5N7KvjFfxow19kCnPl0nx7Mah8pK0uG/preview].

19 *See* FAR 31.205; Def. Cont. Audit Agency, *Selected Area of Cost Guidebook: FAR 31.205 Cost Principles* ch. 34 (Mar. 6, 2019), https://www.dcaa.mil/Guidance/Selected-Area-of-Cost-Guidebook/ [https://web.archive.org/web/20210127041627/https://www.dcaa.mil/Portals/88/Documents/Guidance/Selected%20Area%20of%20Cost%20Guidebook/Chapter34.pdf?ver=2019-03-06-135648-533] [hereinafter *Selected Area of Cost Guidebook*] ("Insurance Costs").

20 *See supra*, section I.B.

1. *Katie Arrington's 2019 Statement Regarding Cybersecurity as an Allowable Cost*

On June 13, 2019, Katie Arrington, the Chief Information Security Officer for the Office of the Under Secretary of Defense (Acquisition and Sustainment), impactfully stated at a Professional Services Council ("PSC") meeting in Arlington, Virginia:

> "I need you all now to get out your pens and you better write this down and tell your teams: Hear it from Katie Arrington, who got permission to say it from Mr. [Kevin] Fahey [then the assistant secretary of Defense for Acquisition in the Office of the Under Secretary of Acquisition and Sustainment] ***security is an allowable cost. Amen, right***?" . . . "Now, what you need to do as industry is help me, help you. I'm not the enemy. I'm literally the one person in government who said, 'Hi, I'm here to help,[‘] and I'm legit here to help."[21]

Accordingly, it is generally expected that costs related to implementing necessary cybersecurity protocols aligned with CMMC requirements will be deemed allowable costs for DoD contracts. This position makes sense, as several other costs necessary for conducting business and complying with DoD requirements are likewise allowable costs.[22]

---

21 Jason Miller, *Why DoD's Decision to Make Cybersecurity an 'Allowable Cost' Matters*, FEDERAL NEWS NETWORK: REPORTER'S NOTEBOOK (June 17, 2019), https://federalnewsnetwork.com/reporters-notebook-jason-miller/2019/06/why-dods-decision-to-make-cybersecurity-an-allowable-cost-matters/[https://web.archive.org/web/20201208010047/https://federalnewsnetwork.com/reporters-notebook-jason-miller/2019/06/why-dods-decision-to-make-cybersecurity-an-allowable-cost-matters/] (quoting Arrington at the PSC Federal Acquisition Conference on June 13, 2019) (some alterations in original) (emphasis added).

22 *See* FAR 31.205; *see also* Off. of the Under Sec'y of Def. for Acquisition & Sustainment, *CMMC FAQ's*, CYBERSECURITY MATURITY MODEL CERTIFICATION (Dec. 10, 2020), https://www.acq.osd.mil/cmmc/faq.html [https://web.archive.org/web/20210106111917/https://www.acq.osd.mil/cmmc/faq.html] ("The costs associated with implementing CMMC requirements, supporting the CMMC assessment, and contracting with the C3PAO will be considered an allowed cost.").

2. *Is Cyber Insurance an Allowable Cost?*

The next question, of course, is whether the premiums paid to procure cyber insurance could also be an allowable cost. While there is some guidance as to whether cybersecurity costs are an allowable cost (including Arrington's statement *supra*, section II.A), Defense Contract Audit Agency ("DCAA") guidance, as well as FAR and DFARS requirements, are mum as to whether cybersecurity insurance costs are likewise an allowable cost.[23]

Currently, cyber insurance is not a requirement for DoD contractors.[24] As such, maintaining cyber insurance is not necessarily a cost of compliance that could otherwise be reimbursable as an allowed cost. That said, however, FAR may provide an avenue by which cyber insurance could be deemed an allowable cost. Specifically, FAR 31.205-19 provides, in pertinent part, that "[t]he cost of insurance to protect the contractor against the costs of correcting its own defects in material and workmanship is unallowable. However, insurance costs to cover fortuitous or casualty losses resulting from defects in materials or workmanship are allowable as a normal business expense."[25]

In short, FAR explains that to the extent a contractor maintains liability insurance to provide coverage for claims of defects in material and workmanship, such as through a professional liability policy, the premiums for such policies are not an allowable cost. In the context of cyber insurance, however, if a contractor—or more specifically a contractor's data—is the subject of a cyber attack, the resulting loss and harm is typically financial in nature including the payment of ransom, loss of income, loss of use of computer networks, the cost of breach response and notice to individuals affected. Such losses (putting aside the possibility of negligence in maintaining such systems) are generally not due to the

---

23 See Selected Area of Cost Guidebook, supra note 19; FAR 31.205.

24 *See supra*, section I.E; *but see* Cyberspace Solarium Comm'n, *Final Report*, at 83 (Mar. 11, 2020), https://www.solarium.gov/report [https://web.archive.org/web/20200314183755/https://drive.google.com/file/d/1ryMCIL_dZ30QyjFqFkkf10MxIXJGT4yv/view] (recommending that, "[u]pon the development of cybersecurity insurance policy certifications . . . , U.S. government contractors maintain a certified level of cybersecurity insurance and explore whether the Cybersecurity Maturity Model Certification should be updated to require cybersecurity insurance").

25 FAR 31.205-19(e)(3).

contractor's defective material and workmanship. Rather, such losses are fortuitous and purchasing cyber insurance is a normal business expense. Over the next few years, we will likely learn more about whether the DoD and the DCAA consider the cost of cyber insurance to be an allowable cost.

C. War Exclusions

Cyber insurance policies generally exclude from coverage losses that are considered uninsurable, such as losses due to war. While war exclusions can apply to any kind of insured, they have particular relevance for the defense industry. And, as explained below, they are especially difficult to interpret and apply in relation to cyber attacks.

1. Purpose of Exclusions

War is an "actuarial nightmare."[26] It is difficult to predict, and the damage can quickly aggregate (rather than dilute) across many insureds.[27] Where risks are hard to assess, premiums are hard to compute.[28] Moreover, to insure war-risks creates a "moral hazard" problem—if insurers were

---

26 Jon Bateman, *War, Terrorism, and Catastrophe in Cyber Insurance: Understanding and Reforming Exclusions*, at 9 (Carnegie Endowment for Int'l Peace, Working Paper Oct. 5, 2020), https://Carnegieendowment.org/files/Bateman_-_Cyber_Insurance_-_Final.pdf [https://web.archive.org/web/20201217080538/https://carnegieendowment.org/files/Bateman_-_Cyber_Insurance_-_Final.pdf]; *see also* Letter from W. T. Sherman to the Mayor and City Council of Atlanta (Sept. 12, 1864), *in* 39-2 THE WAR OF THE REBELLION: A COMPILATION OF THE OFFICIAL RECORDS OF THE UNION AND CONFEDERATE ARMIES, SER. NO. 1, at 418, (Robert N. Scott *et al.* eds., 1892) http://collections.library.cornell.edu/moa_new/ waro.html [https://babel.hathitrust.org/cgi/pt?id=coo.31924077730210&view=1up&seq=420] ("War is cruelty and you cannot refine it . . . .").

27 *See* STEVEN PLITT ET AL., 10A COUCH ON INSURANCE § 152:1 (3d ed. 2019) ("systemic catastrophic-type losses"; "large loss that has a substantial impact upon disparate lines of insurance").

28 *Id.*

responsible for covering the cost of war, governments would have less incentive to pursue peace.[29]

For these reasons, most property policies, including those for cyber insurance, expressly exclude coverage for losses due to war.[30] War exclusions are not new. Insurers have been including them since at least 1720.[31] Recently, courts have begun to interpret war exclusions in the context of cyber attacks.

2. *The NotPetya Cyber Attack*

The NotPetya Cyber Attack ("NotPetya") was the "most destructive and costly cyber-attack in history" and has generated substantial litigation regarding the application of war exclusions.[32,33] Because the story of NotPetya has been more fully reported by others,[34] this chapter will briefly outline only the facts salient for discussing the war exclusion.

---

29 Bateman, *supra* note 26, at 10; *see also infra*, section III.E (discussing a federal backstop for losses to terrorism).

30 Sasha Romanosky *et al.*, *Content Analysis of Cyber Insurance Policies: How Do Carriers Write Policies and Price Cyber Risk?* 16 (Mar. 7, 2017), https://papers.ssrn.com/sol3/papers.cfm?abstract_id=2929137 [https://web.archive.org/web/20200327000540/https://papers.ssrn.com/sol3/papers.cfm?abstract_id=2929137] ("over half of the [cyber insurance] policies we examined excluded any claims related to war, military action, or terrorist action").

31 *See* Pan Am. World Airways, Inc. v. Aetna Cas. & Sur. Co., 505 F.2d 989, 1009 n.11 (2d Cir. 1974).

32 White House, Statement from the Press Secretary (Feb. 15, 2018), https://www.whitehouse.gov/briefings-statements/statement-press-secretary-25/ [https://web.archive.org/web/20210116171428/https://www.whitehouse.gov/briefings-statements/statement-press-secretary-25/].

33 *See, e.g.*, *infra*, section III.C.

34 *See, e.g.*, Andy Greenberg, *The Untold Story of NotPetya, the Most Devastating Cyberattack in History*, WIRED (Aug. 22, 2018), https://www.wired.com/story/notpetya-cyberattack-ukraine-russia-code-crashed-the-world/ [https://web.archive.org/web/20210123060548/ https://www.wired.com/story/notpetya-cyberattack-ukraine-russia-code-crashed-the-world/]; Katherine S. Wan, Comment, *NotPetya, Not Warfare: Rethinking the Insurance War Exclusion in the Context of International Cyberattacks*, 95 WASH. L. REV. 1595, 1611-13 (2020), https://digitalcommons.law.uw.edu/wlr/vol95/iss3/12/ [https://digitalcommons.law.uw.edu/cgi/viewcontent.cgi?article=5135&context=wlr].

In June 2017, a series of malware infections crippled computer systems of numerous companies operating in Ukraine. The attacks irreversibly destroyed data of banks, transport agencies, even the Chernobyl Nuclear Power Plant.[35] Because some of the affected companies operate internationally, NotPetya had a global effect.[36] The U.S. government estimated that the damage totaled more than $10,000,000,000.[37] The identities of the hackers remain unknown. Nonetheless, the governments of seven different nations—the U.S., the U.K., Australia, Denmark, Lithuania, Estonia, and Ukraine—blamed the Kremlin.[38] Complicating matters are that even Russian businesses were affected (including Rosneft, the state-controlled oil company) and that the malware used an exploit developed by the U.S. National Security Agency (the "NSA").[39] Russia denied any involvement,[40] and for purposes of the

---

35 Greenberg, *supra* note 34; Andrew Griffin, *'Petya' Cyber Attack: Chernobyl's Radiation Monitoring System Hit by Worldwide Attack*, THE INDEPENDENT (June 27, 2017), https://www.independent.co.uk/news/world/europe/chernobyl-ukraine-petya-cyber-attack-hack-nuclear-power-plant-danger-latest-a7810941.html [https://web.archive.org/web/20210110013646/https://www.independent.co.uk/news/world/europe/chernobyl-ukraine-petya-cyber-attack-hack-nuclear-power-plant-danger-latest-a7810941.html] (Early reports identified the malware as "Petya," which had been discovered in 2016. Only later did Kaspersky Lab's informal name "NotPetya" catch on to differentiate the malware as a distinct variant of Petya. *See* Marvin the Robot, *New Petya / NotPetya / ExPetr Ransomware Outbreak*, KASPERSKY DAILY (June 27, 2017), https://usa.kaspersky.com/blog/new-ransomware-epidemics/11710/[https://web.archive.org/web/20210113112546/ https://usa.kaspersky.com/blog/new-ransomware-epidemics/11710/].).

36 *See* Greenberg, *supra* note 34 ("The weapon's target was Ukraine. But its blast radius was the entire world.").

37 *Id.* (citing "a White House assessment confirmed . . . by former Homeland Security adviser Tom Bossert").

38 *See NotPetya*, COUNCIL ON FOREIGN RELATIONS: CYBER OPERATIONS TRACKER (July 2017), https://www.cfr.org/cyber-operations/notpetya [https://web.archive.org/web/20210111230201/https://www.cfr.org/cyber-operations/notpetya] [hereinafter *CFR Tracker*].

39 *See* Greenberg, *supra* note 34.

40 *Kremlin Slams "Russophobic" Allegations That Pin NotPetya Attack on Russia*, RUSSIAN NEWS AGENCY TASS (Feb. 15, 2018), https://tass.com/politics/990154 [https://web.archive.org/web/20190426092559/ http://tass.com/politics/990154].

war exclusion, the extent to which the cyber-attack was state-funded or state-directed may be critical depending on the precise language of the policy.

3. Mondelez v. Zurich

One affected company was Mondelez International, one of the world's largest snack companies.[41] Mondelez's losses from NotPetya exceeded $100,000,000, including, but not limited to, rendering 1,700 servers and 24,000 laptops dysfunctional, which in turn led to complete disruption of its supply chain and other consequential losses.[42] Mondelez filed a claim with its all-risk property insurer, Zurich.[43] Zurich denied the claim, citing the policy's "hostile and warlike action" exclusion, which stated as follows:

> This policy excludes loss or damage directly or indirectly caused by or resulting from . . . hostile or warlike action in time of peace or war, including action hindering, combating or defending against an actual, impending or expected attack by any:
>
> (i) government or sovereign power (de jure or de facto);
> (ii) military, naval, or air force; or
> (iii) agent or authority of any party specified in i or ii above.[44]

Mondelez sued Zurich for breach of contract in Illinois state court asserting that the war exclusion was ambiguous (and thus should be construed in favor or the insured) and that the exclusion should be applied

41 Complaint at ¶ 4, Mondelez Int'l, Inc. v. Zurich Am. Ins. Co., No. 2018L011008 (Ill. Cir. Ct. Oct. 10, 2018), 2018 WL 4941760 [hereinafter *Mondelez Complaint*].

42 *Id.* at ¶ 10.

43 *Id.* at ¶¶ 6-7, 11. It is important to note that Mondelez filed its claim on a *property* policy, not a *cyber* policy. One reason to prefer true, standalone cyber policies is that the exclusions—including those for war and terrorism—can be written with cyber risks in mind. More certainty attends exclusions that are written with reference to more-clearly foreseen risks.

44 *Id.* at ¶ 13.

narrowly only to the traditional concept of "war" as an armed conflict between nation states.[45]

As the insurer, Zurich will bear the burden of proving the applicability of the exclusion and, thus, will need to prove: (1) that NotPetya constitutes "hostile or warlike action"; and (2) that NotPetya was committed by either a government or agent acting for a government. Here, to attribute NotPetya to Russia poses both taxonomic problems ("What counts?") and evidentiary problems ("How to prove it?") for Zurich.[46]

Mondelez v. Zurich appears to be the first litigated case in which an insurer has invoked an act-of-war exclusion to deny coverage for a cyber attack. How courts have addressed application of the war exclusion in similar cases may forecast how the *Mondelez* court could decide the case.

(a) Taxonomic/Policy Language Application Problems

Consider Hamas. Hamas is a Sunni Islamist group that refuses to accept any recognition of the State of Israel.[47] The U.S. State Department has listed Hamas as a "Foreign Terrorist Organization" since 1997.[48] Universal Cable Productions lost money when its filming operations in Jerusalem were disrupted by Hamas.[49] When its insurer denied coverage for the losses citing exclusions for "war" and "warlike action by a military force," Universal Cable filed suit for breach of contract.[50] The Ninth Circuit held the war exclusion in this television production insurance policy could not apply to Hamas, because it was neither a *de jure* nor a *de*

---

45 *Id.* at ¶¶ 1, 23-38. Another company which had its NotPetya-related claims denied was Merck, which has also sued its insurers, in New Jersey state court. *See* Wan, *supra* note 34, at 1613 n.159. (citing Complaint, Merck & Co., Inc. v. Ace Am. Ins. Co., No. UNN-L-002682-18 (N.J. Super. Ct. Law Div. Aug. 2, 2018), which the present authors have not viewed).

46 *See generally* Bateman, *supra* note 26.

47 *See generally* JIM ZANOTTI, CONG. RSCH. SERV., IF10644, THE PALESTINIANS: OVERVIEW AND KEY ISSUES FOR U.S. POLICY (updated Jan. 28, 2021), https://crsreports.congress.gov/product/pdf/IF/IF10644.

48 Designation of Foreign Terrorist Organizations, 62 Fed. Reg. 52650, 52650 (Oct. 8, 1997).

49 Universal Cable Prods., LLC v. Atlantic Specialty Ins. Co., 929 F.3d 1143, 1149-50 (9th Cir. 2019).

50 *Id.* at 1149-51.

facto sovereign.[51] While the war exclusion in *Mondelez* is explicitly broader than the exclusion at issue in *Universal Cable*, the difficulty of classifying a "Foreign Terrorist Organization"[52] as a government or sovereign state, exemplifies the kinds of questions courts must grapple with when interpreting war exclusions.

Even characterizing NotPetya as hostile or warlike is problematic. Traditionally, war involved physical damage, either to property or to people. Courts could rule that "war" does not include merely corrupting data or interrupting communications. War was also usually directed towards a particular adverse sovereign. But NotPetya had global effects, including on companies run by the same Russian government being blamed for the attack.[53] And kinetic war could be understood to be limited in time by victory, defeat, or surrender whereas many cyber attacks persist over long periods of time that might otherwise be characterized as peaceful.

Finally, characterizing any event as "war" can bring heavy consequences. When President Obama characterized the Sony Pictures hack as mere "cybervandalism," some commentators complained that the U.S. had missed an opportunity to "send a message."[54] It is interesting, however, to note—especially in the context of this article—that it has since

---

51 *Id.* at 1154-55, 1162 (citing Pan Am. World Airways, Inc. v. Aetna Cas. & Sur. Co., 505 F.2d 989, 1005 (2d Cir. 1974) ("[F]or there to be a 'war' a sovereign or quasi-sovereign must engage in hostilities.")).

52 *See Universal Cable*, 929 F.3d at 1159 ("[T]he [U.S.] Secretary of State has consistently designated Hamas as a Foreign Terrorist Organization since 1997."); *see also* 62 Fed. Reg. at 52650.

53 *See* Greenberg, *supra* note 34.

54 *E.g.*, David Rothkopf, *The Sony Hack Is Not 'Cybervandalism'*, CARNEGIE ENDOWMENT FOR INTERNATIONAL PEACE (Dec. 22, 2014), https://carnegieendowment.org/2014/12/22/sony-hack-is-not-cybervandalism-pub-57596 [https://web.archive.org/web/20201217131618/ https://carnegieendowment.org/2014/12/22/sony-hack-is-not-cybervandalism-pub-57596]; *see also* Adam Satariano & Nicole Perlroth, *Big Companies Thought Insurance Covered a Cyberattack. They May Be Wrong.*, NEW YORK TIMES (Apr. 15, 2019), https://www.nytimes.com/2019/04/15/technology/cyberinsurance-notpetya-attack.html [https://web.archive.org/web/ 20210103154802/ https://www.nytimes.com/2019/04/15/technology/cyberinsurance-notpetya-attack.html] ("That label was sharply criticized by Senators John McCain and Lindsey Graham, who called the hack 'a new form of warfare' and 'terrorism.'").

been reported that "the Obama administration had worried, in part, that the use of 'cyberwar' would have triggered the liability exclusions and fine print that Mondelez is now challenging . . . ."[55] So, as with attribution, even governmental characterizations of an action as war (or not) are suspect in the courts.

In addition, the taxonomic problems raised in cyber attacks are further complicated by the variety of relationships that governments may have with cyber attackers. The war exclusion in *Mondelez* expressly provides that it applies to exclude coverage where a non-state actor may act as agent of a state.[56] Some countries allow, encourage, or even reward attackers without explicitly directing them—at what point does a hacker in such a scenario become an agent of the government?[57] As Bateman suggests, "governments might provide general guidance but not oversee individual operations, state-affiliated cyber actors could sometimes act on their own initiative or moonlight on the side, and both parties may use subtle forms of coercion or enticements to influence the other."[58]

For example, Bateman discusses APT41, an important group of Chinese cybercriminals.[59] Though not "official" state agents, "some of

55 Satariano & Perlroth, *supra* note 54 (citing an interview with "John Carlin, the assistant attorney general at the Justice Department at the time").

56 *Mondelez Complaint*, *supra* note 41, at ¶ 13 ("attack by any . . . agent or authority of any party specified . . . above").

57 Minority Staff of S. Comm. on Foreign Rels., Putin's Asymmetric Assault on Democracy in Russia and Europe: Implications for U.S. National Security, S. Prt. No. 115-21, app. D, at 181 (2018) ("Russia's security services have worked with and provided protection to criminal hackers for decades . . . . Despite a wealth of evidence, Putin has long denied any connection between Russia's security services and cyberattacks on foreign institutions."). The same report goes on to explain that the Kremlin protects the activity of cyber criminals in exchange for their services. *E.g.*, *id.* at 182 ("Despite his most-wanted status in the United States and several other countries, [cybercriminal Evgeniy] Bogachev is living openly in a Russian resort town on the Black Sea . . . .").

58 Bateman, *supra* note 26, at 15.

59 *Id.*; see U.S. Dep't of Just. Off. of Pub. Affs., Seven International Cyber Defendants, Including "Apt41" Actors, Charged in Connection with Computer Intrusion Campaigns Against More Than 100 Victims Globally, Press Release No. 20-942, JUSTICE NEWS (Sept. 16, 2020), https://www.justice.gov/opa/pr/seven-international-cyber-defendants-including-apt41-actors-charged-connection-computer [https://web.archive.

these criminal actors believed their association with the [People's Republic of China] provided them free license to hack and steal across the globe."[60] Similarly, in February 2021, three North Korean computer programmers where indicted by a grand jury in California for conspiring to steal and extort more than $1 billion in cyberattacks against banks, entertainment companies, and cryptocurrency traders.[61] It was reported that the hackers were, "pursuing strategic and financial goals of the country's leader, Kim Jong Un" and were working on behalf of a North Korean military agency, the Reconnaissance General Bureau, authorities. Determining whether a hacker constitutes an agent of the state could raise evidentiary issues.

(b) Evidentiary Problems

Generally, interpretation of insurance policies is limited to the four corners of the policy itself. In limited circumstances where the language of a policy is ambiguous, courts may consider extrinsic evidence to aid in interpretation. As of the date of publication of this chapter, the *Mondelez* court has not yet issued a ruling regarding its interpretation of the war exclusion. Such interpretation, of course, must be performed within the context of the Illinois standard policy-interpretation framework that exclusions should be narrowly construed and that ambiguities should be construed against the insurer and in favor of the insured.[62]

---

org/web/20210120171424/https://www.justice.gov/opa/pr/seven-international-cyber-defendants-including-apt41-actors-charged-connection-computer] [hereinafter APT41 Press Release].

60 *APT41 Press Release*, *supra* note 59 (quoting Michael R. Sherwin, Acting U.S. Attorney for the District of Columbia); *see also id.* (quoting Deputy Attorney General Jeffrey A. Rosen warning that "the Chinese communist party has chosen a … path of making China safe for cybercriminals so long as they attack computers outside China and steal intellectual property helpful to China").

61 *North Korean Military Hackers Indicted in Cyber Plot To Rob Banks, Attack Companies; https*://www.latimes.com/california/story/2021-02-17/ north-korea-indictment-cyberattacks-banks-sony.

62 *See, e.g.*, Outboard Marine Corp. v. Liberty Mut. Ins. Co., 607 N.E.2d 1204, 1212, 1217 (Ill. 1992) ("[I]f the words in the policy are . . . ambiguous [they] will be construed in favor of the insured and against the insurer who drafted the policy. . . . This is especially true with respect to exclusionary clauses.") (citations omitted).

In support of its position that the exclusion applies, Zurich will likely seek to introduce evidence of the determinations, both by the U.S. Department of State and by the governments of other countries, that NotPetya was carried out by Russia. Mondelez, on the other hand, will present evidence regarding Russia's denial of any official involvement. Just like in baseball, where the tie goes to the runner—under the traditional rules of insurance-policy interpretation that require narrow interpretation of exclusions and construe ambiguities in favor of the insured, a "tie" regarding responsibility for NotPetya may go to Mondelez.

Thc difficulties of cyber attribution were described by the Office of the Director of National Intelligence as follows:

> Establishing attribution for cyber operations is difficult but not impossible. No simple technical process or automated solution for determining responsibility for cyber operations exists. The painstaking work in many cases requires weeks or months of analyzing intelligence and forensics to assess culpability. . . . [T]he accuracy and confidence of the attribution will vary depending on the available data.[63]

Courts interpreting applicability of the war exclusion may, thus, rely on a "battle of the experts."[64] Further complicating this evidentiary issue, civilian "experts" may not have full access to the knowledge and tools available to DoD or Department of Homeland Security. And the United States government might—for a multitude of reasons—not even disclose its own attribution, even if it makes one. NotPetya was very unusual in having a coordinated, multi-national, declared attribution to Russia.[65]

Moreover, when governments do make an attribution, it will be difficult to use that as evidence in court. First, the government relies on evidence which might not be entered into the court record. Even under

---

63 OFF. OF THE DIR. OF NAT'L INTEL., A GUIDE TO CYBER ATTRIBUTION, at 2 (Sept. 14, 2018), https://www.dni.gov/files/CTIIC/documents/ODNI_A_Guide_to_Cyber_Attribution.pdf [https://web.archive.org/web/ 20201223233721/ https://www.dni.gov/files/CTIIC/documents/ODNI_A_Guide_to_Cyber_Attribution.pdf].

64 *See* Bateman, *supra* note 26, at 14 ("In high-stakes litigation, each side has ample incentive to find friendly experts—or at least someone who can cast doubt on the other side's position.").

65 See CFR Tracker, supra note 38.

seal, the NSA is not likely to give details of all that it used to make an attribution.[66] Second—lest one expect that even a naked governmental attribution would be strong evidence in court—nations have geopolitical motives for both attribution and non-attribution.[67,68]

---

66 The government could be especially hesitant in light of "an apparent compromise of the confidentiality of the [Case Management / Electronic Case Files] system due to . . . a known compromise involving SolarWinds Orion products." U.S. Cts., *Judiciary Addresses Cybersecurity Breach: Extra Safeguards to Protect Sensitive Court Records*, JUDICIARY NEWS (Jan. 6, 2021), https://www.uscourts.gov/news/2021/01/06/judiciary-addresses-cybersecurity-breach-extra-safeguards-protect-sensitive-court [https://web.archive.org/web/20210126203246/https://www.uscourts.gov/news/2021/01/06/judiciary-addresses-cybersecurity-breach-extra-safeguards-protect-sensitive-court] (quotation marks and citations omitted); *see also* U.S. DEPT. OF HOMELAND SEC., CYBERSECURITY & INFRASTRUCTURE SEC. AGENCY, MITIGATE SOLARWINDS ORION CODE COMPROMISE, EMERGENCY DIRECTIVE 21-01 (Dec. 13, 2020; updated Jan. 6, 2021), https://cyber.dhs.gov/ed/21-01/ [https://web.archive.org/web/20210127075029/https://cyber.dhs.gov/ed/21-01/].

67 *E.g.*, Raphael Satter, *U.S. Treasury Confirms SolarWinds Hack as More Officials Blame Russia*, REUTERS (Dec. 21, 2020), https://www.reuters.com/article/global-cyber/u-s-treasury-confirms-solarwinds-hack-as-more-officials-blame-russia-idUSL1N2J11HU [https://web.archive.org/web/20201231220137/https://www.reuters.com/article/global-cyber/u-s-treasury-confirms-solarwinds-hack-as-more-officials-blame-russia-idUSL1N2J11HU] (Top U.S. officials blame Russia for the SolarWinds hack, but "[t]he Kremlin has denied any involvement and President Donald Trump, who has spent much of his term in office defending Russia from various allegations of hacking and interference, downplayed the breach and raised the possibility that China might be involved.").

68 The Stuxnet worm that damaged Iranian nuclear facilities in 2010 is widely attributed to the U.S. and Israel—but neither has acknowledged any responsibility. *See* N.J. Cybersecurity & Commc'ns Integration Cell, *Stuxnet: NJCCIC Threat Profile* (Oct. 10, 2017), https:// www.cyber.nj.gov/threat-center/threat-profiles/ics-malware-variants/stuxnet ("Stuxnet is a computer worm, reportedly developed and launched by the United States and Israel . . . ."); Ronen Bergman & Mark Mazzetti, *The Secret History of the Push to Strike Iran*, THE NEW YORK TIMES MAGAZINE (Sept. 4, 2019), https://www.nytimes.com/2019/09/04/magazine/iran-strike-israel-america.html [https://web.archive.org/web/20210125070213/https://www.nytimes.com/2019/09/04/magazine/iran-strike-israel-america.html] (Cooperation between the U.S. and Israel "culminate[d] in the Olympic Games operation,

Zurich might feel confident in attributing NotPetya to Russia—*i.e.*, "a government or sovereign power."[69] Probably no large cyber attack has ever been so unanimously pinned on one state.[70] But the burden of proving the exclusion lies squarely on Zurich.[71] It remains to be seen exactly how helpful a governmental attribution might (or might not) be.

4. *Proposals*

In addition to the risks that could be covered through a privately insured cyber insurance program, other proposals include a (now partially implemented) federal backstop for cyber insurance.[72] Insurance policy language generally, and coverage exclusions specifically, evolve in response to historical events and circumstances. For example, following the attacks of September 11, insurers introduced new terrorism specific exclusion to preclude coverage for similar September 11-like losses. Claims for losses associated with NotPetya or the more recent SolarWinds attack, will likely lead to similar revisions in policies, including, but not limited to, changes in the language of act-of-war exclusions.

In response to the terrorism-related exclusions following September 11, Congress enacted the Terrorism Risk Insurance Act ("TRIA"), which effectively created a federal re-insurance program for certain officially-designated terrorist attacks. TRIA has been reauthorized several times since it was enacted in 2002, most recently through the Terrorism Risk Insurance Program ("TRIP") Reauthorization Act of

---

which deployed sophisticated computer malware, including the Stuxnet virus, to sabotage Iranian nuclear facilities.").

69 See Mondelez Complaint, supra note 41, at ¶ 13.

70 *But see supra*, note 67 (Stuxnet is widely attributed to the U.S. and Israel.).

71 Steven Plitt *et al.*, 10A COUCH ON INSURANCE § 254:12 (3d ed. 2019) ("The insurer bears the burden of proving the applicability of policy exclusions and limitations . . . after the insured has sustained its burden and made its prima facie case [of coverage].").

72 *See, e.g.*, Aaron Klein & Scott R. Anderson, *A Federal Backstop for Insuring Against Cyberattacks?*, BROOKINGS (Sept. 27, 2019), https://www.brookings.edu/blog/techtank/2019/09/27/a-federal-backstop-for-insuring-against-cyberattacks/ [https://web.archive.org/web/20201030021156/https://www.brookings.edu/blog/techtank/2019/09/27/a-federal-backstop-for-insuring-against-cyberattacks/].

2019.[73] This reauthorization requires the U.S. Government Accountability Office to study cyberterrorism risks including analysis of the potential costs of cyberterrorism, whether the private market is able to price cyber risks adequately, and whether the TRIA structure may be appropriate for allocation of the risks associated with cyber terrorism. In further implementation of TRIP, proposed Treasury Department rules would make certain definitional changes to incorporate the department's prior cyber coverage guidance into the TRIP regulations.[74]

Robust cyber insurance may be critical to boosting the cyber hygiene of the defense industry.[75] While cyber insurance policies continue to develop and evolve, defense contractors should understand unique cyber risks—particularly where, unlike Mondelez, defense contractors are always preparing for war and certainly may be targets for cyber attacks from nation states. In working with an experienced broker and coverage counsel, defense contractors can negotiate for comprehensive coverage of their unique cyber risks.

---

73 Terrorism Risk Insurance Program Reauthorization Act of 2019, Pub. L. No. 116-94, §§ 501-502, 133 Stat. 2534, 3026-27 (Dec. 20, 2019) (extending TRIP through Dec. 31, 2027).

74 Terrorism Risk Insurance Program; Updated Regulations in Light of the Terrorism Risk Insurance Program Reauthorization Act of 2019, and for Other Purposes, 85 Fed. Reg. 71588, 71590 (Nov. 10, 2020) (proposed rule at the time of writing; comment period closed on Jan. 11, 2021, with eighteen comments).

75 *See generally* Cyberspace Solarium Comm'n, *Final Report* (Mar. 11, 2020), https://www.solarium.gov/report [https://web.archive.org/web/20200314183755/https://drive.google.com/file/d/1ryMCIL_dZ30QyjFqFkkf10MxIXJGT4yv/view].

Chapter 13

Technology*

A. An Industry Whose Time Has Arrived and Much More

In this chapter, we will review the progression and the magnitude of what is now considered "technology" and the risks attendant to the use and misuse of technology. We will review how cyber insurance responds to many of these risks, where technology enterprises face expenses or losses related to attacks, disruptions or even as the result of their own negligence. We also will discuss whether some of the challenges for technology companies may be outside the scope of the insurance world, which despite some past criticism from the tech sector, has made strides to meet their challenges, but cannot, and maybe, should not rush to embrace every shiny new tech advance.

B. What is Technology?

Currently, the consensus suggests that "technology" encompasses hardware, software, applications, servers, systems, networks, devices, equipment, components, designs, skills, methods and beyond. Where to begin with that array of concerns? Let's go with "how it began versus how it's going."[1]

---

* By Peggy Reetz.

1 Joe Berkowitz, *'How it Started vs. How It's Going' Has Become the All-Purpose Meme of 2020,* FAST COMPANY (October 30, 2020); https://www.fastcompany.com/90570574/how-it-started-vs-how-its-going-has-become-the-all-purpose-meme-of-2020.

1. A Series of Tubes[2] *and Many Other Wondrous Things*[3]

The initial concept of the internet reportedly goes back as far as 1961.[4] Common attribution is also given to the U.S. Defense Department's Advanced Research Projects Agency Network (ARPANET), which funded development of many of the protocols still in use.[5] The first "link" to be established was between UCLA and SRI (Stanford Research Institute) in September 1969.[6] Margaret Hamilton, a renowned mathematician and computer science pioneer, first coined the term *software engineering.*[7] The discipline was distinguished from hardware engineering and other kinds of engineering, and it became an essential part of the Apollo program. In addition to the formal emergence of software engineering, came the related field of *information technology*, which is defined as "technology involving the development, maintenance, and use of computer systems, software, and networks for the processing and distribution of data."[8]

---

2 Sarah Kliff, *The Internet Is, In Fact, a Series of Tubes*, THE WASHINGTON POST (September 20, 2011) (quoting Sen. Ted Stevens (AK) "viral" remark that the "Internet is a series of tubes").

3 *See* In re Doubleclick Inc. Privacy Litigation, 154 F. Supp. 2d 497, 498 (2001) ("The World Wide Web ('the Web' or "WWW") is often mistakenly referred to as the Internet. However, the two are quite different. The Internet is the physical infrastructure of the online world: the servers, computers, fiber-optic cables and routers through which data is shared online. The Web is data: a vast collection of documents containing text, visual images, audio clips and other information media that is accessed through the Internet.")

4 Jesse Emspak & Kim Ann Zimmermann, *Internet History Timeline: ARPANET to the World Wide Web*, LIVE SCIENCE (June 27, 2017), https://www.livescience.com/20727-internet-history.html.

5 *Id.*

6 Gil Press, *A Very Short History of The Internet And The Web*, FORBES (Jan. 2, 2015), https://www.forbes.com/sites/gilpress/2015/01/02/a-very-short-history-of-the-internet-and-the-web-2/?sh=22ea2c2c7a4e

7 Lori Cameron, *What to Know About the Scientist Who Invented the Term "Software Engineering"*, COMPUTER https://www.computer.org/publications/tech-news/events/what-to-know-about-the-scientist-who-invented-the-term-software-engineering/ ("Problems began when the computer was overloaded with commands. . .Hamilton. . .programmed the computer to prioritize tasks according to importance not sequence.")

8 "Definition of *information technology*, Merriam-Webster.com; https://www.merriam-webster.com/dictionary/information%20technology;

2. *Tech Needs Cover*

Once the age of personal computing and the internet were in full bloom, insurers started to identify a marketplace to provide coverage for specific risks relating to information technology, and to recognize an important need to segregate those risks from other types of coverage.[9] Of course, much of the groundwork for how *information* was to be transmitted grew from advances in the telecommunications industry. Thus, some of the risks are defined in direct relation to those earlier systems (interfaces between systems) and some of the risks are defined in distinction to the earlier advances (the move to cloud-based services as compared to on premises machines).

---

some opine that "information" "technology" goes back centuries. P. Kamkarian, "A Brief History of IT," IT Computer Technical Support Newsletter, Vo. 2, No. 29 (May 23, 2016), Southern Il. Univ., College of Educ. and Human Services; https://ehs.siu.edu/_common/documents/IT%20newsletter/vol-2-no-29.pdf. For purposes of the technology errors and omissions discussion, the focus relates to advances in computing following IBM's introduction of the first large-scale computer in 1944 but really attention to these risks begin, as noted, with advances in personal computing and the invention of the World Wide Web and the internet, which were as of 1989 and 1991, respectively. *Id.*

9 Policyholders first turned to commercial general liability (CGL) carriers seeking coverage for incidents involving disruptions of systems, or disclosures of information but these scenarios did not always fall neatly within those terms and disputes often arose. *See*, NMS Servs., Inc. v. Hartford Ins. Co., 62 F. App'x 511, 514 (4th Cir. 2002) (describing property coverage with a computer and media endorsement and finding that acts of destruction by employees did not preclude coverage). Ward Gen. Ins. Servs., Inc. v. Emp'rs Fire Ins. Co., 114 Cal. App. 4th 548, 554–55 (Cal. Ct. App. 2003) (finding no coverage for costs of recovery of data or business interruption because there was no loss of, or damage to, tangible property; loss of a computer database was not a direct physical loss or damage to covered property under a first-party insurance policy, and rejecting the idea that "*information, qua* information, can be said to have a material existence, be formed out of tangible matter, or be perceptible to the sense of touch").

C. Computers at Risk or Computers Are the Risk—Machines Have Feelings, Too

With the recognition that their clients' business practices were largely online and involved network security, insurance agents and brokers identified that errors or omissions arising out of such day-to-day activity may not be picked up under general liability forms.[10] The early technology professional liability claims arose out of some familiar but almost mundane circumstances:

- Network security administrator wipes out electronic medical records for provider
- Software consultant allegedly does not perform upgrades to client system per specifications
- Denial of service attack disrupts sellers' access to online market platform
- Website developer uses copyrighted material on a client's site
- Negligent acts in creating software products or failure of products to meet certain standards
- Coding errors that result in a failure of product or service[11]

With the rise of digital platforms, social media, and the use of more and different devices means that the professionals who are responsible for setting up and managing these systems or applications have an expanded surface of potential exposures.[12] The latest challenges include managing and storing cloud-based client data, upgrades that fail to timely implement or the installation of defective or malware-exposed software or applications. The last example may be painfully illustrated on a global

---

10 Stephanie K. Jones, *Cyber Insurance: An Evolutionary Coverage*, INS. J. (Dec. 21, 2015), https://www.insurancejournal.com/magazines/mag-features/2015/12/21/391961.htm.

11 Zoom interview with Tammy Kocher, Assistant Vice President, Cyber Underwriting, BCS Financial Corporation, January 27, 2021 (notes on file).

12 "The Rise in Mobile Apps and Need for Tech E&O Insurance," Insurance Market Source (Sep. 19, 2018); https://www.insurancebusinessmag.com/ca/news/specialty-insurance/the-rise-in-mobile-apps-and-need-for-tech-eando-insurance-111638.aspx

scale in light of reports regarding SolarWinds' security products and similar "supply chain" challenges.[13]

D. Dynamic Designs, Displays and Some Downsides

The earliest concerns over how technology was taking over a sector involved financial institutions and the healthcare sector. All that data and the speed with which information needed to be acquired, accessed, managed and stored resulted in many of the information technology developments that soon transformed retail, transportation, media and almost every other aspect of commercial and residential life. If Domino's was going to track orders and deliveries via an app downloaded to customers' phones, they first needed someone to develop the software to locate their stores, their product offerings, the geolocation of their customers in relation to the closest store and to tie all of that into their payment systems. This, of course, means that there are various vulnerabilities along the way: Did the geolocation application function for its intended purpose? Did the application connect to the payment service timely and accurately? Does the design of the application follow the specifications Domino's set out? Does the application include copyrighted information not authorized for use by Domino's?

Given the ubiquity of these applications, it is easy to forget the long and winding road they take to get implemented. The latest in a long line of issues facing these applications and websites are lawsuits alleging that

---

13 On December 13, 2020, Reuters reported that "hackers believed to be working for Russia have been monitoring internal email traffic at the U.S. Treasury and Commerce departments." The reporting suggests that attackers were believed to have tampered with updates released by a software firm called SolarWinds, which serves government customers but also has clients across the U.S. Fortune 500 including MasterCard, Symantec, telecoms, health insurers, accounting firms, and others. See, https://www.reuters.com/article/BigStory12/idUSKBN28N0PG.
SolarWinds Security Advisory stated that they were made aware of a cyberattack on their systems, that inserted a vulnerability within the SolarWinds Orion Platform software; https://www.solarwinds.com/securityadvisory (updated December 15, 2020). The company stated they have been advised that the incident was likely the result of a highly sophisticated, targeted, and manual supply chain attack by an outside nation state, but that they have not independently verified the identity of attacker.

they are not compliant with the Americans with Disabilities Act.[14] While many technology professional liability policies may exclude discrimination claims, whether the design of a system or application was in accordance with compliance specifications potentially is an error or omission by the consultants or designers, thus triggering coverage. Similar issues appear to arise when it comes to making sure devices are BIPA or TCPA compliant.[15]

E. Coverages Can and Have Evolved to Meet Tech Where It's At

For technology enterprises, one essential part of any cyber policy is inclusion of coverage for their own "technology services" or relating to the failure of their "technology products." A review of those terms and comparison to the other coverage grants is a good place to start in evaluating a tech companies' needs.

---

14 *See, e.g.,* Robles v. Domino's Pizza LLC, 913 F.3d 898 (9th Cir.), *cert. denied* (U.S. Oct 7, 2019); Domino's and many other companies have faced class litigation where plaintiffs allege that websites and mobile apps do not work with common screen-reading software. A. Robert, "SCOTUS Rejects Pizza Delivery Company's Appeal Over Web and Mobile App Accessibility," ABA JOURNAL, October 7, 2019, 12:54 PM CDT, https://www.abajournal.com/news/article/supreme-court-rejects-dominos-appeal-over-web-and-app-accessibility.

15 *See, e.g.*, HUB Parking Tech. USA, Inc. v. Ill. Nat'l Ins. Co., No. 2:19-cv-00727-MJH (W.D. Pa. June 19, 2019) (a coverage suit arising from the tender of the class action complaint alleging violations of the Telephone Consumer Protection Act (TCPA), where the maker of parking access and revenue control systems was joined in litigation by the airport parking operator for the allowing computer-generated parking receipts to display eight digits of a credit card; the coverage litigation only addressed security and privacy liability issues but any negligence to properly design the application potentially implicates a tech e&o coverage; similarly, litigation arising under BIPA, the Illinois Biometric Information Privacy Act, potentially could end up with the fingerprint device manufacturer for any failure to properly gain consent for the collection of personal information.

1. *Won't Computers Just Solve All These Problems?*

In the early days of cyber insurance, there were some skeptics. "Why do we need insurance? We know our risks and can solve them better than any insurance company," was a more common refrain than not. While tech companies were some of the earliest takers with respect to purchasing "cyber" coverages, they usually thought in terms of disruptions to an online platform.[16] Most believed they were able to handle the small disruptions but needed some form of backstop. Thus, many of the earlier forms addressed network security issues and technology errors and omissions ("tech e&o"). The forms also responded, in a limited way, to "privacy" allegations, where for example, class action Plaintiffs alleged that their information (e-mail, name, addresses) were being collected by cookies, in violation of certain federal statutes.[17]

2. *Responding to a "Tech" Wrongful Act*

The tech e&o forms initially introduced were patterned after miscellaneous errors and omissions policies, as described in earlier chapters.[18] The initial insurance products, as previously noted, were tailored toward addressing denial of service attacks, unauthorized access

---

16 Bethan Moorcraft, *The Evolution of Cyber Insurance-Where Are We Now?* INSURANCE BUSINESS MAGAZINE)6 February 2019) (Quoting James Burns of CFC Underwriting: "Business interruption is almost like the prodigal son of the cyber insurance market," he said. "If you look right back to the 1990s / early 2000s when cyber insurance policies were first developed, there was no meaningful privacy legislation, even in the US. At that point cyber insurance was all about business interruption. It was developed for the first breed dot-com companies, who were trading online and therefore had big exposure to system downtime. . .The product really took off in the US because privacy is quite an easy concept for consumers to understand and for brokers to sell.")

17 *See supra,* note 3, In re Doubleclick Privacy Litigation; Plaintiffs alleged violations of the Electronic Communications Privacy Act; Court found that the cookies' identification numbers fell outside of the statute's scope.

18 Mark Camillo, *Cyber Risk and the Changing Role of Insurance*, 2 J. CYBER POL'Y 53, 53 (2017); *see also*, *Tech E&O is a must for technology firms*, https://www.insuretrust.com/cyber-liability/technology-eo/ (last visited Jan. 28, 2021).

and unauthorized use of information.[19] These were "named perils" that were formatted to address technology errors and omissions.[20] The terms included a basic "pay on behalf of" insuring agreement, and then the scope of the coverage would be tied to key definitions like "computer system," "professional services," and the list of perils reflected under "wrongful act." The earlier list of "wrongful acts" often included libel/slander, invasion of privacy, misappropriation of ideas, liability for failure to prevent hacks, liability for negligence in respect of media content, denial of service attacks, negligent transmission of viruses, and/or misuse of confidential information. Many of those "wrongful acts" would subsequently find a place under separate coverage grants in what would become cyber policies.

In light of a changing regulatory environment, the risk profile relating to privacy and network challenges proved to be too much to fit into a single "wrongful act" definition or insuring provision. As a result, addressing specific technology errors and omissions have, for the most part, been likewise subsumed into a list of insuring provisions, along side security, privacy, regulatory, breach response, media and then other first party loss provisions now standard in the true "cyber" forms. In other words, the privacy, security, media and other wrongful acts would evolve to have their own insuring agreements and the tech e&o now sits along side these coverage grants.[21] Some forms are broken into sections, or modules, for the sake of further setting apart what is a "technology professional service." While stand-alone tech e&o forms are more the exception than the rule these days, some insureds or brokers prefer this approach for the sake of clarity regarding their particular services or products.

As a result, technology errors and omissions forms (or insuring agreements) will include the following typical coverage provisions:[22]

We will pay those sums that the insured must pay as "damages" . . . resulting from a claim alleging a wrongful act . . .

---

19 Jones, *supra* note 6.

20 *Id.*

21 R. DeNatale & B. McDonald, *The Guide to Cyber Investigations: Insurance*, Global Investigations Review (19 June 2019); https://globalinvestigationsreview.com/guide/the-guide-cyber-investigations/first-edition/article/insurance.

22 *See, e.g.*, Travelers Prop. Cas. Co. of Am. v. Fed. Recovery Servs., Inc, 156 F. Supp. 3d 1330 (D. Utah 2016).

"Wrongful act" means any negligent act, error or omission in the insured's performance of "technology professional services" for others . . . [for a fee][23]

"Technology professional services" means those services described . . . in endorsement . . .

The services also may be listed or spelled out in a policy endorsement, typically following how the insured described "professional services" in the application for coverage. The basic framework is close to miscellaneous errors and omissions terms, except with greater specificity relating to the "technology" aspect of the professional service. For example, the form definitions may include a list of services provided or activities involving: the creation, development, distribution, license, lease, sale or training of any information technology, data processing, information services, installation, design, development, integration or configuration of a computer system; training, consulting, data collecting, software programming, maintenance of computer equipment, products, components, networks or systems. Some policyholders insert specific types of services or activities to highlight the service or product that falls just inside or outside one of these general types of descriptors (e.g., application developer for a unique sector or industry).[24]

3. Data Is Gonna Data

Amazon Web Services (AWS) reportedly stores over 100 trillion objects.[25] About one-third of all daily internet users will access a website built on AWS infrastructure at least once a day. The estimated number of servers for the top tech companies is 1.4 million for Amazon, 1 million

---

23 Some policies leave out the "for a fee" language. For example, see AIG's Specialty Risk Protector®, a copy of which was disclosed as part of the docket in a customer data breach class action, *In re SuperValu, Inc., Customer Data Security Breach Litigation*, 870 F.3d 763 (8th Cir. 2017). *See also,* New Hotel Monteleone, LLC v. Certain Underwriters at Lloyd's of London, No. 2:16-cv-00061 (E.D. La. dismissed Aug. 17, 2016) (copy of Ascent™ CyberPro US v1.4, effected by Underwriters at Lloyd's of London; policy disclosed in pleadings);

24 *See* Travelers and New Hotel Monteleone, *supra.*

25 Liam Tung, *AWS: S3 Storage Now Holds over 100 Trillion* Objects, ZDNET (March 15, 2021); https://www.zdnet.com/article/aws-s3-storage-now-holds-over-100-trillion-objects/.

plus for Google, 1 million plus for Microsoft, hundreds of thousands for Facebook and the list goes on.[26] So, great; that's for the big boys. What about your small and medium business enterprises? Managed Service Providers ("MSPs) are the type of vendor smaller organizations will depend upon for managing their day-to-day technology needs.[27] Their most popular services are hosting and storage/backup.[28] As more and more organizations accept that they have a lower level of tolerance for managing in-house hardware and all other manner of IT infrastructure, reliance on MSP services will continue to rise. Using MSP or outsourced IT does not always relieve an organization of its responsibility (or liability) with respect to managing customer or client information. However, this does mean that as a "tech" provider, the MSPs are on the frontlines of data security and privacy issues.

In this regard, in addition to a "technology" problem, having coverage for the costs related to privacy breaches, including response expenses and any regulatory inquiry is another key to managing their risk exposure. The MSPs and outside IT providers typically have terms of service with clients that address standards for transferring, handling or storing data and capacity for continuity of services. This may include acting as business associates for covered entities (healthcare providers) in accordance with HIPAA requirements. This may also include adhering to NIST compliance guidelines, if acting on behalf of any type of critical infrastructure.[29]

---

26 Daniel Price, Infographic: How Much Data Is Produced Every day, Adeptia; https://cloudtweaks.com/2015/03/how-much-data-is-produced-every-day/; as of 2018, Forbes reported that there were 2.5 quintillion bytes of data created each day; *see*, Bernard Marr, *How Much Data Do We Create Every Day? The Mind-Blowing Stats Everyone Should Read*, FORBES (May 21, 2018). "The amount of the new created data in 2020 was predict to grow 44X to reach 35 zettabytes (35 trillion gigabytes)." Gil Press, *6 Predications About Data in 2020 And The Coming Decade*, Forbes (January 6, 2020); https://www.forbes.com/sites/gilpress/2020/01/06/6-predictions-about-data-in-2020-and-the-coming-decade/?sh=72306a284fc3.

27 *The Growth of Managed Service Providers: Why are they Necessary?* https://blog.etech7.com/the-growth-of-managed-service-providers-why-are-they-necessary.

28 Kimberly Mlitz, *Managed Services Market Size Forecast Worldwide 202-*2026, STATISTA (June 8, 2021); https://www.statista.com/statistics/590884/worldwide-managed-services-market-size/.

29 Jackson Barnett, *New Guidelines from NIST on How To Avoid Cyberattacks From a Nation State*, FEDSCOOP (February 5, 2021); https://

Speaking of data, what if it goes "missing?" If you are the entity responsible for your client's or customer's data assets, having data asset loss coverage or a similar first party provision is another significant way to manage the risk. Losing a client's data probably is not a great marketing scheme but having the ability to recover financially from such a calamity is critical. This type of coverage will define the asset as that which is owned or in the care, custody or control of the insured, or that for which they are legally responsible (including where such care, custody or control is outsourced by the vendor). Thus, the good news is that those who rely upon you for holding their data, and those that you rely upon, hopefully can benefit if the assets are gone for good.

4. A Not-So-Social Network

In light of this challenging environment, tech companies big and small should benefit from network security and privacy liability coverages available in most popular cyber forms. Again, even the best and the brightest will require the assistance of outside counsel and vendors in the event of an attack or disruption. The in-house teams at the tech companies are well aware that bringing an incident response team, with forensic expertise, is the best way to ensure evidence is preserved and the post-incident activities are in accordance with other regulatory and compliance frameworks. Given that the data may be stored with another service provider, a covered entity or the client of the provider may actually send out notification letters to their clients or customers but ultimately, the vendor likely will be liable for the costs.

As recent history illustrates, the bad actors are targeting the providers and vendors that serve the needs of large financial institutions, retailers, healthcare providers, utilities, and even governmental agencies. Having

---

www.fedscoop.com/nist-800-172-cybersecurity-guidelines/ (In new guidelines, issued in the wake of the SolarWinds incident, the National Institute for Standards and Technology has new advice for contractors that handle sensitive information, which should have been in place for federal government contractors, e.g., implementing strong password protocols, multifactor authentication, automated tracking of unauthorized users on a network.) (See discussion *infra*, at paragraph F.)

robust extortion coverage in place is a necessary for those entities that are at the heart of these "supply chains."[30]

5. *Down But Not Out*

Given this inter-reliance and interconnectedness, the vendors and providers try to have their own redundancies and work-arounds in the event that there is an attempt to take them "offline." Even if they think they can keep their clients' access to systems and data up and running, invariably, there are disruptions to the smooth operations of their data management and applications. In that regard, these are the entities that should take full advantage of available first party business loss coverages. The goal is to have coverage for total and partial failures, suspensions, interruptions or even measureable deterioration or degradation in their systems, and even for *their* dependent systems. It may be that they continue to "service" their clients but they may be dragged down by having to decrypt systems, revert to back-ups, and deploying other assets and tools.

6. *Thick as a Brick*

Some malware has the ability to disable a device altogether. Seems pretty sci-fi but it is a "thing."[31] This is another in a list of first party coverages where cyber insurers pricked up their ears to their policyholders and responded. In that regard, where an electronic device, from desktop to laptop, from digital cameras to game systems, can be rendered useless due to malware, there are many policies that will respond to that as a "loss." The coverage may include recovery for costs to replace a component of a computer system (including hardware or electronic equipment). Usually this relates to where the data is stored, for purposes of identifying why the hardware is part of the organization's essential infrastructure. The

---

30 Leeann Nicolo, *Monitoring Cyber Insurance Supply Chain Risks*, PROPERTY AND CASUALTY 360 (March 23, 2021); https://www.propertycasualty360.com/2021/03/23/monitoring-cyber-insurance-supply-chain-risks/?slreturn=20210631104235 ("In a cyber supply chain, third parties own every piece of a company's technology.").

31 Robert Earl Wells III, *What Does Bricking a Device Mean?,* LIFEWIRE (updated January 6, 2020); https://www.lifewire.com/what-does-bricking-a-device-mean-4685834.

coverage may be triggered on the basis that such equipment is no longer operable or functional. The coverage typically will not apply to what may be deemed "updates" or "upgrades," although some insurers have introduced "betterment" coverages in recent years.[32]

7. *We Know Better Than That*

While most technology companies or MSPs are likely being targeted as a way to get to their clients, and to extort or disrupt their activities generally, there is a chance that these "smart guys" are not immune from the social engineering tactics that plague thc rest of us. Most of the tech companies are well aware that their technologies are being used for great and not-so-great purposes.[33] Some of these same companies though have accounting departments and personnel who handle everyday supplier and payroll transactions. Hopefully, their protocols are as stringent as any when it comes to verifying requests for changes in payment instructions. But, they call it "social engineering" for a reason—the attackers do their best to dupe even the most sophisticated organizations. In that regard, MSPs, IT providers, tech companies big and small would be wise (and at the level of most of their customers) if they procured coverage for fraudulent funds transfer incidents and other scams that divert funds from authorized parties.

---

32 Mia Wallace, *Travelers Reveals How Its Enhanced Cyber Product Came* About, INSURANCE BUSINESS MAGAZINE (07 May 2020); https://www.insurancebusinessmag.com/uk/news/cyber/travelers-reveals-how-its-enhanced-cyber-product-came-about-221810.aspx.

33 Mark Latonero, *Opinion: AI For Good Is Often Bad,* WIRED (November 19, 2019); https://www.wired.com/story/opinion-ai-for-good-is-often-bad/; David Campbell, *Pandemic Has Shown Us The Good and Bad of Technology,* THE SYDNEY MORNING HERALD (January 31, 2021); https://www.smh.com.au/lifestyle/life-and-relationships/pandemic-has-shown-us-the-good-and-bad-of-technology-20210117-p56us8.html; University of Plymouth *Tech Companies Not Doing Enough To Protect Users from Phishing* Scams, SCIENCE DAILY (30 July 2019); https://www.sciencedaily.com/releases/2019/07/190730083656.htm.

F. Tech is Everywhere But Not Everything Is Covered

Most cyber policies exclude bodily injury and property damage claims. However, there are carve-backs in some forms when it comes to "emotional distress" relating to a privacy incident, and more recently, some broad cyber forms address specific types of property loss as noted above ("bricking," for example)[34] arising out of security incidents. Likewise, any tech e&o form or clause would be subject to the bodily injury and property damage exclusions. Originally, the tech e&o forms were specifically written as a way to distill the coverage for liability arising out of data hosting, processing, analysis, network services and software programming.[35] The insurers were not looking to replace hardware (property damage); and, indeed, before the internet of things,[36] there was little expectation that a programming error would result in bodily injury but the exclusion was an appropriate fit in the professional liability context.[37]

---

34 C. Hoffman, *What Does 'Bricking' a Device Mean?*, HOW-TO-GEEK (Sep. 26, 2016, 5:36 PM EST); https://www.howtogeek.com/126665/htg-explains-what-does-bricking-a-device-mean/.

35 T. Finger, *General Liability Insurance vs. Errors & Omissions Liability*, ILLINOIS TECH.ORG/NEWS (Sept. 16, 2016), https://www.illinoistech.org/news/374981/General-Liability-Insurance-vs.-Errors--Omissions-Liability.htm.

36 D. Turgel, *How the IoT Presents a New Path for Insurance*, PROPERTY CASUALTY 360 (Jan. 29, 2020, 12:00 AM), https://www.propertycasualty360.com/2020/01/29/how-the-iot-presents-a-new-path-for-insurance/?slreturn=20210028204845 (The "internet of things" or "IoT" is in reference to connected devices that d not require human intervention to respond to or adapt to the physical environment, or in reaction to changing data. S. Ranger, *What is the IoT? Everything You Need to Know about the Internet of Things Right Now*, ZDNET (Feb. 3, 2020 14:45 PM GMT), https://www.zdnet.com/article/what-is-the-internet-of-things-everything-you-need-to-know-about-the-iot-right-now/.

37 *Compare*, Am. Guarantee & Liab. Ins. Co. v. Ingram Micro, 2000 WL 726789 (D. Ariz. Apr. 18, 2000) (power outage knocked out systems, causing loss of data, software functionality; court found there was "property damage" per CGL terms; *see also*, America Online, Inc. v. St. Paul Mercury Ins. Co., 347 F. 3d 89 (4th Cir. 2003) discussion regarding whether data, information or instructions are "tangible property" and "impaired property" under exclusion for loss of use of tangible property that is not physically damaged. Some policy forms use.

As in the rest of the cyber forms, and other miscellaneous errors/omissions forms, intentional or dishonest acts are excluded but a defense is allowed prior to a "final" decision on that act. The breach of contract exclusion typically will include a carve-back for "unintentional" breaches of contract for "technology professional services," and some terms mention breach of a privacy policy is also carved-back.

Defining the "insured" in the policy also is a way to include or exclude various employees, part-time employees, contractors, or sub-contractors who may be involved in any development of a service or product. To the extent that the insured's in-house team needs to rely on a contractor for data processing, analysis, systems design or configurations, the insured likely will assume that coverage would extend to these professionals as well. However, to avoid capturing an entirely separate entity or professional, often the policy terms will specify that contractors or agents must be acting on behalf of the named insured, at their direction and under their control. Where a policyholder has a formal joint-venture arrangement for a particular service or product, they may seek to add their joint-venture partner as an additional insured to avoid any confusion about the scope of the risk.[38]

Government investigations (except maybe for privacy-related issues, as noted above) or enforcement actions are not typically covered.[39] However, for technology issues, there is a carve-back for those claims brought by a government entity if in fact the insured entered into a contract for the provision of technology services.

Terrorism is always a consideration when it comes to various cyber events and there is always a concern about whether exclusions for "acts of terrorism" would swallow up the coverage because many malicious acts and attacks are reportedly perpetrated by groups controlled or sponsored by states like Russia or North Korea.[40] In the case of technology

---

38 J. Buchanan, M. Gallozzzi, *Top Tips and Traps for Cyber Insurance Buyers*, INSIDE PRIVACY, Covington & Burling (Nov. 2, 2017), https://www.insideprivacy.com/data-security/cybersecurity/top-tips-and-traps-for-cyber-insurance-buyers/.

39 DeNatale *supra* note 16.

40 A great deal of ink gets spilled about the need for "reform" or clarity following the news of major attacks like NotPetya and now in the aftermath of the SolarWinds disclosure. *See*, A. Klein, S. Anderson, *A Federal Backstop for Insuring Against Cyber Attacks*, Brookings Institute, TECHTANK (Sept. 27, 2019); *Encouraging Clarity in Cyber Insurance*

professional services, to the extent that a vendor or sub-contractor has been specifically targeted by "state sponsors" of terrorism, this can be a significant issue.[41] Most often, "attribution" to a particular actor is a significant hurdle to claiming that an incident or attack is an "act of terrorism." Also, the standard terrorism exclusions include varying definitions to qualify the act as "terrorism" (separate and apart from TRIA,[42] which defines terrorism for purposes of triggering specific federal intervention).[43] Was the act by force? Was it committed with a political, religious or ideological purpose to influence government or the public? For those consultants and vendors charged with designing and implementing various software programs, and in particular, security applications and programs, more and more they may be perceived as gateways to larger organizations, or organizations with more valuable information. Many insurers recognize that their policyholders would be concerned about getting caught up in such events and as a result, technology professionals and their brokers will look for those policies that include a carve-back for "cyber terrorism," or maybe language that carves-back acts "perpetrated electronically."[44]

Coverage, https://www.brookings.edu/blog/techtank/2019/09/27/a-federal-backstop-for-insuring-against-cyberattacks/; OECD (2020), Encouraging Clarity in Cyber Insurance Coverage: The Role of Public Policy and Regulation, www.oecd.org/finance/insurance/Encouraging-Clarity-in-Cyber-Insurance-Coverage.pdf.

41 Y. Vindman, *Is the SolarWinds Cyberattack an Act of Ware? It Is, If the United States Says It Is*, LAWFARE BLOG, (Jan. 26, 2021, 1:24 PM); https://www.lawfareblog.com/solarwinds-cyberattack-act-war-it-if-united-states-says-it.

42 *Terrorism Risk Insurance Act (TRIA)*, The Center for Insurance Policy and Research, National Association of Ins. Comm'rs (Dec. 15, 2020); https://content.naic.org/cipr_topics/topic_terrorism_risk_insurance_act_tria.htm.

43 J. Wolfe, B. Pierson, *Suspected Russian Hack of U.S. Government: Espionage or Act of War?* INSURANCE JOURNAL (Dec. 21, 2020), https://www.insurancejournal.com/news/national/2020/12/21/594810.htm.

44 R. Anderson, *Does Your Cybersecurity Policy Cover Cyberterrorism?* ADVISEN NEWS (June 5, 2014), https://www.advisenltd.com/2014/06/05/does-your-cybersecurity-policy-cover-cyberterrorism/.

G. "Who Are Those Guys?"[45]

One refrain from forensic investigators is that the bad actors will not stop looking for ways to exploit a system or an application.[46] In addition to keeping up with their internal demands, organizations are often tasked with keeping up with various industry standards either because of a regulatory or compliance framework, or because one of their business partners or stakeholders has insisted on it. If your organization is in any way involved with the U.S. defense contractor sector, for instance, you may have been asked whether you are NIST compliant. This is in reference to the National Institute of Standards and Technology framework for computer security guidance for the private sector.[47] These types of standards do tend to trickle down to various contractors, vendors, agents, facilitators, and the like. Whether some of these protocols are always achievable and whether insurers can expect full compliance is a moving target. Other regulatory standards contain slightly more straightforward guidance but still leave room for interpretation.[48]

---

45 This was the constant refrain from Paul Newman as Butch Cassidy in scenes from *Butch Cassidy and The Sundance Kid* (Campanile Products, Newman-Foreman Company; released by 20th Century Fox 1969); Butch and Sundance cannot seem to shake the scent of a posse of presumed law enforcement in chase.

46 H. Pasha, *What Should CISOs Do in the Post-COVID Era?* SECURITY ROUNDTABLE (Sep. 28, 2020), https://www.securityroundtable.org/what-should-cisos-do-in-the-post-covid-era/ ("The COVID-19 pandemic has created new opportunities for bad actors. . .[but] we would be foolhardy to assume that the attacks will stop.").

47 H. Sekara, *NIST Cybersecurity Framework—The Key to Critical Infrastructure Cyber Resiliency*, TRIPWIRE (Jan. 24, 2021), https://www.tripwire.com/state-of-security/ics-security/key-critical-infrastructure-cyber-resiliency/.

48 D. Silver, C. Tucciarello, *NYDFS Files First Enforcement Action Under Reg 500*, THE NATIONAL LAW REVIEW, Vol. XI, No. 29 (Aug. 17, 2020), https://www.natlawreview.com/article/nydfs-files-first-enforcement-action-under-reg-500 regarding compliance with NYDFS cybersecurity guidelines; see also, gaps in HIPAA privacy framework discussed, J. Harrod, D. Utter, *Health Data Privacy: Updating HIPAA to Match Today's Technology Challenges*, HEALTH DATA PRIVACY BLOG, The Graduate School of Arts and Sciences, Harvard University (May 15, 2019), http://sitn.hms.harvard.edu/flash/2019/health-data-privacy/.

These standards and guidelines, however closely an entity can adhere to them, at the very least provide a backdrop for what is expected regarding data security and privacy, especially when acting on behalf of another organization. Despite what appears now to be a well-trod path toward mitigating risks, many CISOs seem skeptical that cyber insurance is a critical part of that toolkit.[49] The insurers, of course, continue to look for evidence of more controls, and more detection or monitoring systems.[50] Insurers will want details regarding indemnification terms, testing frequency, how customers are allowed to log in and log off, how a client may seek recourse for a failed product or service and whether security is embedded in the first instance.[51] There is more accountability being required from the customer (some may be old enough to remember when 'tech never worked.')

H. The More Things Change, the More They . . . Never Stay the Same

While there seems no end to innovations in the digital and electronic space, there is a through line to these risks. The SolarWinds news seems to have gained the attention of board rooms and news outlets but the seasoned cyber underwriter will remind them that they have always had an eye out for vendor issues.[52] Cyber insurers have been talking about vendor exposure for a long time. They are well aware that rather than the hospital system handling their electronic medical records in-house, it became cheaper and more reliable to use the expertise of a data storage company (we used to call this "outsourcing" but there are now supply-chain vendor management issues to keep CISOs up at night). More

---

49 D. Raywood, *CISOs: Cyber Insurance Fails to Cover Modern Threats and Remote Workforces*, INFOSECURITY MAGAZINE (23 Jul 2020), https://www.infosecurity-magazine.com/news/cisos-cyber-insurance-cover/.

50 *Id.*

51 Kocher, *supra* note 8.

52 Kocher, *supra* note 8. J. Miller, C*an the SolarWinds Incident Spur More Action, Less Talk About Supply Chain Security?* FEDERAL NEWS NETWORK (Jan. 25, 2021 4:31 pm); https://federalnewsnetwork.com/reporters-notebook-jason-miller/2021/01/can-the-solarwinds-incident-spur-more-action-less-talk-about-supply-chain-security/.

recently, these are harder placements for brokers to make.[53] The market has been hardening for the technology industry and the claim activity has been high.[54] The most difficult insureds remain those servicing healthcare and financial services entities. Managed service providers, those firms that can provide the "cloud" services platforms, as discussed more and more have been targeted for attacks and disruptions.[55] Often the outside provider or vendor is seen as a choke point for what is happening on the front lines for these high-profile sectors. In addition, there are so many new access points and more systemic issues to consider.[56]

Gone are the days when the focus for insurers was on the tech start-up world and that start-up they were underwriting only developed one neat thing. It used to be enough to worry about negligent design and distribution. There is a great deal of overlap now amongst the risks—which bucket does it fall into—security, privacy, or technology?[57] The insureds get the benefit of the doubt in most data security incident scenarios. However, given that playing field, it is hard to ignore the redundancy in some of these terms and the situations that potentially implicate the terms.

In addition, even if an underwriter assumed that the insured was not primarily in the business of technology, many companies use off-the-shelf software to develop products or services in-house, without the assistance of an outside developer or designer. If the company finds success in-house, they may find they have a niche product or service to offer to their clients and customers. They are not a tech company. They do not have a huge staff. But along the way they developed something marketable. It may only be by reading press releases that an underwriter would know to quiz the insured on the technology behind what they are offering since they do not consider themselves "tech."

These same firms will be required to have some form of insurance to get in the door with the larger organizations. Some of the concerns may be

---

53 Telephone interview with Chris Cotterell, Chief Executive Officer/Founder, Safeonline, January 27, 2021 (notes on file).

54 *Id.*

55 L. Whitney, *US Secret Service Warns About Increased Cyberattacks against MSPs*, TECH REPUBLIC (Jul. 8, 2020, 5:30 AM PST), https://www.techrepublic.com/article/how-managed-service-providers-can-pose-a-risk-to-their-customers/.

56 Kocher, *supra* note 8.

57 Kocher, *supra* note 8.

old but some of the ways bad actors are getting in are more and more sophisticated. Most large organizations now outsource much of their IT, data storage and other related services. As these entities try to squeeze their budgets, it means that there are more vendors, contractors and sub-contractors to track. Hopefully, most of their errors or omissions can be captured in meaningful insurance policy terms.

Chapter 14

Cyber Risk Management and Insurance for Telecommunication Companies*

A. Industry Introduction and Overview

Telecommunications ("Telecom") includes all data and communications transmitted outside of direct human-to-human verbal communication. This chapter focuses on the businesses that shape our telecommunications infrastructure and the unique data and cyber risks they carry.

The Telecom industry began in the 1830s[1] with the introduction of the telegraph. Revolution struck the industry in 1979[2] with the introduction of the first current day cellular network, also known as 1G (First-Generation). Commercial mobile phones originated in the US in 1983.[3] 2G's introduction in 1991[4] brought about the ability to transfer data packets such as text messages and remains the backbone of coverage in many rural areas. The introduction of 3G in 1999[5] provided vastly increased data transfer speeds, enabling internet browsing on mobile devices and subsequently created the smartphone market. 4G increased the

---

* By Dennis Logan Jr.

1 History.com Editors, "Morse Code & the Telegraph," History.com (A&E Television Networks, November 9, 2009), https://www.history.com/topics/inventions/telegraph.

2 "1G." Wikipedia. Wikimedia Foundation, January 24, 2021. https://en.wikipedia.org/wiki/1G.

3 "Cell Phone Development," Motorola Solutions USA—Motorola Solutions, accessed February 1, 2021, https://www.motorolasolutions.com/en_us/about/company-overview/history/explore-motorola-heritage/cell-phone-development.html.

4 "2G," Wikipedia (Wikimedia Foundation, January 12, 2021), https://en.wikipedia.org/wiki/2G

5 "3G," Wikipedia (Wikimedia Foundation, January 12, 2021), https://en.wikipedia.org/wiki/3G.

upload/download speeds by three times 3G in 2009,[6] making voice through data possible. 5G[7] capable devices have been created with the infrastructure and applications to use the increased bandwidth capabilities of 4-10 times 4G speeds quickly developing. Near future capabilities may include truly autonomous driving cars/drones, remote robotic surgery, and replacement of traditional Wifi (Home broadband).

Telecom regulations have been written with much ambiguity, particularly regarding data collection. The Radio Acts of 1912[8] and 1927[9] are the framework for most communications laws[10] to date; which required radio stations to carry licenses and be "in the public interest, convenience, or necessity," respectively. The Communications Act of 1934 established the Federal Communications Commission (FCC) with the intent to prevent telephone and radio monopolization. The Communications Act of 1996 sought to "let anyone enter any communications business—to let any communications business compete in any market against any other."[11]

The first acts to make a national impact regarding data privacy for consumers were the Privacy Act of 1974,[12] Health Insurance Portability and Accountability Act (HIPAA,1996[13]), Gramm-Leach-Bliley Act

---

6 "4G," Wikipedia (Wikimedia Foundation, January 12, 2021), https://en.wikipedia.org/wiki/4G.

7 "5G," Wikipedia (Wikimedia Foundation, January 31, 2021), https://en.wikipedia.org/wiki/5G.

8 "Radio Act of 1912," Wikipedia (Wikimedia Foundation, August 25, 2020), https://en.wikipedia.org/wiki/Radio_Act_of_1912.

9 "Radio Act of 1927," Wikipedia (Wikimedia Foundation, April 8, 2020), https://en.wikipedia.org/wiki/Radio_Act_of_1927.

10 Sean Ross, "Government Regulated Impact on the Telecommunications Sector," Investopedia (Investopedia, August 29, 2020), https://www.investopedia.com/ask/answers/070815/how-does-government-regulation-impact-telecommunications-sector.asp.

11 "Telecommunications Act of 1996," Federal Communications Commission, December 30, 2014, https://www.fcc.gov/general/telecommunications-act-1996.

12 "Privacy Act of 1974," The United States Department of Justice, January 15, 2020, https://www.justice.gov/opcl/privacy-act-1974#:~:text=The%20Privacy%20Act%20of%201974,of%20records%20by%20federal%20agencies.

13 "Health Insurance Portability and Accountability Act of 1996 (HIPAA)," Centers for Disease Control and Prevention (Centers for Disease Control and

(1999,[14] 15 U.S.C. § 6801), and Children's Online Privacy Protection Act (COPPA, 2000). These provided data protection guidelines for government agencies, financial sector, healthcare and children. They did not, however, address the enormous amount of new data about individuals that would be created and stored by Telecom.

The Net Neutrality Act of 2015 was enacted to prevent internet service providers from "intentionally blocking, slowing down, or charging"[15] consumers money for specific online content. California's Consumer Privacy Act (2018) protects "how data is collected, managed, shared and sold by companies and entities doing business with or compiling information about California residents."[16] Given no company would like to exclude California residents from its potential customer base, the CCPA is the first customer data privacy act with national implications. Additional states[17] have proposed new bills similar to CCPA, however currently there is disagreement among states on the definition of Personal Identifiable Information (PII), sensitive data and the penalty for breached privacy.

B. Internet Service Providers and Telecommunications Carriers

Service providers and Telecom carriers coordinate all the physical infrastructure, digital signal processing hardware and software needed to communicate data from one device to another. Because they handle the subscriber and payment information, they are high profile targets for cyber attacks. Attackers seek to directly affect Telecom operations or target their

---

Prevention, September 14, 2018), https://www.cdc.gov/phlp/publications/topic/hipaa.html.

14 Gramm–Leach–Bliley Act. (2021, January 05). Retrieved February 01, 2021, from https://en.wikipedia.org/wiki/Gramm%E2%80%93 Leach%E2%80%93Bliley_Act.

15 Net neutrality in the United States. (2021, January 15). Retrieved February 01, 2021, from https://en.wikipedia.org/wiki/Net_neutrality_in_the_ United_States.

16 Oct 28, 2. (n.d.). Your Data Is Shared and Sold . . . What's Being Done About It? Retrieved February 01, 2021, from https://knowledge.wharton.upenn.edu/article/data-shared-sold-whats-done/.

17 3/29/2020, A. (2020, March 30). Complete Guide to Privacy Laws in the US: Varonis. Retrieved February 01, 2021, from https://www.varonis.com/blog/us-privacy-laws/.

subscribers, with assistance of additional social engineering data gained from the providers' systems.

There have been lawsuits related to privacy of customer information,[18] which focus on safekeeping of other telecommunication carriers, equipment manufacturers, and customers[19] as a result of carrier data breaches. However, the CCPA's guidelines do not apply specifically to providers or carriers. It only states that businesses must "implement and maintain reasonable security procedures and practice."[20] "While these alleged failures may constitute technical violations of the CCPA, under a plain reading of the statute, they do not give rise to a private right of action."[21]

C. Cell Towers

The physical infrastructure of cell towers is relatively similar across all cellular generations. Towers are key components of telecommunication; they are used to magnify the signals transmitted by cellular devices. The radio waves are differentiated by bandwidth (i.e. 2G, 3G, 4G) and by service provider. The towers are constructed by companies that acquire real estate, design, engineer, construct and manage the tower site. The slots or cells are then rented out by service providers. The towers transmit/receive the signals and, in some cases, use fiber optic cables to transfer the signal to another tower to finally transmit the signal to the subscriber. Fiber optic transmissions travel at a slower rate than radio waves, increasing latency but capable of maintaining larger bandwidths.

18 LII / Legal Information Institute. 2021. *47 U.S. Code § 222—Privacy of customer information.* [online] Available at: <https://www.law.cornell.edu/uscode/text/47/222> retrieved 8 August 2021.

19 47 U.S. Code § 222—Privacy of customer information. (n.d.). Retrieved February 01, 2021, from https://www.law.cornell.edu/uscode/text/47/222.

20 Spelman, K. (2020, October 20). Class Actions Seek to Test the Limits of the CCPA's Private Right of Action. Retrieved February 01, 2021, from https://www.law.com/therecorder/2020/10/20/class-actions-seek-to-test-the-limits-of-the-california-consumer-privacy-acts-private-right-of-action/?sl return=20210101000736.

21 Spelman, K. (2020, October 20). Class Actions Seek to Test the Limits of the CCPA's Private Right of Action. Retrieved February 01, 2021, from https://www.law.com/therecorder/2020/10/20/class-actions-seek-to-test-the-limits-of-the-california-consumer-privacy-acts-private-right-of-action/.

Tower companies do not take ownership of the transmitted data, they only record the subscriber's location details on the device used. This data has been used by one insurance company[22] to attempt to deny a property damage claim. Law enforcement-only approved devices like Stingray[23] can trick subscribers' phones into connecting with the cell tower-mimicking device instead of the designated local tower. This can be used to track a suspect's location and/or communicate messages. It has been used to manipulate multi-factor authentication.

In 2018, *Carpenter v. United States*[24] set a safeguard for citizens by requiring a warrant for the collection of tower data history. This is in contrast to the 1979 *Smith v. Maryland*[25] decision, which "held that information voluntarily shared with a third party is not protected by the Fourth Amendment."[26]

Towers have not faced much data and cybersecurity litigation. Litigation more often occurs regarding bodily injury, property damage and land-rights disputes. Cell tower management companies still have cyber liability exposures similar to any public or private company where software and the internet are used for communications, client management and business operations.

D. Satellites

Satellites are also an integral part of the Telecom industry. They are mostly managed by private parties or national entities like NASA. To date there have been no confirmed successful cyber attacks on orbiting satellites or ground stations., resulting in interruption or physical damage.

---

22 Docket for *Bentley v. State Farm Fire & Cas. Co.*, No. 3:15-cv-00052. Retrieved February 01, 2021, from https://www.courtlistener.com/docket/4619992/bentley-v-state-farm-fire-and-casualty-company/.

23 Newman, L. (n.d.). One Small Fix Would Curb Stingray Surveillance. Retrieved February 01, 2021, from https://www.wired.com/story/stingray-surveillance-cell-tower-pre-authentication/.

24 *Carpenter v. United States*. 138 S.Ct. 2206 (2018).

25 *Smith v. Maryland*, 442 U.S. 735 (1979).

26 *Id.* at 744; Supreme Court Holds Search Warrant Needed To Obtain Cell Tower Location History. (n.d.). Retrieved February 01, 2021, from https://www.greenspunlaw.com/blog/search-warrant-needed-to-obtain-cell-tower-records.cfm.

Experts agree it is a matter of when, not if an event will occur. James Turgal, managing director of Cyber Risk Services at Deloitte and Touche advises that "the main areas of concern have to be the human factor and the supply chain."[27] Human error is the number one cause of cyber claims for all industries. Turgal continues "satellites and systems are made from thousands of parts manufactured in places both inside and outside the U.S., vulnerabilities can be built in by threat actors—which can cause greater levels of access to the satellite system as a whole."[28]

On September 17, 2020, the United States Department of Justice indicted three Iranian hackers for computer intrusions at United States satellite companies. "The defendants successfully compromised multiple victim networks, resulting in the theft of sensitive commercial information, intellectual property, and personal data from victim companies, including a satellite-tracking company and a satellite voice and data."[29] Andy Davis adds, "the trend of cheaper Commercial Off The Shelf (COTS) hardware, open source software and new initiatives such as Ground Stations-as-a-Service . . . increases the likelihood of a cyber-attack significantly."[30] "The industry has proved to be proactive, adopting defense practices . . . that provide an air-gapped hyper-realistic environment to test, "vulnerabilities, misconfigurations and software bugs on precise network replications."[31]

---

27 Holmes, M. (2019, October 14). The Growing Risk of a Major Satellite Cyber Attack. Retrieved February 01, 2021, from http://interactive.satellitetoday.com/the-growing-risk-of-a-major-satellite-cyber-attack/ ("Holmes").

28 *Id.*

29 Nine Iranians Charged With Conducting Massive Cyber Theft Campaign on Behalf of the Islamic Revolutionary Guard Corps. (2018, March 23). Retrieved February 01, 2021, from https://www.justice.gov/opa/pr/nine-iranians-charged-conducting-massive-cyber-theft-campaign-behalf-islamic-revolutionary.

30 Holmes.

31 Thompson, L. (2020, June 12). ManTech 'Space Range' Simulates Cyberattacks On Satellites & Ground Stations To Bolster Defenses. Retrieved February 01, 2021, from https://www.forbes.com/sites/lorenthompson/2020/06/12/mantech-space-range-simulates-cyberattacks-on-satellites--ground-stations-to-bolster-defenses/?sh=52ce752240f7.

E. Fiber Optics

Optic cables are used in a number of industries from automotive to medical. They are versatile in that they are as thin and can be as cheaply produced as copper wires and transmit data through light. This means they can be used to illuminate a car or human body with minimal invasion. Specifically for telecommunications, fiber optic cables vastly increased the ability to transmit large amounts of data, 60 Tbps+ compared to 10Gbps using copper.[32] Fiber optic cables quickly became a cornerstone of communications networks both locally and intercontinental with lines running underground and underwater. Not unlike traditional telephone cords (made of copper) with the correct hardware and software, fiber optic lines are also tappable, often without little to no interference or knowledge to the authorized parties.

Fiber optics litigation, similar to cell towers, thus far, have involved land rights disputes. There have been allegations of government-sponsored and targeted fiber optic splicing attacks, however, there has been no public litigation regarding resulting data breaches.

F. Digital Signal Processing Hardware

The signal transferred from the sender's device travels through satellite, cell towers, and/or fiber optic cables, finally reaching the receiver's digital signal processing hardware. Hardware is responsible for the amount of data a device can process and how quickly. Digital Signal Processing (DSP) hardware is used in several industries most notably in cellular telecommunications. For example, Apple developed its own DSPs labeled 'bionic' chips, claiming to provide increased security with top performance capabilities. In the Android market, the 'Snapdragon' DSP chip[33] is used by Google, Samsung and many other manufacturers in their smartphones.

---

32 Copper vs. Fiber—Which to Choose? (n.d.). Retrieved February 01, 2021, from https://www.multicominc.com/training/technical-resources/copper-vs-fiber-which-to-choose/.

33 1, R. (2020, November 06). Top 5 Mobile Processor Companies List. Retrieved February 01, 2021, from https://www.techgeek360.com/top-5-mobile-processor-companies-list/.

The 'Snapdragon' chip came under heavy global scrutiny after vulnerabilities were exposed that allowed unauthorized parties to access and disable users' devices without their consent. The vulnerabilities have been addressed, however, each of the billion[34] vulnerable users needed to update their phone. Given the lack of education and awareness regarding cybersecurity, millions of devices may continue to be highly vulnerable.

G. Software

After the data is communicated to the DSP it is translated into the correct software application or "app." These apps may process, store, or transmit data on the device or through the cloud. The regulations on data storage for app creators apply according to the data they collect. Many applications may use a single cloud with different processes. Although the term cloud endears no physical storage, it is the opposite in practice. Clouds are collections of numerous physical servers that communicate stored data through the internet. The origin of cloud storage was intended for large file storage or computing. The physical servers may be managed by a separate entity from the app provider or, in the case of Apple/iCloud, they are managed by the same entity.

H. The Cloud

Cloud providers face, possibly, the most cyber liability exposure because they are highly desirable targets given their vast amounts of diverse data and internet reliant services. Emetic reported that according to surveys from 300 CISOs, 80% suffered "at least one cloud data breach in the past 18 months, and 43% reported 10 or more breaches."[35] The breach of Blackbaud is an example of the systemic loss a single breach can

---

34 Dan Goodin—Aug 8, 2. (2020, August 08). Snapdragon chip flaws put 1 billion Android phones at risk of data theft. Retrieved February 01, 2021, from https://arstechnica.com/information-technology/2020/08/snapdragon-chip-flaws-put-1-billion-android-phones-at-risk-of-data-theft/.

35 Nearly 80% of Companies Experienced a Cloud Data Breach in Past 18 Months. (2020, June 05). Retrieved February 01, 2021, from https://www.securitymagazine.com/articles/92533-nearly-80-of-companies-experienced-a-cloud-data-breach-in-past-18-months.

cause. Blackbaud "managed, maintained, and secured" the data and servers for "schools, healthcare providers, non-profits, and other organizations."[36] The breach resulted in several lawsuits against Blackbaud including accusations of "negligence, invasion of privacy, breach of express contract, breach of implied contract and negligence per se."[37]

Risk-averse insurance markets are reluctant to offer coverage to cloud providers due to the systemic business interruption loss and notification costs that the breach of a single cloud provider could cause. Coverages will vary greatly depending on the data stored, security posture and risk mitigation tools used. Multiple carriers and high retentions may be needed to cover necessary exposures even for low revenue cloud provider applicants.

United States consumer law is being crafted to protect consumers and establish clear indemnification methods for data breaches, but insurance policies have not yet responded.

I. Coverage Grants

As claim severity and frequency increases across all industries, Telecom industries have not been left out. At this time, any company in the Telecom supply chain should be able to obtain coverage for all agreements found in existing cyber insurance policies. Carriers and underwriters are just beginning to truly differentiate coverages and limits by industry. Notification costs, business interruption, and regulatory defense will likely become sub-limited or excluded entirely as they are the largest loss drivers across all industries. Given the massive systemic nature of telecommunications, notification costs, (cyber) business interruption and regulatory defense may be covered better by, or in tandem with, stand-alone notification costs, (cyber) business interruption and regulatory defense policies. The costs for these stand-alone policies can be cost inhibitive for smaller companies, particularly for software and hardware

36 Errick, K., By, & Errick, K. (2020, September 15). Cloud Software Company Blackbaud Sued Over Ransomware Attack And Data Breach—Tech. Retrieved February 01, 2021, from https://lawstreetmedia.com/ tech/cloud-software-company-blackbaud-sued-over-ransomware-attack-and-data-breach/.

37 *Id.*

companies as their systemic reach, and therefore exposure, may outreach their anticipated budget.

Cyber extortion is also on the list of coverages that will likely soon be sub-limited or excluded from existing cyber insurance policies due to severe losses across all industries. The policy language regarding network security/privacy liability should be reviewed thoroughly and should include coverage for breaches caused or originating by vendors. Acts of terrorism should be kept in mind as well when reviewing policy language; as the cyber warfare is becoming more evident, it is more likely the government may declare an attack as an act of terrorism, which has coverage implications that varies by carrier.

Chapter 15

Hospitality and Leisure Industry*

Because of the personalized nature of the hospitality and leisure industry, the industry presents unique cybersecurity vulnerabilities. This chapter addresses those unique vulnerabilities, as well as case law regarding liability for data breaches in the industry and risk mitigation through insurance and best practices.

A. Unique Data-Based Aspects of the Hospitality Industry

The hospitality industry is a highly competitive field that relies on customer satisfaction and brand loyalty, which is often fostered through creating a more personalized experience for each guest. In order to personalize each guest's visit, the hospitality industry collects personal and financial data through its loyalty programs and reservation systems. Each reservation may result in the collection of personal data, credit card information, passport numbers, driver's license numbers, and loyalty program numbers. In order to provide customers with an expected personalized experience, the industry not only collects personal data but also provides integrated services in order to furnish the customer with a seamless experience. Therefore, hotels have numerous access points to their customer data, including the reservation system, hotel restaurants, spas, and stores.

It is this very trove of personal and financial information and data that makes the hospitality industry an attractive target for cyber criminals. In fact,

> [a]ccording to PwC's [PricewaterhouseCoopers'] *Hotels Outlook report 2018-2022*, the hospitality industry has the second-largest number of cybersecurity breaches after the retail sector. According to Trustwave Holdings, Hospitality was the third-most targeted industry in 2018, after Retail and Finance. Almost all major hotel brands were affected by a data breach in the past several years. This is the new alarming reality, in which

---

* By Deborah W. Yue and Debbie Sines Crockett.

customers' personal information is being stolen and often sold on dark web black markets.[1]

A few examples of the unique vulnerabilities of the hospitality industry to cybersecurity breaches include:

- Point of Sales (POS) systems;
- Reservation system;
- Loyalty programs;
- Interconnected electronic services;
- Ransomware and malware;
- Spearfishing attack;
- Phishing;
- WiFi network; and
- Human threats.

B. Liability Concerns in the Hospitality Industry

The fact that the hospitality industry is data-based and interconnected exposes those in the industry to a number of cyber threats. Those threats, and the potential liability exposure for the businesses as a result, are well illustrated by a number of litigation matters that have arisen as a result various types of cybercrime.

1. *Exposure Related to Data Breaches in the Hospitality Industry*

One of the first notable data breaches in the hotel industry involved the Wyndham Worldwide Corporation. Between April 2008 through January 2010, the Wyndham experienced three separate breaches. In the case of *FTC v. Wyndham*,[2] the Federal Trade Commission ("FTC") filed suit against the organization for the data breaches that resulted in a landmark ruling in favor of the FTC. In fact, Wyndham had practically no

---

1 *Cyber Threat Report Leisure & Hospitality Industry*, Intsights Defend Forward, http://wow.intsights.com/rs/071-ZWD-900/images/Cyber%20Threat%20Report%20Gaming%2C%20Leisure%20%26%20Hospitality%20Industry.pdf.

2 799 F.3d 236 (3d Cir. 2015).

security measures in place in that the hotel stored customer credit card information in readable text, allowed remote access into hotel systems using easily guessed passwords, and failed to use available firewalls to limit access to Wyndham's corporate network.[3] Compounding on the lack of adequate and appropriate data security, Wyndham was accused of deceptive practices and misleading its customers because its own published privacy policy misrepresented its cybersecurity.[4] The FTC alleged that, "contrary to [Wydham's published privacy policy, it] did not use encryption, firewalls, and other commercially reasonable methods for protecting consumer data."[5] Though not an insurance coverage dispute, this case confirmed the FTC's broad authority to regulate cybersecurity in private industries—like hotels.

Since the Wyndham breaches, nearly every major hotel brand has experienced data breaches. One of the largest breaches on record is the Marriott International breach. Starting in 2014 and continuing through the Fall of 2018, the data breach compromised the personal information of nearly 400 million customers who made reservations at Starwood-branded hotels, which Marriott acquired in 2016, making Marriott the world's largest hotel chain and making this data breach one of the largest in U.S. history.[6] Hackers exploited vulnerabilities in the hotel's network to access the guest reservation system and stole customer data.[7] Though Marriott discovered the breach in September 2018, Marriott did not publicly disclose it until November 2018. At that time, Marriott admitted that there had been unauthorized access to the guest reservation database which contained personal customer information, including names, mailing addresses, phone numbers, email addresses, over 5 million unencrypted passport numbers, over 20 million encrypted passport numbers, loyalty program account information, dates of birth, gender, arrival and departure dates, reservation dates, communication preferences, credit card numbers

---

3 *Id.*

4 *Id.* at 241.

5 *Id.*

6 In Re: Marriott Int'l, Inc. Customer Data Breach Sec. Litig., 440 F.Supp.3d 447, 454-455 (D. Md. 2020).

7 *Id.*

including expiration dates and information needed to decrypt cardholder data.[8]

As a consequence of this breach, in January 2019, a putative nationwide data breach class action suit, *In Re: Marriott Int'l, Inc. Customer Data Breach Sec. Litig.*,[9] was filed against Marriott International, Inc. on behalf of 176 Plaintiffs from all fifty states, the District of Columbia, Puerto Rico, and the Virgin Islands.[10] Like the *FTC* case against Wyndham, while not an insurance coverage dispute case, it is notable because in such cases throughout the country, standing has been an insurmountable hurdle for the plaintiff. In *In Re: Marriott*, on February 21, 2020, Judge Grimm largely denied Marriott's motion to dismiss, thereby allowing Plaintiffs to move forward with their post-data breach consumer class action against Marriott, specifically finding that Plaintiffs had standing in that their allegations of having suffered injury-in-fact were sufficient.[11]

2. Exposure Related to Multiple Access Points

In addition to the volume of data collected by the hospitality industry through its reservation system and loyalty programs, the hospitality industry is uniquely interconnected and, therefore, allows for a number of access points to its data. As an added convenience for its guests, often the hotel gift shop or hotel restaurant are connected to the hotel's payment processing system to allow guests to charge their restaurant bill to their hotel room. These point-of-sale (POS) breaches have impacted a number of hospitality brands, from the Hyatt to Kimpton Hotels & Resorts.

One of the earliest POS breaches was in 2015, when White Lodging Services Corporation, which is an independent hotel management company, announced that its point of sales system at its hotel restaurants and lounges suffered a malware attack.[12] In 2016, the Intercontinental

---

8 *Id.*; *Marriott International News Center*, MARRIOTT.COM, (Nov. 30, 2018), https://news.marriott.com/news/2018/11/30/marriott-announces-starwood-guest-reservation-database-security-incident.

9 In Re: Marriott, 440 F.Supp.3d 447 (D. Md. 2020).

10 *Id.* at 454-455.

11 *Id.* at 457.

12 Nicole Perlroth, *Latest Sites of Breaches In Security Are Hotels*, NY TIMES, Jan. 31, 2014, https://www.nytimes.com/2014/02/01/technology/latest-sites-of-breaches-in-security-are-hotels.html.

Hotels Group (IHG) announced that the POS system at its managed restaurants at 12 of its U.S. properties were attacked by malware. As a result, over 1000 of its hotels were affected and customers' credit card payment data were exposed.[13] While theft of personal and financial information is not new and has impacted other industries, the Sabre Hospitality Solutions hack in 2017 was a wakeup call to the hospitality industry. While many hospitality brands had taken some steps to protect its customers' personal data, it is worth noting that some of the hotel operators themselves may not retain their customers' financial data and, instead, opted to utilize third party vendors, such as Sabre Hospitality Solutions, to process their reservations.

In the Sabre Hospitality hack, Sabre's reservation system, SynXis Central Reservation system, was breached. As a result, it impacted several global properties of Hard Rock Hotels & Casinos, Four Seasons Hotels and resorts, Trump Hotels and Lowes Hotels. In Sabre's investigation, the data breach lasted approximately 7 months.[14]

3. *Exposure Related to Use of Technology*

In addition to cybersecurity threats to customers' personal and financial data, unlike many other industries, the hospitality industry is particularly reliant upon technology in its day-to-day operation of each property. Therefore, the industry faces a number of unique cybersecurity threats that impact not only data but also their physical properties. Having electronic key card access to guest rooms, parking lots, and garages is commonplace. Many properties, however, also have connected technology that controls the HVAC system, elevators, plumbing, lights, and sprinklers.

In 2017, guests at the Romantik Seehotel Jaegerwirt, a 111-year-old historic lakeside hotel in the Austrian Alps, were locked out of their hotel rooms by a cyberattack on the hotel's computer system. Although this was the second time the hotel was hacked, the hackers were able to access the

---

13 Steven Musil, *Scope of Data Breach at InterContinental Hotels Expand*, www.cnet.com, Apr. 19, 2017, https://www.cnet.com/news/scope-of-data-breach-at-intercontinental-hotels-expands/.

14 Esther Hertzfeld, *Sabre's Data Breach Expands to Four Seasons, Trump Hotel*, HOTEL MANAGEMENT (July 13, 2017, 12:13 P.M.), www.hotelmanagement.com, https://www.hotelmanagement.net/sabres-data-breach-hits-four-season-trump-hotels.

hotel's key card system and installed ransomware to prevent guests from accessing their rooms. The hackers demanded the equivalent of $1,800.00 in Bitcoins as ransom, which the hotel chose to pay in order to avoid inconveniencing their guests. In response to the ransomware attack, the hotel considered returning to physical keys instead of electronic key cards.[15]

4. Exposure Related to Human Threats

While the Romantik Seehotel Jaegerwirt ransomware incident demonstrates the unique cybersecurity vulnerabilities of the hospitality industry, the largest security threat to the hospitality industry, as with many other industries, is the human threat. Ninety-five percent of cybersecurity breaches are caused, intentionally or unintentionally, by humans. The hospitality industry employs hundreds of thousands of workers around the world, many of whom are seasonal workers, and experiences a high turnover rate. Therefore, the hospitality industry faces cyberthreats such as ransomware and malware from an employee clicking on a malicious link or data thefts from a disgruntled employee at a rate that may be higher than many other industries.

A common threat to the hospitality industry is a spearfishing attack. In these attacks, a hacker calls the hotel complaining that they are unable to make a reservation on the website and, instead, asks to email their reservation details. When the hotel employee opens the file, the malware is released into the hotel's computer system.

On March 31, 2020, Marriott International announced that it discovered another data breach through the use of login credentials of two employees at a franchise property. The 2020 breach may affect up to 5.2 million customers' data.[16] Data breaches in the hospitality industry, however, are not limited to hotels but extend into the cruise industry.

---

15 Dan Bilefsky, *Hackers Use New Tactic at Austrian Hotel: Locking the Doors*, THE NEW YORK TIMES (Jan. 30, 2017), https://www.nytimes.com/2017/01/30/world/europe/hotel-austria-bitcoin-ransom.html.

16 *Marriott International News Center*, MARRIOTT.COM, (March 31, 2020), https://news.marriott.com/news/2020/03/31/marriott-international-notifies-guests-of-property-system-incident.

In March 2020, Norwegian Cruise Line announced a data breach through a travel agent partner's portal.[17] That same month, Carnival Corporation announced that two of its cruise lines, Holland America and Princess Cruises, experienced data breaches when its staff fell victim to phishing emails that resulted in the exposure of personal data of its customers and workers contained in employee emails. The breaches occurred between April and July 2019. In October 2020, Carnival Corporation announced another data breach caused by ransomware.[18]

The shared hospitality industry, such as Airbnb, is not immune from cybersecurity breaches. As with traditional hospitality brands, Airbnb customers are subject to phishing scams as well as fake host accounts. In addition, Wi-Fi networks at Airbnb sites are a source of data thefts. Cybercriminals need only access to the Airbnb host's router to reset the password or install malware or monitoring software. Recently, Airbnb hosts had their information exposed as a result of internal software issues at Airbnb.[19]

C. Insurance Coverage Cases in the Hospitality Industry

The cyberthreats in the hospitality and leisure industry, and breaches that resulted, have been the subject of various lawsuits filed against the hotel brands, owners and operators. The notable insurance coverage cases involving disputes about insurance coverage for cyberattacks and the hospitality industry are *New Hotel Monteleone, LLC v. Certain*

---

17 Davey Winder, *Norwegian Cruise Line Hit By Data Breach As COVID-19 Continues to Impact Travel Industry*, FORBES (March 20, 2020, 10:09 A.M. EST), https://www.forbes.com/sites/daveywinder/2020/03/20/ norwegian- cruise-line-hit-by-data-breach-as-covid-19-continues-to-impact-travel-industry/?sh=376f518a5ecd.

18 *Carnival Corporation & Plc Identified Ransomware Incident*, https://www.carnivalcorp.com/news-releases/news-release-details/carnival-corporation-plc-identifies-ransomware-incident.

19 Charlie Osborne, *Airbnb May Be Exposing Private Host Inbox Messages, Bookings and Earnings Data, ZDNet (Sept. 25, 2020, 10:56 GMT)*, https://www.zdnet.com/article/airbnb-security-incident-may-be-leaking-host-inbox-messages-bookings-information.

Underwriters at Lloyd's of London,[20] and *St. Paul Fire & Marine Ins. v. Rosen Millennium, Inc.*[21]

1. *Hospitality Insureds Beware: Understand Your Coverage*

New Hotel Monteleone involved disputes about whether fraud recovery, operational reimbursement, and case management fee losses resulting from a cyber-attack were covered under the cyber policy under the "Payment Card Industry Fines or Penalties Endorsement" ("PCI").[22] Hotel Monteleone's complaint alleged that it had been family-owned for more than a century, had been the target of at least two cyberattacks—security breaches that compromised credit and debit card numbers, and had been exposed to hundreds of thousands of dollars in liabilities.[23] Hotel Monteleone pleaded that the first cyberattack was in 2013, which "resulted in liabilities assessed against Hotel Monteleone in the form of operational fraud and operational reimbursement" in excess of $200,000.00.[24] The Hotel Monteleone complaint further asserted that it "has been held liable for multiple types of losses as a result of the 2014 cyberattack," including "fraudulent charges" and the cost of replacing credit and debit cards.[25] Hotel Monteleone did not have a cyber-insurance policy at the time of the 2013 attack, but later purchased one, wanting to make certain that it would have coverage against "fraudulent charges and the costs of replacing payment cards as a result of a cyberattack."[26]

The cyber policy that Hotel Monteleone purchased was called a "Cyberpro Insurance Policy" from Ascent Underwriting, a specialist managing general agent underwriting on behalf of a number of Lloyd's Syndicates.[27] For the next series of cyberattacks it incurred, Hotel Monteleone expected that the full policy limit of $3 million would be available to cover its alleged losses, which included not only PCI fines and assessments, but also fraudulent charge reimbursement and card

20 2:16-cv-00061 (E.D. La. Jan. 15, 2016).
21 337 F.Supp.3d 1176 (M.D. Fla. 2018).
22 New Hotel Monteleone, LLC v. Certain Underwriters at Lloyd's of London, 2:16-cv-00061 (E.D. La. Jan. 15, 2016).
23 *Id.*
24 *Id.*
25 *Id.*
26 *Id.*
27 *Id.*

replacement.[28] In response, the insurer asserted that the $200,000.00 limit in that endorsement applied to all claims arising from a cyberattack against the hotel.[29] Following removal to federal court, the placing broker brought a third-party action against the wholesaler, alleging that it had advised the wholesale broker of the earlier attack involving "fraud recovery and operational reimbursement" from credit card brands, and that it relied on wholesaler's expertise regarding cyber coverage.[30] On August 17, 2016, the case was dismissed with prejudice, and no significant opinions or rulings ever resulted in that case.[31]

An important lesson from the case is that, although Hotel Montelone believed the cyber policy it purchased was sufficient, and relied upon insurance brokers and agents it trusted had the proper expertise, its coverage claims were denied, as a result of the actual terms of the policy issued. This case is merely one example to demonstrates that policyholders are looking to their brokers to guide them through the cyber insurance marketplace, yet there is still much confusion and misunderstanding about the scope of cyber insurance, the products available, and the types of coverages (and exclusions) applicable. When a business selects an agent or broker to place such coverage, it is important to ensure that the agents and brokers actually understand the policyholder's business and the unique threats to that business. At the same time, it is equally imperative for policyholders to educate themselves about cyber security, so that they can defend their business against it, as well as understand the coverage that may be afforded by cyber policies they purchase.

2. *Service Providers Beware: Verify the Scope of Coverage*

In 2016, the hotel chain Rosen Hotels & Resorts, Inc. discovered a data breach at one of its hotels that affected its customers' credit cards used at the hotel.[32] The data breach resulted from the installation of malware on the hotel chain's payment network by a third party.[33]

---

28 *Id.*

29 *Id.*

30 *Id.*

31 *Id.*

32 St. Paul Fire & Marine Ins. v. Rosen Millennium, Inc., 337 F.Supp.3d 1176 (M.D. Fla. 2018).

33 *Id.* at 1180.

The policyholder was Rosen Millennium, Inc., an information technology company, that performed IT services for the hotel chain.[34] The policyholder provided a Notice of Claim to the insurer, inquiring whether the policy provided insurance coverage for the data breach which the hotel chain was asserted resulted from the insured's negligence in providing services.[35] In response, St. Paul sent a reservation of rights letter disclaiming coverage for the loss, and then filed a declaratory judgment action against Millennium, seeking a judgment to determine whether St. Paul had a duty to defend Millennium from the hotel chain's claims.[36]

The court first ruled that, because the policyholder did not make a claim for property damage or the costs incurred for complying with notification statutes in its Notice of Claim, the issue of whether the commercial general liability ("CGL") policies would cover those claims was not ripe.[37] With respect to the policyholder's remaining claims under the personal injury provisions of the policies, the court found that since St. Paul never admitted the existence of coverage, it did not waive its ability to deny coverage.[38]

The court then concluded that the plain language of the CGL policy did not require St. Paul to defend the policyholder because the hotel chain's claims were not covered under the personal injury provisions of the policies.[39] Specifically, the CGL provided coverage for "personal injury," defined as an "injury, other than bodily injury or advertising injury, that's caused by a personal injury or offense," including "[m]aking known to any person or organization covered material that violates a person's right of privacy."[40] Although the policies did not define the term "making known," the parties agreed that the term meant "to publish."[41] The interpretation and application of the policy language "making known" was dispositive for the court.[42] The court found because the alleged injuries resulted from the actions of third parties, not the actions of the policyholder, the personal injury claim was not covered under the CGL

---

34 *Id.*

35 *Id.* at 1181.

36 *Id.*

37 *Id.* at 1182-1183.

38 *Id.* at 1183-1184.

39 *Id.* at 1185-1186.

40 *Id.*

41 *Id.*

42 *Id.*

policy, and St. Paul had no duty to defend the insured IT company, Millennium.[43] Because it was not the policyholder, Millennium, that had "made known" the information, but rather a third party, there was no coverage under the policy for Millennium.[44]

D. Cases Discussing a Hotel's Liability to Its Customers

There are a number of cases that illustrate the scope of risk and exposure that hotel have to their own customers when customer data is stolen through cyberattacks on the hotel's computer files and databases. These cases are helpful to understand, once again, the scope of exposure that hotels face in the context of cyber attacks.

Driscoll v. Trump Int'l Hotels Management LLC,[45] was a class action filed against Trump International alleging that it failed to keep payment information secure, enabling data hacks of his personal and financial data. Trump International acknowledged that hackers had gained unauthorized access to the plaintiff's credit card data by hacking the computer network that processed credit card transactions.[46] The plaintiff alleged that in addition to failing to prevent the data breach, Trump International failed to take action in response to the hack and failed to timely and adequately notify its customers.[47] The case was dismissed by stipulation in December of 2015, without any disclosed settlement terms or any other information.[48]

Walters v. Kimpton Hotels & Rest. Grp., LLC,[49] was also a class action case filed by customers whose credit card information was stolen. In August 2016, Kimpton Hotel disclosed that malware had been installed on its servers by hackers and mailed notification letters to those guests who used their credit cards during that period.[50] The breach resulted in unauthorized charges that had been used at a Kimpton hotel restaurant.[51] The plaintiff was a guest at a Kimpton Hotel during the relevant time and

---

43 *Id.*

44 *Id.*

45 3:15-cv-01089-DRH-SCW (S.D. Ill. Oct. 2, 2015).

46 *Id.*

47 *Id.*

48 *Id.*

49 6-CV-05387-VC, 2017 WL 1398660 (N.D. Cal. Apr. 13, 2017).

50 *Id.*

51 *Id.*

alleged that after his stay, his credit card information was stolen. After learning of the breach, the customer alleged that he expended time and effort to monitor his credit, and that he faced increased risk of identity theft due to the breach.[52]

The court rejected Kimpton Hotel's motion to dismiss a proposed class action arising from a data breach, finding that the named plaintiff sufficiently alleged imminent harm to establish standing notwithstanding the failure to allege that his personal information had actually been misused.[53] The court explained that a plaintiff did not need to "actually suffer the misuse of his data or an unauthorized charge before he has an injury for standing purposes," and that allegations of imminent harm due to his personal information being at risk of being stolen were sufficient to establish standing.[54]

The plaintiff alleged damages of paying for credit-monitoring services and suffering other out-of-pocket expenses, which the court determined were actual damages sufficient to allow claims of breach of implied contract, negligence, and a violation of California's unfair competition law to survive.[55] The court found that efforts to monitor one's credit following identity theft was sufficient to demonstrate injury-in-fact.[56] Eventually, a settlement was reached which included, *inter alia,* Kimpton's agreement to implement new security measures to safeguard consumer data and prevent further data breaches.[57]

Lastly, the case of *Dugas v. Starwood Hotels & Resorts Worldwide, Inc.,*[58] was also a class action filed by customers whose credit card information was stolen. In April 2014, the customer systems of Starwood Hotels and Resorts Worldwide, Inc. ("Starwood") had malicious software installed which led to a data breach that affected hundreds of thousands of customers of the Starwood hotel system."[59] The data was not discovered by Starwood until about a year later, and even then Starwood did not notify its customers or regulators of the data breach until about 6 months later when Starwood revealed "that hackers had breached its database

---

52 *Id.*
53 *Id.*
54 *Id.*
55 *Id.*
56 *Id.*
57 *Id.*
58 16-cv-00014-GPC-BLM, 2016 WL 6523428 (S.D. Cal. Nov. 3, 2016).
59 *Id.*

containing sensitive records including: names, credit card numbers, security codes and expiration dates."[60]

The court dismissed all but one of the plaintiff's data breach claims against Starwood in a proposed class-action lawsuit over a 2014 data breach.[61] As to that one remaining claim, the court found that Plaintiff sufficiently alleged in his complaint, at the pleading stage, a legal duty and a corresponding breach as to inadequate security measures.[62] The plaintiff alleged that he was injured by Starwood's violation of the California Customer Records Act (§1798.81.5) in that its cybersecurity was deficient, and, more specifically that "Starwood, among other things, failed to 'appropriately encrypt customers' data in its possession."[63] The plaintiff also pleaded that Starwood's "security systems and protocols" should have been designed, implemented, maintained, and tested "consistent with industry standards and requirements."[64] The court determined that the plaintiff made a plausible showing, sufficient for pleading purposes, to demonstrate that his injuries are "fairly traceable" to the Starwood breach.[65]

Notably, the court stated, "where the plaintiff did not assert that he suffered any unreimbursed losses from the unauthorized use of his credit card or that he was unable to use credit thereafter, and merely alleged that he was 'exposed' to economic losses," the plaintiff did not demonstrate injury-in-fact.[66] Moreover, the court explained that, "where sensitive personal data, such as names, addresses, social security numbers, and credit card numbers are improperly disclosed or disseminated into the public—thereby increasing the risk of future harm to the plaintiff—injury-in-fact has been sufficiently alleged." In the case, the personal information stolen was limited to plaintiff's name, address, and credit card information, and because the credit card has since been cancelled (and no social security numbers were compromise), the court found that the plaintiff did not sufficiently allege a credible threat of future identity theft, which was needed in order to plead injury-in-fact for his causes of action.[67] The court

60 *Id.*
61 *Id.*
62 *Id.*
63 *Id.*
64 *Id.*
65 *Id.*
66 *Id.* at *4.
67 *Id.* at *4 and *5.

went on to further explain that "alleging theft of PII [personal identifying information], without more, is inadequate to demonstrate a harm that qualifies as an injury in fact for standing purposes."[68]

In a slight twist, the court acknowledged and ultimately determined that "[p]laintiff alleged that his credit card information was stolen and misused and that he arranged to cancel and reissue the compromised credit card after learning that his [personal identifying information] was misused," and that plaintiff who mitigated his exposure to fraudulent charges and potential identity theft had a resulting loss of productivity. As a result, the court found that those allegations "presented a concrete, non-speculative harm that befell Plaintiff as a result of the Starwood breach. Accordingly, to the extent Plaintiff seeks relief for the loss of time and money spent to avoid losses caused by the data breach, his allegations are sufficient to state an injury in fact."[69]

E. Risk Management and Insurance Considerations in Hospitality

All of the hospitality-industry cases highlight the liabilities and responsibilities of the hospitality brands, owners, and operators for cybersecurity and data breaches, as well as the importance of maintaining a comprehensive risk management program. The hospitality industry's business model is complex, with third party vendor agreements and franchise agreements that attempt to shift and allocate risk liabilities and costs. Many such agreements include a provision where the hotel operator indemnifies the hotel owner for willful or gross negligence, which may not include cybersecurity breaches. Therefore, it is important for the hotel owner and hotel operator to carefully review and negotiate the terms of the contract in order to allocate responsibility for third party claims, including investigation cost, minimum cyber insurance requirements and breach responses.

A comprehensive risk management program should also include cyber liability coverage for first-party and third-party claims. First-party liability coverage addresses the policyholder's own damages from cybercrime or data breach, and may or may not include cost for notification, regulatory compliance, or penalties. There may also be additional coverages for risks such as cyber extortion, loss to physical and non-physical assets, and

---

68 *Id.* at *6.

69 *Id.*

reputational damage. Both the hotel owner and hotel operator should purchase cyber insurance products to protect itself from these and other losses related to data breaches involving its customers and employees.

Inasmuch as a majority of data breaches are the result of human actions, a comprehensive risk management program must include the development and implementation of ongoing training for employees. As technology evolves, cybersecurity issues will also evolve. Given the hospitality and leisure industry's collection of a large amount of personal and financial data for millions of individuals, and the particular reliance on interconnected technology as well as third parties, it is essential for the industry to embrace and continuously update its risk management program on cybersecurity and data privacy in order to maintain a competitive edge.

Chapter 16

The Financial Services Industry*

This chapter focuses on the financial services industry. While there may be different definitions of what entities might fall within the definition of financial services, we will use the definition contained in the New York Department of Financial Services Cybersecurity Regulation ("NYDFS Cyber Reg"),[1] which includes companies subject to New York's 1) insurance laws, 2) banking laws, and 3) financial services laws.[2] Financial services providers face increasing exposure to cyber attacks because the types of information these companies collect and use to provide services to their business and personal customers is of high value. This chapter explores the risks facing the financial services industry and how these companies are addressing the challenges. While we have included insurance companies in the definition for purposes of this chapter and cover at some level insurers, many (at least property and casualty insurers) are not buyers of specific cyber insurance policies or self-insure for such risks.[3]

---

* By Daniel Cotter.

1 23 N.Y.C.R.R. § 500, https://govt.westlaw.com/nycrr/Browse/Home/NewYork/NewYorkCodesRulesandRegulations?guid=I5be30d2007f811e79d43a037eefd0011&originationContext=documenttoc&transitionType=Default&contextData=(sc.Default).

2 23 N.Y.C.R.R. § 500.1(c).

3 While insurance companies do have substantial amounts of sensitive data, the end product, insurance policies, are not readily transferrable or usable by unrelated third parties. Some of the big attacks in the insurance arena have been against the health (Anthem for example), life and disability (Aflac) insurers.

---

* By Deborah W. Yue and Debbie Sines Crockett.

A. The State of Cyber Risks in the Financial Services Industry

Financial services companies were one of the first focuses of the insurance industry when it began writing policies directed at cyber risks.[4] The focus was on the financial institutions' "electronic connection to customers."[5] Attacks on financial services companies continue to occur with greater frequency. Each year, for the last number of years, the law firm of BakerHostetler[6] has put out an annual data security incident response report. The report includes an industries affected section.[7] For 2019 data, "Finance & Insurance" was listed as the third most affected industry, with 16% of the 2019 incidents impacting that industry.[8] One reason this industry is vulnerable is the type of information that the organizations collect. If someone signs up for a loan or opens a bank account, information such as the person's social security number, drivers' license number, and other sensitive information is collected. Financial advisors and tax preparation companies often have financial account numbers, tax information including social security numbers, and other sensitive types of data. For insurance companies, depending on the type of policy procured, the organization collects additional information, such as driving records, personal health information including medication information.

All of this sensitive data and information is not easily changed or cancelled. Financial services companies "operate large, mission-critical networks that process seemingly endless volumes of sensitive

---

4 In an interview with Tracey Vispoli, currently President of Berkley Cyber Risk Solutions, on November 23, 2020, by the author, Vispoli discussed her time at Chubb Insurance and the early 2000s. She stated in the interview, "Around 2000, real cyber insurance started. People will tell you 1990s, may have been technologyesque policies back then, but what we see today, real roots of what we are seeing today began in early 2000. Chubb was focused on financial institutions exposures." Telephone Interview with Tracey Vispoli, President, Berkley Cyber Risk Solutions (Nov. 23, 2020) (hereinafter, "Vispoli Interview").

5 *Id.*

6 BakerHostetler, https://www.bakerlaw.com/ (last visited Jan. 24, 2021).

7 *See, e.g.,* BakerHostetler, *2020 Data Security Incident Response Report,* https://f.datasrvr.com/fr1/620/24943/2020_DSIR_Report_(003).pdf.p.3 [hereinafter *2020 Response Report*].

8 *Id.*

information."[9] Due to the COVID-19 pandemic, more people began to work from home and the world became more virtual as more individuals than ever accessed the internet to complete their financial services transactions. Not surprisingly, financial services companies faced increased cyber attacks.[10]

One of the motivations for attacks on financial services companies is the collection of the sensitive information discussed above. Another reason for the vulnerability is the outdated systems that are used by those entities to collect and store the sensitive information.[11]

Finally, hackers attack the financial services industry because these organizations possess not only sensitive information that is hard to change for the victims, making it more valuable, but massive amounts of financial assets that can be stolen.[12] With respect to the third reason financial services companies are victims of an increasing number of thefts, it reminds one of the bank robberies that Willie Sutton committed in the 1930s. When he was asked why he repeatedly robbed banks, Sutton replied, "Because that's where the money is."[13] Cyber hackers are using a

---

9 SYMANTEC WHITE PAPER, *Cyber Security for Financial Services: Strategies that Empower your Business, Drive Innovation and Build Customer Trust*, https://docs.broadcom.com/doc/cybersecurity-for-financial-services-en.

10 *See, e.g.*, Deloitte, *Impact of COVID-19 on Cybersecurity*, https://www2.deloitte.com/ch/en/pages/risk/articles/impact-covid-cybersecurity.html.

11 *See, e.g.*, Adrian Nish, Saher Naumaan, & James Muir, *Enduring Cyber Threats and Emerging Challenges to the Financial Sector*, CARNEGIE ENDOWMENT FOR INTERNATIONAL PEACE (Nov. 18, 2020), https://carnegieendowment.org/2020/11/18/enduring-cyber-threats-and-emerging-challenges-to-financial-sector-pub-83239 ("One vector all of these groups use is the targeting of outdated and legacy technology within enterprise networks (see box 1).")

12 *Id.* ("Some of the most significant threats to the financial system come from state or organized criminal groups seeking to steal funds.")

13 Wille Sutton, *History*, Federal Bureau of Investigation, https://www.fbi.gov/history/famous-cases/willie-sutton#:~:text=One%20victim%20said%20witnessing%20one,that's%20where%20the%20money%20is.%E2%80%9D. Sutton wrote a memoir about his bank robbery exploits. *See* Willie Sutton, *Where the Money Was: The Memoirs of a Bank Robber*, (1976), https://smile.amazon.com/Where-Money-Was-Memoirs-Hardcover/dp/B011W95EE4/ref=tmm_hrd_swatch_0?_encoding=UTF8&qid=1610819367&sr=8-2.

very similar approach to cyber theft, going to industries such as financial services and paying homage to the Sutton statement.

1. Recent Incidents in the Financial Services Sector

Consistent with the statements above, many financial services firms have experienced some type of a cyber attack in the recent past. According to one report, 65% "of large financial services companies have suffered a cyber-attack in the past year, while 45% have experienced a rise in attack attempts since the start of the COVID-19 pandemic."[14] Since 2007, hackers have attacked financial institutions approximately 200 times.[15] Because financial institutions have substantial assets that, if breached, can lead to asset transfer, and because a large majority of all data breaches are motivated by financial gains,[16] the impact on financial institutions is significant, with the "cost of cyberattacks in the banking industry reach[ing] $18.3 million annually per company."[17]

Cyber attacks in the financial services sector happen to institutions of all sizes. In 2019, a major cyber attack impacted CapitalOne. The company disclosed the breach on its website, informing the public, "The government has stated they believe the data has been recovered and that there is no evidence the data was used for fraud or shared by this individual."[18] According to CapitalOne, the "event affected approximately 100 million individuals in the United States and approximately 6 million in Canada"[19] with reports that the "individual also obtained the following data: [a]bout 140,000 Social Security numbers of our credit card customers

---

14 James Coker, *Two-Thirds of Financial Services Firms Suffered Cyber-Attack in the Past Year*, INFO SECURITY (Nov. 5, 2020), https://www.infosecurity-magazine.com/news/two-thirds-financial-services/.

15 CARNEGIE ENDOWMENT FOR INTERNATIONAL PEACE, *Timeline of Cyber Incidents Involving Financial Institutions*, https://carnegieendowment.org/specialprojects/protectingfinancialstability/timeline.

16 *See, e.g.*, G. Dautovic, *Top 25 Financial Data Breach Statistics for 2020*, FORTUNLY (published Sept. 30, 2020), https://fortunly.com/statistics/data-breach-statistics/#gref ("71% of all data breaches are financially motivated").

17 *Id.*

18 CAPITALONE, *Information on the Capital One Cyber Incident*, (updated Sept. 23, 2019), https://www.capitalone.com/facts2019/.

19 *Id.*

[and] [a]bout 80,000 linked bank account numbers of our secured credit card customers."[20]

First American Title Financial Corp.[21] also learned of a major cyber breach dating back to as far as 2003.[22] According to reports, the breach went back for many years and reports "indicate that First American's website exposed approximately 885 million files, the earliest dating back more than 16 years. No authentication was required to read the documents."[23] Many other financial institutions suffered major attacks in 2019 as well.[24]

The Securities and Exchange Commission ("SEC")[25] became so concerned about the increasing attacks on financial institutions that on July 20, 2020, it issued a "Cybersecurity: Ransomware Alert."[26] The Office of Compliance Inspections and Examinations ("OCIE") warned financial institutions:

> Recent reports indicate that one or more threat actors have orchestrated phishing and other campaigns designed to penetrate financial institution networks to, among other objectives, access internal resources and deploy ransomware. Ransomware is a type of malware designed to provide an unauthorized actor access to

---

20 *Id.*

21 The NYDFS recently filed a statement of charges against First American.

22 *See* Krebs on Security, *First American Financial Corp. Leaked Hundreds of Millions of Title Insurance Records* (May 24, 2019), https://krebsonsecurity.com/2019/05/first-american-financial-corp-leaked-hundreds-of-millions-of-title-insurance-records/.

23 *Id.*

24 *See, e.g.*, Brian Thomas, *Financial Data Breaches 2019: Capital One, First American, Desjardins, More*, BITSIGHT (Oct. 1, 2019), https://www.bitsight.com/blog/financial-data-breaches-2019-capital-one-first-american-desjardins-more (describing various financial institutions breaches in 2019).

25 U.S. Securities and Exchange Commission, www.sec.gov (last visited Jan. 24, 2021).

26 Office of Compliance Inspections and Examinations, U.S. Securities and Exchange Commission, *Cybersecurity: Ransomware Alert*, RISK ALERT (July 10, 2020), https://www.sec.gov/files/Risk%20Alert%20-%20Ransomware.pdf. [hereinafter *Ransomware Alert*].

> institutions' systems and to deny the institutions use of those systems until a ransom is paid.
>
> OCIE has also observed an apparent increase in sophistication of ransomware attacks on SEC registrants, which include broker-dealers, investment advisers, and investment companies. The perpetrators behind these attacks typically demand compensation (ransom) to maintain the integrity and/or confidentiality of customer data or for the return of control over registrant systems. In addition, OCIE has observed ransomware attacks impacting service providers to registrants.[27]

In addition to the increased ransomware attacks, the OCIE has discovered during examinations of "SEC-registered investment advisers and brokers and dealers"[28] a substantial increase in "credential stuffing."[29] Credential stuffing is "a method of cyber-attack to client accounts that uses compromised client login credentials, resulting in the possible loss of customer assets and unauthorized disclosure of sensitive personal information."[30]

2. *Data Breach Litigation Summary in the Financial Services Sector*

(a) *Bessemer System Federal Credit Union v. Fiserv Solutions, LLC*

While the number of incidents of cyber attacks in the financial services industry have increased, the number of lawsuits filed against financial institutions for those attacks remains relatively quiet. However, in a lawsuit filed in May 2019, *Bessemer System Federal Credit Union v.*

---

27 *Id.*

28 Office of Compliance Inspections and Examinations, U.S. Securities and Exchange Commission, *Cybersecurity: Safeguarding Client Accounts against Credential Compromise*, RISK ALERT (Sept. 15, 2020), https://www.sec.gov/files/Risk%20Alert%20-%20Credential%20Compromise.pdf.

29 U.S. Securities and Exchange Commission, https://www.sec.gov/ocie/announcement/risk-alert-credential-compromise (last visited Jan. 24, 2021).

30 *Id.*

Fiserv Solutions, LLC,[31] a small credit union, Bessemer System Federal Credit Union,[32] sued Fiserv,[33] alleging that the provider of technology services to credit unions and other financial institutions had engaged in "widespread, systemic misconduct."[34] Bessemer alleged that Fiserv had a long "history of failing to protect confidential information."[35] Bessemer filed claims against Fiserv in connection with a 2016 breach that Fiserv experienced, alleging among other things that Fiserv inaccurately reported member account records and information, failed to secure confidential member information and financial records against access by unauthorized third parties and that Fiserv threatened to take civil and criminal actions against the credit union.

On June 30, 2020, Judge Robert J. Colville issued an order addressing several motions filed by Fiserv.[36] Bessemer had asserted that the negligence in providing security services by Fiserv were separate and apart from the contractual obligations under a master service agreement that Bessemer had with Fiserv.[37] The court disagreed, holding:

> As such, Bessemer's negligence claim, which relies on allegations of Bessemer's deficient security practices, is barred by the gist of the action doctrine. The Court finds that amendment as to Bessemer's negligence claim would be futile. Accordingly, the

---

31 The docket can be found at Pacer. *See Bessemer Sys. Fed. Credit Union v. Fiserv Solutions, LLC,* 19-cv-00624 (May 28, 2019), https://www.pacermonitor.com/public/case/28352330/BESSEMER_SYSTEM_FEDERAL_CREDIT_UNION_v_FISERV_SOLUTIONS,_LLC (last visited Jan. 24 2021).

32 Bessemer System, https://www.bessfcu.com/ (last visited Jan. 24, 2021).

33 According to its website, "Fiserv enables money movement for thousands of financial institutions and millions of people and businesses in a world that never powers down." FISERV, https://www.fiserv.com/en/about-fiserv.html?rdf=/en/about-fiserv/about.html&rdc=2020-12-04&rdr=2021-06-04 (last visited Jan. 21, 2021).

34 CUTIMES, *Complaint in Civil Action*, Civil Div. No. 2018-01130, ¶ 1, https://images.cutimes.com/contrib/content/uploads/documents/413/157987/Bessemer-Filed-and-Stamped-Complaint4823414.1.pdf.

35 *Id.* at ¶ 32.

36 Judicial Caselaw, https://judicialcaselaw.com/courts/pawd/cases/2_19-cv-00624-RJC/15717473252 (Dkt. 69) (last visited Jan. 21 2021).

37 *Id.*

> Court will grant Fiserv's Motion to Dismiss as to this claim and dismiss Bessemer's negligence claim with prejudice.[38]

The court also dismissed the negligent misrepresentations count, but refused to dismiss the fraudulent inducement claim and some other claims.

(b) *In the Matter of: First American Title Insurance Company*

In a second action related to financial institutions and cybersecurity, the NYDFS recently filed its first enforcement action under the NYDFS Cyber Reg, consistent with its enforcement powers.[39] In the action, *In the Matter of: First American Title Insurance Company,* No. 2020-0030-C,[40] the NYDFS accused First American of exposing its clients' data to anyone with a web browser as a result of "a known vulnerability on Respondent's public-facing website."[41] According to the Statement of Charges, First American's "mishandling of its own customers' data was compounded by its willful failure to remediate the Vulnerability."[42]

The NYDFS Cyber Reg broadly defines "nonpublic information" as:

> (g) . . . all electronic information that is not publicly available information and is:
>
> (1) business related information of a covered entity the tampering with which, or unauthorized disclosure, access or use of which, would cause a material adverse impact to the business, operations or security of the covered entity;
>
> (2) any information concerning an individual which because of name, number, personal mark, or other identifier can be used to identify such individual, in combination with any one or more of the following data elements:
>
> (i) social security number;

---

38 *Id.*

39 23 CRRNY § 500.20 (May 2020).

40 *In the Matter of: First American Title Insurance Company,* No. 2020-0030-C, Statement of Charges and Notice of Hearing, https://www.dfs.ny.gov/system/files/documents/2020/07/ea20200721_first_american_notice_charges.pdf.

41 *Id.,* ¶ 2.

42 *Id.,* ¶ 5.

(ii) drivers' license number or non-driver identification card number;
(iii) account number, credit or debit card number;
(iv) any security code, access code or password that would permit access to an individual's financial account; or
(v) biometric records;

(3) any information or data, except age or gender, in any form or medium created by or derived from a health care provider or an individual and that relates to:

(i) the past, present or future physical, mental or behavioral health or condition of any individual or a member of the individual's family;
(ii) the provision of health care to any individual; or
(iii) payment for the provision of health care to any individual.[43]

The NYDFS filed an amended complaint against First American, with the same basic allegations.[44]

The action by the NYDFS against First American likely will not be the last. It will be interesting to watch how entities covered by the NYDFS Cyber Reg will be held accountable in the future.

B. Survey of Unique Issues to Financial Services

1. Overview of Unique Issues

Financial services companies have long been subject to enhanced privacy and cybersecurity obligations. All financial services organizations are subject to an extensive regulatory framework and that oversight by regulatory bodies has long extended to privacy and data security. This industry has been subject to privacy regulation and data security oversight for more than twenty years. In November 1999, the Gramm-Leach Bliley

43 23 CRR-NY 500.1(g) (May 2020).

44 The DFS filed an amended complaint, https://www.dfs.ny.gov/system/files/documents/2021/03/ea20200721_first_american_notice.pdf. [hereinafter, *Amended Complaint*].

Act ("GLB"),[45] also known as the Financial Services Modernization Act of 1999, became law. While the primary focus of GLB was to repeal part of the Glass-Steagall Act of 1933,[46] Title V of GLB addressed privacy.[47] Privacy was reportedly added to GLB due to a "confluence of international and domestic events."[48] GLB was one of the early laws at the state or federal levels addressing privacy and data security.[49] It was the first known industry-specific privacy law in the United States.[50] GLB does not clearly define what is a financial institution. However, Section 505 of GLB[51] lists the agencies that have enforcement powers and subject covered entities to privacy obligations, including:

1. Federal banking agencies;[52]
2. National Credit Union Administration;[53]
3. Brokers and dealers under the Securities & Exchange Commission ("SEC") Act of 1934;[54]

45 GRAMM-LEACH-BLILEY ACT, Pub. L. No. 106-102 (Nov. 12, 1999), https://www.govinfo.gov/content/pkg/PLAW-106publ102/pdf/PLAW-106publ102.pdf.

46 *See* Federal Reserve History, *Banking Act of 1933 (Glass-Steagall)*, https://www.federalreservehistory.org/essays/glass-steagall-act#:~:text=June%2016%2C%201933,Roosevelt%20in%20June%201933.

47 *Amended Complaint, supra* note 44, at Title V.

48 Electronic Privacy Information Center, *The Gramm-Leach-Bliley Act*, https://epic.org/privacy/glba/#:~:text=The%20GLBA%20primarily%20sought%20to,brokerage%20companies%2C%20and%20insurance%20companies (reporting several major instances of financial institutions not protecting consumer information).

49 For example, *see* California's Security Breach Information Act, or Senate Bill 1386 (SB1386), which California passed in 2002, which was the first state law to address companies' obligations to provide notice when a data breach occurred that impacted its customers, https://leginfo.legislature.ca.gov/faces/billTextClient.xhtml?bill_id=200120020SB1386.

50 *But see* the HEALTH INSURANCE PORTABILITY AND ACCOUNTABILITY ACT OF 1996, Pub. L. 104-191 (Aug. 21, 1996), https://www.govinfo.gov/content/pkg/PLAW-104publ191/pdf/PLAW-104publ191.pdf (addressing health information and privacy).

51 GRAMM-LEACH-BLILEY ACT, Pub. L. 106-102, Title V, § 505 (codified at 15 U.S.C. § 6805).

52 15 U.S.C. § 6805(a)(1).

53 15 U.S.C. § 6805(a)(2).

54 15 U.S.C. § 6805(a)(3).

4. Investment companies under the Investment Company Act of 1940;[55]
5. Investment advisors subject to the Investment Advisors Act of 1940;[56]
6. Underwriters and producers subject to the insurance laws of the states;[57]
7. Any other financial institution not included in the prior six categories that are under the jurisdiction of the Federal Trade Commission;[58] and,
8. Any financial institution subject to the Consumer Financial Protection Bureau.[59]

If an entity falls within any of the above categories, then the financial institution must adhere to GLB's several requirements in order to demonstrate compliance with the mandates of GLB: 1) the privacy rule; 2) the safeguards rule; and, 3) the pretexting rule.[60]

The GLB privacy rule requires a financial institution to "provide a clear and conspicuous disclosure to such consumer, in writing or in electronic form or other form permitted by the regulations"[61] when establishing a relationship with a customer and annually thereafter. In 2015, the section was amended to provide that, if the information collected and practices of the financial institution had not changed its activities, the annual notice was not required.[62]

The safeguards rule says a financial institution "has an affirmative and continuing obligation to respect the privacy of its customers and to protect the security and confidentiality of those customers' nonpublic personal information"[63] and requires the responsible agency over the financial

55 15 U.S.C. § 6805(a)(4).
56 15 U.S.C. § 6805(a)(5).
57 15 U.S.C. § 6805(a)(6).
58 15 U.S.C. § 6805(a)(7).
59 15 U.S.C. § 6805(a)(8).
60 *See, e.g.,* Portland Community College, *Gramm-Leach-Bliley Act (GLBA)*, INFORMATION TECHNOLOGY, https://www.pcc.edu/technology/security/glba/ (last visited Jan. 21, 2021).
61 15 U.S.C. § 6803(a).
62 15 U.S.C. § 6803(f).
63 15 U.S.C. § 6801(a).

institution to "establish appropriate standards,"[64] permitting such agency to enforce the regulation for such security measures.[65] For those financial institutions that are subject to the jurisdiction of the Federal Trade Commission ("FTC"), for example, the safeguards rule can be found at 16 CFR 314.[66] Finally, the pretext rule prohibits financial institutions from obtaining customer information by false pretense by "false, fictitious, or fraudulent statement or representation."[67]

Financial services are highly regulated. In addition to GLB, which imposes the three rules outlined above on entities subject to GLB's broad application, on March 1, 2017, the NYDFS Cyber Reg became effective.[68] The NYDFS Cyber Reg:

> requires all DFS regulated entities, subject to certain exemptions, to adopt the core requirements of a cybersecurity program, including a cybersecurity policy, effective access privileges, cybersecurity risk assessments, and training and monitoring for all authorized users, among other requirements. The regulation also requires the establishment of governance processes to ensure senior attention to these important protections.[69]

For insurance companies subject to state insurance laws, in the 4th quarter of 2017, after much discussion and in large part based on the NYDFS Cyber Reg, the National Association of Insurance Commissioners ("NAIC") Executive/Plenary adopted the Insurance Data Security Model Law ("NAIC Cyber Law").[70] Prior to 2020, eight states had adopted the NAIC Cyber Law. The eight states that adopted the NAIC Cyber Law before 2020 are:

---

64 15 U.S.C. § 6801(b).

65 15 U.S.C. § 6805.

66 E-CFR, *16 C.F.R. § 314*, https://www.ecfr.gov/cgi-bin/text-idx?c=ecfr&sid=1e9a81d52a0904d70a046d0675d613b0&rgn=div5&view=text&node=16%3A1.0.1.3.38&idno=16.

67 15 U.S.C. § 6821.

68 Maria T. Vullo, *Memorandum to CEOs of DFS Regulated Industries*, New York Dep't. of Fin. Servs. (Dec. 21, 2018), https://www.dfs.ny.gov/system/files/documents/2019/01/cyber_memo_12212018.pdf.

69 *Id.*

70 Insurance Data Security Model Law, *Model Laws MDL-668*, NAIC MODEL LAWS, REGULATIONS, GUIDELINES AND OTHER RESOURCES—4TH QUARTER (2017), https://content.naic.org/sites/default/files/inline-files/MDL-668.pdf.

1. South Carolina[71];
2. Ohio[72];
3. Michigan;[73]
4. Mississippi;[74]
5. Alabama;[75]
6. Connecticut;[76]
7. New Hampshire;[77] and
8. Delaware.[78]

During 2020, three additional states adopted the Model Law: Virginia on March 10, 2020;[79] Indiana on March 20, 2020;[80] and, Louisiana on June 11, 2020.[81] At least five other states are considering adopting the Model Law.[82]

2. *Discussion of Unique Elements to Consider When Evaluating Endorsements and Standalone Policies*

While the standalone cyber market has grown substantially in recent years,[83] the market for cyber insurance as part of a broader policy and addressed via endorsement continues to be a large part of the overall market.[84] The same remains true in the financial services industry. With risks facing financial services organizations such as ransomware and

71 S.C. CODE ANN. §§ 38-99-10 to 38-99-100 (2018).

72 OHIO REV. CODE ANN. §§ 3965.01 to 3965.11 (2018).

73 MICH. COMP. LAWS §§ 500.550 to 500.565 (2018).

74 MISS. CODE ANN. §§ 83-5-801 to 83-5-825 (2019).

75 ALA. CODE §§ 27-62-1 to 27-62-12 (2019).

76 CONN. GEN. STAT. ANN. § 38a-38 (2020).

77 N.H. REV. STAT. ANN. §§ 420-P:1 to 420-P:14; §§ 309:2 to 309:3 (2019).

78 DEL. CODE ANN. tit. 18, §§ 8601 to 8611 (2019).

79 VA. CODE ANN. §§ 38.2-621 to 38.2-629 (2020).

80 IND. CODE ANN. §§ 27-2-27-1 to 27-2-27-32 (2020).

81 H.B. 614 (2020).

82 *Implementation of Model Act #668*, INSURANCE DATA SECURITY MODEL LAW (status as of June 16, 2020), https://content.naic.org/sites/default/files/inline-files/Model_%23668_Map06.17.20.pdf.

83 *See Chapter 1.*

84 *Id.*

"phishing[85] attacks aiming to steal login credentials and DDoS[86] attacks trying to sabotage online payments,"[87] some of the biggest issues facing financial services organizations is penetration and control of their systems by hackers, including ransomware demands, and vulnerabilities created by substantial reliance on third parties as part of their services and offerings. For example, many financial institutions outsource some or most of their computer services. According to one report by the Office of the Comptroller of the Currency ("OCC") on third parties and financial institution responsibilities, the number and complexity of such relationships includes:

- outsourcing entire bank functions to third parties, such as tax, legal, audit, or information technology operations.
- outsourcing lines of business or products.
- relying on a single third party to perform multiple activities, often to such an extent that the third party becomes an integral component of the bank's operations.
- working with third parties that engage directly with customers.
- contracting with third parties that subcontract activities to other foreign and domestic providers.
- contracting with third parties whose employees, facilities, and subcontractors may be geographically concentrated.
- working with a third party to address deficiencies in bank operations or compliance with laws or regulations.[88]

Financial services, as noted, have legacy systems and are heavily dependent on third party vendors for the provision of services.[89] Each

---

85 Phishing refers to a method of trying to gather personal information using deceptive e-mails and websites.

86 DDos refers to a distributed denial of service.

87 MK CS Team *Cyber Security in BFSI—Challenges and Solutions*, MK CYBER SERVICES (Dec.19, 2020), https://www.mkcyberservices.com/cyber-security-in-bfsi-challenges-solutions/. The acronym, BFSI, refers to banking, financial services, and insurance.

88 OCC Bulletin 2013-29, *Third-Party Relationships: Risk Management Guidance* (Oct. 29, 2013), https://www.occ.gov/news-issuances/bulletins/2013/bulletin-2013-29.html.

89 *See above.* As noted in the Bulletin, "Banks continue to increase the number and complexity of relationships with both foreign and domestic third parties,

regulator has issued guidance and examination principles for third party vendor due diligence. For example, the NYDFS included in the NYDFS Cyber Reg a section on third party service providers that says:[90]

> Each covered entity shall implement written policies and procedures designed to ensure the security of information systems and nonpublic information that are accessible to, or held by, third party service providers. Such policies and procedures shall be based on the risk assessment of the covered entity and shall address to the extent applicable:
>
> (1) the identification and risk assessment of third party service providers;
> (2) minimum cybersecurity practices required to be met by such third party service providers in order for them to do business with the covered entity;
> (3) due diligence processes used to evaluate the adequacy of cybersecurity practices of such third party service providers; and
> (4) periodic assessment of such third party service providers based on the risk they present and the continued adequacy of their cybersecurity practices.[91]

The importance of third party vendor assessments might best be demonstrated by the Target breach in 2013, that occurred as a result of access gained through its HVAC vendor.[92] However, in 2020, a major breach also took place in the financial services industry that involved a third party vendor. On July 25, 2020, a breach occurred when hackers published data and personal information of 7.5 million users of the

---

such as outsourcing entire bank functions to third parties, such as tax, legal, audit, or information technology operations."

90 23 CRR-NY 500.11 (May 2020).

91 23 CRR-NY § 500.11(a) (May 2020).

92 Target, 8-K (Feb. 26, 2014), https://www.sec.gov/Archives/edgar/data/27419/000002741914000006/a2013q48k.htm.

"Dave"[93] app.[94] Dave, in turn, "said the security breach originated on the network of a former business partner, Waydev, an analytics platform used by engineering teams."[95] The breach demonstrates that third party partners might well expose the financial institution to hackers.

One additional vulnerability for financial institutions that is not unique to financial institutions, but that many cyber insurance policies respond to, is fraudulent phishing emails. For example, in 2020, the National Futures Association ("NFA") issued a bulletin to the U.S. derivative industry warning the members of an increase in "fraudulent phishing emails which purport to be from the institution or the institution's employees."[96] In an ironic twist, a year later, the NFA sent a warning that many complaints had been received about emails purporting to be from the NFA.[97]

C. Future Issues and Concerns that Will Confront the Financial Services Industry

One of the biggest issues confronting the financial services industry for cyber risks and insurance is the extent to which certain fines and penalties might be insurable. Recent laws enacted that impact the financial services industry, such as the NYDFS Cyber Reg,[98] impose such fines. Often, cyber insurance policies contain exclusions for regulatory fines and penalties. For example, in New York, fines and penalties are generally not

---

93 Dave is a banking app, named after the David in David v. Goliath. *See* DAVE, https://dave.com/about (last visited Jan. 21, 2020).

94 Catalin Cimpanu, *Tech unicorn Dave admits to security breach impacting 7.5 million users*, ZERO DAY, ZDNET (July 26, 2020), https://www.zdnet.com/article/tech-unicorn-dave-admits-to-security-breach-impacting-7-5-million-users/.

95 *Id.*

96 NFA, Notice I-20-21, *Increase in Fraudulent Phishing Emails Warrants Member Vigilance* (May 13, 2020), https://www.nfa.futures.org/news/newsNotice.asp?ArticleID=5226.

97 Notice I-21-10, *NFA warns of fraudulent phishing emails purporting to be from NFA* (Mar. 3, 2021), https://www.nfa.futures.org/news/newsNotice.asp?ArticleID=5331.

98 23 N.Y.C.R.R. § 500, https://govt.westlaw.com/nycrr/Browse/Home/NewYork/NewYorkCodesRulesandRegulations?guid=I5be30d2007f811e79d43a037eefd0011&originationContext=documenttoc&transitionType=Default&contextData=(sc.Default)

insurable as a matter of public policy.[99] The reasoning is that "no one shall be permitted to profit by. . .or to take advantage of his own wrong" and "the sting of. . .penalties is not to be soothed by permitting its payment out of an insurance pool rather than directly by the wrongdoer."[100]

California caselaw also strongly cautions against insurability of fines and penalties. Several case decisions from California support the notion that civil penalties are uninsurable as a matter of California public policy. For example, in *Bulluck v. Maryland Casualty Company,*[101] the insured filed a bad faith lawsuit against the defendant, asserting bad faith for refusing to defend the insureds in an action brought by a city seeking to compel the insured to comply with a city ordinance pursuant to which the city sought civil penalties. The insured argued that "the penalties were 'damages' because they would compensate the city for an injury to the 'public fisc.'"[102] However, the court rejected that argument, citing California Insurance Code § 533.5[103] for the proposition that the payment of a penalty was not "damages" within the meaning of a liability insurance policy under California law. [need a citation here].

Financial services organizations also must consider their substantial exposure to hackers as a result of their services becoming increasingly digital. There are opportunities not only to find rich resources in direct financial assets, but also the value of the voluminous amount of data the industry maintains: "The banking, financial services, and insurance (BFSI) sector is an obvious target for attackers. However, malicious actors can walk away with more than just money. The sheer volume of data held by companies in the BFSI arena makes the sector all-the-more exciting for attackers."[104] Cybercrime exposures will continue to be one of the larger exposures facing the financial services industry, given these factors.

---

99 *See Silverman Neu, LLP v. Admiral Insurance Company,* 933 F. Supp. 2d 463 (E.D.N.Y. 2013) *(quoting Drexel Burnham Lambert Group, Inc. v. Vigilant Insurance Company,* 595 N.Y.S.2d 999, 1010 (N.Y. Sup. Ct. 1993)).

100 *Id.*

101 85 Cal. App. 4th 1435 (Cal. Ct. App. 2001).

102 *Id.*

103 CAL. INS. CODE, § 533.5.

104 Rema Farhan, *What are the main cybersecurity challenges the BSFI sector faces?*, ENTERPRISE MANAGEMENT 360 (published Apr. 20, 2020), https://em360tech.com/continuity/tech-features-featuredtech-news/bfsi-cybersecurity-challenges.

As noted, financial services organizations are one of the most vulnerable organizations.[105] Recent attacks continue. On April 10, 2018, the Federal Financial Institutions Examination Council ("FFIEC")[106] issued a joint statement "to provide awareness of the potential role of cyber insurance in financial institutions' risk management programs."[107] The FFIEC advised entities that are covered by the inter agencies:

> The increasing number and sophistication of cyber incidents affect financial institutions of all sizes, and remediation of cyber incidents can be costly. Traditional insurance policies for general liability or basic business interruption coverage may not fully cover cyber risk exposures without special endorsement or by exclusion not cover them at all. Coverage may also be limited and not cover incidents caused by or tracked to outside vendors. Cyber insurance may offset financial losses from a variety of exposures, such as data breaches resulting in the loss of sensitive customer information.
>
> The cyber insurance marketplace is growing and evolving in response to the increasing cyberattack frequency, severity, and

105 *2020 Response Report, supra* note 7.

106 The FFIEC is comprised of the principals of various agencies. Per its website, "[t]he Council is a formal interagency body empowered to prescribe uniform principles, standards, and report forms for the federal examination of financial institutions by the Board of Governors of the Federal Reserve System (FRB), the Federal Deposit Insurance Corporation (FDIC), the National Credit Union Administration (NCUA), the Office of the Comptroller of the Currency (OCC), and the Consumer Financial Protection Bureau (CFPB), and to make recommendations to promote uniformity in the supervision of financial institutions. In 2006, the State Liaison Committee (SLC) was added to the Council as a voting member. The SLC includes representatives from the Conference of State Bank Supervisors (CSBS), the American Council of State Savings Supervisors (ACSSS), and the National Association of State Credit Union Supervisors (NASCUS)." FEDERAL FIN. INSTITUTIONS EXAM. COUNCIL (FFIEC), https://www.ffiec.gov/ (last visited Jan. 21, 2021).

107 FFIEC, *Joint Statement: Cyber Insurance and Its Potential Role in Risk Management Programs* (Apr. 10, 2018), https://www.ffiec.gov/press/pdf/FFIEC%20Joint%20Statement%20Cyber%20Insurance%20FINAL.pdf.

related losses. Many aspects of the cyber insurance marketplace, such as terminology, claims history, legal precedents, and risk modeling continue to evolve and are shaping the nature and scope of cyber insurance.[108]

As noted, the OCIE became so concerned about the rise in cyber attacks on financial institutions that it issued a risk alert on July 10, 2020.[109] OCIE and the FFIEC are not alone in stressing to regulated financial institutions the risk that they face from cyber hackers. On January 16, 2020, the Federal Deposit Insurance Corporation ("FDIC") and the OCC issued a "Joint Statement on Heightened Cybersecurity Risk"[110] that warned their regulated organizations:

Heightened risk from cybersecurity threats, such as increased geopolitical tensions and threats of aggression, may result in cyber attacks against U.S. targets and interests. In recent years, disruptive and destructive attacks against financial institutions have increased in frequency and severity. Cyber actors often use malware to exploit weaknesses in a financial institution's computers or networks. They often obtain access to financial institution systems and networks by compromising user credentials and introducing malware through social engineering financial institution employees and contractors with phishing or spear phishing attacks. Another method of attack is to introduce infected external devices to computers and networks through removable media.[111]

Another emerging issue for financial services organizations is the business email compromise ("BEC"), which has been reported as a "top threat to financial services."[112] A BEC attack:

---

108 *Id.*

109 *Ransomware Alert, supra* note 26.

110 Federal Deposit Insurance Corporation—Office of the Comptroller of the Currency, *Joint Statement on Heightened Cybersecurity Risk* (Jan. 16, 2020), https://www.occ.gov/news-issuances/bulletins/2020/bulletin-2020-5a.pdf. [hereinafter *Joint Statement*].

111 *Id.*

112 Armen Najarian, *Email Security Blog, Business Email Compromise (BEC) Scams: COVID-19 Related Email Attacks Top Threat to Financial Services*, AGARI, (Apr. 30, 2020), https://www.agari.com/email-security-blog/business-email-compromise-bec-scams-covid-19-financial-services/.

begins with a cybercriminal hacking and spoofing emails to impersonate your company's supervisors, CEO, or vendors. Once in, they request a seemingly legitimate business payment. The email looks authentic, seems to come from a known authority figure, so the employee complies. Typically, the fraudster will ask for money to be wired or checks to be deposited, whatever the usual business practice. However, this scam has evolved not even to involve money.[113] [114]

Another emergent risk that financial services organizations face is island hopping, "an attack where supply chains and partners are commandeered to target the primary financial institution."[115] According to a recent report, one-third of the surveyed respondents admitted they had suffered an island hopping event in the last twelve months.[116]

While the risks financial services organizations face from cyber attacks continue to evolve and grow as a threat, the organizations are not required to purchase cyber insurance. While that might be a decision that the companies can make, it is ill advised to go naked for cyber risks. The nature and complexity of the cyber attacks in the financial services arena continues to evolve.

D. Conclusion

The issues in cyber insurance for the financial services sector will continue to grow and emerge. Financial services companies "are being disproportionately targeted by threat actors because of their rich financial and data assets, and a percentage are successful due to their specific

---

113 WESTSTAR, *BEC Attacks: What They Are and How to Protect Yourself*, https://www.weststarbank.com/our-info/bec-attacks--what-they-are-and-how-to-protect-yourself (last visited Jan. 21, 2021).

114 *See, e.g.*, FFIEC, *Joint Statement—Cyber Insurance and Its Potential Role in Risk Management Programs*, https://www.ncua.gov/newsroom/other/2018/joint-statement-cyber-insurance-and-its-potential-role-risk-management-programs ("Use of cyber insurance may offset financial losses resulting from cyber incidents; however, it is not required by the agencies").

115 Tom Kellermann & Ryan Murphy, *Modern Bank Heists 3.0*, VMWARE AND CARBON BLACK (May 2020), https://cdn.www.carbonblack.com/wp-content/uploads/VMWCB-Report-Modern-Bank-Heists-2020.pdf.

116 *Id.*

cybersecurity challenges, yielding an overall higher number of attacks."[117] Given the substantial assets that the financial services industry manages and maintains, and the large exposures they face from resourceful hackers attempting to penetrate and control what are, in many cases, legacy systems, Willie Sutton's statement will continue to hold true for many decades, given the volume of assets the industry holds and the vulnerabilities to such attacks. As one report stated, "the bank heist has evolved significantly—from stickups to cyberspace—but the fundamental motivation behind the attacks has remained: money."[118] The financial services industry companies must take steps to review their cyber insurance coverages and make sure they havc adequate protections to address the ever present vulnerabilities and exposures they face.

117 Rod Holmes, *Hackers Keep Hitting Financial Services Despite Hefty Cyber Spend*, FORBES (Sept. 22, 2020), https://www.forbes.com/sites/forbestechcouncil/2020/09/22/hackers-keep-hitting-financial-services-despite-hefty-cyber-spend/?sh=722bb60ea614.

118 *Joint Statement, supra* note 110.

Chapter 17

Cybersecurity in the Energy Sector*

The energy sector has long been a target of physical threats from a variety of actors, including geopolitical adversaries and domestic and foreign terrorists. The reason for these threats is fairly straightforward—energy systems play a vital role in modern society, such that even temporary disruptions can cause turmoil for a nation and its citizenry, and the scale and nature of energy systems carry the potential for catastrophic destruction and loss. While industry members must remain cognizant of physical threats, those threats have been compounded in recent years by the emerging threat of cyber attacks—a threat that looks likely to grow more pronounced in the years ahead.

As the energy sector increasingly relies on a mix of complex computer systems and automated processes alongside legacy industrial control systems, malicious cyber actors are becoming more sophisticated in their approaches to attacking systems and facilities within the energy sector. As with physical security threats, the malicious actors who threaten the energy sector consist of a range of individuals and entities, including highly sophisticated nation-state actors, domestic and international terrorist groups, politically motivated individual "hacktivists," and cyber criminals acting independently as well as those who are part of organized cyber crime syndicates. As automated processes and internet-facing connections increase the attack surface of energy sector companies and energy infrastructure components, malicious cyber actors are more motivated and able than ever to exploit human error and the weaknesses of flawed or insufficiently guarded computer systems for sinister purposes. Moreover, the proliferation of readily available cyber tools, which are difficult to control and contain, has lowered the barrier to entry.

This chapter provides a primer on cybersecurity in the energy sector. Section A provides a background on the cyber threat landscape by briefly examining three major incidents impacting the energy sector in Turkey, Ukraine, and the United States, and the U.S. government's response to these incidents. Section B discusses common themes of cybersecurity threats in the energy sector. Section C details the operative regulatory

---

* By April Falcon Doss and Albert F. Moran. The authors thank John R. Dixon for his research support.

framework and outlines the cybersecurity regulations and guidance that impact the interstate electric sector, the natural gas pipeline sector, and the nuclear power sector. Section D discusses three categories of legal risk associated with energy industry cyber incidents: catastrophic incidents, litigation risks, and regulatory enforcement risks. In closing, Section E offers various practical considerations and tips for industry members to deal with cyber threats proactively.

A. Background on the Cyber Threat Landscape

Since the beginning of the twenty-first century, security experts, policy researchers, and government departments have been warning of the risk of cyber attacks on the energy sector in the United States.[1] Over the past two decades, those threats have accelerated and grown, leading to the issuance by federal government agencies of cybersecurity threat advisories aimed specifically at the energy sector.[2] This chapter takes a brief look at three twenty-first century case studies which powerfully illustrate the threats posed by lax or defective cybersecurity in the energy industry as well as the severe physical-world consequences that can result from cyber attacks. At the time this book was being prepared for publication, the most recent of these was a major incident in 2021 involving a ransomware attack on fuel distribution company Colonial Pipeline, which quickly became one of the most high-profile energy sector incidents in the United States.[3] Before examining the implications of that incident, however, it is worth examining two previous cyber events involving the energy sector.

---

1 *See, e.g.*, "*Critical Infrastructure: Control Systems and the Terrorist Threat,*" Report for Congress, CONGRESSIONAL RESEARCH SERVICE (Jan. 20, 2004), https://www.everycrsreport.com/reports/RL31534. html.

2 *See, e.g.*, *Alert (TA18-074A) "Russian Government Cyber Activity Targeting Energy and other Critical Infrastructure Sectors*," (March 16, 2018) FEDERAL BUREAU OF INVESTIGATION and DEPARTMENT OF HOMELAND SECURITY, CYBERSECURITY AND INFRASTRUCTURE AGENCY, https://us-cert.cisa.gov/ncas/alerts/TA18-074A; and *Alert (AA21-201A), "Chinese Gas Pipeline Intrusion Campaign, 2011 to 2013*," (July 21, 2021), Joint Cybersecurity Alert, FEDERAL BUREAU OF INVESTIGATION and DEPARTMENT OF HOMELAND SECURITY CYBERSECURITY AND INFRASTRUCTURE AGENCY, https://us-cert.cisa.gov/ncas/alerts/aa21-201a.

3 David Sanger, Clifford Kraus, Nicole Perlroth, *Cyberattack Forces a Shutdown of a Top U.S. Pipeline,* NEW YORK TIMES (May 8, 2021),

In August 2008, a major explosion and fire in Refahiye, Turkey forced the Baku-Tbilisi-Ceyhan crude oil pipeline ("BTC Pipeline") to cease operations for twenty days. While the Kurdistan Workers Party claimed responsibility for the incident, circumstantial evidence has arisen that suggests that the explosion and fire were caused by a Russian cyber attack.[4] The BTC Pipeline was built to be extremely secure given the longstanding political unrest in the region, but the pipeline's security "was no match for the digital intruders who injected malicious software into the control network, allowing them to tamper with the system and cause an explosion."[5] Unfortunately, the explosion destroyed much of the evidence, but Bloomberg has suggested that the attack was the result of a hack on the computers managing the pipeline.[6] According to some accounts, the pipeline's security cameras provided the critical attack vector, as their operating system contained vulnerabilities that allowed malicious cyber actors to gain entrance to the pipeline's control network and cause the resulting explosion.[7] Although there hasn't yet been definitive proof of whether the 2008 explosion was caused by cyber or kinetic means, the incident proved to be a wake-up call for an industry that had long recognized the theoretical risk of cyber attacks leading to physical damage. If nothing else, this incident demonstrated a stark use case of the ways in which malicious cyber actors could plausibly gain control of, and damage or destroy, vital physical structures involved in energy generation, storage, or transmission.

---

https://www.nytimes.com/2021/05/08/us/politics/cyberattack-colonial-pipeline.html.

4 Joshua Kucera, *U.S. Intelligence: Russia Sabotaged BTC Pipeline Ahead of 2008 Georgia War*, EURASIANET (Dec. 11, 2014), https://eurasianet.org/us-intelligence-russia-sabotaged-btc-pipeline-ahead-of-2008-georgia-war.

5 Elizabeth Corner, *Cyber Attack Caused 2008 Pipeline Explosion?*, WORLD PIPELINES (Dec. 12, 2014), https://www.worldpipelines.com/business-news/12122014/cyber-attack-caused-2008-pipeline-explosion/.

6 Jordan Robertson and Michael Riley, *Mysterious '08 Turkey Pipeline Blast Opened New Cyberwar*, BLOOMBERG (Dec. 10, 2014), https://www.bloomberg.com/news/articles/2014-12-10/mysterious-08-turkey-pipeline-blast-opened-new-cyberwar.

7 Ariel Bogle, "*A Cyber Attack May Have Caused a Turkish Oil Pipeline to Catch Fire in 2008,*" SLATE *(Dec. 11, 2014*). https://slate.com/technology/2014/12/bloomberg-reports-a-cyber-attack-may-have-made-a-turkish-oil-pipeline-catch-fire.html.

In December 2015, the target was a different component of the energy sector: hackers compromised information systems of three energy distribution systems in Ukraine and temporarily disrupted the electric supply to consumers.[8] This attack—believed to be the first cyber attack on a power grid—impacted approximately 230,000 people, who lost power for hours during the middle of the Eastern European winter—and leaving Ukrainian energy control centers compromised for months. Unlike the 2008 pipeline incident, this attack has been widely and credibly attributed to Russian government cyber actors.[9] According to representatives of one of the companies that was attacked, the attacks were conducted from computers with IP addresses located in Russia.[10] At least one investigation concluded that the attack had intended to cause far more damage.[11]

More recently and closer to home, when one of the largest pipeline operators in the U.S. was hit by a ransomware attack in May, 2021, the disruption was swift and severe. Colonial Pipeline, a major distributor of gasoline on the eastern seaboard of the United States, was hit by a ransomware attack that infected the pipeline company's corporate networks.[12] The ransomware had been launched by a group known as DarkSide that offered ransomware-as-a-service: an increasingly popular business model among cybercriminals, groups like DarkSide offered to make cyber exploitation and encryption tools available to third parties who used the tools to carry out attacks on unsuspecting victims; the

---

8 Kim Zetter, *Inside the Cunning, Unprecedented Hack of Ukraine's Power Grid*, WIRED (Mar. 3, 2016), https://www.wired.com/2016/03/inside-cunning-unprecedented-hack-ukraines-power-grid/.; Dustin Volz, *U.S. Government Concludes Cyber Attack Caused Ukraine Power Outage*, REUTERS (Feb. 25, 2016), https://www.reuters.com/article/us-ukraine-cybersecurity/u-s-government-concludes-cyber-attack-caused-ukraine-power-outage-idUSKCN0VY30K.

9 *Id.*

10 Kim Zetter, *Everything We Know About Ukraine's Power Plant Hack*, WIRED (Jan. 20, 2016), https://www.wired.com/2016/01/everything-we-know-about-ukraines-power-plant-hack/.

11 Andy Greenberg, *New Clues Show How Russia's Grid Hackers Aimed for Physical Destruction*, WIRED (Sept. 12, 2019), https://www.wired.com/story/russia-ukraine-cyberattack-power-grid-blackout-destruction/.

12 David E. Sanger and Nicole Perlroth, *"Pipeline Attack Yields Urgent Lessons About U.S. Cybersecurity,"* NEW YORK TIMES (May 14, 2021, updated June 8, 2021), https://www.nytimes.com/2021/05/14/us/politics/ pipeline-hack.html.

ransomware-as-a-service operator consulted on penetration tactics and techniques and provided the necessary tools in exchange for a cut of the profits gained by the third party when the victim paid the ransom in order to have their data and systems unlocked. There was no indication that the pipeline company's operational control systems were directly impacted. And in one respect, the Federal Bureau of Investigation had an unprecedented success: it was able to seize roughly half of the cryptocurrency that Colonial Pipeline had paid to the cyber criminals.[13] However, the impact to the business networks crippled the company's ability to supply gasoline and jet fuel,[14] leading to panic-hoarding of gasoline at fuel pumps up and down the East Coast.[15]

The above-referenced attacks and other cyber threats to the energy sector have commanded the attention of the U.S. Department of Homeland Security ("DHS") and the Federal Bureau of Investigation ("FBI"). With respect to the Ukraine attack, DHS issued a press release affirming that it was committed to working with "critical infrastructure owners and operators to raise awareness of cyber threats."[16] The FBI has for years briefed pipeline industry leaders on national security threats to energy infrastructure, including cyber threats, and has warned that Russia is

---

13 "*Department of Justice Seizes $2.3 Million in Cryptocurrency Paid to the Ransomware Extortionists Darkside,*" (June 7, 2021) Press release, U.S. Department of Justice, https://www.justice.gov/opa/pr/department-justice-seizes-23-million-cryptocurrency-paid-ransomware-extortionists-darkside; and Vanessa Romo, "*How a New Team of Feds Hacked the Hackers and Got Colonial Pipeline's Ransom Back,*" (June 8, 2021), NPR, https://www.npr.org/2021/06/08/1004223000/how-a-new-team-of-feds-hacked-the-hackers-and-got-colonial-pipelines-bitcoin-bac.

14 David E. Sanger, Clifford Kraus, and Nicole Perlroth, "*Cyberattack Forces a Shutdown of a Top U.S. Pipeline,*" NEW YORK TIMES, (May 8, 2021, updated May 13, 2021), https://www.nytimes.com/2021/05/08/us/politics/cyberattack-colonial-pipeline.html.

15 Vanessa Romo, "*Panic Drives Gas Shortages after Colonial Pipeline Ransomware Attack,*" NPR (May 11, 2021), https://www.npr.org/2021/05/11/996044288/panic-drives-gas-shortages-after-colonial-pipeline-ransomware-attack.

16 Andy Ozment and Greg Touhill, *DHS Works with Critical Infrastructure Owners and Operators to Raise Awareness of Cyber Threats*, U.S. DEPARTMENT OF HOMELAND SECURITY (Mar. 7, 2016), https://www.dhs.gov/blog/2016/03/07/dhs-works-critical-infrastructure-owners-and-operators-raise-awareness-cyber-threats.

probing energy sector cyber systems.[17] And most recently, joint FBI-DHS alerts in 2021 have included narratives of Chinese cyber threats to pipelines, advisories on the DarkSide ransomware used in the Colonial Pipeline attack.[18] With respect to the Chinese cyber intrusion campaign, the joint FBI-DHS alert noted that Chinese state-sponsored actors had been targeting U.S. oil and natural gas pipeline companies between 2011 and 2013 with some success: "Of the known targeted entities, 13 were confirmed compromises, 3 were near misses, and 7 had an unknown depth of intrusion."[19]

B. Industry Context

The major cybersecurity threats today may be divided into categories of "enduring threats" and "emerging and sector-specific threats." "Enduring threats" include the data-related cyber threats that may be suffered by any organization; these are not unique to the energy sector, and may include data breaches (encompassing, for example, unauthorized disclosure of personally identifiable information ("PII"), intellectual property, and financial data); compromises of business email that can lead to misdirected funds in cyber-facilitated wire fraud schemes; ransomware; and website defacement. "Emerging and sector-specific threats" include information operations and related harassment, weaponization of

---

17 *FBI and Federal Partners Brief Pipeline Industry Leaders on National Security Threats to Energy Infrastructure*, U.S. FED. BUREAU OF INVESTIGATION (Nov. 7, 2019), https://www.fbi.gov/contact-us/field-offices/houston/news/press-releases/fbi-and-federal-partners-brief-pipeline-industry-leaders-on-national-security-threats-to-energy-infrastructure; *see also* Robert Walton, *FBI Warns Russia Is Probing Energy Sector Cyber Systems as Threat to Industrial Control Technology Grows*, UTILITYDIVE (Aug. 21, 2020), https://www.utilitydive.com/news/fbi-warns-russia-is-probing-energy-sector-cyber-systems-as-threat-to-indust/583929/.

18 "*Alert (AA21-131A), Joint CISA-FBI Cybersecurity Advisory on DarkSide Ransomware,*" (May 11, 2021), Federal Bureau of Investigation and Department of Homeland Security Cybersecurity and Infrastructure Agency, https://us-cert.cisa.gov/ncas/alerts/aa21-131a.

19 *Alert (AA21-201A), "Chinese Gas Pipeline Intrusion Campaign, 2011 to 2013,*" (July 21, 2021), Joint Cybersecurity Alert issues by Federal Bureau of Investigation and Department of Homeland Security Cybersecurity and Infrastructure Agency, https://us-cert.cisa.gov/ncas/alerts/aa21-201a.

information, and the physical or kinetic harms that can be caused by cyber incidents and that are uniquely tied to the energy sector, such as personal injury, property damage, and environmental harm.

Cybersecurity threats to the energy industry can manifest in different ways for different components of this diverse sector, as different computer systems control facilities such as interstate electric grids, pipelines, nuclear power facilities, and other energy systems and infrastructure. However, there are some common features of energy industry threats, three of which are discussed below: (1) high-value targets for nation-state adversaries; (2) 'energy systems' increasing attack surface as systems become increasingly complex from a geographic and technological standpoint; and (3) older systems that have limited ability to be patched or upgraded. Data-related threats that are not unique to the energy sector, such as theft of privacy-protected information, intellectual property, and encryption of data through the use of ransomware, are discussed further below.

1. Geopolitical Adversaries

It should come as no surprise that ambitious and technologically savvy nation-states can, and do, target the energy systems of their geopolitical adversaries. As DHS has advised, certain nation-states "have the ability to leverage sophisticated tools to target other nation-states with the intent of driving geopolitical outcomes."[20] These nation-states use tools like malware to target companies and key executives and may seek to steal login credentials, keystrokes, confidential communications, and sensitive documents. Nation-state actors pose a particularly serious threat because the cyber threats they pose may be deployed in coordination with military tactics. Two powerful nation-states that have shown a willingness and propensity to use cyber attacks for political purposes are China and Russia.

A key distinction may be drawn between "established" nation-state actors and "emerging" nation-state actors. According to DHS, the hallmark of "emerging" actors is that their attempts to stage cyber attacks are not as consistently successful as those of established actors. "These groups have the beginning of organizational maturity, and are on the cusp

---

20 *Commodification of Cyber Capabilities: A Grand Cyber Arms Bazaar*, 2019 PUBLIC-PRIVATE ANALYTIC EXCHANGE PROGRAM 9, https://www.dhs.gov/sites/default/files/publications/ia/ia_geopolitical-impact-cyber-threats-nation-state-actors.pdf (last accessed Jan. 25, 2021).

of developing the products, processes, and people necessary to contend with the 'established' actors."[21] "Emerging" nation-state actors may look to "established" nation-states for ideas and tactics.

Energy facilities are particularly attractive targets for nation-states who are interested in cyber attacks. As James Clapper, a former Director of National Intelligence, has explained:

> Politically motivated cyber attacks are now a growing reality, and foreign actors are reconnoitering and developing access to U.S. critical infrastructure systems, which might be quickly exploited for disruption if an adversary's intent became hostile. In addition, those conducting cyber espionage are targeting U.S. government, military, and commercial networks on a daily basis.[22]

The 2021 joint cybersecurity publications from the FBI and DHS have underscored the prominence of the nation-state threat, as they have specifically called out the threats from Russia and China.[23] These nations are not the only geopolitical threats, however. In 2013, Iranian cyber actors gained access to the industrial control network for a dam in Rye, New York—a level of access that would have enabled the cyber actors to release the dam's floodgates had the system not been manually disconnected at the time of the attack.[24] Although that dam was a small

---

21 *Id.* at 10.

22 James R. Clapper, *Statement for the Record, Worldwide Cyber Threats, House Permanent Select Committee on Intelligence*, OFFICE OF THE DIRECTOR OF NATIONAL INTELLIGENCE 3 (Sept. 10, 2015), https://www.dni.gov/files/documents/HPSCI%2010%20Sept%20Cyber%20Hearing%20SFR.pdf.

23 *See, e.g., Alert (TA18-074A) "Russian Government Cyber Activity Targeting Energy and other Critical Infrastructure Sectors,"* (March 16, 2018) FEDERAL BUREAU OF INVESTIGATION and DEPARTMENT OF HOMELAND SECURITY, CYBERSECURITY AND INFRASTRUCTURE AGENCY, https://us-cert.cisa.gov/ncas/alerts/TA18-074A; and *Alert (AA21-201A), "Chinese Gas Pipeline Intrusion Campaign, 2011 to 2013,"* (July 21, 2021), Joint Cybersecurity Alert, FEDERAL BUREAU OF INVESTIGATION and DEPARTMENT OF HOMELAND SECURITY CYBERSECURITY AND INFRASTRUCTURE AGENCY, https://us-cert.cisa.gov/ncas/alerts/aa21-201a.

24 Mark Thompson, "*Iranian Cyber Attack on New York Dam Shows Future of War,*" TIME (March 24, 2016), https://time.com/4270728/iran-cyber-attack-dam-fbi/.

one, and designed for flood control rather than hydroelectric power generation, it provides yet another stark example of the ways in which foreign adversary governments have targeted—and likely will continue to target—the types of critical infrastructure associated with the energy sector.

2. The Increasing Complexity of Energy Sector Systems

The increasing complexity of energy systems has opened more doors for potential cyber attacks. Accidents are inevitable in extremely complex systems, and multiple failures that interact with each other may become magnified, despite best efforts to avoid them. While automation and digitation may assist certain sectors of the energy industry to remain afloat in the years ahead, these same technologies present potential cybersecurity vulnerabilities.[25] Further, the technological advances in the energy industry track rapid leaps in technology and interconnectedness more generally in society—the growth of big data, machine learning, and artificial intelligence continue to be transformative in business operations, while physical plants used for energy generation, storage, and transmission often continue to rely on older industrial control systems that often are not easily updated and in some cases may not be possible to migrate to more secure software platforms.[26]

Somewhat counterintuitively, increasingly complex automated systems also give rise to human errors that may in turn produce

---

25 *See, e.g.*, Dany Palmer, *Cybersecurity Warning: 10 Ways Hackers Are Using Automation to Boost Their Attacks*, ZDNET (Mar. 25, 2020), https://www.zdnet.com/article/cybersecurity-warning-10-ways-hackers-are-using-automation-to-boost-their-attacks/.

26 *See, e.g.,* Brad Plumer, "*Pipeline Hack Points to Growing Cybersecurity Risk in the Energy System,*" New York Times (May 13, 2021) https://www.nytimes.com/2021/05/13/climate/pipeline-ransomware-hack-energy-grid.html; and Tucker Bailey, Adam Marayuma, and Daniel Wallance, "*The energy-sector threat: How to address cybersecurity vulnerabilities,*" McKinsey (Nov. 3, 2020) https://www.mckinsey.com/business-functions/risk-and-resilience/our-insights/the-energy-sector-threat-how-to-address-cybersecurity-vulnerabilities# ; "Industrial Control Systems in the Energy Industry Highly Vulnerable to Cyber Attacks," Emergency Preparedness Partnerships, https://emergencypreparednesspartnerships.com/industrial-control-systems-in-the-energy-industry-highly-vulnerable-to-cyber-attacks/.

cybersecurity vulnerabilities. Indeed, human error has been cited as the cause for up to 80 percent of all incidents and accidents in complex, high-risk systems that exist in the petrochemical and nuclear power industries,[27] and human error has been cited as being the root cause of 9-17% of electrical outages.[28] The causes for human error are varied, and may include fatigue, stress, and lack of experience or knowledge. While some degree of human error is likely inevitable, the risk of catastrophic consequences can be hedged through sound risk management practices, including the incorporation of checks for certain high-risk processes and decisions and allocating critical decisions to more experienced personnel.

3. *Aging Industrial Control Systems*

Computer systems in the energy industry are frequently built on hard-coded industrial control systems that require physical access to hack. However, these systems are frequently retro-fitted to allow remote monitoring and operation, and are often controlled from, or connected to, computer systems connected to internet-enabled devices. These upgrades introduce new vulnerabilities to cyber attacks carried out from afar.

Additionally, older computer systems are prime targets for hackers and other bad actors. As such, obsolescence of computer systems is a critically important issue—the longer software or hardware has been available, the longer bad actors have had to find and exploit their weaknesses.[29] Fortunately, obsolescence can be monitored—most vendors publish the life cycle for support that they offer, so users are aware of the date that support such as security patches will be phased out.

Another practical problematic effect of old computer systems is that legacy systems may only be able to be serviced by one vendor or a small

---

27 James Merlo, *Protecting the Grid in a Time of Increasing Complexity*, TDWORLD (Dec. 19, 2018), https://www.tdworld.com/transmission-reliability/article/20972051/protecting-the-grid-in-a-time-of-increasing-complexity.

28 Mehdi Tavakoli & Mehdi Nafar, *Human Reliability Analysis in Maintenance Team of Power Transmission System Protection*, PROTECTION AND CONTROL OF MODERN POWER SYS. (Nov. 25, 2020), *available at* https://pcmp.springeropen.com/articles/10.1186/s41601-020-00176-6.

29 Alex Ruiz, *Your Old Computer Is A Security Risk*, THE SAFE: INFORMATION SECURITY—EXPLAINED (July 24, 2018), https://sites.northwestern.edu/thesafe/2018/07/24/your-old-computer-is-a-security-risk/.

number of vendors.[30] These vendors may not prioritize updating security systems, and when a lapse occurs, there may be a delay in identifying the cause of the lapse and getting the system back online. While any computer system will slowly become obsolete as time marches on, energy companies should be keenly aware of the age of their computer systems, the risk associated with them, and newer technologies that may be worth the investment for the additional security they provide.

In recognition of these challenges, the U.S. Department of Energy launched an initiative in 2021 aimed at enhancing the security of electric utilities' industrial control systems,[31] the White House issued an Executive Order on Improving the Nation's Cybersecurity[32] that may have beneficial impacts on the cyber resilience of the energy sector, and a National Security Memorandum on Improving Cybersecurity for Critical Infrastructure Control Systems,[33] another effort aimed at enhancing the long-term cybersecurity of key systems that are widely used in the energy sector.

C. Regulatory Context

The regulatory web surrounding cybersecurity risks is complex and includes not only federal and state data security laws, but other criminal and civil statutes, as well as potential exposure to common law claims that

---

30 Tucker Bailey et al., *The Energy Sector Threat: How To Address Cybersecurity Vulnerabilities*, McKinsey & Co. (Nov. 3, 2020), https://www.mckinsey.com/business-functions/risk/our-insights/the-energy-sector-threat-how-to-address-cybersecurity-vulnerabilities#.

31 "*Biden Administration Takes Bold Action to Protect Electricity Operations from Rising Cyber Threats,*" Department of Energy (April 20, 2021) https://www.energy.gov/articles/biden-administration-takes-bold-action-protect-electricity-operations-increasing-cyber-0.

32 *Executive Order on Improving the Nation's Cybersecurity*, (May 12, 2021) https://www.whitehouse.gov/briefing-room/presidential-actions/2021/05/12/executive-order-on-improving-the-nations-cybersecurity/.

33 *National Security Memorandum on Improving Cybersecurity for Critical Infrastructure Control Systems* (July 28, 2021), https://www.whitehouse.gov/briefing-room/statements-releases/2021/07/28/national-security-memorandum-on-improving-cybersecurity-for-critical-infrastructure-control-systems/.

may arise after cybersecurity breaches.[34] Relevant regulations are also promulgated by a variety of different federal and state agencies. A brief overview of the regulatory framework, as well as background on the level of security specifically expected for different components of the energy sector, follows below.

1. Federal and State Data Security Laws

At the time of this writing, the United States does not have a general federal statute that expressly requires the security of personal information across all industries and sectors. There are a patchwork of laws that impose data security requirements on particular sectors, including, for example, the Gramm-Leach-Bliley Act for financial institutions and the Health Insurance Portability and Accountability Act for health plans, healthcare clearinghouses and providers and their business associates.[35] As cybersecurity incidents have grown more common, there have been increased calls for federal legislation. These include proposals for federal data breach notification laws such as the draft Cyber Incident Notification Act, which would require companies in critical infrastructure sectors report cyber incidents to the government,[36] as well as calls for federal data privacy legislation which, in some instances, might also require notification of cybersecurity incidents.[37]

Certain data security mandates apply to the interstate electric and nuclear power industries, as explained below in Section III.E.

---

34 Jeff Kosseff, *Hacking Cybersecurity Law*, 2020 U. ILL. L. REV. 811, 815 (2020).

35 *See id.* at 815-16.

36 Lauren Feiner, "*New bill would make some companies report cyberattacks to the government*," CNBC (July 21, 2021), https://www.cnbc.com/2021/07/21/new-bill-would-make-some-companies-report-cyber-attacks-to-government.html.

37 Phillip Bezanson, "*The Battle of the Bills: Proposed Federal Data Privacy Legislation Aims to End Patchwork Problem but Increases Enforcement*," NATIONAL LAW JOURNAL (March 18, 2021) https://www.natlawreview.com/article/battle-bills-begins-proposed-federal-data-privacy-legislation-aims-to-end-patchwork.

2. *State Data Security and Data Breach Notification Laws*

All major U.S. jurisdictions (the fifty states, District of Columbia, Puerto Rico, Guam, and the Virgin Islands) have enacted state data breach laws which require notification to individuals when there has been a digital compromise of personal information or personally identifiable information about the jurisdiction's residents.[38] Although these law vary in their details, they have common attributes: a definition of protected information, which often includes details such as an individual's Social Security number and financial account information; a definition of data breach, compromise, or unauthorized access; an obligation to notify individuals and/or state consumer protection regulators such as Attorneys General; and exemptions (such as for encrypted data).[39] At the time of this writing, over twenty states have enacted general data security statutes. At least thirteen states simply require "reasonable" protection or policies for the personal information of their residents. Certain other states require more specific safeguards like encryption. Moreover, some state agencies have promulgated targeted regulations toward the industries they regulate, and this trend may increase as state regulators take a more active role vis-à-vis the federal government with respect to industry regulation.[40]

In some jurisdictions, these laws focus solely on notification obligations; in other instances, however, these state laws also impose obligations to covered entities (generally commercial businesses and other non-governmental entities) to maintain "reasonable security procedures and practices" with respect to their handling of personal information or personally identifiable information.[41]

Although much of this chapter focuses on the elements of cybersecurity risk that are unique to the energy sector, it is important to note that businesses in the energy sector are generally subject to all of the same state data security and data breach laws that apply to other types of businesses. Thus, if an energy sector company suffers a breach—

---

38 *Security Breach Notification Laws* (April 15, 2021), National Conference of State Legislatures, https://www.ncsl.org/research/telecommunications-and-information-technology/security-breach-notification-laws.aspx.

39 See *id.*

40 *See id.* at 815.

41 "*Data Security Laws: Private Sector,*" National Association of State Legislatures (May 29, 2019), https://www.ncsl.org/research/telecommunications-and-information-technology/data-security-laws.aspx.

unauthorized access or disclosure—of personal information of its employees or its customers, it will need to assess its obligations to carry out timely incident investigation and notification to impacted employees, customers, or others under applicable state data security and data breach notification laws.

3. *Cyber Threat Information-Sharing Arrangements*

The U.S. government has attempted to partner in some respects with the private sector to achieve goals relating to cybersecurity. For example, the Cybersecurity Act of 2015 provides limited immunity for companies to share cybersecurity threats and defensive measures with the federal government. Additionally, the National Institute of Standards and Technologies ("NIST") has developed various voluntary cybersecurity standards that have been implemented by a number of private sector companies and public entities.[42] The NIST standards are based around a framework consisting of "five concurrent and continuous functions" whereby stakeholders are encouraged to "identify," "protect," "detect," "respond," and "recover."[43]

While these threat-sharing arrangements represent a potentially useful alternative to more conventional regulatory and enforcement approaches, they are imperfect. As one commentator has noted, "[m]any of these laws have been on the books for many decades, and have not been substantially updated to account for the many technological changes of the modern Internet era."[44] There has been a call to modernize these laws, but legislative action does not seem imminent.

4. *Level of Security Expected*

In addition to any obligations to comply with state data security laws, businesses in the energy sector must be mindful of government regulations that may apply. The Department of Energy ("DOE") is the lead agency overseeing cybersecurity in the energy sector, including taking charge of

---

42 *See id.* at 818.

43 *Framework for Improving Critical Infrastructure Cybersecurity Version 1.1*, NAT'L INST. OF STANDARDS AND TECH. 6 (Apr. 16, 2018), https://nvlpubs.nist.gov/nistpubs/CSWP/NIST.CSWP.04162018.pdf.

44 *See* Kosseff, *supra* note 18, at 818.

protecting the nation's energy infrastructure from threats.[45] In 2018, DOE established the Office of Cybersecurity, Energy Security, and Emergency Response. Within this office is the Cybersecurity for Energy Delivery Systems Division, which leads research and development to improve the security of the nation's critical energy infrastructure from cyber threats.

Aside from general compliance with the foregoing statutes and other legal authorities, specific levels of security are required, or recommended, for different components of the energy sector. Three of these sectors—the interstate electricity sector, natural gas pipelines, and nuclear power facilities—are discussed below.

(a) Electric

The interstate electricity sector, also known as the Bulk Power System, must comply with the Critical Infrastructure Protection ("CIP") Standards promulgated by the North American Electric Reliability Corporation ("NERC"). NERC was established by the Federal Energy Regulatory Commission ("FERC") and is dedicated to reducing risks to the reliability and security of the interstate electric grid.[46] NERC's CIP Standards were developed in 2003 "to establish a baseline set of security measures across the sector" and became mandatory for the Bulk Power System in 2008.[47] The NERC CIP Standards include twelve controls that are actively being enforced.[48] These include requirements pertaining to:

- the categorization of cyber systems (CIP-002-5.1a);
- security management controls (CIP-003-8);
- personnel and training (CIP-004-6);
- electronic security perimeters (CIP-005-6);
- physical security of cyber systems (CIP-006-6);

---

45 See Katherine Sauter, Pipe Dreams: Streamlining Cybersecurity Regulatory Authority Over The Energy Industry to Increase National Security, 72 ADMIN. L. REV. 507, 514 (2020).

46 *See id.* at 522. The Energy Policy Act of 2005 expanded FERC's authority to approve mandatory cybersecurity reliability standards and associated penalties. *Id.* at 517.

47 *Id.* at 521.

48 *See CIP Standards*, N. AM. ELEC. RELIABILITY CORP., https://www.nerc.com/pa/Stand/Pages/CIPStandards.aspx (last accessed Jan. 25, 2021).

- system security management (CIP-006-6);
- incident reporting and response planning (CIP-008-6);
- recovery plans for cyber systems (CIP-009-6);
- configuration change management and vulnerability assessments (CIP-010-3);
- information protection (CIP-011-2);
- supply chain risk management (CIP-013-1); and
- physical security (CIP-014-2).[49]

Four additional CIP Standards have been filed and are pending regulatory approval (CIP-002-6; CIP-005-7; CIP-010-4; and CIP-013-2), so the regulatory context for electrical systems is in flux and should be closely monitored by electric industry members.[50]

Notably, the standards do not apply to certain types of electric infrastructure, as facilities used in the local distribution of electric energy are not included. These facilities are regulated by state or local authorities.[51]

(b) Natural Gas Pipelines

Unlike the electricity sector, regulators do not currently require natural gas pipelines to meet any industry-specific cybersecurity standards.[52] However, DHS's Transportation Security Administration ("TSA")—which is charged as the primary regulator for security in all modes of transportation, including interstate pipeline systems—has promulgated pipeline cybersecurity guidelines, which are periodically updated. These guidelines include, among other things:

- The development and implementation of a "risk-based corporate security program" by each pipeline operator to address and document the organization's policies and

49 See *id.*

50 *See id.* at "Filed and Pending Regulatory Approval" tab.

51 Richard J. Campbell, *Cybersecurity Issues for the Bulk Power System*, CONG. RESEARCH SERV. 2 n.9 (June 10, 2015), *available at* https://fas.org/sgp/crs/misc/R43989.pdf.

52 *See* Sauter, *supra* note 25, at 508.

procedures for managing security related threats, incidents, and responses;

- Ensuring that sufficient resources, including trained staff and equipment, are provided to effectively execute the corporate security program;
- Ensuring identified security deficiencies have appropriate financial resources allocated in the corporate budgeting and purchasing processes;
- Assigning a qualified primary and alternate staff member to manage the corporate security program;
- Developing and maintaining a cyber/Supervisory Control and Data Acquisition ("SCADA") security plan, or incorporate cyber/SCADA security measures in the corporate security plan;
- Developing and maintaining security elements within the corporate incident response and recovery plan;
- Implementing appropriate threat level protective measures upon receipt of a pertinent National Terrorism Advisory System ("NTAS") Bulletin or Alert; and
- Notifying TSA of security incidents meeting certain specified criteria as soon as possible.[53]

Commentators have noted that while "the TSA's voluntary Pipeline Security Guidelines incorporate most of the best practices from the NIST Framework for Improving Critical Infrastructure Cybersecurity, the TSA did not incorporate all principles, and it has no documented process for reviewing and revising its voluntary guidelines in the future."[54] Additionally, in May 2019, the U.S. Government Accountability Office ("GAO") performed a study to identify weaknesses in the TSA Pipeline Security Guidelines and concluded that the Guidelines did not include all of the elements of the current NIST framework and that the TSA did not have an identifiable process for reviewing and revising the Guidelines on a regular basis.[55]

---

53 *Pipeline Security Guidelines*, U.S. TRANSP. SEC. ADMIN. 2, (Mar. 2018), https://www.tsa.gov/sites/default/files/pipeline_security_guidelines.pdf.

54 See Sauter, *supra* note 25, at 522-23.

55 Critical Infrastructure Protection: Actions Needed to Address Weaknesses in TSA's Pipeline Security Program Management, Highlights, U.S. GOV'T

Perhaps unsurprisingly then, calls have been made for mandatory cybersecurity guidelines to be promulgated.[56] Industry members should be aware of and monitor this possibility, particularly as the policy prerogatives of the Biden administration take shape.

(c) Nuclear Facilities

Regulation of cybersecurity for nuclear facilities are shared by the U.S. Nuclear Regulatory Commission ("NRC") and the DOE.

The NRC originally issued cybersecurity requirements for licensed operators of nuclear facilities following the September 11, 2001 terrorist attacks and formalized the requirements in 2009.[57] The requirements, which are set forth in the Code of Federal Regulations, include the general requirement that "a licensee must provide high assurance that digital computer and communication systems and networks are adequately protected against cyber attacks."[58] A guidance document from the NRC further provides as follows:

> [L]icensees must protect from cyber attacks digital computer and communication systems associated with certain categories of functions and support systems and equipment, which, if compromised, would adversely impact the [safety, security, or emergency preparedness] functions of a nuclear facility. These functions include safety-related and important-to-safety functions, security functions, and emergency preparedness functions (including offsite communications). The rule specifies that digital computer and communication systems and networks associated

ACCOUNTABILITY OFFICE (May 1, 2019), https://www.gao.gov/products/GAO-19-542T.

56 *See, e.g.*, Mariam Baksh, *Leading Manufacturers Urge Senators to Establish Mandatory Cybersecurity Standards for Natural Gas Pipelines*, INSIDE CYBERSECURITY (Feb. 13, 2019), https://insidecybersecurity.com/ daily-news/leading-manufactures-urge-senators-establish-mandatory-cybersecurity-standards-natural.

57 *Nuclear Power Plants to Complete Cyber Security Programs by End of Year*, DAILY ENERGY INSIDER (Jan. 25, 2017), https://dailyenergy insider.com/news/3036-nuclear-power-plants-complete-cyber-security-programs-end-year/.

58 10 C.F.R. 73.54.

with these functions must be protected from cyber attacks that would adversely impact the integrity or confidentiality of data and software; deny access to systems, services, or data; or provide an adverse impact to the operations of systems, networks, and associated equipment.[59]

NRC documents require a detailed list of specific measures, including defense-in-depth strategies, vulnerability mitigation plans, personnel training, and the integration of cybersecurity programs with existing physical security protocols.[60] Licensees must also develop a cyber security plan that addresses: (1) how the requirements of 10 C.F.R. 73.54 will be implemented and must account for the site-specific conditions that affect implementation; (2) measures for incident response and recovery for cyber attacks; and (3) how the licensee will "maintain the capability for timely detection and response to cyber attacks," correct "exploited vulnerabilities," and "restore affected systems, networks, and/or equipment affected by cyber attacks."[61]

In addition to C.F.R. 73.54, the "Nuclear Security Recommendations on Physical Protection of Nuclear Material and Nuclear Facilities" Order promulgated by the International Atomic Energy Agency ("IAEA") states that nuclear facilities need to focus on the protection of computer-based systems associated with physical protection and nuclear material accounting and control.[62] Because computer-based systems are crucial elements of the physical protection system, as well as the control system, if these computer-based systems are compromised by malicious actors, other protection and control systems could also be at risk.

---

59 *Regulatory Guide 5.71: Cyber Security Programs for Nuclear Facilities*, NUCLEAR REGULATORY COMM'N 8 (2010), http://www.nrc.gov/docs/ML0903/ML090340159.pdf.

60 Regulatory Guide 1.152: Criteria for Use of Computers in Safety Systems of Nuclear Power Plans, NUCLEAR REGULATORY COMM'N (2010), https://www.nrc.gov/docs/ML1028/ML102870022.pdf; Regulatory Guide 5.71: Cyber Security Programs for Nuclear Facilities, NUCLEAR REGULATORY COMM'N (2010), http://www.nrc.gov/docs/ML0903/ML090340159.pdf.

61 10 C.F.R. § 73.54(e).

62 Nuclear Security Recommendation on Physical Protection of Nuclear Material and Nuclear Facilities (INFCIRC/225/Revision 5), INT'L ATOMIC ENERGY AGENCY (FOREWORD), https://www-pub.iaea.org/MTCD/Publications/PDF/Pub1481_web.pdf.

D. Legal Risks And Mitigations Associated with Energy Sector Incidents

The marriage of complex technologies, high-profile targets, and extensive regulations in the energy industry combine to create significant legal risks with respect to cybersecurity. Three such risks—catastrophic incidents, litigation risks, and regulatory enforcement risks—and mitigation strategies are discussed below. When it comes to cyber risk, money spent on mitigation measures—personnel training, technical cybersecurity measures, and relevant insurance coverage as a means of risk management—can result in significant cost savings over time, by reducing the likelihood of significant cyber incidents occurring and by reducing the likely costs of those incidents when they occur. When it comes to managing budgets and investment in cybersecurity risk mitigation measures, "Pay now, or pay more later" is a sound maxim to bear in mind.

1. *Catastrophic Incidents*

The most consequential legal risk associated with cyber threats in the energy industry is the risk that cyber intrusions could result in catastrophic physical impacts such as environmental damage, property damage, and loss of life. While there have been a number of recent catastrophic incidents resulting from the physical failures of energy facilities—including, by way of example, the 2010 Deepwater Horizon oil spill in the Gulf of Mexico and the 2011 Fukushima I nuclear accidents in Japan—the threat of catastrophic cyber attacks may well become the more profound threat moving forward. Indeed, a 2017 study commissioned for a global insurer estimated that a major cyber attack on the United States interstate electric grid could cause more than $1 trillion in economic impact and cripple the American economy.[63]

The threat of catastrophic incidents, and the astronomical potential exposure and reputational harm associated with the same, favor diligent monitoring of cybersecurity systems and robust accountability systems, as well as the maintenance of appropriate cybersecurity, property, casualty,

---

63 *Cyber Attack on U.S. Power Grid Could Cost Economy $1 Trillion*, REUTERS (July 8, 2015), https://www.reuters.com/article/us-cyberattack-power-survey/cyber-attack-on-u-s-power-grid-could-cost-economy-1-trillion- report-idUSKCN0PI0XS20150708.

and directors and officer's liability insurance coverage. However, this insurance landscape can be complex. General liability policies frequently contain exclusions for cybersecurity incidents. However, there is often enough ambiguity regarding potential scope of "silent" coverage that the UK's top insurance regulator carried out a comprehensive review of its impact, and Lloyds of London made news throughout the insurance world in 2019 when it called for all insurance and reinsurance policies to contain explicit language clarifying whether the policies did, or did not, cover losses caused by cyber incidents.[64] This issue of "silent cyber" liability has been a growing area of concern within the insurance industry in recent years, as some courts have held that many types of losses (e.g., business interruption, physical damage to equipment) must be covered under general liability and other types of policies that are not specifically sold or designated as "cyber" policies if those policies do not contain explicitly exclusions for cyber-caused losses.[65]

As a general matter, cyber insurance policies tend to provide coverage for the costs of outside counsel to serve as an incident response advisor or "breach coach" as well as forensic investigation of a potential data breach and associated notification costs if a breach of personally identifiable information has occurred. Cyber policies might include coverage for negotiation and to pay ransom for decryption or restoration of files in ransomware incidents, but they often do not pay for the replacement of devices or systems (such as backup storage servers) that may have been rendered inoperable or consequential damages associated with the permanent loss of data that cannot be recovered or restored.[66] The scope of coverage that may be applicable in a particular scenario will depend on

---

64 *"Lloyd's of London Calls for Cyber Cover Clarity in Insurance Policies,"* (July 4, 2019) REUTERS, https://www.reuters.com/article/us-cyber-insurance-lloyds-of-london/lloyds-of-london-calls-for-cyber-cover-clarity-in- insurance-policies-idUSKCN1TZ19J.

65 Bethan Moorcraft, "*What is silent cyber risk?,*" INSURANCE BUSINESS (26 Nov. 2018), https://www.insurancebusinessmag.com/us/guides/what-is-silent-cyber-risk-117150.aspx.

66 Larry P. Schiffer, Kristin Bryan, Ann LaFrance, Glenn Brown, "*CGL Exclusions for Cyberattacks and Loss of Electronic Data: Is There a Gap in Your Coverage?*" AMERICAN BAR ASSOCIATION (Sept. 2, 2020). https://www.americanbar.org/groups/tort_trial_insurance_practice/publications/the_brief/2019-20/summer/cgl-exclusions-cyberattacks-and-loss-electronic-data-there-gap-your-coverage/.

the precise wording of the policy and its exclusions and any applicable riders; reviewing these policies is crucial to understanding the scope of coverage, as policies can vary widely from one carrier to another.

2. *Litigation Risks*

While there do not appear to be any reported decisions on cybersecurity in the energy industry, litigation in the cybersecurity space more generally suggests that a variety of litigation theories may be advanced following a cyber attack. These legal theories include: breach of contract; breach of fiduciary duty; waste of corporate assets; unjust enrichment; unfair competition; property misappropriation; tort; and state and federal statutes that create a private right of action.[67] Because many private lawsuits are initiated after a company is charged by the government for a security violation, energy industry members should be cognizant of the fact that a government charge may beget more litigation.[68]

Energy industry members should also be on guard for class action lawsuits that attempt to assert the above-referenced theories. The number of class action lawsuits filed over the past several years has been rising,[69] and the potential exposure associated with these suits, as well as the cost to defend against them, can be particularly high.[70] Class action suits may

---

67 Perry E. Wallace, et al., Cybersecurity Regulation and Private Litigation Involving Corporations and Their Directors and Officers: A Legal Perspective, THE CHANGING FACES OF CYBERSECURITY GOVERNANCE 20-21 (2016), available at https://www.american.edu/kogod/research/cybergov/upload/cybersecurity-regulation.pdf.

68 *See id.* at 21 ("[M]any private lawsuits are commenced after a government agency has charged a company with a cybersecurity violation – especially if the government eventually wins, but even if there is merely a settlement. Why? One reason is that where the government has chosen to go forward with charges, there is at least an implicit assumption that there has been a thorough preliminary investigation, by an expert agency, in which substantial incriminating evidence has been uncovered.").

69 Abbie Bennett, *Class Action Lawsuits Are On The Rise*, COLUMBIA REGIONAL BUSINESS REPORT (Apr. 30, 2019), https://columbiabusinessreport.com/news/law/76380/.

70 *See* Daniel S. Wittenberg, *Class Action Spending Reaches 10-Year High*, AM. BAR ASS'N BUS. OF LAW (Sept. 26, 2019), https://www.americanbar.org/groups/litigation/publications/litigation-news/business-litigation/class-action-spending-reaches-10year-high/; *Class Action Defense*

attempt to assert a diverse array of legal theories, ranging from tort-based causes of action like negligence, to shareholder derivative actions, to statutory claims under consumer protection statutes. Energy sector companies, like those in other industries, should carefully consider the scope of their directors and officers liability coverage, as there is increasing precedent for the possibility of holding corporate directors and officers personally liable for cybersecurity incidents that take place during their tenure.[71]

3. *Regulatory Enforcement Risks*

Finally, regulatory enforcement risks present a considerable threat for certain sectors of the energy industry. Companies in the interstate electric sector and the nuclear power sector in particular may face regulatory scrutiny for cybersecurity lapses.

By way of example, in 2019, NERC fined Duke Energy a record $10 million for 127 violations of the CIP Standards.[72] Thirteen of the violations listed were rated as a "serious risk" to the operation of the Bulk Power System and 62 were rated a "moderate risk." Together, the "collective risk of the 127 violations posed a serious risk to the reliability of the [Bulk Power System]," NERC wrote. Duke later agreed to pay the fine and

---

Costs Rising; Wave of Cyber Actions Predicted, INS. JOURNAL (April 22, 2019), https://www.insurancejournal.com/news/national/2019/04/22/524334.htm.

71 Freya K. Bowen, "Recent Developments in Yahoo and Equifax Data Breach Litigation Suggest Increasing Risk of Personally Liability for Directors and Officers for Cybersecurity Incidents," TECH RISK REPORT (Feb. 6, 2019), https://www.techriskreport.com/2019/02/recent-developments- yahoo-equifax-data-breach-litigation-suggest-increased-risk-personal-liability-directors-officers-cybersecurity-incidents/; see also generally Benjamin P. Edwards, "Cybersecurity Oversight Liability," UNIVERSITY OF NEVADA LAS VEGAS LAW REVIEW (2019), https://scholars.law.unlv.edu/cgi/viewcontent.cgi?article=2246&context=facpub.

72 Elizabeth Montalbano, *Secrecy Reigns as NERC Fines Utilities $10M Citing Serious Cyber Risks*, THE SEC. LEDGER (Feb. 1, 2019), https://securityledger.com/2019/02/secrecy-reigns-as-nerc-fines-utilities-10m-citing-serious-cyber-risks/; *see also* Iulia Gheorghiu, *Duke Fined $10M for Cybersecurity Lapses Since 2015*, UTILITYDIVE (Feb. 4, 2019), https://www.utilitydive.com/news/duke-fined-10m-for-cybersecurity-lapses-since-2015/547528/.

reached a settlement with the NERC that included increased training, oversight, restructuring of roles, and addition of management and compliance tools.[73] NERC fined another utility company $2.7 million in 2018 for a data security breach following a finding that data were publicly available online that appeared to be protected information associated with the utility.[74]

Although the NRC's cybersecurity rules were implemented more than ten years ago, it has not yet completed its first round of inspections of nuclear plants to confirm compliance with the rule.[75] While there do not appear to have been any public records regarding fines or other penalties for violation of the NRC's cybersecurity rules, the NRC is empowered to issue sanctions for violations of the cybersecurity regulations,[76] and given the increased scrutiny in this space, a more aggressive enforcement approach may be on the horizon.

As discussed above, the cybersecurity guidance issued by the TSA pertaining to pipelines is advisory, rather than mandatory. If, however, calls are heeded to transform the guidance and recommendations into mandates, regulatory scrutiny and enforcement efforts will likely follow.

---

73 *Id.*

74 Eduard Kovacs, *U.S. Energy Firm Fined $2.7 Million Over Data Security Incident*, SEC. WEEK (March 14, 2018), https://www.securityweek.com/us-energy-firm-fined-27-million-over-data-security-incident; *see also NERC Full Notice of Penalty Regarding Unidentified Registered Entity*, FERC Docket No. NP18-_-000, N. AM. ELEC. RELIABILITY CORP. (Feb. 28, 2018), *available at* https://elibrary.ferc.gov/eLibrary/idmws/common/opennat.asp?fileID=14831147.

75 U.S. Nuclear Regulatory Commission Defense Nuclear Facilities Safety Board, Audit of NRC's Cyber Security Inspections at Nuclear Power Plans, OFFICE OF THE INSPECTOR GEN. (June 4, 2019), https://www.oversight.gov/sites/default/files/oig-reports/OIG-19-A-13-Audit%20of%20NRC%27s%20Cyber%20Security%20Inspections%20at%20Nuclear%20Power%20Plants%20Final%20Report%28BXK%29.pdf; see also Memorandum—Inspection Guidance During Transition from COVID-19 Telework, U.S. NUCLEAR REGULATORY COMM'N (May 28, 2020), https://www.nrc.gov/docs/ML2014/ML20141L766.pdf.

76 *See* 10 C.F.R. 50.111 (providing for criminal sanctions).

E. Conclusion—Practical Considerations and Tips

The complexity of cybersecurity issues in the energy industry cannot be overstated. Moreover, the stakes are high, as the consequences of breaches or failures may be catastrophic. There are, however, a number of straightforward steps industry members may take to begin dealing with cyber threats proactively and meaningfully with the assistance of sophisticated counsel. In closing, we offer the following practical considerations and tips:

1. How to Think about Cyber Defense

- Cyber threats may come from nation-states, organized cyber crime groups, or individual "smash-and-grab" hackers. The tactics and goals of the threats may differ. Be mindful of, and prepared for, both types of threats.

2. Enterprise Approach

- Cultivate an organizational culture that is cognizant of the risks posed by cyber threats. This should include board-level engagement. An effective cybersecurity program requires strong processes and technologies, but the most important driver of success is people.

3. Legal Frameworks

- Know your potential exposure if an incident occurs. This can help drive effective decision-making in terms of oversight and resource allocation.

4. Cyber Preparedness

- It is far better to be proactive than reactive in this space, and this is particularly true when it comes to potential costs. Develop and implement a cyber incident response plan and conduct tabletop exercises and other training on this plan. Model potential risk scenarios and adapt processes and systems accordingly.

5. *Privacy Programs*

- Laws relating to data security and data privacy are constantly evolving. From a data privacy and data protection perspective, start with the basics: ensure that sensitive data are protected and work from there to create robust accountability and compliance systems. Develop data governance policies and invest in training and awareness.

6. *Vendor Liability*

- Review contracts with information-technology vendors and update them as necessary to reflect modern realities. Do not assume that a historic relationship with a vendor means that the relationship continues to make good business sense at this juncture.

7. *Risk Tiering*

- Focus initial efforts on protecting the company's "crown jewels." In the energy sector, these may include protecting personally identifiable information of employees and customers and protecting industrial control systems from penetration. Implementing the strongest protections for the areas that carry the most significant risks can be an effective way to prioritize cybersecurity resources and planning.

8. *Risk Mitigation*

- Successful and focused risk-mitigation can be accomplished in ways that are cost-effective and practical, and include employee training, technical cybersecurity defenses, incident response plans and tabletop exercises, reassessing and ensuring appropriate insurance coverages are in place, and other proactive measures. View risk mitigation as an investment, rather than a cost of doing business.

9. *Multi-Pronged Approach*

- Cybersecurity preparedness should include personnel training, technical defenses, and sound and effective policies and procedures. The very best technical measures cannot eliminate, or compensate for, all possible forms of human error. Policies and procedures that provide clear guidance, and regular training on those policies, as well as on the constantly changing cybersecurity threat environment, are critically important components of any holistic approach to cybersecurity defense.

10. *Interdisciplinary Approach.*

- Planning and execution of cyber risk mitigation planning and cybersecurity defense implementation in the energy sector, as with other sectors of the economy, is most effective when conducted by interdisciplinary teams that can bring together expertise and perspectives from business units, information technology departments, human resources, legal, risk, compliance, finance, and other key stakeholders within an organization.

Chapter 18

Professional Services*

Professional liability insurance, also commonly referred to as Errors & Omissions ("E&O") or malpractice insurance, is designed to respond to claims alleging a breach of one's duty of care. Black letter law long established that such duty of care is measured against an industry standard of care, weighing factors such as client and patient expectations, local community standards, and the type of professional services being performed.[1] These standards of care are also heavily influenced by state licensing requirements, rules of conduct, and oversight committees.[2]

---

* By Renier P. Pierantoni.

1 *See, e.g., Toogood v. Owen J. Rogal, D.D.S., P.C.,* 573 Pa. 245, 254, 824 A.2d 1140, 1145 (2003) ("[M]edical malpractice can be broadly defined as the unwarranted departure from generally accepted standards of medical practice resulting in injury to a patient, including all liability-producing conduct arising from the rendition of professional medical services."); *LaMarca v. United States,* 31 F. Supp. 2d 110, 125 (E.D.N.Y. 1998) ("By not following the admitting physician's orders, the Hospital departed from generally accepted standards of care in the community thereby breaching its duty of care. . . ."); *see also, Gleason v. Title Guarantee Co.,* 317 F.2d 56, 60 (5th Cir. 1963) ("[P]hysician's duty is to exercise skill 'according to the standard of those who are qualified by training and experience to perform similar services in the community.'"); *Palmer v. Nissen,* 256 F. Supp. 497, 501 (D. Me. 1966) ("The parties agree that defendant's duty, as an attorney, to plaintiffs, as his clients, must be measured by the standards of professional conduct prevailing in the community in which he did his work.").

2 *See, e.g., Teague v. St. Paul Fire & Marine Ins. Co.,* 2006-1266 (La. App. 1 Cir. 4/7/09), 10 So. 3d 806, 825, writ denied, 2009-1030 (La. 6/17/09), 10 So. 3d 722 (the "Rules of Professional Conduct may be relevant in defining the particular standard of care imposed upon attorneys in most circumstances, they do not provide an independent basis upon which to impose liability upon an attorney for legal malpractice.") and *Gilles v. Wiley, Malehorn & Sirota,* 345 N.J. Super. 119, 125–26, 783 A.2d 756, 760 (App. Div. 2001), which held, similar to other jurisdictions, that "while we recognize that a cause of action for malpractice cannot be based exclusively on the asserted breach of an *R.P.C.,* nevertheless it is clear that the *R.P.C.*s may be relied on as prescribing the requisite standard of care and the scope of the attorney's duty to the client." *Baxt v. Liloia,* 155 *N.J.* 190, 201, 714 *A.*2d 271 (1998); *Davin,*

Indeed, it is because of the potential for accidents and unintentional errors in judgment by the professional that insurance is needed to protect the insured against not only "first-party" losses (*i.e.,* the insured's losses for business income loss, expenses to repair and restore operations, *etc.*), as well as third-party losses (*i.e.,* claims asserted by clients and patients for their losses) arising from malpractice claims.

To that extent, the scope of professional liability ("PL") policies has sought to evolve to address the professional's need for first and third-party claims related to cyber breaches. This is especially so in the context of unauthorized exposure of personally identifiable information ("PII") or Personal Health Information ("PHI"). The insurance industry's change to meet the demands for expanded and particularized cyber coverage is, in large part, due to the ever-expanding privacy regulations affecting the professional's duty of care and those preventive mechanisms to avoid or minimize the inadvertent or unauthorized disclosure of PII/PHI related confidential communications, health records, and financial data.

As a result, professionals are required, more so than ever before, to abide by a duty of care that necessarily mandates the professional's obligation to proactively implement protective measures as required under the Health Insurance Portability and Accountability Act ("HIPAA"), American Bar Association ("ABA") Model Rules, and related federal state and local ethical rules and guidelines. Though these rules and procedures may have been, at one time, considered extraordinary as preventive measures, the advent and use of online technology, social media, and cloud programs have become commonly used tools used by professionals today.[3]

L.L.C. v. Daham, 329 *N.J. Super.* 54, 74 n. 3, 746 *A.*2d 1034 (App. Div. 2000). Thus, violation of an *R.P.C.* has essentially the same status and function in a malpractice action as a statute that prescribes a standard of conduct as in a negligence action. Its breach is evidential of the defendant's failure to comply with the required standard of care. *See, e.g., J.S. v. R.T.H.,* 155 N.J. 330, 348, 714 A.2d 924 (1998)."

3 Indeed, the modern-day professional's duty of care now includes protecting PII/PHI at pretty much all costs—including their transmission through (i) the Internet of Things "IoT" devices (the term is used here to describe the interaction between medical professionals, patients, insurers, and third-party vendors in transferring data through integrated software and hardware programs over networks through mostly handheld devices, essentially replacing the stand-alone desktop model); (ii) online storage programs, such as Google Drive and Dropbox, and (iii) cloud-based "service as service"

Instead, todays professional—especially one serving in the capacity of a confidant or fiduciary—often handles, stores, and transmits extremely sensitive PII/PHI. Consequently, when PII/PHI is breached, it will necessarily subject the professional to costly first-party claims and embarrassing (and more expensive) third-party liability claims due to a departure from the standard of care. However, despite these protections, and judging from growing litigation concerning first- and third-party data compromise due to business email compromise, ransomware, and other cyber threats, no preventive measures are ever fully guaranteed.[4]

Accordingly, while professional liability policy renewals over the past 5 to 10 years have evolved to provide coverage for risks of unauthorized PII/PHI disclosure, insurance industry actuaries nonetheless seem to be still struggling to address the evolving cyber risks present to the professional. As a result, professionals should not assume the PL policies of yesterday will protect them against the modern-day cyber threats of today and tomorrow. Instead, professionals should ensure they have the coverage needed to both protect against potential liabilities for malpractice in the traditional sense and comply with more stringent and demanding rules governing the protection of their clients' and patients' privacy—an

---

("SaaS") or "platform as a service" ("PaaS") third-party data protection encryption platforms.

4 Ransomware is a particularly sinister and common form of malware. It targets weaknesses in a company's overall networking and human resource structure by locking and making inaccessible critical company and client information, thus "preventing staff from performing work and, as a consequence, shutting down operations for a substantial period of time." BECs are no less devious, presenting themselves as fraudulent email scams, such as phishing, that focus on professionals and business entities involved in transferring assets and funds. Source: Federal Bureau of Investigation (FBI) Internet Crime Complaint Center, *Internet Crime Report*, pp. 14 (2019); see also Lawyer Monthly, THE GROWING CYBER THREAT FACING THE LEGAL SECTOR, by Andy Pearch (October 22, 2019) at https://www.lawyer-monthly.com/2019/10/the-growing-cyber-threat-facing-the-legal-sector/; National Law Review, *3 Cyberattacks and 3 Practical Measures Lawyers Can Take to Protect Themselves*, Volume X, Number 357 (May 13, 2020) at https://www.natlawreview.com/article/3-cyberattacks-and-3-practical-measures-lawyers-can-take-to-protect-themselves.

approach to disclaiming coverage for cyber-related claims that insurance carriers will most certainly rely upon.

On that front, for solo practitioners and small professional offices reading this publication are (hopefully) aware of coverage options available for cyber risks, it may be a foolhardy decision to continue to cut corners on coverage based on a self-convinced certainty they have nearly foolproof protective measures and systems in place. As Benjamin Franklin once said: "In this world, nothing can be said to be certain, except death and taxes."

While it may be stating the obvious that such practitioners who do not implement the most basic security measures, such as "strong passwords with two factor authentication, encrypting email and files," nor obtain a suitable level of cyber coverage, represents the ideal "low hanging fruit" for the hacker, the following message nonetheless bears reinforcement here:[5] When it comes to insurance coverage—whether as a stand-alone cyber policy, by endorsement to a PL policy, or as one of several modules within packaged commercial policy protection, *the cost of not protecting oneself from the increasing risk of data exposure of PII and PHI due to cyber vulnerabilities likely outweighs the savings*. As such, all professionals should assume their PL policies will not protect them in the event of a cyber threat until further review with a broker, risk manager or insurance coverage counsel. Together, they should carefully read the provisions of their PL policies—including so-called comprehensive cyber endorsements that may have been pitched to you as "good enough" for cyber-attacks—rather than standing on assumptions that could find the professional deprived of coverage down the road.

A. Professional Obligations Regarding PII, PHI & Technology

Professionals must ensure they comply with strict state and federal and ethical rules and laws regulating PII/ the storage and transmission of PII/PHI and related data. Those requirements further buttress the common law duties of care by lawyers, medical practitioners, accountants,

---

5 Janet Falk, *Solos and Small Firms: Conduct Your Cybersecurity Check-up*, 226 NJLJ 2565 (October 12, 2020) (quoting Ryan J. Cooper, Esq. of Cooper, LLC).

expanding their responsibilities to include a knowledge of complex and somewhat onerous privacy laws and rules to protect client data. In addition, the professional is also expected to not only protect such client and patient data, but are ascribed the obligation to be knowledgeable about the associated risks that come from the use of technology in storing and transmitting PII and PHI. As such, the days of simply storing such data in office file cabinets and local hard drives and servers may not be enough. The professional must now familiarize herself/himself with technology that, ironically enough, encourages the storage of such data outside what was once considered the safe confines of a traditional office environment. By being required to use external sources of protection, such as cloud-based programs and third-party data protection companies. The professional is arguably *more* susceptible to hacking and, thus, increasing its confidential files to cyber risks and ensuing liabilities due to the compromise of the same.

Legislative efforts across the country have resulted in businesses and professions that collect, store, and transmit PII for their clients and patients to abide by strict regulations concerning cybersecurity safeguards to protect the same. In addition to the most commonly understood privacy regulation, HIPAA, there is a growing legislative movement towards allowing private rights of action under state cybersecurity regulations. Illustrative of these efforts is the California Consumer Privacy Act ("CCPA"), the Illinois Biometric Information Privacy Act ("BIPA"), and New York's Stop Hacks and Improve Electronic Data Security ("SHIELDS") Act.[6] To that extent, many professionals, including

6 For example, the SHIELD Act focuses on entities maintaining computer records containing PII on New York State residents, and established cybersecurity standards around data protection. See, e.g., Arctic Wolf White Paper, *New York State's SHIELD Law: Is Your Business Ready?* (October 29, 2019) at https://arcticwolf.com/resources/legal/shield-law-is-your-business-ready. Similarly, HIPPA (and its companion regulation, the HITECH Act)[6] requires a medical professional or organization experiencing a cyberattack to take immediate steps to both fix the technology loophole and engage in measures to "mitigate any impermissible disclosure of protected health information, which may be done by the entity's own information technology staff, or by an outside entity brought in to help (which would be a business associate, if it has access to protected health information for that purpose)." *Id.* Specifically, HIPAA Privacy Rule at 45 CFR Part 160 et seq. and 45 CFR Part 64 (Subparts A and E) sets forth "national standards to protect individuals' medical records and other personal health information and

attorneys, are required to be reasonably informed and take reasonable measures in diligently protecting such data through the use of technology vendors and IT staff.[7]

---

applies to health plans, health care clearinghouses, and those health care providers that conduct certain health care transactions electronically." See, Daniel Solove (July 2, 2020), *How Cyberinsurance Is Responding to Ransomware: An Interview with Ken Suh, Mark Singer, and Marcello Antonucci* at https://www.linkedin.com/pulse/ how-cyberinsurance-responding-ransomware-interview-ken-daniel-solove/; see also, https://www.hhs.gov/hipaa/for-professionals/privacy/index. html#:~:text=The%20HIPAA%20Privacy%20Rule%20establishes,certain%20health%20care%20transactions%20electronically.

7 *See, e.g.,* ABA Model Rule of Professional Conduct 1.4 and 1.6(c), Comment 18, one of several ABA rules and opinions requiring lawyers to use "reasonable efforts" to prevent unauthorized access to and disclosure of client data and "take special security precautions to protect against the inadvertent or unauthorized disclosure of client information when required by an agreement with the client or by law, or when the nature of the information requires a higher degree of security." LAWYERS' OBLIGATIONS AFTER AN ELECTRONIC DATA BREACH OR CYBERATTACK, ABA Formal Op. 18-483. In an ironic twist, this essentially means that files kept digitally to avoid office-related disasters become equally susceptible to another type of disaster: cyberattacks that target client files kept in the cloud. To that extent, the ABA reports that little more than 25% of all U.S. law firms with 100 or more lawyers experience a data breach resulting in a compromise of not only their operational and financial databases, but electronically stored client files as well. *See, e.g.,* Law 360, *1 In 4 Law Firms Are Victims of A Data Breach*, September 22, 2015 at https://www.law360.com/articles/705657/1-in-4-law-firms-are-victims-of-a-data-breach.

Similarly, ABA Formal Opinions 18-482 and 18-483, which seek to minimize professional risks to disaster scenarios that might compromise client files, specifically require lawyers who use cloud-based servers holding client files to apply a level of technological expertise that may elude some of us in the profession without hiring an outside vendor. ABA Formal Opinion 18-483 ("to understand technologies that are being used to deliver legal services to their clients [and] maintain those technologies in a manner that will reasonably safeguard property and information that has been entrusted to the lawyer."). ABA Formal Opinion 18-483 and various state rules and ethics opinions regarding the use of electronic devices that contain confidential client information, and the obligations of a lawyer in the event

While these privacy focused rules and regulations may not dictate that a professional exhibits perfection in being reasonably informed about data security and implementing proper data security systems, they do serve influence the scope of a standard by which tribunals (and insurance carriers) have relied upon in determining whether there was a departure from the duty of care.

B. Most Common Cyber Risks for the Professional

The risk of unauthorized disclosure of PII, PHI, or other sensitive and confidential information due to a cyber breach is the same regardless of the size of the professional practice, with over half of all small businesses experiencing some form of cyberattack.[8] Indeed, according to at least one Federal Bureau of Investigation report, losses from cybercrimes totaled $3.5 billion in 2019, with over 340,000 complaints filed with the FBI from socially engineered hacks occurring on average each year since 2014.[9]

As alluded to earlier, ransomware and BECs represent the most common forms of cyber threats to professionals. Concerning ransomware, one of the most infamous events, the "WannaCry" virus, targeted IoT medical devices used in England's national healthcare

---

of actual or suspected unauthorized access by third parties to confidential client information. *See also,* U.S. Department of Health & Human Services, Office of Civil Rights Cyber Security Checklist at https://www.hhs.gov/sites/default/files/cyber-attack-checklist-06-2017.pdf.

8 Insurance Information Institute White Paper, *Protecting against #cyberfail: Small Business and Cyber Insurance*, p. 3, (November 2017) at https://www.iii.org/white-paper/protecting-against-cyberfail-small-business-and-cyber-insurance-103017.

9 Federal Bureau of Investigation (FBI) Internet Crime Complaint Center, *Internet Crime Report*, pp. 5, 15 (2019). As to the effect on small businesses, not only do the increasing and more sophisticated cyber-attacks result in approximately $100,000 in losses to small businesses, on average, as the result of IT and financial network data and information breaches, with over 20% of any stolen monies never recovered by the FBI. Moreover, an additional $100,000 in business interruption losses is lost on average for small businesses.

service.[10] [11] In another major ransomware incident, "NotPetya," DLA Piper suffered a cyber-attack in 2017 that started in its overseas Ukrainian offices during an upgrade to its payroll software. As a result, DLA Piper employees globally were not able to access the firm's work laptops and office computers, as well as the firm's telephones and email systems.[12] Though DLA Piper was not the original target of the NotPetya virus, and did not lose any data, it is reported that the attack cost the firm several million dollars, including approximately 15,000 hours of paid overtime for their IT staff to fix the problem (leading the firm to rebuild its Windows-based data).

Equally notorious are two prominent socially engineered cyber breach insurance coverage cases involving BECs—*Medidata* and *American Tooling*[13]—both of which involved computer fraud coverage under crime policies. Nonetheless, these cases are worthy of a brief discussion here due to their potential impact on professionals and often misplaced "comfort from having purchased both "cyber" and "computer fraud" coverage,

---

10 According to Advisen, one of the leading data and solution providers to insurance industry stakeholders and other professional service providers, slightly more than 50% of BEC related losses occur in the finance and information systems sector, and less than 2% take place in the professional service industry. *See* Advisen's 2019 Cyber Guide at https://www.advisenltd.com; *see also*, *Ransomware in Health Care: An Insurance-Based Analysis,* by Kristen Psaty and Christina Terplan (August 30, 2017) at https://www.americanbar.org/groups/litigation/committees/insurance-coverage/articles/2017/summer2017-ransomware-healthcare/.

11 CNET, *Ransomware froze more cities in 2019. Next year is a toss-up*, by Alfred Ng (December 5, 2019) at https://www.cnet.com/news/ransomware-devastated-cities-in-2019-officials-hope-to-stop-a-repeat-in-2020/.

12 Arctic Wolf White Paper re: The Top 8 Legal Industry Cyberattacks, August 17, 2020 at https://arcticwolf.com/resources/legal/top-8-legal-industry-cyberattacks.

13 Medidata Solutions, Inc. v. Federal Insurance Company, 268 F. Supp. 3d 471 (S.D.N.Y. 2017); American Tooling Center, Inc. v. Travelers Casualty and Surety Company of America, 895 F.3d 455 (6th Cir. 2018); see also, Principle Sols. Grp., LLC v. Ironshore Indem., Inc., No. 1:15-CV-4130-RWS, 2016 WL 4618761 (N.D. Ga. Aug. 30, 2016), aff'd, 944 F.3d 886 (11th Cir. 2019) (where the court found policy language to be ambiguous, and thus the claim covered, regarding a multimillion-dollar loss from a fraudulent transfer BEC scheme similar to Medidata).

believing that such policies most certainly protect and cover for such losses."[14] In *Medidata*, the Southern District found coverage for nearly $5 million in fraudulent wire transfer losses through external "spoof" emails from a hacker posing as the president of Medidata under the crime segment of the company's business policy. Coverage was found despite the carrier, Federal, arguing that sending external, fraudulent messages did not constitute a breach and accessing of Medidata's computer systems. Similarly, in *American Tooling*, the U.S. Court of Appeals reversed a Michigan federal district court decision that held there was no coverage for a BEC attack under the computer fraud provision of the company's policy. That is because, as the Court found, American Tooling did not suffer a "direct loss" due to intervening events. The Court of Appeals found that the intervening. temporal period, as well as any other perceived difference between the fraudulent emails and wire transfer to the hacker's bank account, to represent a distinction without a difference.[15]

Lastly, the well-known Panama Papers leak of over eleven million confidential documents from the Panama-based law firm Mossack Fonseca, and its ultimate demise less than two years later, was the direct result of a breach of its email server. The breach led to the global disclosure of how the firm advised its clients regarding the protection and creation of shelters and schemes other efforts to minimize or avoid tax consequences. This disclosure leads to the launching of numerous investigations and lawsuits alleging financial wrongdoings in the form of the laundering of money, dodging of sanctions and illegal evasion of tax laws, and the resignations of prominent government leaders and condemnation of powerful figures and celebrities.[16] The success of the email server breach was likely because Mossack Fonseca was seen by

---

14 International Risk Management Institute ("IRMI") Insurance law Essentials—*Deep Dives: Insurance Coverage For "Phishing" Losses—Make Sure Your "Net" Is Adequate Before You Get Caught*, February 2018 (Lisa M. Campisi—Blank Rome, LLP).

15 The Sixth Circuit also rejected the insurer's argument that the "electronic data" exclusion applied, and the phrase "use of a computer" required, the actual manipulation of computer keys to effectuate the fraudulent transfer pursuant to so-called "instructions or directions" by a person. *American Tooling*, 895 F.3d at 460-464 (6th Cir. 2018).

16 BBC News Service, *Panama Papers: Leak firm Mossack Fonseca 'victim of hack'* (April 6, 2016) at https://www.bbc.com/news/world-latin-america-35975503.

hackers as the very "low hanging fruit" discussed earlier, likely due to its not being subject to the more stringent cybersecurity regulations in place for U.S. and EU based law firms.

Again, the lesson to be learned here is that you must carefully review your PL and any gaps in other policies in consultation with brokers, risk managers, and outside insurance counsel to obtain more expansive and superior coverage grants for ransomware, BEC and similar cyber-attacks unique to professionals.[17] Even when understood, the policy language may not adequately address the individual professional risks and, in any event, is a new and growing area of coverage such that policy terms may not be interpreted and (predictably) applied by courts in coverage actions. This may not be as much of an issue for larger professional practices since they typically maintain a risk manager who is tasked with ensuring the firm, organization or association is not bereft of cyber coverage for present and anticipated malware attacks. However, under any scenario, there is no escaping what the professional's obligation may be to purchase cyber coverage to minimize potential liability from a cyber incident. As such, an examination of some of the policy forms available to provide coverage for such cyber related losses is warranted here.

17 In addition to the added cost of maintaining cyber insurance, when added to the evolving world of cyber coverage – many of which are still being written as manuscript policies, i.e., policies specifically tailored to the insured's needs and risks—many professionals, unfortunately, choose to maintain coverage under their PL policies in the hope that it covers malware claims as part of professional services. Even when specific cyber coverage is purchased, either as part of a package, an endorsement or standalone policy, to fill in the gaps left by PL policies or traditional business property insurance, it may become victimized a second time to the denial of a malware type claim. Per the Insurance Information Institute White Paper on Protecting against #cyberfail: *Small Business and Cyber Insurance*, p. 3, (November 2017) at https://www.iii.org/white-paper/protecting-against-cyberfail-small-business-and-cyber-insurance-103017, "[e]ndorsements are added to packages and policies that these small businesses already buy, such as their Business Owners' Policy (BOP) or commercial property policy. These endorsements add various coverages not already addressed in the existing policy."

C. Potential Under Policies Other than Cyber-specific Policies

1. Coverage Through "Silent Cyber"

IT networks, including hardware and software storage and processing systems, are often the target of hackers resulting in losses arguably covered under "all risk" business property or "package" policies. However, insurers—in response to coverage decisions over the past few years finding "silent cyber" coverage under those policies—have taken to either explicitly excluding coverage for "electronic data" for purposes of limiting coverage under traditional PL policies for cyber related claims."[18] Regardless, a basic understanding of professional liability terms and conditions is needed before the professional can glean whether coverage is—unintentionally or not—available under a traditional PL or E&O policy, no less what additional coverage may be needed for cyber threats.[19]

---

18 Various non-cyber policies limit coverage, as such, have resorted to both general and detailed definitions of electronic data. Compare, "shall mean any data stored electronically on a Computer Network, including Confidential Information" (Professional Liability and Network Security and Privacy Policy form EP-MPL-001-08/2017) vs. "information, facts or programs stored as or on, created or used on, or transmitted to or from computer hardware, including systems and applications software, hard or floppy disks, CD-ROMs, tapes, drives, cells, data processing devices, or any other media which are used with electronically controlled equipment" (ISO Form CG 00 01 04 13).

19 On a related note, as to what constitutes "Property" in the context of PII/PH, due to technology's greater integration of software and hardware software in data storage, handling, and dissemination on behalf of the professional, the "tangible"/ "non-tangible" distinction has become blurred. As discussed earlier, there are vulnerabilities to storing PII/PHI locally and, as such, such data is encouraged to be stored in a cloud-based program, many times through a third-party vendor. But what do we make of the unauthorized access of PHI through a medical IoT, *i.e.,* "turnkey," device? Or a request made through a Microsoft program to the accounting department of a law firm purporting to authorize the transfer of client funds? In each of these circumstances, the professional's losses from PII/PHI data breaches may be found to be more akin to "hardware" ("tangible") rather than commonly excluded "software" property damage. Renier P. Pierantoni, *Vendor's Products Liability Coverage: An Option for Malware-Based* Cyber *Breaches*, Law.com (Online) / New Jersey Law Journal (December 13, 2019) at https://www.law.com/njlawjournal/2019/12/13/tapping-into-a-vendors-

2. *Potential Coverage for Cyber Claims under Traditional PL Policies*

There are typically three questions in determining whether a professional potentially has coverage under a traditional PL policy for first or third-party claims: (1) how is a "Wrongful Act" defined; (2) how are "Professional Services" defined; and (3) how is "Loss" defined? Though PL and E&O policies are purportedly negotiated and drafted to meet the needs of the particular industry or profession, and their proportional risks, you will often find the coverage grants and exclusions to be pretty formulaic. For example, with regard to third-party PL policy claims, almost always written on a "claims made" basis, an insurer will typically promise to pay, on behalf of the insured professional, for "Loss" or "Damages."[20] that the professional is "legally obligated to pay" as the result of a claim made within the policy (or extended) reporting period.[21] Typically, the types of "loss" or "damage" that fall within the scope of many such provisions are compensatory judgments, settlements, awards, pre-judgment and post-judgment interest, defense costs and certain punitive or exemplary damages, fines or penalties, sanctions. Moreover,

---

products-liability-coverage-an-option-to-consider-for-malware-based-cyber-breaches/.

20 The insured professional is encouraged to closely examine how these terms are defined in the PL and E&O policies, as the scope of what constitutes a "loss" or damage varies outside of the standard coverage for compensatory judgments, settlements, awards, pre-judgment and post-judgment interest, defense costs and certain punitive or exemplary damages, fines or penalties, sanctions. *Compare* Asset Management Liability Policy Form EP-ASM2020-POL-05/2020 and Design Professionals Liability Policy Form NAV DPL 1001 (01 10).

21 This is distinguished from "occurrence" based claims, where the Colorado Supreme Court elucidates on the distinction between the two as follows: "occurrence policies and claims-made policies are almost the mirror image of each other: an occurrence policy provides coverage for events that happen during the policy period, even if the claim is brought many years in the future; a claims-made policy provides potential coverage for claims brought against the insured during the policy period, even if the underlying event giving rise to liability occurred many years in the past." *Craft v. Philadelphia Indem. Ins. Co.*, 343 P.3d 951, 957 (Colo. 2015), *opinion after certified question answered*, 599 F. App'x 846 (10th Cir. 2015).

the Loss/Damage must be caused by a "Wrongful Act" that took place during the insured's rendering of "Professional Services."[22]

One PL policy designed and tailored towards an asset management company is somewhat illustrative of traditional PL policies across many professions in defining a "Wrongful Act" as follows:

> "any actual or alleged act, omission, error, misstatement, misleading statement, neglect or breach of duty in the rendering or failure to render Professional Services for others by or on behalf of an [Insured], including any person or entity for who's Wrongful Acts in the rendering or failing to render Professional Services such [Insured] is vicariously liable."[23]

Though the same policy goes on to define the scope of "Professional Services" in terms of the services typically offered by an asset management company (e.g., "(i) advice regarding investments in securities, (ii) investment, management, back-office services and asset allocation services performed; (iii) the selection, monitoring and supervision of unaffiliated asset managers, third-party funds or third-party service providers; and (iv) the publication of written material pertaining to any of the activities and services outlined above), the gist of these services can be similarly categorized in the context of scope of services and advice to a client, oversight of those services, and publication of materials relating to such services, such as the case is with a PL policy issued to an attorney or law firm (e.g., services "performed or advice given as a lawyer"; services performed by the lawyer "in the course of a lawyer-client relationship advice given or services performed. . . although such services could be performed wholly or in part by non-lawyers"; the "publication or presentation of legal research papers or similar legal materials.").[24]

---

22 Some PL policies do not define the term "Wrongful Act", instead providing coverage for a "Claim. . . arising out of any act, error, omission or Personal Injury in the rendering of or failure to render Professional Services" by the insured professional. *See, e.g.,* Markel Insurance Company Lawyers Professional Liability Insurance Policy form MLP 0001 07 13.

23 *See, e.g.,* Asset Management Liability Policy Form EP-ASM2020-POL-05/2020.

24 Lawyers Professional Liability Platinum Protection Policy Form LPL—100 (09/10). Note that the parallel drawn between these two PL policy forms, or any other PL/E&O policies, should not be interpreted as taking a

3. *Policy Language Obstacles/Limitations to Coverage for Cyber Events*

To better understand the difficulties presented in seeking coverage under a traditional PL policy for a cyber related loss, even where there is no exclusionary language or endorsement for cyber, let us examine the likelihood of coverage for a third-party claim base on the unauthorized disclosure and fraudulent transfer of funds from a law firm's trust accounts through a phishing scam. More specifically, the phishing scam took place from a fake client email address requesting confirmation of the client's retainer deposited in an IOLTA account, and a response by an attorney or the firm's accounting department unintentionally provided the scammer backdoor access to the law firm's Clio program that stored the requested account information. One question is whether this constitutes a "loss" under the PL forms previously discussed (none of which contain an "electronic data" or similar exclusion).[25] As defined, assuming the hypothetical claim is and or can be brought to judgment as a compensatory loss, then the stolen funds arguably constitute a "loss".

However, the nub is whether the "loss" was caused by a "wrongful act" during the law firm's rendering of "professional services." An insured professional might assume there is a valid basis for coverage because there was an "actual or alleged act, omission, error" (e.g., the attorney's response to a spoof client email providing the hacker credentials for the trust account through Clio). Moreover, the firm's retainer agreement may specifically contemplate the use of the third-party SaaS such as Clio in the providing of services or, perhaps more significantly, necessarily contemplates the use of an external, third-party program due to the

---

lackadaisical approach to an insured's analysis of its own PL/E&O policy. Instead, the comparisons are generally drawn to elucidate on the gaps in coverage for cyber risks that likely exist under traditional and, even technology—PL and E&O policies. Moreover, leaving aside whether the "loss" or "damage" falls within the defined term, many coverage disputes will nearly always focus on whether a "wrongful act" took place in a professional's providing "professional services. Indeed, the properly defined pairing of a "wrongful act" with "professional services" will likely be critical to the professional's ability to access coverage for not just first and third-party claims for cyber-attacks, but first and third-party coverage for any claim unique to that profession.

25 As pointed out through some of the form policies cited to in this chapter, for many third-party claims, the Loss would likely include defense costs.

mandates of the very privacy and ethics rules and regulations discussed earlier in this chapter. After all, is there any doubt that an attorney, in rendering "professional services" to a client, is expected to include as part of those services the accurate entry of time entries? Or a tickler/calendar system to track deadlines? In fact, any integration with other legal applications often used by attorneys (*e.g.,* PACER, eDiscovery and data management programs, and web-based applications that used to digest and tag deposition testimony) that solely serve to meet the needs of the client and the matter being handled? One would think not.

Then again, query whether the insurer might nonetheless disclaim coverage? For example, is it unreasonable to imagine the insurer asserting a reservation of rights (am insurer's letter to an insured that coverage for a claim may or may not apply, subject to further investigation) for the third-party claim because there is still an open question as to whether there was a "wrongful act" since the term contemplates an act performed during the actual rendering of legal advice or services, and the attorney responding to the spoof email was doing neither by simply answering a question as to the deposit of client funds? Perhaps, but what is clear is that coverage—whether it applies, can be disclaimed or otherwise delayed—will turn on the language of the policy and its defined terms and conditions. As such, analyzing your PL and E&O coverage should be done with the cooperation of an experienced broker or insurance coverage counsel, and never assumed when it can instead be clarified by obtaining express endorsements and policy add-ons that focus on not only cyber coverage in general, but specific cyber attacks of which there are myriad choices.

Viewed another way, in the context of obtaining the right amount of coverage for cyber claims, would you rather retain to the services of savvy, experienced policyholder counsel, willing to engage in costly insurance coverage litigation, to seek coverage for a cyber related claim that is neither expressly excluded under a PL policy, but also not (as counsel for an insurer will no doubt argue) purportedly contemplated under the PL policy, especially given the availability of companion cyber insurance programs, endorsement and modules that were available to the insured to complement, or "gap fill," such provisions.[26] Accordingly, coverage for a

26 One particular insurance company cautioned insureds that coverage for third-party cyber claims compromising a clients' privacy and security MAY 'un-intentionally' BE AVAILABLE on some Professional Liability Policies, this

cyber related loss under PL and E&O policies—as is the case for any claim for any loss under any policy—will be dictated by devil in the details—here, what type of cyber attack took place?

D. Insurance Coverage Disputes Over Coverage for Cyber Claims

As discussed earlier, the two most common cyber threats facing professionals are BECs and ransomware; however, in the context of insurance coverage disputes, the two might as well be as different as oil and water. Where ransomware nearly always involves first party coverage given the insured is being threatened with the loss of *company* data, BECs also target insureds, but may involve accessing client PII/PHI and funds—not surprisingly disguised as client email addresses. This potential of client data and fund exfiltration will necessarily implicate third-party coverage under a PL and E&O policy.

Examining again *Medidata*, which began with the crime policy carrier's attempt to disclaim coverage for the loss of bank funds due to a phishing scheme the carrier asserted fell outside the scope of "Computer Fraud" coverage, which as defined as "the unlawful taking or the fraudulently induced transfer of Money, Securities or Property resulting from a Computer Violation." The policy defined "Computer Violation" as: "the fraudulent: (a) entry of Data into . . . a Computer System; [and] (b) change to Data elements or program logic of a Computer System, which is kept in machine readable format . . . directed against an Organization."[27] The court nonetheless recognized the phishing scam as just another, more advanced form of fraudulent transfer covered under the policy.[28] But, what

---

'unintended coverage' is NOT ADEQUATE for a Data Breach, Malware or Extortion/Ransomware."

27 *Medidata*, 268 F. Supp. 3d at 474.

28 *Id.* Indeed, professionals should not be fooled by some cyber policies that specifically provide coverage for something termed "funds transfer fraud", but which focuses on coverage for the loss of insured's funds, not the clients. *See, e.g.,* Technology Professional and Cyber Advantage Form 912-5000 10 19 ("FUNDS TRANSFER FRAUD: We will pay "your" loss of "money" or "securities" directly resulting from a "funds transfer fraud" that: a. First occurs during the "policy period"; and b. A "described authorized person" first discovers during the "policy period" and first reports to us during the "policy period" or within 90 days after the end of the "policy period").

if the policy implicated was a PL or E&O policy containing the definitions of "loss," "wrongful act" and "professional services" discussed herein?

Another point to be made here that some insurers, rather than focusing on how a policy should provide coverage for the insured, oftentimes seeks to do quite the opposite, posing disclaimer arguments that strain incredulity to avoid paying for an otherwise legitimate and covered loss. That approach should be no less ignored by insureds in the context of cyber claims—whether under traditional PL, tech E&O or standalone (or module) cyber policies.

On a related note, where hardware and software purchases (or licensing of the same) involve turnkey transactions, as is the case with IoT devices, recent decisions have trended toward finding software to be "goods," and thus covered as a tangible item.[29] Similarly, in the context of whether malware impacting third-party software affects a "service" (as opposed to a tangible good or product), and whether resulting liability from the cyber event constitutes "property damage," the trend is to find the traditional "software" vs. "hardware" coverage argument as amounting to a distinction without a difference.[30]

---

29 It is also interesting to note that, according to at least the New Jersey appellate court, the term "turnkey" does not necessarily mean the simultaneous integration of software with hardware, and one can follow the other in time. *See, Dreier Co. v. Unitronix Corp.*, 218 N.J. Super. 260 (App. Div. 1986).

30 *See, e.g.,* N.J. Rev. Stat. § N.J.S.A. 12A:2-313.2 (2013); Food and Drug Administration, *Guidance for the Content of Premarket Submissions for Software Contained in Medical Devices* (May 11, 2005), pp. 6, 8, 15 ("Blood Establishment Computer Software" defined as a "software product"; development of software device and revisions as "product development"); *Eyeblaster, Inc. v. Fed. Ins. Co.,* 613 F.3d 797, 801-802 (8th Cir. 2010) (ruling that allegations of a computer OS being rendered inoperable as the result of the installation of new software constituted the "loss of use of tangible property."); *Retail Sys., Inc. v. CNA Ins. Companies,* 469 N.W.2d 735 (Minn. Ct. App. 1991). In a recent decision by the U.S. District Court in Maryland specifically addressed that issue, finding that a Businessowners Special Form Computer Coverage endorsement provided coverage for a ransomware attack that resulted in a "direct physical loss of or damage to" its computer software and stored data—all of which the company's hardware needed in order to properly function. *See Nat'l Ink & Stitch, LLC v. State Auto Prop. & Cas. Ins. Co.*, No. SAG-18-2138, 2020 U.S. Dist. LEXIS 11411, at *3-6, 13 (D. Md. Jan. 23, 2020).

As we continue to engage in commerce through the increased use of smart devices via the IoT—devices that necessarily integrate software with hardware, thus arguably rendering the idea of "standalone" software a relic of the past—so too do we increase the risk of cyberattacks which can take the form of the viruses infecting software that also do harm to hardware. This is undoubtedly the case when it comes to the theft of PII/PHI stored "in the cloud." With regard to PL and E&O coverage in these circumstances, the insurance industry has sought to write coverage to protect specific risks related to cyber events, such as "technology" PL/E&O policies.[31] Such policies market to computer software and hardware vendors and manufacturers, website developers, and related companies to protect them for third-party claims related to their data protection products and services.[32]

Finally, what of the professional and her/his PL policy cyber risk endorsements or "modes" seeking to purportedly address coverage for the various types of electronic data coverage otherwise excluded under the insured's business property and commercial liability policies?

E. Filling PL and E&O Coverage "Gaps" with Cyber Insurance

Even an insured professional holding a technology PL/E&O policy should not necessarily count on standard form cyber insurance policies, given many cyber liability insurance tends to be written and issued as third-party coverage for data breaches that implicate confidential information not authorized to be exposed or stolen. Instead, though standard form cyber insurance may be pitched by brokers to risk managers and insureds as a gap filler to address underinsured business property or commercial general liability policies—all of which will likely contain electronic data exclusions—such professionals should not assume that the cyber policies pitched actually do the job of providing coverage for each and every cyber related risk.

Given the now prevalent cyber related exclusions (e.g., for "electronic data" and "technical services") in PL policies that should be protecting the professional against client, patient and/or third-party claims that arise out of cyber related negligence, wrongful acts, errors and omissions that may

---

31 IRMI website defining Cyber and Privacy Insurance terms at https://www.irmi.com/term/insurance-definitions/cyber-and-privacy-insurance.

32 *Id.*

occur in providing professional services, how do cyber endorsements and cyber policy "modules" best interact with PL and E&O coverage? Take, for example, how best to provide coverage for losses associated with ransomware. While such coverage may be available as companion cyber-extortion coverage under cyber insurance policies, will such coverage also cover BECs? As a result, insured professionals should expect insurance carriers issuing PL coverage to review and investigate not only the facts alleged supporting a data breach claim to see if they fall within the coverage part that is written to expressly cover that particular cyber claim.

As a result, the insurance industry has a variety of cyber policy forms and modules that should provide coverage for specific cyber risks, in the form of third-party claims[33] and first party (the insured's) property losses,[34] that could affect anything from "customers' personal information, such as Social Security or credit card numbers, [] exposed or stolen by a hacker or other criminal who has gained access to the firm's electronic network. The policies [also] cover a variety of expenses associated with data breaches, including notification costs, credit monitoring, costs to defend claims by state regulators, fines and penalties, and loss resulting from identity theft. . . . website media content, as well as property exposures from: (a) business interruption, (b) data loss/destruction, (c) computer fraud, (d) funds transfer loss, and (e) cyber extortion."[35]

---

33 Such third-party claims are those that result from the insured's failure to protect and have released (or threatened to be released) as the result of an unauthorized network and data security breach a client's or patient's personally identifiable information ("PII") and sensitive financial data and medical information. Source: Insurance Information Institute at https://www.iii.org/white-paper/protecting-against-cyberfail-small-business-and-cyber-insurance-103017; *see also,* NJSBA Annual Meeting Presentation, *What is Cyber Insurance & How is the Market Responding?* The Hanover Insurance Group (2019).

34 First party claims that typically fall into this category relate to crisis management (e.g., regulatory compliance with privacy laws, training, monitoring, and public relations), business interruption (resulting in operation and network interruption as the result of malware, ransomware, and similar distributed denial of service (DDoS)), fines & penalties, digital and network security replacement and restoration expenses, and defense costs. Source: Insurance Information Institute at https://www.iii.org/white-paper/protecting-against-cyberfail-small-business-and-cyber-insurance-103017. *Id.*

35 Cyber extortion policies provide coverage for defense costs and indemnity/settlement of an extortion threat against a company's network, as well as the

One type of cyber coverage drafted by a major insurance carrier serves as part of a package policy protecting professionals, called "modules."[36] Under the Specialty Risk Form, each module is dedicated to the specific cyber risk from which the insured seeks to be protected, such as "Media Content", which defines a similarly worded "wrongful act" discussed earlier herein as limited to acts that result in "infringement of [various IP claims]. . . plagiarism, piracy or misappropriation or theft of ideas. . . invasion, infringement or interference with [various privacy rights," defamation, libel, slander" etc. Note that this particular mode may not provide coverage for a phishing or ransomware scam, such as the one that took place in *Medidata* and *DLA Piper*, respectively, and as such, allows for a multitude of various, other modes and endorsements that can change the scope of coverage (indeed, this particular specimen policy contained no less than 42 endorsements). The "Media Content" module sets out three pages of exclusions seeking to insure (i) coverage for a "silent cyber" event does not exist and (ii) the insured purchases another mode of coverage that best fits the type of risk for which the professional needs coverage.

Under a separate mode of the Specialty Risk Form, coverage is provided specifically for so-called "Security Failure" or a "Privacy Event," as those terms are defined. More relevant to the professional seeking coverage for cyber threats, the Specialty Risk form provides a module terms "Specialty Professional Liability Insurance" that provides E&O coverage for "professional services" as that term is defined pursuant to a separate endorsement. Notably, one endorsement titled, "Internet Professional Services Coverage Endorsement" seems to specifically cover the hypothetical raised earlier concerning a breach due to a hacker's access of client funds through Clio or similar SaaS platform.[37] By drafting coverage in the form of modules, the presumption is that the insurance

---

cost of hiring a security firm to track down and negotiate with blackmailers. International Risk Management Institute website at https://www.irmi.com/term/insurance-definitions/cyber-and-privacy-insurance.

36 Specialty Risk Protector Policy Specimen Form 101013 (12/13) ("Specialty Risk Form").

37 Redefining "Professional Services" as inclusive of "Internet Professional Services", which provides coverage for services provided by the insured professional that encompass "internet hosting services", "e-commerce transactions", "web portal services", and "cloud computing services." Specimen module form 103526 (12/09) as part of the Specialty Risk Form.

industry allows the insured professional freedom to define the scope of her/his professional services, cyber risks its faces, and coverage sought for those risks.[38]

Other insurers provide more broad stroked coverage for cyber threats that can be grouped together as "social engineering fraud" by way of endorsements to PL policies.[39] One such endorsement defines "social engineering fraud" in the context of s PL policy as "the transfer, payment or delivery of an **Insured's Money** or **Securities** from the **Premises** or **Transfer Account** by: (i) an **Employee** acting on good faith reliance upon a telephone or written instruction that purported and reasonably appeared to have been issued by a **Vendor**, **Client**, or **Employee** authorized by an Insured to approve and direct such payment, transfer or delivery, but in fact, was issued by a **Third-party** not so authorized; or (ii) a **Financial Institution** as instructed by such **Employee**."[40] Given these policies are written to fill in the gaps to or otherwise buttress existing CGL, E&O and PL coverage lines, it is incumbent upon the professional to carefully review whether the present PL and E&O coverage adequately meets cyber risk protection needs.

---

38 Some endorsements are for (i) adding a "Cyberterrorism Coverage and War Exclusion"; (ii) redefining the terms "Privacy Threat" and "Security Threat" to include "cyberterrorism"; (iii) physical theft of hardware; (iv) redefining security failure to include "theft of a password or access code"; and, (v) redefining "confidential information," "privacy event," and "regulatory action" to include GDPR (General Data Protection Regulation) issues.

39 "Social engineering" is a term used to describe a cyber incident where a hacker induces a company staff member or employee to fraudulently transfer funds to the hacker's account through the use of a spoof email, i.e., an email that leads the victim to believe it comes from a trusted vendor, client, or executive/administrative superior at their purported direction.

40 Policy Form CR 0301 (09-15); compare, Policy Form FB 02 43 1216, which defined "social engineering fraud" as "the intentional misleading of an Employee through the fraudulent misrepresentation of a material fact which is relied upon by an Employee believing it to be genuine. This fraudulently mispresented material fact must be received by the Employee directly from the perpetration of the fraud and not from any person, intermediary or source." Indeed, even the insurer sought to fill in gaps for cyber threats that was discussed earlier with what it terms a "Professional Liability and Network Security and Privacy Policy" (Form EP-MPL-001-08/2017) by covering liabilities from "Electronic Data" and "Technology Services," as those terms are defined therein.

F. Conclusion

The reality is that, for many professionals, whether it be the result of cost savings, assumptions about coverage, or simply a lack of attentiveness to the cyber perils that await, they still provide services to their customer, clients and patients without adequate coverage in place to protect against cyber risks.[41] As a result, I am reminded by sound advice given to me as a young lawyer by a senior partner: "On day one, you're an attorney—subject to the same rules, the same expectations, the same standards—as the client would expect of me, so prepare, advise and take responsibility accordingly." Similarly, in the world of cyber, whether large or small, lucrative, or struggling, pennywise or pound foolish, cyber threats make no distinction between the fully protected professional and the professional who cut corners on coverage.

As such, it is the wise professional who will take extra time from what is likely a busy schedule in order to work cooperatively with experienced brokers or policyholder counsel to ensure an adequate level of cyber coverage is obtained to protect against first and third-party losses *before* they arrive in the form of BECs, ransomware or other cybersecurity attack. With so many small and mid-sized firms not having dedicated IT professionals, it may be worth noting that many policies come with consulting services that policyholders can access for no additional cost or little additional cost. The "take rate" on these services is low, but is well-worth the time when professionals may be risking a professional negligence claim for failing to safeguard information.

---

41 According to the American Bar Association's Legal Technology Resource Center, only one-third of law firms and attorneys responded as having cyber insurance in place. See 2019 ABA Legal Technology Survey Report at https://www.americanbar.org/groups/law_practice/publications/techreport/abatechreport2019/cybersecurity2019/; *see also*, Insurance Information Institute White Paper, *Protecting against #cyberfail: Small Business and Cyber Insurance* at p. 3.

Chapter 19

The Transportation Industry*

The transportation industry allows for the movement of people, goods, and things within a variety of regions. These systems include the combinations of vehicles, infrastructure, and operations that facilitate such movement.[1] The United States transportation network includes but is not limited to automotive, aviation, and shipping transit. These systems are crucial to the U.S. economy and are a way of life. Unfortunately, the automotive, shipping, and aviation industries are not commonly considered cybersecurity target markets. However, these industries have become increasingly digitized over the years, relying more and more on computer software, codes, and online platforms to manage various parts of their businesses. With the increasing advancement of information technology and the interconnectivity of networks within these transportation infrastructures, the risks associated with their cyber systems have also increased. Secure transportation infrastructure is essential for safety and continuity within the transportation industry.[2]

While cyber coverage is evolving in the industries covered in this chapter, the topic of insurance is essential to any discussion of cybersecurity. As the use of alternative intelligence through cyber systems evolves, cybersecurity will become more critical for protecting the businesses operating within these industries. It is essential to remember that this digital dependence opens these businesses up to attacks, not just from independent actors but also from those acting on others' behalf. Cyber insurance is designed to provide compensation to individuals and

---

* By Daniel B. Garrie and Dr. Bonnie Reagan-Aylor.

1 *See* Andrew Cox, Fynnwin Prager & Adam Rose, *Transportation Security and the Role of Resilience: A Foundation for Operational Metrics*, 18 TRANSP. POL'Y 307-17 (2011), https://www. sciencedirect.com/ science/article/abs/pii/S0967070X10001137?via%3Dihub.

2 Barry C. Ezell, et al., *Cyber Risk to Transportation, Industrial Control Systems, and Traffic Signal Controllers*, 33 ENV'T SYS. & DECISIONS 508-16 (2013), https://www.researchgate.net/publication/263176807_ Cyber_ risk_to_transportation_industrial_control_systems_and_traffic_signal_contr ollers. As these attacks increase, cyber adversaries are becoming more and more persistent, skilled and technologically savvy. *See id.*

organizations for damages that occur because of cybercrime.[3] Cyber insurances are formed by expert cyber security organizations and computer repair, data recovery organizations, to offer a full array of expertise during such a time that an attack occurs.[4] Some cyber insurances reduce the overall cost of repairs and recovery by negotiating a smaller ransom and then paying it.

After all, wars are fought using more than just physical weapons.[5] As such, we must understand what technological developments have been made, how those developments have improved the operation of businesses in each industry, and where the possible vulnerabilities exist. We then need to consider the impact of a cyber incident on the company and evaluate whether current industry practices are sufficient to protect businesses against cyber threats. Finally, but significantly, where there are gaps, cyber insurance policies need to be considered a hedge to those risks and minimize potential damages.

A. Summary of the State of Cyber Risks in the Automotive, Shipping and Aviation Industries

Below is a discussion of the state of cyber risks facing the automotive, shipping, and aviation industries. The summary below reflects the current state, but new threats will undoubtedly emerge in the coming months and years.

---

3 Dwight Weingarten, *Ransomware can hold cities hostage. Will cyber insurance help?,* CHRISTIAN SCIENCE MONITOR, (Dec. 18, 2019), https://www.csmonitor.com/Technology/2019/1218/Ransomware-can-hold-cities-hostage.-Will-cyber-insurance-help (last visited Sept. 25, 2021).

4 Sean Michael Kerner, *Cisco, Apple, Aon, Allianz Partner on Cyber-Risk Management,* EWEEK (Feb. 5, 2018) https://www.eweek.com/security/ cisco-apple-aon-allianz-partner-on-cyber-risk-management/ (last visited Sept. 25, 2021).

5 Tom O'Conner, Naveed Jamali & Fred Guterl, *Are We Headed for a Cyber Pearl Harbor?* NEWSWEEK GLOBAL, (July 2-9, 2021), at 20-31, https://www.magzter.com/stories/Business/Newsweek/ARE-WE-HEADED-FOR-A-CYBER-PEARL-HARBOR (last visited Sept. 25, 2021).

1. *Survey of the Current State of Cybersecurity in the Automotive Sector*

Autonomous vehicles and connected cars are great examples of the drastic technological advances the automotive industry has made over the years. Unfortunately, while these advances are desirable from a consumer point of view, they also make vehicles more prone to cyber-attacks. The automotive industry, especially auto dealerships, has been a favorite target of cybercriminals due to the massive amount of sensitive customer information they collect, process, and store across their networks. A 2019 report from Automotive News noted that an average of 153 viruses and eighty-four malicious spam emails were detected and blocked on a dealership's network daily.[6] While this is not an all-encompassing statistic, it is certainly sufficient to raise concern.

Malicious or phishing emails,[7] often used by cybercriminals as a delivery mechanism for ransomware and other malware, can be quite costly for businesses that fall victim to them. Opening an attachment or clicking on a link included in these emails can lead to a shutdown of the business's systems, causing it to come to a complete halt. For example, in 2020, when an unsuspecting employee opened an email that appeared to be from a coworker, most of the computers across Arrigo Automotive Group's multiple dealerships were compromised and ransomed.[8] It cost the dealerships upwards of a half of a million dollars to remediate this ransomware incident.[9] While the cost of repair, replacement, and recovery can be expensive after a ransomware attack, cyber insurance has developed solutions to directly pay the ransomer to reduce the cost. Instead of having to replace equipment and go through channels to recover data,

6 John P. Rondini, *Michigan Auto Dealerships Are at Risk of Cyber Attacks During the COVID-19 Crisis—Here's How to Combat Against the Threats*, LEXOLOGY (Apr. 20, 2020), https://www.lexology.com/library/detail.aspx?g=c3fbb887-367e-4f80-b21d-9bb6627dabc0.

7 Phishing emails are just one example of how dangerous cyber incidents could be to the automotive industry.

8 Stu Sjouwerman, *Auto Dealership Becomes Latest Victim of Ransomware Attack Costing Up to $500,000*, KNOWBE4 (Jan. 13, 2020), https://blog.knowbe4.com/auto-dealership-becomes-latest-victim-of-ransomware-attack-costing-up-to-500000.

9 *Id.*

the ransom is paid, and repair is minimal.[10] Most insurances come with a team of experts that can repair, recover, and use high customer support to get the word out to affected people. It's a great cost saver.

There continues to be a concern for how data is stored and shared across platforms for automotive businesses.[11] In recent years, the automotive industry has suffered multiple massive data leak incidents. First, in 2018, approximately 47,000 files containing factory records from companies such as Tesla, Toyota, Volkswagen, Fiat, Ford, and General Motors were part of a data leak that exposed blueprints and factory schematics, contracts, invoices, work plans, client materials, and various nondisclosure agreements which described the sensitivity of the leaked data.[12] Then, in 2019, a data leak resulted in 198 million car buyers' records being compromised.[13] The information, ranging from phone numbers to addresses and more, was exposed to the public, in plain text, on the internet because the database they had been stored on was not secure. Perhaps the worst part of this incident is that it was not detected internally by the company itself. Instead, a security researcher from a different firm discovered, traced, and reported the affected company's breach.[14] The sheer volume of data compromised in these two incidents alone evidences the need to develop cybersecurity protocols, ensure adequate insurance coverage, and protections in the automotive industry.

A current trend in dealing with this cybersecurity trend is to mix cyber insurance with a cyber risk management service. This is a great option for optimizing the full array of protections against data breaches, intrusions, and trojans. There are insurance benefits in the form of discounts, and some insurances even require a risk management plan or service to

---

10 S. Limmroth, *Cyber Insurance: An Insider's Guide to Why You Should Have Coverage*, 22 J. OF HEALTH CARE COMPLIANCE 51, at 51-69 (2020).

11 In addition, some states, such as Massachusetts, are in the process of amending laws which, if approved, would weaken vehicle manufacturers' ability to ensure the safety of their vehicles.

12 Alexa St. John, *Massive Data Breach Hits Several Automakers, Report Says*, AUTOMOTIVE NEWS (July 20, 2018), https://www.autonews.com/article/20180720/OEM06/180729931/massive-data-breach-hits-several-automakers-report-says.

13 *Id.*; *see generally* Lynn Rohland, *Navigating Complex Data Privacy Terrain*, AUTOMOTIVE NEWS (Mar. 9, 2020), https://www.autonews.com/commentary/navigating-complex-data-privacy-terrain.

14 *See id.*

approve a cyber insurance application. However, a 2019 study found that the most prevalent of the measures is the insurance regardless of the risk management plan, which oftentimes comes with packages to manage the cyber risk without consulting an external plan.[15] In this regard, while a cyber risk management plan may be a good way to round out the safety of using cyber interfaces, the cyber insurance prevails as the option that is most helpful and most in need of refinement for future evolutions of cyber advancement.

Autonomous and technologically advanced vehicles, on the other hand, give rise to a new set of concerns due to some of the latest connectivity conveniences that they offer. In 2015, a vehicle was hijacked over the internet by hackers.[16] By tapping into the vehicle's connectivity features, hackers were able to gain control over its functions, including the steering wheel, brakes, and even the engine.[17] This incident never would, or could, have happened before the digitization of vehicles. However, it is now a serious threat that needs to be evaluated and accounted for as businesses in this industry build cyber incident protection and response plans.

The interplay of the car dealership coupled with the introduction of autonomous cars has begun to create a lot of new implications related to gaps and new coverage needs among the automobile insurance industry. Implications arise over multiple types of insurance needs—that which automobile consumers buy to cover their purchase as well as themselves, and that which manufacturers and car dealers purchase to cover defects, hacking, and vender mess-ups. Car manufacturing companies purchase special insurance to cover any unknown defects, currently undetected with the automobile being sold. While dealers are required to obtain their own insurance policies, those policies are minimal. While most dealer policy requirements vary by state, the most prevalent requirements could be

---

15 Alessandro Mazzoccoli & Maurizio Naldi, *Robustness of Optimal Investment Decisions in Mixed Insurance/Investment Cyber Risk Management,* 40 Risk Analysis: An Int'l J. 550, at 550-564 (Oct. 15, 2019), https://doi.org/10.1111/risa.13416.

16 *Cyber readiness: Are Auto Companies Prepared to Counter the Risk of a Cyber Attack?* PwC, https://www.pwc.com/us/en/industries/industrial-products/library/automotive-cyber-readiness.html (last visited Feb. 26, 2021).

17 *Id.*

upgraded to address the complications of computerized cars and out of shop access by those who engage in cybercrime.

There is another prevalent conversation among the automobile industry that effects how insurance is administered. This concerns questions of who owns the data along the chain, which entity is responsible for the security of data, who is ultimately responsible to safeguard against hackers, and who is required to inform consumers of a breach? Other questions include what type of IoT errors will need to be reported to safety commissions, and who along the chain needs to report them? Also, when will defects need to be reported, what will trigger the requirement of a non-routine report?[18] Are these questions that can be answered through insurance? Are the increasing requirements for internal, external, or insurance agency monitoring for insurance policy approval a good starting point?

(a) Manufacturer Liability and Inclusions for the Changing Auto Industry

With the new atmosphere of autonomous, semi-autonomous, and smart safety features in automobiles, manufacturers are becoming increasingly more liable when accidents do occur. In fact, there is a decrease in the number of claims towards individual automobile insurance because the safety features in the automobiles activate in response to programmed code instead of humans, taking the fault away from the auto owner and displacing it back to the manufacturer.[19] In response, manufacturers now must rely on another type of insurance that directly deals with mishaps to the automatic features. Autonomous vehicle features become vulnerable to cyberattacks the second the software within the automobile becomes a resting app in wait for a user to purchase the automobile. The applicable insurance now becomes a package of Cyber Insurance with Technical Errors and Omissions plus Cyber Gap insurance.

The first of these insurances that a business would attempt to cover cyber-attacks with is general Cyber Insurance. Cyber insurance is coverage for data breaches and identity fraud. It covers services for the

---

18 H.M. O'Brien, *The Internet of Things: A Mosaic*, 10 J. OF MULTIDISCIPLINARY RES. (1947-2900) 81, at 81-104 (2018).

19 Shauhin Talesh, *Data breach, privacy, and cyber insurance: How insurance companies act as "compliance managers" for businesses,* 43 L. & SOC. INQUIRY, 417, 417-440 (Dec. 27, 2018).

mitigation and resolution of a breach. It covers client's identity protection plus any data recovery. It also covers internal damage to a business that occurs during a cyber-attack or virus in reaction.[20]

Although cyber risk insurance appears to cover exactly what is missing from general liability, there are a few typical exclusions that make the insurance null and void. For instance, a failure to maintain minimum security requirements which could relate to industry standards, or else a service prescribed minimum required security practice, may cancel any ability to recover from the policy. For an insurance company that provides their own security software, the wording may create the need for a consumer to have to use that specific security protocol, without directly stating it. The risk management requirement is oftentimes indirectly enforced using a contingent commission that an agent earns when the insured company has a reduction in losses after being insured.[21] Some policies require an insured to apply for a policy and then require that the insured use the approved protocol described in the insurance application. It is imperative that a business representative or attorney review the wording concisely to properly implement the requirements mentioned in the exclusion. An attorney can request removal of certain parts of an exclusion and review an application prior to submittal to ensure submitted protocols are something that can be continuously implemented.

Many cyber insurance policies include bodily injury and property damage. A common claim after a cyber-attack is damages due to mental anguish, mental injury, shock, emotional distress, and humiliation that stem from a data breach.[22] However, oftentimes these types of injuries are excluded from cyber insurance. It is important to make sure emotional injuries are included so that the company does not become vulnerable to an uncovered claim.

---

20 Sean M. Kerner, *Lloyd's Estimates the Impact of a U.S. Cloud Outage at $19 Billion,* EWEEK (Jan. 24. 2018), at 1, https://www. eweek.com/cloud/lloyd-s-estimates-the-impact-of-a-u.s.-cloud-outage-at-19- billion/ (last visited Sept. 25, 2021).

21 *New England Sys. v. Citizens Ins. Co. of Am.*, No. 3:20-cv-01743 (JAM), 2021 U.S. Dist. LEXIS 93601, at 3 (D. Conn. May 17, 2021).

22 *Wengui v. Clark Hill, PLC*, 440 F. Supp. 3d 9, at 15 (D.D.C. 2020) (Plaintiff contends that the damages related to him were persecution and harassment by means of the data being published on social media and then people protesting his ability to stay in this country.)

Another common exclusion is for prior acts. Cybercrime sometimes takes a few months or longer to become evident. If an insurance company can prove that the crime started before the policy did, it won't matter when the result of the crime took place—the prior acts exclusion keeps the insurance company from having to pay for it.[23] One thing to look for when purchasing cyber insurance is the retroactive date of any inclusions. Also, check that the insurance does cover for criminal acts since a common exclusion is that such acts are not covered, entirely cancelling the policy for true cyber-attacks. Reading the wording carefully will let you know if there is room for a prior, undetected crime to be covered.[24] The exclusion is not always a problem for those renewing their insurance because the retroactive date will usually revert to a time under the previous policy term. However, for those switching insurance or subscribing to new insurance, this may be a concern that should be reviewed.

Another common exclusion in all types of insurance, not just cyber insurance, is the war exclusion. The war exclusion is #6 in the top ten exclusions for cyber insurance.[25] This exclusion means there is no coverage for invasions, revolutions, military coups, and terrorism. This could mean that most cyber risks might not be covered if the insurance company can produce convincing evidence that the attack came from a related entity. Currently countries such as the United States, Russia, Israel, Iran, China, the United Kingdom, and North Korea can commit

---

23 TechTarget Contributor, *What is Cybersecurity Insurance (Cyber Liability Insurance)?,* TechTarget.com, Security Policies -> Threat Management (July 2021), https://searchsecurity.techtarget.com/definition/cybersecurity-insurance-cybersecurity-liability-insurance#:~:text=TechTarget%20Contributor%20Cybersecurity%20insurance%2C%20also%20called%20cyber%20liability,transfers%20some%20of%20the%20risk%20to%20the%20insurer.

24 Sasha Romanosky, Lillian Ablon, Andrea Kuehn & Therese Jones, *Content Analysis of Cyber Insurance Policies*, RAND CORP WR-1208, 3, 14, https://www.ftc.gov/system/files/documents/public_events/1223263/panel012_cyberinsurance_policies.pdf.

25 *Id.*

cyber warfare, with some already intensely engaged in such warfare.[26] [27] It's critical to make sure that the overall insurance package includes coverage for warfare somewhere.

Since cyber insurance exists to cover when the company experiences a data breach or comes under a cyber-attack, auto manufacturers still need insurance to cover software errors or omissions in the car. The the coverage gap creating the need for errors and omissions is similar between autonomous cars and generalized technology as this need is a universal liability in the cyberworld. When an automobile fails because the wrong part was included or the vendor's airbags won't deploy, etc., then the manufacturer will use general Errors and Omissions ("E&O") insurance to cover the loss. Here, when the company uses software in their automobiles that end up with a glitch, maybe misreading a distance calculation or discovering an object the wrong way, even failing to see a line for lane departure, they can be covered by the E&O insurance.[28] For software and artificial intelligence ("AI") in autonomous vehicles, such insurance is called Technology Errors and Omissions.

E&O insurance can cover claims for negligence. One example is if a customer tries to allow the car to go fully autonomous instead of using a pilot and the car causes an accident. The customer may be partially to blame because fully autonomous operation is not yet permitted. However, the error in determining the correct driving decision is also the responsibility of the car's software manufacturer installed by the car's manufacturer. Responsibility lies with the car's manufacturer to test the software prior to putting the car into production. In a partial fault state, the automobile manufacturer will need the E&O to cover for a related claim. Other states may determine the manufacturer to be the most at fault, making the need for Tech E&O even stronger.[29] However, even E&O

---

26 Ruth Taplin, *Cyber Risk, Intellectual Property Theft and Cyberwarfare: Asia, Europe and the USA*, Routledge (2020).

27 Anang Setiyawan & Jamal Wiwoho, *Strengthening Indonesia's Policy On National Cyber Security To Deal With Cyberwarfare Threat*, 32 INT'L & COMP. L. REV 303, 303-311 (2018).

28 Toni S. Reed, *Cybercrime and Technology Losses: Claims and Potential Insurance Coverage for Modern Cyber Risks*, 54 TORT TRIAL & INS. PRAC. L.J. 153, 153-209 (2019).

29 Alfred R. Cowger, Jr., *Liability Considerations When Autonomous Vehicles Choose The Accident Victim*, 19 THE J. OF HIGH TECH. L. 1, 1-60 (July 1, 2018), https://www.thefreelibrary.com/LIABILITY+CON-

policies have exclusions and limitations. Read the policy carefully. Sometimes a manufacturer can recover for all damages, sometimes only for those that are listed as included or not listed as excluded.[30] Regardless, a Tech E&O policy is a necessity to compliment the Cyber Risk/Cyber Liability policy.

Within the autonomous automobile industry, competition leads companies to constantly improve features to make the vehicle a tad safer than all the others. Amid this, some companies may unknowingly infringe on the copyrights of others. Innovation is volatile, and consumers enjoy the benefits of the extra safe upgrades. This has led to an inclusion in Tech E&O insurance to cover for accidental infringement, defamation claims, and trademark and domain name infringement. Keep in mind that there are also several E&O claims that have gone through summary judgement in court, entirely throwing out the case, due to the ability for the insurance company to prove that the covered incident was not accidental.[31] [32]

Tech E&O insurances vary by carrier covering different items and excluding others. One issue of extreme importance to manufacturers is the ability to have new items covered under the same insurance policy. Some Tech E&O policies only cover the products developed at the time that the insurance goes into effect. Manufacturers will need to sign on to a policy that will allow the continuous improvement of products and services by way of new innovations designed as new products and services.[33] For instance, if GM's Driverless Cruise vehicle suddenly goes from a regular to an autonomous vehicle that turns into an air taxi, GM will want this new feature covered under their Tech E&O in case something unexpected goes wrong with it.

SIDERATIONS+WHEN+AUTONOMOUS+VEHICLES+CHOOSE+THE +ACCIDENT...-a0571681134.

30 *TRAX, LLC v. Cont'l Cas. Co.*, No. 10-CV-6901, 2011 U.S. Dist. LEXIS 145869, at 4 (N.D. Ill. Dec. 14, 2011).

31 *Eyeblaster, Inc. v. Fed. Ins. Co.*, 613 F.3d 797, at 798 (8th Cir. 2010).

32 Pinchas Huberman, *Tort Law, Corrective Justice and the Problem of Autonomous-Machine-Caused Harm*, 34 CANADIAN JOURNAL OF LAW AND JURISPRUDENCE, 105-147 (Feb. 2021), link.gale.com/apps/doc/A660122660/AONE?u=mnawebl&sid=bookmark-AONE&xid=137885d4 (last visited Sept. 12, 2021).

33 Christopher P. Holland & Daniel John, *HUK-COBURG: Innovation and Change in the Automotive Insurance Market using Artificial Intelligence (AI) and Telematics* (Mar. 22, 2021), https://papers.ssrn.com/sol3/papers.cfm?abstract_id=3803180.

Another issue to look for in Tech E&O insurance is the and/or policy. Manufacturers should pay attention to whether the policy covers negligence *and* breach of contract or if it covers negligence *or* breach of contract. Many times, a claim will include both and some policies only cover one or the other.[34] Also make sure the policy handles delays in services. Many E&O claims derive when the manufacturer tries to avoid delays in services, so having an inclusion for coverage when a delay does occur is an indirect incentive to avoid an error or omission.[35] A delay could be a lesser harm.

Currently, manufacturers of autonomous vehicles do not have an individualized cyber gap option. There is cyber gap insurance in the cyber insurance industry, and there may be gap insurance for autonomous owners, however, there currently is none for manufacturers of autonomous vehicles.[36] Energy companies in the U.K. began to use Cyber Gap Insurance to cover exclusions and ransomware incidents. Even with the gap coverage, policyholders need to pay attention to the wording in the policy to be sure that they know what gaps are covered so that they don't rely on a null claim.

(b) Consumer Autonomous Automobile Insurance

Consumer insurance is a vast playing field where insurances become a marketplace for customization. It ranges from incentives for the extra safety controls that come with autonomous and semi-autonomous, to add-on individual cyber insurances. Incentive programs come in the form of initial discounts for advanced safety features all the way to user activated insurance.[37] The user activated insurance comes with hardware in the car that detects the activation of the automated safety features. The rate each month is adjusted according to whether those safety features were

---

34 *Crum & Forster Specialty Ins. Co. v. DVO, Inc.*, 939 F.3d 852, 854 (7th Cir. 2019).

35 Reed, *supra*, note 28, at 11.

36 Talesh, *supra*, note 19, at 7.

37 Amirreza Nickkar, Nashid Khadem & Hyeon-Shic Shin , *Willingness to Pay for Autonomous Vehicles: An Adaptive Choice-Based Conjoint Analysis Approach*, INTERNATIONAL CONFERENCE ON TRANSPORTATION AND DEVELOPMENT 2020, at 1-14 (Aug. 31, 2020), https://ascelibrary.org/doi/10.1061/9780784483138.001.

activated.[38] [39] There are two ways insurance can be provided in these automobiles—by the manufacturer of the vehicle as a part of the purchase package, or else by a third party insuring the vehicle but having nothing to do with its creation. However, some of the insurances packages provided by the manufacturer through the dealer are actually underwritten by the third party insurer. The insurer has an incentive for doing this since they experience an increase in profits due to the reduction in accident expenditures.

A positive aspect of consumer insurance is that settlements are greatly reducing because of the advanced safety of the autonomous designs. This means that most of the liability for any of these accidents, if there are any at all, are going to the manufacturer.[40] The domestic civilian sector is being kept off the negative insurance grid. However, some insurance agencies don't believe in the safety of autonomous vehicles just yet. In the United Kingdom, automobile insurance companies use a single insurer model where policyholders are found liable for damages caused while the vehicle was moving driverless, but not if the damages were incurred because the owner allowed the vehicle to drive in an area that was inappropriate or where the automobile failed to install critical updates.[41] [42] These kinds of accidents, also considered a form of negligence, and are typically attributed to the car's manufacturer.

What if I get in my car, start driving it down the road, then suddenly someone sends a malicious code through the dash via a connected device?

---

38 Fabrizio Lamberti, Valentina Gatteschi, Claudio Demartini, Matteo Pelissier, Alfonso Gomez & Victor Santamaria, *Blockchains can work for car insurance: Using smart contracts and sensors to provide on-demand coverage*, IEEE CONSUMER ELECTRONICS MAGAZINE, (June 15, 2018), at 72-81.

39 Alzbeta Krausová & Jan Matejka, *Autonomous vehicles and in-vehicle data in the context of motor insurance,* 10 THE LAWYER QUARTERLY No. 2 (2020), at 153-169.

40 Huberman, *supra*, note 32, at 12.

41 James Davey, *By Insurers, For Insurers: The UK's Liability Regime for Autonomous Vehicles*, 13 JOURNAL OF TORT LAW 163, 163-188 (2020), https://doi.org/10.1515/jtl-2020-2010.

42 Tracy Hresko Pearl, *Compensation At The Crossroads: Autonomous Vehicles & Alternative Victim Compensation Schemes*, 60 WILLIAM AND MARY L.R. 1827, 1883 (Apr. 2019), link.gale.com/apps/doc/A590762799/AONE?u=mnawebl&sid=bookmark-AONE&xid=748732ea (last visited Sept. 12, 2021).

Say it allows them to take my car like a remote. The Halloween vision comes true while this remote person drives my car around in the parking garage, turns on the Halloween station on Siri, allows the doors to open and close, the inside lights to dim and brighten, and the outside lights to stay on as if a sneering, sinister face. The car then drives around a pedestrian and mocks it, telling it not to be afraid even with the Halloween music. The pedestrian ends up getting an anxiety attack each time he or she goes by the garage in the future because of the memory and the speed of their heart palpitating.

Who would be liable for such an incident? Would it be the car's owner? With current updates in autonomous car coverage, this would be up to the manufacturer since the manufacturer oversees continuous updates to the car and monitoring. There is an anomaly in products that are vendor-related regarding the liability for their mishaps, or even those that are located on the cloud as -aaS type infrastructures.[43] The anomaly is that hackers tend to engage in their activities while apps and api's are latent.[44] This is called a resting state when they are not being monitored and no system is cleaning them.[45] The malicious actors find the code, inject it and go on their way undetected. As soon as the resting structure is turned on, the malicious code is deployed. The malicious actors may also insert an alarm that will notify the system once the code is activated.

Should liability be placed on the manufacturer since the product was not in service when the code was inserted? Should the dealers be liable since they could have kept the system on an alert platform to test and monitor it until it was sold? Or should liability be placed on the customer for lack of due diligence or knowledge or for simply starting the vehicle? These are hard questions to answer. This is an area of consumer insurance that has not yet been fully addressed. Currently, it is the manufacturer's

---

43 Chandana Roy, Chandrani Chowdhury, Sudip Misra, S. & Jhareswar Maiti, *DQ-Map: Dynamic Decision Query Mapping for Provisioning Safety-as-a-Service in IoT*, IEEE INTERNET OF THINGS J. 1, 1-11 (2021).

44 Kyle Porter, *Analyzing the DarkNetMarkets subreddit for evolutions of tools and trends using LDA topic modeling*, 26 DIGITAL INVESTIGATIONS87, S87-S97 (July 2018).

45 Jinfeng Li (2020). *Vulnerabilities mapping based on OWASP-SANS: a survey for static application security testing (SAST)*, 4 ANNALS OF EMERGING TECHNOLOGIES IN COMPUTING (AETIC), No. 3, 1, 1-8 (2020), http://aetic.theiaer.org/archive/v4/v4n3/p1.pdf.

responsibility to produce error free software in their product.[46] However, the mechanics of liability may shift in the future to generate a new type of insurance which places liability on another entity. Automobile drivers currently have the option to purchase uninsured motorist insurance—in the future, there may be an option for "uninsured cyber-hack insurance" if that sounds better.

(c) Consumer, Dealer, and Manufacturer Related Ransomware Insurance

Consider this scenario: A customer purchases the vehicle but an anti-rights activist group targets the consumer. The group wants to use the consumer as an example of who should or should not be allowed to own property based on the consumer's private lifestyle decisions. The activist group then uses advanced technology to inject a virus and takes over the car. This allows them to essentially kidnap the car through a hack, taking full control using a remote command base somewhere to program the cars activity through the hack. The group uses their control to make demands for the return of the vehicle to the dealer, similar to a ransomware attack on a pc. This type of scenario may be easily covered under ransomware insurance, however there may be no exact rule written for it yet since it's regarding hardware on an automobile.

There are a few companies that will pay a ransom for the return of useability to computer hardware when the computer gets interrupted, but only a few. Governments are debating whether to continue to allow this type of insurance.[47] Since the inception of this type of insurance, there have been cases where malicious ransomware groups have targeted consumers that have information showing they have insurance on the dark web. They know that if they interrupt these devices, indirectly interrupting operations that stem from them, they can get paid.[48] Such devices become the main target, and ransomware attacks have increased as a result.

---

46 Cowger, *supra*, note 29, at 11.

47 Kyle D. Logue & Adam B. Shniderman, *The Case for Banning (and Mandating) Ransomware Insurance,* U. OF MICH. LAW & ECON. RES. PAPER NO. 21-040 1, 1-59 (Aug. 18, 2021)

48 Anirudha Balasubramanian, *Insurance against Ransomware*, [name of publication], [xx], [xx-xx] (2021).

2. *Survey of the Current State of Cybersecurity in the Shipping Industry*

Similar to the automotive industry, while digitization has proved beneficial in the shipping industry, it has also broadened the scope of possible cyber threats. This industry's shift towards "smart" shipping has streamlined logistics and made many business functions more efficient; however, it has also inherently increased its exposure to cyber threats.

Over the past five years alone, the shipping industry has suffered many large-scale cyber incidents. In 2019, the United States Coast Guard revealed that a large commercial vessel headed to New York had been hit with a malware attack that had degraded functionality after the on-board network had been targeted.[49] More recently, the Mediterranean Shipping Company was the target of a malware attack that caused a total network outage.[50] However, perhaps the most devastating incident of all was the 2017 NotPetya malware attack on shipper Maersk. This attack crippled ports, terminals, and cargo handling operations, forcing the company to disconnect completely and rebuild its entire global network. The damages were estimated to be nearly $300 million.[51] While these cyber incidents are just a few of many that the shipping industry has fallen victim to in recent times, the loss and damage incurred indicate an immediate need for companies to invest in cyber protection measures and closely review their coverages.

Historically, cyberattacks have been covered by a company's property and liability insurance. Companies like PanAm and Cadbury were successfully able to obtain coverage from their insurance companies for

---

49 *Shore-Based Infrastructure and Prospect of Conflicts Top Cyber Concerns for the Shipping Industry*, ALLIANZ (July 15, 2020), https://www.agcs.allianz.com/news-and-insights/expert-risk-articles/shipping-2020-cyber-concerns.html.

50 *Id.*

51 *Id.*; *see generally DCSA Implementation Guide for Cyber Security on Vessels v1.0*, DIGITAL CONTAINER SHIPPING ASSOCIATION (Oct. 3, 2020), https://dcsa.org/wp-content/uploads/2020/03/DCSA-Implementation-Guideline-for-BIMCO-Compliant-Cyber-Security-on-Vessels-v1.0.pdf; *see generally* Mike McQuade, *The Untold Story of NotPetya, the Most Devastating Cyberattack in History*, WIRED (Aug. 22, 2018), https://www.wired.com/story/notpetya-cyberattack-ukraine-russia-code-crashed-the-world/.

cyberattacks costing them millions of dollars in services.[52] Former President Obama deliberated over and decided to name a Sony attack cyber vandalism to avoid negative outcomes related to the term cyberwar.[53] However, in 2017 Mondolez was denied coverage under the NotPetya attack based on the attack being considered a cyberwar and the insurance having included a war exclusion in their policy.[54] This was the beginning of the wartime exclusion regime in cyber insurance coverage. However, the question remains as to what will be considered cyberwar, where to draw the lines between cyberwar and cyber-attacks, and what the difference is between cyber war and cyber terrorism.

The shipping industry has similar coverage options to the manufacturing industry; including cyber insurance, Technical E&O coverage, and cyber gap insurance options.[55] For a manufacturer, insurance must cover product malfunction and the many different types of damages that result. Shipping and logistics companies must have coverage for loss of goods when their shipments go awry, or when a calamity strikes that destroys the inventory aboard a cargo device. However, regular liability insurance has historically been successful at creating exclusions for cyberattacks. Even so, many cyber insurance companies can use peril of the sea for cyber piracy to avoid the exclusion.[56] Cyber insurances are also beginning to include cyber physical risks, such as bodily injury or injury to cargo.[57]

---

52 Adam Satariano & Nicole Perlroth, *Big Companies Thought Insurance Covered a Cyberattack. They May Be Wrong.* NEW YORK TIMES (Apr. 15, 2019), https://www.nytimes.com/2019/04/15/technology/cyberinsurance-notpetya-attack.html.

53 *Id.*

54 Russ Banham, *Cyber Coverage Confusion*, RISK MANAGEMENT Oct. 3, 2019, at 20-25, https://www.russbanham.com/2019/10/03/cyber-coverage-confusion/.

55 Abigail Chase, *The Evolution of Cyber Risk and the Cyber Insurance Market*, Senior Theses, Scholar Commons (Spring 2021), https://scholarcommons.sc.edu/cgi/viewcontent.cgi?article=1416&context=senior_theses.

56 Julia Constantino-Chagas-Lessa, & Belma Bulut Şahin, *A New Era A New Risk: A Study on the Impact of the Developments of New Technologies in the Shipping Industry and Marine Insurance Market*, INSURTECH- A LEGAL AND REGULATORY VIEW (Dec. 5, 2019), at 313-361.

57 Aristeidis Farao, Sakshyam Panda, Sofia Anna Menesidou, et al., *SECONDO: A platform for cybersecurity investments and cyber insurance*

A unique feature of shipping and logistics companies is the rising ability to render services on a just-in-time basis using block chain. Cargo devices are tracked using blockchain administered by gps maps in real time, orders are updated and paid on the spot with unbending knowledge of the status of supplies as well as the movement. Insurance companies have begun to move their platforms to the blockchain.[58] In doing so, they have also begun to enlist a use case platform where the insurance kicks in as the covered carriers and covered shipments are moved about—on an as needed basis.[59] The insurance also adds benefit to data validators for securing the network because the policyholder pays the premium while the insurance covers the validators.[60] [61] The benefit that the shipping company insurers are getting out of the blockchain includes almost real time updates on policies and paperwork, and they know where shipments are at all times. The benefit to policyholders is that the immutable memory of the blockchain allows for claims processing to take place in almost no time, with a claim check distributed at close to the same time that a claim is approved. Blockchain has become a huge benefit to shipping companies and their insurers.[62]

---

decisions, INTERNATIONAL CONFERENCE ON TRUST AND PRIVACY IN DIGITAL BUSINESS, Sept. 2020, at 65-74, https://www.manospanaousis.com/papers/farao2020secondo.pdf.

58 Jia Xu, Yongqi Wu, Xiapu Luo & Dejun Yang, *Improving the efficiency of blockchain applications with smart contract based cyber-insurance*, 2020 IEEE International Conference on Communications, June 2020, *at* 1-7.

59 T. Lepoint, G Ciocarlie & K. Eldefrawy, *Blockcis—a blockchain-based cyber insurance system,* 2018 IEEE International Conference on Cloud Engineering (IC2E), April 2018, at 378-384.

60 Jing Li, Dusit Nivato., Choong Seon Hong, et al., *A contract-theoretic cyber insurance for withdraw delay in the blockchain networks with shards*, ICC IEEE International Conference on Communications (ICC), Sept. 2021, at 1-7.

61 Jing Li, Dusit Niyato, Choong Seon Hong, et al., *Cyber Insurance Design for Validator Rotation in Sharded Blockchain Networks: A Hierarchical Game-Based Approa*ch 18 IEEE TRANSACTIONS ON NETWORK AND SERVICE MANAGEMENT, Sept. 2021, at 3092-3106.

62 Charles Tim Battista Garrocho, Matteus Coelho Silva, Celio Marcio Soares Ferreira, et al., *Real-Time Systems Implications in the Blockchain-Based Vertical Integration of Industry 4.0*, 53 COMPUTER, Sept. 2020, at 46-55.

3. *Survey of the Current State of Cybersecurity in the Aviation Industry*

Like the automotive and shipping industries, currently, the aviation industry relies heavily on cyber-enabled technology to increase air transport safety and efficiency.[63] The increased digitization, interconnectivity, and dependence on technology bring about a new set of risks. For example, the computer-based systems often used in the aviation industry are interconnected to control everything from airport grounding systems to onboard aircraft control and even air navigation. This interconnectivity increases the risks such that a potential attack could affect the air traffic control centers or online booking systems and the airlines and possibly even the passengers.

Fortunately, cyber incidents impacting the aviation industry have not yet gotten to the level of remote hijacking like the automobile incident mentioned above or the shipping cyber incident involving Maersk. However, there have been multiple large-scale incidents that have caused airlines and customers significant losses and inconveniences. While many of these attacks were data breaches, one was a distributed denial of service (DDoS) attack. The DDoS attack targeted LOT Polish Airlines by crippling their computers and flight plan information technology (IT) system, disabling them from carrying out their normal functions.[64] The incident resulted in a five-hour disruption which caused ten flight cancellations and additional flight delays.

However, the aviation industry's data breach incidents have unfortunately caused significantly more damage than the DDoS attack. For example, British Airways was targeted by hackers who stole over 380,000 customers' data, including personal and payment information, based on flight bookings.[65] Further, when Cathay Pacific Airlines suffered a data breach in 2018, 9.4 million global customers were impacted. Data including names, passport information, addresses, and more were

---

63 These emerging technologies in the aviation industry are inevitably increasing the potential "attack surface."

64 Gary Moran, et al., *Cyber Resilience in the Aviation Sector*, AON (2018), https://www.aon.com/getmedia/475a36e5-fae0-484b-b333-a7507c13b62b/cyber-sellsheet-aviation.aspx.

65 *Id.*

compromised.[66] Most surprising, however, is the data breach incident involving Heathrow Airport in 2017. In that incident, a USB stick with 76 folders and more than 1,000 files containing customers' sensitive personal information was misplaced by an employee.[67] The USB stick was neither password-protected nor encrypted, causing all of the information contained within it to be exposed.[68] Though the severity of these cyber-attacks is not on the same scale as a remote hijacking or complete crippling of a company's global network, they illustrate gaps in cybersecurity measures that need to be addressed and rectified. Costs relating to such incidents are great.

Cyber insurance coverage for the aviation industry is slightly different than manufacturing, shipping, and consumer vehicles. While aviation insurance does cover data breaches, viruses, and malicious coding, there are some characteristics of the aviation industry that are unique to that industry. Consumer automobiles are sold through a dealership. Manufacturers typically sell automobiles directly to partnership dealers through internal transactions. Shipping companies operate in a similar way. For avionics, services are offered on an open platform to the general body of citizens.[69] [70] [71] This creates a different type of vulnerability because industry players work with payment systems, consumer data, and marketing platforms.[72] Data is transferred from a publicly accessible web

---

66 Eimer McAuley, *All of the Big Data breaches in the UK Aviation Industry*, RIGHTLY (Oct. 13, 2020), https://www.rightly.co.uk/blog/all-big-data-breaches-uk-aviation-industry/.

67 *Id.*

68 *Id.*

69 Christopher B. Watkins & Randy Walter, *Transitioning from federated avionics architectures to integrated modular avionics*, 2007 IEEE/AIAA 26th Digital Avionics Systems Conference, Oct. 2007, at 2-A.

70 G.A. Chuyanov, V.V. Kosyanchuk, N.I. Selvesyuk & E.Y. Zybin, *Advanced avionics equipment on the basis of second generation integrated modular avionics,* 29th Congress of the International Council of the Aeronautical Sciences, ICAS, 2014, at 2014.

71 Z. Toth, C. Kowalkowski, A. Sklyar, D. Sörhammar, B. Tronvoll & O. Wirths, (2020). *A paradox theory approach to tensions in digital servitization: the case of the aerospace and maritime industries*, ADVANCED SERVICES FOR SUSTAINABILITY AND GROWTH, 2020, at 96.

72 Bjoern Annighoefer, *An open source domain-specific avionics system architecture model for the design phase and self-organizing avionics,* SAE

interface to an internal system, offering room for vulnerability as each transaction is completed. Further, many aviation companies offer membership services with rewards points, sometimes coupled with payment cards. These rewards systems also present vulnerabilities as they move between public platforms to internal data structures. Cyber insurance must be designed to cover this advanced level of vulnerability.

In the aviation industry you may find insurance packages that include an al la carte level of services. The base package covers the same breach protection as any other cyber insurance—public relations announcements, consumer identity protection, data recovery, and court costs. The packages in the aviation industry, however, need an additional level of coverage for investigations that are meant to detect the vulnerability while gathering the forensic data required to prosecute the perpetrator of the breach.[73] Aviation insurance must cover for third party payment card systems while also covering multiplatform internal systems. Unlike in the automobile dealership, manufacturing, or consumer automobile industry, the aviation industry may experience massive downtime in employment when a cyber-attack occurs since the avionics industry runs almost entirely on the cyber forefront. Cyber insurance must cover for lost wages during such downtimes.[74]

One way that insurance companies attempt to reduce expenditures towards insurance plans for clients is through catastrophic data modeling[75]. This allows the insurance company to confidently predict a range of costs from catastrophes, including cyber-attacks, and determine the chances that such a catastrophe will happen. This data is used to set prices. However, this type of modeling is less available to the aviation industry because the range of catastrophes that could affect flying disasters are manmade cyber incidences as opposed to natural disasters that can be

---

International Journal of Advances and Current Practices in Mobility, Mar. 3, 2019, at 429-446.

73 Toth, Kowalkowski, Sklyar, Sörhammar, Tronvoll, & Wirths, *supra*, note 71.

74 Marianne Bonner, *What Does Cyber Liability Insurance Cover?*, The Balances MD, (Mar. 12, 2021), www.thebalancesmb.com/what-is-covered-under-a-cyber-liability-policy-462459.

75 Banavar Sridhar, Kenneth Freeman, & Gano Broto Chatterji, Simulation and Modeling Concepts for Secure Airspace Operations, AIAA Aviation 2021 Forum, 2021, at 3008.

better predicted.[76] [77] [78] However, insurance companies can still generate a range of catastrophic simulations to price cyber liability insurances.[79] Some companies may benefit by creating their own data models by keeping past data and then compiling it into a simulation to provide results to the insurance company. The insurance company may provide an incentive, and the modeling will help set a better rate for the insured.

Aviation personnel sometimes use portable electronic flight bags that are not affixed to the aircraft. These are also vulnerable to cyber-attack and used for the general operation of a safe flight. Examples include iPads for data collection, GPS units for navigation, and avionics devices.[80] A typical airflight cyber liability policy will not cover these devices. They are more like individual devices and need their own plan. They can be covered by insurance; however, the insuring policy will be device specific and run with the individual owner of the device.[81] These are not commercial insurances. Where an electronic flight bag needs licensing to be used during flight, the insurance company may require proof of such licensing, however they will still insure the product on an individualized one single owner basis.[82]

---

76 Vladyslav Chernysh, *Model of Functional Hazard Assessment in Air Traffic Management System Regarding Information Security Threats*, 4 ADVANCED INFORMATION SYSTEMS, 2020, at 120-127.

77 Savino Dambra, Leyla Bilge, & Davide Balzarotti, *SoK: Cyber insurance—technical challenges and a system security roadmap*, 2020 IEEE Symposium on Security and Privacy, May 18-21, 2020, at 1367-1383.

78 Banavar Sridhar, Kenneth Freeman, & Gano Broto Chatterji, *Simulation and Modeling Concepts for Secure Airspace Operations*, AIAA Aviation 2021 Forum, 2021, at 3008.

79 Dambra, Bilge & *Balzarotti*, *supra*, note 76.

80 Michelle Yeh, Joseph Jaworski & Stephanie Chase, *Pilot Perceptions on the Integration of Electronic Flight Bag Information in New Flight Deck Designs*, 63 Proceedings of the human factors and ergonomics society annual meeting, Nov. 1, 2019, at 91-95.

81 Navid Kagalwalla & Prathamesh Churi, *Cybersecurity in aviation: An intrinsic review*, 2019 5th International Conference On Computing, Communication, Control And Automation (ICCUBEA), Sept. 2019, at 1-6.

82 Peter Skaves, *Software & Airborne Electronic Administration Hardware Standardization Conference: Electronic Flight Bag (EFB) & Security*, Federal Aviation Administration (Aug. 20, 2008), http://www.microwaysystems.com/FAA-08/Presentations/Skaves%20EFB%20Security%208-20-08%20Rev%20A.pdf.

While much of the insurance needs along the automotive, shipping, and aviation industries mirror that of the general cybersphere, they also have unique issues. These issues will be discussed further in the remaining parts of this chapter.

B. Survey of Unique Issues to the Automotive, Shipping, and Aviation Industries

The cyber risk landscape within the automotive, shipping, and aviation industries is continuously evolving. Thus, businesses need to be aware of such risks to implement systems to prevent and reduce the likelihood of cyber-attacks. Critically, transportation managers should prepare financially for the possible losses resulting from a cyber incident by ensuring that they have the appropriate insurance coverage.[83]

1. The Automotive Industry

In recent years, the automotive industry has seen growth in autonomous driving, connected cars, electric vehicles, and shared mobility.[84] As these innovations have "built on the digitization of in-car systems, the extension of car IT systems into the back end, and the propagation of software, the hacking of connected cars has increased."[85] This industry has become increasingly dependent on advancing computer technologies to enhance various features in its products. As a result, the security of these technologies is now a critical matter.

There are currently two main cyberthreat opportunities in the automotive industry. First, as vehicle electronic systems continue to grow

---

83 *See generally* Costis Toregas & Nicolas Zahn, *Insurance for Cyber Attacks: The Issue of Setting Premiums in Context*, GEO. WASH. U. CYBER SEC. & RES. INST. (Jan. 7, 2014), https://cspri.seas.gwu.edu/sites/g/files/zaxdzs1446/f/downloads/cyberinsurance_paper_pdf_0.pdf.

84 *See generally* Francois Charbonneau, et al., *Cybersecurity in Automotive, Mastering the Challenge*, ALTRAN, https:// www.altran.com/as-content/uploads/sites/5/2018/01/cybersecurity-in-automotive_position-paper.pdf (last visited Feb. 26, 2021).

85 Ondrej Burkacky, et al., *Cybersecurity in Automotive: Mastering the Challenge*, MCKINSEY&CO. : AUTOMOTIVE & ASSEMBLY (June 22, 2020), https://www.mckinsey.com/industries/automotive-and-assembly/our-insights/cybersecurity-in-automotive-mastering-the-challenge.

in complexity, these systems' vulnerabilities also increase. Innovation and market demand represent substantial drivers in pushing the electronic systems' complexity in vehicles, for example, consumers prefer the safety of an electronic driver assistance system (e.g., parking and speed regulation) over their own self-driving.

The law and the market require that these new vehicle systems be secure and safe. For example, the embedded system that controls the brakes can become corrupted by malware. This can lead to an accident with consequences impacting the vehicle, the vehicle manufacturer, and the driver. Accordingly, the security of vehicle systems and passengers' safety must be considered together to ensure proper risk mitigation measures are taken.

The law still requires autonomous and semi-autonomous vehicles to be insured the same way that other vehicles are insured. Owners are required to maintain property liability insurance and are strongly encouraged to keep bodily injury insurance. However, many insurance companies have exclusions in their policies from audio, video, and data and electronic equipment. These exclusions were created to minimize the coverage for sound systems and third-party additions to the vehicle.[86] With autonomous vehicles, visual, as well as audio, signals are a major part of the way the vehicle operates for safety. Further, the vehicles are constantly collecting data about the use of the car and how devices are implemented that helps the company update products and create a safer atmosphere for drivers.[87] Insurers will have to negotiate around these exclusions so that autonomous safety features are not excluded when an accident is caused by the failure of one to work.

Another critical general liability exclusion for automobiles is weather exclusions. Many insurance policies don't consider weather related mishaps to be an excuse for liability insurance because drivers are required to understand how to drive through weather hazards or else stay off the

86 Insurance Services Offices Inc, *Personal Auto Policy*, DOI.NV.GOV, 1-12 at 8 https://doi.nv.gov/uploadedFiles/doinvgov/_public-documents/Consumers/PP_00_01_06_98.pdf.

87 Shunxi Li et al., *Policy Formulation for Highly Automated Vehicles: Emerging Importance, Research Frontiers and Insights*, 124 Transportation Research Part A: Policy and Practice 573, 573-586 (2019).

road at the time that they sign for their license.[88] There are even weather precautions included on driver's tests.[89] However, in an autonomous or semi-autonomous vehicle, weather could interfere with the camera or set off the cellular signal that connects it to infrastructure.[90] In fact, just a small drop of water is notorious for setting off the vision in the cameras, while also interfering with the measurement the cameras are programmed to perform that increases the safety of the camera.[91] Insurers will also need to negotiate around this exclusion to make sure that weather related signal interference for these types of products are included.

As insurers become more knowledgeable about autonomous controls, the coverages change. In fact, insurance premiums for cyber cars are getting more expensive to cover new devices that may be needed for the computerized controls, such as cameras, lidars, GPS units, receivers, or hardware computer data systems.[92] Some insurers are also changing the structure of their policies. Such changes include the use of by-the-use devises that cover data collected on each use and charge accordingly per use, or else exclusions in the form of safety feature discounts.[93] However, the newest concerns dealing with hacking and malicious software have required a different type of addition, namely cyber insurance, ransomware insurance, or technical errors and omissions insurance, leading to that increase in cost.[94]

---

88 Adley Law Firm, *Who is at Fault for an Accident Caused by Weather?* (2019)adleylzawfirm.com https://adleylawfirm.com/who-is-at-fault-for-a-car-accident-caused-by-bad-weather/.

89 *North Carolina Free Practice Test*, DMV.com (Jan. 24, 2019), www.dmv.com/nc/north-carolina/free-practice-test.

90 Bridget Clerkin, *Can Autonomous Cars Weather the Weather?*, DMV.ORG (Mar. 27, 2018), www.dmv.org/articles/weather-impact-on-self-driving-cars.

91 Andrew Baker-Campbell, *Fair Weather Friend: How Do LiDAR Systems Cope In Rain & Fog?* |, AutoVision News (Dec. 18, 2020), www.autovision-news.com/sensing/sensor-technology/lidar-systems-rain-fog/.

92 De Jong Yeong et al, *Sensor and Sensor Fusion Technology in Autonomous Vehicles: A Review*, 21 MDPI 1-37 (2021).

93 Martina F. Baumann et al, *Taking Responsibility: A Responsible Research and Innovation (RRI) Perspective on Insurance Issues of Semi-Autonomous Driving*, 124 Transportation Research Part A: Policy and Practice, 557-572 (2019).

94 Michael Costonis, *Driverless Cars Will Change Auto Insurance. Heres How Insurers Can Adapt*, Harvard Business Review (Dec. 5, 2017),

Collectively, the vehicle safety laws, and the market is fueling a rapid expansion in the complexity of the automotive electronic architectures. A modern high-end car's software can have up to 100 million lines of code.[95] Due to the complexity of the computer systems involved in automobiles and the rapidly changing threat landscape, there is no way to achieve perfect security. Also, vehicle systems that have been disconnected, exclusively within a car, are now connected to a litany of internet-enabled devices, introducing many new potential threat actors.[96]

With this changing platform of vehicle mobility, insurances will need to transform to cover areas that manufacturers are not eligible for. Consumers will need to be able to add some type of mobility cyber insurance to their vehicles. As laws change to transfer liability to driverless vehicle owners when they are not driving, and away from manufacturers or dealerships, owners will need some way to compensate when their devices cause harm to others. Currently, insurers can provide technology insurance for any device that uses a connected format or has a technology infrastructure, which switches the liability to a third party other than the owner[97] However, since many of the complications with automobiles are unique and extremely hazardous, personal liability insurances may begin to evolve the wording in their exclusions to allow coverage for cyber-attacks on automobiles and software malfunctions; after all, the computer is only as good as its owner teaches it to be.[98] However, insurers may also require strict security protocols for any insured device and can exclude devices that were not following those security protocols at the time of any incident pertaining to a claim.

---

hbr.org/2017/12/driverless-cars-will-change-auto-insurance-heres-how-insurers-can-adapt.

95 *See generally* Robert N. Charette, *This Car Runs on Cod*e, IEEE SPECTRUM (Feb. 1, 2009), https://spectrum.ieee.org/transportation/ systems/this-car-runs-on-code.

96 *See generally*, Tao Zhang, Helder Antunes & Siddhartha Aggarwal, *Defending Connected Vehicles Against Malware: Challenges and a Solution Framework*, 1 IEEE INTERNET OF THINGS J. 10 (2014), http://www.cse.msu.edu/~cse914/Sp2019/Papers/Paper3-Zhang2014-malwareCars.pdf.

97 Li, Niyato, Hong & Park, *supra*, at note 61.

98 Cowger, *supra*, note 29.

2. *The Shipping Industry*

The shipping industry, like the automotive industry, has recently experienced several cyber technological advancements.[99] These advancements include the access, connectivity, and networking of a ship's systems. This has led to an increase in cyber security threats and potential risks.[100] More cyber threats emerge as today's shipping industry increasingly depends on digitalization[101], integration of operations, and automation. Cyber-attacks pose a threat to all parts of the shipping industry; however, the shore-based offices are the hackers' central target. This risk is amplified because many ship-owner victims of cyber-attacks are often reluctant to share information for fear of bad publicity and the damage that it would cause to their brand. According to the World Economic Forum's Global Risks Report 2020, cyber-attacks on shipping rank as the fifth top risk globally in 2020 concerning infrastructure.[102]

Hackers in the shipping industry come with a slew of motives. First, the shipping industry becomes a supplier access to a chain of data systems. Hackers can use one vulnerable entry point to search through systems to find where orders lie, then hop through the orders to another system to find data on all the consumers of that single shipment order. This is combined

---

99 Some of these technological advancements have integrated Information Technology and Operational Technology on board ships through networking and connecting to the internet. This increased dependence on computers and software opens up threats of cyber attacks in the shipping industry as geopolitical risks increase ("war is not only fought with physical weapons"). Allianz, *supra* note 13.

100 The International Maritime Organization (IMO) defines Maritime cyber security risk as "a measure of the extent to which a technology asset is threatened by a potential circumstance or event, which may result in shipping-related operational, safety or security failures as a consequence of information or systems being corrupted, lost or compromised". *Maritime cyber risk,* INT'L MAR. ORG., https://www.imo.org/en/OurWork/Security/Pages/Cyber-security.aspx (last visited Feb. 26, 2021).

101 *See generally* Poulis, Konstantinos, et al., *Value Migration: Digitalization of Shipping as a Mechanism of Industry Dethronement*, 5 J. SHIPPING & TRADE 9 (2020), https://jshippingandtrade.springeropen.com/articles/10.1186/s41072-020-00064-0#citeas.

102 Emilio Granados Franco, et al., *The Global Risks Report 2020*, WORLD ECON. F., https://www.weforum.org/reports/the-global-risks-report-2020 (last visited Feb. 26, 2021).

with several shipping orders per shipment, that provides a rich atmosphere for a hacker to find several datapoints for a massive data exploitation.[103] Other reasons involve incentives commonly known as terrorism.[104] It could be an anti-authority group against whatever entity is shipping the product, or it could be an environmental front group protesting a chemical in a shipment and desiring to find out the location of shipments, or it could be a smuggling entity hoping to hijack the shipment to smuggle goods into it.[105] These are only a few of the possible motives that hackers have for exploiting the shipping industry. This is a reason that the shipping industry requires advanced security along with healthy insurance options.

The three most common vulnerabilities associated with cyber-attacks in the shipping industry are a lack of awareness, ineffective policies and procedures, and an underdeveloped cyber risk management culture.[106] As there have not been many significant incidents involving vessels, there is a lack of timely response to technical vulnerabilities, which allows the industry to remain complacent about the risks associated with potential cyber incidents.[107] However, the risks are numerous, requiring logistics companies to exercise diligence rather than complacency.[108] Insurance structures are beginning to conform to this desire by requiring policy holders to submit diligent security protocols before they will ensure them.

---

103 Toth, Kowalkowski, Sklyar, Sörhammar, Tronvoll, & Wirths, *supra*, note 71.

104 Elliot A. Anderson, *It's a pirate's life for some: the development of an illegal industry in response to an unjust global power dynamic*, 17 IND. J. GLOBAL LEGAL STUD., 319, 319-339 (Summer 2010), https://www.repository.law.indiana.edu/cgi/viewcontent.cgi?referer=&httpsredir=1&article=1425&context=ijgls.

105 Michael Miller, *Cyberspies: Inside the World of Hacking, Online Privacy, and Cyberterrorism* 67 SCH. LIBR. J., at 118, 1-120 (Mar. 2021), link.gale.com/apps/doc/A654790415/AONE?u=mnawebl&sid=bookmark-AONE&xid=81add185 (last visited on Sept. 17, 2021).

106 *Q&A: Cyber Risk on the Rise in Shipping*, ALLIANZ, https://www.agcs.allianz.com/news-and-insights/expert-risk-articles/ cyber-risk-on-the-rise-in-shipping.html (last visited Feb. 26, 2021); *see generally* Anastasios Arampatzis, *The Biggest Challenges and Best Practices to Mitigate Risks in Maritime Cybersecurity*, TRIPWIRE (Aug. 2, 2020), https://www.tripwire.com/state-of-security/security-data-protection/biggest-challenges-best-practices-mitigate-risks-maritime-cybersecurity/.

107 Julia Constantino-Chagas-Lessa & Belma Bulut, , INSURTECH—A LEGAL AND REGULATORY VIEW, at313-361 (Dec. 5, 2019).

108 Li, Niyato & Hong, *supra*, note 60.

Modern technologies have integrated IT and operational technology ("OT") onboard ships through networking and connectivity to the internet.[109] Unfortunately, the policies associated with this integration are weak because there is no process to account for upgrades. Moreover, there is also an urgent need to secure critical systems as most shipping attacks have been directed at breaching corporate security, resulting in loss of essential data, financial loss, or IT problems, rather than gaining actual control of a vessel itself.

In March 2020, the Digital Container Shipping Association (DCSA) published the DCSA Implementation Guide for Cyber Security on Vessels.[110] This guidance focused on assisting shipping companies seeking to comply with the International Maritime Organization ("IMO") Resolution MSC. 428 (98) on Maritime Cyber Risk Management in Safety Management Systems.[111] These protocols are also gaining implementation into cyber liability insurances such that insurers are requiring documentation of adhering security protocols to allow companies to obtain a policy.[112] [113] Further, the insurance innovation market is evolving such that they are literally changing their platforms to the distributed ledger and blockchain so that they can view the blockchain

---

109 *Building A Sustainable Maritime OT Cyber Security Program*, FORTRESS, https://fortressinfosec.com/building-a-sustainable-maritime-ot-cyber-security-program/ (last visited Feb. 26, 2021).

110 *DCSA Implementation Guide for Cyber Security on Vessels v1.0*, DIGITAL CONTAINER SHIPPING ASSOCIATION (Oct. 3, 2020), https://dcsa.org/wp-content/uploads/2020/03/DCSA-Implementation-Guideline-for-BIMCO-Compliant-Cyber-Security-on-Vessels-v1.0.pdf. The Guide provides shipping companies with a "management framework that can be used to reduce the risk of cyber incidents that could affect the safety or security of the vessel, the crew, or the cargo." *Id.*

111 Maritime Safety Committee Res. 428(98), annex 10, Maritime Cyber Risk Management in Safety Management Systems (June 16, 2017), https://wwwcdn.imo.org/localresources/en/KnowledgeCentre/IndexofIMOResolutions/MSCResolutions/MSC.428(98).pdf.

112 Lauri Floresca, *Cyber 101: Obtaining Cyber Insurance The Process I*, Woodruff Sawyer (Dec. 18, 2014), woodruffsawyer.com/cyber-liability/obtaining-cyber/.

113 *Cybersecurity Insurance*, CISA www.cisa.gov/cybersecurity-insurance.

data of their clients to monitor for mishaps.[114] [115] This way, the insurance company can alert their insured when they see something in the system that needs a change that will reduce the risk of a claim occurring in the future.

3. *The Aviation Industry*

Much like the unique issues surrounding the automotive and shipping industries, the aviation industry also faces cybersecurity-related challenges. As the aviation industry also embraces new technologies, cybersecurity is an increasingly essential component of delivering airplanes.[116]

New operational functions and the streaming of inflight entertainment to passengers have significantly increased the data being transferred between the aircraft and the ground.[117] These streams of communication create vulnerabilities. Two such vulnerabilities are the rise of online attacks due to the increase in real-time aircraft connectivity and the Federal Aviation Administration's ("FAA") modernization of air traffic control. As real-time aircraft connectivity continues to grow, the surface area for potential cyber-attacks also increases.[118] The FAA's Next Generation Air Transportation System or NextGen's purpose is to improve network efficiency by using a global positioning system ("GPS") that is software-based and connected to the internet.[119] This transition is needed to modernize the air traffic control systems; however, such a system will bring more security and safety threats. These two vulnerabilities

---

114 Lepoint, Ciocarlie & Eldefrawy, *supra*, note 59.

115 Xu, Wu & Luo & Yang, *supra*, note 58.

116 *See generally Airline Modernisation Raises New Cybersecurity Risks*, OXFORD ANALYTICA (Aug. 24, 2020), https://www.emerald.com/insight/content/doi/10.1108/OXAN-DB254767/full/html.

117 According to a survey conducted by PwC in 2015, 85% of airline CEOs expressed concern about the cybersecurity risk in the aviation industry. *Aviation perspectives 2016 special report series: Cybersecurity and the airline industry*, PwC, https://www.pwc.com/us/en/industrial-products/publications/assets/pwc-airline-industry-perspectives-cybersecurity.pdf (last visited Feb. 26, 2021).

118 *Id.*

119 This system is to replace the current system that is 40 years old and provides limited connectivity, as it relies on radar.

demonstrate the need for lawyers in the aviation space to consider cyber security insurance's value to manage these new threats and risks.

Aside from the traditional types of aviation, the industry now occupies unmanned aircraft that may be propelled by a remote but may also be pre-programmed to propel itself according to a course within its navigational system.[120] Such crafts are being found in the airplane industry, the space flight industry, and entertainment industry in the form of drones. One noted space mishap occurred in one of the newest commercial line space capsules, Boeing's Starliner, when they attempted their first test flight and the software timing pushed itself way off course due to a system failure.[121] The company has not reported it as a hack; however, the space industry is very competitive and filled with protesting bodies that think that spaceflight is anti-environmental and bound to cause human destruction. This alone can indicate the possibility of detrimental hacks. Just like an unmanned Thunderbird flying in an airshow suddenly being hacked and reprogrammed by an enemy force, or a drone suddenly chasing off its owner due to a bored hacker, the re-controlling of new aviation technologies can be a dangerous venture if not secured by anti-hacking protocols and liability insurances.

The aviation industry does require similar insurances for pilots as vehicle owners do in the domestic driving industry. Aircraft owners are required to have the personal injury and property damage liability insurances.[122] [123] However, there are many exclusions to the risks

---

120 Alexandra Conn, *Who's Protecting Whom? An Analysis oftThe Newest Federal Aviation Administration's Unmanned Aerial Vehicle Regulations and Restrictions and Their Hindrance to Technological Advancement*20 THE J. OF HIGH TECH. L., at 304, xxx-xxx (July 2020), link.gale.com/apps/doc/A627515910/AONE?u=mnawebl&sid=bookmark-AONE&xid=c36955b6 (last visited Sept. 17, 2021).

121 *Boeing delays Starliner spacecraft launch again over technical issues*, CNN WIRE (Aug. 4, 2021), link.gale.com/apps/doc/A670655116/AONE?u=mnawebl&sid=bookmark-AONE&xid=9be79a05 (last visited Sept. 17, 2021).

122 John Bowman, *Federal agency evaluates general aviation insurance requirements*, 51 TRIAL, at 52, xx-xx (Feb. 2015), link.gale.com/apps/doc/A401379354/AONE?u=mnawebl&sid=bookmark-AONE&xid=f9ac18ee (last visited Sept. 17, 2021).

123 Jon Doolittle, *Renter's Insurance: Affordable, But Limited*, 50 THE AVIATION CONSUMER, at 14, xx-xx (April 2020), https://link.gale.com/apps/doc/A620471001/AONE?u=mnawebl&sid=bookmark-AONE&xid=975f7bd1.

associated with putting a vehicle in the air and hoping it continues to fly until landed. There have been exclusions for those who are not licensed or are driving the craft in any way besides what is regulated as the way to operate.[124] There have also been terrorism exclusions added after the 9/11 attacks. Take note that liability insurance is to cover the general safety of the passengers aboard the plane.[125] If the owner must pay medical bills, chances are the regulated operation exclusion would be void in the name of justice. Further, the government began taking partial blame for terrorist attacks on aircraft after the enactment of 49 U.S.C.S. §403, making it void where insurance companies try to exclude coverage for such activity related to the 9/11 terrorist attacks.[126] Since most cyber-attacks are considered terrorist attacks, an insurance policy could not exclude coverage for airline passengers. Further, an insurance company cannot claim exclusions against that the controller or pilot of the aircraft during an invasion, even though they may not have been operating according to regulations since the safety of passengers supersedes any related exclusions.[127]

However, to be on the safe side, aircraft owners are still beginning to purchase individual cyber liability insurance.[128] Since the property and personal injury insurances are already packaged to the aircraft owner, the likelihood of an aircraft owner to need the Tech Errors and Omissions

---

124 John Kelly, *Flight to quality: since organizations that rent or hire aircraft can be liable for significant non-owned aircraft exposures, risk managers must develop methods for managing these risks*, 42 RISK MANAGEMENT at 53, xx-xx (Sept. 1995), link.gale.com/apps/doc/A17437211/AONE?u=mnawebl&sid=bookmark-AONE&xid=082192b1 (last visited Sept. 17, 2021).

125 Berard, M. G. (2012). Flying cars: The reconciliation of aircraft and automobile insurance policies. *Tort Trial and Insurance Practice Law Journal, 47(2),* 781-802.

126 Patrick J. Keating, Kevin R. Sutherland, Gerald V. Cleary, III, & Timothy J. Walsh, *Recent developments in aviation and space law*, TORT TRIAL & INSURANCE PRACTICE LAW JOURNAL, 205, 205-238 (Winter 2003).

127 *Anonymous, Pilot/Controller Roles and Responsibilities*, Federal Aviation Administration, www.faa.gov/air_traffic/publications/atpubs/aim_html/chap5_section_5.html.

128 Juliann Walsh, *Protecting Flying Computers Increased reliance on technology makes aviation safer but increases the importance of cyber security.*, Rick & Insurance (July 5, 2016), https://riskandinsurance.com/cyber-risk-aviation/.

insurance is greatly reduced.[129] Cyber Gap policies are still a great compliment to regular gap policies and may be a wealthy addition in the future.

C. Discussion and Unique Elements to Consider When Evaluating Endorsements and Stand-Alone Policies

A cyber insurance policy's purpose is to protect businesses and consumers from possible liability arising from a cyber incident. However, cyber insurance is still somewhat new, so policy inclusion for many insurance companies will vary. Cyber insurance coverage in the automotive, shipping, and aviation industries may be tricky to handle. Consequently, businesses in these industries must know their policy's specifics to understand what is and is not covered.

As a starting point, here are some general considerations to keep in mind when looking for a cyber insurance policy.[130] These considerations will help select a provider and ensure the policy provides coverage that fits the business's specific needs.

Not all providers and policies are equal. While there are some commonalities among most policies, such as a "Standard Cyber Insurance Coverage," it is crucial that businesses understand the details of the policy they choose. For example, standard policies typically include customer notifications, customer protections, extortion coverage, system recovery services, and digital forensics.[131]

When selecting a policy, companies should also look beyond coverage details to determine whether the deductibles associated with a policy are financially feasible for the organization. For example, selecting a policy with a deductible of $300,000 would not be possible for an organization that would be unable to pay that deductible in the event of a cyber incident, as they would not be able to leverage their insurance coverage to help them.

---

129 Vitaly S. Guzhva et al, *Liability Insurance*, Science Direct (2019) https://www.sciencedirect.com/topics/social-sciences/liability-insurance.

130 Oscar Minks, *6 Do's and Don'ts When Selecting Cyber Insurance Coverage*, FRSECURE (Feb. 12, 2021), *https*://frsecure.com/blog/cyber-insurance-coverage/.

131 *Id.*

Infrastructure improvements and proactive services are two main things that insurers do not usually cover.[132] It will be imperative for businesses to read the fine print to understand what is excluded in most policies and then create a plan for protection around that.

Confirm whether the insurer allows businesses to work with preferred vendors. It is recommended that companies engage with a cyber security partner. This security partner can help to prepare for a cyber incident and assist in working through proactive services.[133]

As discussed previously, the automotive, shipping, and aviation industries have overlapping yet unique concerns regarding cybersecurity. For example, in the aviation industry, aviation insurance is considered one of the world's most comprehensive insurance coverages.[134] However, cyber coverage remains a complicated area because certain cyber risks, such as network business interruption exposures, may not be included in aviation insurance policies.[135]

Similarly, cyber insurance for cars continues to be a developing market. However, there are still many security complexities and challenges across the entire supply chain.[136] The safety of connected vehicles concerning cybercrime is challenging for insurance companies. In recent years, several high-profile hacks in vehicles have resulted in safety recalls and reputational damage for high-end manufacturers. As such, it is more crucial than ever in this industry for insurance providers to understand and account for a new range of risks such as ransomware.

Cyber insurance in the shipping industry, on the other hand, has evolved to offer more coverage. One global advisory, broking, and solutions company disclosed a new type of cyber insurance product for shipowners that re-designs standard cyber policies to better navigate the

---

132 Infrastructure improvements include costs to remediate deficiencies identified in a business' systems when responding to a cyber incident. Examples of proactive services, on the other hand, include tabletop exercises and proactive testing (vulnerability scanning and penetration testing). *Id.*

133 *Id.*

134 Juliann Walsh, *Protecting 'Flying Computers'*, RISK & INSURANCE: AVIATION SAFETY (July 5, 2016), https://riskandinsurance.com/cyber-risk-aviation/.

135 *Id.*

136 *Who is Responsible for Securing the Connected Car?,* NTT SECURITY, https://www.nttsecurity.com/docs/librariesprovider3/resources/gbl_thought_leadership_connected_car_insurance_uea (last visited Feb. 26, 2021).

risks for ship operators in the digital era.[137] This new product allows ship owners to protect their businesses against the cost of non-compliance with new regulations, including lost revenue resulting from ship detainment. It will also enable shipowners to reinforce protection against specific threats that are unique to their businesses.[138] This new product was designed by cyber and maritime experts. It addresses cyber threats more broadly, including losses that occur from cyber-related business disruptions even when the cyber event originates with a third-party IT service provider. This product provides for organizations that can be the unintended victims of cyber-attacks and compensation for cyber-related business interruptions which can include loss of gross profit and increased working costs (including payments on account to help with cash flow, which is a first in cyber).[139]

D. Conclusion

In conclusion, aircrafts, automobiles, and ships will continue to evolve in complexity. They continue to be the by-products of years of technological prowess that have significantly advanced our daily lives.[140] However, this growth in advanced technologies has exposed otherwise secure industries to new cyber vulnerabilities as they embrace the technologies.[141] To mitigate damages caused by a possible cyber incident, all players within these industries need to explore cyber insurance policies and determine what best suits their businesses' needs.

---

137 Ben Abraham, *New Customized Cyber Insurance Product for Shipowners*, SEATRADE MARITIME NEWS (Apr. 28, 2020), https://www.seatrade-maritime.com/finance-insurance/new-customised-cyber-insurance-product-shipowners.

138 *Id.*

139 *Id.*

140 Helene Duchamp, Ibrahim Bayram & Ranim Korhani, *Cyber-Security, a New Challenge for the Aviation and Automotive Industries*, HARVARD BLOGS (June 30, 2016), https://blogs.harvard.edu/cybersecurity/files/2017/01/Cybersecurity-aviation-strategic-report.pdf.

141 On June 30th 2016, a Tesla self-drive car user was killed when the system failed to detect a turning truck. Danny Yadron & Dan Tynan, *Tesla Driver Dies in First Fatal Crash while using Autopilot Mode*, THE GUARDIAN (June 30, 2016), https://www.theguardian.com/technology/2016/jun/30/tesla-autopilot-death-self-driving-car-elon-musk.

Chapter 20

Retail and Consumer Products*

The retail and consumer products industry is difficult to define because of its broad nature and relationship with other industries. For this book, the retail and consumer products industry can be described as encompassing every item an individual can purchase, which includes food, beverages, software, electronics, appliances, cosmetics, and other generic household items. Consumer packaged goods (CPG) companies manufacture products and sell them to retailers. Retailers sell finished goods to consumers through brick-and-mortar stores, kiosks, mail and the internet.

The business landscape for CPG companies and retailers has changed drastically within the last 20-30 years. The internet, by its very nature, has changed the way consumer products are manufactured, produced and distributed to retailers. The internet has also changed the way retailers advertise, market, sell and deliver their products to consumers. To compete in the digital age, CPG companies and retailers are investing in technologies, strategies and processes to bolster their supply chains, including cloud-based platforms, artificial intelligence-driven analytics and Internet of Things (IoT) sensors that reduce forecasting errors, provide real-time insights into machine functioning, and track assets along the supply chain. The 2020 coronavirus pandemic exposed how vital the internet and other technologies have become to ensure business resiliency. Scholars and business executives may debate this point, but an industrial revolution is on the horizon—one that marries advanced manufacturing techniques with IoT, robotics, AI and cognitive technologies.

With the use of data-driven functionality, such as supply chain, resource allocation, individual-specific marketing, and time-sensitive price modifications based on customer demand, there is the continued existence of sensitive information in the care, custody and control of CPG companies and retailers. Wrongdoers such as nation-states, opportunistic criminals (hackers), and disgruntled employees prey on CPG companies and retailers because they have a treasure trove of consumer confidential and personally identifiable information (PII) that is very valuable for various reasons.

---

* By Robert Stines.

A. Critical Information Stored in Binary Format on Storage Devices

With the advent of IoT, e-commerce, online payments, social media and targeted marketing to consumers, CPG companies and retailers are handling, storing and exchanging volumes of sensitive consumer information, maintained in binary format (1's and 0's) on storage devices in multiple locations. That information may include names, phone numbers, addresses, debit and credit card information, account credentials and individual preferences for items purchased.

CPG companies and retailers may also have human resources departments that possess sensitive information such as employee social security numbers, salaries and health information. If CPG companies or retailers are using IoT technology in their products, they might also track customer location through GPS, IP addresses, biometrics and other forms of PII.

When a company holds PII, whether a consumer's or an employee's, various states require the company to take measures to protect and secure the PII that is stored in electronic form.[1] In the event of a data breach, all states including the District of Columbia and U.S. territories require that the breached company notify each individual whose personal information was accessed as a result of the breach. The cost of taking measures to protect PII or notifying consumers in the event of a data breach could prove extremely expensive for some companies.

Another concern for CPG companies and retailers in the digital age is protecting intellectual property and trade secrets from theft or unauthorized disclosure. Patents, proprietary software, plans, designs and client lists are now stored on servers, desktops and mobile devices. It is arguably easier for competitors and nation-states to surreptitiously access company trade secret and intellectual property. Such access is considered a cyber trespass—the act of crossing invisible, yet established, boundaries of ownership in online environments.[2]

Almost every retailer has an online presence to compete in today's market. A company's website might replace a brick-and-mortar location and is almost always the first place a consumer will visit to research a company. Motivated by a political agenda or to express dissatisfaction,

---

1 *See e.g.*, Fla. Stat. § 501.171(2) (2020).

2 Thomas J. Holt & Adam M. Bossler, Cybercrime in Progress (Crime Science Series) (Taylor and Francis) (Kindle Edition).

individuals may attempt to vandalize websites through web defacements[3] that will cause reputational harm to the company.

B. Case Studies

Data Breach

The FBI informs a retailer that there was a recent discovery of credit card information and user account credentials on the dark web. The FBI believes the source of the data is from the retailer's e-commerce website. An insurance company could assist the retailer with hiring a forensic investigator to determine if the website was compromised and the source of the data on the dark web. If necessary, the insurance company could assist with notifying customers of the data breach. If there is a class-action lawsuit against the insured, an insurance company could pay for the defense of the lawsuit and cover any settlements to resolve the lawsuit.

DDoS Attack

An e-commerce retailer who relies almost exclusively on online sales through its website had a major website outage for 30 minutes causing minimal lost revenue. The retailer is not concerned because it was only a 30-minute outage. The retailer then received emails from a known hacking group who threatens to return with a larger attack which would render the website inoperable for 24 hours unless the hackers receive 10 Bitcoin. The retailer would lose all of its online sales without an operable website. The retailer does not have access to Bitcoin and does not know whether it can trust the hackers. An insurance company could provide guidance and arrange for services to assist in the event of a larger attack. Insurance companies have relationships with specialists to harden the retailer's website and possibly negotiate with the hackers, if necessary.

3 *See id.*

Ransomware Attack

Employees at a CPG company turn on computers at the beginning of a workday to find that they cannot access any files. Instead, there is a digital note on every computer screen informing the employees that all files have been encrypted and will eventually be erased if the company does not pay 100 Bitcoin within 72 hours. The CPG company cannot access files that show product orders, deliveries, payments to vendors, payroll etc. With the proper type of cyber insurance, the company can report the situation to the insurer who will step in to hire forensic specialists, attorneys, and negotiators to mitigate the situation. In some scenarios, the insurer will pay the ransom on behalf of the company.

Point-of-Sale (POS) Attack

A brick-and-mortar retailer believes that its POS system is infected by malware that has compromised payment cards. An insurance carrier can arrange panel counsel and a forensic firm for the retailer. If necessary, the insurance carrier can cover the cost to notify customers that their payment cards were compromised and arrange for credit monitoring.

Portable Device Theft

A laptop was stolen from the human resource manager's vehicle. The laptop was encrypted and held files containing employee information, such as names, address, SSN and salary information. An insurance carrier can retain forensics and privacy counsel to determine whether the retailer is obligated to notify and provide credit monitoring for the employees.

C. Types of Cyber-Related Risks

As the case studies reflect, there are various types of cyber risks that may cause harm to CPG companies and retailers. Some of those risks include:

a. **Data Breaches**—The acquisition, access, or disclosure of PII or confidential corporate information by an unauthorized third party.
b. **Distributed Denial of Service (DDoS) Attack**—An attack that floods a targeted system's functions or connection to the internet. Consumers are then denied access to the target system such as a retailer's website. Attackers distribute the overwhelming traffic across multiple sources, often using botnets of thousands or millions of machines that access the internet.
c. **Fraudulent Funds Transfer**—Typically occurs when a financial institution receives instructions, which purport to have been transmitted by an authorized account holder but is actually from an unauthorized person, to transfer, pay, or deliver money or securities from one account to another. Depending on the language in the policy, this may also cover a client's vendor receiving a spoofed email posing as the client and requesting a change in ACH information, which causes the vendor to send payments to the fraudster's bank account.
d. **Malware**—Malicious software, including viruses and worms, that is programmed to attack, disrupt, and/or compromise computer networks or systems.
e. **Ransomware**—A type of malware that restricts access to a target system and demands payment in return for regular service.
f. **Stolen portable computer devices that contain sensitive information**—Laptops, smartphones, tablets and USB drives can store gigabytes of data that equate to millions of documents. These portable devices may contain sensitive or confidential information that would trigger notification laws if unauthorized individuals took possession or gained access.

If a CPG company or retailer is the victim of any of these types of cyber events, the company may encounter several types of financial losses and costs that could become extremely expensive. These costs include:

- legal costs, including attorneys' fees, experts, and electronic discovery;
- costs to conduct computer and digital forensics;
- costs to comply with regulatory and state notification laws;
- call centers to provide customer service and assistance to concerned customers;

- credit monitoring and identity protection services for customers or employees;
- crisis management and public relations;
- bricking costs (partial loss of hardware and the costs to replace it);
- business interruption;
- cyber extortion;
- Payment Card Industry (PCI) Fines and Assessments; and
- Data Recovery costs.

D. The Rise of Cyber Attacks Against CPG Companies and Retailers

News of cyber attacks against retailers and CPG companies permeate the media. It was not the first cyber attack against a retailer, but the timing and the vast volume of data that was exposed caused a media frenzy when in December 2013, Target was the victim of a cyber attack that impacted data on POS systems and exposed thousands of consumer's payment card information. Shortly after, in 2014, Home Depot confirmed that a cyber attack struck its payment systems, impacting customers across the United States and Canada. Macy's, eBay, Heartland Payment Systems, Sears, Adidas, Saks Fifth Avenue, StockX, and Starbucks are just some of the recognizable brands that have been victims of cyber events and the list continues to grow. While it may seem that only major brands or companies are targets for cyber-attacks, hackers do not discriminate as to the size of the company. Small and medium-sized companies are also victims of cyber events and may have greater risk due to lack of financial resources to implement robust cybersecurity measures.[4]

The consumer goods industry suffered from a major cyber incident when the NotPetya malware infiltrated thousands of companies in 2017. Mondelez, one of the largest confectionery, food and beverage companies in the world, was the victim of NotPetya that rendered 1700 of its servers and 24,000 laptops "permanently dysfunctional."[5] NotPetya also affected Maersk, the world's largest shipping group, that crippled some ports.

---

4 Verizon, *Does size matter? A deep dive into SMB breaches*, Verizon 2020 Data Breach Investigations Report (2020).

5 *Mondelez International, Inc. v. Zurich American Insurance Company*, In the Cir. Ct. of Cook Cty., Ill., Cty. Dep't, Law Div., Case No. 2018L011008, Compl. ¶ 9.

Hundreds of companies across the globe suffered from the attack that caused expensive business interruption losses. In total, NotPetya caused more than $10 billion in total damages.[6]

The rise of ransomware has become a threat that no company should ignore. Understanding that companies rely on computer systems and networks to operate, hackers are infecting these systems with ransomware for an easy and relatively risk-free payout. Companies are then faced with the unenviable decision of whether to pay wrongdoers to resume business operations, or completely replace systems from scratch.

To understand the dollar value of some of these cyber events, the Ponemon Institute in partnership with IBM Security published a report that quantified the average cost of a data breach in the retail industry at $2.01 million and the average cost in the consumer products industry at $2.59 million.[7] Based on these numbers, some companies may not survive a cyber event without assistance from insurance. In fact, according to the Ponemon report, cyber insurance most often covered the cost of some types of cyber events. For this reason, it is critical that decisionmakers in the consumer product and retail industry at least consider cyber insurance to mitigate some of the risk related to cyber events.

E. Why Cyber Insurance for CPG Companies and Retailers?

Cyber insurance serves two main purposes, (1) risk transference for the insured, and (2) to fill gaps left by existing insurance policies.

According to the Ponemon Institute, in 2017, there was a 27.7 percent probability that an organization would have a material data breach within twenty-four months.[8] With a 1 in 4 chance, companies should not ignore the risk of being the victim of a cyber event such as ransomware, data breaches, fraudulent payments, or DDoS attacks. Considering the high-risk landscape, it is prudent to mitigate some of the risk. While there are operational changes that could reduce the risk of an adverse cyber event, such as cyber awareness training and cybersecurity protocols, insurance is a cost-efficient method to transfer cyber risks.

---

6 Andy Greenberg, *Sandworm: A New Era of Cyberwar and the Hunt for Kremlin's Most Dangerous Hackers* 198 (Anchor Books 2019) (Kindle Edition).

7 Ponemon Institute, *Cost of a Data Breach 2020*, 25, Fig. 11 (2020).

8 Ponemon Institute, *Cost of a Data Breach 2017*, 1 (2017).

Cyber insurance is also used to fill the gaps which conventional insurance policies leave open. CPG companies and retailers may assume that their existing insurance policies will respond to the full range of cyber risks they may encounter. In reality, many conventional insurance policies do not respond to the broad and expanding cyber events that cause harm to companies. In addition, conventional insurance policies may contain exclusions relating to cyber losses that may expose a company to financial loss caused by a cyber risk.

F. Types of Coverage to Consider

A cyber insurance policy may cover the financial costs and losses associated with an adverse cyber event. When considering the forms of coverage, a CPG company or retailer may desire, it is important to appreciate the difference between first party and third party losses.

1. First Party

First party losses occur when there is loss and/or damage to a company's own business or data because of a cyber incident. For example, losses arising from business interruption, loss or damage to digital assets, reputational harm, theft, ransom demands or incident response costs. It is not always the case, but first party sections of a cyber insurance policy are typically written on an occurrence basis. This means that the policy will respond to cyber events that occur during the policy period. Sometimes insurance is provided on a discovery basis (this is important for cyber incidents that could remain undiscovered for a long time such as data breaches). This type of insurance policy will cover events that are discovered during the policy period. This alleviates concerns over a lack of coverage for historical hacks, provided they could not be identified until after inception of the policy. First Party Coverage may include the following:

- **Business interruption/extra expense**: For the time that the business could not operate during or immediately after a cyber incident. Recent cyber incidents impacting CPG companies, such as the NotPetya malware attack, has exposed the need for business interruption coverage as a result of a cyber incident. Business interruption may also include reimbursement for lost revenue and expenses caused by a technology failure, computer system outage, or cyber attack, with the option to include coverage for contingent business interruption resulting from a third party/supply chain event.

- **Cyber extortion**: Whereas the business interruption section(s) under a cyber policy will cover the loss of profits and increased costs of working associated with the unavailability of computer systems resulting from such attacks, the cyber extortion section of the policy will cover specialist cyber extortion advisers' costs, as well as, ransoms that are typically demanded in cryptocurrencies such as Bitcoin.
- **Information asset protection**: Costs to recreate or reconfigure information and electronic data assets, with the option to include cost to replace hardware or to rebuild systems.
- **Breach/event management**: Costs for notification and investigation of privacy and data security incidents, including breach coach (legal) and forensic services.
- **Bricking Cost:** This may cover partial loss of hardware that resulted from a cyber incident.
- **Cyber Crime**: This may cover losses resulting from funds transfer fraud or social engineering.
- **Claims, expenses, fines**: This type of coverage is beneficial to cover claim expenses, damages, or penalties because of a regulatory proceeding initiated against the company, as well as PCI fines and assessments because of a claim made against the company.
- **Dependent Business Interruption**: Some policies may cover business interruption where the insured organization was not the target of a cyber attack but rather a third party entity was attacked and that entity provided outsourced business processes or information technology services for the insured organization.
- **Consumer privacy violations**: The improper collection or retention of PII or the misuse of PII.
- **Reputational harm**: Losses due to the organization's loss of clients, customers or sales resulting from damage to the organization's reputation or brand.
- **System failure**: In situations where a cyber event has not been identified but there is an unintentional or unplanned outage of the organization's computer systems.

2. *Third Party*

In contrast to first party, third party losses occur when there is (alleged or actual) damage or loss to others, such as a CPG company's or retailer's clients or customers as a result of a cyber event. Third party coverage may cover losses due to payments to customers for a breach of personal data controlled by the organization. It may also include liability in contract or tort to business partners arising out of cyber events. The third party liability sections of a cyber insurance policy are typically written on a claims made basis (similar to professional liability insurance). This means that the policy will cover claims that are made against the insured during the effective dates of the policy. Third Party Coverage may include the following:

- **Privacy Liability**: Failure to prevent breaches of PII or to disclose a data breach event that caused the unauthorized disclosure of PII;
- **Network Security Liability**: Actual or alleged failure of computer security to prevent or mitigate an IoT or computer attack;
- **Regulatory Defense**: Costs to defend regulatory actions and for certain fines and penalties;
- **Payment Card Information**: Fines and penalties for PCI industry settlements, fraud recoveries, chargebacks, and forensic investigations.

G. Provisions to Consider

An insurance policy is a contract between the insurance carrier and the company (insured) to provide indemnification and a defense under very specific circumstances. Like any contract, the language in the document determines each party's duties and obligations. It is a mistake to assume that because the insurance carrier is providing a "cyber" insurance policy this automatically means that every type of cyber incident will trigger the insurance carrier's obligation to indemnify or defend the company.

One of the critical components to any insurance policy is the exclusions. Insurance carriers can provide specific coverage but then restrict or exclude aspects of the same coverage. For this reason, it is advisable to review and understand the exclusions section of a policy.

A common type of exclusion is claims or regulatory actions under the Children's Online Privacy Protection Act (COPPA).[9] If a CPG company or retailer offers products to children under 13, then a COPPA exclusion might change the nature of the insurance provided to the company. For example, the company may believe it has coverage for consumer privacy violations, which covers the improper collection or retention of PII or the misuse of PII, but then there is a COPPA exclusion that does not cover the improper collection of information related to children under 13.

Another exclusion that might change coverages is an exclusion for social engineering resulting from the use of an organization's computer system by a person authorized to access the computer system. In other words, losses resulting from compromises to the computer system because of insiders (employees or agents), might be excluded. For example, an employee sends an email to the accounting department to send funds to an account. It is later discovered that the employee was siphoning funds. With a social engineering exclusion, or something similar, this type of event may not trigger coverage under a cyber policy.

Another important aspect of the insurance contract are sub-limits. A CPG company or retailer may believe a policy provides maximum limits of X dollars (typically identified on the declarations page of the policy), but may not then realize there is a sub-limit for certain type of coverages. For example, a cyber insurance policy may have $1 million in data breach coverage, but only $50,000 in business interruption coverage or only $25,000 to pay for cyber extortion.

Often overlooked, but very important, is whether defense costs erode the policy limits. In some insurance policies, defense costs are paid by the carrier over and above the coverage limits of the policy. For example, the policy has $100,000 in limits, and after being sued, the legal fees amount to $150,000. The defense costs are separate and apart from the coverage limits; therefore, the $100,000 is still available to pay the claimant. In this situation, the defense costs are outside the limits. The other situation is where defense costs erode the policy's coverage limits. In our example with the $100,000 in limits, if defense costs reach the limit, there are likely no funds available from the carrier to pay the claimant. This is typically known as defense within limits or an eroding policy. Many cyber insurance carriers offer eroding policies.

---

9 Children's Online Privacy Protection Act, 15 U.S.C. §§ 6501–6505 (2020).

H. How Much Insurance?

The question that many CPG companies and retailers may ask is "how much insurance is enough" or "what should be the policy limits." Unfortunately, the best answer to this question is "it depends on a multiple of factors." Two of those factors are (1) the organization's budget and (2) the organization's appetite for risk. For an e-commerce company that relies on computers and the internet, business interruption insurance may prove critical and purchasing the most insurance within the budget is advisable. For a brick-and-mortar company, the analysis is different.

One factor to consider is how much PII does the company store on its servers. The Ponemon Institute reported that 80% of breached organizations stated that customer PII was compromised during the breach and the average cost per lost or stolen record was $150 for breaches involving PII.[10] Based on this information, companies with volumes of customer data may desire a policy with the data breach coverage and higher limits that fit within the company's budget. Another factor to consider is how long the company can survive without access to computer systems. Every company should discuss with their broker and insurance carrier how to best appreciate the risks and discuss limits that meet the needs of the company.

I. Risk Mitigation and the Insurance Application

One of the purposes of cyber insurance is to transfer risk; however, in addition to transferring risk, companies should also consider risk mitigation. CPG companies and retailers should consider reasonable methods to protect against or respond to cyber events. Insurance carriers may require that companies take certain precautions to reduce risks associated with cyber events. As an incentive, some insurance companies may provide discounts or credits for companies that implement cybersecurity protocols. Similar to premium discounts on home insurance when the homeowner purchases a security or sprinkler system, cyber insurance carriers provide discounts for applicants that implement cybersecurity systems. For this reason, during the application process, insurance carriers may ask questions such as:

---

10 *See Cost of a Data Breach 2020* at 8.

- Does the applicant use firewall or Anti-Virus protection?
- Does the applicant have policies or procedures concerning the encryption of internal and external electronic communications?
- Who is responsible for privacy and information security within the organization?
- Are there regular cyber security assessments of systems?
- Is the applicant compliant with data security standards issued by financial institutions?
- Does the applicant encrypt data stored on laptop computers and portable media?
- Does the applicant back up computer system data and how is it stored?
- What kind of sensitive client or customer information does the applicant collect and store?
- Is there a Business Continuity or Disaster Recovery Plan in place that covers cyber events?
- If you experience network disruption, how long will it take to become fully operational?

These types of questions demonstrate that CPG companies and retailers should proactively implement cybersecurity protocols and procedures not only to protect themselves but also to qualify for cyber insurance and possibly obtain better premiums. CPG companies and retailers should therefore consider whether the information technology department is accountable for cybersecurity measures. If not, why? In some situations, CPG companies and retailers may consider the need for a Chief Information Security Officer (CISO) or a Chief Information Officer (CIO). In other situations, retaining a managed security service provider (MSSP) to outsource some of the tasks associated with cybersecurity is beneficial. If anything, an MSSP may assist with understanding the company's cyber risk exposures and provide proof to insurance carriers that security measures have been implemented.

Whether the CPG company or retailer relies on the IT department, CISO or MSSP, all companies should strongly consider regular cyber security assessments, encryption of data, Anti-Virus protection and update Business Continuity and Disaster Recovery Plans. Additionally, companies should provide training to employees on cyber awareness and cyber-hygiene.

J. Final Thoughts

Companies in the retail and consumer products industry rely on technology, such as computer systems and the internet, to compete in the digital age. Disruption or denial of access to these technologies could cause significant financial harm to these companies. Cyber threats that deny access to a company's computer systems has increased and has become more expensive to protect against and recover from.

For many CPG and retail companies, their business model relies on collecting and storing sensitive customer and employee information that have value to cyber-wrongdoers. This information includes, payment card information, SSNs, confidential online account credentials, and other private data. The risk of an adverse cyber event that causes the unauthorized access or disclosure of this information is high.

Considering the threat landscape, it is prudent to implement procedures, protocols and measures to mitigate risks associated with a cyber event. Cyber insurance that meets the needs of the particular company is one cost-efficient method to transfer some of the financial exposure related to cyber risk.

Chapter 21

Manufacturing and Industrial Products*

Many have said the world is experiencing the Fourth Industrial Revolution, caused by a combination of inventions and developments, including Artificial Intelligence, the Internet of Things, big data analytics, cloud computing, and biometrics.[1] The rapid digitization of nearly every aspect of most industries is both a result and a perpetuating cause of this revolution.

Manufacturers still face many of the same cyber threats as other businesses, including ransomware, theft of employee information, distributed denial of service attacks, and so on. Additionally, many of the threats to today's manufacturing industry are either fairly unique or, at the very least, heightened due to the current industrial revolution and the accompanying changes in the modern industrial data ecosystem.[2] Control systems common in manufacturing operations are distinctly different from many information systems in other industries, complete with their own vulnerabilities and risks.[3] Manufacturers face a different threat landscape than companies in other industries for a number of reasons, including the integrated ecosystem of the supply chain, massive networks of connected sensors and controllers increasingly involved in manufacturing, and the connectivity of the products created. Furthermore, manufacturers face challenges regarding cyber liability coverage for such events as personal injury, property damage, and contractual obligations.[4] Manufacturers also face increased risks from third parties through integrated supply chain

---

* By J. Paul Zimmerman.

1 See, e.g., https://www.purdueglobal.edu/education-partnerships/fourth-industrial-revolution-is-your-workforce-ready/ (last visited Mar. 17, 2021).

2 Deloitte & MAPI, *Cybersecurity for Smart Factories*, MAPI, https://www.mapi.net/sites/default/files/cybersecurity-for-smart-factories-mfg.pdf (last visited Mar. 18 2021).

3 Joe Wiess, *Don't Overlook the Most Consequential Control System Cyber Events of 2020*, CONTROL (Jan. 18, 2021), https://www.controlglobal.com/blogs/unfettered/dont-overlook-the-most-consequential-control-system-cyber-events-of-2020/ (last visited Jan. 20, 2021).

4 2 Robert Persons & Ken Brownlee, EXCESS LIABILITY: RIGHTS & DUTIES OF COMMERCIAL RISK INSUREDS & INSURERS §14:8 (4th ed. 2020). *See also* Deloitte & MAPI, *Smart Factories*, *supra* note 2.

information systems.[5] Depending on the circumstances, some manufacturers face tremendous risk of reputational harm.

In this chapter, manufacturing includes not only manufacturers of end products, but also the supply chain leading to the end product—after all, most companies in a manufacturer's value chain are manufacturers as well. This discussion also applies to supply chain logistics, for two reasons. First, because the data and ecosystems of many supply chains are tightly integrated, including as to logistics, the entire network includes suppliers and logistics companies. A primary vulnerability for manufacturers can be third parties, including both suppliers and logistics vendors, with access to the manufacturer's systems and data. By one survey, 57% of manufacturers have experienced a vendor breach in the previous twelve months.[6] Second, a disruption in a manufacturer's supply chain can have similar results as a disruption of the manufacturer's own operation, regardless of whether the disruption originates with a supplier or a logistics provider.

Also, as will become evident in considering the coverages needed in many manufacturing operations, "supply chain" entails the company's value chain—the companies involved in supplying and incorporating components into a finished product. Some insurance policies treat these suppliers and relationships separately from a manufacturer's infrastructure and business process vendors, such as data hosting, software vendors for operational systems, and other vendors providing services to the operation as opposed to providing raw materials or component parts for the manufacturer's products. This distinction can be seen in various scenarios.[7]

---

5 *See* Deloitte & MAPI, *Smart Factories*, *supra* note 2.

6 BlueVoyant, *BlueVoyant Research Reveals Four in Five Firms Have Suffered a Cybersecurity Breach Caused By a Third-Party Vendor*, CISION PR NEWSWIRE (Sept. 23, 2020), https://www.prnewswire.com/news-releases/bluevoyant-research-reveals-four-in-five-firms-have-suffered-a-cybersecurity-breach-caused-by-a-third-party-vendor-301136072.html (last visited Jan. 29, 2021).

7 For example, a cyber policy may specifically define "outsourced provider" as "[a]ny third party, including a cloud service provider, to which an Insured has contracted to provide a business process on behalf and for the benefit of an Insured." Thus, the policy distinguishes contractual supply chain providers from "outsourced [process] providers" for many coverages and exclusions. Some may even specifically further limit "outsourced provider" to "outsourced IT provider" or "outsourced BPO provider." Policies containing

This chapter will outline prevalent and emerging cyber liability coverage issues relating to manufacturers and industrial environments, beginning with an overview of increasingly common equipment in the digital manufacturing environment, ecosystem, and process. Primarily, the use and generation of data in increasingly complex networks of sensors and controllers makes the manufacturer's potential cyber and related insurance needs unique. Then those unique considerations are discussed. Finally, coverages and related considerations that must be examined in managing first- and third-party risks to today's manufacturer are explored. Obviously, no categorical rules or recommendations exist in identifying and quantifying a manufacturer's cyber risks and insurance needs because manufacturers occupy a spectrum from decades old (or older) equipment and processes to cutting edge facilities that were not possible just a decade ago, some utilizing or making smart devices not in production a decade ago. This chapter, therefore, identifies potential issues and pitfalls, along with developing trends, in order to assist in a thorough examination of the manufacturer's risks and cyber insurance needs while evaluating policies.

A. Overview of the Manufacturing Environment

Today's manufacturers rely more and more on efficient and integrated supply chains, using increasingly connected information systems. Furthermore, manufacturing processes require increasingly interconnected sensors and actuators that generate and provide a wealth of data and analysis about both the manufacturing process and the finished product. The sharing of information systems between supply chain partners and the explosion in the use of sensors and controlled devices complicate the threat landscape of today's manufacturers and, ultimately, their insurance requirements. Additionally, the National Counterintelligence and Security Center identifies high-end manufacturing, such as those involving or relating to 3D printing, advanced robotics, electric motors, foundational manufacturing equipment, integrated circuits, and specialized materials, as having particular interest to foreign intelligence collectors.[8]

---

such distinctions should be reviewed with the effect of this distinction as a consideration.

8 National Counterintelligence and Security Center, Report on Foreign Economic Espionage in Cyberspace, National Counterintelligence and

The environment in which any company operates impacts nearly every aspect of its cyber security and coverage needs. Many manufacturers use systems originally designed and built for safety and efficiency; in other words, legacy systems that pre-date the modern cyber threat landscape. Supply chains are now designed to be responsive and efficient, allowing such practices as just-in-time inventory and continuous process improvement. Many older operations and supply chains were not built with cybersecurity as a primary consideration, and even many new components in a manufacturer's network did not incorporate security by design. Furthermore, to the extent that devices are added to a manufacturer's existing system, they are often implemented and maintained by an operations group rather than IT/IS, thus creating gaps in system controls, design, management, and surveillance.[9] Collectively, these various conditions all affect the manufacturer's coverage needs.

Manufacturing continues to incorporate, at a still-increasing rate, a growing network of sensors, controllers, and other connected "smart" devices. The various devices are intended to assist manufacturers with process improvement, maintenance, inventory tracking, customer service, and other analytics capabilities. Some manufacturing facilities now use thousands, or even millions, of connected devices. Such "Operational Technology" ("OT") devices often connect wirelessly via the facility's network. They send and receive data to each other and to one or more databases or servers. Those various information systems may be controlled, hosted, or at least accessed, by multiple third parties.

Because these devices are at the center of the modern manufacturing operation, ownership of their implementation, set up, and maintenance often falls to operations rather than IT or IS. As a result, IT and IS often are not involved in vetting and testing these devices and systems. Indeed, it may not even have an inventory of these devices or be involved in

---

Security Center (2018). Found at https://www.dni.gov/index.php/ncsc-newsroom/item/1889-2018-foreign-economic-espionage-in-cyberspace.

9 Operational Technology Cyber Security Alliance, New Operational Technology Cyber Security Alliance Launces to Deliver Comprehensive Cyber Security Guidelines for Operational Technology (Oct. 22, 2019), https://www.businesswire.com/news/home/20191021005857/en/New-Operational-Technology-Cyber-Security-Alliance-Launches-to-Deliver-Comprehensive-Cyber-Security-Guidelines-for-Operational-Technology (last visited Feb. 2, 2021).

patching and updating schedules or needs. Every such device is another connection to a network and another potential vulnerability.

Much of the data shared by or with these devices is accessible from outside the company. A contractor or vendor often monitors and analyzes the data generated by these devices.[10] The data may also be available to other companies in the manufacturer's supply chain (whether upstream or downstream). Furthermore, sensor data is only the beginning of the access and data exchanges among partners within a supply chain.[11] Obviously, intrusion into one network may lead to or facilitate intrusions into other networks, whether within the same operation or between networks within the same supply chain.

Reputational harm to a manufacturer following a data breach or attack should not be underestimated, particularly as to manufacturers that are considered "critical infrastructure."[12] Often the data at risk—specifications, formulas, processes, and so on—belong to a customer. Jeopardizing a client's data can jeopardize the relationship with the client. For manufacturers that are part of a supply chain, the manufacturer may have a limited number of customers it supplies, thus increasing the impact of the reputational harm in the event of a security incident. Manufacturers that are government contractors could suffer prolonged fallout from data security incidents, given the limited markets for their products and the increasingly stringent controls that are required.

While most manufacturers do not generally hold significant amounts of personal consumer information,[13] a growing exception is data obtained from smart devices. Consumer and commercial products increasingly have

---

10 Michael Hamilton, *IT, OT, and IoT: Existential Technology Lifecycle Management*, CRITICAL INFORMATICS (June 6, 2018), https://www.csoonline.com/article/3279545/it-ot-and-iot-existential-technology-lifecycle-management.html (last visited Feb. 2, 2021).

11 Adam Robinson, *How Supply Chain Systems Integration Is a Game Changer*, INDUSTRY WEEK (Jul. 3, 2018), https://www.industryweek. com/supply-chain/article/22025901/how-supply-chain-systems-integration-is-a-game-changer (last visited Feb. 2, 2021).

12 CYBERSECURITY & INFRASTRUCTURE SECURITY AGENCY, NATIONAL CRITICAL FUNCTIONS SET, https://www.cisa.gov/national-critical-functions-set (last visited Jan. 15, 2021).

13 *But see* Juliana De Groot, *Biggest Manufacturing Data Breaches of the 21st Century*, DIGITAL GUARDIAN (Aug. 7, 2020), https://digitalguardian.com/blog/biggest-manufacturing-data-breaches-of-the-21-century (last visited Mar. 16, 2021).

the ability—and indeed, the functionality—to provide the manufacturer with feedback regarding the device's use and environment. This data may or may not be stored in an anonymized condition. Such feedback may also include, and be connected to, account information that is required in order for the customer to use the product. Examples include smart speakers and various electronics for which the purchaser sets up a customer account relating to the device. Therefore, while most manufacturers do not hold consumer data in the classic sense (e.g., credit card information, financial information, etc.), other forms of customer and consumer data, which are likely protected under various privacy laws, can lead to third-party data breach liability for manufacturers.[14] The ever-increasing capabilities for re-identifying previously anonymized data must be considered as a potential future tort liability, even if the anonymization met regulatory requirements in effect at the time it was collected.[15]

B. Manufacturing Hardware and Systems

The manufacturing landscape is changing rapidly, with increasingly automated systems that self-monitor. These systems contain far more devices than just a few years ago, each involving hardware, software and firmware, connections, and data storage. Multiple components in a typical manufacturing system are potential vulnerabilities. An understanding of the various components of a "smart factory" is necessary in identifying needed coverages and limits.

---

14 See, e.g., Megan Wollerton, *Aibo's Dark Side: Why Illinois Bans Sony's Robot Dog*, CNET (Apr. 1, 2019), https://www.cnet.com/news/what-sonys-robot-dog-teaches-us-about-biometric-data-privacy/ (discussing the implications of Illinois' Biometric Information Privacy Act on Aibo, a robotic dog with a camera, and Ring doorbell cameras) (last visited Mar. 16, 2021); https://www.theguardian.com/technology/2020/mar/08/how-to-stop-your-smart-home-spying-on-you-lightbulbs-doorbell-ring-google-assistant-alexa-privacy (last visited Mar. 29, 2021).

15 Mauricio Paez & Mike La Marka, Cyber-Security Issue: Article: The Internet of Tmngs: Emerging Legal Issues for Businesses, 43 N. KY. L. REV. 29, 39 (2016); Natasha Lomas, Researchers Spotlight the Lie of 'Anonymous' Data, TechCrunch (July 24, 2019) (found at https://techcrunch.com/2019/07/24/researchers-spotlight-the-lie-of-anonymous-data/) (last visited Mar. 31, 2021).

1. IoT

Today's manufacturing facilities include massive networks of interconnected devices, many of which are web-enabled—the smart factory. Many of those sensors and devices are connected to computer systems, other devices, or both, and are referred to as the internet of things ("IoT").[16] IoT uses include traditional scenarios such as access control, HVAC systems, inventory/component tracking, and countless applications in the manufacturing process. Motors, valves, actuators, pressure vessels, and so on, are built or refitted with sensors that transmit data about their condition, performance, and use.[17] Sensor data are collected to monitor all aspects of production. Production facilities may include networks of thousands or even millions of IoT devices, all of which are network enabled. While segmented networks and systems can mitigate unauthorized access, countless IoT connections to the same network and the data obtained from or sent to those devices may reside in the same database.

IoT networks provide many benefits in manufacturing.

> The industrial IoT encompasses connected sensors and actuators associated with kinetic industrial processes, including factory assembly lines. . . Whilst these sensors and actuators have always been prevalent in the context of operational technology (OT), connectivity and the data processing opportunities offered by cloud technologies mean that deeper insight and near real-time feedback can further optimize industrial processes. As a consequence, industrial IoT is seen as core to the digitalization of industry.[18]

Rather than waiting until parts or components fail before diagnosing a problem, then ordering parts and installing them, manufacturers can

---

16 Gilad David Maayan, *The IoT Rundown for 2020: Stats, Risks, and Solutions*, SECURITY TODAY (Jan. 13, 2020), https://www.industryweek. com/supply-chain/article/22025901/how-supply-chain-systems-integration-is-a-game-changer (last visited Feb. 2, 2021).

17 *Id.*

18 Andy Jones, *Securing the IoT: Taming the Connected World*, INFORMATION SECURITY FORUM (2019), https://www.securityforum.org/research/securing-the-iot-taming-the-connected-world/ (last visited Jan. 7, 2021).

identify wear or fatigue before it becomes problematic, order the needed parts based on actual conditions, and schedule a minimal shutdown if needed. For example, IoT systems can allow real time monitoring of conditions in component seals, allowing the operation to engage in predictive maintenance rather than reactive or scheduled maintenance.[19] Whereas manufacturers were once faced with either stockpiling critical parts "just in case" or facing long lead times in ordering specialized or customized parts, manufacturers can now delay expenditures until a potential or developing problem is recognized by the system and minimize associated disruptions thanks to insights obtained through IoT deployment. This capability mitigates the risk of prolonged or unanticipated disruptions.[20]

While the term "IoT" is generally meant to refer specifically to devices that are web enabled,[21] some of these devices transmit or receive data through other means, including Bluetooth transmission, RFID signals, or other radio frequencies.[22] However, simply because a device connects to other devices or to computer devices through means other than the internet does not mean they do not present cyberliability risk. At some point, the data and the control systems are nearly always accessible via internet connection, and these systems are often accessible from outside the network.[23]

Three basic types of devices among the unique threats manufacturers face are supervisory control and data acquisition ("SCADA") systems, industrial control systems ("ICS"), and programmable logic circuits ("PLC").[24] All of these systems implicate a manufacturer's cyber security,

---

19 See Justin Bass, *Predictive Maintenance Programs Can Increase the Longevity of Wear Parts*, PUMPS & SYSTEMS (Nov. 29, 2018), https://www.pumpsandsystems.com/how-use-iot-improve-mechanical-seal-reliability (last visited Mar. 18, 2021).

20 See, e.g., Peter Fretty, *IIoT Enables CommScope to Avoid Costly Downtime*, INDUSTRY WEEk (Mar. 2, 2021), https://www.industryweek.com/technology-and-iiot/article/21156606/iiot-enables-commscope-to-avoid-costly-downtown (last visited Mar. 24, 2021).

21 See Maayan, The IoT Rundown, supra note 16.

22 S.W. Mohad & Rohit S. Deshmukh, *Internet of Things for Industrial Monitoring and Controls Applications*, 71 INT'L J. OF SCI. ENG'G RES. Iss. 2, Feb. 2016, at 494, 496.

23 *Id.*

24 Josh Fruhlinger, *What is Stuxnet, Who Created It and How Does It Work?*, CSO ONLINE (Aug. 22, 2017)("PLCs are how computers interact with and

providing potential entry points into a network, generating data that are subject to manipulation, being accessed improperly for any number of reasons, and potential points of failure.[25]

2. *Proliferation of Devices (and Risks)*

By one estimate, there are 31-35 billion devices connected to the internet.[26] A significant percentage of these are IoT devices in manufacturing facilities: 80% of manufacturing facilities were anticipated to have added industrial IoT devices during 2020, and adoption could continue at a rate of 127 devices per second.[27] That is a large number of potential targets for internal threats and external hackers.

With this substantial number of devices comes increased and more common risks. First, the firmware and software programmed into these devices often incorporate "off the shelf" security modules, which is a common and not necessarily improper practice. That said, many IoT devices contain firmware that originates from an era when cybersecurity was not widely recognized as a top concern, and may have been built on older open source or unsecured operating systems.[28] Any exploitable vulnerability in a device's software or firmware security modules creates

---

control industrial machinery like uranium centrifuges."), https://www.csoonline.com/article/3218104/what-is-stuxnet-who-created-it-and-how-does-it-work.html (last visited Feb. 2, 2021).

25 *See, e.g.*, CYBERSECURITY & INFRASTRUCTURE SECURITY AGENCY, ICS ALERT 17-206-01 (viewable at https://us-cert.cisa.gov/ics/alerts/ICS-ALERT-17-206-01 (last visited Jan. 31, 2021)(regarding malware targeting certain ICS systems allowing control of switches and circuit breakers)[hereinafter ICA ALERT 17-206-01]. *See also* AJ GALLAGHER, https://www.ajg.com/us/news-and-insights/2019/12/insuring-cyber-emerging-risks-physical-damage-and-bodily-injury/ (last visited Jan. 13, 2021) [hereinafter AJ Gallagher Blog] ("Attacks are made on SCADA and ICS not just through brute force and insiders, but also through advanced persistent threats, spear phishing, SQL injection, distributed denial of service, and social engineering attacks.").

26 See Maayan, The IoT Rundown, supra note 16.

27 See Maayan, The IoT Rundown, supra note 16.

28 Jason G. Weiss, *How the Healthcare Industry Can Fight Rising Cyber Attacks*, Cybersecurity Law & Strategy (Dec. 1, 2019).

a vulnerability in any system incorporating that device.[29] Furthermore, updating these IoT devices presents challenges. The sheer number, and potentially constant or near constant use, makes pushing out patches and updates difficult, and that is assuming that the devices are set up to be able to accept patches and updates, which is not always the case. Thus, patching vulnerabilities in potentially millions of IoT devices incorporated into an operation is not consistent and often is not timely, if performed at all.

Second, IoT devices of numerous types are subject to being maliciously re-assigned to such tasks as DDoS attacks or other bot nets. Improper operation or configuration of manufacturing IoT devices can lead to whatever problems would arise from the devices not working, such as inefficient operations, improper operations, unmonitored wear and tear, and so on. This can result in unanticipated production outages that the devices are designed to predict, prevent, or mitigate.

Third, the data sent to or obtained from IoT devices is subject to manipulation. Not only can the devices themselves be misappropriated or somehow impaired in their designated functions, but the integrity of the data associated with these devices is another possible risk. An example of how the data is at risk can be seen in recent threats to cargo data held by shipping container brokers.[30] When a seller needs shipping capacity for its goods, it can order capacity on a ship through a broker's online portal.[31] The customer provides information such as the weight, volume, and type of cargo. The broker forwards this information to the shipping company, which incorporates it into the ship's manifest data and loading/unloading plan. In 2017, one or more brokers were hacked, and the hackers changed load data on the broker's system. A ship could have sunk due to unauthorized changes in the data regarding cargo weight.[32] Obviously, a

---

29 See, e.g., Brandon Vigliarolo, *IBM Finds Vulnerability in IoT Chips Present in Billions of Devices*, TECHREPUBLIC (Aug. 19, 2020), https://www.techrepublic.com/article/ibm-finds-vulnerability-in-iot-chips-present-in-billions-of-devices/ (last visited Feb. 2, 2021). *See also* Doug Olenick, *Even in Test Mode, New Mirai Variant Infecting IoT Devices*, DATA BREACH TODAY (Oct. 26, 2020).

30 Ken Munro, *Sinking Containing Ships by Hacking Load Plan Software* (Nov. 16, 2017), https://www.pentestpartners.com/security-blog/sinking-container-ships-by-hacking-load-plan-software/ (last visited Jan. 31, 2021).

31 Munro, Sinking Container Ships, supra note 30.

32 Munro, Sinking Container Ships, supra note 30.

potential catastrophe without any data being "stolen" in the classic sense of hacking.

A similar risk was seen with the Stuxnet worm, which was designed to attack uranium enrichment operations in Iran.[33] The malware targeted ICS components, which changed the rotation speed of centrifuges. This sabotaged the uranium being produced and damaged the equipment.[34] If data relating to SCADA, ICS, PLCs, and IoT devices is improperly manipulated, any number of results can be seen, including damaged equipment, defective products, or dangerous conditions.

3. *Cloud Platforms*

The explosion of data, including as a result of OT, is leading to continued expansion in the use of cloud platforms, whether simply for data storage, or in some variation of Software as a Service, Platform as a Service, or Infrastructure as a Service models.[35] Cloud systems add a layer of complexity to securing data and systems and in adequately insuring the added risks,[36] particularly through the contract provisions between the manufacturer and the outsourced provider relating to ownership, access, integrity, and protection of data.

4. *Robotics.*

Robotics present another broad impact on insuring risk.[37] The need for insurance coverage regarding robotics will only grow based on estimates that factories could already be using up to 3 million robots.[38] From

33 Munro, Sinking Container Ships, supra note 30.

34 Munro, Sinking Container Ships, supra note 30.

35 Steve Ranger, *What Is Cloud Computing? Everything You Need to Know About the Cloud Explained*, ZDNET (Dec. 13, 2018), https://www.zdnet.com/article/what-is-cloud-computing-everything-you-need-to-know-about-the-cloud/ (last visited Feb. 2, 2021).

36 Persons & Brownlee, EXCESS LIABILITY, *supra* note 4.

37 *See*, e.g., ICA ALERT 17-206-01, *supra* note 25 (regarding a vulnerability in robot motion servers that, along with network access and knowledge of the robotics system, could allow data exfiltration and partial control over a robot's motion).

38 Michelle Kerr, *9 Critical Risks Facing the Manufacturing Industry*, Risk & Insurance, https://www.ajg.com/us/news-and-insights/2019/12/

worker's compensation claims as a result of mobile robots causing injuries, to robot systems on an assembly line causing losses due to altered data fed to the robots, these systems can be the focus of bodily injury claims, property damage losses, or the cause of various other losses or liabilities.

5. Digital Twins.

A fascinating development in industrial systems is the "digital twin," which is a digital representation of an actual physical system.[39] Large numbers of sensors within physical systems, such as power plants and factory equipment, can monitor the conditions inside various components of the system and feed that data to a server that generates a digital representation of the equipment. The company can better monitor conditions inside the system based on the real time digital representation.[40] However, with the connectability of this network of sensors and the servers assembling, hosting, and analyzing the digital twin data, the company faces the risk of incorrect or incomplete data depriving the company of the benefit of that information. Worse yet, incorrect information could lead the company to incorrect conclusions concerning the state of the system, allowing failures that should have been detected, but were not, or to decisions that have unintended consequences.

6. Siloed IT and OT

Legal, risk management, and the technical departments responsible for both OT and IT should review coverage options, and even insurance policies, due to the intricacies of the OT and IT inherent in manufacturing and the complexity of related risks, threats, and vulnerabilities.[41] Furthermore, manufacturers that face product liability claims, particularly

---

insuring-cyber-emerging-risks-physical-damage-and-bodily-injury/ (last visited Jan. 17, 2021).

39 Christy Pettey, *When IT and Operational Technology Converge*, GARTNER (Jan. 13, 2017), https://www.gartner.com/smarterwithgartner/when-it-and-operational-technology-converge/ (last visited Feb. 2, 2021).

40 Pettey, IT and Operational Technology, *supra* note 39.

41 Steven R. Gilford & Marc E. Rosenthal, Proskauer on Privacy: A Guide to Privacy and Data Security Law in the Information Age §16:3.2, at 16-42 to -43 (Kristen R. Mathews ed., 2d ed. Supp. 2019).

on a class action basis, should note whether an insurance policy's third-party coverage requires a breach of the manufacturer's system, rather than the product's security, before a covered "occurrence" has taken place, particularly due to exclusion of cyber risks in the manufacturer's CGL policies.[42]

C. Cyber Risks in Manufacturing

The unique vulnerabilities and the broad range of potential losses in today's manufacturing sectors present unique challenges in assembling an effective insurance portfolio.[43] Granted, third-party risks in manufacturing do not ordinarily include class action tort claims over large bodies of personal data, which is a common circumstance necessitating large towers of coverage for industries such as healthcare and retail. However, third-party risk is not to be disregarded entirely in manufacturing. Possible losses can relate to tort liability arising from defective products[44] (resulting, for example, from inaccurate sensor data in the manufacturing process), contractual liability to customers,[45] or regulatory penalties. That being said, risks particular to manufacturing should not cause risk managers to lose sight entirely of many risks common across commercial operations, such as payment card liability (PCI DSS), employee liability relating to personal information (and the attendant statutory notification requirements), and ransomware.

One survey of manufacturing executives found the following as their top concerns, in order from greatest to least:

---

42 Gilford & Rosenthal, PROSKAUER ON PRIVACY §16:3.2, at 16-66, *supra* note 41.

43 Maria Korolov, *Supply Chain Attacks Show Why You Should Be Wary of Third-Party Providers*, CSO ONLINE (Feb. 4, 2021), https://www.csoonline.com/article/3191947/supply-chain-attacks-show-why-you-should-be-wary-of-third-party-providers.html (last visited Feb. 2, 2021).

44 Jeffrey F. Addicott, Impact of Data on Litigation: Enhancing Cybersecurity in the Private Sector By Means of Civil Liability Lawsuits—The Connie Francis Effect, 51 U. RICH. L. REV. 857, 892 (Mar. 2017).

45 Margaret A. Reetz et al., *Cyber Risks: Evolving Threats, Emerging Coverages, and Ensuing Case Law*. 122 PENN. ST. L. REV. 727, 734-35 (2018).

1. Theft of intellectual property
2. Phishing, pharming and other related variants
3. Increasing sophistication and proliferation of threats
4. Security breaches involving third parties
5. Social engineering
6. Employee errors and omissions
7. External financial fraud involving information systems
8. Employee abuse of IT systems and information
9. Mobile devices (e.g., smartphones, tablets)
10. Attacks exploiting mobile network vulnerabilities
11. Attacks exploiting vulnerabilities due to unsecured code
12. Attacks exploiting vulnerabilities of endpoint devices
13. Theft of goods or products
14. Exploits of vulnerabilities in emerging technologies (e.g., Web 2.0)
15. Organized crime
16. Compromise and exploitation of plant assembly machines or industrial controls
17. Non-intentional loss of sensitive information (i.e., information leakage)
18. Zombie networks (e.g., bots)
19. Foreign state-sponsored spies or espionage
20. Regulatory fines and penalties
21. Attacks targeting specific senior executives' sensitive data
22. Personnel safety[46]

Assessments of these issues and quantifying the risks and consequences they present for a given manufacturer are necessary and should account for the degree to which insurance coverage is needed in light of other preventative and mitigating controls in place.

One study identified the following as the greatest vulnerabilities in IoT devices specifically, which would include those in industrial and manufacturing settings:

---

46 DELOITTE & MAPI, CYBER RISK IN ADVANCED MANUFACTURING 7-8 (2016), https://www2.deloitte.com/content/dam/Deloitte/us/Documents/manufacturing/us-manu-cyber-risk-in-advanced-manufacturing.pdf (last visited Jan. 30, 2021).

1. Weak or default passwords
2. Insecure network services
3. Insecure ecosystem interfaces
4. Lack of secure update mechanisms
5. Insecure or outdated components
6. Insufficient privacy protection
7. Insecure data transfer and storage
8. Lack of device management
9. Insecure default settings
10. Lack of physical hardening.[47]

The vectors in manufacturing operations and the results of cyber threats can be varied. While manufacturers do not generally hold tremendous amounts of payment, financial, and personal data, much of the data held by manufacturers belongs to other entities; thus, among the greatest risks from a cyber attack is a manufacturer's violation of contractual obligations regarding data owned by other entities. That said, do not lose sight of customer data sent to the manufacturer via smart products it produces, as discussed above.[48]

1. Supply Chain Risks

Supply chain networks integrate various companies and systems. Third parties have access to manufacturing data and systems, and data is regularly exported to third parties through automated systems. Third parties often monitor various IoT and ICS units if the third party is charged with maintenance of that equipment. The Target breach clearly demonstrates the risks involved in third-party access to a company's information system because experts have established that the bad actors gained access to Target's computer systems through credentials given to

---

47 THE OPEN WEB APPLICATION SECURITY PROJECT, https://owasp.org/www-pdf-archive/OWASP-IoT-Top-10-2018-final.pdf (last visited Jan. 29, 2021).

48 As to such data, ownership of that data pursuant to any terms of use could affect coverage for a breach of such data, depending on the language of the policy. In *P.F. Chang's China Bistro, Inc. v. Fed. Ins. Co*, 2016 WL 3055111 (D. Ariz. May 31, 2016), the court agreed with the insurer that no injury, as defined by the policy, occurred because the data at issue belonged to payment card holders, which was not subject to coverage under a policy providing coverage for the insured's data.

the company's HVAC vendor.[49] Many other circumstances in manufacturing involve the exchange of data between a given company and its vendors. Ordering and tracking of components, specifications, and various other operational data are regularly exchanged among companies, leading to ongoing system and data access by third parties. Thus, compromised third parties are a risk to any manufacturer's information system to which that third party has access.

Supply chain risks may not end when the contractual relationship between the manufacturer and the third party ends.[50] If the manufacturer's data remains on the information system of a vendor after the relationship between them terminates, the risk to the manufacturer continues,[51] and insurance coverage may hinge, in part, on the policy language regarding the relationship between the manufacturer and vendor at the time of the occurrence or loss. Furthermore, regulatory proceedings (and the need for coverage pertaining to the same) concerning the manufacturer's treatment of data at termination in its vendor management program present additional potential coverage gaps.

The numerous risks associated with third parties present unique coverage challenges for manufacturers. The degree to which the manufacturer's information system is integrated with systems of vendors and supply chain partners presents underwriting challenges that can be reflected in the manufacturer's premiums. Due to the expense of insuring against these third-party risks, the manufacturer must additionally engage in significant supply chain and vendor management efforts, including contractual security requirements, audit rights, the imposition of contractual indemnity, and insurance coverage requirements. Even then, coverage for business interruption and contingent business interruption due to interruptions of the insured's supply chain can present difficult

---

49 Rajender Singh, *Supply & Demand: Outsourcing Can Come at a Much Higher Cost After You Sign That Vendor Contract*, 12 INFOSECURITY PROFESSIONAL 5, 27 (2019), https://www.isc2.org/-/media/ISC2/Member-Resources/Infosecurity-Professional-Magazine/2019/Sep-Oct-Files/Sept-Oct-2019_ISP-pdf.ashx.

50 Korolov, Supply Chain Attacks, supra note 43.

51 Korolov, Supply Chain Attacks, supra note 43.

challenges,[52] and failing to reasonably delineate the risks being insured against can impact premiums and coverage.[53]

2. *Tightening Operations Through IoT and Supply Chain Management*

The insurability of losses and liabilities relating to supply chains depends greatly upon the contractual allocations of liability, data, tasks, indemnity, and so on, associated with this ecosystem that can involve numerous companies. A disruption of data, such as through ransomware, a lack of data integrity, etc., involving one company within a supply chain can have ramifications for many other companies throughout the manufacturing chain, even those several steps away. As companies continue to improve the efficiency of and lower costs associated with supply chains, these coverage challenges will only increase.

Manufacturers are experiencing increasing pressure to improve supply chain security as a result of numerous standards and schema. CMMC, Sarbanes-Oxley, NIST, and other frameworks, standards, and regulations, are imposing greater requirements on companies to assess, monitor, and audit as part of their vendor management programs.[54] Where possible, companies are imposing standards contractually, meaning supply chain entities face breach of contract claims in the event of a breach causing

---

52 Doris Mühlmann-Burger, *Business Interruptions Due to Cyber Events*, MUNICH RE (Sept. 25, 2018), https://www.munichre.com/topics-online/en/digitalisation/cyber/business-interruptions-due-to-cyber-events.html (last visited Jan. 20, 2021) ("It is crucial that the risk situation of the suppliers concerned be transparent and that the risk be assessable. For this reason, it is wise to include only contingent business interruption losses for direct contractual partners of the insured, and to explicitly exclude second- and third-tier suppliers."). *But see* Matthew Foy & Jonathan Schwartz, *Sony's Interview Quagmire*, In-House Defense Q, Spring 2015, at 73, 81 ("Policyholders should be highly attuned to whether a cyberliability insurance policy covers misconduct by a vendor, subcontractor, or other independent contractor whom they retained or with whom they have contracted.").

53 *Id.*

54 Dawn Bailey, *Lumberjacks and Supply Chain Cybersecurity: Take Time to Prepare*, NIST (Aug. 2, 2018) https://www.nist.gov/blogs/blogrige/lumberjacks-and-supply-chain-cybersecurity-take-time-prepare (last visited Jan. 17, 2021).

exposure or loss to a downstream entity. Companies within a manufacturing supply chain that are under contractual obligations as to data security and privacy practices should consider whether their cyber insurance policies will provide third-party coverage due to such claims.[55] Such contract claims are often excluded from cyber policies unless liability exists separately from any contract between the entities.[56]

3. *Trips*

The opportunities for manufacturers to experience complete disruptions in their operations are numerous. The smart factory, as part of a multi-partner network containing all manner of IoT devices, SCADA and ICS systems, can be brought to a complete shutdown—a "trip"—through any number of vulnerabilities, both internal and external. Eliminating all single sources of failure is nearly impossible. This is one of the reasons that cyber coverage is a challenge for manufacturers: shutdowns can occur not only due to an incident involving its own OT, but also through loss or alteration of data or a breach experienced by a supply chain partner that leads to a shutdown of the manufacturer or an upstream supplier. A trip leads to business interruption losses, along with the potential for property damage and remediation costs.[57] Furthermore, a manufacturer operating in certain industries can have significant reputational losses, depending on the sensitivity and nature of customer data in the control of the manufacturer.

---

55 Toni Scott Reed, Cybercrime and Technology Losses: Claims and Potential Insurance Coverage for Modern Cyber Risks, 54 TORT TRIAL & INS. PRAC. L.J. 153, 167 (2019).

56 *See, e.g., Spec's Family Partners, Ltd. v. Hanover Ins. Co.*, 739 Fed. App'x 233 (5th Cir. 2018) (analyzing the effect of a D&O policy exclusion for liability based in contract after a breach of payment card data).

57 Tom Finan & Annie McIntyre, *Cyber Risk and Critical Infrastructure: The Role of Insurance in Driving Better Security*, WILLISTOWERSWATSON (Mar. 8, 2021), found at https://www.willistowerswatson.com/en-US/Insights/2021/03/cyber-risk-and-critical-infrastructure (last visited Mar. 31, 2021).

D. Coverage and Related Issues to Address

Categorizing typical coverages and exclusions seen in cyber insurance policies,[58] regarding both first- and third-party coverages, can help begin the analysis of coverage concerns particular to manufacturers by revealing potential mismatches in types of coverage.

Coverage Type	Description
Data Breach and Responsive Measures	Coverage for specified expenses arising from a data breach involving personally identifying information of affected individuals. Affected individuals may be customers, clients, members, directors or employees of the insured entity.
Cyberattack Computer System Repair	Coverage for expenses to investigate cause of cyberattack on computer system and remove malware. Coverage will likely *not* include custom software design or replacement of computer system
Public Relations After Cyberattack	Coverage for public relations expenses to repair business reputation injured by cyberattack
Programing Errors	Coverage for loss caused by businesses programming errors
Identity Recovery	Coverage for identity recovery and repair caused by data disclosure first discovered during the policy period. May include coverage for credit monitoring

58 Paul E.B. Glad et al., 4 NEW APPLEMAN INSURANCE LAW PRACTICE GUIDE §45A.08[2][a] (2020).

Coverage Type	Description
Business Interruption Losses	Coverage for loss of business revenues caused by cyberattack and may include denial of service attacks
Cyber Extortion	Coverage for ransomware losses, Coverage for the cost of an investigator retained in connection with the extortion threat and coverage for any amount paid by the insured in response to the threat.
Credit Card Fraud	Coverage for losses from use of fraudulent credit card information

As can be readily seen when first-party coverages are outlined, some are generally more important to manufacturers than others (e.g., credit card fraud and identity recover are generally smaller risks to a manufacturer than programming errors).

1. *Insuring Provisions*

Coverage language suited for manufacturing entities may be drastically different from coverage appropriate for other industries. For example, the following could prove highly inadequate for a manufacturer:

> Network and Information Security Wrongful Act means any of the following actual or alleged actions:
>
> 1. Failure to prevent unauthorized access to, or use of, electronic or non-electronic data containing identity information;
> 2. Failure to prevent the transmission of a Computer Virus through a Computer System into a computer network, any application software, or a computer operating system or related network, that is not rented, owned, leased by, licensed to, or under the direct operational control of, the Insured Organization;

3. Failure to provide any authorized user of the Insured Organization's website or Computer System with access to such website or Computer System; or
4. Failure to provide notification of any actual or potential unauthorized access to, or use of, data containing private or confidential information of others if such notification is required by any Security Breach Notification Law,

By, or asserted against, an Insured Person, in his or her capacity as such, or the Insured Organization.[59]

This provision provides coverages that many manufacturers do not need, such as breach of consumer data and requirements imposed by data breach notification laws. Actions (1) and (4) have little application to most manufacturers. While actions (2) and (3) address events that manufacturers face, such as propagating or spreading viruses to another system or denial of service attacks, manufacturers face too many risks not addressed here, such as contractual obligations as to data security and mitigation, business interruption of supply chain partners, attacks on data integrity, and so on. This is but one example illustrating the need to align a cyber insurance policy's insuring language to the manufacturer's needs.[60] Similarly, the suitability of exclusions and definitions regarding occurrences, contractual liabilities,[61] property, and causes of interruptions are critical in selecting coverages for manufacturers. Many of those provisions, such as those pertaining to the location of an occurrence, stored data, and damaged property, can be affected by the existence of multiple locations involved in an occurrence or loss.

---

59 Reed, *Cybercrime* at 176 (and notes therein), *supra* note 55.

60 Some insurers are coordinating the coverage offered by their various policies in an effort to minimize gaps. *See, e.g.,* CHUBB, https://www.chubb.com/us-en/business-insurance/integrity-by-chubb.html (last visited Jan. 29, 2021)("Integrates with Chubb's General Liability and Property/Business Income insurance to help minimize gaps.").

61 A typical exclusion for contractually assumed liabilities would state: "Any express warranties or guarantees or any liability you assume under contract unless you would have been legally liable in the absence of such contract." Provisions such as this require heightened scrutiny if the manufacturer has contractual supply chain or information system contracts.

2. *Personal Injury/Property Damage Resulting From Cyber Incidents*

Insuring against bodily injuries and property damage resulting from cyber incidents is among the emerging issues manufacturers face.[62] CGL policies exclude damages and losses resulting from many computer-related incidents and do not cover first-party losses.[63] Therefore, while a manufacturer may intend to look to commercial property policies for such coverage, most of these policies were not created for cyber events and crimes, so coverage may be doubtful.[64] Often, computer devices or "data processing equipment" are excluded from coverage under commercial property coverage.[65] Likewise, cyber insurance policies traditionally exclude personal injury and property damage,[66] with the occasional exception for damaged computer systems and devices (e.g., bricking). That being said, some courts have found coverage for loss of computer equipment under first-party property policies.[67] Regardless, attention to the definitions relating to both property and perils covered by the policy is crucial given the unsettled landscape, both in terms of policy language and case law.[68] To varying degrees, many first-party property policies have been modified to more clearly exclude computer-related losses.[69] While

62 *See* Leta Gorman, *The Era of the Internet of Things: Can Product Liability Laws Keep Up?*, 84 DEFENSE COUNSEL JOURNAL 3 (Feb. 2020)(cataloging product liability cases predicated on data breach and cyber breach theories), https://www.iadclaw.org/defensecounseljournal/the-era-of-the-internet-of-things-can-product-liability-laws-keep-up/ (last visited Mar. 24, 2021).

63 Persons & Brownlee, EXCESS LIABILITY, *supra* note 4; Larry P. Schiffer et al., *CGL Exclusions for Cyberattacks and Loss of Electronic Data*, 49 SUM Brief 48, 49 (2020).

64 Reed, *Cybercrime* at 169, *supra* note 55.

65 Persons & Brownlee, EXCESS LIABILITY, *supra* note 4. *See also* Gilford & Rosenthal, PROSKAUER ON PRIVACY §16:2.1, at 16-11, *supra* note 41.

66 Reetz, et al., *Cyber Threats* at 757, *supra* note 45; Schiffer et al., *CGL Exclusions for Cyberattacks* at 53, *supra* note 63.

67 Gilford & Rosenthal, PROSKAUER ON PRIVACY §16:2.1, at 16-11, n.28, *supra* note 41.

68 Gilford & Rosenthal, PROSKAUER ON PRIVACY §16:2.1, at 16-11, *supra* note 41.

69 Gilford & Rosenthal, PROSKAUER ON PRIVACY §16:32.1, at 16-11, n.29, *supra* note 41; AJ Gallagher Blog, *supra* note 25 (listing marine, terrorism, property, and CGL policy forms excluding property damage).

inland marine insurance may be a natural direction to turn for "direct physical loss" and related extra expense, such policies often exclude physical damage caused by viruses, hacking, and illegal acts.[70] This creates a clear, and increasingly dangerous, potential gap in coverage within a manufacturer's insurance portfolio.[71]

The risks manufacturers face from such gaps are increasing. STUXNET disrupted the timing of critical parts in centrifuge equipment, which may have resulted in damage to the equipment.[72] In 2000, an individual was able to control numerous ICS components of a wastewater treatment plant in Australia.[73] More recently, bad actors took control of PLCs at a water treatment plant and controlled the chemicals being added to the water.[74] Perhaps the clearest example of the threat of physical damage occurred at a German steel mill in 2014.[75] Hackers took control of ICS components for a blast furnace by gaining access to the mill's business network, and then moving laterally to a production network.[76] Even when a vulnerability is addressed, repeat attacks through different or additional vulnerabilities are possible, as seen in the power grid in Ukraine, which went down twice—the second time in an attack on SCADA systems coupled with a simultaneous DDoS attack to make recovery more difficult.[77]

Manufacturers face the same issues with regard to bodily injury. Instances of personal injury, or at least potential injury, have already been seen. In short, if a malfunction of industrial equipment or a web-enabled manufactured product can cause a personal injury, then the risk of such an event through a cyber attack exists. The above-referenced takeover of ICS

---

70 Persons & Brownlee, EXCESS LIABILITY, *supra* note 4.

71 *But see* Schiffer et al., *CGL Exclusions for Cyberattacks* at 53, *supra* note 63 (noting a narrow exception in ISO endorsement CG 21 06 05 14 provides limited CGL coverage for bodily injury caused by data-related perils).

72 Jay P. Kesan & Carol M. Hayes, Strengthening Cybersecurity with Cyber Insurance Markets and Better Risk Assessment, 102 MINN. L. REV. 191, 197-98 (2017).

73 Kevin E. Hensley & Ronald E. Fisher, *History of Industrial Control System Cyber Incidents* at 4-5, IDAHO NAT'L LAB'Y (Dec. 31, 2018) (available at https://www.osti.gov/biblio/1505628-history-industrial-control-system-cyber-incidents)(last visited Jan. 11, 2021).

74 Hensley & Fisher, *History of ICS Incidents* at 17, *supra* note 73.

75 Hensley & Fisher, *History of ICS Incidents* at 14-15, *supra* note 73.

76 *Id.*

77 Hensley & Fisher, *History of ICS Incidents* at 18, *supra* note 73.

components in the German steel mill prevented a proper shutdown of the furnace.[78] The attack not only created conditions inside the furnace that damaged equipment, but also could have further caused disastrous injuries.[79] In fact, many examples of cyber attacks that result in physical damage could easily result in bodily injuries as well, such as the New York dam takeover[80] and wastewater treatment plant hacks.[81] While many recent attacks that resulted in property damage or that could have resulted in bodily injuries were not on manufacturing facilities, the similarities in ICS and SCADA systems and the use of PLCs on a broad scale show that manufacturing facilities are certainly attractive targets that could have similar outcomes.

One possibility for manufacturers is the ISO Commercial Property (CP 00 10 10 12) form, which applies to business personal property and includes computer hardware "if damaged by a covered or non-excluded peril."[82] This coverage extends only to electronic data as provided under an Additional Coverage clause.[83] However, a remaining gap in such coverage is the expense to replace or restore data.[84] Adding Business Income and Extra Expense coverage (CP 00 30 06 07) can include coverage for loss from interruption of computer operations, but only if covered under the property form.[85] Acts by employees may not be included, and with internal threats being a significant issue for manufacturers, additional coverage such as a cyber crime policy may be needed as well.

Larger systems may be covered by Equipment Breakdown coverage (formerly a Boiler & Machinery policy).[86] The Fourth Circuit found coverage for business interruption and extra expense for a software

---

78 Kim Zetter, *A Cyberattack Has Caused Confirmed Physical Damage for the Second Time Ever*, WIRED (Jan. 8, 2015), https://www.wired.com/2015/01/german-steel-mill-hack-destruction/ (last visited Feb. 2, 2021).

79 *Id.*

80 *Id.*

81 Cynthia Brumfield, *Attempted Cyberattack Highlights Vulnerability of Global Water Infrastructure*, CSO ONLINE (May 7, 2020), https://www.csoonline.com/article/3541837/attempted-cyberattack-highlights-vulnerability-of-global-water-infrastructure.html (last visited Feb. 2, 2021).

82 Persons & Brownlee, EXCESS LIABILITY, *supra* note 4.

83 Persons & Brownlee, EXCESS LIABILITY, *supra* note 4.

84 Persons & Brownlee, EXCESS LIABILITY, *supra* note 4.

85 Persons & Brownlee, EXCESS LIABILITY, *supra* note 4.

86 Persons & Brownlee, EXCESS LIABILITY, *supra* note 4.

company under a property policy after a former employee hacked its system.[87] Specifically, a rogue former employee was able to override security controls and gained access to unencrypted system passwords.[88] The Fourth Circuit found that property damage occurred, thereby triggering coverage for suspended operations for a period of time relating to a period of restoration.[89] While this case, like many others, found "property damage" to have occurred, subsequent form revisions have further delineated the bounds of coverage under such property policies.[90] These former provisions and network outage policies have similarities that manufacturers should review.[91] The manufacturing industry cannot underestimate the potential harm from rogue employees. Indeed, many attacks seen in recent years could be worse if launched by hackers with knowledge of industrial systems.[92]

Increasingly, some commentators and even insurers are promoting coverage for bodily injury, property damage, or both, due to cyber attacks, under policies that heretofore have excluded such coverage.[93] Because most cyber insurance policies have developed exclusions for property damage and physical injury to others, carriers that offer such coverages

---

87 *See NMS Services, Inc. v. The Hartford*, 62 Fed. App'x 551, 2003 U.S. App. LEXIS 7442 (4th Cir. Apr. 21, 2003).

88 Kathryn M. Guinn, 1 INSURANCE COVERAGE FOR IP CLAIMS §5.13[b] (2019).

89 *NMS Services, Inc.*, 62 Fed. App'x 511 (4th Cir. Apr. 21, 2003).

90 *See generally* Albert Küller & Caroline Dunn, *Lloyd's Market Insight: Cyber Risk Cover, Physical Damage* (December 2016)(available at https://www.lloyds.com/~/media/files/news-and-insight/risk-insight/class-of-business/cyber-physical.pdf)(last visited Mar. 31, 2021).

91 Kathryn M. Guinn, 1 INSURANCE COVERAGE FOR IP CLAIMS §5.13[b] (2019).

92 Hensley & Fisher, *History of ICS Incidents* at 17, *supra* note 73.

93 Bethan Moorcraft, *AGCS Global Cyber Head Explains Stance on Silent Cyber*, INSURANCE BUSINESS AMERICA (OCT. 23, 2019), https://www.insurancebusinessmag.com/us/news/cyber/agcs-global-cyber-head-explains-stance-on-silent-cyber-189414.aspx (last visited Jan. 29, 2021); Michael Sampson, *When Cyber Attacks Result in Physical Damage: Important Insurance Considerations*, THE LEGAL INTELLIGENCER (Aug. 21, 2020), https://www.law.com/thelegalintelligencer/2020/08/21/when-cyber-attacks-result-in-physical-damage-important-insurance-considerations/ (last visited Jan. 29, 2021).

are specifically touting them as distinguishing their coverage from others.[94]

3. *Operational Technology*

Deployment of many devices unique to manufacturing can create vulnerabilities before the manufacturer even deploys the devices. Because operations and plant facilities personnel deploy many IoT devices and other OT, IT may not have conducted its usual due diligence and testing before deployment. Thus, many vulnerabilities relating to these devices can exist without the company's awareness of them. To the degree that such OT are monitored or maintained by vendors, manufacturers should consider imposing contractual requirements for Technology E&O coverage in the event the manufacturer suffers an event because of an act by the vendor.[95] As with cyber insurance and cyber crime policies, the definitions and exclusions in a Technology E&O policy can greatly affect whether the policy provides necessary coverage for a manufacturer, including the intent and nature of the wrongful act or error at issue.[96]

How many of these property and casualty policies will ultimately cover cyber attacks, incidents, and their resulting losses is not entirely clear. While it does not involve a cyber insurance policy, the outcome of *Mondelez Int'l v. Zurich Amer. Ins. Co.*, Cook Co. No. 2018-L-11008, 2018 WL 4941760 (Ill. Cir. Ct., Cook Cty., Oct. 10, 2018), could be problematic for manufacturers. In *Mondelez*, a food manufacturer made a claim under its property policy's cyber endorsement for losses relating to the NotPetya cyber attack. Zurich denied the claim pursuant to the policy's war and warlike acts exclusion. While no cyber policy has seen a similar dispute yet (indeed, many cyber policies cover war risks), the potential need for manufacturers to turn to smaller endorsements in other types of policies makes the outcome of this litigation a concern.

---

94 See, e.g., https://www.aig.com/content/dam/aig/america-canada/us/ documents/business/cyber/cyber-cover-guide.pdf (last visited Feb. 4, 2021) (offering coverage for property damage to the insured and to third parties).

95 Reed, *Cybercrime* at 173-74, *supra* note 55.

96 Reed, *Cybercrime* at 180, *supra* note 55.

4. *Business Interruption*

Serious consideration and analysis must be devoted to the amount of business interruption coverage a manufacturer needs. As is clear at this point, the risks of a trip, or total shutdown, may be significant, especially due to occurrences originating within supply chain partners.

Purchase considerations include not only the tangible assets to be protected on the property and casualty side, and the nature of the products being manufactured on the liability and business interruption side, but also many other considerations that impact the terms and limits needed for the various cyber coverages.[97] Recovery time objective (the amount of downtime the organization can tolerate for a given system) and recovery point objective (the amount of data the organization must re-enter or withstand losing since the system's last backup)[98] have implications in deductibles and waiting periods for business interruption and contingent business interruption coverage. This information may be available in or determined from the organization's disaster recovery plan. Other contractual risk transfers, as both indemnitor and indemnitee, should be examined for requirements and conditions precedent. Furthermore, as to indemnity agreements, is there risk that contractual indemnitors will not have the financial ability to meet their obligations to the manufacturer? The risk and consequence of supply chain disruption obviously impacts business interruption needs. Inventory the data in need of protection, preferably via a data map, to address issues as to both its location and environment.

Determining the amount of business interruption coverage a manufacturer needs requires advanced planning and analysis. The manufacturer must be able to quantify and substantiate its business interruption losses in the event of a claim. Being able to calculate the company's loss from a lack of operation is one issue, but a second issue involves controlling for compounded causes, cyclical fluctuations, unrelated sales trends, and so on. Litigation surrounding these claims clearly teaches that a claim for business interruption or contingent business

---

97 Glad et al., APPLEMAN § 45.02, *supra* note 58.

98 SOLARWINDS MSP, *Reducing RPO and RTO with SolarWinds Backup* (Apr. 3,2019), (https://www.solarwindsmsp.com/blog/rto-vs-rpo#:~:text=When%20there%20is%20a%20system,how%20frequently%20you%20take%20backups.&text=Recovery%20Time%20Objective%20(RTO)%20is,downtime%20a%20business%20can%20tolerate)(last visited Jan. 20, 2021).

interruption coverage is not as simple as examining past financials and arriving at a net loss per day during the time the plant was not operating.[99] Such claims raise many issues, and the manufacturer would be wise to undertake considerable planning regarding how it will approach such claims. This analysis plays an important role in identifying coverage needs.

For example, when would a decline in revenue appear on the books as a result of various types of interruptions, and how does that relate to the indemnity period defined in the policy? Some business interruptions will have more lag time in the company's revenue cycle than others. This can be an issue when it comes to any waiting period under a policy before an insured manufacturer has a business interruption claim.[100] Business interruption coverage invariably does not begin until after a waiting period set out in the policy declarations, usually in terms of hours, but sometimes days, depending upon the policy. This waiting period essentially operates as a deductible.[101] In evaluating coverage, the waiting period before business interruption coverage becomes available should be viewed in connection with the insured's Recovery Time Objective (RTO).[102] Generally, if the RTO is not met, significant losses begin to occur. Similarly, the insured's Recovery Point Objective (RPO) is an issue to consider in selecting data recovery expense coverage. With data recovery expense coverage being subject to a deductible,[103] that deductible should take into account the manufacturer's RPO and the revenue associated with any data that could be loss in that interim period.

---

99 *See* Brad Murlick, Marshall Gilinsky, and Pamela D. Hans, *How to Recover Business Interruption Losses*, COVERAGE, Fall 2016; Daniel Torpey, *The Essential Equation: A Formula for Determining Business Interruption Loss*, IRMI, found at https://www.irmi.com/articles/expert-commentary/the-essential-equation-a-formula-for-determining-business-interruption-loss (last visited 04/19/2021); *Pennbar Corp. v. Ins. Co. of N. Amer.*, 976 F.2d 145 (3rd Cir.1992).

100 *See, e.g., Pennbar Corp. v. Ins. Co. of North America*, 976 F.2d 145 (3rd Cir. 1992)(discussing the effect of existing inventory that the insured was able to sell and requirements regarding alternative facilities in a business interruption claim arising from an earthquake at the insured's production facility).

101 Bert Wells et al., 4 NEW APPLEMAN ON INSURANCE §29.03(1)(a)(ii) (2020).

102 AMAZON, https://docs.aws.amazon.com/wellarchitected/latest/reliability-pillar/plan-for-disaster-recovery-dr.html (last visited Jan. 11, 2021).

103 See, e.g., XL Catlin Form TRD 050 0717.

5. *Cyber Crime and Social Engineering*

Because of the nature of insurance policy language, the devil can be in the details as to whether certain threats or losses are covered. Particular attention to policy definitions and exclusions is required in order to align coverage with the manufacturer's needs.[104] The best example of this is in cases involving cyber crime, particularly fraudulent wire transfers. Due to the language found in many policies, courts have had to scrutinize details regarding the events that connect the fraud to the event culminating in the insured's loss.[105] Where a policy requires "direct loss" or a loss "directly caused by the use of a computer," outcomes regarding coverage can vary in situations where fraudulent use of a computer leads an employee of an insured to take action, such as wiring money.[106] Because a court may determine that the resulting harm is too many steps removed from the improper or criminal act,[107] note the language in coverage provisions connecting the two. The connection between deceptive computer use and the resulting action that leads to a loss is important, although some courts have simply looked for a natural result.[108]

Where policy provisions require "direct" loss, insurers have argued that the decision to wire funds was not a direct loss when the fraudulent email caused a company employee to take steps to initiate a wire transfer. These cases involve step-by-step dissection of the chain of events that led to the loss in an effort to determine if the losses claimed were a "direct" result of the covered occurrence, yet courts have still arrived at opposite conclusions in some cases.[109] In addition to possible coverage questions

---

104 *See, e.g., Miss. Silicon Holdings, L.L.C. v. Axis Ins. Co.*, 2021 U.S. App. LEXIS 3112, No. 20-60215 (5th Cir. Feb. 4, 2021).

105 Reetz, et al., *Cyber Risks* at 746, *supra* note 45.

106 Reetz, et al., *Cyber Risks* at 748-49, *supra* note 45.

107 See Interactive Communications Int'l, Inc. v. Great Am. Ins. Co., 731 F. App'x 929 (11th Cir. 2018).

108 Reetz, et al., *Cyber Risks* at 750-51, *supra* note 45.

109 Cf. *American Tooling Center, Inc. v. Travelers Casualty and Surety Co. of America,* 895 F.3d 455 (6th Cir. 2018) (finding coverage because the mistaken transfer of money induced by fraudulent emails "directly caused" a "direct loss.") with *Interactive Communications Int'l*, 731 F. App'x 929, 2018 WL 2149769 (holding that a step-by-step analysis of the sequence of events shows that a lack of immediate temporal connection between events shows that the loss claimed did not result "directly" from the computer fraud, even though an unbroken chain of events was shown).

regarding fraudulent transfers, manufacturers must consider the potential coverage issues relating to whether harmful manufacturing decisions were caused by computer fraud.

6. *Decisions Based on False Data*

A similar scenario could be seen with a manufacturer's digital twin technology or other OT systems. Compromised data could give false indications that no problem exists, leading to an unforeseen operational failure. Conversely, a digital twin system may indicate, through improperly altered data, that a problem exists when no problem is present. Either way, a lack of data integrity provides the company with false information and the company makes decisions based on that information. Those decisions could lead to losses of a type covered by a cyber liability or cyber crime policy, such as business interruption, property damage, and so on. Given the courts' scattered decisions in the social engineering context regarding whether the cyber incident "directly" caused the losses claimed, questions will arise as to whether the manufacturer can show that the losses were directly caused by an occurrence that triggers coverage when decisions are made based on false or fraudulent system data.

Examine the coverage language regarding computer crimes in the context of decisions based on manipulated sensor data. For example, manipulated sensor data can lead to decisions regarding mixtures, temperatures, pressures, speeds, timing, and so on, in the manufacturing process. Whether a policy covers such various resulting harms should be analyzed.[110] Given the systematic analysis in cases such as *Interactive Communications Int'l*,[111] which found that the wire transfer losses at issue were not directly related to computer fraud, a similar dissection of events could be part of the coverage analysis where manufacturing decisions are based on fraudulently manipulated sensor data.

A lack of data integrity can disrupt manufacturing operations in a number of ways. To summarize, altered data can alter product and process specifications, leading to the production of defective products, damaged

---

110 *Cf. Miss. Silicon Holdings*, 2021 U.S. App. LEXIS 3112, No. 20-60215, *with Realpage, Inc. v. Nat'l Union Fire Ins. Co. of Pittsburgh, PA, et al.*, 3:19-CV-1350-B (N.D. Tex. Feb. 24, 2021) (analyzing differences in cyber crime and computer fraud coverages, namely, based on plain language meaning of "hold" or "without knowledge.").

111 See note 107.

equipment, or injured employees. Manufacturers can also experience business interruption claims, data restoration expenses, contractual warranty liability to customers, and consumer class actions. Examine insuring provisions to determine if they are consistent with the manufacturer's approach to risk management.

7. *International issues*

Geographic expansion of manufacturers, both as to information systems and physical operations, can cause problems for the insured manufacturer as to the situs of either information systems involved or the location of property damage, particularly when these locations are in different countries from each other.[112]

8. *Holding Third-Party Data*

While manufacturers do not usually have the third-party consumer risks that retailers, financial services, and other industries may have via consumer information, third-party claims are still a concern. This is especially true for manufacturers that operate under private label arrangements, manufacture component parts, or otherwise have a third party's manufacturing data, such as product specifications, formulas, processes, and so on. Third-party losses in an attack on a manufacturer can include the theft or corruption of customer data in the control of the manufacturer or the passing on of malware to a supply-chain partner.[113] The manufacturer's possession of third-party information or its access to a third party's information system is likely pursuant to a contractual relationship. Ideally, the manufacturer's third-party coverage would include contractual liability, in addition to the tort claims generally seen in data breach litigation. However, contractual liability is often excluded. Losses can include the cost of rebuilding the client's data, remediating a supply chain partner's system,[114] and, of course, lost profits. Any significant third-party liability for theft of personal information will generally relate to the manufacturer's employees,[115] since manufacturers

---

112 Küller & Dunn, Lloyd's Market Insight, supra note 90.

113 Reed, *Cybercrime* at 166-67, *supra* note 55.

114 *Id.*

115 *Id.*

rarely have large repositories of personal or account information of people other than employees.

9. Class Action Warranty Claims

Do not lose sight of the possibility of widespread, even class action, warranty claims as a result of a product alleged to have defective security.[116] For example, malware programmed into the firmware of chips that are then incorporated into a product can lie dormant and be triggered once in the hands of the buyer, leading to defective product and warranty claims against the manufacturer.[117] While such claims do not appear to have been successful to date, warranty claims may be excluded from third-party coverages.[118]

10. Lack of Vendors Endorsements[119] *in Cyber Policies*

A common downstream client's demand when negotiating supply chain contracts is a requirement that an upstream partner include the downstream client as an additional insured or to have a vendors endorsement in cyber policies. While vendors endorsements are common in traditional third-party coverages such as CGL and product liability policies, vendors endorsements are not generally seen in cyber coverage, and these should not be expected when demanded. In a product liability claim, the law often makes distributors and retailers liable for a defect that traces to an act by the manufacturer. In such a case, the liability of a distributor or retailer often arises merely because the defective product passed through that company's control on the way to market without the distributor or retailer contributing to the defect.[120] The liability of the supply chain partner is passive and is not generally increased by any action of the supply chain partner.[121]

---

116 Reetz, et al., *Cyber Risks* at 757-58, *supra* note 45.

117 Maureen Wallace, *Mitigating Cyber Risk in IT Supply Chains*, 6 GLOBAL BUS. L. REV. 1, 9 (2016).

118 Reetz, et al., *Cyber Risks* at 757-58, *supra* note 45.

119 See https://www.irmi.com/term/insurance-definitions/vendors-coverage (last visited Jan. 31, 2021).

120 Douglas R. Richmond, *Understanding Vendors Endorsements*, 31 INS. LITIG. REP. 401 (July 27, 2009).

121 *Id.*

The risks presented by a supply chain partner in the cyber liability realm are completely different. Under many circumstances, any liability on the part of a supply chain partner to a manufacturer for a data incident will arise because of the partner's action or inaction. Given the difficulty in measuring the insurer's risk presented by an entity other than the insured, and the degree to which such risk could even exceed the risk presented by the insured, the insurer will not provide a vendors endorsement on a cyber policy.[122] As such, dependent or contingent business interruption coverage is necessary for many manufacturers.[123] This provides business interruption coverage to the insured in the event of a disruption of the insured's operation resulting from an interruption in a contractor's operation.

11. Other Pitfalls

Examine deductibles, limits, and sublimits with IT, OT, operations, finance, and legal, particularly as to ransomware attacks. Again, OT, rather than IT, often maintains components in a manufacturing facility. While the following basic questions apply to any purchaser of cyber coverage, they should be considered in the context of the various types of losses that are unique to or of particular concern in manufacturing:

Does the policy apply to acts by this person?
Does the policy cover this act?
Does the policy bar coverage because of this person's intent?
Does the policy cover this injury?
Does the policy limit coverage to losses that computer activity caused "directly?"[124]

---

122 *Cf. Hartford Fire Ins. Co. v. St. Paul Surplus Lines Ins. Co.*, 280 F.3d 744, 747 (7th Cir. 2002) (noting that vendor endorsements "are cheap add-ons to products liability policies" because the reality is that such supply chain participants are not in a position to impose significant added risk).

123 See, e.g., XL Catlin Form TRD 437 0917 ("Dependent Business Interruption Coverage Endorsement").

124 Stephen Embry & Amanda M. Leffler, Cyber and Social Engineering Fraud: Staying on the Cutting Edge of Coverage Disputes in an Evolving Insurance Landscape, 49 BRIEF 36, 39 (2020) (footnotes omitted, cases cited therein).

The overall response of the insurance market to increasing numbers and sizes of claims has resulted in diversified, rather than consolidated, policy language.[125] Indeed, by some accounts, the market currently provides over 100 policy forms, many of which are manuscripted.[126] Continued evolution of the policies, threat landscape, and business environments—including manufacturing—should certainly allow for bargaining and negotiation regarding coverage provisions to suit the manufacturer's needs and goals.[127]

---

125 Reed, *Cybercrime* at 181, *supra* note 55 ("As for potential coverage of cyber losses under cyber-risk policies, the wide variation in insuring agreements, exclusions, and definitions means that any potential application to cybercrime depends on the individual policy.").

126 Gilford & Rosenthal, PROSKAUER ON PRIVACY §16:3, at 16-36, *supra* note 41.

127 Gilford & Rosenthal, PROSKAUER ON PRIVACY §16:3, at 16-36, *supra* note 41.

Chapter 22

Construction*

The construction industry includes not only general contractors and other builders but also subcontractors and subconsultants; architects, designers, and engineers; professional service providers; developers; and owners. This diverse group has different exposures to cyber risk. But there are far more cyber exposure commonalities within the construction industry.

For those businesses in the construction industry, this chapter is meant to serve as a guide for placing, renewing, and negotiating cyber insurance. To achieve that goal, this chapter has four parts. The first part reviews the cyber risks and exposure within the construction industry, considering emerging and existing risks unique to construction as well as other risks. Second, this chapter focuses on key cyber coverage grants that are necessary for those in the construction industry. Third, the chapter reviews exclusions, limitations, and conditions on coverage to avoid. Finally, this chapter discusses other risk transfer and mitigation strategies beyond cyber insurance.

A. Cyber Risk and Coverage Overview for the Construction Industry

Cyber exposure in the construction industry is changing rapidly. The technology revolution is still in its early stages for construction.[1] Productivity in many construction sectors has actually decreased over the past dozen years.[2] Many technological advances, however, are increasing

---

* By Andrew Deutsch.

1 *See Construction Outlook 2021: Prepare for Bumps in the Road*, HUB INTERNATIONAL, https://www.hubinternational.com/insights/outlook-2021/construction/ (accessed Mar. 15, 2021).

2 *Labor Productivity and Costs—Focus on Productivity: Construction Industries*, US BUREAU OF LABOR STATISTICS, OFFICE OF PRODUCTIVITY AND TECHNOLOGY, Sept. 29, 2020, https://www.bls.gov/lpc/construction.htm. From 2007 to 2019, the latest year that figures are available, single-family residential, multi-family residential, and highway,

productivity through drones, robotics, automated on-site processes and equipment, and back-office and design software.[3] Craft and other workers may use wearable devices or telematics to provide real-time information and track movement and work.[4] Smart, interconnected devices can detect fire, smoke, electrical problems, water leaks, and other hazards.[5] These technological innovations can reduce risk. But they also provide valuable data and ease of access that can increase exposure to cybersecurity or privacy breaches.

1. Emerging Technology and Changing Risks Present Exposures and Risks Unique to Construction

Broadly speaking, technology used in the construction industry tends to fall into three different categories.[6] Technology can increase productivity by facilitating scheduling and managing equipment and supplies, improve worker safety by monitoring and identifying unsafe behavior, and monitor job sites for potential risks and losses. These emerging technologies take many different shapes and forms. The list of these technologies is too numerous to review in detail here. But it is worth mentioning some recent developments to give context for the changing exposures for the construction industry. Those developments include:

- Drones, which builders, owners, and others, now commonly use for photography, monitoring, inspection, data collection, and myriad other uses;[7]

---

street, and bridge work decreased by 1.2%, 1.3%, and 0.3%, respectively, on an average annual basis. Only industrial building saw average annual gains of 0.7% over that period.

3 *See Construction Outlook 2021: Prepare for Bumps in the Road.*

4 Elana Ashanti Jefferson, *The construction insurance market faces rising uncertainty*, PROPERTYCASUALTY360, Oct. 16, 2020, https://www.propertycasualty360.com/2020/10/16/the-construction-insurance-market-faces-rising-uncertainty/?slreturn=20210018210624.

5 *Id.*

6 *See* Joseph Cleaves, Jr., *Artificial Intelligence in Construction Part II: Image Recognition and Sensors-on-Site*, TAFT LAW BULLETIN, Oct. 15, 2020, https://www.taftlaw.com/news-events/law-bulletins/artificial-intelligence-in-construction-part-ii-image-recognition-and-sensors-on-site.

7 Drones used on construction sites raise a host of legal and contractual issues beyond insurance. *See* Jacqueline DeCamara and Daniel D. McMillan, *Use*

- Devices and equipment for 3D printing using concrete and other building materials;
- Artificial intelligence ("AI") to analyze images and data from sensors;[8]
- Automatic and semiautonomous equipment and robots that use global positioning systems ("GPS"), lidar, and other technology to piledrive, drill overhead, and perform many other tasks;[9]
- Autonomous earth moving equipment, including excavators and bulldozers;[10] and
- Autonomous robots that document construction progress, move or deliver supplies or tools, monitor hazards, and perform measuring and other tasks.[11]

These technologies often increase speed, accuracy, and safety, potentially resulting in fewer quality defects and injuries. But they also often collect, store, and transmit large amounts of data and may be used for novel purposes. And even as they reduce hazards, they can introduce new exposure in the form of risks to property and people.

---

of Drones on Construction Projects: Legal and Contractual Considerations, UNDER CONSTRUCTION—WINTER 2019, Dec. 9, 2019, https://www.americanbar.org/groups/construction_industry/publications/under_construction/2019/winter2019/use-of-drones-on-construction-projects/. Drones have become so important to the construction industry that they also have a separate section below regarding key cyber coverage grants.

8 Joseph Cleaves, Jr., *Artificial Intelligence in Construction Part II: Image Recognition and Sensors-on-Site.*

9 *E.g., Automated Pile Driver from Orteco Uses Altus APS-U for Machine Control*, GPS WORLD, Feb. 3, 2015, https://www.gpsworld.com/automated-pile-driver-from-orteco-uses-altus-aps-u-for-machine-control/; *New Release—Jaibot Drilling Robot*, HILTI USA, https://www.hilti.com/content/hilti/W1/US/en/engineering/industry---trade-solutions/construction-automation/jaibot.html (accessed Mar. 15, 2021).

10 Zachary Phillips, *Built Robotics Releases 1st Fully Autonomous Construction Machinery in US*, CONSTRUCTION DIVE, Feb. 26, 2020, https://www.constructiondive.com/news/built-robotics-releases-1st-fully-autonomous-construction-machinery-in-us/573057/.

11 Cory Stieg, *This $75,000 Boston Dynamics robot 'dog' is for sale—take a look*, CNBC, June 22, 2020, https://www.cnbc.com/2020/06/22/75000-boston-dynamics-robot-dog-for-sale-take-a-look.html.

New and existing technologies have also affected construction through building information modeling ("BIM")[12] and virtual design and construction ("VDC").[13] Stakeholders—including owners, architects, engineers, general contractors, subcontractors, and suppliers—use BIM and VDC to collaborate and share complex models, information, and data with each other. BIM and VDC can bring new opportunities and result in increased efficiency. But they also expand the potential for cyber losses that could delete, corrupt, or encrypt data that is crucial for the business. That creates not only potential liability for the business to other stakeholders but also increases possible first-party business income losses.

2. *Some Cyber Exposures Are Not Unique to Construction*

Even a "traditional" construction firm that is not using advanced or new technologies discussed above almost certainly used the same types of technology that are susceptible to cyber risks and exposures. Network infrastructure, across connected computers and mobile devices, contains data related to payroll, accounts payable and receivable, employees, and more. Remote project sites may require network capabilities onsite and to communicate and share data with those at the office. Connecting multiple jobsites, whether related to the same project or not, requires collecting and sharing information across multiple locations.

Of course, construction firms, like other industries, have a wealth of employee data that might be subject to legal protections, regulatory regimes, and fines and penalties for breaches, not just in the United States

---

12 "Building information models (BIMs) are three-dimensional, digital, construction blueprints. BIMs allow numerous project participants to view and modify the same model. They are generally highly detailed, allowing users to access information on each building." Joseph Cleaves, Jr., *Artificial Intelligence in Construction: Part III*, TAFT LAW BULLETIN, Nov. 13, 2020, https://www.taftlaw.com/news-events/law-bulletins/artificial-intelligence-in-construction-part-iii.

13 The term "virtual design and construction" defies an easy explanation and there is no single, widely accepted standard or definition for VDC. VDC is more than BIM, however. VDC uses technology not just for models but also to bring together stakeholders throughout the construction process in estimating, design and preconstruction, construction, and after completion. *See, e.g., Knutson Construction—Virtual Design and Construction*, https://www.knutsonconstruction.com/services/virtual-design-construction-vdc/ (accessed Mar. 15, 2021).

but around the world. Data collected on customers will vary based on the nature of the business model as business-to-consumer, business-to-business, or a mix of both. Data accessed or stored by the firm may include personally identifiable information ("PII"), third-party confidential information, budgets, strategic plans, and other sensitive or non-public information.

B. Key Cyber Coverage Grants for the Construction Industry

With this context in mind, this section will address key cyber coverage grants to consider in the construction industry. Before discussing key coverage grants, though, this section first considers insurance markets themselves.

1. Challenges and Opportunities for Construction Firms in the Insurance Market

Although cyber coverage has experienced many years of increased capacity, greater coverage, and flat or declining premium rates, those days are gone. The Covid-19 pandemic, increased cyber losses generally, and specific losses from data breaches and ransomware have driven premium rates higher.[14] Insurance capacity is also shrinking, resulting in reduced coverage, smaller or new sublimits, additional exclusions, and co-insurance requirements.[15]

While these trends are not unique to the construction industry, they will significantly affect the ability to place coverage for those with construction exposure.[16] Cyber insurance is often an afterthought for the construction industry.[17] Even now, many firms in the construction industry

---

14 *Insurance Marketplace Realities 2021—Cyber Risk*, WILLIS TOWERS WATSON, Nov. 18, 2020, https://www.willistowerswatson.com/en-US/Insights/2020/11/insurance-marketplace-realities-2021-cyber-risk.

15 *Id.*

16 *Insurance Marketplace Realities 2021—Construction*, WILLIS TOWERS WATSON, Nov. 18, 2020, https://www.willistowerswatson.com/en-US/Insights/2020/11/insurance-marketplace-realities-2021-construction.

17 *Id.*

are buying their first cyber insurance policy.[18] And that initial purchase is often reactive as new technologies are adopted, contract provisions require cyber coverage, or the board of directors mandates purchasing a cyber insurance policy.[19]

2. *Specialized Cyber Insurance for the Construction Industry*

There are programs and coverages tailored and marketed to construction risks.[20] Brokers and insurers offer coverage marketed to the construction industry. Solutions focused on the construction industry can offer ready-made products.

Even with a product made for the construction industry, it is still prudent to understand key coverage grants and compare any offering to the actual exposures and risk. Those key coverage grants are discussed below. By necessity, these key coverage grants are not meant to provide an exhaustive list of all potential coverage for all policyholders. But focusing on these specific coverage grants will go a long way toward securing the most robust cyber insurance policy available.

As always, it is important to carefully review the policy to ensure that it covers all identified exposures and that any uncovered risks are understood and transferred, avoided, or mitigated where possible. Working with a skilled broker familiar with the construction industry and insurance markets will greatly assist this process. Similarly, coverage counsel can be an asset in providing coverage reviews and comparisons as

---

18 Joseph Salazar, et al., *U.S. Construction Industry Risk Outlook*, AON, Feb. 2019, https://www.aon.com/getmedia/43a3cc9b-7b6b-45fe-ae85-f22cd215809b/2019-US-Construction-Risk-Outlook-Report.aspx.

19 *Id.*

20 Victor Insurance Managers (formerly known as Victor O. Schinnerer & Company, Inc.) provide cyber coverage for architects and engineers in coordination with the American Institute of Architects. *Cyber Risk Kit for Architects and Engineers*, https://www.victorinsuranceus.com/aecyber/. Willis Towers Watson offers CyCon, "a tailored cyber insurance solution for the construction industry." *Product CyCon*, https://www.willistowerswatson.com/en-US/Solutions/products/cycon. And Zurich, a prominent insurer for the industry, offers extensions and endorsements to provide coverage for construction exposures. *Zurich Cyber coverage for the construction industry*, https://www.zurichna.com/-/media/project/zwp/zna/docs/kh/const/zurich-cyber-for-construction.pdf.

well as drafting policy wording for manuscript coverage. No policyholder should go it alone in attempting to obtain the best possible cyber coverage.

3. Special Considerations Related to Drones, Including Cybersecurity and Privacy Liability

While cybersecurity and privacy liability coverage are core requirements for any cyber policy, a cyber policy might not cover construction industry risks without an appropriate affirmative coverage grant. One of those risks are potential claims involving drones used on a project site or property by the owner, contractor, subcontractor, architect, engineer, or others.[21] An aircraft policy can offer hull or physical damage coverage for a drone as well as liability coverage for bodily injury, property damage, and personal and advertising injury.

But aircraft and cyber policies typically do not insure liability for drone use resulting in a cybersecurity breach or a release of data resulting in privacy exposure.[22] Even if an aircraft liability policy provides personal and advertising injury coverage, that policy will almost certainly use the standard ISO[23] definition of "personal and advertising injury." Under that

---

21 Drone use on construction sites raise a host of legal and contractual issues beyond insurance. *See* Jacqueline DeCamara and Daniel D. McMillan, *Use of Drones on Construction Projects: Legal and Contractual Considerations*, UNDER CONSTRUCTION—WINTER 2019, Dec. 9, 2019, https://www.americanbar.org/groups/construction_industry/publications/under_construction/2019/winter2019/use-of-drones-on-construction-projects/. *See also* Ronnie R. Gipson Jr., *The Rise of Drones and the Erosion of Privacy and Trespass Laws*, THE AIR & SPACE LAWYER, VOL. 33, NO. 3, 2020, https://www.americanbar.org/content/dam/aba/publications/air_space_lawyer/fall2020/asl_v033n03_fall2020_gipson.pdf.

22 Jennifer Walker, *A Bird's-Eye View: Insuring Drones in the Construction Industry*, AMWINS, Aug. 22, 2019, https://www.amwins.com/insights/article/a-bird-s-eye-view-of-insuring-drones-in-the-construction-industry_8-19.

23 ISO is the Insurance Services Office, which provides insurers with policy language and services such as statistical, actuarial, underwriting, and claims information. *See Insurance Services Office*, Verisk, https://www.verisk.com/insurance/brands/iso/ (accessed Mar. 15, 2021). ISO was formed by an association of insurers as a not-for-profit advisory and rating organization, but is now a subsidiary and brand of Verisk Analytics, Inc.

definition, coverage exists for injury arising out of an offense of "oral or written publication, in any manner, of material that violates a person's right of privacy."[24] While there is some case law finding that data breaches can fall within that enumerated offense, many of those cases have addressed non-standard language and the cases have been anything but uniformly decided.[25]

So rather than relying on uncertain outcomes from past coverage disputes, confirm cyber coverage for drones under the cyber insurance policy. The insuring coverage grant should be broad enough to include drone exposures. Also consider any defined terms used in the policy such as those related to the policyholder's systems. Particularly, definitions regarding computers, servers, or similar devices can result in coverage too narrow to apply to drones. Those definitions should either affirmatively include drones or, at a minimum, not exclude drones.

In addition, consider whether the triggering events are broad enough to include a breach involving a drone. The policy should not limit a cyber

---

Form 10-K Annual Report, Feb. 23, 2021, http://d18rn0p25nwr6d.cloudfront.net/CIK-0001442145/9670a126-b3d7-4975-9916-b0cbc6b7e846.pdf.

24 Commercial General Liability Coverage Form, Insurance Services Office, CG 00 01 04 13.

25 It is no stretch to state that there is no majority position or trend on whether cyber breaches constitute "personal and advertising injury." *See* Karin S. Aldama, Tred R. Eyerly, and Rina Carmel, *Seeing Around the Cyber Corner: What's Next for Cyber Liability Policies?,* INSURANCE COVERAGE LITIGATION SPRING 2018, VOL. 28 NO. 2, June 18, 2018, https://www.americanbar.org/content/dam/aba/publications/litigation_committees/insurance/spring2018.pdf. *See also* Lorraine A. Armenti and Steven D. Cantarutti, *The Evolution of Cyber Coverage Law: A Survey of Critical Decisions and the Market's Response*, INSURANCE COVERAGE LITIGATION FALL 2016, VOL. 26 NO. 4, Nov. 21, 2016, https://www.americanbar.org/content/dam/aba/publications/litigation_committees/insurance/fall2016.pdf (discussing differing results for data breach coverage as "personal and advertising injury"); Stephen Embry and Amanda M. Leffler, *Cyber and Social Engineering Fraud: Staying on the Cutting Edge of Coverage Disputes in an Evolving Insurance Landscape*, THE BRIEF—WINTER 2020, Feb. 7, 2020, https://www.americanbar.org/groups/ tort_trial_insurance_practice/publications/the_brief/2019-20/winter/cyber-and-social-engineering-fraud-staying-the-cutting-edge-coverage-disputes-an-evolving-insurance-landscape/ ("Case law also has been mixed, and highly fact specific, on questions involving the personal injury offense of publication of material that allegedly violates a person's right of privacy.")

event that triggers coverage to those computers or devices on the policyholder's network if the policyholder uses drones off the network. Regardless of whether drones are a part of the network, the policy should confirm that a cyber event affecting a drone is within the coverage grant.

4. *Cyber-Physical Losses and the Potential Gap in Cyber and Commercial General Liability Insurance*

Cyber attacks that result in physical losses are a real concern. The International Risk Management Institute, Inc. ("IRMI") defines a "cyber-physical attack" as "a security breach in cyber space that impacts on the physical environment. A malicious user can take control of the computing or communication components of water pumps, transportation, pipeline valves, etc., and cause damage to property and put lives at risk."[26] When it comes to the construction industry, these types of losses could result in property damage or bodily injury that may not be covered by standard cyber insurance. Additional coverages are necessary to fill this gap.

(a) Contingent Cyber Coverage for Property Damage and Bodily Injury Liability

Property damage and bodily injury liability results from a loss for which the policyholder is liable to others. Typical cyber insurance policies do not apply to property damage or bodily injury.

As discussed above, many new and emerging technologies have introduced the real possibility of damage to property and injury to persons. Although builder's risk coverage may apply to any physical damage to the project itself, that coverage typically does not cover damage to others' property. And bodily injury is a real risk for any construction project. For the construction industry, this introduces a potentially significant gap in coverage.

Imagine a hacked drone or autonomous robotic equipment that causes damage to property of others. This could happen on a construction site in an urban location, where space is at a premium and there is little room to maneuver. Or a cyber loss could cause damage another contractor's, or a subcontractor's, equipment or vehicles. Worse yet, a hacked drone or autonomous equipment could cause injury to a person. These are all

---

26 *Glossary*, IRMI, https://www.irmi.com/term/insurance-definitions/cyber-physical-attack (accessed Mar. 15, 2021).

hypothetical examples. But real-world incidents have shown that cyber attacks can result in physical losses.[27] It therefore makes sense to assume that a cyber-physical loss could occur in the construction context.

Contingent property damage or bodily injury coverage ills this potential gap in coverage for a cyber-physical loss. This contingent coverage is meant to protect against potential cyber-physical losses that another policy would not cover—thus, the modifier "contingent."

Existing cyber insurance markets have taken different approaches to this property damage and bodily injury exposure. Some insurers will exclude any claim arising out of or involving property damage or bodily injury. Avoid this approach if possible as it creates a gap in coverage.

Short of a complete exclusion, sublimited coverage for property damage or bodily injury liability will provide at least some protection in the event of a cyber loss. Some insurers, including some of those providing policies specific to the construction industry, may give back coverage through an endorsement or an exception to the property damage or bodily injury exclusions.

While some coverage is obviously better than no coverage, sublimited coverage can create additional issues. Structuring a cyber insurance program with one or more layers of excess coverage could mean that some excess insurers are not willing to drop down to provide coverage. Other excess insurers might provide drop-down coverage on a sublimited basis. Again, getting additional coverage, even if sublimited, is better than nothing. But this approach could still leave the policyholder without enough coverage for cyber-physical losses.

The best approach, of course, is to obtain full limits coverage for contingent property damage and bodily injury liability. Some insurers are willing to provide full limits for property damage and bodily injury coverage. The policy might provide coverage on an implied or express basis. Implied coverage relies on a broad insuring agreement and a lack of a property damage or bodily injury exclusion. Express coverage will state that coverage applies to loss resulting in or arising from property damage or bodily injury. Either can be an acceptable solution. But consider both

---

27 *See* John Buchanan and Dustin Cho, *Cyber-Physical Risks: Are You Covered?*, COVINGTON CLIENT ALERT, Dec. 14, 2016, https://www.cov.com/-/media/files/corporate/publications/2016/12/cyber_physical_risks_are_you_covered.pdf (citing examples of derailed trains, raw sewage pumped onto public and private property, and other losses caused by hackers).

options for any impact on excess coverage. Excess markets may not be willing to follow an express grant of coverage for property damage or bodily injury. In those circumstances, it could make sense to structure coverage in the cyber insurance tower on the same basis—implied or express. Doing so can help avoid different coverage decisions from the insurers in the tower due to differences in policy wording.

(b) First-Party Property Coverage for Cyber Losses

First-party coverage for property damage arising out of a cyber loss applies to damage to the insured's systems or property resulting from cyber incidents. Just as a cyber loss can result in damage to others' property, a cyber loss can cause damage to the policyholder's own property. While a property insurance policy covers physical injury to tangible property, that policy might not cover cyber losses for various reasons. There might be no, or limited, coverage for non-physical damage to computer systems, hardware, data, and software that a cyber policy could insure. Cyber losses could be an excluded cause of loss under an all-risk policy or not a covered peril under a specific perils policy.

A typical cyber policy provides first-party coverage for things such as breach notification costs, credit monitoring, breach response, forensic expenses, data recovery or restoration, extortion or reward payments, fraud and social engineering, and business interruption. Missing from that list, however, is coverage for damage to the insured's systems or property resulting from a cyber event. A cyber policy might also expressly exclude, or sublimit, any cyber-physical losses resulting in damage to the policyholder's own property.

To avoid this potential gap, use a similar strategy for first-party coverage as that used for coverage for potential cyber-physical liability. As with those liability exposures, coverage for first-party property damage under a cyber policy could include an implied or express coverage grant and might be sublimited. But securing that coverage can avoid an unintended gap between the property and cyber insurance policy.

5. *Business Interruption Coverage for Contractors Should Include Missed Bid Coverage*

Missed bid coverage applies if a security incident results in a bid not being timely submitted. If a computer system breach or interruption delays or prevents submission of a bid, the contractor could lose an opportunity for the customer to select it for the project. And without that selection, the contractor has lost out on the potential income and profit from starting and completing the project. A cyber insurance policy does not typically cover this type of loss. To understand why requires a brief review of cyber business interruption coverage.

A typical cyber insurance policy provides business interruption coverage. But that coverage usually applies to the net profit or loss that would have been earned or incurred during the indemnity period and resulting from a cyber event. Because a missed bid results in an inability to compete for business, the actual loss is at least one step removed from a straight profit or loss calculation. This potentially places a missed bid outside the scope of business interruption coverage. Affirmative coverage for lost income due to a missed bid is therefore necessary.

Many insurers will offer missed bid coverage either as part of business interruption, a separate coverage grant, or a separately defined first-party event. Missed bid coverage is typically subject to a sublimit. Insurers will also qualify or condition coverage for missed bid coverage to ensure that the policyholder has actually suffered a loss that would have resulted in coverage. This may require that the policyholder demonstrate that it was not able to submit the bid through other than electronic means. The policyholder might also need to prove that it was reasonably likely that the customer would select it for the project if the bid had been submitted. Even with these conditions, missed bid coverage will help to eliminate a potentially significant risk from a cyber loss that falls outside standard business interruption coverage.

6. Social Engineering

Secure affirmative coverage for social engineering under the cyber policy. Social engineering exposure is not unique to the construction industry. Indeed, most business face some risk of loss due to the good faith or voluntary transfer of funds induced by a cybercriminal. But these losses may be more difficult to prevent, or more likely to occur, for an owner, general contractor, or design-builder making payments to many different parties including other contractors, architects, engineers, subconsultants, subcontractors, suppliers, and vendors. The number of parties receiving payments from a construction business increases the likelihood that social engineering might result in a loss. This makes social engineering coverage an important cyber coverage for those in the construction industry.

Social engineering coverage might be available in a crime policy.[28] Depending on the limits sought for social engineering, it is possible to find more favorable terms in the crime policy compared to a cyber policy. Cyber coverage for social engineering is usually an add-on coverage that is narrower than what might be available under a crime policy. This is so because cyber insurance policies often provide social engineering coverage subject to a sublimit, in excess of other insurance, and only if a verification process is used to obtain a second form of authentication.[29] Nonetheless, it can be cost effective to negotiate broad terms and limits for social engineering under the cyber policy in addition to a crime policy.

Coordinating social engineering coverage between multiple policies also becomes important. While a traditional crime policy might offer higher limits or better terms, the price for that coverage could be more expensive. Coordinating coverage between multiple policies therefore requires considering where to place sufficient coverage most efficiently and whether, or to what extent, coverage might overlap.

7. *Electronic Vandalism Extensions Under Property Policies Might Provide Coverage but Should Not Be Relied on In Lieu of a Cyber Insurance Policy*

As discussed above, property policies insure physical risk of loss to tangible property. A common extension for a property policy is electronic vandalism or similar coverage. This coverage may be available under different types of property policies, including builder's risk, commercial property, course of construction, inland marine, or other property insurance policies. Each of these policies therefore could provide coverage for a potential cyber loss that constitutes electronic vandalism.

But relying on electronic vandalism coverage under a property policy could unduly restrict coverage. Policy definitions for "electronic vandalism"—or similar terms including "computer virus"—will limit coverage to an intentional attack that damages or results in loss to property.

Typical wording for an electronic vandalism coverage extension might state as follows:

---

28 Bob Bregman, *Cyber Risk: Understanding How Multiple Polices Intersect*, IRMI D&O COMPASS, Sept. 2018, p. 18, *available at*: https://www.irmi.com/free-resources/white-papers/cyber-risk-free-report.

29 *Id.*

> We will pay for direct physical loss or damage to electronic hardware, software, programs or data caused by or resulting from:
> (1) Malicious code, computer virus, malware, denial of service attack or other electronic vandalism;
> (2) Willful or malicious electronic alteration, manipulation, tampering or destruction; or
> (3) Mysterious disappearance of code.[30]

The electronic vandalism coverage extension might also provide extra expense coverage for the reasonable and necessary expense incurred to conduct a forensic investigation, remove the threat vector, or protect data or hardware from additional harm.

Although the electronic vandalism coverage in a property policy is a potential source of coverage for intentional acts resulting in loss or damage to hardware, software, or data, it should not be relied on as a primary source for cyber coverage. Electronic vandalism coverage may not be available from all markets. And where it is available, it will be sublimited, often to minimal amounts. For these reasons, relying on a property policy for this coverage can result in much narrower or limited coverage than that which is available under a cyber policy.

8. *OCIPs and CCIPs—Future Sources of Coverage?*

Owner Controlled Insurance Programs ("OCIPs") and Contractor Controlled Insurance Programs ("CCIPs")[31] have not, so far, included cyber coverage. That may change, however. Cyber coverage will likely become more widely adopted within the construction industry. Contractual requirements for cyber coverage are also likely to become more common. If insurance markets are willing to provide cyber coverage for a specific project, it is at least possible that cyber insurance could

---

30 This wording is an amalgamation of different policy wordings to provide an example.

31 OCIPs and CCIPs are also often referred to as "wrap ups" because they wrap up coverage in a single program for a project—or occasionally multiple projects—to insure the owner, contractors, and subcontractors. OCIPs and CCIPs will, at a minimum, provide coverage for CGL and umbrella or excess coverage and oftentimes also include worker's compensation. A more comprehensive wrap up program might include coverage for builder's risk, contractor's pollution liability, and professional liability.

become available as part of a wrap up insurance program. But it is too early to know with any certainty whether that will occur.

C. Exclusions, Limitations, and Conditions to Avoid for the Construction Industry

Avoid exclusions, limitations, and conditions to try to maximize coverage. These restrictions include not only traditional policy exclusions or limitations but also defined terms that could narrow or reduce coverage and create potential uninsured exposures.

1. Any Definitions Tied to Computer Systems or Networks Should Be as Broad as Possible

Depending on how a cyber insurance policy defines computer systems and networks, it could result in potentially uninsured exposure. Narrow definitions of computer systems or networks could exclude coverage for use of third-party service providers, or shared tools or data as part of BIM or VDC. Many cyber policies contain definitions of the systems, devices, or networks covered. When the policy uses those definitions, carefully consider them in conjunction with the scope of the policyholder's activities. For a policyholder that shares data across networks with external parties, coverage could be unduly restricted if policy definitions only apply to systems or networks owned by, or in the care, custody, or control of, the insured. That could exclude coverage for data or information exchanged with third parties.

Similarly, construction firms or owners with exposures at job sites or other locations should make certain that the cyber policy encompasses the use of third-party platforms, products, and services. This includes not only cloud providers or software as a service ("SaaS") but also communication networks and other technology solutions used on the project site.

An optimal solution is to find a cyber policy that does not restrict or limit the covered computer systems. This results in the policyholder having coverage available for liability to another party, or a first-party loss, caused by a cyber event, regardless of what systems were affected by the event. If that coverage cannot be obtained, carefully reviewing and considering the applicable definitions is necessary to make sure that coverage aligns with the exposure.

2. *The Definition of "Insured" Should Include Any Affiliates That Do Not Have Separate Coverage, as Well as Those for Whom the Policyholder is Responsible*

Include within the definitions of "insured" or "subsidiary" any affiliates that do not have coverage available under other cyber insurance policies. The policy should apply to those affiliates through a broad form named insured endorsement or as a specifically named insured. Those in the construction industry that participate in joint ventures, have diversified operations, or minority ownership of other entities should pay particularly close attention to which entities qualify for coverage.

As with any insurance policy, joint ventures can present particularly difficult issues. Cyber insurance policies, like other insurance policies, often do not include, or even specifically exclude, joint venture entities from definitions of the "insured," "subsidiary," or the similar terms.

For a business with diversified operations, the cyber policy should not be restricted to a part of the business or only certain operations. The cyber policy should cover all aspects of the policyholder's business and operations.

Another potential trap is for any entities that a policyholder has a minority interest in or over which the policyholder does not have management responsibility. If these types of entities need coverage, include them within the relevant definitions or scheduled as named insureds on the policy.

If the policyholder manages, owns, or develops property for others, the definition of insured should include the owner and others with interests in the property to the extent the policyholder has liability for those other parties' losses. Any provisions in contracts or operating agreements should specify which party will carry insurance coverage for the other parties. Then align coverage under the cyber insurance policy with the contractual responsibilities.

It may not always be possible to obtain cyber coverage for subsidiaries, affiliates, or other entities that have a risk profile different than the policyholder or are too far removed from, or not subject to, the policyholder's control. In those cases, a separate cyber policy should be procured to provide any necessary coverage.

Keep in mind that the key to obtaining coverage for other entities is understanding what additional coverage is needed and presenting the relevant information to the underwriters. This will be necessary whether adding specific entities to an existing policy, broadening wording to cover other entities, or obtaining a separate policy. Underwriters may be willing to include coverage for other entities when coverage is requested if the risk is materially the same as the policyholder's exposure or can be adequately documented or quantified. But underwriters will also be wary of providing duplicative or overlapping coverage or aggregating exposure. Working with a qualified broker that is familiar with the policyholder's business, as well as underwriting appetites and proclivities, can help ensure success in navigating these issues.

3. *Consider Any Exclusion or Limitation on Professional or Design Services Provided to Others*

As discussed in the first section of this chapter, the construction industry has changed and involves more collaboration and sharing of data, tools, and services than ever before. For some in the construction industry, those changes include providing software or services that modify software or data for customers. If the firm provides these types of software or professional services, review to make sure that the cyber policy does not exclude the policyholder's operations.

Some cyber policies do not provide coverage for contractual liability that the policyholder has to others. Some policies might also exclude coverage for services related to designing or providing software to others. Most cyber policies will also exclude risks that go along with software or related work, such as trademark or patent infringement. For firms providing software or data to others, this can be a potentially significant exposure.

If possible, remove or narrow any contractual liability or software exclusion that implicates the policyholder's business or services. It might not be possible, however, to remove or narrow those exclusions if the risk is outside of the insurer's construction industry target or appetite. Depending on the nature of services provided, it could be prudent to obtain a separate professional liability policy or a combined professional and cyber liability policy. Those policies can align coverage for exposures or services that the cyber policy does not cover.

4. Exclusions for Contractual Penalties Can Result in Significant Uninsured Exposure

For many construction projects, it can be difficult to know or quantify all the potential consequential losses if a project is not completed on time. This can result in liquidated damage provisions in construction contracts that avoid open-ended consequential damages and bring some certainty to damages for delays. Once the delay has met a threshold number of days, each additional day of delay can result in liquidated damages. A cyber loss that delays a project could thus result in significant uncovered losses for liquidated damages owed to customers.

But potentially significant uninsured exposure can result if the cyber policy has an exclusion for contractual penalties. Removing any exclusion, or providing affirmative coverage for, contractual penalties can help provide a buffer for liquidated damages resulting from a cyber event. Unfortunately, most insurers are not likely to provide coverage for contractual penalties, which are often deemed uninsurable or within the policyholder's ability to control. Insurance markets focused on the construction industry may be willing to provide some coverage for contractual penalties. But that coverage is certain to be subject to a sublimit. As a result, it may not be possible to adequately insure contractual penalties arising from a cyber loss.

5. Review the Policy for Exclusions for Human Error, Such as Negligence or Failure to Patch

Exclusions for human error or failure to patch were common in early cyber insurance policies. Those exclusions have become less common. But some policies marketed to small or medium businesses still contain these exclusions, however. If the policy has this type of exclusion, consider modifying the policy to limit the exclusion. It might also be possible to negotiate coverage without these exclusions. Whether a policyholder has a minimal or complex cybersecurity program in place, mistakes happen. Those mistakes might eliminate insurance coverage for a cyber loss if the policy has this type of exclusion.

As discussed above, there are times that conditions for verification, which are potentially subject to human errors, might exist in coverage for social engineering. Those types of limitations can be mitigated in different ways. For example, additional coverage could be available under a crime policy if that social engineering coverage is not subject to a verification condition. If a limitation requiring a second form authentication cannot be removed, consider whether a sublimit might instead apply if that authentication process is not followed. This can provide at least some coverage for losses that the policy might otherwise exclude. And if all else fails, clearly communicate the need to follow verification procedures for financial transactions to avoid jeopardizing insurance coverage.

6. Remove Exclusions That Limit Potential Cyber Coverage Under Other Policies

Seek to limit or remove cyber exclusions from other policies such as commercial general liability, professional liability, executive risk (directors and officers), crime, property, builder's risk, and contractor's equipment. This exercise is becoming increasingly more difficult with trends in the insurance markets. The current trends are for insurers to no longer provide so-called silent cyber coverage and to expressly exclude cyber coverage for non-cyber policies. But even when an exclusion cannot be removed from another policy, a close review of those policies informs whether coverage might exist for a cyber loss.

D. Other Risk Transfer or Mitigation Strategies for the Construction Industry

So far, this chapter has focused on strategies for obtaining the best possible cyber insurance coverage. But what happens if, despite best efforts, cyber coverage cannot be procured? There are still other solutions available.

First, contractual risk transfer in the construction industry is a must to ensure that contracts appropriately shift responsibility to others for their acts, errors, or omissions. Any business in the construction industry that supervises, manages, oversees, hires, or contracts with others has third-party cyber exposure. Appropriately shifting responsibility to those third parties means not only requiring cyber insurance but also cybersecurity policies and privacy protections that meet applicable legal and regulatory requirements. Sound contractual risk transfer helps mitigate exposure to the policyholder.

Second, prepare for incidents by having written policies, guides, or playbooks in place and engaging in tabletop exercises. A good defense to security and privacy incidents begins with having a procedure in place and being prepared for when—not if—a cyber loss occurs. Most insurers also expect that policyholders will have these processes in place or will require it before providing insurance. Being proactive avoids a scramble that might occur when placing, renewing, or negotiating cyber insurance.

Third, collaborate across the organization to ensure successful risk mitigation and preparation for the cyber insurance application. Individuals across the organization may need to provide information necessary for the cyber insurance application.[32] Security and privacy breaches occur not only when systems and process fail but also when individuals fail to take, or unintentionally engage in, actions that result in a cyber loss. Collaboration should include stakeholders from information technology, legal, and risk management. Consider also involving those engaged with environmental, health, and safety ("ESH"); vendor management; finance and accounting; and other areas throughout the organization. Each of those areas involves potential cyber exposures best understood before, not after, a cyber loss.

Fourth, identify any potential gaps in cyber coverage as well as the possibility for coverage under non-cyber policies. Other policies might provide silent cyber coverage because there are no cyber exclusions or limitations that apply to those policies. Although silent cyber coverages are becoming less common, they do still exist. Other policies might provide affirmative cyber coverage grants, including those policies discussed above. Carefully review commercial general liability, property, directors and officers, crime, and all other policies to determine where cyber coverage does or might exist for a claim. That exercise can also identify potential changes to make to an insurance program—not just the cyber policy—to align, broaden, or coordinate coverage across policies.

Last, large self-insured retentions or captive insurance can be a solution for mature firms with significant premiums, well-understood exposures, and the ability to handle functions such as actuarial, claims, and reserving. While self-insurance and captive insurance are beyond the

---

32 "The application process is a multi-disciplinary exercise." John G. Buchanan and Marialuisa S. Gallozzi, *Kicking the Tires on a New Cyber Policy: Top Tips and Traps*, ABA SECTION OF LITIGATION—INSURANCE COVERAGE COMMITTEE ARTICLE, Jan. 22, 2018, https://www.americanbar.org/groups/litigation/committees/insurance-coverage/articles/2017/cyber-policy-tips-traps/.

scope of this chapter, there are many resources available that provide guidance on how to approach these issues.[33]

E. Conclusion

This chapter has provided an overview of the opportunities and pitfalls for cyber coverage for those in the construction industry. By focusing on key coverage issues and undesirable exclusions or limitations, an effective risk transfer can occur from the policyholder to the cyber insurer. In instances where cyber coverage is not available, other risk transfer or mitigation options might be used instead. Taken together, these strategies will help obtain the best possible cyber insurance coverage while identifying and avoiding or mitigating potentially uninsured losses.

---

33 *See, e.g.,* Matthew Queen and Light Townsend, *Modern Captive Insurance*, ABA TORT, TRIAL & INSURANCE PRACTICE, 2019. The ABA Tort, Trial & Insurance Practice Section also has a Self-Insurers and Risk Managers committee, available online at: https://www.americanbar.org/groups/tort_trial_insurance_practice/committees/sirm/.

Chapter 23

Public Sector Cyber Insurance—State and Local Government*

Governmental entities face unprecedented uncertainty in a dynamic and fluid cyber insurance market, more persistent and viral cyber threats, and severe budgetary restrictions.[1] Yet, even as public bodies try to protect a host of different systems and applications from intrusions, employees and citizens alike want their data conveniently available with seamless functionality. Unsurprisingly, the transformation to digitized government with effective cybersecurity is elusive.

The allocation of scarce resources challenges governmental leaders to make hard choices, and the increasing cost of cyber insurance is a difficult issue.[2] Insurance is only part of a layered defense; it offers only post-security incident risk transfer protection to enable an insured to recover unavoidable costs and resume normal functions.[3] Cyber insurance also offers vital response and mitigation experience for dealing with crisis

* By Glenn E. Davis.

1 Joint Biennial Report, *States at Risk: The Cybersecurity Imperative in Uncertain Times*, Deloitte and the National Association of State Chief Information Officers (NASCIO) at 4 (6th ed. 2020) (Deloitte/NASCIO Report), https://www2.deloitte.com/us/en/insights/industry/public-sector/nascio-survey-government-cybersecurity-strategies.html (last visited Jul. 27, 2021); Dan Lohrmann, 2020: The Year the Covid-19 Crisis Brought a Cyber Pandemic at 1, https://www.govtech.com/blogs/lohrmann-on-cybersecurity/2020-the-year-the-covid-19-crisis-brought-a-cyber-pandemic.html (last visited Jul. 27, 2021).

2 *Pandemic Amplified Security Gaps for Public Sector Cyber Officials*, INSURANCE JOURNAL at 1 (October 19, 2020), https://insurancejournal.com/news/national/2020/10/19/587058.html (last visited Jul. 27, 2021).

3 Samantha A. Schwartz, *What Industry Gets Wrong About Cyber Insurance,* at 1 (Oct. 31, 2019), https://www.ciodive.com/news/what-inudsry-gets-wrong-about-cyber-insurance/566080 (last visited Jul. 27, 2021).

situations.[4] Unlike private entities, governments do not have the option to fold—they provide essential services on which their constituents rely.[5]

The sophistication of cyber defenses among state governments varies widely.[6] The level of defense varies even more among local county and city or municipal governments, as well as K-12 public school systems, government-owned electric, gas, and water utilities, and local public transportation entities. Nevertheless, the dependence of public bodies on electronically stored and communicated data has grown exponentially in recent years, and will only increase.[7] Meanwhile, with the explosion of ransomware and other cyber-attacks,[8] the existential threats to essential government operations and finances continue to outpace technological defenses and available funds. And these conditions have been amplified by the Pandemic, with 35 states reporting more than half of their employees working remotely and 9 states with more than 90% of their workforce operating remotely.[9]

Meanwhile, the insurance market has hardened. Insurance companies usually base their pricing on decades of loss experience data. With cyber risk, carriers have not had such longitudinal benchmark data, but nevertheless profited from cyber insurance policies for years, even in an

---

4 Andrew Simpson, *Putting Municipal Ransomware Attacks—and Cyber Insurance—in Context*, INSURANCE JOURNAL at 1 (March, 9, 2019), https://www.insurancejournal.com/news/national/2019/09/03/538635.html (last visited Jul. 27, 2021).

5 Whitepaper, *The Economic Impact of Cyber Attacks on Municipalities*, at 7 KnowBe4 (2020), https://www.knowbe4.com/hubfs/Cyber-Attacks-on-Municipalities-White-Paper.pdf (last visited Feb. 8, 2021).

6 Simpson, *supra* note 4 (Less than 40% of the states have a line item budget appropriation dedicated to cybersecurity.).

7 Lisa Thompson, *Cybersecurity Best Practices for Municipalities,* at 1, https://www.nhmunicipal.org/town-city-article/cybersecurity-best-practices-municipalities (last visited Jul. 27, 2021).

8 The FBI reports that the most common cyberthreats to state and local governments are ransomware, payroll account hijacking, unauthorized wire transfers, unauthorized access to IoT devices, and insider threats. *Local Governments Must Address Cybercrime Vulnerabilities,* https://www.emiia.org/about/46/view-news-item.html (last visited Jan. 27, 2021).

9 Deloitte/NAICS Report, *supra* note 1.

uncertain segment.[10] The loss ratio for U.S. cyber policies was about 35 percent in 2018 compared with 62 percent for property and casualty insurance policies. Thus, for every premium dollar collected, insurers paid out roughly 35 cents in claims; cyber insurance was nearly twice as profitable as other types of insurance.[11] Yet, most cyber carriers "offer only low coverage limits and high deductibles, and they may limit coverage in areas like business interruption, because cyber risk is difficult to estimate and price accurately."[12] This in part explains why some estimate that only 31% of private sector firms secure cyber insurance.[13]

Increasing attacks, including higher ransomware demands and threatened release of data exfiltrated during ransomware attacks, as well as the proliferation of regulatory regimes have driven premiums in primary markets up 5-10% with higher increases expected in excess lines.[14] In a March 2020 report one insurer reported a 131% increase in ransomware attacks on its insureds in 2019, with far larger ransom demands to de-encrypt clients' data.[15] Brokers are showing low double-digit rate increases across the board and higher increases for accounts

---

10 Interview, Kevin Kalinich, Global Collaboration Leader, Intangible Assets, Aon Commercial Risk Solutions, (Dec. 18, 2020) (Insurance companies usually base their pricing on 25-40 years of actuarial, loss experience data.).

11 Srini Subramanian, Doug Powers & Pete Renneker, *Ransoming Government: What State and Local Governments Can Do to Break Free of Ransomware*, DeLoitte Insights (Mar. 11, 2020) https://www2.deloitte.com/us/en/insights/industry/public-sector/government-ransomware-attacks.html (last visited Jan. 30, 2021).

12 Jon Bateman, *Working Paper: War, Terrorism and Catastrophe in Cyber Insurance: Understanding and Reforming Exclusions*, CARNEGIE ENDOWMENT FOR INT'L PEACE, at 6 (Oct. 5, 2020), https://carnegieendowment.org/2020/10/05/war-terrorism-and-catastrophe-in-cyber-insurance-understanding-and-reforming-exclusions, (last visited Jul. 28, 2021).

13 Molly Corbett, *Ransomware, COVID-19 and Cyber Insurance—The Big Disconnect*, at 1 https://www.genre.com/knowledge/blog/contributors/molly-corbett.html (last visited Jul. 28, 2021).

14 Judy Greenwald, *Ransomware Attacks Add to Market Strain*, BUSINESS INSURANCE (Nov.10, 2020), https://f.hubspotusercontent10.net/hubfs/5139161/BI_1120_BB%2011%202%2020.pdf (last visited Jan. 30, 2021).

15 Judy Greenwald, *Businesses Try to Keep Pace with Hackers*, BUSINESS INSURANCE (May 2020).

with prior losses according to a recent Moody's Investor Services report.[16] These trends have continued unabated in 2021.[17]

Carriers are monitoring new business, adding new underwriting criteria, reducing limits, and raising attachment points.[18] The potential accumulation of risk when multiple policyholders are impacted by the same cyber event raises concerns for insurers.[19] Insurers also continue to struggle with so-called "silent cyber coverage," which may be found in policies they did not design to cover cyber risk.[20]

---

16 Claire Wilkinson, *Cyber Insurance Prices Increase on Ransomware Claims,* BUSINESS INSURANCE (Feb. 5, 2021), https://www.businessinsurance.com/article/20210205/NEWS06/912339618/Cyber-insurance-prices-increase-on-ransomware-claims-Moodys?utm_campaign= BI20210205.

17 *Cyber Insurers Hike Rates But Worry About Prices Long-Term As Losses Mount: Fitch,* at 1 INSURANCE JOURNAL (May 27, 2021), https://www.insurancejournal.com/news/national/2021/05/27/616176.htm (last visited Jul. 28, 2021) (Council of Insurance Agents & Brokers recent market survey pegged renewal pricing on cyber coverage at 18%): Judy Greenwald, *Cyber Insurance Rates to Increase 20-50% this Year: AON*, BUSINESS INSURANCE (Mar. 4, 2021), https://www.businessinsurance.com/article/20210304/NEWS06/912340248/Cyber-insurance-rates-to-increase-20-50-this-year-Aon (last visited Jul. 28, 2021).

18 New York has announced a new Cybersecurity Insurance Risk Framework to provide guidance to insurers writing cyber insurance. https://www.dfs.ny.gov/reports_and_publications/press_releases/pr202102041 (encouraging a data-driven approach to measure insureds' risk and vulnerabilities and steps to eliminate "silent cyber" coverage).

19 *Id.*

20 See Chapter 3. To deal with the "silent cyber" problem ISO has clarified its Commercial Property and Businessowner forms with two new endorsements: the Cyber Incident Exclusion and the Cyber Incident Exclusion (CP 1075 12 20 and BP 15 60 02 21) with Ensuing Cause(s) of Loss Exceptions (CP 10 76 12 20 and BP 15 61 02 21). ISO Circular LI-CF-2020-51. For a discussion of these changes, *see* Christine Unger, *ISO's Cyber Incident Exclusion Endorsements—A Solution for the Silent Cyber in Commercial Property Forms?* https://www.genre.com/knowlege/blog/isos-cyber-incident-exclusion-endorsements-a-solution-for-the-silent-cyber-in-commercial-property-forms-en.html.

There are many sources to evaluate the technical steps, training, and basic cyber hygiene public organizations can implement to try to manage cyber risk and exposure.[21] By comparison, other than help from a qualified broker with cyber expertise, there is very little guidance for government Chief Information Security Officers ("CISO"s), risk managers, or CFO's on how to secure appropriate cyber insurance.

For government entities, the insurance picture is more challenging than the private sector. Fewer insurers are willing to write governmental cyber risk policies, and those that are impose not only higher premiums but heightened eligibility and representation requirements.[22] In the past, cyber coverage may have been available without the insured having full encryption, two-factor authentication, or a comprehensive incident response plan, but that is certainly no longer true. Some carriers are specifically cutting back on writing cyber coverage for public entities.[23] Nevertheless, while effective insurance is not a complete solution, it is an indispensable part of risk management for cyber threats. Ironically, the emergence of coverage for certain types of attacks, such as ransomware, has contributed to the dramatic growth in ransomware attacks.[24]

This chapter describes the primary cyber insurance issues governmental entities confront today, both in terms of the risks and the procurement and coverage issues government entities must address.

---

21 *State and Local Partnerships for Cybersecurity, A State by State Analysis*, at 11-20__ https://www.nlc.org (including extensive list of resources for state and local governments) (last visited Jul. 28, 2021) [hereinafter *State Analysis*].

22 Although there are other players, the primary carriers remain AIG, Beazley, Travelers, Chubb and XL Catlin. *Seven Questions to Ask Cyber Insurance Prospects*, INSURANCE JOURNAL (Mar. 16, 2017), https://www.insurancejournal.com/news/national/2017/03/16/444609.html.

23 John H. Jones, *Beazley Scales Back on Cyber for US Entities*, INSURANCE INSIDER (Oct. 29, 2020), https://insuranceinsider.com/p-and-c/articles/136485/beazley-scales-back-on-cyber-for-us-public-entities (last visited Feb. 8, 2021).

24 *Id.* Critics characterize insurance companies as "ransomware enablers" for facilitating payments to cyber criminals. *Cities Warned Not to Rely on Cyber Insurance Alone*, WALL STREET JOURNAL https://www.wsj.com/articles/cities-warned-not-to-rely-on-cyber-insurance-alone-11571995801 (Oct. 25, 2019) (last visited Jan. 22, 2021).

A. Broad Scope of Risk and Attack Vectors

Government entities present all of the attack surfaces and significant vulnerabilities cyber criminals exploit. Email, particularly email spear phishing or email with malware loaded attachments, remains the number one attack vector. Other attack surfaces include web pages, unnecessarily open ports, unpatched VPN's, online servers with weak password protection, pop-up windows, instant and text messages, social engineering, and untested third-party vendors. The lack of unified systems deployed by public bodies makes consistent technical defenses all the more difficult.[25]

The government of today features more remote users with a proliferation of user applications and hardware, as well as increasing use of "Internet of Things" ("IoT") devices. Connected traffic cameras, police cars, ambulances, trash trucks, parking meters, and metering devices illustrate the wide array of endpoints connected to state and local government networks.[26] The "smart" government of the future will feature more data and reliance on computer network systems.[27] With the increase in web-based platforms and functions, such as electronic applications, payment card transactions, and smart city initiatives, the volume of data in movement and at rest will increase exponentially.[28] Breach of street light

---

25 *Cities Turn to Insurance in Fight Against Growing Cyber Risk*, INSURANCE BUSINESS MAGAZINE, https://www.insurancebusinessmag.com/us/news/cyber/cities-turn-to-insurance-in-fight-against-growingcyber-risk-111975.aspx (noting wide variance in infrastructure across government departments) (last visited Jan. 22, 2021).

26 DeLoitte Insights, *Government Ransomware Attacks*, ww2.deloitte.com/us/en/insights/industry/public-sector/government_ransomware-attacks.html.

27 Cybersecurity and Privacy Advisory Committee (CPAC) Public Working Group, *A Risk Management Approach to Smart City Cybersecurity and Privacy,* https://pages.nist.gov/GCTC/uploads/blueprints/2019_GCTC-SC3_Cybersecurity_and_Privacy_Advisory_Committee_Guidebook_July_2019.pdf; *Smart Cities: Threat and Countermeasures*, https://www.rambus.com/iot/smart-cities (depicting attack vectors); Judy Greenwald, *Smart Cities Face Web of Cyber Challenges,* BUSINESS INSURANCE (2020).

28 *The Foundation of Smart City Success,* https://www.pwc.com/us/en/industries/capital-projects-infrastructure/library/foundation-of-smart-city-success.html (describing 7 layers of smart data governance); *Beazley Scales Back on Cyber for US Entities*, INSURANCE INSIDER (Oct. 29, 2020).

systems or other interconnected IoT smart devices can lead to access to servers and on to citizen personal identifiable information ("PII") or financial data.[29]

B. Recent Attacks and the Rise of Ransomware

Loss experience is a major factor in negotiating cyber insurance coverage. While the Solarwinds penetration of federal and some state and local agencies drew significant media attention,[30] state and local governments' biggest threat remains ransomware. Major ransomware attacks have generated significant adverse publicity for government leaders.[31] Ransomware attacks on public entities have also fueled interest in cyber insurance. For example, the City of Houston, Texas, recently paid a premium in excess of $470,000 to acquire $30M in cyber coverage.[32] Others, like Seattle, are self-insured while municipal pools have arisen as an alternative to traditional policies.[33]

Recent ransomware attacks on cities, schools, transportation systems, and other public entities are cautionary tales on the high stakes involved.[34] Consider the following examples.

---

29 https://www.pwc.com/us/en/services/consulting/cybersecurity/library/broader-perspectives/smart-cities.html.

30 Nation-state hacking attempts that can potentially affect state and local governments are nothing new. *See, e.g., Malicious Russian Cyber Activity is Targeting Government Networks,* https://www.nlc.org/article/2018/04/17/malicious-russian-cyber-activity-is-targeting-government-networks/. (Apr. 17, 2018).

31 Simpson, *supra* note 4.

32 *U.S. Cities Turn to Cyber Insurance in Response to Hackers*, https://quandarypeak.com/2018/10/u-s-cities-turn-to-cyber-insurance-in-response-to-hackers/ (providing examples of major cities' approaches to insuring against cyber risk) (last visited Jan. 26, 2021).

33 For general information on municipal risk pools, *see* State Municipal League Risk Pools, https://www.nlc.org/wp-content/uploads/2020/10/State-League-Risk-Pools-NLC-RISC-MemberPartnerEngagement-Bifold-v9.pdf.

34 It is estimated that the number of ransomware variants increased by 50% during 2020 alone. Whitepaper, *How Local Government Can Reduce Cyber Security Risks,* (Nov.12, 2020), https://ontech.com/local-government-cyber-security (last visited Jan. 27, 2021).

In May 2019, the city of Baltimore, Maryland experienced a severe ransomware attack using the so-called "RobbinHood" ransomware strain.[35] The City lost approximately $18.2 M in uncollectible or delayed revenue, not including the direct costs incurred to restore functionality. The attack shut down all city credit card payment system transactions, such as water bill collections, disabled municipal processes for collecting property taxes, real estate fees, and fines, effectively halting all real transactions.

When Baltimore's Mayor received the ransom demand of about $76,000 in Bitcoin, the city made the hard decision to refuse payment and incur over $5 million in data recovery and system repairs and upgrades.[36] Among the impacts: first responders were unable to access computer-aided dispatch systems, forcing police, fire, and ambulance services to rely on telephone communications while the situation evolved.[37]

An audit of Atlanta's network systems, prior to a ransomware attack in 2018, revealed 2,000 network vulnerabilities.[38] When it struck, the ransomware attack disrupted many critical aspects of the state capital's functions as well as the nation's busiest airport.[39] The incursion significantly impacted law enforcement, forcing police to write incident reports by hand, and blocking access to archived in-vehicle video, forcing manual processing of Atlanta Municipal Court cases, and halting payment of tickets, water bills, and business licenses and renewals. Atlanta had incident response plans to perform services in an analog way while the incident unfolded and Atlanta declined to pay the $55,000 in Bitcoin ransom demand. The city lost a decade of legal documents and video

---

35 White Paper, *Ransomware,* https://media.bitpipe.com/io_15x/io_150503/item_2092497/Ransomware%20White%20Paper%20v04.pdf. (the malware is executed through an "sc. exe stop" command: cmd.exe /c sc.exe stop AVP /y.) (last visited Jan. 31, 2021).

36 Dwight Weingarten, *Ransomware Can Hold Cities Hostage. Will Cyber Insurance Help?* BALTIMORE BUSINESS JOURNAL https://www.bizjournals.com/baltimore/news/2020/10/27/city-reup-20m-cyber-insurance-post-ransomware.html.

37 *Cyber Attacks Smart Cities,* https://www.dilitrust.com/en/blog/cyber-attacks-smart-cities/ (last visited Jan. 31, 2021) [hereinafter *Attacks*].

38 DeLoitte Insights, *supra* note 26.

39 *What Can We Learn from Atlanta,* https://www.govtech.com/security/What-Can-We-Learn-from-Atlanta.html (last visited Jan. 31, 2021).

evidence.[40] Nevertheless, media reports revealed Atlanta's costs would exceed $17 million.

Other public bodies have elected to pay the ransom. In June 2019 Lake City, Florida chose to pay $460,000 in ransom to decrypt its systems, which had been shut down for two weeks. Public employees were locked out of their email accounts. Cyber insurance covered the ransom payment, after the City paid its $10,000 deductible.[41] Riviera Beach, Florida endured three weeks of chaos before its City Council decided to meet the ransom demand for $600,000. Riviera Beach diverted capital funds earmarked for technology improvements to pay the ransom. Key Biscayne, Florida had a similar experience. Jackson County, Georgia officials agreed to pay $400,000 to restore their systems. Jackson County paid the ransom entirely from their own funds.[42]

In the public transportation sector, thieves crippled Vancouver, British Columbia's transportation agency, TransLink, through a ransomware attack. The attack, which occurred in December 2020, left Vancouver residents unable to use pre-purchased Compass metro cards or pay for new tickets at TransLink's Compass ticketing kiosks.[43] San Francisco experienced a similar public transportation attack in 2016, when hackers forced the city to turn off ticket vending machines for the city's public transportation system.[44] While San Francisco has a $50 million cyber insurance policy for its health systems, it is now exploring coverage for the entire city government.

Public education entities, from K-12 systems to state universities, are also under attack. For example, a cybercriminal published private data belonging to thousands of students following a failed attempt to extort a ransomware payment from Clark County Nevada School District.[45] When

---

40 *Id.*

41 DeLoitte Insights, *supra* note 26.

42 Luke Irwin, *The Five Biggest Ransomware Pay-Outs of All Time,* https://www.itgovernance.co.uk/blog/the-5-biggest-ransomware-pay-outs-of-all-time (10/2/2019).

43 Ransomware Attack Cripples Vancouver Public Transportation Agency, https://www.zdnet.com/article/ransomware-attack-cripples-vancouver-public-transportation-agency (last visited Jan. 31, 2021).

44 *Attacks, supra* note 37.

45 *Nevada School District Refuses to Submit to Ransomware Blackmail—Hacker Responds by Publishing Student Data,* https://www.zdnet.com/

the district refused to pay, the ransom sponsor retaliated by releasing the student data.

By contrast, the University of Utah decided to pay $457,059 in ransom to avoid having hackers leak student information online.[46] Like other recent "double extortion" attacks, the criminals exfiltrated files before encrypting the University's files, threatening to release the files if they refused to pay. Initially, the University thought that by restoring data from back-ups it had avoided a major ransomware attack, with only 0.02% of the data stored on its servers accessed and encrypted. The second threat led the University to reconsider and pay the ransom to ensure the student data was not released to the internet or sold on the dark web. The University acknowledged that insurance paid a significant portion of the ransom.

The stakes may be even higher when patient care, university research and intellectual property is at stake. In January 2021, the University of California San Francisco ("UCSF") found malware in the UCSF School of Medicine's IT systems. Network administrators attempted to isolate the infection and prevent the ransomware from traveling to the core UCSF network. Although UCSF represented the cyberattack did not affect patient care or the university's campus network, the school of medicine servers were encrypted. According to dark web reports, the attackers initially demanded $3 million but UCSF negotiated payment of $1.14 million to recover locked-down research files, but the servers remain locked.[47]

There are success stories. In 2019, the Lubbock County Texas IT department realized that user reports of desktop icons changing in real time meant an attack was occurring. The staff quickly isolated the computers and stopped a ransomware attack before it affected critical systems.

---

article/nevada-school-district-refuses-to-submit-to-ransomware-blackmail-hacker-responds-by-publishing-student-data/ (last visited Jan. 31, 2021).

46 *University of Utah Pays $457,000 to Ransomware Gang,* https://www.zdnet.com/article/university-of-utah-pays-457000-to-ransomware-gang/ (last visited Jan. 30, 2021).

47 *University of California San Francisco Pays Ransomware Hackers $1.14 Million to Salvage Research,* https://www.zdnet.com/article/university-of-california-sf-pays-ransomware-hackers-1-14-million-to-salvage-research/ (last visited Jan. 30, 2021).

However, it appears that Lubbock County was one of twenty-three Texas local governments averting a coordinated attack in a one-month period.[48]

The pressure on public entities to pay ransom, particularly when they have extortion coverage for such events, is high despite law enforcement recommendations to refuse payment. The following chart illustrates the impact gap between paying ransom and the cost of recovery:[49]

City Population Affected	Demand (USD)	Recovery Cost ($USD)
619,493 Maryland	$76,000	$10-18 Million
619,968 Colorado	$51,000	$1.5 Million
523,738 Georgia	$55,000	$17 Million
390,144 Louisiana	Unknown	$7-10 Million

C. Cyber Risk Profile for Public Entities

The cyber-attacks on state and local governments—libraries, schools, courthouses, hospitals, police and fire and other government service agencies—vary in severity by the type of data each institution uses and holds. The cybersecurity breach costs for U.S. states range between $665,000 and $40.53 Million.[50] The median costs varied from $60,000 to $1.87 million. Over fifty percent of the governmental attacks target local cities and school systems.[51] Fifteen percent of all targeted attacks are on government entities.[52] Government offices are frequent ransomware targets of financially-motivated attackers, with ransomware accounting for about 61% of malware incidents.[53]

---

48 DeLoitte Insights, *supra* note 26.

49 Whitepaper, *The Economic Impact of Cyber Attacks on Municipalities*, KnowBe4, Inc. at 3 (2020), https://info.knowbe4.com/economic-impact-of-cyber-attacks-municipalities.

50 Whitepaper, *supra* note 49.

51 *Id.* (citing Report to the Whitehouse, *The Cost of Malicious Cyber Activity to the U.S. Economy,* THE COUNCIL OF ECONOMIC ADVISERS (Feb. 2018).

52 Whitepaper, *supra* note 35.

53 The Data Breach Investigations Report, Fig. 92 (Verizon 2020) (based largely on data from federal administrative offices) (download available at www.verizon.com).

Notably, state and local governments must manage the risks associated with owning or leasing a wide variety of buildings. Many house highly sensitive information, networks or systems, including office buildings, national guard installations, courthouses, health facilities, law enforcement, and fire and other first responder facilities. Cyber-related property management includes protection of sector assets with access control systems and closed-circuit television systems. Industrial control systems used in state or local facilities are subject to attack and manipulation.[54] The facilities house the work of individuals who perform essential governmental functions.[55]

Not all protected information breaches are the product of criminal attacks. Significant losses also come from mis-delivery of information, misconfiguration of data sets in transit, and lost or stolen assets.[56] Insider errors are a major source of data exposure that can create liabilities. The Illinois Department of Employment Security ("IDES") recently acknowledged unintentional exposure of private information of independent contractors and self-employed persons who apply for unemployment benefits.[57] The IDES attributed the security incident to a new system inadvertently exposing names, social security numbers, phone

54 The U.S. Department of Homeland Security's (DHS), National Cybersecurity and Communications Integration Center (NCCIC), with assistance from the Industrial Control System Joint Working Group (ICSJWG), have developed important resources to support communication and improve critical infrastructure cybersecurity practices. https://us-cert.cisa.gov/sites/default/files/FactSheets/NCCIC%20ICS_FactSheet_ICS_Cybersecurity_C-Level_S508C.pdf. (last visited Jan. 24, 2021). The NCCIC is a 24x7 cyber situational awareness, incident response, and management center that is a national nexus of cyber and communications integration for the federal government, intelligence community, and law enforcement. *See generally* http://www.dhs.gov/national-cybersecurity-communications-integration-center.

55 *See* Critical Infrastructure Sectors, Government Facilities Sector, CISA, https://www.cisa.gov/government-facilities-sector. (last visited Jan. 24, 2021).

56 *Id.* at Fig. 93.

57 Illinois Blames "Glitch" for Exposure of Applicant Social Security Numbers and Private Data, https://www.zdnet.com/article/illinois-blames-glitch-for-exposure-of-applicant-social-security-numbers-private-data/ (last visited Jan. 31, 2021).

numbers, addresses, and other data points.[58] A business owner who applied for benefits noticed she was able to view others' confidential information. The Governor's office acknowledged the problem, noting the state was working to remedy the situation immediately. Fortunately, although thousands of individuals' PII was exposed, the gap was fixed within hours; how many applicants were impacted is unknown.

All of these risks bear on assessment of appropriate cyber coverage, as well as risks associated with other functions, such as human resources management and the vital responsibilities state and local governments assume for election infrastructure security.[59]

1. State Government

Given the vast quantity of confidential data state agencies, judicial systems, and legislative bodies possess, they are frequent targets of hacker probes seeking login webpages, Wordpress® sites, and other vulnerable assets.[60] States offer digitized transactional services with online payment of taxes, fees, and fines. This, as well as voluminous and detailed tax data, imposes payment data protection and privacy protection obligations.[61]

States are becoming more mature in technical cyber protection. They benefit from a variety of organizations that provide resources and support.[62] For example, the Multi-State Information Sharing and Analysis Center provides 24/7 incident response services, cybersecurity advisories and notifications, malicious domains identification, table-top exercises

---

58 The IDES website was set up to enable workers to access funds if they lost their jobs due to the COVID-19 pandemic. The new system, known as the Pandemic Unemployment Assistance (PUA), had over 44,000 claim applicants within the first 24 hours.

59 *See generally Critical Infrastructure Sectors, Election Infrastructure Security, CISA*. https://www.cisa.gov/election-security (last visited Jan. 24, 2021).

60 *State and Local Government Security Report* at 15 (BlueVoyant, August 2020), https://www.bluevoyant.com/state-and-local-gov-security-report (last visited Jan. 26, 2021).

61 *Id.* at 9.

62 The National Governors Association is one example. *See* Resource Center for State Cybersecurity, https://nga.org/statecyber/; Task Force Memorandum, https://nga.org/wp-content/uploads/2019/09/Task-Force-Memo-Final.pdf (analyzing state governance bodies addressing cyberthreats).

and training, and secure document sharing.[63] A number of states have consolidated information technology agencies.[64] Fifteen states have dedicated CISOs established by statute, and others have established CISOs by executive order, to provide oversight and management of state IT resources and security.[65] And there is increasing federal-state cooperation.[66] For example, DHS will partner with states to scan their websites and internal systems for vulnerabilities.[67]

2. Municipalities

Between 2017 and 2020, experts estimate that the average ransom paid by cities was $125,697.[68] A city's cybersecurity risks include lost or stolen confidential PII, theft of credit card or financial account information, access to personal healthcare information ("PHI") protected by HIPPA. These are typically insider risks, which could occur when protectible

---

63 https://www.cisecurity.org/ms-isac/.

64 *See, e.g.,* Colorado (C.R.S. §24-37.5-103 et seq.); Minnesota (MINN. STAT. § 16E.01); N. Carolina (N.C. STAT. § 143B-1325); Ohio (OHIO REV. CODE § 125.18); Oklahoma (62 OKL. ST. § 35.1 et seq.); Texas (TEX. GOV'T CODE § 2054.062); Utah (UTAH GOV'T CODE 63F-1-101 et seq.); Virginia (VA. CODE § 2.2-2005 et seq.); Washington (RCW § 43.105.006.

65 *State Statutes Creating Chief Information Security Officer (CISO) Positions in State Government,* https://www.ncsl.org/research/telecommunications-and-information-technology/state-statutes-creating-chief-information-security-officer-ciso-positions-in-state-government.aspx (last visited Jan. 18, 2021).

66 Congress has passed S. 1846 that authorizes the DHS to continue to coordinate with state and local governments to enhance the cybersecurity of their information systems. Under the bill, the DHS-NCCIC would continue to provide assistance to state and local governments, including conducting cybersecurity exercises, providing training, and notifying officials of cybersecurity threats. *State and Local Cybersecurity Act of 2019*, S.B. 1846, 116TH CONG. (2019-2020). The bill also authorizes DHS to implement an initiative to help state and local governments detect and prevent malicious network traffic on non-federal information systems.

67 *Iowa Secretary of State puts $1M Toward Election Cybersecurity*, https://www.govtech.com/security/Iowa-Secretary-of-State-Puts 1M-Toward-Election-Cybersecurity.html (DHS and state CISO work on state counties election security and transition of all Iowa counties to .gov domains) (last visited Jan. 30, 2021).

68 *Id.*

information is compromised by personnel via carelessness, mistake, or sabotage. Additionally, external hacking on city systems can damage equipment and software, requiring expensive replacement costs.

The financial and legal implications for a city that experiences a cyberattack are significant.[69] Cyber intrusions may involve significant losses from financial fraud, or other damage to financial systems. City and county court records contain a trove of PII and PHI, as well as non-public data on juveniles, and other vital information, such as tax, real estate transaction, and commercial license records. There may be third-party related risks, such as exposure for failure to take reasonable steps to protect commercial partners' information, personnel, or property. Subject to possible immunity defenses, there is risk of private litigation for negligence and potential penalties for compliance failures.

Breaches may also create significant second or third-party risks, including disruption of water, waste management, and electric service as well as environmental damage. Attacks on fire, emergency medical response, and police dispatch and communications, and traffic control systems threaten lives, and a wide range of damage to residents, visitors, employees and property.[70] On February 5, 2021, unidentified hackers remotely accessed a computer system used to monitor a city water treatment plant in Oldsmar, Florida.[71] The criminals accessed an industrial control system to increase lye levels in water to dangerous levels.

Not all consequences are obvious. Increasingly, underwriters are requiring municipalities to disclose cybersecurity risks in municipal bond offering documents. A cyberattack could result in a lower municipal credit rating,[72] although the S&P has yet to downgrade a municipal credit rating

---

69 *What Cities Should Know About Cybersecurity,* https://www.nlc.org/resource/new-report-what-cities-should-know-about-cybersecurity/ (last visited Jan. 26, 2021).

70 Duncan Greatwood, *Developing Comprehensive Cyberinsurance for Tomorrow's Cities—Today*, SECURITY MAGAZINE (January 9, 2020), https://www.securitymagazine.com/articles/91514-developing-comprehensive-cyberinsurance-for-tomorrows-cities---today (last visited Jan. 30, 2021).

71 *Hacker Changed Chemical Level in Florida City's Water System,* WALL STREET JOURNAL (Feb. 8, 2021), https://www.wsj.com/articles/hacker-changed-chemicals-level-in-florida-citys-sater-system-11612827672.

72 Lisa Thompson, *Cybersecurity Best Practices for Municipalities,* https://www.nhmunicipal.org/town-city-article/cybersecurity-best-practices-municipalities (last visited Jan. 27, 2021).

specifically because of a cyberattack. However, one bank has declared a covenant violation caused in part by a ransomware attack on a public hospital, and required notice of the violation to its bondholders.[73] Although the ransomed data did not include PHI, the attack caused Pleasant Valley Hospital, in West Virginia, to spend in excess of $1 million on new network infrastructure and computer equipment. In public finance, analysts and underwriters are questioning governmental entities about their readiness to deal with a cyberattack.

3. *County Government*

County governments typically use networks controlling county police and fire dispatch functions. County public health systems store a wide variety of personal and public health information, which may include substantial PHI and immunization records. Counties frequently maintain all of the important real estate transaction records for real property transactions and title records, as well as real estate tax records that may include PCI, through widespread use of credit cards. Many counties maintain county court as well as juvenile and criminal justice systems, with sensitive non-public data.

4. *K-12 School Systems*

Public school systems also maintain a large volume of confidential and private student health and performance records. Any school receiving federal funds has express privacy obligations on preservation of confidentiality and accessibility of student data.[74] Increasingly, K-12 schools also host parent-teacher organizations and private fund-raising foundations which maintain financial information on private donors and financial account information. School systems engage in a myriad of vendor and supplier relationships, ranging from major construction projects and large-scale food service providers to small school supply vendors. Moreover, in the wake of school shooting incidents many schools

---

73 *Hospital's Ransomware Attack Exposes New Risk for Muni-Bond Issuers*, INSURANCE JOURNAL (Feb. 26, 2020) https://www.insurnejournal.com/news/national/2020/02/06/557539.html.

74 *See* The Family Educational Rights and Privacy Act (FERPA), 20 U.S.C. § 1232g (Federal law protecting the privacy of student education records); 34 CFR Part 99; https://www2.ed.gov/policy/gen/guid/fpco/ferpa/index. html.

have implemented electronically controlled entry and lock-down security systems, which could be disabled or misused to access networks.

Since 2016 over 1105 school districts have experienced a cyber breach, with 221 reported to have had more than one.[75] There were 348 in 2019 alone, nearly three times the number in 2018.[76] An unfortunate side impact is that 519 of these incidents have drawn extensive media coverage. In the education environment, phishing attacks account for 28% of the breaches, followed by stolen credentials at 23%.[77] Ransomware is by far the most predominant malware variety.[78] Verizon reports that education is the only sector in which malware distribution to victims more commonly came from websites than email, likely due to use of stolen credentials, unmonitored email accounts, and Bring Your Own Devices ("BYOD"s) connected to shared networks. Most threats are external but a full 33% are internal, fueled by profit motives. Even inadvertent incidents impose liability.[79]

School cybersecurity is taken seriously given that schools are responsible for the safety of students in several dimensions, including: physical safety (from active shooters, abductors, and physical harm), online safety (from online predators, cyberbullying, pornography and online human trafficking), and data safety (student PII & PHI stolen for identity theft).[80] Yet, the cyberattacks that plague the education sector are only intensifying. The increased use of technology for remote classrooms during the Pandemic contributes to schools' vulnerability to cyberattacks. As a leading expert noted: "With more teachers and students online,

---

75 K12 Cyber Resource Center, https://K12cybersecure.com (last visited Jan. 15, 2021).

76 The impact on education is likely underreported due to the absence of data on private and parochial schools.

77 Verizon Report, *supra* note 53 (Educational Services).

78 *Id.* at Fig. 65 (over 80% of reported incidents; up from 48% only one year ago).

79 Cybersecurity for Schools Fact Sheet, *Readiness and Emergency Management for Schools*, (REMS), Technical Assistance Center, https://rems.ed.gov/docs/Cybersecurity_K-12_Fact_Sheet_508C.PDF (accidental posting of PII on a school website prompted class action against a Florida school district school board).

80 *What is Cybersecurity's Impact on K-12 Education Today,* EDTECH MAGAZINE (Aug. 2020) https://edtechmagazine.com/k12/article/2020/08/what-cybersecuritys-impact-k-12-education-today (last visited Jan. 23, 2021).

particularly if they're doing it from less controlled environments outside of the school, the attack surface of the school community is increased."[81]

While cybersecurity is the top priority of education IT leaders,[82] despite many resources for K-12 schools on developing cyber defenses,[83] how to assess risks to secure appropriate cyber coverage as part of a holistic protection program is less clear.[84]

5. *Government Healthcare*

The focus on privacy and confidentiality of healthcare data is not new and the challenges for government-run entities are largely the same as private healthcare entities.[85] The number of data breaches in this sector continue to increase, driven by attackers seeking PHI and PII to sell or ransom.[86] In this category, a high number of security incidents may be tied to human error and loss of assets (such as a misplaced unencrypted laptop).[87]

Government officials can access a host of resources to guide development of healthcare information security programs. Resources from NIST, HHS, OCR, HSCC, and others can support the development of

---

81 Cyberattacks Increasingly Threaten Schools, Here's What We Know, EDTECH MAGAZINE (June 2020), https://edtechmagazine.com/k12/article/2020/06/cyberattacks-increasingly-threaten-schools-heres-what-know-perfcon (quoting Doug Levin, founder and president of EdTech Strategies, which runs the K-12 Cybersecurity Resource Center) (Coronavirus pandemic provided hackers with new opportunities as schools shifted to remote learning.).

82 *Id.* (citing 2020 educational technology leadership survey conducted by the Consortium for School Networking (CoSN), *EdTech Leaders Cite Cybersecurity as No. 1 Priority, Critical IT Infrastructure Updates Needed,* https://www.cosn.org/about/news/edtech-leaders-cite-cybersecurity-no-1-priority-critical-it-infrastructure-updates-needed) (last visited Jan. 23, 2021).

83 *See Joint Advisory on Warning on Cyber Threats to K-12 Schools*, FBI, CISA and MS-ISAC, https://us-cert.cisa.gov/ncas/alerts/aa20-345adendum (containing extensive list of network, user, ransomware defense, and policy and procedures best practices).

84 *See* COSN, *Cyber Insurance: Do You Meet the Requirements for a Payout,* https://cosn.org/sites/default/files/Cyber%20Insurance%202-pager_0.pdf.

85 *See* Chapter 11.

86 Verizon Report, *supra* note 53.

87 *Id.* at Fig. 70.

cybersecurity plans.[88] For example, the Department of Health and Human Services (HHS) has issued numerous guides.[89] HIPAA establishes national standards to protect individuals' electronic personal health information that is created, received, used, or maintained by a covered entity.[90]

6. *Transportation and Transit Authorities*

Government cyber risk in transportation ranges widely, with vulnerabilities such as computer controlled light rail switches, websites, and credit card information taken in ticket systems or even payment card skimmers. If internet fronting applications are used there is risk of financially motivated attacks.[91] In 2016, San Francisco experienced a hack of its transportation agency's system, which shut down its ticket vending machines for a lengthy period.[92] Government transportation systems may include mass transit terminals, operational systems, and supporting infrastructure for bus, subway or metro light rail, and vanpool/rideshare services. The federal Cybersecurity & Infrastructure Security Agency ("CISA"), Department of Homeland Security ("DHS"), and Department of Transportation ("DOT") provide sector specific guidance and information-sharing resources for transportation systems.[93]

---

88 https://healthitsecurity.com/news/top-healthcare-cybersecurity-resources-from-nist-hhs-ocr-hscc (last visited Jan. 26, 2021).

89 *See, e.g., Health Industry Cybersecurity Practices: Managing Threats and Protecting Patients*, https://www.phe.gov/Preparedness/planning/405d/Documents/HICP-Main-508.pdf (last visited Jan. 26, 2021).

90 45 C.F.R. PART 160 & PART 164 SUBPARTS A & C. The Security Rule requires appropriate administrative, physical and technical safeguards to ensure the confidentiality, integrity, and security of electronic protected health information. The Privacy Rule establishes permitted and uses and disclosures of personal health information (PHI), individual rights for individuals as to their PHI, and administrative, technical and physical safeguards to access PHI.

91 Verizon Report, note 53, *supra,* at Fig. 106-108.

92 *See Cities Turn to Cyber Insurance*, *supra* note 25.

93 *See Critical Infrastructure Sectors, Transportation Systems Sector, CISA,* https://www.cisa.gov/transportation-systems-sector (last visited Jan. 24, 2021); *Surface Transportation Cybersecurity Toolkit,* https://www.tsa.gov/for-industry/surface-transportation-cybersecurity-toolkit; *Transportation Systems Sector Cybersecurity Framework Implementation Guidance,*

7. *Utilities*

Municipal electric systems are interconnected with investor-owned utilities and the regional power grids. Computers control the network of generation, transmission and distribution infrastructure—power lines, transformers, and other equipment—that powers a region. Utilities increasingly rely on remotely accessible equipment and mobile devices. However, vulnerabilities stemming from unsecure access or connection to critical systems via remote tools and devices are often the source of frequent cyber incidents.[94]

Various federal and state cyber security regulatory requirements or voluntary industry recommendations guide U.S. utilities on practices to incorporate cyber security into risk management practices. The North American Electric Reliability Corporation ("NERC"), which is supervised by the Federal Energy Regulatory Commission ("FERC"), is currently the only regulatory body with mandatory standards, but they apply only to certain Bulk Electric Systems ("BES"). Some state public utility commissions, including those of Pennsylvania, Texas, and Missouri, independently require utilities under their jurisdiction to meet specific cyber security standards for facilities that are not subject to the NERC standards.[95] City utilities also increasingly rely on remote industrial controls.

In May and July 2021, in response to the ongoing threat to pipeline systems, the DHS Transportation Security Administration ("TSA") issued security directives. The May 2021 Security Directive requires critical pipeline owners and operators to (1) report actual or potential

---

https://www.cisa.gov/sites/default/files/publications/tss-cybersecurity-framework-implementation-guide-2016-508v2_0.pdf (June 26, 2015) (DHS/CISA use of NIST Framework adapted to transportation) (last visited Jan. 24, 2021).

94 *Cyber Threat and Vulnerability Analysis of the U.S. Electric Sector*, Mission Support Center, Idaho Nat'l Lab. (August 2016).

95 *Cybersecurity and the North American Electric Grid: New Policy Approaches to Address an Evolving Threat,* Bipartisan Policy Center (Feb. 2014) (CIP Standards and NERC Reliability Standards) http://www.nerc.com/pa/Stand/Pages/CIPStandards.aspx. Additional state measures include requirements for secure meter technology and emergency response plans for cyber incidents, or impose federal standards such as NERC CIP.155. *See also supra* note 75, and accompanying text.

cybersecurity incidents to DHS' Cybersecurity and Infrastructure Security Agency ("CISA"); (2) identify a continuously available Cybersecurity Coordinator; (3) review current practices; and (4) identify gaps and remediation measures to address cyber-related risks and report the results within 30 days. The second Security Directive requires owner/operators of critical pipelines to "implement specific mitigation measures to protect against ransomware attacks and other known threats to information technology and operational technology systems, develop and implement a cybersecurity contingency and recovery plan, and conduct a cybersecurity architecture design review."[96]

D. Common Insurance-Related Challenges for Public Entities

1. *Budgetary Constraints*

State and local governments confront extraordinary demands in the face of volatility driven by the COVID-19 pandemic. According to AON's Katie Sabo "[t]he current pandemic is projected to result in more than $500 billion in budget deficits from 2020 to 2022 and affect public sector budgets more significantly than the Great Recession."[97] Governmental entities must fund mandatory programs, such as education, healthcare and long-term liabilities before discretionary funding on IT improvements and cyber protection. Yet, these funding challenges are occurring while criminals increase cyberattacks, capitalizing on dislocation of people and IT equipment with remote workers, over-taxed healthcare resources, and remote school programs.

2. *Lack of Personnel*

As noted above, local governments have difficulty maintaining competent IT workers well-trained in cyber defense. Public entity IT

---

96 Press Release, *DHS Announces New Cybersecurity Requirements for Critical Pipeline Owners and Operators*, (July 20, 2021), Department of Homeland Security, https://www.dhs.gov/news/2021/07/20/dhs-announces-new-cybersecurity-requirements-critical-pipeline-owners-and-operators (last visited Jul. 28, 2021).

97 Interview, Katie Sabo, Aon Public Sector Partnership, State and Local Leader (Dec.17, 2020).

personnel have traditionally focused on keeping networks and software running rather than implementing defenses against outside attackers.[98] There is a well-known capacity constraint for capable workers even beyond the public sector, increasing the demand and complicating governments' ability to meet the pay scale. A recent survey of IT department leaders rated inability to pay competitive salaries for cybersecurity personnel as the largest severe barrier to achieving cybersecurity.[99] In some cases, this has led to outsourcing or use of off-site or cloud data storage. Even with use of sophisticated cloud storage service providers, such as Blackbaud, school and local government records may still be exposed and require incident response expertise and cost recovery.[100]

3. *Third-Parties, Vendors and Related Risks*

Government networks are interconnected with vendors, other government entities, and the public. Like private industry, state and local governments are in the procurement business to acquire necessary goods and services to perform their functions. Many of the same best practices to limit cyber exposure through vendor management practices, such as those developed by NIST, can be employed. Demonstrable implementation of such processes may improve a government's risk rating and improve potential terms during underwriting.

Evaluation of supplier risk indicators[101] can inform government buyers whether contractors or suppliers can deliver on time and without

---

98 *Cities Turn to Insurance in Fight Against Growing Cyber Risk*, INSURANCE BUSINESS MAGAZINE, https://www.insurancebusinessmag.com/us/news/cyber/cities-turn-to-insurance-in-fight-against-growing-cyber-risk-111975.aspx.

99 Whitepaper, *supra* note 49.

100 Blackbaud is a leading provider of cloud-based solutions with over 45,000 customers across the world in non-profit, education, healthcare, and other sectors. Blackbaud announced a May ransomware attack with notifications beginning in July 2020, concerning the criminals' access to and promised destruction of customer data. *See* https://www.blackbaud.com/securityincident.

101 The primary supplier risk criteria typically include: financial risks, location risk, business continuity and time to recovery risks, and operational risks. Information security practices are interwoven in all of them.

disruption.[102] Use of standardized vendor questionnaires are increasingly used to gather information on vendor security practices. For example, a non-profit industry association, known as Shared Assessments, publishes the "Standardized Information Gathering (Questionnaire)" ("SIG"), a detailed set of third-party information security and privacy questions. Shared Assessments updates the SIG questionnaire annually in light of new security and privacy challenges, regulatory changes, and new trends and best practices in third-party risk management.[103] SIG is currently used mostly by large commercial and financial service entities at a significant cost, but prior versions of questionnaires are publicly available for review.[104] A detailed vendor risk management plan will favorably influence underwriting decisions.

---

102 Conference Materials, *Best Practices in Supply Chain Cyber Risk Management*, https://csrc.nist.gov/CSRC/media/Projects/Supply-Chain-Risk-Management/documents/briefings/Workshop-Brief-on-Cyber-SCRM-Vendor-Selection-and-Management.pdf. Vendor management best practices for government procurement may include:

- Proactive identification and correction of vulnerabilities in the supply chain.
- IT, security, engineering, and operations personnel involvement in sourcing decisions.
- Use of standardized security terms and conditions in all requests for proposals (RFPs) and contracts, adjusted for particular functional or business needs.
- Direction to minimize and assign responsibility for exceptions to security guidelines.
- Careful review of any risk assessments that depend on supplier self-evaluation and seek verification of security criteria compliance.
- Pilot programs or test periods for new suppliers in high risk areas.
- Approved vendor lists.
- Periodic reviews of supplier performance by the relevant stakeholder group.
- Annual meetings with vendors on any performance issues, concerns and security priorities and to reinforce the primacy of cybersecurity protection.

103 *See* https://sharedassessments.org/sig/. SIG is indexed to many industry standards (ISO 27002:2013, FFIEC Appendix J, FFIEC CAT, PCI, FFIEC IT Management Handbook, NIS SP 800-53 Rev 4, NIST CSF, HIPAA and GDPR) and users can tailor their questionnaire to their industry.

104 *See* 2017 General Questionnaire, https://community.broadcom.com/HigherLogic/System/DownloadDocumentFile.ashx?DocumentFileKey=fea

4. *Governmental Immunity Considerations*

If governmental immunity eliminates or reduces risk for particular claims, that consideration will influence determination of coverage needs. Various sovereign and governmental immunity doctrines or statutes provide state and local governments immunity from tort-based claims, with important exceptions to or waivers of that immunity. Generally, a state government is immune from tort suits by individuals under the doctrine of sovereign immunity. Generally, "sovereign immunity" protects the State and its divisions, including agencies, boards, hospitals, and universities; while "governmental immunity" technically only protects political subdivisions of the State including cities, counties, towns, villages, and school districts. Local governments, municipalities, and political subdivisions of the state are generally immune from tort suits by governmental immunity, because the state grants them immunity.

However, lawsuits against states, their officers, and employees are frequently asserted under federal laws.[105] Prior to the Federal Tort Claims Act[106] ("FTCA"), states and municipalities had near total immunity from civil liability. While many laws and decisions have eroded governmental immunity, claimants still must generally establish their claims fall within a recognized immunity exception. With respect to data breaches, plaintiffs continue to attack sovereign and governmental immunity and expand privacy rights claims.

For example, in a federal matter, multiple class actions were filed following the U.S. Office of Personnel Management's ("OPM") massive breach in 2014.[107] Following consolidation of numerous class action complaints in the District of Columbia, the district court granted defendants governmental immunity.[108] The District of Columbia Circuit

---

97e02-114d-4607-9a42-c39942f05318&forceDialog=0 (last visited Jan. 23, 2021).

105 *See, e.g.,* 42 U.S.C. § 1983.

106 28 U.S.C. § 2674.

107 In re Office of Personnel Management Data Security Breach Litigation, 928 F.3d 42, 50-51 (D.C. Cir. 2019) (involving data breach in which hackers allegedly used stolen contractor credentials to steal almost 21.5 million background investigation records and over 4 million federal employees' personnel files.).

108 The district court found the plaintiffs lacked Art. III standing and the court lacked subject matter jurisdiction because the Arnold Plaintiffs failed to plead

of Appeals reversed, holding that a federal agency and its private contractor were not entitled to sovereign immunity and derivative sovereign immunity, respectively.[109]

Specifically, the panel opinion found that The Privacy Act[110] "safeguards the public from unwarranted collection, maintenance, use, and dissemination of personal information collected in agency records" and thus "waives sovereign immunity by expressly authorizing a cause of action for damages against federal agencies that violated its rules. . . ."[111] According to the panel, the history of agency data breaches and failure to comply with critical information security standards[112] showed that OPM's conduct was "willful" or "intentional," as required to waive sovereign immunity.[113] Nevertheless, the panel affirmed the district court's refusal to recognize a constitutional right to privacy claim when a third-party steals information voluntarily submitted to a government agency.

In a recent case with implications for privacy claims against government entities, the Eighth Circuit held that there is no clearly established due process right to informational privacy.[114] The court reversed the denial of qualified immunity to city and county officials who had disclosed highly confidential and sensational information about the

---

the actual damages necessary to bring them within the Privacy Act's waiver of sovereign immunity. 928 F.3d at 53. To satisfy the Privacy Act's waiver of sovereign immunity and state a cognizable claim for damages, a plaintiff must allege that (i) the agency "intentional[ly] or willful[ly]" violated the Act's requirements for protecting the confidentiality of personal records and information; and (ii) she sustained "actual damages" (iii) "as a result of" that violation. 5 U.S.C. § 552a(g)(4).

109 *In re Office of Personnel Management*, 928 F.3d at 68.

110 5 U.S.C. § 552a.

111 928 F.3d at 61-62.

112 It is noteworthy that the General Accounting Office has criticized audited federal agencies' failure to apply basic cyber protection standards. GAO 19-234 *CYBERSECURITY, Agencies Need to Fully Establish Risk Management Programs and Address Challenges* (July 2019), https://www.gao.gov/assets/710/700503.pdf. The report provides detail on federal agencies failure to fully establish a cybersecurity risk management strategy for risk-based decisions, agency- and system-level policies for assessing, responding to, and monitoring risk, and a process for assessing agency-wide cybersecurity risks based on an aggregation of system-level risks.

113 928 F.3d at 52-53 & 62-63.

114 *Dillard v. O'Kelley*, 961 F.3d 1048 (8th Cir. 2020) (en banc).

plaintiffs. The district court denied the individual defendants' motions to dismiss the Section 1983 claims based on qualified immunity and the state-law claims based on official immunity under a state statute.[115] The individual defendants appealed, and an Eighth Circuit panel affirmed.[116]

On rehearing, the Eighth Circuit reversed the denial of qualified immunity, holding that the asserted due process right to informational privacy was not clearly established. The majority analyzed right to privacy precedent and concluded that, notwithstanding many decisions assuming the existence of such a right, a 2011 Supreme Court decision called into question "whether the right Defendants are alleged to have violated even exists."[117]

Still, most federal courts of appeal recognize "a constitutional right to the privacy of medical, sexual, financial, and other categories of highly personal information, grounded in the Fourteenth Amendment right to substantive due process."[118]

E. The Market for Public Entity Cyber & Privacy Coverage

As noted, the market for cyber insurance has hardened. The constriction in the market and increased pricing for public entities is illustrated by the Baltimore experience. In 2019, Baltimore carried $20 million in coverage from two carriers, which cost $835,103, for cyber incident response, business interruption loss and expense, digital recovery, and network extortion loss. Seventeen insurers participated in a competitive bid process for the 2019 package. The Baltimore Board of Estimates recently approved renewal of $20 million in coverage for a total premium of $949,172. This time, only ten carriers participated in the bidding.[119]

As the severity of ransomware attacks increased, the total cost of ransomware payments doubled through the first six months of 2020 as

---

115 *Dillard v. City of Springdale*, No. 5-17-CV-5089 (W.D. Ark. Sept. 29, 2017).

116 *Dillard v. City of Springdale*, 930 F.3d 935 (8th Cir. 2019).

117 *Dillard v. O'Kelley*, 961 F.3d at 1053.

118 *Dillard*, 961 F.3d at 1053.

119 *Baltimore Renews $20M in Cyber Insurance Cover*, BUSINESS INSURANCE 10/28/2020. https://www.businessinsurance.com/article/20201028/ NEWS06/ 912337422.

compared to 2019,[120] and the severity of incidents reported were generally more complex. Today's cyber extortion events are much more likely to involve threat actors who exploit access to networks, install highly persistent malware, target backups, exfiltrate stolen data, and threaten to sell it for profit rather than just encrypt it for ransom.[121] In fact, almost half of ransomware cases in the third quarter of 2020 included the "double extortion" threat to release exfiltrated data along with encrypted data; 22% higher than the second quarter. Beazley reported that ransomware attacks against its clients increased 25% overall between last year's fourth quarter and this year's first quarter. Another major carrier reported a 260% increase in the frequency of ransomware attacks, with ransom demands increasing by 47%, in the first half of 2020.[122]

F. Types of First Party and Third-Party Government Entity Coverage Available[123]

The elements of a comprehensive cyber policy include network security, privacy liability, network business interruption, media liability, and errors and omissions. Most policies contain multiple insuring agreements. There are no underwriting standards or uniform policy or endorsement forms for cyber coverage. Further, there are few separate policy forms for state and local government bodies[124] but no industry-accepted common policy forms. Accordingly, it is critical for governmental entities to understand exactly what is covered by a proposed policy. Exclusions and sub-limits require careful attention. Some insurers may exclude certain high-risk incidents from coverage. For example, a

---

120 Beazley, *Breach Insights Q3 2020* (Dec. 20, 2020), https://www.beazley.com/news/2020/beazley_breach_insights_q3.html.

121 *Id.*

122 Catalin Cimpanu, *Ransomware Accounted for 41% of all Cyber Insurance Claims in H1 2020,* https://www.zdnet.com/article/ransomware-accounts-to-41-of-all-cyber-insurnce-claims/ (last visited Feb. 1, 2021).

123 For more detailed discussion of first-and-third party coverage available, *see* Chapter 2.

124 Travelers®, for example, offers a CyberRisk for Public Entities Program, which includes separate coverage descriptions for Municipalities and counties, K-12 public schools, transit authorities, and other subclasses. These are available on their website: travelers.com/cyber-insurance/public-sector.

breach stemming from an unencrypted smartphone in an office with a BYOD policy might not be covered. Cyber insurance policies often contain multiple sub-limits that usually are not found in traditional insurance policies. The sheer number of sub-limits and even sub-limits within sub-limits can lead to confusion. The potential for misunderstanding is greater when cyber coverage is provided through an endorsement without a declaration page listing the limits available for the endorsed coverage.

Some carriers require audits, warranties, or ongoing compliance representations on cyber defense measures. Government cyber policy buyers should ensure prospective audit rights are reasonable and not one-sided and negotiate for an independent expert to perform the audit review. Cyber policy warranties and representations often require insureds to warrant they are maintaining proper administrative and complex technical security controls. Buyers often fail to understand the warranties or the implications of signing them. Often the warranties on standards or use of specific cyber defenses are in the fine print and can result in unexpected denials of claims.[125] Finally, government insurance buyers should not rely on the "silent cyber" approach and hope that coverage may be secured from other policies, such as CGL, Professional Liability, Director & Officer Liability, Employment Practices, Crime and other Liability Policies.[126]

First party coverage generally includes reimbursement for costs incurred as a result of a breach, including payment for privacy notification, crisis management, and usually credit monitoring services. Separate first party coverages may also provide for cyber extortion, business interruption, and data restoration costs. Accordingly, first party breach response coverage generally provides for security incident investigation and response costs, privacy breach notification and communication expense, and remediation services for those whose data is exposed.[127]

---

125 James Rundle, *Cities Warned Not to Rely on Cyber Insurance Alone*, WALL STREET JOURNAL (Oct. 25, 2019), https://www.wsj.com/articles/cities-warned-not-to-rely-on-cyber-insurance-alone-11571995801.

126 *See* Chapter 3.

127 *See* Chapter 2. The policies typically provide a variety of breach response services to assist insureds, including:

- Legal services;
- Computer forensic services;
- Privacy breach notification services;

Note, however, that all of the policy's multiple limits will be available for breach response.

Depending on the specific policy provisions, first party breach coverage may also provide for recovery of: business interruption loss from security breach or system failure; dependent business interruption loss from security breach or system failure; cyber extortion loss; PCI/DSS assessments; data recovery loss; data and network liability; funds transfer theft; network interruption loss; and data, hardware, and software restoration or replacement. Other forms of first party coverage may be sought, such as Cyber Crime Coverage, for first party losses to the insured for events such as: computer fraud; funds transfer fraud; social engineering fraud; telecommunications theft; defamation and reputational harm; invasion of privacy; and injuries from stolen data.

Third-party coverage addresses liability risks for third-party claims. Third party liability policies cover privacy liability, network security, media liability, and regulatory actions, often imposing sub-limits. Specifically, third-party cyber liability coverage may address the potential for privacy and security claims, regulatory fines or penalties, and private actions for damages, including potential class actions.

G. Evaluating and Securing Coverage

For a public entity, the exercise of securing cyber insurance is an opportunity, regardless of the final decisions, to assess thoroughly its vulnerabilities and exposure to financial loss and unbudgeted costs from cyber security incidents and breaches. Cyber insurance itself is only a risk transfer component of a holistic information security program.[128] Risk

---

- Call center services;
- Remediation services, such as credit monitoring, identity monitoring or other personal fraud or loss prevention solutions; and
- Public relations and crisis management expenses.

128 Public bodies should employ other forms of risk transfer for cyber exposure, including indemnification provisions in vendor agreements, limitation of liability provisions in contracts, disclaimers of incidental and consequential damages, and specific requirements for contracting parties to carry cyber insurance and include the entity as an additional insured. These protections are especially important for cloud services and software suppliers. Websites,

transfer requires assessment of operational risks, those areas in which the public body is dependent on technology and harm results from interruption.[129] There are also privacy risks, found in regulations and contractual commitments to constituents and third parties. Finally, there are security risks, when a cyber-attack can inflict financial harm.[130] As noted, risks and coverage vary considerably from insurer to insurer, which suggests the need for specialized assistance to help evaluate specialized policy forms and endorsements, in consultation with the public bodies' most knowledgeable risk managers and IT leadership.

1. Determining the Need

State and local governments must carefully assess what risks they must address with cyber insurance. A recent survey of government IT managers indicates that 78% of their employers have some form of cyber insurance, but there is a mix of responsibility for determination of what is needed.[131] Only 32% determine needs with a combination of risk management and IT executives, and only 34% are fully knowledgeable of their insurance requirements.[132] All risk managers in the city, county or state entity should be involved in a process, with a capable broker to

---

in addition to privacy notices, may also include disclaimers and user assumption of risk statements.

129 White Paper, *Cyber Liability Insurance: A Buyer's Guide,* Woodruff-Sawyer & Co. (Jul. 15, 2020), https://woodruffsawyer.com/cyber-liability/cyber-liability-buying-guide-2020/ (last visited Feb. 4, 2021).

130 *Id.*

131 *Cybersecurity Remains Top Priority for Cities and Counties as Threats and Attacks Continue to Disrupt Vital Public Services,* https://www.comptia.org/advocacy/news/comptia-advocacy-news/2020/10/29/cybersecurity-remains-top-priority-for-cities-and-counties-as-threats-and-attacks-continue-to-disrupt-vital-public-services; https://comptiacdn.azureedge.net/webcontent/docs/default-source/advocacy-documents/2020-pti-cybersecurity-national-survey.pdf?sfvrsn=b0488502_2 (last visited Jan. 30, 2021). PTI, the Public Technology Institute, supports local government through research, education, professional development, and consulting services, in conjunction with The Computing Technology Industry Association (CompTIA).

132 *Id.* at 4.

identify what coverage to prioritize.[133] Qualified brokers can also provide important information as to what peer cities, counties or states are doing and there are many sources to obtain requests for proposals or quotations for network security services and cyber insurance.[134]

This process will include a review of all other insurance with potential coverage for cyber-related losses. This is a moving target. The ISO Commercial Lines program is undergoing change.[135] As noted above, new endorsements are being implemented to eliminate any implied coverage for cyber risk in traditional commercial liability policies.[136] The change also involves use of only two proposed cyber policy forms, one for enterprises with under $250 million in annual revenue, and one for larger entities and financial institutions with revenue over $250M. New endorsements are also anticipated for auto risk policies to cover damage to on-board vehicle computers caused by hacks and related ransomware.

Cyber insurance policies and endorsements have not gravitated to common, widely-accepted forms. Government buyers need to understand each company's terms and conditions and not make assumptions on accepted practices.[137] Cyber coverage must also be put in context of any primary, excess and self-insurance layers it may maintain.

---

133 Memo on State Cybersecurity Governance Bodies, *Meet the Threat, States Confront the Cyber Challenge: Cyber Liability Insurance for States,* National Governors Association (Sep. 2019) https://www.nga.org/wp-content/uploads/2019/09/Task-Force-Memo-Final.pdf (last visited Feb. 10. 2021).

134 *See, e.g.*, https://www.bristoltn.org/DocumentCenter/View/8789/RFP-20003-Cyber-Liability-Insurance-Coverage?bidId= (City of Bristol, TN); http://www.state.wv.us/brim/RFPs/2014%20Cyber%20Liability%20Insurance%20Broker%20RFP/CyberLiability%20Insurance%20Broker%20RFP%20FINAL%202014,%201-2014.pdf (State of W. Virginia); https://www.findrfp.com/it-information-technology-bids/computer-security-network-security.aspx;https://govdirections.com/bids/sitemap/none/288/IT:%20Security%20-%20Cyber,%20Firewall,%20Technology%20Related%20RFP's/;

135 *See generally* Visualize Monthly, *Five Big Changes Coming to ISO Commercial Lines Insurance Programs*, https://www.verisk.com/insurance/visualize/five-big-changes-coming-to-iso-commercial-lines-insurance-programs/ (last visited Jan. 14, 2021).

136 *State Analysis, supra* note 21.

137 A public university, for example, may have Comprehensive General Liability (CGL), Directors and Officers (D&O), Educators Legal Liability (ELL),

For example, crime policies, most of which promise coverage for losses resulting from "computer fraud," are often a presumed source of coverage. This is an unsafe assumption; the coverage cases yield many different results.[138] Carriers have denied or resisted coverage when the computer system itself was not compromised even if used to commit fraud; when a fraud or crime is committed by authorized users; when sophisticated scams are directed to insureds; or if the insureds' negligence contributes to the fraud occurrence.[139]

There must be an inventory of the government systems themselves and all types of data that flows in and out of them. Identifying and understanding the nature and extent of a government entity's unique risks, as well as statutorily-imposed data protection or privacy requirements, is crucial. Only then can you tailor coverage to meet specific needs that are not otherwise adequately protected. The requirements of publicly available policy application forms, and ongoing compliance requirements, are a starting point.[140]

2. *Underwriting Process*[141]

Currently, government bodies seeking cyber coverage are typically required to provide detailed information on their cyber defenses and any

---

Employment Practices Liability (EPL), First Party Property Insurance, Automobile Liability Insurance, Disaster Insurance, Athletic Insurance, Medical Malpractice Insurance, and Fidelity Policies, some of which might be interpreted to cover some types of information security or cyber related events. *See* note 47-48, *supra.*

138 *See* Sanderina, LLC v. Great Am. Ins. Co. of Pittsburgh, Pa., 2019 WL *3 (D. Nev. Sep. 11, 2019) (analyzing cases finding and rejecting coverage for computer fraud losses).

139 Joshua Gold, *Crime Insurance is Failing to Keep Up With Cyber-Criminal Innovation,* NEW YORK LAW JOURNAL (Oct. 2, 2020) https://www.law.com/newyorklawjournal/2020/20/02/crime-insurance-failing-to-keep-up-with-cyber-criminal-innovation/ (last visited Jan. 30, 2021).

140 The SERFF Filing Access System provides access to policy forms filed with state regulators. www.serff.com. *See* White Paper, *Meet the Threat—States Confront the Cyber Challenge, Cyber Liability Insurance for States,* National Governors Association (Sep. 2019), https://wp-content/uploads/2019/09/Cybersecurity-Insurance-Two-Pager-Final.pdf (last visited Feb. 4, 2021).

141 *See* Chapter 6.

relevant loss history. Current applications and questionnaires seek details on: (i) the type of personal information and number of records by category (i.e. social security numbers, payment card information, protected health information, and biometric information); (ii) how response resources are organized; (iii) the volume of payment card transactions per year, and whether the prospective insured encrypts PCI data at the time of transactions and is otherwise compliant with PCI standards; (iv) the computer and network security plans and systems in place (written policies, process for timely updates and patches, firewalls, network intrusion detection systems, internal and external testing of defenses, appropriate training); and (v) prior security incidents or loss experiences.[142] Insurers are requiring governmental entities, however, to complete even more detailed supplemental questionnaires and respond to more pointed questions. This is a concern for any insured because any error in responsive information could result in a denial of coverage.

The application and follow-on underwriting discussions, including interviews, are critical for obtaining the cyber coverages sought and procuring the best possible pricing. The preceding sections describe, only in part, the many forms of cyber risk that merit consideration of cyber specific coverage. The needs of a K-12 school district differ dramatically from a local transit authority, but many of the same requirements must be met. The goal, working with a broker who is knowledgeable and experienced with cyber risk, is to tailor a program that proactively protects the specific exposures faced. This presupposes that the public entity has done a thorough audit or assessment of its specific risks, what impact they might have, and how they are protected. To achieve that goal, the government entity must prioritize what is most important and deal first with the threats that present the greatest risk.

During underwriting, the public entity must demonstrate preparedness to face and minimize cyber threats through real information security protection and incident response plans. It is advisable, in this regard, to demonstrate to carriers that the government's data systems have been audited, are subject to regular pen testing, are connected to industry best practices through associations or other resources, are supported by strategic training and user awareness surveys. It is even better if the government information security group can demonstrate these factors

142 *See, e.g.,* Beazley Breach Response Application and Beazley InfoSec Application, www.beazley.com.

objectively through certifications, such as ISO 27001, HITRUST, or Baldridge, or show compliance with NIST standards.

Other favorable considerations include: cloud-first practices, segregation of data, maintenance of end-point controls, secure network configurations for network firewalls, routers and switches, systematic patching, and continuous vulnerability assessment and management.[143] Basic cyber hygiene elements, such as a strong password management policy, multi-factor authentication, encryption of data in motion and at rest, timely updates and patches, third-party and vendor management plans, and systematic back-up of data are a given but must be demonstrated.[144]

These actions bear a cost. However, as the Baltimore experience has shown, the cost of recovery and restoration more than justify the cost of hardening the defenses and insurance. This is where hard choices need to be made despite budgetary pressure.[145]

Another problem in evaluating coverage (and its cost) is determining the value of the potential loss a government entity is trying to insure.[146] There is potential financial statement harm, and calculation-defying harm that may be different than damage to intangible assets in private industry.[147] How do you place an estimated dollar value on disruption of

---

143 *See generally* 2020 Verizon Report, *supra* note 53, at Critical Security Controls.

144 Use of tools widely used by public entities is a must, including: anti-virus software, intrusion detection systems, network traffic analysis and monitoring, automated malware protection and firewalls, multi-factor/biometric authentication, and secure virtual private networks. *See Cybersecurity: Protecting Local Government Digital Resources*, *supra* note 70. These are expected, not aspirational future goals.

145 The main reasons surveys show entities do not buy cyber insurance include: insurance limits do not match exposure (44%); premiums are too high (41%); and there are too many exclusions and uninsurable risks (34%). *See* 2020 Aon-Ponemon Global Report, *Financial Impact of Intellectual Property & Cyber Assets Report*, at 26, Aon & Ponemon Institute (Global Ed. 2020).

146 *See generally* Ian Barker, *The Economic Costs of Being Hacked*, BetaNews, Inc., (Feb. 10, 2016), http://betanews.com/2016/02/10/the-economic-costs-of-being-hacked/; Cyberecurity Programs and Policies, https://gsa.gov/portal/content/129686.

147 There are models to assess severity and frequency of financial harm to tangible and certain intangible assets. *See* 2020 Aon-Ponemon Global Report, note 168, *supra* at 5.

an election? Dissemination of citizens' stolen PII on the dark web? The loss of reputation of a school district on the eve of a tax levy vote? Such damage may be *sui generis* and more difficult to prove.

Intangible government reputation and public confidence values may have little to do with getting an entity back on its feet and paying its hard recovery costs. Identifiable first-party risks and many third-party risks can be modeled.[148] Cyber insurance decisions can be informed by data from prior breaches and insurance pay outs. The anticipated first-party costs can be estimated by analyzing other peer governments' average response and remediation costs from actual breaches. Determining the adequacy of limits sought may be difficult.

Once again, evaluating what the cyber application requires and developing careful responses sharpens the focus. Government entities normally will use some form of bid process to evaluate alternative offers to develop coverage and pricing alternatives. The request for proposals or quotations (RFP/Q) must carefully explain the specific risks for which cyber coverage is sought and elicit responses that permit comparison of terms and conditions. The RFP/Q should include desired coverage limits for each category sought. For example, one medium-sized city[149] with 16 departments and 350 employees sought renewal coverage as depicted on Exh. A in the chapter addendum. A similar description of one insurer's Cyber Program is included as Exh. B for comparison. These and similar forms set out the coverages for public bodies to evaluate.

Finally, the overall quote should state all costs, including premiums, fees, surplus lines taxes, if any, for all services and insurance provided.[150] The RFP/Q should require the insurer to provide a clear description of all related support services that come with the cyber policy and any associated fees or expenses beyond the premium, including any optional incident response services.

Many cyber policies separate coverage into subcategories, such as data theft remediation, extortion payments, identity theft and fraud protection. There may be areas to avoid the cost of cyber insurance for public bodies.

---

148 White Paper, *supra* note 140, at 5-7 (describing modeling tools including breach calculators, business interruption worksheets, comparative document statistics by sector).

149 City of Bristol, TN, *see supra* note 157.

150 *See, e.g.*, Mississippi Public Universities, Request for Proposals Cyber Insurance and Brokerage Services & Insurance Quotes, http://www.ihl.state.ms.us/rm/downloads/rfps_rfqs/cyber.pdf.

For example, a state or city that has determined it will refuse to pay ransom, may decide to forego extortion payment coverage.[151] Similarly, some public entities have no payment card usage and thus PCI liability coverage may be excluded from consideration.

3. *Exclusions & Loss Limits*

The broker and the insurer should be able to clearly state the applicable coverage limits, applicable sub-limits and coverage exclusions. Public entities should understand the triggers of coverage and how the limits apply, such as whether defense costs are included in the aggregate limit for each claim. If an insurer provides alternative quote levels, the limits and exclusions relevant to each proposal must be compared closely.

Cyber policy or endorsement "Definitions" are critically important. Caution should be exercised to define the "Insured" very carefully, to include a complete list of affiliated governmental departments, divisions or entities to avoid any confusion as to the "Covered Entities" or "Named Insured(s)" under a proposed policy. Most cyber forms define named insureds in terms more appropriate to describe commercial entities and their personnel.

"Breach," "Security Breach," or "Data Breach" should be broadly defined to include any failure to protect data, including unauthorized access to data as well as unlawful dissemination or use.[152] "Network"

---

151 Whitepaper, *supra* note 149.

152 One current Breach Response Policy defines "security breach" as "a failure of computer security to prevent:

1. unauthorized access or use of computer systems, including unauthorized access or use resulting from theft of a password from computer systems or from any insured;
2. a denial of service attack affecting computer systems;
3. with respect to coverage under the Liability insuring agreements, a denial of service attack affecting computer systems that are not owned, operated, or controlled by an insured; or
4. infection of computer systems by malicious code or transmission of malicious code from computer systems.

"Unauthorized access or use" and "unauthorized disclosure" are separately defined. "[U]nauthorized access or use means the gaining of access to or use of computer systems by an unauthorized person(s) or the use of computer systems in an unauthorized manner." "[U]nauthorized disclosure means the disclosure of (including disclosure resulting from phishing) or access to

should include any networks, whether shared or in-house or cloud related, in which the state or local government entity transmits, receives or holds data. It should be broad enough to include any breaches of cloud storage that might expose the entity's data. "Data Loss" should include the loss, partial loss or corruption of data, or decrease in its value. Multiple claims or losses from a series of related acts, errors or omissions normally are considered a single loss under most policy forms.[153]

Exclusion and loss limit terms vary considerably and must be read in detail and understood. The policy should ideally cover losses from access to and disclosure of confidential data for any reason, such as from a network breach, a lost lap top, or an insider release of confidential information. The policy should apply to all "security incidents" not simply outside attacks. Coverage should exist for negligent or intentional release of data, perhaps by an IT department error in maintenance or failure of an HR department to protect employment data. Evaluate "claim" definitions as used in exclusions carefully.[154]

"Severability" or "non-imputed to another" provisions require care to avoid an act of an employee triggering an exclusion for the entity. "Insured vs. Insured" exclusions are common; if present, a public entity should try to obtain a carve-out for employee lawsuits against the entity arising out of a cyber breach. Similarly, if there is an unauthorized theft of funds involving computers, crime policies and fidelity bonds have been interpreted to apply only to external access to and misuse of data. Negotiators should specifically seek coverage for social engineering scheme losses. Insider threats, including when an attacker fools an

---

information in a manner that is not authorized by the insured organization and is without knowledge of, consent or acquiescence of any member of the control group." https://policies.dppl.com/policy? policy_number=BBR-5A8ED7A3-8OEF (last visited Dec. 17, 2020).

153 *Id.* (definitions of "Claim" and "Loss").

154 Many exclusions eliminate coverage for "any claim" arising out a variety of subjects, including: contractually assumed liabilities or warranties, coverage under Professional Liability or other policies, employment-related matters that do not involve privacy violation claims, willful or deliberate or acts, sabotage by employees, acts of war or terrorism, insured vs. insured claims, and others. *See, e.g.,* NorthStar Mutual Cyber Liability Insurance Coverage Part Endorsement, at 3-7, https://www.northstarmutual.com/UserFiles/File/forms/policyforms/Current/CF-2123%2003-16.pdf.

employee into causing a breach, should be covered.[155] Extortion provisions should include all costs to respond to ransom threats, not simply ransom payments.

Disruption of some governmental functions, such as emergency response and fire and police dispatch, can lead to injuries or death. Many cyber policies exclude coverage for physical injuries arising out of security incidents.[156] Finally, given the rise of nation-state attacks, provisions excluding coverage or limiting liability for acts of war or terrorism are common.[157] Cyber policies vary in this regard and many policies are silent; very few provide coverage.

It bears emphasis that state and local governments need an effective broker with cyber insurance expertise, which is essential to secure cyber coverage that addresses the institution's specific needs. Public entities should use a broker with a comprehensive grasp of the scope of government organizations' cyber risk, who can fully explain how this risk is quantified, and provide recommendations on insurance carriers or policies that fit the organization's needs with appropriate coverage and favorable pricing.

H. Conclusion

No government official can predict if or when an attack may occur. Cyber insurance is an integral part of a public entity's integrated approach to protecting itself and its constituents from potentially catastrophic loss from cyber threats. While the cost is significant, the costs public entity victims of ransomware and other attacks have incurred, illustrate its usefulness. The temptation to attempt to insure every risk is unlikely to succeed, even if the funds were available to acquire the most comprehensive primary and excess coverages. State and local government entities are well-advised to secure the assistance of a broker or consultant with government sector cyber experience to work with a team of risk

---

155 Whitepaper, *supra* note 149.

156 *Id.*

157 *Cyber Security, Cyber Governance, and Cyber Insurance,* https://corpgov.law.harvard.edu/2014/11/13/cyber-security-cyber-governance-and-cyber-insurance (Nov. 13, 2014).

managers, IT professionals, and finance personnel to evaluate the coverages specifically needed and possible within budgetary constraints.

Chapter 24

Educational Institutions*

In running a charter school for nearly ten years, one of the most significant issues (and, for all practical purposes, fears) was how best to prepare for, and protect against, the disruption of a safe learning environment and day-to-day operations. Part of that concern was an effort to minimize (since one can never entirely prevent) any unauthorized access to the school's operational and financial systems, human resource files, medical records, and student academic and special education files—nearly all of which were stored and maintained electronically. For some of our concerns, they were rooted not in the expectation of an external threat through a hack or other form of cyber security threat, but rather in what took place in the context of ordinary, day-to-day school operations. These threats to the disruption of school operations ranged from student interaction in the hallways to classroom misbehavior to incidents of harassment, intimidation, and bullying ("HIB"), both on school premises and online.[1]

Nevertheless, despite the constant vigilance administrators, teachers, parents, and staff maintain towards keeping disruptive occurrences like HIB in check, studies and reports have shown that the effort to keep such distractions in check has not been equal to addressing the potential for disruption caused by cyber threats. While more attention has been paid by school and district information technology ("IT") staff, third-party educational technology ("edtech") vendors, and through the implementation of incident response plans, security protocols, and other proactive measures, they are only as effective as the attention paid by the millions of stakeholders. Teachers, students, parents, guardians, board members, administrators, staff, and vendors are all susceptible to the growing number of cyber vulnerabilities facing schools today.[2] Indeed, it

---

* By Renier P. Pierantoni and Lauren D. Godfrey.

1 Co-author Renier P. Pierantoni previously served as the Executive Director and Academic Compliance Leader for one of the most successful charter schools in New Jersey and shares his practical experience in that role to communicate better the essential legal issues addressed in this chapter.

2 David Saleh Rauf, *Cyberattacks on Ed-Tech Companies Rare, But Hugely Disruptive, Report Finds*, Education Week Market Brief, (Nov. 16, 2020)

is because of the element of human error, whether it be due to inattentiveness, negligence, or innocent mistake, committed while performing and engaging in the familiar, everyday tasks that we have insurance. However, in the context of formalized learning, there exists a dearth of cyber coverage to protect against the risks posed by cyber threats, due in no small part to the all too common and unfortunate refrain regarding education today: a lack of funding and concern about accountability.[3]

A. The Regulatory Framework

As mandates issued by the United States Department of Education ("DOE"), and state and local education departments, to institutions of higher education ("IHEs") and school districts across the country to increase protection against cyber attacks grows—much to the dismay of school business administrators ("SBA"s), administrators and board

---

("The Government Accountability Office, an independent watchdog agency that conducts investigations for Congress, was asked to look into the vulnerability of student, teacher and administrator data as more schools than ever before utilize online tools because of the mass shift to distance learning following the COVID-19 Pandemic. In one report, the agency analyzed 99 school data breaches over the past four years that compromised the personal information of K-12 students in about 287 districts. In doing so, the GAO also acknowledged the 99 data breaches it counted more than likely underrepresents the total number of successful hacks that occurred during that period.")

3 Leo Duran, *Ransomware Attacks Force School Districts to Shore Up—or Pay Up*, Education Week (Jan. 10, 2017), https://www.edweek.org/technology/ransomware-attacks-force-school-districts-to-shore-up-or-pay-up/2017/01 ("Some districts have been forced to weigh the ethics of paying a few thousand dollars to untrustworthy and anonymous criminals against surviving for weeks without access to lesson plans, learning software, or student records." "Paying the ransom was not a philosophical decision, but a business decision," said Charles Hucks, the executive technology director for South Carolina's Horry County schools. "What's it worth per day to not have access for our 43,200 students?" After his district was critically hit by a ransomware attack last school year, Hucks immediately shut his servers down to stop the spread of the virus. He then urged his bosses, who oversee a half billion-dollar yearly operating budget, to pay the nearly $10,000 ransom.)

members seeking to keep costs under control—there is simply no guarantee of being 100% hackproof. Well-known regulations that stand out in this regard are the Family Educational Rights and Privacy Act of 1974 ("FERPA"),[4] the Graham-Leach-Bliley Act ("GLBA"),[5] and the Children's Online Privacy Protection Act of 1998 ("COPPA"),[6] not to mention the myriad of state laws that address data privacy and security protection for all persons in general.[7] These regulations are further buttressed by the fact that compliance is directly tied to federal student aid programs, *e.g.,* money—a factor often serving as the strongest incentive for compliance with pretty much any regulation.

Regarding FERPA, the DOE applies FERPA to address the privacy of personally identifiable information ("PII") maintained in student information systems ("SIS") by educational institutions receiving funds through a DOE administered program. Under FERPA, the term "education records" is broadly defined to include all records directly related to a student and maintained by a school or by a party on behalf of a school, including grades, academic records, financial aid records, and disciplinary records.[8] Disclosure of education records is permitted only if the information is not personally identifiable, the student has given consent, the disclosure is made to the student directly, the information is merely directory information, or a specific statutory exception applies.[9] Unauthorized disclosure of education records could lead to a potential investigation by the DOE.[10] However, the DOE's authority under FERPA focuses solely on the privacy aspect of education records and, as such, is

---

4 20 U.S.C.A. § 1232g (West 2020); 34 C.F.R. Part 99.

5 15 U.S.C.A. §§ 6801, 6809, 6821, and 6827 (West 2020); 16 C.F.R. Part 313.

6 15 U.S.C.A. §§ 6501-6505 (West 2020), *et seq.*; 16 C.F.R. Part 312.

7 *See, e.g.,* the California Consumer Privacy Act, CA Civ Code § 1798.192 (2018) ("CCPA"); Illinois Biometric Information Privacy Act, 740 ILCS/14 ("BIPA"), and New York's Stop Hacks and Improve Electronic Data Security ("SHIELDS") Act, N.Y. G.B.L. § 899 *et seq.*; *see also* on the federal level, the Health Insurance Portability and Accountability Act of 1996 ("HIPAA") at 45 CFR Part 160 and Subparts A and E of Part 164 and the Health Information Technology for Economic and Clinical Health Act ("HITECH") at 42 U.S.C. § 139w-4(0)(2) (Feb. 2009).

8 *See* 20 U.S.C. § 1232g(a)(4)(A); 34 C.F.R. Subpart A.

9 *See* 20 U.S.C. § 1232g(b); 34 C.F.R. Subpart D.

10 *See* 20 U.S.C. § 1232g(g); 34 C.F.R. Subpart E

not granted oversight power to address incidents involving a cyber threat compromise to a district's educational technology, for example.[11]

The DOE's Office of Financial Student Aid ("FSA"), however, imposes certain contractual obligations upon IHE's if the IHE accepts Title IV funding which include breach reporting,[12] maintaining a written information security program,[13] and contracting with third party suppliers who can also maintain safeguards.[14] The DOE can fine an institution for violating an applicable statutory provision related to Title IV up to $55,907 per violation.[15]

COPPA, which is overseen by the FTC, issues and enforces regulations concerning children's right to privacy.[16] Due to these privacy

---

11 GAO Report to the Republican Leader, Committee on Education and Labor, House of Representatives, *Data Security: Recent K-12 Data Breaches Show That Students Are Vulnerable to Harm*, p. 6 (Sept. 2020).

12 *See* 2020-2021 FEDERAL STUDENT AID HANDBOOK, *School Eligibility and Operations*, Vol. 2, Ch. 7, at 2-209 (Feb. 25, 2021), https://fsapartners.ed.gov/sites/default/files/attachments/2021-02/2021FSAHbkVol2Ch7.pdf. The DOE has reminded institutions of their breach reporting obligations through numerous Dear Colleague letters, electronic announcements, and the annual FSA Handbook. *See, e.g.*, GEN-15-18, Dear Colleague Letter, Protecting Student Information (July 29, 2015), https://fsapartners.ed.gov/knowledge-center/library/dear-colleague-letters/2015-07-29/protecting-student-information; *see also* GEN-16-12 Dear Colleague Letter, Protecting Student Information (July 1, 2016), https://fsapartners.ed.gov/knowledge-center/library/dear-colleague-letters/2016-07-01/gen-16-12-subject-protecting-student-information.

13 *See* GLBA Safeguards Rule, 16 C.F.R. Part 314.3.

14 2020-2021 FEDERAL STUDENT AID HANDBOOK, Vol. 2, Ch. 7 at 2-210 (The FTC requirements apply to Title IV third-party servicers, so colleges must use servicers that are capable of maintaining such safeguards and must require servicers by contract to implement and maintain those safeguards.)

15 *See* 20 U.S.C. 1094(c)(3)(b); 83 Fed. Reg. 2062, 2063 (Jan. 16, 2018), https://www.federalregister.gov/documents/2018/01/16/2018-00614/adjustment-of-civil-monetary-penalties-for-inflation.

16 Other relevant (but no less complex) privacy laws and regulations that school districts must kept abreast with or otherwise be aware of are the Children's Internet Protection Act, or "CIPA" (a federal regulation to address a child's access to offensive content over the internet on school premises), Protection of Pupil Rights Amendment, otherwise referred to as the Hatch Amendment or "PPRA" (a federal law providing rights to parents of minor students concerning surveys asking personal questions) and, when applicable, the European Union General Data Protection Regulation ("GDPR"), which seeks

laws, schools, districts, and third-party edtech vendors—all of whom provide, operate and/or maintain websites, cloud and online programs that collect PII on educational stakeholders in some way or another, are required to provide notice that PII is being collected and, where necessary, obtain consent to do so. Depending on the information collected, PII may contain sensitive information about not just students, parents, and guardians, but family members and even friends.[17]

However, though these regulations seek to provide students and parents with a sense of comfort concerning their rights of privacy and protection, as well as schools and school districts with a belief there has been compliance, there remains a genuine concern over the unknown and inevitable cyber threat. Furthermore, where ensuing losses and liabilities that follow from even the most advanced and protective of security data systems occur, one thing will always be clear: students (and, as to minor students, parents) have the right to expect schools will prevent the disclosure of sensitive information contained in their record, and will blame the school, the district, its leaders, its board members, and its IT staff for not doing enough.[18] Enter: cyber insurance, which—unlike traditional commercial general liability and property insurance—is specifically tailored to provide coverage for first-party losses (*i.e.,* the insured's losses for business income loss, expenses to repair and restore operations, *etc.*) and third-party liabilities (*i.e.,* claims and lawsuits that

---

to protect the processing and storage of PII or any other information relating to an identified or identifiable natural person. *Id.* at pp. 5-6, 13.

17 Take, for example, where a school requires the PII of a relative or family friend to confirm parental authorization to pick up a student from school or participate in extracurricular activities. *See also* the GAO Report to the Republican Leader, Committee on Education and Labor, House of Representatives, *Data Security: Recent K-12 Data Breaches Show That Students Are Vulnerable to Harm*, p. 6 (Sept. 2020) and Commission's 1999 Statement of Basis and Purpose as "expect[ing] that operators will keep confidential any information obtained from parents in the course of obtaining parental consent or providing for parental access pursuant to COPPA." Children's Online Privacy Protection Rule, 64 Fed. Reg. 59888, 59902, 64 Fed. Reg. 59888-01, 59902 n.213.

18 34 C.F.R. § 99, *et seq.*; however, schools are allowed what is often referred to as an "administrative exemption" to disclose—without parental consent (but with notice to parents and students)—basic information such as a student's name, address, telephone number, date and place of birth, honors and awards, and dates of attendance.

may be asserted by parents and students for their harm) in the event of a cyber event affecting data privacy and security.[19] Cyber insurance seeks to "fill in the gaps" that exist under traditional liability coverage, much of which is either questionable or non-existent to protect against cyber vulnerabilities. However, much of the data stored on SIS is some of the most "highly sought after" PII "on the black market, and most schools lack the resources to adequately protect the data."[20] Accordingly, because of the most basic (and unintentional) errors in judgment by even the most experienced and prepared IT departments and edtech vendors, cyber insurance is a "necessary evil" despite the added costs associated with the same.

B. Cyber Threats Common to Educational Institutions

The most common vulnerabilities to data maintained by educational institutions come mainly from

- internal, unauthorized access incidents (such as students and disgruntled employees who know the school operating and tech systems) that steal, destroy or publicly post school files, student data and other confidential information—some of which is stored not only on school computer programs and servers, are also shared (unintentionally or not) on IoTs.[21] personal laptops, cloud

19 Though separate terms of art, "data privacy" and "data security" are interconnected in that data privacy represents the collecting, using, and handling of PII (primarily the focus, as mentioned earlier, of FERPA), whereas data security is the process of maintaining the confidentiality and integrity of such PII.

20 Malia Herman, *Threat of Data-Privacy Litigation Fuels District Insurance Purchases*, Education Week (Oct. 19, 2015), https://www.edweek.org/technology/threat-of-data-privacy-litigation-fuels-district-insurance-purchases/2015/10.

21 IoT means "Internet of Things," or handheld devices (such as iPhones, Androids, and other smart devices) that engage multiple parties in interacting with each other by transferring data via integrated software and hardware programs over networks, essentially replacing the standalone desktop model.

applications, social media and file-sharing sites (*e.g.*, Dropbox, Google Drive or OneDrive);[22]

- external "cybercriminals" and hackers—who at times are disgruntled employees from trusted third-party vendors—that seek to steal SIS stored PII through phishing (a business email compromise, or "BEC" type of fraudulent email solicitation where an email is sent to the school by a hacker posing as a trusted vendor or other "reputable person or business"), ransomware (defined by the GAO as "an attempt to block access to a data system until a fee is paid) or other social engineering or security exploit, such as a trojan horse, computer virus/worm, etc.;[23] or,
- both.

Moreover, such attacks are not limited to students and parents. For example, concerning a BEC or spoofing attack, such as phishing, the Federal Bureau of Investigation ("FBI") and Internal Revenue Service ("IRS") have tracked such incidents and issued warnings to school business administrators of phishing scams which have victimized scores of school districts since 2017, and many of which target employee W-2 form information stored on school payroll systems "in an effort to have them release employees' confidential information. . . ."[24] As for ransomware, according to the FBI, IHEs are more susceptible than K-12 systems because "universities tend to have larger networks and more financial wherewithal to pay ransom demands."[25]

---

22 Jacey Fortin, *Student Charged in Cyberattacks at Miami-Dade Schools*, New York Times (Sept. 8, 2020), https://www.nytimes.com/2020/09/03/us/miami-dade-school-cyberattack.html?module=inline, where a 16-year-old student had successfully implemented Distributed Denial-of-Service ("DDoS") cyber attacks to the school district networks.

23 GAO Report to the Republican Leader, *Committee on Education and Labor, House of Representatives, Data Security: Recent K-12 Data Breaches Show That Students Are Vulnerable to Harm*, p. 5 (Sept. 2020).

24 Michael Molnar, *Education Week Market Brief, Phishing Scammers Target Schools for Employee Info*, Market Brief (Feb. 8, 2017), https://marketbrief.edweek.org/marketplace-k-12/phishing-scammers-target-schools-for-employee-info-school-association-says/.

25 Leo Duran, *Ransomware Attacks Force School Districts to Shore Up—or Pay Up,* Education Week (Jan. 10, 2017), https://www.edweek.org/technology/ransomware-attacks-force-school-districts-to-shore-up-or-pay-up/2017/01.

Weighed with the costs associated with safeguarding against these cyber vulnerabilities should also be the purchase of cyber insurance to reduce the exposure to losses stemming from these threats. According to respected insurance industry sources, and an analysis of over twelve million third-party losses from cyber-related data claims, industries worldwide have suffered billions in losses each year, and due to the proliferation of IoT devices, is expected to exceed $21 billion in losses from cyber vulnerabilities this year.[26] An insured's exposure to the costs associated with what are typically termed "first party losses" under a liability policy, such as: (i) post-breach investigation costs (including forensic analyses to determine the past, present and future consequences, and which typically involve third-party security firms, legal counsel and law enforcement); (ii) business loss (the costs related to "data loss recovery, potential closure, crisis management, and repairing reputation damage"); (iii) the expenses associated with customer and client notification; and in the context of third party losses, (iv) ensuing lawsuits that will necessarily incur legal expenses (*e.g.*, defense costs, settlements and judgments) and regulatory fines.[27]

Following the increase in educators working from home due to the COVID-19 pandemic, it was reported that "the average number of weekly attacks per organization in the academic sector in July-August [2020] increased by 30% from 468 to 608 when compared to the previous two months. The general increase when you consider all sectors in the USA is only 6.5%."[28] 2020 presented the most significant number of reported

---

26 *See, e.g.,* Fred Smith, *Understanding Cyber Liability Insurance*, eSchool News (Apr. 3, 2019), https://www.eschoolnews.com/2019/04/03/understanding-cyber-liability-insurance/; *see also* Bethan Moorcraft, *Cyber: The big 'back to school' risk that can't be overlooked*, Insurance Business America (Sept. 3, 2020), https://www.insurancebusinessmag.com/us/news/cyber/cyber-the-big-back-to-school-risk-that-cant-be-overlooked-232618.aspx; *see also* Insurance Information Institute, *Cyber risk: Threat and Opportunity*, p. 8 (Oct. 2016), https://www.iii.org/sites/default/files/docs/pdf/cyber_risk_wp_102716-92.pdf.

27 *Id.*

28 National Law Review, *Dealing with Two Schoolyard Bullies: Schools Are Forced to Contend with Cyber-attacks While Also Trying to Manage Covid-19 Crisis*, (Nov. 4, 2020), https://www.natlawreview.com/article/dealing-two-schoolyard-bullies-schools-are-forced-to-contend-cyber-attacks-while; *see also*, Check Point Blog, *Not for higher education: cybercriminals target academic & research institutions across the world*, Sept. 15, 2020,

cyber threats through learning via Zoom conferencing, in addition to a growing number of incidents of cyberbullying.[29] A new term to describe this form of HIB, Zoom bombing,[30] along with denial-of-service attacks (DoS), phishing campaigns and more, became more common. In addition, the following cyber incidents affecting school districts and IHEs over the past several years have become more commonplace and worthy of mention:

- In mid-November 2020, the Baltimore County public school system was shut down by what was described as a "catastrophic" ransomware attack that brought online classes being held during the COVID-19 pandemic to a complete shutdown, disrupting the learning of 115,000 students;[31]
- On June 1, 2020, the University of California San Francisco's ("UCSF") School of Medicine was the victim of a ransomware attack that encrypted some of its servers for its medical research facility. While the attack did not impact patient care or its COVID-19 research, the University paid $1.14 Million to decrypt its

---

https://blog.checkpoint.com/2020/09/15/not-for-higher-education-cybercriminals-target-academic-research-institutions-across-the-world/.

29 The GAO recently issued a report stating, "[w]hen the Coronavirus Disease 2019 (COVID-19) pandemic forced the closures of schools across the nation and the sudden transition to distance learning, attention to cybersecurity heightened, as notable incidents such as Zoom Bombing were widely reported" See, GAO Letter to the Republican Leader, Committee on Education and Labor, House of Representatives, *Data Security: Recent K-12 Data Breaches Show That Students Are Vulnerable to Harm* (Sept. 2020).

30 The GAO report defined "Zoom bombing" as the "disruption of teleconferences and online classrooms, often with pornographic or hate images and threatening language. The term is derived from the Zoom video conferencing platform but is used to describe disruptions to video conferencing more generally."

31 McKenna Oxenden, *Baltimore County schools suffered a ransomware attack. Here's what you need to know*, Baltimore Sun (Nov. 30, 2020), https://www.baltimoresun.com/maryland/baltimore-county/bs-md-co-what-to-know-schools-ransomware-attack-20201130-2j3ws6yffzcrrkfzzf3m43zxma-story.html.

information to regain access to its other crucial medical research being conducted for the public good;[32]

- In the first week of school for more than 118,000 students, the Hartford Public School district's SIS, which contained personal data, academic records and schedules, was effectively shut down due to a ransomware attack that targeted the software delivering real-time information on bus routes as part of the city's more than 200 government-operated servers;[33]
- Another ransomware attack led to hackers publicly posting student and employee PII stolen from Fairfax County Public Schools servers;[34] and,
- In the Montgomery County public school system in Maryland, a third-party educational technology service provider used to collect more than 6,000 students' test scores and other sensitive data suffered a data breach through a hacker's use of a script to repeatedly log into accounts where the user ID and passwords were the same.[35]

Given the amount of PII, such as social security numbers, medical records, payroll information, special education evaluations, etc. that school districts keep on file, when paired with the lack of funding dedicated towards preventive measures, it is not surprising that schools and districts are fertile ground for the hacker. Indeed, at the time of the

---

32 Davey Winder, *The University of California Pays $1 Million Ransom Following Cyber Attack,* Forbes (June 29, 2020).

33 Michael Gold, *First Pandemic, Now Ransomware: Attack Forces Hartford to Postpone School*, New York Times (Sept. 8, 2020), https://www.nytimes.com/2020/09/08/nyregion/hartford-schools-ransomware.html.

34 The attack was the 63rd school district in the nation last year to be impacted by a cyber incident. Joe Heim, *Hackers post stolen information from Fairfax school district*, (Oct. 10, 2020), https://www.washingtonpost.com/local/education/hackers-post-stolen-information-from-fairfax-school-district/2020/10/10/edf5f050-0b1a-11eb-859b-f9c27abe638d_story.html.

35 Joel Schwarz, *The Cyber-Security Problem Schools and Ed. Tech Need to Face*, Education Week (Jan. 30, 2020), https://www.edweek.org/technology/opinion-the-cyber-security-problem-schools-and-ed-tech-need-to-face/2020/01; *see also* [35] David Saleh Rauf, *Cyberattacks on Ed-Tech Companies Rare, but hugely Disruptive, Report Finds*, Education Week Market Brief (Nov. 16, 2020).

writing of this book, at least one educational technology expert warned that, unless IT experts become intricately involved in the remote learning process, a continued "spike in the number of COVID-related phishing scams, and malware can be introduced through the sites that users have visited, the links they have clicked on, or the material they've downloaded—and also through home routers that aren't very secure."[36]

As such, the following message bears repeating: when it comes to insurance coverage, *the cost of not protecting against the increased risk of unauthorized data exposure due to cyber vulnerabilities likely outweighs the savings*. Moreover, as discussed further below, schools and districts should not even assume their "blanket cyber" policies will protect them in the event of a unique type of cyber threat, no less their general liability protection.[37] Instead, in partnership with brokers, SBAs should carefully read the provisions of their liability policies—even including so-called comprehensive cyber endorsements—to ensure they are not deprived of coverage down the road for cyber attacks.

C. Cyber Coverage for Cyber Threats

How best can a school or district or IHE address the fallout from cyber attacks? One possible way is to place the cart before the horse by dedicating the funding needed to purchase cyber insurance to ensure that the costs associated with cyber attacks are minimized if not obviated altogether. Seen another way, an SBA positing there is no funding to purchase additional coverage for cyber attacks will not suffer fools gladly. As one prominent brokerage firm servicing school districts pointed out,

> victims of crimes usually get sympathy, but if a school is the victim of a cybercrime attack, it will not get such sympathy. It will

---

36 Dennis Pierce, *Here's why cybersecurity experts are concerned about remote learning*, eSchool Week (July 16, 2020), https://www.eschoolnews.com/2020/07/16/heres-why-cyber-security-experts-are-concerned-about-remote-learning/.

37 As alluded to earlier, cyber attacks come in several forms, and may/may not be covered under a cyber policy without examining the coverage in detail. Some examples of cyber attacks are: brute-force attacks; password guessing; spoofing/phishing; BEC's; rootkits; trojan horses; computer viruses, etc.—each of which may have its own or categorized lines of coverage.

be instantly labeled as irresponsible, get investigated and questioned about what it did to prevent the attack from happening, and if the answer is not adequate, it will be found liable, face serious fines and lawsuits—*even if the district relied on a trusted third party vendor or an outsourced IT support company to protect it*. Claiming ignorance is not an acceptable defense, and this giant, expensive, and reputation-destroying nightmare will land squarely on its shoulders. In short, your bank is not required to replace funds stolen due to cyber attacks, and unless you have a specific type of insurance policy, any such financial losses will be denied coverage under the school's liability policies.[38]

As such, the answer is for SBAs and school districts to get on board with the purchase of first- and third-party cyber coverage for theft of SIS/PII data. Such coverage can address and provide coverage for pre-breach education and training costs, as well as breach response expenses (e.g., legal fees, forensic investigation, data restoration, etc.). Specifically, cyber insurance can serve as a gap filler to its general liability and property insurance already in place, compensating the district for expenses incurred by making the required notifications in the event of a data breach, including the cost of regulatory proceedings related to a data breach, media liability (e.g., invasion of privacy, IP infringement, plagiarism, and negligence), cyberextortion/ransomware, and BEC incidents. Such cyber coverage will also include third party coverage to protect the district in the event of a claim or lawsuit stemming from a cyber related breach.[39] As such, a district's insurance coverage program should incorporate cyber insurance as part and parcel of its risk management portfolio.

Given the availability of such coverage, an SBA seeking to impress the school board by taking a "penny wise; pound foolish" approach to keeping costs down by not obtaining the same may be placing the district

38 Interview with Mitchell Mund, President and CEO of Fortitude Insurance Group, Florham Park, New Jersey (Jan. 27, 2021).

39 As to cost, typically, the premium to be paid for additional cyber coverage is usually measured against factors such as the total number of employees, overall (and past) risk exposure, level of IT and data security systems in place, and overall student population. As such, if a district pays approximately $800,000 in worker's compensation, general liability, and property insurance coverage, it can expect to pay an additional $25,000 to $30,000 for added cyber coverage, arguably making as one SBA stated, a "no brainer" to obtain.

in the position of hundreds of thousands of dollars in liabilities from uncovered losses. Whatever the losses, they will most certainly impact funding to a greater extent than had cyber coverage not been purchased, and may lead to the closure and cessation of district operations altogether, not to meniton the ensuing crisis management and exposure to potential third party claims from victims as the result of a cyber attack. That is not to mention exorbitant fines, penalties, and a public relations fallout that will almost certainly adversely affect the district's reputation for years to come—a dire and irreparable consequence at a time when learning has become a competitive marketplace for students and parents.[40] Accordingly, however "expert" an SBA might believe herself/himself to be on cyber risks and a district's need for cyber coverage, it would be prudent to work with an experienced cyber broker in getting a solid understanding of what coverage exists under traditional liability policies for cyber claims.

However, what cyber coverage may be needed to address cyber threats adequately?[41] In analyzing cyber coverage, educational institutions should be mindful that not all cyber coverage is created equal, and issues such as how a cyber "loss" is defined, what specific coverages are available and whether they fit into the institution's overall risk assessment, and whether there are any exclusions to certain types of cyber threats, should be addressed in policy analysis. A typical formulation of coverage under a cyber policy can be found in one policy form which provides one or more

---

40 It should be noted that, in the context of fines and penalties, those that are punitive or based on intentional or willful conduct (i.e., not negligent) may not be covered or, at best, will nonetheless be disclaimed by the insurer.

41 For example, and as alluded to in the chapter on professional liability insurance, there has been growing insurance coverage litigation on the issue of what constitutes covered "property" in the context of PII related losses under liability and property policies. Usually, the dispute centers around technology's increased use of IoT ("IoT") devices using data that insurers often argue is "non-tangible", and thus, not covered "property." Given that many districts are encouraged to use cloud-based programs, many times through a third-party "edtech" vendor, the SBA should ensure there is protection against cyber threats that might compromise data systems, whether stored as hardware or software. *See,* Renier P. Pierantoni, *Vendor's Products Liability Coverage: An Option for Malware-Based Cyber Breaches*, Law.com (Online) / N.J.L.J. (Dec. 13, 2019), https://www.law.com/njlawjournal/2019/12/13/tapping-into-a-vendors-products-liability-coverage-an- option-to-consider-for-malware-based-cyber-breaches/.

"insuring clauses" or modules of coverage for cyber-related losses, such as:

- Multimedia Liability
- Network Security and Privacy[42]
- Data Recovery & Business Interruption[43]
- Crisis Management & Customer Notification
- Data Extortion
- Payment Card Industry Fines or Penalties

Each of these individual "Insuring Agreements" all set forth the carrier's promise to "pay . . . all damages and claims expenses . . . which [the institution] become legally obligated to pay because of any claim . . . during the policy period. . . ."[44] They differ in what "activities" each clause covers that results in "any actual or alleged wrongful acts".

Take, for example, the following "Network Security & Privacy Liability" third party insuring clause, which reads in two parts as

---

42 In many cyber policies, this type of coverage usually seeks to protect the insured against security breaches and can include coverage for data breach, cyber extortion, ransomware, and data restoration coverage, as well as privacy-related losses arising out of privacy law violations.

43 This coverage in most policies protects against losses related to operational risk events, such as lost profits and fixed expenses resulting at the time operations were impacted by the cyber incident. Some of the coverage disputes in this area center around the distinction between a cyber incident implicating the insured's computer network or a third-party network (such as a trusted vendor providing services to the insured). Other disputes focus on an analysis of whether the type of security failure (i.e., transmission of malware, DDoS attack, unauthorized access to the network, etc.) that lead to the business interruption claim was—in itself—covered (i.e., social engineered attacks vs. ransomware, for example, and some of which are not covered and obtained as a separate endorsement to the cyber policy).

44 This, as is the case with nearly all cyber policies, provides for "claims made" coverage, i.e., requiring the claim to be submitted to the carrier during the policy period (or other designated reporting period). This is distinct from an "occurrence" based policy, which provides coverage for events (not claims) during the policy period, "even if the claim is brought many years in the future. . . ." *See, e.g., Craft v. Philadelphia Indem. Ins. Co.,* 343 P.3d 951, 957 (Colo. 2015), *opinion after certified question answered,* 599 F. App'x 846 (10th Cir. 2015).

covering—first—any "**security breach** on **your computer network(s)** or **privacy breach** which results in any actual or alleged wrongful acts, which for this agreement shall mean" that result in—second—certain cyber incidents. The latter including the "failure to prevent or hinder unauthorized access to or unauthorized use of a **computer network**; failure to prevent physical theft, or loss of information, or **hardware** controlled by you, your people, or processes; security failures; false communications designed to trick the user into surrendering personal information (commonly known as 'phishing' or 'pharming') that results in":

a. "The alteration, copying, corruption, destruction, deletion, or damage to electronic **data** on a **computer network**";
b. "Unauthorized disclosure of commercial, personal, or private information or **data**";
c. "failure to disclose a breach of security affecting" PII; and
d. "The failure to prevent transmission of **malicious code** or **computer virus** from a **computer network** to third party computers or systems."[45]

Similarly, the first party insuring clause for "Data Recovery and Business Interruption" promises to "indemnify" (e.g., reimburse or pay for first-party liabilities) for "**first-party costs and expenses** . . . and for **loss of business income** . . . as a result of a **first-party insured event** incurred by [the institution]. . . ."[46] The bold terms and phrases are defined elsewhere in the policy, which may present to the institution and, even in some cases, the broker, some puzzling questions related to coverage. Take, for example, how the phrase "**computer network(s)**" is defined:

---

45 Other "wrongful acts" covered (and mostly defined) under the policy are privacy breaches, security breaches or other breach of privacy regulations; DDoS attacks; and loss of employee PII.

46 The form policy defines "**first-party costs and expenses**" as not including "loss of profits or **loss of business income**", where the latter is separately defined as "net income. . . which would have been earned had no first-party event occurred. . . or [r]easonable, continuing, and normal operating expenses that were incurred and affected by a first-party insured event." The form policy further defines a "**first party insured event**" as requiring a "monetary loss sustained. . . at the [school's/district's] premises, or . . . external backup, data center or storage facilities. . . ."

Computer network(s) means interconnected electronic, wireless, web, or similar systems (including all **hardware** and software) used to process **data** or information in an analog, digital, electronic or wireless format including, but not limited to, computer programs, electronic data, operating systems, servers, media libraries, associated input and output devices, mobile devices, networking equipment, websites, the internet of things (IoT), extranets, off line storage facilities (to the extent that they hold electronic data), and electronic backup equipment.

Let us examine an actual incident: the multiple cyber attacks by a 16-year-old student that led to the shutdown of Miami-Dade's online classes for the first three days of the district's virtual classes in September 2020. According to at least one news report, the "student admitted to using a tool called a 'Low Orbit Ion Cannon (LOIC),' . . . [a] software that is easy to download and can be used to disrupt websites, [and is] the same tool that the hacker group Anonymous used a decade ago to cripple companies such as MasterCard, Visa and PayPal. The program is designed to overwhelm a system with what's known as a 'distributed denial of service attack,' or DDoS attack, which uses a slew of random computers to overwhelm a website with packets of data."[47]

While the foregoing policy form example specifically provides coverage for DDoS attacks under one of the sub-provisions in the "Network Security & Privacy Liability" insuring clause, what if the attack were not DDoS? What if the attack instead came in the form of a "spoof" email to an administrator that was unsuspectingly opened and led to not only the shutdown of operations, but the unauthorized dissemination of sensitive student data that was maintained only minimally on the school's network, and kept mainly by a third-party IT service provider? Let us add that the policy form could have provided coverage via an endorsement that expanded the term "**computer network**" to include the outsourcing of the school network to a third-party IT service provider; however, the SBA, in an attempt to save money after having been constrained to purchase cyber coverage at all, decided not to purchase the endorsement.[48]

---

47 Colleen Wright & David Ovalle, *Student arrested for cyberattack against Miami schools used 'easy to prevent' program*, Miami Herald (Sept. 3, 2020), https://www.miamiherald.com/news/local/education/article245461020.html.

48 *See* "Outsource and IT Service Provider Extension for Busines Interruption" endorsement form RPSDependantBI (Feb. 2019).

Working with these assumptions for purposes of our hypothetical, at first glance to an SBA, it appears coverage exists under both the "Network Security & Privacy Liability" third-party and "Data Recovery and Business Interruption" first-party insuring clauses, respectively, for the district's losses. However, regarding third party coverage, was there was a breach of the school's (*e.g.*, "your") "**computer network**" where the network was—as the carrier will be sure to argue—outsourced to and operated by a third-party IT service provider? While the SBA might be convinced—correctly so—there should be no bar to coverage for third party claims because the term "**computer network**" expressly contemplates the use of "off line storage facilities (to the extent that they hold electronic data), and electronic backup equipment," can the SBA know for sure? Especially since the SBA, to save a few dollars, decided not to obtain the endorsement because she/he saw little use for it in the context of business interruption losses in a federally and state funded non-profit school setting?[49] In this context, was the minimal amount in savings worth the potential legal battle over coverage with the carrier?[50] Should the SBA have consulted insurance coverage counsel to consider whether to purchase the "Outsource and IT Service Provider Extension for Business Interruption" endorsement? Experienced coverage counsel could have advised the SBA that the absence of the endorsement might be weaponized by the carrier to argue it reflected the SBA's decision to not extend coverage to outsourced technology edtech providers for the district's third-party losses. This is one of many instances where experienced policyholder counsel can advise the SBA and school district that carriers—when given the opportunity—may seek to focus efforts on disclaiming or otherwise avoiding coverage for cyber claims, and rely on the insured's purchasing decisions to do so. In short, an insured should never assume coverage when there may be a doubt as to the same.

---

49 This would include the SBA paying little attention to the fact that "business interruption loss" is defined to include "reasonable, continuing, and normal operating expenses."

50 It is recognized that the claim in our hypothetical may be covered, nonetheless, as a privacy breach or breach of privacy regulation. However, as pointed out earlier in this chapter, careful attention should be paid to ensure provisions provide the coverage sought, and where an SBA seeks to do so without the advice of savvy coverage counsel or an experienced broker, then the question for the SBA becomes whether she or he is aware of that which she/he is not aware or knows what she/he does not know.

D. Conclusion

To be sure the right level of coverage is obtained, consultation with an experienced broker expert in cyber coverage is necessary. An experienced broker can guide school administration through the quandary of coverage, exclusions, exceptions to exclusions, and numerous endorsements to best tailor coverage to address an educational institutions' unique cyber risks. To not do so may be a foolhardy decision that may leave the school, district, and, most importantly, its students without the protection needed to make learning successful.

Chapter 25

Sports and Entertainment*

A. All the World's a Stage Though the World Is (Still) Not Enough[1]

Despite your brother-in-law's slavish fealty to the Chicago Cubs, for purposes of reviewing cyber risks, sports (professional and amateur) are most often treated as an extension of the entertainment industry. (The Cubs are *entertainment*, not real life, Bill—we digress). If it seems that sports are everywhere though, there is some data to back up that perception. The market for sports makes up a significant proportion of amounts spent on entertainment as a whole.[2] It seems like this trend will continue and the turf (forgive the pun) is under relentless renovation and renewal, given how teams, venues and programs maximize opportunities for engagement with fans and participants.[3] The entertainment industry proper, of course, knows a little something about audience engagement. These industries

---

* By Peggy Reetz and Greg Mantych.

1 Number nineteen in the James Bond film series starred Piece Brosnan in *The World is Not Enough* (Danjaq, Eon Productions, Nov. 19, 1999)

2 Scott Roxborough, *Sports Rights Now Make up 26 Percent of Global Content Spend*, THE HOLLYWOOD REPORTER (Oct. 16, 2019), https://www.hollywoodreporter.com/news/sports-rights-now-make-up-26-percent-global-content-spend-1247865.

3 *See* Pete Giorgio, 2021, *Outlook for the US Sports Industry*, DELOITTE CENTER FOR TECHNOLOGY, MEDIA & TELECOMMUNICATIONS, https://www2.deloitte.com/us/en/pages/technology-media-and-telecommunications/articles/ sports-business-trends-disruption.html ("One of the biggest sources of alternative revenue for US sports organizations in 2021 could be data monetization, particularly in the areas of fan engagement, player and team performance, and sports betting."); *see also* Kim Lyons, *CBS All Access App Had Technical Difficulties at the Start of the Super Bowl*, THE VERGE (Feb. 7, 2021); Mike Snider, *Super Bowl 2021: How to Watch and Stream, Including with Friends on Yahoo Sports App*, *USA Today* (Feb. 5, 2021, updated 10:39 am ET Feb. 7, 2021), available at https://www.usatoday.com/story/tech/2021/02/05/super-bowl-2021-how-watch-stream/4386968001/ (The nickname for [Super Bowl LV) could be the "Super 'Streaming' Bowl.")

likewise also tend to be early adopters of the latest technology, which can create its own set of challenges.[4] It is with these expanded platforms in mind that we review the cyber risks facing such high profile sectors.

For the sake of trying to package the very disparate mediums and spaces involved in sports and entertainment, this chapter broadly will review cyber risks and exposures within this sector, including an attempt to capture emerging and unique risks to these endeavors. Next, there are some cyber coverage grants that have gained particular relevance to sports and entertainment, which will be highlighted here. Finally, there may be strategies beyond insurance and even cybersecurity for these industries to consider when managing such an extensive spectrum of issues.

B. Scale of the Potential Exposure: You're Gonna Need a Bigger Boat . . . and Better Field Vision

To put their numbers in context, the sports and entertainment industries produced two of the top fifteen largest data breaches in recent history—Zynga and My Fitness Pal.[5] In September 2019, the creator of Farmville, Zynga, was hacked, with the perpetrator claiming to have gained access to 218 million accounts registered with the site. Zynga confirmed that email addresses, hashed passwords, phone numbers and user names or identifications were stolen.[6] In February of 2018, the UnderArmor-owned fitness app MyFitnessPal was breached, compromising user names, email addresses, and hashed passwords for 150 million customers. MyFitnessPal required users to change their passwords.[7]

---

4 *See* Rosenbach v. Six Flags Entertainment, 129 N.E.3d 1197 , 2019 IL 123186 (2019) (allegations that amusement park violated Illinois' Biometric Information Privacy Act, BIPA, when Six Flags took plaintiff's son's fingerprint as part of his purchase of a season pass to the amusement park).

5 D. Swinhoe, *The 15 Biggest Data Breaches of the 21st Century*, CSO ONLINE (Jan. 8, 2021), https://www.csoonline.com/article/2130877/the-biggest-data-breaches-of-the-21st-century.html.

6 *Id.*

7 *Id.*

1. *Lights? Off. Camera? Off. Action On!*

Some of the most extraordinary data breaches have involved entertainment giants. In 2014, Sony Pictures Entertainment was hacked by a group calling itself the Guardians of Peace. Reportedly, the group had ties to North Korea.[8] The hackers went on to release a huge amount of information, which was mostly sensitive and some of it proved to be embarrassing to the executives involved. The confidential sensitive information included employee salary and performance details. The perpetrators also released five movies, four of which had been previously unreleased. In an even more peculiar twist to these events, one of the movies released was *The Interview*, a satirical comedy involving a CIA plot to assassinate the leader of North Korea. North Korean officials had even complained about the film to Sony executives in Japan.[9] Following the unauthorized disclosure, Sony initially decided not to officially release the movie but then agreed to release it in an online version via on-demand platforms. Due to this decision, independent movie theaters who had agreed to show it pulled out. The result was a loss to the studio—a film produced for $44 million grossed about $36 million.[10]

---

8 Apparently, that claim may just be another part of the "story." *Tatiana Siegel, Five Years Later, Who Really Hacked Sony?* THE HOLLYWOOD REPORTER, (Nov. 24, 2019) https://www.hollywoodreporter.com/features/ five-years-who-hacked-sony-1257591 (". . .22 days of massive data dumps that exposed embarrassing executive email exchanges. . .trade secrets. . .and five upcoming full-length films. . .") [hereinafter *Sony*].

9 E. VanDerWerff, T. B. Lee, *The 2014 Sony Hacks, Explained*, VOX (Jun. 3, 2015), https://www.vox.com/2015/1/20/18089084/sony-hack-north-korea.

10 *Id.* "In the case of Sony Pictures, the attackers got quite a bit. The entertainment company has reportedly lost control of more than 100 terabytes of data without the company, or its security measures, detecting the breach. SPE's security teams' inability to catch the attackers in the act of stealing so much data is a direct result of its lack of focus on security, according to a paper by security-services firm Thinkst, outlining the lessons learned from the attack." *See also* R. Lemos, *Unprecedented' Cyberattack No Excuse for Sony Breach, Pros Say*, ARS TECHNICA (Dec. 9, 2014), http://arstechnica.com/security/2014/12/unprecedented-cyberattack-no-excuse-for-sony-breach-pros-say/; Sony settled the class action that followed this incident with terms finalized in October 2015, and approved by the court in April 2016. The class included over 15,000 current/former employees, freelancers and celebrities with contracts with Sony. The settlement included

Sony, of course, has also been the victim of other attacks on their gaming platform, PlayStation.[11] In April 2011, gamers were locked out of the network and then Sony revealed that an unauthorized person had access to users' names, addresses, emails, birthdates, passwords, logins, and security questions amongst other things.[12] Not to be outdone by their film and gaming soul mates, U.S. professional sports teams have had a string of notorious data security incidents—electronic play stealing; victims to phishing scams; hacking into competitor's records.[13] These issues are not restricted to U.S. "games" or "entertainment," when in 2019, the gaming company EA disclosed that the personal information for registrants to the *FIFA 20* global series had been compromised.[14]

2. One-Man Bands and Switch Hitters

These stories highlight the scope of vulnerabilities related to managing data, information and content in these conspicuous sectors. It also

---

funds for up to $10,000 for each claimant for identity theft losses and a $1million fund for up to $1,000 for each with respect to credit-fraud protection services; attorneys' fees were approved of approximately $2.6 million. See, Corona v. Sony Pictures Entertainment, Inc., Case No. 14-CV-09600-RGK-E (Oct. 19, 2015); Warwick Ashford, Sony $8m Breach Settlement Underlines Need to Secure Personal Data, Computer Weekly (Oct. 22, 2015), https://www.computerweekly.com/news/4500255929/Sony-8m-breach-settlement-underlines-need-to-secure-personal-data.

11 R. Trenholm, S. Rosenblatt, *Sony Hacked Again, This time the PlayStation Network*, CNET (Dec. 8, 2014), https://www.cnet.com/news/sony-hacked-again-this-time-the-playstation-store/.

12 John Gaudiosi, *Why Sony Didn't Learn from Its 2011 Hack*, FORTUNE (Dec. 24, 2014), https://fortune.com/2014/12/24/why-sony-didnt-learn-from-its-2011-hack/ ("The Company reported a hard cost of $171 million. . . Sony and Microsoft. . .have experienced smaller breaches of their online gaming networks, including another PlayStation Network attack in October 2011 and a PlayStation Store attack [in December 2014]. But the April 2011 attack stands alone for its size and scope.")

13 Nathaniel Grow & Scott J. Shackelford, *The Sport of Cybersecurity: How Professional Sport Leagues Can Better Protect the Competitive Integrity of Their Games*," 61 B.C.L. REV. 473 (2020), available at https://law digitalcommons.bc.edu/bclr/vol61/iss2/3.

14 Taylor Lyles, *EA Discloses Massive Data Breach Affecting Thousands of Competitive FIFA Players*, DIGITAL TRENDS (Oct. 4, 2019), https://www.digitaltrends.com/gaming/ea-fifa-data-breach/.

illustrates how even for operations like live events, there is a growing reliance on digital applications and the collection of data and information critical to producing the event.[15] While the music, film and gaming sectors may be particular targets for bad actors, some suggest that these industries have a long way to go to meet the momentous cybersecurity challenges presented, especially given the scale of valuable content created, collected, re-packaged, refined and distributed.[16]

If content is king,[17] then perhaps streaming is the crown prince. Television, film, music, and sports have been dramatically caught up and

---

15 The 2020 Tokyo Olympics was supposed to present new streaming opportunities. Steve Impey, *Revenue Streams Will Multiply: How the Olympics' Postponement can Boost the Sports Tech Industry,* SPORTS PRO MEDIA (Jul. 13, 2020), https://www.sportspromedia.com/analysis/tokyo-2020-olympics-wimbledon-digital-revenue-remote-technology-ibm-alibaba ("[T]technologies that were due to be trialled this summer could now be scaled into more powerful tools by the time the event is due to reconvene in Japan next year."). The stakes remain high as news reports surfaced that the Tokyo Olympics were also potential targets for disruption. *See, e.g.,* Ami Miyazaki, Jack Tarrant, *Japan Will Take Steps to Guard Against Olympics Cyberattacks*, REUTERS (Oct. 20, 2020), https://www.reuters.com/article/olympics-2020-cyber-russia-idUSKBN2750IN. *See also* Catalin Cimpanu, *UK says Russia Was Preparing Cyber-Attacks against the Tokyo Olympics*, ZDNET (Oct. 19, 2020), https://www.zdnet.com/article/uk-says-russia-was-preparing-cyber-attacks-against-the-tokyo-olympics/ ("Targets included the Games' organizers, logistics services, and sponsors. . .In February 2018, Russian hackers deployed the OlympicDestroyer that crippled web servers during the opening ceremony of the 2018 Winter Olympics.").

16 *Media and Entertainment Industry Unprepared for Cyber Risks,* SECURITY MAGAZINE (Sept. 13, 2018), https://www.securitymagazine.com/articles/89404-media-and-entertainment-industry-unprepared-for-cyber-risks.

17 Bill Gates wrote an essay in 1996 published on the Microsoft website entitled "Content is King," in reference to the transformative possibilities of the internet (". . .the broad opportunities for most companies involve supplying information or entertainment. . .Opportunities are remarkable, and many companies are laying plans to create content for the Internet." Heath Evans, *Content is King*, MEDIUM (Jan. 30, 2017), https://medium.com/@HeathEvans/content-is-king-essay-by-bill-gates-1996-df74552f80d9; Luis Congdon, *Why What Bill Gates said about the Internet in 1996 is Truer than Ever Today*, ENTREPRENEUR (Dec. 5, 2017), https://www.entrepreneur.com/article/305300; Jonathan A. Knee, *Why*

in some cases swept away by the streaming tide.[18] But this may be where the content providers face their cyber Waterloo. The services have to address multiple cyber fronts as they have been targets for distributing malware, stealing passwords and launching spam and phishing attacks.[19] For many, there is no going back—both for those producing the content and for those consuming it.[20] Securing those platforms for the protection and integrity of what is being delivered, as well as who it is being delivered to, may be the coin of the realm.

Probably because of the amount of money involved, or the stature of these enterprises, not surprisingly the entertainment and sports worlds have also generated their own share of coverage disputes relating to cyber incidents or data issues.[21] Given that much of the media content produced in these areas is consumed on ever more devices and media offerings,

---

Content Isn't King, THE ATLANTIC (July/August 2011 Issue), *available at* https://www.theatlantic.com/magazine/archive/2011/07/why-content-isnt-king/308551/ (quoting from a Kaspersky research article, *The Streaming Wars: A Cybercriminal's Perspective*, (Jul. 16, 2020), https://securelist.com/the-streaming-wars-a-cybercriminals-perspective/97851/).

18 Katie Dwyer, *Critical Risks Facing the Entertainment Industry*, *Risk and Insurance* (Aug. 2, 2018), https://riskandinsurance.com/6-critical-risks-facing-the-entertainment-industry/ ("Streaming services. . .are reliant on uninterrupted service. A cyber attack that renders those platforms inaccessible could anger advertisers seeking a certain amount of visibility and will certainly frustrate viewers paying a monthly membership fee for on-demand content.")

19 Macy Bayern, *Cybercriminals Disguising as Top Streaming Services to Spread Malware*, TECH REPUBLIC (Jul. 16, 2020), https://www.techrepublic.com/article/cybercriminals-disguising-as-top-streaming-services-to-spread-malware/.

20 Brookes Barnes, *The Streaming Era Has Finally Arrived. Everything Is About to Change*, THE NEW YORK TIMES (Nov. 19, 2019), *available at* https://www.nytimes.com/2019/11/18/business/media/streaming-hollywood-revolution.html.

21 Zurich Am. Ins. v. Sony Corp. of Am., No. 651982/2011, 2014 N.Y. Misc. LEXIS 5141, at *67–72 (N.Y. Sup. Ct. Feb. 24, 2014) (describing how an insured sought coverage under CGL terms for alleged transmission of private information by hackers and finding no coverage); *see also* L.A. Lakers, Inc. v. Fed. Ins. Co., 869 F.3d 795, 799 (9th Cir. 2017) (seeking coverage under a directors and officers policy for alleged invasion of privacy allegations where the Lakers reported inappropriately sent out automated texts in violation of the TCPA, Telephone Consumer Protection Act).

identifying all the relevant risks, and managing them appropriately, may give rise to an endless cycle of opening night nerves or pre-game jitters for both front and back offices.

C. Deconstructing that Scene and Diagramming that Play—Risks and Exposures

With these topical scenarios in mind, the risks and potential exposures facing sports and entertainment entities can be broken down into a few categories as a way to understand how the risks are evaluated, which risks present exposure to different sections of a cyber policy and where there may be overlapping considerations in establishing coverage.

1. What Kind of Information Are We Talking About?

Like with the array of where the data can be collected or distributed, the types of data subject to vulnerabilities is just as expansive. These would include:

- audience/fan information (emails, mailing addresses, demographic details, purchasing habits)
- personnel/performer information (personally identifiable information; salary/contractual details; human resources/ management records and communications; biometric data on players)[22]
- financial records
- statistical data (ticket sales, streaming/broadcast details)
- operations details (venues/facilities information)
- digital/electronic content
    - content for broadcast (scripts, film, animation, sound, music)
    - content for live events (visual effects, performance enhancements)
    - content for interactive engagement (gaming, fantasy leagues)

22 Grow and Shackleford, *supra* note 13, at 489.

2. *What's It Worth?*

Not only is the data of all shapes and sizes, the value of that data can be extraordinary. The typical assets at stake include:

- intellectual property rights (created, purchased, packaged or sold)
- performer, player, producer personal and confidential information
- user, fan, audience details and demographics

3. *Where in the World Is It?*

The expanse of what needs to be managed can also be breathtaking. The systems, applications and media to secure can include:

- Specific software created for content/media/venue (music composition; music orchestration; film and music production; facilities operations)
- Apps for fans/audience
- Social media content
- Networks/systems (connectivity; distribution; management)

Some of the risks are well-known to cyber insurers: network security and continuity; confidentiality of private or proprietary information; misappropriation or infringement of another's work. Other risks are just amplified by the magnitude of the potential exposure: unauthorized disclosure of creative content; unauthorized disclosure of celebrity personal or financial records; network disruptions of large-scale live events.[23] Then there is the overlapping nature of the risks: content from players or performers may be incorporated into fan apps or social media promotions (potential limitations on use of images or content); collection of data for diverse purposes (appropriate consent and methods of

---

23 *Sony, supra* note 8; Lyles, *supra* note 14.

collection[24]); impermissible use of authorized media (video replay used to decipher opposing team's signs[25]).

D. From Classic Covers to Zone Defense—Coverages and Limitations

Some of the issues that typically arise in the entertainment and sports realms are readily addressed in insurance coverages that are specific to media risks. To the extent that a cyber policy includes standard "media liability" or any "multimedia" insuring provisions, wrongful acts like libel, slander, plagiarism, piracy, infringement of rights to publicity or commercial appropriation will trigger such provisions.[26] The same may be true where there is an alleged copyright infringement or trademark infringement, which are common allegations in media rights disputes.[27] Those types of high profile media issues do not often involve class

---

24 For example, biometric data that is collected on players for performance or health reasons but then is used in promotional materials. Collection of data on minors, of course, is regulated under federal, state and foreign statutes, including the Children's Online Privacy Protection Act (COPPA). *See* Sara Ovaska-Few, *The Perils of Collecting Children's Data*, FM-MAGAZINE (Oct. 1, 2018), https://www.fm-magazine.com/issues/2018/oct/collecting-childrens-data.html, see also Cecilia Kang, *Toymaker VTech Settles Charges of Violating Child Privacy Law*, THE NEW YORK TIMES (Jan. 8, 2018), *available at* https://www.nytimes.com/2018/01/08/business/vtech-child-privacy.html (VTech settled with the FTC for collecting digital data on children without parents' permission and failed to secure the information).

25 Grow and Shackleford, *supra* note 13, at 491.

26 J. Williams-Alvarez, *Why Celebrities like Lindsay Lohan are Suing Video Game Studios*, ENGADGET (Nov. 18, 2014), https://www.engadget.com/2014-11-18-gaming-likeness-lawsuit-explainer.htm ("In New York, where Lohan's suit was filed, the right of publicity law is codified as part of its Right of Privacy statute. . .provid[ing] protection for a person's name, portrait, picture and voice. . .").

27 *See, e.g.,* copy of Chubb Group of Insurance Companies *Cybersecurity by Chubb*℠ policy disclosed in the case of P.F. Chang's China Bistro, Inc. v. Fed. Ins. Co., No. CV-15-01322-PHX-SMM, 2016 WL 3055111 (D. Ariz. May 31, 2016) (a so-called "content injury").

litigation but, of course, may generate some monetary damage exposure, and maybe more so, reputational harm.[28]

1. Rehearse—and Insure—Like It's Opening Night

Class litigation usually arises out of the disclosure of or misuse use of user information.[29] As discussed in earlier chapters, in those cases, a cyber policy may respond where there was an alleged security failure (an inability to prevent a third party from gaining access to systems). If the user information included passwords or other sensitive details, a cyber policy's privacy liability provisions will be implicated, which terms may include language that even a breach of the online privacy policy provisions would be considered a breach of privacy.[30] Of course, if there is personal information exposed, then notification costs (and the preliminary investigation costs) will implicate a cyber policy's first party provisions. To the extent that such a disclosure also means that the organization will have to review various statutes and regulations, and respond accordingly,

---

28 The Associated Press, *$60 Million Settlement Approved in N.C.A.A. Video Game Lawsuit*, (Jul. 2015) (plaintiffs alleged that the N.C.A.A. and the gaming company Electronic Arts illegally used college football and basketball players' names and likenesses in video games for years). The exception may prove the rule, however, where former UCLA star basketball player led an antitrust case against the NCAA and EA Sports, as well as the Collegiate Licensing Company for wrongfully using college athletes' images commercially. *See also*, K. Sweeney, *Why Did EA Sports Stop Making NCAA Football Video Games?* SPORTS ILLUSTRATED (Feb. 2, 2021), *available at* https://www.si.com/college/2021/02/02/ncaa-football-ea-sports-stopped-making-games.

29 *Supra* note 10. *See also*, *supra*, note 21, *L.A. Lakers, Inc.*; *see also*, allegations in the Sony PlayStation breach actions, *In re Sony Gaming Networks & Customer Data Sec. Breach Litig.*, MDL 11MD2258 AJB MDD, 2014 WL 223677 (S.D. Cal. Jan. 21, 2014).

30 For example, in *In re Premera Blue Cross Customers Data Security Breach Litigation*, No. 3:15-md-2633 SI, 2017 WL539578 (D. Or. Feb. 9, 2017) (plaintiffs alleged amongst other things that the entity violated Oregon consumer protection statutes because they were deceived by the privacy notices provided).

then any coverage for regulatory investigations also should be covered under most current cyber policies.[31]

As such, the most prominent insuring agreements within cyber coverages may be the most significant "assets" in the event of a ransom attack or misuse of information for any high profile entity whose management is worried about a) responding and investigating a "crisis" event like ransomware and b) ensuring they have resources to respond to any regulatory inquiry or third-party liability. For example, in one of the Sony hack scenarios, Sony sued its commercial general liability (CGL) insurer[32] seeking defense and indemnification for data breach claims, which included responding to over 50 class action complaints. The suit sought coverage under the Coverage B, personal and advertising injury coverage section of that CGL policy and the insurer disputed coverage arguing in part that there was no "publication" as a result of the breach. Under usual CGL terms, coverage may apply where "publication in any manner of the material. . .violates a person's right of privacy."[33] Sony would have had no such hurdle if it sought coverage under a cyber policy that included today's most market competitive wording.[34] (In fact, Sony

---

31 See discussion of cyber insurance policy terms in Sasha Romanosky, Lillian Ablon, Andreas Kuehn, Therese Jones, *Content Analysis of Cyber Insurance Policies: How do carriers write policies and price cyber risk?* [Draft], the U.S. Federal Trade Commission (2017), https://www.ftc.gov/system/files/documents/public_comments/2017/10/00012-141437.pdf ("Cyber insurance, like most insurance products, generally distinguishes between two broad loss categories, *first party* and *third party*. . . .first party coverage covers losses for costs incurred directly by the insured [and] includes costs related to investigating the cause of a data breach or security incident, costs associated with restoring business services, the costs of notifying affected individuals, credit monitoring services, costs incurred from public relations and media services in order to communicate the event, extortion and ransom payments, and losses associated with business interruption.").

32 Zurich Am. Ins. v. Sony Corp. of Am., No. 651982/2011, 2014 N.Y. Misc. LEXIS 5141, at *67–72 (N.Y. Sup. Ct. Feb. 24, 2014).

33 Young Ha, *NY.Y. Court: Zurich Not Obligated to Defend Sony Units in Data Breach* Litigation, INSURANCE JOURNAL (March 17, 2014); https://www.insurancejournal.com/news/east/2014/03/17/323551.htm#.

34 Sony settled with its insurer, Zurich, by May 2015under confidential terms. Caitlin Bronson, *Zurich Reaches Settlement with Sony Over PlayStation Hack*, INSURANCE BUSINESS MAGAZINE (1 May 2015);

did have the relevant coverage in "the next hack").[35] In the initial throes of responding to an attack, the first party coverages for breach response costs and services likely would have been triggered as these coverages specifically respond to "data breaches" and likely capture any kind of "security failure," as described in the PlayStation litigation In particular, the first call under either the Sony "gamer" hack or the more notorious "Lazarus Heist" (i.e., the "North Korean" attack)[36] would have been to an outside forensic team to examine what systems were impacted, whether anything had been encrypted, destroyed or exfiltrated, and then the teams would set about reviewing how best to restore and remediate any compromised data and systems. The professional forensic fees and expenses, including legal expenses incurred to oversee these investigations are covered under most current first party breach response provisions.

In order to comply with breach notification statues and in some cases, customer terms and conditions, entities like Sony send out notification letters to users/customers/employees. These costs also would fall within the breach response costs provisions. While Sony definitely came under scrutiny from third parties, their in-house legal and compliance teams likely sought advice on any reporting or potential inquiry from state, federal or foreign regulators. The more comprehensive cyber terms generally outline in a separate insuring agreement that address "regulatory defense and penalties." The breach response costs coverage may pick up legal fees relating to oversight of the forensic investigation while the regulatory coverage leaves no doubt that counsel fees are covered to review the regulatory framework that may apply (whether and which state or foreign regulations apply). Further down the line, the regulatory coverage may also respond to specific fines imposed by a governmental

---

https://www.insurancebusinessmag.com/us/risk-management/news/zurich-reaches-settlement-with-sony-over-playstation-hack-22314.aspx.

35 Tina Amirtha, *This Isn't The First Time Sony Didn't Have Enough Hacker Insurance*, FAST COMPANY (December 22, 2014); https://www.fastcompany.com/3040251/the-sony-disaster-shows-why-companies-need-hacking-insurance (Reportedly, the cyber coverage was only up to $60 million while the fall out from that incident included class action litigation, costs of replacing servers, loss in box office earnings, which was speculated to total somewhere from $80 to $200 million.)

36 *The Lazarus Heist,* Podcast, BBC News, (Released 18 April 2021) https://www.bbc.co.uk/programmes/p09dx4p1.

authority. Note, there may be limitations, however, under the regulatory coverage with respect to costs to comply with injunctive relief, improving security systems or other reporting functions. These provisions likewise may not respond to alleged securities laws violations. The usual intent is to cover legal fees incurred in responding to inquiries like those from state Attorneys General, the Federal Trade Commission or the Office of Civil Rights for the Department of Health and Human Services (for alleged HIPAA violations).

Notably, most standalone cyber coverages also respond directly to costs relating to a ransom demand, including payment of the demand itself. Costs, again, likely relate to attorneys' fees but also would include specific costs incurred in retaining a consultant to negotiate with the threat actor, and any fees or charges associated with payment or those fees. In October 2020, the U.S. Department of Treasury, Office of Foreign Assets (OFAC) issued an advisory in which it sought to highlight that the ransomware payments may be violating anti-money laundering and sanctions regulations, and specifically, for the first time, OFAC mentioned cyber insurers.[37] Given that ransomware was a significant threat to businesses as well as governmental authorities throughout 2020 and 2021,[38] cyber insurers faced pressure to review not only underwriting procedures and protocols but the type and scope of some of these provisions.[39] For

---

37 "Companies that facilitate ransomware payments to cyber actors on behalf of victims, including financial institutions, cyber insurance firms, and companies involved in digital forensics and incident response, not only encourage future ransomware payment demands but also may risk violating OFAC regulations (see, "Advisory on Potential Sanctions Risks for Facilitating Ransomware Payments," October 1, 2020). Then, on February 4, 2021, the New York State Department of Financial Services (DFS) issued additional guidance, which recommended against making such payments but also included the Cyber Insurance Risk Framework—manage/eliminate silent cyber; evaluate system risk; rigorously measure risk by using "data-driven, comprehensive plan;" educate insureds/producers, hire knowledgeable personnel; require insureds to notify law enforcement (Insurance Circular Letter No. 2 (2021).

38 Matt Stieb, *What's Driving the Surge in Ransomware Attacks?*, NEW YORK MAGAZINE (June 11, 2021); https://nymag.com/intelligencer/article/ransomware-attacks-2021.html.

39 Frank Bajak, *In Crosshairs of Ransomware Crooks, Cyber Insurers Struggle,* AP NEWS (July 5, 2021). https://apnews.com/article/kaseya-ransomware-attack-0705-4c2272cdd428ddfa1f3644d513566c06 ("In a bid to turn back

entertainment and sports giants though, avoiding the headlines of a cyber extortion event is likely worth the ounce of prevention recommended by their cyber insurer as well as coverage of at least costs related to responding to such a cataclysm (see comments on reputational harm below).

2. Girl, [Your System Is] Interrupted and That Is the Day Your Earth Stood Still[40]

Disruptions to a live event due to a ransomware attack or other network security failure would be covered in many cyber policies, although underwriting and pricing for such risks may come with its own unique level of scrutiny, as discussed above. Most cyber insurers offering business interruption coverage anticipate that the enterprise will do its best to be back up-and-running within a short time frame, and thus there are built in "waiting period" retentions.[41] The period of time between when an insurer believes the entity should be back online may range from six to twenty-four hours.[42] In the case of a live concert or sporting event, it would seem the length of the "wait" would be measured in minutes rather than hours.[43]

---

ransomware-related losses [reportedly amounting to 40% of North American cyber claims for 2020], policy renewals are carrying new, stricter rules or lowered coverage limits" in addition to premium increases).

40 *Girl, Interrupted* (Released December 21, 1999; Columbia Pictures, Red Wagon Entertainment) (starring Winona Ryder, Angelina Jolie, Brittany Murphy, Elisabeth Moss, amongst others); *The Day the Earth Stood Still* (Released September 18, 1951, 20th Century Fox).

41 *Business Interruption: The unexpected Costs of a Cyber Incident*, Advisen blog; https://www.advisenltd.com/business-interruption-the-unexpected-cost-of-a-cyber-incident/.

42 *Id.*

43 Anne Freedman, *Cyber Business Interruptions*, RISK AND INSURANCE (Apr. 7, 2017), https://riskandinsurance.com/cyber-business-interruption/ (". . .in October 2016. . .a massive distributed denial of service (DDoS) attack assaulted Dyn, a company that controls much of the internet infrastructure. . .[which] brought down major sites including Netflix, CNN, Spotify, Airbnb, Twitter and many others. . .to add more uncertainty, came the outages on Feb. 28 connected to Amazon Web Services. Although this was due to human error—apparently a coding error—rather than maliciousness, the result was the same: Companies, large and small,

Given that there remains a level of variety of how cyber terms are spelled out, as noted in earlier chapters, the business interruption piece, given its relative newness to the market, is in a particular state of innovation. Some terms include detailed requirements relating to proofs of loss for the insured to submit its losses, which usually is a page taken out of the property adjuster's handbook. Other business interruption loss provisions are more forgiving to the insured, in likely anticipation that the insured and the insurer will be able to come to a good faith understanding about the length of time the business was down, and the numbers to be factored into resolving the "loss" piece. The business interruption terms are usually quite specific, however, that there is a time limitation on the period in which losses can be included as related to the interruption.[44] Some cyber insurers rely on outside consultants to perform a post-loss "review" of the proof of loss submitted by the insured while other insurers have set up in-house adjusters to perform that function.

One factor that inures to the benefit of the sports and entertainment industry in this regard is their overriding reputational credibility that likely drives any disruption to last minutes rather than months, weeks or hours, as may be less the case for a manufacturer or pharmaceutical company who also must weigh quality control considerations following a shutdown. When the lights go out at Major League Baseball,[45] it can last up to half an hour, but query whether they really lose any beer and hotdog sales, if the emergency concourse lights guide the way.

---

including Netflix, Airbnb, the Securities and Exchange Commission and Expedia, became inaccessible or their sites ran like molasses.").

44 Andrew G. Simpson, *5 Ways Cyber Business Interruption Differs from Traditional Business Interruption: RIMS*, INSURANCE JOURNAL (May 19, 2021) ("up until a few years ago, much of the focus for cyber insurance was on data breach or data privacy issues and how many records relate as a result of an incident. Now there's much more focus on the actual financial disruptions that these cyber events are causing and the resulting business interruption that comes along with them," quoting Chris Mortifoglio, CPA/CFE).

45 *Power Outage Causes 25-Minute Delay at Dodger* Stadium, ASSOCIATED PRESS (September 26, 2020) https://www.washingtonpost.com/sports/mlb/power-goes-out-at-dodger-stadium-in-6th-inning/2020/09/26/4b2bf9ce-0074-11eb-b0e4-350e4e60cc91_story.html.

3. *It's the Pictures That Got Small*[46]

When the music stops and the lights go out, what happens to my street cred? Is there an app for that? One part of robust cyber coverage that will may help alleviate these concerns are the latest provisions for "reputational harm." These terms are tie closely into other first party losses and expenses like the retention of crisis management and public relations firms but also the disruption caused to the organization and its customers (audience). The terms may reimburse a franchise or studio for an earnings loss suffered "for a period of indemnity" (i.e., up to six months post-incident). The goal is to identify the difference in what would have been the gross revenues received absent the "incident" and the gross revenues actually received. Some of the terms key off of the date that the event was publicized, as compared to the date of the actual "breach." There are many factors to be considered in analyzing the events, the appropriate comparison figures (seasonal variations, venue variations) or how and to whom the events became known or "notorious. The sporting and event worlds again may have relevant experience to draw on with respect to event cancellation insurance, and up-to-the-minute statistics regarding ticket sales that could be used to spotlight the true impact of a disruptive data security disruption or breach.

4. *No-Shows and Also-Rans*

Given the above tales, the imperative for procuring the most up-to-date cyber coverage for entertainment and sports productions seems indisputable. However, there are also some claims, expenses or losses, like all insurance policies, where the cyber coverage may not respond. In certain circumstances, some consumer type of claims may not be covered, or there may be some limitations on coverage.[47] Because the sports and

---

46 Quote from *Sunset Boulevard* (Released August 10, 1950, Paramount Pictures) (struggling screenwriter Joe Gillis unwittingly enters the surreal world of faded silent film star Norma Desmond; in response to Mr. Gillis' opening remark to her, "You used to be big," Norma replies "I am big. It's the pictures that got small.").

47 Doctors Direct Ins., Inc. v. Bochenek, 38 N.E.3d 116, 119 (Ill. App. Ct. 2015) (even some policies that reference "privacy wrongful acts" may not respond to certain consumer fraud statutes, like the Telephone Consumer Protection Act of 1991, TCPA). *See also*, potential exclusions relating to "biometric"

entertainment fields rely specifically on "consumers," a close look at any regulations or statutes that are excluded, or not specifically referenced, is a worthwhile analysis. Moreover, because the large entertainment companies are publicly traded, there is always the potential that a data breach or data/privacy security event could result in shareholder actions.[48] Most cyber policies are explicit in excluding securities type of actions.[49] Similarly, cyber coverages will exclude claims against directors or officers in their basic forms, but some insurers may be explicitly trying to capture any perceived "gaps" there.[50]

Finally, since the Sony "hack" dominated the news cycle circa 2015, once an insurer invoked the "war" exclusion following a data breach, many commentators pondered the fate of entities similarly targeted.[51] As

---

data although many cyber coverages will be explicit on this point. Jeff Bowen, *Employee Biometric Data: Are You Covered for Collecting or Using It?* TECH RISK REPORT (Jan. 13, 2020), https://www.techriskreport.com/2020/01/employee-biometric-data-are-you-covered-for-collecting-or-using-it/.

48 *See, e.g.*, suit involving a glitch-plagued video game release , Carolyn Casey, *Cyberpunk 2077 Investor Files Securities Class Action Lawsuit Against Game Developers*, EXPERT INSTITUTE (Jan. 20, 2021), (https://www.expertinstitute.com/resources/insights/cyberpunk-2077-investor-files-securities-class-action-lawsuit-against-game-developers/ ("Shortly after its release, Cyberpunk 2077 was criticized for widespread technical issues. . .company shareholders felt similarly bewildered by the release—resulting in the current class action.")

49 *Supra* note 27, the Chubb policy disclosed in the *P.F. Chang's China Bistro* case ("[c]ompany shall not be liable for any **Loss** on account of any **Claim** or for any **Expense**. . .based upon. . .the underwriting, securitizing, syndicating, promoting, or market making. . .[per the SEC] of any debt or equity security. . .").

50 *Cyber and D&O Liability Increasingly Interlinked*, AIRMIC (Jan. 11, 2018), https://airmic.com/news/guest-stories/cyber-and-do-liability-increasingly-interlinked.

51 *See*, Adam Schniderman, *Prove It! Judging the Hostile-or-Warlike-Action Exclusion in Cyber Policies*, THE YALE LAW JOURNAL FORUM (Oct. 15, 2019), https://www.yalelawjournal.org/pdf/Shniderman_ProveIt_46vzsvqt.pdf (discussing the case of *Mondelez Intl. Inc. v. Zurich Am. Ins. Co.*, No. 2018-L-11008, 2018 WL 4941760 (Ill. Cir. Ct., Cook Cty., complaint filed Oct. 10, 2018), in which Zurich invoked a "war exclusion" to avoid expenses stemming from the NotPetya virus ; *see also*, Jon Bateman, *War, Terrorism,*

in the early days of cyber insurance though, cyber insurers may look for ways to respond to market forces, and provide at least a variation on a "carve-back" for "cyber terrorism," given that so many incidents are the result of some kind of organized criminal, or potentially state-sponsored, element.[52]

Considering the above specialty risk considerations that may—or may not—apply to a sports or entertainment sector-based policyholders, ensuring proper coverage will necessarily require a case-by-case assessment based on a number of factors specific to each entity. Distilling the above, some preliminary considerations thus include:

- "Crisis" Coverage: Ensure adequate coverage for "crisis events" (e.g. costs for legal and forensic parties aka "first responders") and eventual notice to regulators and/or individuals that may stem from an incident. Consider the geographic reach and amount of data being handled (a further and wider reach may translate into greater response costs). A policyholder will not want to have to look for this coverage elsewhere after the fact.

---

and Catastrophe in Cyber Insurance: Understanding and Reforming Exclusions, CARNEGIE ENDOWMENT FOR INTERNATIONAL PEACE (Oct. 5, 2020), https://carnegieendowment.org/2020/10/05/war-terrorism-and-catastrophe-in-cyber-insurance-understanding-and-reforming-exclusions-pub-82819; and Jordan Rand, *A Tale of Two Carriers—Disparate Views of War/Terrorism Exclusion*, CYBERINSURANCE LAW BLOG (Mar. 2, 2019), https://www.databreachninja.com/a-tale-of-two-carriers-disparate-views-of-war-terrorism-exclusion/; and, in another timely example, reportedly there was a cyber attack on a water supply in proximity to Super Bowl venue; *see*, Frances Robles, Nicole Perlroth, *Danger Stuff: Hackers Tried to Poison Water Supply of Florida Town*, THE NEW YORK TIMES (Feb. 8, 2021), *available* at https://www.nytimes.com/ 2021/02/08/us/oldsmar-florida-water-supply-hack.html?referringSource= articleShare.

52 Mirza Salam Ahmed, Ben Dyson, *Cyber Insurers Wrestle with War Exclusions as State-Sponsored Attack Fears Grow*, S&P GLOBAL, MARKET INTELLIGENCE (Jan. 30, 2020), https://www.spglobal.com/market intelligence/en/news-insights/latest-news-headlines/cyber-insurers-wrestle-with-war-exclusions-as-state-sponsored-attack-fears-grow-56743302 ("William Wright, partner at Paragon International Insurance Brokers, said his company tries to ensure that in addition to a clear war exclusion, a cyber-terrorism carve-back is in place to ensure there is cover for events where war has not been declared or an attack cannot be attributed.")

- Business Interruption: Consider the time-sensitive nature of the business operations (Are hours *more* valuable here than for others?) and whether there are any inherent metrics that may calibrate coverage terms for interruptions accordingly.
- Be mindful of the gaps: Considering the consumer engagement and corporate structures underlying the sports/entertainment field, third-party claims arising under consumer statutes or shareholder agreements may be more common than other industries. If not coverable in a standalone cyber policy, ensure coverage elsewhere (e.g. a Directors & Officers liability policy)

E. Coming Attractions and Scouting Reports

Like many industries, the sports and entertainment fields have many and varied contractors, sub-contractors, part-time employees, freelancers, suppliers and vendors.[53] The seasonal and freelance nature of the work might provoke some concern relating to oversight and business continuity. In that regard, attaining cyber coverage that accounts for all of these attendant and frequently distant and global players may be a heavier lift than in other more focused, provincial industries. Also, given vigorous advertising and marketing efforts of their products or the experience, social media promotions can be taken to extremes.[54] Despite some of these provocative narratives, this may not necessarily mean these industries are inherently bigger risk headaches.[55] Especially now that your favorite tech company is also now your favorite television, film and music producer (e.g., Amazon, Apple).[56]

---

53 Even supposedly sophisticated advisors are potential sources of risk. *See*, Todd Spangler, *Hacked Law Firm Informs Clients Like Lady Gaga and Bruce Springsteen of Data Breach*, VARIETY (May 11, 2020), *available at* https://variety.com/2020/digital/news/law-firm-hacked-clients-lady-gaga-bruce-springsteen-1234603831/.

54 Michael Baggs, *Fyre Festival: Inside the World's Biggest Festival Flop*, BBC (Jan. 18, 2019), https://www.bbc.com/news/newsbeat-46904445.

55 Telephone interview with Christopher Keegan, Senior Managing Director, Cyber & Technology National Practice Leader, Beecher Carlson Insurance Services, LLC (January 29, 2021) (notes on file).

56 And innovate they do and will; invest they do and will. R. Lawler, *Apple TV+ subscribers can expect ad-free original shows and movies this fall.* ENGADGET (March 25, 2019) (Oprah is "expected" "to join forces" to

As for any consumer-facing financial transactions, the industries generally rely on back-end payment systems, so that risk presumably is ring-fenced.[57] There may be some valuation issues when it comes to the intellectual property at issue, but like in the case of the unauthorized release of the Sony films, there are also some obvious available revenue metrics.[58] Also, their practices in collecting data should be comparably sourced as would be the case with most large retail outfits. Like online retailers, their reward, loyalty and promotional programs should benefit from specialized outsourcing arrangements. There are some additional dynamics to these sectors that potentially take them to a different level than even the highly data-centric healthcare and financial services industries, such as performer or player confidential contractual terms, publishing or distribution rights, and the pervasive rankings and ratings nature of such lofty pursuits. On the plus side, perhaps any network or digital disruption can be readily remedied or compensated for given redundancies in the platforms and the fact that eventually everything ends up online for consumption sooner or later. Sports and entertainment organizations may strive to be first-to-the-finish, top of the heap, in all ventures so perhaps there is a glimmer of hope, that these entities will apply that same drive to their cybersecurity practices and when it comes to their digital assets, they won't "*wait til next year*!"

"service this moment."); Kif Leswing, *Apple is spending $6 billion on original shows and trying to beat Disney+ to market, reports FT,* CNBC (August 19, 2019) https://www.cnbc.com/2019/08/19/apple-spending-6-billion-on-shows-trying-to-beat-disney-ft.html; Annie Palmer, *Amazon spent $11 billion on video and music content last year, up from $7.8 billion in 2019,* CNBC (April 15, 2021) https://www.cnbc.com/2021/04/15/ amazon-spent-11-billion-on-video-and-music-content-last-year.html.

57 *Id.*

58 *Sony, supra* note 10.